Opening Bazin

Postwar Film Theory and Its Afterlife

EDITED BY

Dudley Andrew

WITH

Hervé Joubert-Laurencin

OXFORD
UNIVERSITY PRESS

OXFORD
UNIVERSITY PRESS

Oxford University Press, Inc., publishes works that further
Oxford University's objective of excellence
in research, scholarship, and education.

Oxford   New York
Auckland   Cape Town   Dar es Salaam   Hong Kong   Karachi
Kuala Lumpur   Madrid   Melbourne   Mexico City   Nairobi
New Delhi   Shanghai   Taipei   Toronto

With offices in
Argentina   Austria   Brazil   Chile   Czech Republic   France   Greece
Guatemala   Hungary   Italy   Japan Poland   Portugal   Singapore
South Korea   Switzerland   Thailand   Turkey   Ukraine   Vietnam

Copyright © 2011 by Oxford University Press, Inc.

Published by Oxford University Press, Inc.
198 Madison Avenue, New York, New York 10016

www.oup.com

Oxford is a registered trademark of Oxford University Press

Library of Congress Cataloging-in-Publication Data
Opening Bazin : postwar film theory and its afterlife / edited by Dudley Andrew; with Hervé Joubert-Laurencin.
         p.   cm.
Includes bibliographical references and index.
ISBN 978-0-19-973388-0 (cloth : alk. paper) — ISBN 978-0-19-973389-7 (pbk. : alk. paper)
1. Bazin, Andr?, 1918–1958—Criticism and interpretation. 2. Motion pictures—Philosophy.
I. Andrew, Dudley, 1945– II. Joubert-Laurencin, Hervé.
PN1998.3.B39O64   2011
791.43092—dc22
[B]
2010019161

Printed in the United States of America
on acid-free paper

Contents

A Binocular Preface

New Haven: Dudley Andrew

The oeuvre of André Bazin (April 1918–November 1958) goes well beyond the particular genre of its expression, film criticism, reaching out to the full history of the twentieth century and to a variety of theories of art. As a child of the photographic revolution, cinema transformed the century it chronicled, a century of artistic modernism of which it has been the most troubling case. Bazin intuited its special place between art and history, positioning himself as a philosophical observer of the world and the world's inhabitants seen through the screen. Never a flaneur, he was both systematic surveyor and militant cinephile, a daily critic of the hundreds of films on Paris' screens during the most crucial period of this art, a man who never let a new film or a new idea escape him. Writing without interruption for fifteen years (1943–1958) and producing some 2,600 articles, he must be considered the sound film's master-thinker and the first to register the effervescence of a cinematic modernism that began to come to prominence during his professional life. We are fifty years beyond Bazin and have entered another century. Yet rather than dreaming about him, we can dream with him, for "each epoch dreams the one to follow," according to Jules Michelet. But to dream with Bazin we must delve into his oeuvre where the man still lives, opening an archive that needs to be opened out to the questions of concern to us today. *Ouvrir Bazin!* Let us open André Bazin. He has much to tell us.

We should all be ashamed—I more than anyone—that it took the fiftieth anniversary of his passing to goad us into genuinely exploring André Bazin. Did we believe that we possessed all we needed in the collection he put together on the eve of his death? Were the fifty-two articles (twenty-six in the standard English translation) comprising *Qu'est-ce que le cinéma?* sufficient to fund his brand of film theory, letting us stand him up against Eisenstein in some battle of the titans? For that is effectively what we've done for four decades. In the modest preface he composed for *Qu'est-ce que le cinéma?* Bazin consigned most of his writing to ephemera, as he "reviewed" everyday films or ordinary moments few of which merited resurrection. However, each moment did demand that he take a position, and we've come to value those positions and learn from many of those moments. His friends and followers eventually gathered additional collections of his writing (on Renoir, on Chaplin, on Welles, on the Occupation and Liberation, on French cinema, and, most intriguingly, on "The Cinema of Cruelty"). Counting everything available in the various French and English anthologies brings us 204 pieces. The persistent student can locate some of these at the bookstore and all of them through diligent use of inter-library loan. What would it be like to open up the lesser known of these articles to their history or to new interpretations? And what about the uncollected Bazin, the rests of the 2,600 pieces in the bibliography on Yale's and Amien's Web sites? What would it be like to open *le tout Bazin*, 90 percent of which has remained invisible and unread after a fleeting appearance in one or another flimsy newspaper or journal? This challenge was met by the scholars in this volume who heard and answered the invitation sent out by me and my co-enthusiast, Hervé Joubert-Laurencin, an invitation to "Open Bazin" wide and dig deep to see what was there, either in the essays we had all read for decades and mistakenly thought we understood, or in the fugitive pieces amassed in our offices, the Bazin "archives."

Bazin was surely an original, a gift without a donor showing up on cinema's doorstep just as it was striding out to take up new responsibilities after the war. Some thought him an angel, arriving unbidden to point filmmakers and spectators to the promised land of cinematic modernism. He would have been the last to appreciate this compliment, for he was a staunch evolutionist and surely saw himself as product and conduit of multiple lines of thought running through him, lines to which he gave his own twist as demanded by the "situations" (Sartre) he participated in. Digging into and underneath Bazin, we expose roots and tendrils, delicate threads of intellectual life that the contributors to this anthology, especially in the first of its four parts, tug at and follow out. They disentangle, from a teeming thicket of ideas, those that make up a line of thought, a lineage.

In a recent manifesto, *What Cinema Is!: Bazin's Quest and Its Charge*, I sketch an aesthetic heritage that begins with Roger Leenhardt at the outset of the sound era, passing through Bazin to the journal he founded and directed. The "*Cahiers* Line," as Serge Daney once dubbed it, is neither perfectly straight, nor is it singular (having many threads), nor is it necessarily tied to this one periodical; however, it does identify an orientation that owes most to Bazin on three fronts: first, the pursuit of "the real" beyond representation and certainly beyond mere images; second, a taste for the interaction of reality and imagination in all sorts of genres, in the play of actors and nonactors before the camera, in the multiple "voices" of the soundtrack, and in the dialectic of technical effects and raw images; third, a concern for the social consequences of "projection," both in the circumstances of exhibition and in the discourse provoked by films, including ultimately the writing of criticism and the *écriture* of subsequent films.

Part two of this anthology goes right at Bazin's thoughts about many of these issues, opening up unresolved aesthetic questions concerning cinema's alleged capture of audiovisual facts in real time, its rhetorical composition of images and sounds, and its claims on our experience of what is ultimately screened. Especially since the advent of the digital image, "authenticity" (another name for cinema's myth) has returned as an inveterate and troubling issue, related dialectically to technology and to the history of cinematic language and effects. Cinema may not have escaped the conditions governing all arts of representation, but its status among (or beside) those arts is genuinely peculiar. Bazin shared cinema's appetite for incorporating (digesting) the other arts; more broadly, with his rare dual attitude—literary/artistic and ethnographic/scientific—he rode the back of cinema in pursuit of the living otherness of animals, of the human body as opposed to the actor's screen persona, and of the bare human face. Bazin's intuitions about cinema's predilections lead in quite novel directions, as he seems to have made a new discovery with every film he reviewed. Paradoxically, "re-viewing" is something he did on the spot, something he found most films doing as well; Joubert-Laurencin believes that cinema's duality produced the "double clutch" that often makes Bazin's perceptions and reflections so startling. Might not a kind of critical stutter serve as cinema's heartbeat, pumping life into those hybrid films that have produced so much writing along the *Cahiers* line all these years?

While a certain postwar "idea of cinema" surely would have emerged in Europe without him, Bazin articulated that idea with such subtlety and consistency that a school of thought could be said to have developed around him. Of course, it was not an academic school; quite the opposite, as he was shut out of the educational system. But it was a school nonetheless, with a range of intellectual and artistic forebears, with tastes and procedures, with a particular rhetoric, and with a legacy stretching into our own day well beyond *Cahiers du Cinéma*, stretching finally into the university where this anthology has gestated. Part I exposes Bazin's ideas to the vast network that nourished him and that he in turn electrified, for films invariably provoked his insatiable curiosity, leading him to draw, without pedantry, on an astoundingly encyclopedic knowledge of the sciences and humanities. How did he keep it all straight? How did he coordinate his knowledge so as to bring to bear what was needed in any given instance? We learn right away that he was an enthusiastic and brilliant student, rising to the top of France's most elite schools. And in that environment he digested and never abandoned the values (as well as the limits) of maps in the spatial realm and evolution in the temporal. Thanks to the Bergsonism that permeated so much of the advanced Catholic thinking of the period, he recoiled from static views; hence his preference for cinema over photography; hence his Bergsonian view of painting as process rather than product. Hence his amateur's enthusiasm for a geology that turns geography into an exteme slow-motion view of a changing earth.

But Bergson was just one philosophical influence (clearly he knew his Plato and Aristotle) and existentialism just one of the current intellectual movements he routinely interacted with. As for his legacy, the contributors to this anthology make a strong case that he was ahead of contemporaries like Sartre, entertaining postclassical notions that resonate intriguingly with those of Barthes and Deleuze (who acknowledge him) as well as of Lyotard, Derrida, and Nancy. How did we ever take him for a naïve realist? And yet he won't let the concerns associated with realism evaporate entirely into the ether of constructivism. As the overviews by Thomas Elsaesser and Colin MacCabe make clear, Bazin spread his arms across the full length of the century in which he was situated exactly at the midpoint.

While he had actual encounters with Sartre, Merleau-Ponty, and Gabriel Marcel—and kept up with philosophy—Bazin trained professionally as a scholar of literature, producing a thesis on Baudelaire. His references to popular and classical literature are so frequent that he must have been an avid reader; however, underneath his eclecticism lies a complex view of literary theory and history. The names of Baudelaire and Malraux authorize us to imagine Bazin's intellectual rapport with Walter Benjamin. For one thing, both thinkers had an ongoing romance with surrealism. Jean-François Chevrier drives the surrealist concern with hallucinations deep into the nineteenth century, to Hippolyte Taine and Gustave Flaubert. At this point Bazin's realism can be seen to be as "naïve" as that of Flaubert, which is to say, sophisticated beyond our comprehension.

As for art history, Bazin's fascination with movement and with automatically produced images made him deviate somewhat from the final direction of Malraux's massively influential *Psychology of Art*, even while he banked on that genius's overarching evolutionary scheme. Once again an imagined rapport with Benjamin helps us put Bazin's values in place. For both men could honor the great painters of the past and of their own day while still preferring to draw attention to the labor of artisans and to the "automatic" images produced in the minor arts of mechanical ornamentation as well as in the various modes of "imprinting" from the molds of ancient times to photography today. Jean-Michel Frodon intimates that Bazin may have helped fund art history's anthropological turn, most visible today in the work of Georges Didi-Huberman.

Speculations on the long history of ideas and of the arts that passed through Bazin and found their way into our twenty-first century should not let us forget that more than any thinker I know, Bazin was literally tied to the day-to-day operations of the film world from 1943 until his death. The contributors to Part III took pains to open the huge bibliography of his daily, weekly, and monthly writings to situate him in his various roles and moments. James Tweedie treats this so-called philosopher of film as a precursor of today's cultural studies scholar. Other contributors depict the acrimonious cold war atmosphere in which every film review could be taken as tendentious. Not just films, but critics had to negotiate the economic and censorship restrictions that constricted an art form eager to be free. They had a better time of it outside the mainstream feature, in documentary and experimental shorts, which, hindsight tells us, foretold the new waves of the sixties. Bazin always kept up with marginal modes, reserving some of his most telling observations for the most fugitive of films: newsreels, science films, films on art. Never snobbish, he followed the growth of French television from its inception, commenting on it increasingly as his deteriorating health kept him home. In this he showed himself to be a popular critic, looking for any means whereby television might promote community. For Bazin believed in the intelligence of the audience and in the value of collective viewing and reflection. Philip Watts insists on this in the finale of his contribution: "The film-viewing experience always consists, for him, of an initial 'shock'—the word reappears throughout his essays—which the critic and spectator must then attempt to negotiate, to understand, to translate as best they can. This 'ethic of realism' also meant that this negotiation with cinema must always be tied to deliberation, to our encounter with others and to the ways in which we live together." Bazin's life in his historical moment was one of constant negotiation with the realities of political and economic determinants, and with the vagaries of the market. But he seems to have negotiated from a secure position, for he was confident in his ideas, confident in the cinema, and confident ultimately in the taste and intelligence of spectators, who, especially in the afterglow of ciné-club discussion, or of critical argument, would come to demand richer, more mature films.

At the end of his life, Bazin could sense a richer cinema on the horizon, in the greater variety of experimental and documentary works he found himself reviewing and in the growing swells of independent features building toward a towering new wave. He heard of, and witnessed, the increasingly important cultural role cinema was playing around the world at the many festivals he attended (in Germany, Czechoslovakia, Uruguay, Belgium, Italy, Brazil). Part IV of this anthology chronicles Bazin's relation to the cinema beyond his own country and his own time. It could have been extended to cover many other countries, but Bazin's relation to the USSR (and later Russia), to Czechoslovakia and Eastern Europe, to Japan and China, and to Brazil helps fill out a picture of the world of cinema that he inflated with the power and spirit of his writing. That writing, as this volume promises to demonstrate, never ceases to open up. Like the man himself, Bazin's ideas show themselves ready to encounter not just new films but new media, as well as the evolving social world which they expose and, in the best scenario, enrich.

Paris: Hervé Joubert-Laurencin

Few intellectuals have suffered a more difficult, contorted, and contradictory reception than has Bazin in his native France these past fifty years. Outside the fractious French arena, Bazin has found a more dispassionate readership and perhaps a broader one. Scholars and students from North America, the United Kingdom, Brazil, Japan, China, and Italy seem to have given him a fairer examination. Still, no matter how precise their studies of his philosophy, critical method, and rhetoric may be, they have treated Bazin as though he lived above the earth in some transcendent cinematic zone. The French, on the other hand, find him perhaps too close to home. French discussions of his writings—whether mawkishly positive or aggressively hostile, essentialist or ideological—have been partial in two senses of the word: they deal with only a fraction of Bazin's corpus, and they almost always approach it from a distinct *parti pris*.

In an issue of the review *Hors-cadre* devoted to the "voice-over," the excellent Lacanian psychoanalyst Jean Allouch mentions the "errance de toute tentative d'enregistrement" (the deviance of every attempted recording). "Errance" suggests both *erreur* (to err) and wandering. In this specific context, Allouch is referring to wrongheaded stabs at recording or transcribing what occurs: for instance, the "taping of what is said in an analysis" for the purpose of coming up with a precise linguistic representation, something he declares a useless, even foolish idea. Allouch in fact points to nothing less than the irreducible distinction between the *signifiant* in the psychoanalytical sense and the linguistic signifier in Saussure's vocabulary. Hence the opposition between reality on the one hand—including the reality of the talking cure—and, on the other hand, any representation of this reality, any attempt at recording it.

The consequences of this for Bazin lie first and crucially in his theory of ontological realism, which was surely his way to get at cinema's unique definition, so distinct from traditional verbal notions of realism. This stance, which Bazin shared with Roger Leenhardt and Maurice Merleau-Ponty, insists that cinema has to be defined apart from the other arts, for *cinema possesses a very specific, very intrinsic link with living reality,* and it stands opposed to that tagline he would eventually append to his famous "Ontology" essay: "Cinema is also a language." So, cinema is defined primordially as a "recording," a "mechanical recording." While this may be a common way to identify Bazin, what is often misunderstood—what Bazin has discovered, together with Robert Bresson and other artist-directors through their filmmaking, and later Serge Daney in his criticism—is that in cinema, recording is not in fact a product of its mechanics. By this I mean that mechanics are necessary but not sufficient for cinematic recording. For during any technical recording, something else occurs, as something is recording and being recorded.

Bazin was not a philosopher but a daily film-screening practitioner, and he wrote out of his experience as a member of the audience; so he realized again and again the distinction between an event and its "mechanical recording." Bresson put it remarkably well in one maxim from his famous *Notes sur le Cinématographe*: "une mécanique fait surgir l'inconnu" (a mechanism gives rise to the unknown).[1] "A thing" happens "in an obscure way" in the "models" (actors, for Bresson) when they find themselves in front of the recording camera: it frees them from so-called "stage mechanics," and it frees cinema itself from "photographic reproduction." We are in the realm not of a reproduction of the same, but of the appearance of "a new mode," a "method of discovery," an appearance of the unknown (which is not necessarily the unknowable nor the divine, nor grace, but simply what is not yet known, not having been perceptible before . . . before the invention of cinema, before the finished film, before the editing of the takes, before the take).

It should be no surprise, then, that Bazin's theory regularly contradicts the standard notion of recording. Just look at his discussion of such things as the negative imprint, the ellipsis, Bresson's blank screen, the true hallucination of the surrealists, Chaplin's *néantisation* (nullification) of Hitler, Fellini's super-naturalization, and so on. Bazin does not care about recording as defined in the dictionary or summed up by those uninterested in it.

Another dimension of the erring/errance of recording applies distinctly to "Bazin," that is, to the fate of his name and his works; for "what Bazin means," has been delivered to us in the present not as talking cure, but as "the erring/errance of every attempted recording." During his life and right up to today, particularly in France, his name has been taken as a convenient shorthand, a kind of vocalized automatic memory, while his writing has been unscrupulously ransacked. High on the list of those who have mistreated him are film professors with their deliberate or unconscious parody of Bazinian categories, especially egregious during the period of his complete rejection after 1968.

That period commenced with Jean Mitry's *Esthétique et psychologie du cinéma* (volume 1 in 1963, volume 2 in 1965, published in the premonitory "Encyclopédie universitaire" series). A highly disputable general survey of theory, this magnum opus was itself immediately critiqued by Christian Metz in his *Essais sur la signification au cinéma*. Metz's views of theory were more scientifically grounded and would quickly foster a dominant trend of thought; yet, like Mitry, the "academic" nature of his film studies seemed to depend on a rejection, or more insidiously, a skillful erasure, of Bazin.

After Mitry, who copiously cited Bazin, a routine of lazy summary started to develop, eventually taking the place of Bazin's actual prose, as if he were merely a position (and one to be overcome) rather than an author who had written a great deal. As film theory became more organized and rigorous in the 1970s, a certain *doxa* took hold. And so it was that Bazin, the greatest writer in the history of our art, the equivalent of Roberto Longhi for painting, has been constantly referred to yet betrayed. Recall the most remarkable historical symptom of this, Jean-Luc Godard's fabrication at the beginning of *Le Mépris*: "'Cinema,' said André Bazin, 'substitutes for our gaze . . .'" You know the rest of this apocryphal citation. This is why today in a new era, we must again go through a mechanical recording of Bazin, so as to dream again with him.

Our first recording device is the "explorer service" put up on the Yale Web site and on that of the University of Picardie Jules Verne in Amiens. The contributors to this anthology could riffle through the titles of all of Bazin's articles, locating every instance where he analyzed or mentioned a director or film. While we await a complete edition of Bazin and the full-text search capability that it would provide, we now at least have a better sense of his amazing breadth and erudition. Of course, even as we follow his manner of following the cinema, we ourselves cannot escape erring (and *errance*), since we are in fact recording his recording of his viewing. Nevertheless, we asked our contributors to meander with and through Bazin. The results, you will see, either dig deeper into familiar ground or explore utterly new territory that no one had expected Bazin to have wandered into.

This recovery effort aims first to return to Bazin's words, for in the short time needed to bring out the four volumes of *Qu-est ce que le cinéma?* (late 1958 to 1962), Bazin became effectively closed off to the future. The publication of his writings did not have a negative effect on its reception; on the contrary, the fatal moment occurred when the recording was interrupted. In sum, we can say that in the cinematic field, the "erring/errance of every attempted recording" goes hand in hand with listening to what is said once the recording device has made "the unknown appear."

Take a paradigmatic example of Bazin's reception: his role in the birth of the New Wave. The phrase "Nouvelle Vague" should be read as a play on words, a historical inversion that transforms the first term into a noun and the second one into an adjective. Thus "New Wave" becomes "vague news," or "uncertain gospel." Indeed what the New Wave directors received in the transmission from Bazin can only be called vague. Truffaut, Godard, Rohmer, Chabrol—all of them disagreed with the Bazinian criteria for cinematic value: don't they champion "small subjects," set against the "important topics" their master had always believed went hand in hand with great cinema? Still, they absorbed his lessons about Renoir and Rossellini (the play of amateurism, the mixture of actors and ordinary people), and they generally agreed with the key principles of his ontological realism.

But how can one stick to so-called Bazinian ideas and yet oppose their historical, sociological, and political consequences? Failing to apply the general idea of cinematic realism in their treatment of individual films, one after the next, the New Wave critics had to remain "vague" if they were to remain Bazinian in any sense at all. This was especially true as their own films moved further from rendering a conception of the world, becoming increasingly focused on a conception of cinema (although Bazin preached that one should not divorce these). Still a larger transmission occurred, larger because much more vague: the transmission of a philosophical idea, which does not personally belong to Bazin, though he knew how to phrase it properly: the idea of mimesis.

Bazin's writing at its most concrete, and in its best passages, offers a reformulation of the ancient question of mimesis specific to the filmic medium. Yet the possibility of a transmission between discursive thought and practical filmmaking requires a translation of the historian's protocols: accumulating objects of transmission is useless since the transmission itself is not equal to the sum of the elements transmitted. Here lies my own small discovery: what is transmitted from Bazin to the New Wave is transmission itself. And nothing could be more important, as Giorgio Agamben came to realize in considering, after other writers and philosophers, the remarkable Katcina rite of passage in the culture of the Pueblos Indians. During this rite, initiates are let in on the secrets of the powerful Katcina figures; but in fact the elders and the gods pass on no secrets whatsoever; instead the initiates are exposed to a more powerful truth, that "there is nothing to transmit except *transmission itself*: the signifying function in itself."[2]

The directors of the New Wave may in fact have misled themselves about Bazin's ideas, may have merely used him for their own purposes, may have passed on bazinism rather than

Bazin to later generations; nonetheless, this fallacious transmission was true in the most important respect: as a transmission it amplified Bazin's own marvelous spirit as transmitter. For the fifteen years of his professional life that spirit transmitted to a public those other spirits that came to him on the screen each night like the visitors from the future in *La Jetée*. Serge Daney was perhaps the first to understand this Bazinian transmission, and for that reason became a *passeur* himself. And so while we cannot deny having inherited an ignoble legacy of misunderstanding André Bazin, we can be glad that his name has been kept alive, even when taken in vain. The tremendous outpouring of scholarship during this anniversary year (which has dwelt not on his dolorous passing but rather on the glorious appearance of *Qu'est-ce que le cinéma?*) has worked to reverse once again the Bazinian transmission and to raise it to a higher power. This anthology is both an inevitably errant recording of that effort of transmission and an instrument of its success.

Notes

1. Robert Bresson, *Notes on the Cinematographer* (New York: Urizen Books, 1977), 32: "GESTURES AND WORDS: Gestures and words cannot form the substance of a film as they form the substance of a stage play. But the substance of a film can be that . . . thing or those things which provoke the gestures and words and which are produced in some obscure way in your models. Your camera sees them and records them. So one escapes from the photographic reproduction of actors performing a play; and cinematography, that new writing, becomes at the same time a method of discovery. *(*It does so because a mechanism gives rise to the unknown, and not because one has found this unknown in advance)."
2. Giorgio Agamben, *Infancy and History: the Destruction of Experience* (London: Verso, 1993), note 13, p.87.

Acknowledgments

It took effort to open Bazin. First came the systematic collection of his articles, begun in the 1990s under Colin MacCabe's initiative with money coming for a time from the BFI before their policies changed. The photocopying was carried out by Nell Andrew working with *Cahiers du Cinéma* (and Claudine Paquot) but especially with Janine Bazin, who left us too soon to have seen all that has come to pass recently, including the filling out of the archive to a state that now appears nearly complete. At the University of Rennes II, Hervé Joubert-Laurencin assembled a working group that undertook the immense task of building from these hundreds of articles an excel database of searchable categories. A grant from Yale's European Studies Council enabled Liam Andrew, assisted by Katy Jarzebowski, to classify the materials until it became a useable "archive," useable, that is, once the Bazin Web site had been uploaded thanks to Yale's ITS team. It was possible at long last to begin to tease out threads of Bazin's ideas and to read what he said about a given film, genre, or topic. The contributors to this anthology were invited to consult all of Bazin's works. So too were graduate students in my Yale seminar and in the parallel seminar directed by Joubert-Laurencin which met at the Institut National de l'Histoire de l'Art where he also had organized these materials.

All this was in preparation for the transatlantic conference "Ouvrir Bazin/Opening Bazin" that is the source of many of the articles in this anthology. American scholars and doctoral students joined French ones at the University of Paris VII (Denis Diderot) during the last week of November 2008. Paris-Diderot (and specifically Martin Rueff, Stéphane Villain, and Frédéric Ogée) supported not just this event but a cycle of international lectures on Bazin held throughout the academic year, several of which were hosted by Columbia University and the University of Florida at Reid Hall. Bazin's vision was exposed to the entire city of Paris when Serge Toubiana, Jean-François Rauger, and Olivier Père of the Cinémathèque Française graciously programmed "le regard de Bazin," a phenomenal series of 160 films that concluded just in advance of the "Ouvrir Bazin" conference. And the conference itself culminated in the Cinémathèque's grand screening room with reflections by Jean Narboni, legendary editor of Bazin's writings. All credit for the Bazinien year in Paris goes to Joubert-Laurencin, who even enticed Jeanne Moreau to open "Opening Bazin" by reading, in her inimitable voice, a selection of the critic's witty prose, and then recounting to us Truffaut's feelings about the man who had formed him.

Act Two of the conference followed immediately in New Haven, with many of the French towed back across the Atlantic to meet additional participants at Yale. This elaborate, thrilling event was made possible through Associate Provost Emily Bakemeier who drew on Kempf and Woodward funds to supplement the budget of the Film Studies Program and the largesse extended by Maria Rosa Menacol, director of the Whitney Humanities Center. Delphine Selles of the French Cultural Services of New York warmly contributed so that additional European scholars could interact with their American counterparts. The presence of Mary Ann Doane, Francesco Casetti, Laura Mulvey, Charles Musser, David Rodowick, Prakash Younger, Dominique Blüher, and especially Raymond Bellour lifted discussion to the highest level of Film Studies imaginable. It was evident that a plateau had been reached, from which we could better understand not just Bazin but the field itself. And it was clear that a set of essays going beyond the conference needed to be produced. New selections were commissioned; presentations were rewritten—every piece but one designed specifically for this collection.

Enter Oxford University Press in the bright presence of Shannon McLachlan, who saw instantly (this is her genius) just how special this anthology could be. Her enthusiasm fed mine and sped the project to completion. Here let me salute the thirty-two authors who accepted my demanding deadlines and presumptuous insistence that they improve their already excellent submissions. Brendan O'Neill saw things through to publication at the press, working with a complicated manuscript that had been shepherded and groomed by Liam Andrew. Liam is also to be credited with translation of the articles by Jean-Michel Frodon, Antoine de Baecque, Marc Vernet, Rochelle Fack, and Kan Nozaki; Sally Shafto translated the article by Jean-François Chevrier and worked on that of Hervé Joubert-Laurencin. Pierre Berthomieu also provided, with scarcely any notice, some textual conversions from French to English. However, I take responsibility for the final version of all these translations and beg the indulgence of the authors (and those two translators) whose work I may well have compromised in certain instances. To minimize infelicities and outright errors, I turned often to Jeremi Szaniawski.

The difficulties presented by translation remind us that this, like all books, is nothing other than language, and Bazin's language—the material object of this anthology—has been particularly underserved to date. Not enough of it is available; that which is available has been neglected, as Hervé Joubert-Laurencin points out in the preface, in favor of the clichés he terms "bazinism." To render Bazin for an English publication like this, I have come up with variable strategies, usually with the consent of each author. Most often the common English versions are cited, especially Hugh Gray's familiar two volumes from the University of California Press. In 2009, however, a competing Canadian selection from *Qu'est-ce que le cinéma?* came out, also titled *What Is Cinema?* Less literary but generally more literally accurate, Timothy Barnard's Bazin sometimes serves us better. The diligent reader will want frequently to return to the French, and should certainly do so in those cases where a given author—or I myself—have provided unofficial renditions of passages from Bazin that have not appeared in English before or that in our opinion have been questionably or anemically translated. An endnote should signal the situation, chapter to chapter.

This book was finalized at the moment of the death of Eric Rohmer, whose declining health had kept him from participating in the way he so wanted in the celebration of Bazin's fiftieth anniversary. Yet Rohmer was not sentimental; with him in mind, I dedicate this work not to the memory of Bazin, but to his future, and to the students who must (and will) encounter a vision of the world that is perpetually sharpened and refreshed through an open yet critical vision of cinema. Reading Bazin, one can only be improved; the same holds, I trust, for reading about him, at least with the intensity and imagination supplied by the contributors to *Opening Bazin*

Dudley Andrew
Thanksgiving, 2010.

Opening Bazin

PART ONE

Lineage

1

A Bazinian Half-Century

Thomas Elsaesser

André Bazin is taken by many to be the undisputed father of modern film studies, the classic whom we make our students read but also the classic to whom we return ourselves. My title alludes to the fifty years since the publication of the first collection of his essays, volume one of *Qu'est-ce que le cinéma?* But "The Bazinian Half-Century" alludes as well to Michel Foucault's notorious prediction that "perhaps one day this [i.e., the twentieth] century will be known as the Deleuzian century."[1] By suggesting that a more realistic estimation might be half this length, and, for our field, to give the honor to Bazin, I nonetheless want to acknowledge Deleuze's part—in addition to Serge Daney's tireless advocacy—in reigniting the discussion around the master's unexpected topicality. In the special Autumn 2007 issue of *Cinémas* titled "La théorie du cinéma – enfin en crise," Bazin, flanked by Roger Leenhardt and the *Cahiers du Cinéma* generation, is situated at the center of a renewal of film theory in the spirit of discovery and disclosure, terms Deleuze would endorse in opposition to aesthetic programs serving social constructivism or cultural studies.

This "finally in crisis" of film theory may sound odd to non-French ears, for when has film theory not been in crisis? In fact—if we think of Arnheim, Balazs, Kracauer, Bazin, Metz, Heath, Daney, Mulvey, and Deleuze—is not film theory the product of the different crises that the cinema has undergone, such as the coming of sound, the trauma of fascism, and the ubiquity of television, not to mention the crisis in the humanities occasioned by structuralism and deconstruction, as well as the crisis of patriarchy highlighted by feminism? Deleuze's theory of the "time-image" responds to the crisis of the "movement-image," when European cinema realized the impossibility after Auschwitz of telling stories or inhabiting a world, of aligning body and mind (perception, sensation, and action) in a coherent continuum. Perhaps film theory has always been a reflection on one or another "death of cinema" (the death of early cinema brought about by classical narrative in the '20s, the death of silent cinema by sound in the '30s, the death of the studio system by television in the '50s, the decay of cinephilia by the closure of neighborhood cinemas in the '70s, the death of projection by the video recorder in the '80s, the death of celluloid by digitization in the '90s). Every film theory may be a funeral as much as a birth announcement.

The present moment stands under the crisis-sign of the digital divide. In a graduate seminar at Yale University called "What Was Cinema," we adopted a set of simple maxims: rather than reading this "what was cinema" as a question, we imagined a full stop, acknowledging the so-called "death of cinema" debate but refusing to presume knowledge about what cinema actually was, or to predicate what it no longer is. The full stop allows for "cinema after cinema," for "cinema next to cinema," and indeed for cinema to redefine itself retrospectively and retroactively, by turning out to have been something slightly different from what we have thought it was. This interrogation of a seemingly entrenched medium takes inspiration from Bazin himself, who in reviewing the first volume of Georges Sadoul's monumental *Histoire générale du cinéma*, concluded that "every new development added to the cinema must, paradoxically, take it nearer and nearer to its origins. In short, cinema has not yet been invented!"[2] A fortiori, this must apply to cinema today: the efflorescence of early cinema studies occurring in parallel to developments in digital media are indeed bringing us closer to the medium's origins.

In the seminar, a second maxim followed directly from the first, namely that we reread Bazin not to ask "what would Bazin have said about the situation of the cinema today?" but "what *did* Bazin say about the situation of the cinema today," and using what vocabulary? So: banned from discussion was the word "digital" and the term often used in relation to Bazin but never used by him, "indexicality." Whether such a counterfactual approach is nothing more than an *exercise de style*, its didactic and heuristic value encourages one (a) to read Bazin more carefully, (b) to think in categories that may have pertinence beyond the present, and (c) to confirm that classics—and Bazin is nothing if not a classic—have to be reread and reinterpreted by every generation anew.

Extending the Range of "What Is Cinema"

Bazin is useful today because he can bridge the often fatal divide between photographic and post-photographic cinema simply by the fact that he did not know it existed. His categories were so well informed by classical philosophy and aesthetics that he makes us look beyond our narrow and local view of changes we take to be radical. At the same time, his key articles were written in a very specific historical context and against a background of often highly polemical debates. The famous "Ontology" essay, for instance, was first published in a volume entitled *Problèmes de la peinture* and therefore engages with painting: classic and modern, but also with baroque art (which Bazin didn't much like, calling it "convulsive catalepsy") and surrealism (which he did appreciate). He defines the cinema as painting's extension as well as its redemption, yet precisely not in terms of its heightened realism or mimesis but rather because of its alternative genealogy: the cinema's family relation with masks and moldings, with the Turin Shroud and the "taking of impressions." Much of recent art history in the spirit of Aby Warburg (from Hans Belting to Georges Didi-Huberman, from Michael Fried to Hal Foster) finds here its confirmation for a way of thinking differently about images in the post-photographic age, by reference to pre-Renaissance art, trying to go beyond debates about "representation" and elaborate an idea of bodily mimesis not trapped by the mirror-metaphor.

Bazin's double position—universalist thinker and local critic, with specific preferences and dislikes—has been used to attack him: one thinks of the polemics in *Cahiers'* rival journal *Positif*, by Robert Benayoun or Gerard Gozlan, or subsequently by critics of the realism-effect, such as Jean-Louis Comolli or Colin MacCabe. Yet he is also enlisted on the side of the argument that would see the post-photographic cinema as not being cinema at all. By endorsing the "death of cinema" one not only mourns its loss but opens the way for the cinema to finally have a history, with a beginning, a middle, and an end, whereupon one can elaborate the proper methodology for its study, work on its canon, and establish an agreed-upon corpus of its auteurs and masterpieces.

Bazin's growing importance is due, however, to the very opposite of the need for closure. Sensing that cinema would change forever our idea of time, linearity, and temporal succession, he extends what cinema is by making us reconsider what it was, revisiting its past so as to open once more this past's own future, rather than foreclose it, while interpreting the present in a way that not only links it to the past but also retroactively contributes to it. As T. S. Eliot argued in "Tradition and the Individual Talent" (1919), the introduction of a new work or a new way of thinking not only changes the future but also the past, because the new work illuminates elements and establishes connections neither noted nor recognized before. For instance, and decisively, with a brilliant stroke Bazin put to rest the long debate about whether the cinema could be an art, since it was based on mechanical reproduction. Arguing against the dominant view, held by Eisenstein, Arnheim, and others ("the formalists"), that for the cinema to be art, there had to be human intentionality and intervention, Bazin famously insists on mechanical reproduction as the key aspect of photographically based film: "For the first time an image of the world is formed automatically, without the creative intervention of man. . . . All the arts are based on the presence of man, only photography derives an advantage from his absence."[3] In the context of a debate that had raged for some twenty years, this was a truly counterintuitive claim, its revolutionary impact usually mitigated by being attributed to his Catholicism. But from today's perspective—where the question "is cinema art?" no longer exercises us in quite the same way—it is an insight that still points forward and reverberates backward. For instance, we usually cite Marey in one breath with Eadweard Muybridge as the inventors of chronophotography and thus as precursors of the cinematic moving image. But Bazin sets Marey and Muybridge at opposite sides. Marey—who knew Henri Bergson, as they both had positions at the Collège de France—had little to do with painting or still photography, which were Muybridge's reference points. Instead, he concentrated on tracking, tracing, and recording movement that emanates from both sentient and natural phenomena: he was as interested in the possibility of recording the shapes of smoke as he was in the movement of humans, as interested in the vibrations of bees' wings as he was in recording blood-pressure, heartbeat, pulse, breath.

Marey's use of the cinematograph, the oscillograph, x-rays, and other evolving technologies of vision aimed at natural or man-made phenomena that previously could not be recorded, stored, or imaged. One might say that he continued the original promise of photography, that of being "the pencil of nature," working without the intervention of the human will or agency. Thanks to the moving image, apparently contingent phenomena could now be visualized, and thereby reveal hitherto undiscovered patterns, their regularities and temporalities: "Photography affects us like a phenomenon in nature, like a flower or a snowflake." Making Marey one of Bazin's predecessors suggests that among his successors are not only Daney and Deleuze, but also Friedrich Kittler and Mary Ann Doane, the latter trying to understand the relation between the inscription and storage of audiovisual data—their registration and legibility for the human eye and ear—in a nonreductive manner, and thereby conceiving of the index and the materiality of the imprint in ways that do not confine them to the special case of photography.

Bazin, in short, can be fruitfully understood to stand at the intersection of several geneal-
ogies of the moving image; helpful for the difference between "cinema" and "film," between
fiction and documentary, he also illuminates other aspects of contemporary visual culture. I
want to outline three intersecting lines that bring us effectively to three Bazins: Bazin the
media-archaeologist ("the delay of cinema"/"the cinema is yet to be invented"), Bazin the aes-
thetician (not the "naïve realist" but the "sophisticated illusionist"), and Bazin the philosopher
of cinema (not the misguided epistemologist, dependent on the "indexicality" of the photographic image).

Bazin as Media-Archaeologist

In "The Myth of Total Cinema," Bazin provides a surprisingly relevant revisionist program and
research agenda. There he demonstrates the impossibility of film history without a history of
other entertainment industries and other moving image practices, exactly as thematized by
recent scholars of early cinema and of its conditions and spaces of reception. Paying due attention to the different media technologies, without attributing to them determining influence, he
carefully balances the idealist vision of cinema as the "fulfillment of mankind's age old dream"
against the contingencies surrounding the inventions of the technologies necessary to bring
about the dream. He mentions the still insufficiently understood "delay" in the implementation
of cinema, the arbitrariness of its eventual definition, as well as the gap between the various
pioneers' goals and the consequences of their labors. Thus he implicitly shows how an archaeo-
logical approach might supplement (if not altogether supersede) what until now we have
understood by film history. In fact, he positions himself not far from those who today argue
that in the competition among media, the eventual victory of cinema or the survival of its apparatus is not a foregone conclusion. Daney has pointed out that Bazin was perfectly capable of
thinking about the "disappearance" of cinema, in the sense of its apparatic contingency, seeing
this not as a death but as an ongoing transformation or consummation of a way of seeing and—
even more so—of being in the world.[4]

Daney's idea of the cinema as "the skin of history" also comments interestingly on Bazin's
remarkably dialectical understanding of the relation between realism, imagination, and illusionism. Consider the statement ". . . cinematic reality could not do without . . . documentary
reality, but if it is to become a truth of the imagination, it must die and be born again of reality
itself."[5] Depending on the meaning we give to each occurrence of the term "reality," the cinema
appears as a transformational agent that either intervenes in a process of change and renewal
through self-effacement, or constitutes an act of appropriation involving the destruction of
what you wish to preserve: a commonly observed fate of "documentary reality." Bazin may not
draw this ultimate conclusion, but the passage shows him anything but a naïve realist, while
much points to the sophisticated advocate of illusionism, concerned with reality and illusion,
truth and belief as mutually interdependent rather than opposed categories. Rereading the
famous article on De Sica's *Bicycle Thieves* (1948), one notices once more how complex and
nuanced Bazin's views on realism actually are; not only does he repeatedly insist that "realism in
art can only be achieved in one way—through artifice,"[6] but he imagines a kind of self-abolition
of cinema in the dialectic between "spectacle" and "event," whose overcoming—rightly or
wrongly—he associates with De Sica's film: "No more actors, no more story, no more sets,

which is to say that in the perfect aesthetic illusion of reality, there is no more cinema."[7] This self-abolition can be read against the neorealist credo it here supports, for it envisages the possibility of artifice taking on a life of its own. When, in "A Note on *Umberto D.*," Bazin suggests enigmatically that "the outside world is reduced to being an accessory to . . . pure action, which is sufficient to itself in the same way that algae deprived of air produce the oxygen they need,"[8] the medium is no longer measured against some a priori "reality" but has the density, agency, and resistance of life itself. But this means, conversely, that the cinema may disappear precisely because, complexly animated and ubiquitous, the cinematic way of seeing and being in the world—its way of picturing the self, its logics of the visible and its narratives of conflict, resolution, and redemption—no longer need actors, plots, or sets, in order to be experienced as our lived reality's signifier of authenticity and "truth." Or as Jean-Luc Nancy would say: "the lie of the image is the truth of our world."[9]

This reading of Bazin differs from that of Daney, who in his early essay on his forebear cites the same passage: "Sometimes [Bazin] declares the limit has been reached: 'no more actors, no more story, no more mise-en-scène, that is to say finally the perfect aesthetic illusion of reality: no more cinema.' Whoever passes through the screen and meets reality on the other side has gone beyond *jouissance*. If he makes it back (but in what state? obsessional for sure) and if he is still speaking, it will be to talk at length about what he has missed the most: the prohibited."[10] In other words, Daney, ever the *ciné-fils*, insists on the cinema's alterity and transgressiveness vis-à-vis contemporary visual culture, but he is not entirely sure if he has Bazin's support.

Bazin and "Indexicality"

Having redefined the reality-status or "ontology" of the image at the outset of his career with two distinct terms—"trace" and "imprint," rather than truth and likeness—Bazin could go on to provide a highly differentiated discussion of specific films and genres, including those of the fantastic and the "marvelous." Take his essay on *Crin blanc* (*White Mane*, 1952) and *Le Ballon rouge* (*The Red Balloon*, 1956) by Albert Lamorisse. For Bazin, the fact that Lamorisse had to use hundreds of red balloons and six different horses to "play" the single object/animal in no way diminishes the realism of these films, for their magical effects succeed because staging and editing give the flow of images a unique "spatial density"—Bazin's very modern term for the cinema's unique form of realism. Shuttling between "documentary" and "fiction," but nonetheless making both a condition of their "truth," these films "owe everything to the cinema [the respect for the unity of space], precisely because they owe nothing to the cinema. . . . If the film is to fulfill itself aesthetically, we are to believe in the reality of what is happening while knowing it to be tricked. . . . The screen reflects the ebb and flow of our imagination, which feeds on a reality for which it plans to substitute. Correspondingly, what is imaginary on the screen must have the spatial density of something real."[11] This passage shows Bazin perfectly capable of defining an "ontology" without restricting it to first-level indexicality; that is, "this space and place" and "this moment in time" can serve as a "substitute."

Although based on photography, Bazin's ontology of cinematic realism is above all a theory about the inscription and storage of time, rather than being dependent on what we usually understand by image, namely mimesis and representation. "Spatial density," while exemplified in Bazin by the long take and depth of field, is not identical with these stylistic options, nor inherently more "natural" or "ontologically grounded," because "spatial density" is always a result of artifice, selection, and design (i.e., mise- en-scène), or alternatively montage of one sort or another. His famous example of the lioness and the child together in the same shot in *Where No Vultures Fly* (1951) insists that realism resides in spatial homogeneity, which in this instance happens to be the opposite of montage. On the other hand, spatial homogeneity and montage are not per se incompatible, as for instance proven in Harun Farocki's *Images of the World and Inscription of War* (1988) or *Schnittselle/Interface* (1995). Likewise, grainy video footage can have spatial density, and so does the high-definition digital image of the opening shot of Michael Haneke's *Caché* (2005), even though it plunges us into an ontological void when we realize that it is in fact a "recording" and not given in "real- time" (and that the footage of the videotape must have been produced "digitally").

Bazin's concerns with time, the interval, and the series play into the debate, still ongoing, between photography and the cinema, stillness and movement, as well as absence and presence. First, he famously distinguished the cinema from photography by arguing that the latter captures "change mummified"; later, in his essay on "Theater and Cinema" he elaborated: "The cinema does something [more] strangely paradoxical [than the photograph]. It makes a molding of the object as it exists in time, and furthermore, makes an imprint of the duration of an object. . . . Hence it is no longer as certain as it was that there is no middle stage between presence and absence. It is likewise at the ontological level that the effectiveness of the cinema has its source. It is false to say that the screen is incapable of putting us 'in the presence' of the actor. It does so in the same way as a mirror—but it is a mirror with a delayed reflection, the tin foil of which retains the image."[12] Most arguments about indexicality (and its loss in digital processes) are fixated on space, not considering the way a temporal index may apply to nonphotographic technical media, as Bazin implies here. Think how important the time-coding of images has become today, in the "real-time" surveillance of human beings (in traffic, train stations, shopping malls), and in the incessant monitoring of nonhuman movements (weather, stock prices, data traffic).

Bazin and Philosophy

Bazin can be considered the alpha and omega of modern film theory, because he stands at its beginning, while he may well preside over its (temporary) end, perhaps even over its rebirth. One could describe this history as the circular movement that has led film theory since 1945 from a focus on "aesthetics" to "anthropology," then from "anthropology" to "psychology" and "ideology," before returning to "aesthetics" at the beginning of the 1990s. A more philosophical vocabulary would suggest this to be a movement from "ontology" to "epistemology" and back to a redefined "ontology."

Bazin stands at the beginning, because he subtly translated the perennial prewar question: "if the cinema is art, what are its uniquely defining characteristics?" into an anthropological inquiry, without foreclosing aesthetic and philosophical dimensions. His "Ontology" essay shifted the terms of the debate as is evident in the work of key figures of the first generation of postwar theorists. The most prominent of these, Edgar Morin, followed Bazin's line of thought in *Cinema or the Imaginary Man* (*Le cinéma ou l'homme imaginaire*, 1956), but in giving a broadly conceived account of cinema in civilization, he also differed from him in the kind of anthropology he appealed to. For Morin this medium is a product of toolmaking, and thus a prosthetic extension of the human senses, providing evolutionary advantages entailed by the disembodied eye in voyages of discovery and conquest; while for Bazin the cinema offers protection against and preservation from death and material decay, aligning it with ancient burial customs, embalming, plaster molds, death masks, and then with portraiture of the high and mighty as well as the family albums of ordinary people. But Morin and Bazin complement each other in indicating the role of cinema as mirror and double, fundamental to the formation and the crises of consciousness and self-reflexivity, while aiding mankind's ambiguous quest for self-creation and self-perfection.

Because of its obsession with death, photographically based theories of the cinema in the wake of Bazin (and Benjamin) have tended to focus on memory, melancholia, and mourning, where the cinema is always already an art of loss and precarious recovery, and where cinephilia compensates as that anxious love of the moment, of transient and evanescent pleasures, tinged with nostalgia and regret, ready to cast itself in a retrospective mode. Such a theory of the cinema is usually called "ontological" because of the title of Bazin's famous essay, but Bazin was neither melancholic nor dystopic with respect to the present state of the world. The most striking characteristic of his anthropological-ontological vision is that it is anti-mimetic, whereas Morin's sociological, more evolutionary approach could be called mimetic, in the sense of "training" survival skills.

Thus, when he discusses Egyptian mummies, the Shroud of Turin, and the memorializing function of early photographs, Bazin stands right in the line of current art history which has moved from connoisseurship and canon-formation to what Hans Belting calls "image-anthropology," conceived as coming to the "end of art-history," while incorporating photography, the cinema, video, and installation art. Regardless of whether this is a friendly or hostile takeover of the cinema by the museum and an enlarged art history, the paradoxes of such rescue operations would have pleased Bazin, and it is clearly a debate he could join easily and effectively. In the same vein, Bazin's anthropological perspective can lead to contemporary debates on modernity, perception, and visuality, like those associated with Walter Benjamin and Siegfried Kracauer, and with disciples of Foucault, such as Jonathan Crary. He also would have had much to contribute to the new phenomenology, evident in titles and terms like "the skin of film," "tactility," the "haptic," and "embodied vision."

Because we have tended to prefer the term "indexicality" to "ontology," Bazin's ontology-driven anthropology made his transit to our era a difficult passage. Indeed, just after his death, his film theory was denounced at *Positif* as "bad ontology," and as "Catholic." Then he came massively under assault by the second generation of film theorists (Christian Metz, Jean-Louis Comolli, Jean-Louis Baudry in France; Peter Wollen, Steven Heath, Laura Mulvey in Britain), whose apparatus theory and psychoanalysis amounted to an epistemology, not an ontology of the cinema. Reality, knowledge, and even subjectivity were taken as "effects" based on miscognition. As a consequence, Bazin's realism was taken as naively pertaining to truth-claims, announcing a correspondence between what was on the screen and what was in the world, clearly a fallacious or "ideological" position. However, Bazin, as we have seen, had always maintained a more nuanced, aesthetic view, arguing that realism is a function of artifice, and that realism comes by way of belief. This is a classically aesthetic stance, which can be linked to post-Kantian aesthetics of "play" and "make-believe" on one side and to an aesthetically grounded pragmatism on the other; in any case Bazin does not seem to have held to straight epistemic realism. His thinking is unique, because in it the anthropological perspective of the social historian is not severed from the aesthetic value judgment of the critic; moreover, his philosophical reflection on the ontology of the photographic image never denies the cinema's epistemological dimension. Recall the final sentence of the "Ontology" essay: "On the other hand, of course, the cinema is also a language."[13] In "The Evolution of the Language of Cinema," language is understood as a practice governed by rules and conventions, where a stylistic "grammar" serves specific purposes: in other words, Bazin accommodates both an argument in favor of "the content of the form" and one amenable to a constructivist view of verisimilitude ("realism in the arts can only be achieved one way—through artifice").

Paradoxically, when in the 1970s the epistemological view of cinema prevailed, the denunciation of Bazin's "realist" ideology as an un-deconstructed "subject-effect" actually amounted less to a break with Bazin than to a manifestation of a disenchanted bazinism. Wishing the cinema to provide "objective" knowledge, the new generation was disappointed that it did not and could not. Psycho-semiotics, apparatus theory, and feminism all subscribed to a Cartesian division of *res cogitans* and *res extensa*—of subject divided from object—however much this Cartesianism may have been inverted to become skeptical and agnostic, sometimes to the point of nihilism. Inverting Bazin's premises, epistemic film theory depended on balancing two sets of assumptions: first, that there is a real world we strive to know through vision, and second, that there is the film-world that serves our demand for knowledge. When brought together, these assumptions resulted in a third: that knowledge can and does change the world, and thus that the cinema can, and indeed should, change the world.

It is this package of implicit assumptions (or "fallacies") that American cognitivists have attacked in "screen theory" or "apparatus theory," arguing that it rested on (false) epistemological premises, notably about the equation of seeing and knowing, together with its mirror inversion in seeing as miscognition. Noël Carroll, David Bordwell, Richard Allen and Murray Smith have variously delegitimized these concepts of illusionism and miscognition as creating false epistemological problems around the nature of perception, and its relation to consciousness and truth.

The philosophical core of their objection revolves around the kind of "seeing" that cinematic perception involves. Apparatus theory treats the spectator-screen relationship as if it were based on a perceptual "illusion" (by suggesting that objects which move on the screen are really there) which in turn assumes that vision is always transitive, in other words, that it is a matter of "seeing something," when it could just as well be aspect seeing, or "seeing-as" (in Wittgenstein's terminology). At the same time, cognitivists and analytical philosophers question the way apparatus theory unwittingly reinforces (bourgeois) ideology's disembodied, decontextualized, dematerialized version of watching movies, while critiquing (with its call for "anti-illusionism") mainstream cinema for producing such alienated, commodified forms of human perception. Why, they ask, should perception, recognition, and apprehension of objects, people, or places in the moving image involve deception or the suspension of disbelief?[14]

Indirect—and as it turned out, unwelcome—support for this cognitivist attack on Grand Theory's epistemology came from a more influential source in the development of film theory,

Gilles Deleuze. Sweeping aside altogether the epistemological questions surrounding the image, the subject, language, and knowledge, Deleuze put ontology back on the agenda. Rather than regarding cinema as a (deceptive) epistemological practice that opposes true/false, appearance/being, body/spirit, Deleuze imagined cinema to be something not in opposition to life but a part of life, open to the Bergsonian universe of energy and process, of becoming, of intensities.

After Deleuze, cinema was no longer about meaning-making, about subjectification, or about the "representation of . . ."; it was now about movement as the manifestation of "life," and about "time" (or its suspension) as the medium in which humans experience life. The Bazinian phrase, "[the cinema] makes a molding of the object as it exists in time,"[15] now sounds remarkably Deleuzian, because in the latter's version the cinema had best be regarded as a unique amalgam of mind *and* matter, beyond any subject-object division. For Deleuze and perhaps for Bazin, this amalgam, like a Spinozist "substance," fills the world, reorganizing the abstract and the concrete, the animate and the inanimate, the actual and the virtual, the general and the particular, necessitating a new classification of what exists, that is to say, a new ontology.

Stanley Cavell would probably nod in agreement, since he has himself, in *The World Viewed: Reflections on the Ontology of Film* (1971), identified the essence of the cinematic as a form of unseeing or perceptive-attentive seeing, whereby films themselves teach us how to look at them and how to think about them. Precisely because the cinema is a technical reproduction, people and things in the cinema are not represented, but present-as-de-presented, and therefore touching us only insofar as we allow ourselves to be equally present in a mode of being other than our usual meaning-making, goal-pursuing selves. As William Rothman and Marian Keene have summed up Cavell's film-ontology: "Coming to know what films are is inseparable from acquiring self-knowledge."[16] Deleuze and Cavell, as well as Jean-Luc Nancy and Giorgio Agamben, intimate that the cinema's ontology is one of presence and appearance, by which reality discloses itself to those who have learned to "look," in the sense of remaining open toward letting something enter before needing to "understand." As thinkers of an always already mediated world, they hold out the prospect of a post-epistemological ontology of the cinema. This seems a philosophically appropriate way of arguing that the cinema is amenable to a critique in terms of belief and trust more than in terms of truth and falsehood or of reality and its simulacrum/manipulation.[17]

We have come full circle. If Bazin's *Qu'est-ce que le cinéma?* can no longer be construed as a question of epistemology, it becomes once more a question of ontology, in the sense of "what cinema is," or even: "cinema is." This in turn implies that we do not have to be "in the cinema" in order to be (i.e., to feel, see, believe, and live) "in the (world of) cinema." Against the background of such an assumption, the question of knowing and of knowledge, of evidence and of meaning (i.e., the question of an epistemology of the cinema), may be posed anew, this time beyond radical skepticism and after constructivism. Here, too, Bazin can come to the rescue, since his belief that the cinema has yet to be invented must mean today that the cinema—neither as reality's copy nor its illusory opposite, but its ever-present potential—always already "knew" what it knew, as well as what it could not have "known." Put differently, and to repeat in conclusion: it is not a matter of asking what Bazin might have said about the new media but what he did say about the new media. Enough reason, then, to read him again, and to conclude that the Bazinian half-century is only just beginning.

Notes

1. Michel Foucault, *Dits et Écrits*, 1954–1988, vol 2 (Paris: Gallimard, 1994), 276.

2. André Bazin, "The Myth of Total Cinema," in *What Is Cinema?* vol. 1, trans. Hugh Gray (Berkeley: University of California Press, 1967), 21.

3. Bazin, "The Ontology of the Photographic Image," in *What Is Cinema?* vol. 1, 13.

4. "For Bazin, the horizon of cinema's history is cinema's disappearance. Until then, this history is indistinguishable from that of a small difference that is the object of a constant negation: I know (that the image is not real) but all the same . . . [the formula for fetishism and disavowal]. With each technical change, the transparency grows, the difference seems to get smaller, the celluloid becomes the skin of History and the screen a window open to the world." Serge Daney, "The Screen of Fantasy (Bazin and Animals)," in *Rites of Realism: Essays on Corporeal Cinema*, ed. Ivone Margulies, trans. Mark A. Cohen (Durham, NC: Duke University Press, 2002), 34.

5. Bazin, "The Virtues and Limitations of Montage," in *What Is Cinema?* vol. 1, 47.

6. Bazin, "An Aesthetic of Reality: Cinematic Realism and the Italian School of the Liberation," in *What Is Cinema?* vol. 2 (Berkeley: University of California Press, 1971), 26.

7. Bazin, "Bicycle Thief," in *What Is Cinema?* vol. 2, 60.

8. Bazin, "De Sica: Metteur en Scène," in *What Is Cinema?* vol. 2, 77.

9. Jean-Luc Nancy, "After Tragedy," a lecture in honor of Philippe Lacoue-Labarthe, at the New School University, April 10, 2008.

10. Serge Daney, "The Screen of Fantasy (Bazin and Animals)," 34.

11. Bazin, "The Virtues and Limitations of Montage," in *What Is Cinema?* vol. 1, 46–48.

12. Bazin, "Theater and Cinema—Part Two," in *What Is Cinema?* vol. 1, 97

13. Bazin, "The Ontology of the Photographic Image," 16.

14. Noel Carroll, *Mystifying Movies: Fads and Fallacies in Contemporary Film Theory* (New York: Columbia University Press, 1988), 89ff.

15. Bazin, "Theater and Cinema—Part Two," in *What Is Cinema?* vol. 1, 97.

16. William Rothman and Marian Keane, Reading Cavell's *The World Viewed* (Detroit, MI: Wayne State University Press, 2000), 18.

17. If the epistemological question in the humanities during the 1970s and 1980s was above all prompted by the negative assumption about the impossibility of secure knowledge and thus was the expression of a radical skepticism, where every ontology and every "order of things" was owed to or based on a historically, ideologically, or technologically determined "episteme," then one might have to reverse Foucault's archaeology of knowledge and argue that every epistemology, every form of knowledge today, already presupposes mediated reality as "evidence" and as "given." Conversely, if cinema is our way of being on the way to a new ontology, then of course this would be the best proof that the cinema is also our episteme, in Foucault's sense, and that the new ontology of the cinema would define our way of knowing and of not knowing the world.

2

Cinema Across Fault Lines

Bazin and the French School of Geography

Ludovic Cortade

Before he became a cinephile and a film critic in the 1940s, André Bazin concentrated on his studies to be a teacher. He later recalled his stay at the École normale d'instituteurs in La Rochelle between 1934 and 1937 in these terms: "My school life, my tastes, the films we could see in the provinces, did not yet incline me towards a passion or serious reflection on cinema."[1] Hence the role of his formative years in shaping his conception of cinema cannot be overestimated. Besides, in the foreword he composed in 1958 for *Qu'est-ce que le cinéma?* Bazin acknowledges the importance of two disciplines central to his education, saying that his texts do not claim to "offer an exhaustive geography and geology of cinema."[2] Based on the articles he wrote between 1941 and 1958, and three sources of archives documenting his formative years, I aim to determine the influence of the French school of geography on Bazin's conception of cinema. Three aspects are discussed: the cartographic origins of the ontological ambiguity of reality, the geology of universalism, and the role of map analysis in the shaping of Bazin's methodology of film criticism.[3]

Cartography, Ontology, and Language

Pierre Teilhard de Chardin was an important influence on Bazin's interest in geology, especially in 1938 and during the Occupation.[4] However, Bazin's practical background in geology came from the strong role geography played in his curriculum during his formative years: between 1934 and 1941, maps, photographs, and possibly pedagogical short films on French landscapes were the first kinds of images Bazin analyzed, even before he began to analyze films as a critic. In July 1934, Bazin passed the *Brevet élémentaire* degree granting him access to the École normale d'instituteurs of La Rochelle where he studied a wide range of disciplines until 1937: history, geography, psychology, physics, natural sciences, mathematics, literature, orthography, drawing, music, sport, sociology, English, and ethics.[5] In contrast to the more specialized education that the young men of the elite received in French universities, the École normale d'instituteurs emphasized both pedagogy and the links between disciplines, two characteristics Bazin exemplified when he later animated ciné-clubs. He passed the *Brevet supérieur* in 1937, enabling him to teach in elementary schools [figure 2.1]. Based on his achievements and the

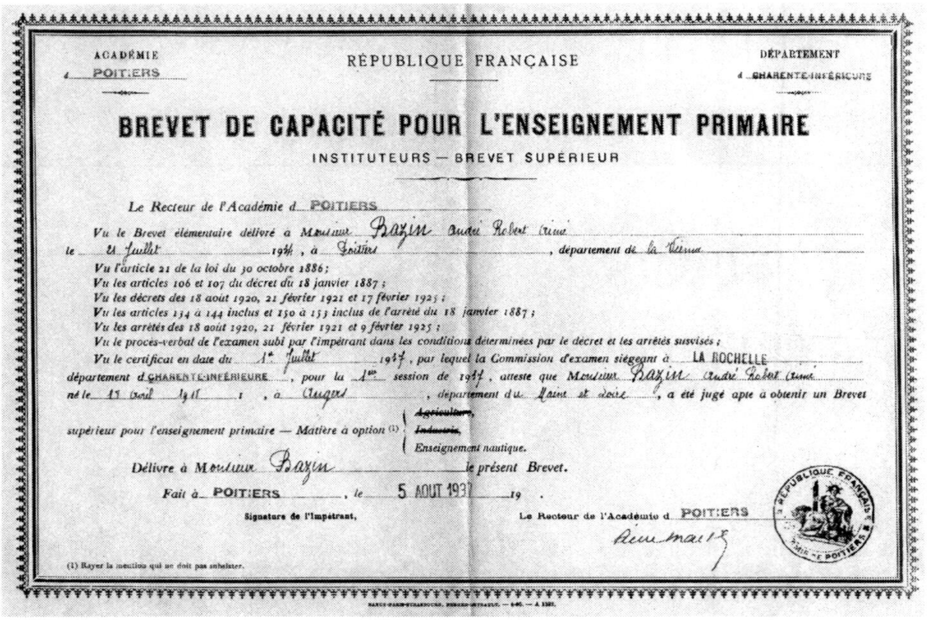

FIGURE 2.1: Bazin's diploma (Archives départementales de la Charente-Maritime, La Rochelle, France;
1 T 1958)

appreciation of the director of the École normale d'institueurs of La Rochelle, he was eligible to apply for a so-called "fourth year," to prepare for the prestigious and highly competitive École normale supérieure of Saint-Cloud, an opportunity Bazin would not miss.[6] The preparation Bazin received in Versailles in 1937 and 1938 was significantly more intense than what he had received in La Rochelle.[7] A decree published in the *Journal officiel* of the French Republic in fall 1937 lists the disciplines and the topics that candidates had to study to be admitted to Saint-Cloud, including literature (six hours a week), history and geography (five hours), philosophy (two hours) and a foreign language (two hours).[8] In contrast to the requirements at the more traditional and famous École normale superieur-Rue d'Ulm, the exam in geography was compulsory at Saint-Cloud. The École normale supérieure of Saint-Cloud was created only a few years after France's humiliation in the Franco-Prussian War, thus fostering a sense of national identity among the *normaliens* (in fact the school's site lies on the former location of one of Napoleon III's palaces, destroyed by Prussia in 1870). During the 1938 school year, candidates were expected to study French regional geography, colonial geography, and physical geography, particularly mountains and rivers [figure 2.2]. In addition, the library register for the École normale of Versailles testifies to the importance of the books by Paul Vidal de la Blache, the founding father of the French school of geography, and his disciple Emmanuel de Martonne, including a significant corpus of maps.[9] Indeed, the instructions published in the *Journal officiel* specify that the oral part of the exam would include map analysis: "In the cases where the candidates' oral exams must specifically be approached using one of the maps shown below, you can, in preparation, draw inspiration from the examples provided by the manuals of the *Geographic Interpretation of Cartography*"[10] [figure 2.3].

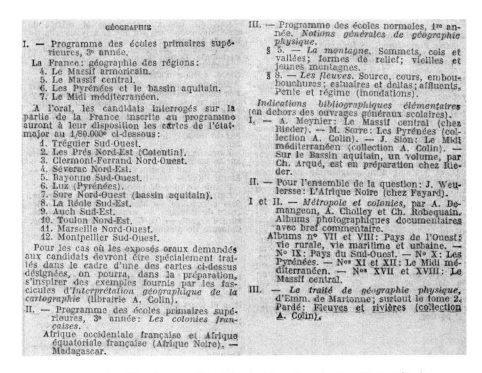

FIGURE 2.2: Geography syllabus. Journal officiel de la République Française, Sept. 29, 1937 (Archives départementales des Yvelines, Versailles, France, 37T 373)

Bazin's overall performance at the selective entrance examinations of Saint-Cloud was outstanding: of the 159 candidates who hailed from the very best Écoles normales across the country, Bazin ranked ninth, obtaining his best grades in literature and geography; he ranked second on the written exam and third on the oral exam in geography, respectively obtaining 13/20 and 14/20 [figure 2.4]. Though his studies were interrupted by the outbreak of the Second World War, the impact of geography on Bazin at Saint-Cloud was twofold: he took the courses of Philippe Arbos, a specialist of the Massif Central region and a disciple of Raoul Blanchard, who had been Vidal de la Blache's student; he was exposed to the rising influence of the École des annales and the figures of Lucien Febvre and Marc Bloch in his history classes. Arbos' former classmate at the École normale supérieure (Rue d'Ulm), Bloch became a professor at Saint-Cloud a few months before Bazin was admitted in the summer of 1938.[11] The influence of the French school of geography on the École des annales cannot be overestimated: maps, landscape analysis, and aerial photographs were extensively used by the cofounders of the École des annales, and Febvre's *A Geographical Introduction to History* [*La Terre et l'évolution humaine*] is an homage to Vidal's geography.[12]

In addition to maps, which have always served as the crux of geography teaching, photographs and films were extensively used at the Écoles normales. Vidal de la Blache's *Tableau géographique de la France* was republished in an illustrated edition in 1908 under the title *La France: tableau géographique* [figure 2.5], a book containing 245 photographs and 58 maps, and it became a staple of geography instruction, along with the volume of photographs edited in

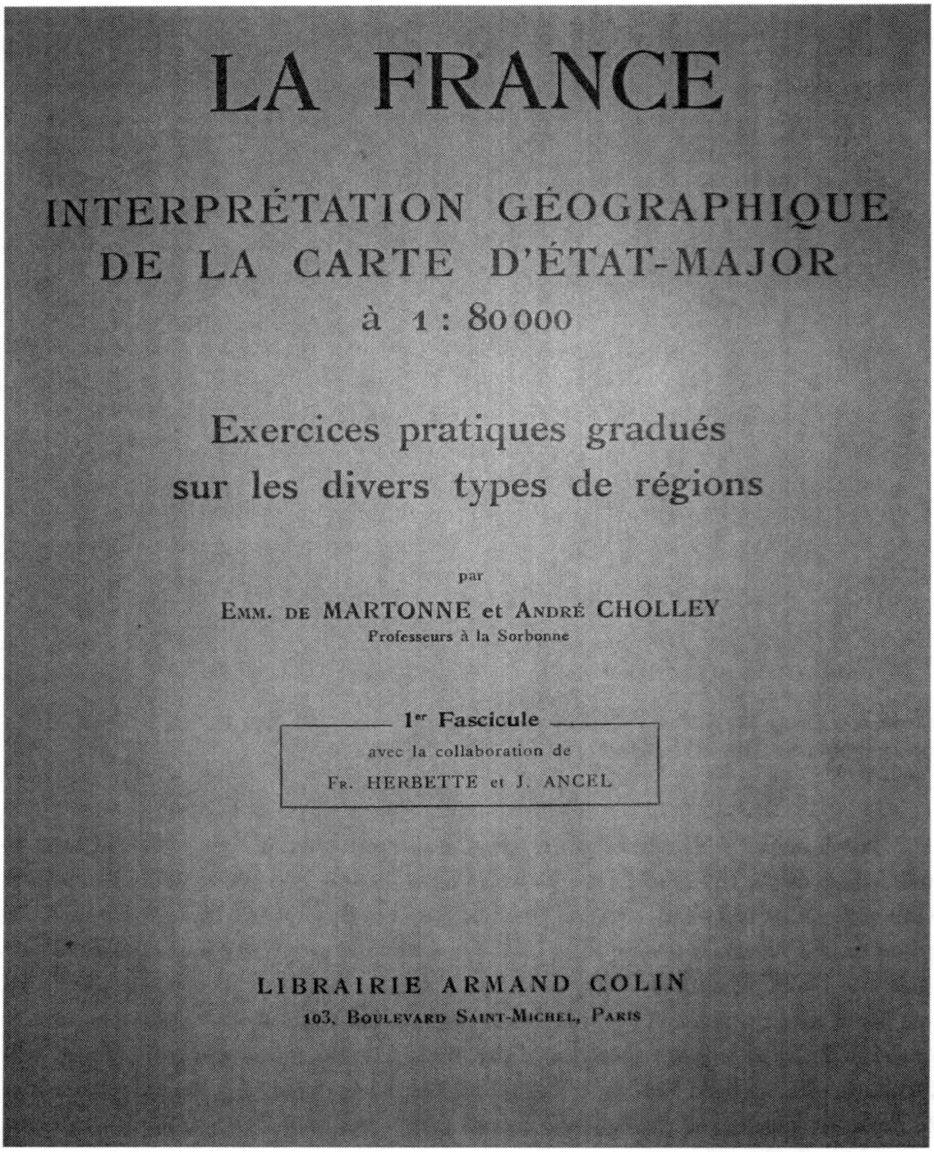

LA FRANCE

INTERPRÉTATION GÉOGRAPHIQUE
DE LA CARTE D'ÉTAT-MAJOR
à 1 : 80 000

Exercices pratiques gradués
sur les divers types de régions

par

EMM. DE MARTONNE et ANDRÉ CHOLLEY
Professeurs à la Sorbonne

1ᵉʳ Fascicule
avec la collaboration de
FR. HERBETTE et J. ANCEL

LIBRAIRIE ARMAND COLIN
103, BOULEVARD SAINT-MICHEL, PARIS

FIGURE 2.3: Emmanuel de Martonne, André Cholley, *La France, interprétation géographique de la carte d'état-major à 1:80 000*. Paris: Librairie Armand Colin, 1934 (courtesy Armand Colin Editeur)

1933 by A. Demangeon, A. Cholley, and Ch. Robequain: *Métropole et colonies*. Moreover, educational films were widely used in France in the 1930s, in the wake of the founding of the Office Cinématographique d'Enseignement et d'Education de l'Académie de Paris in 1928, the Institut International du Cinématographe Educatif under the auspices of the Society of Nations in the same year, the Fédération Nationale des Offices du Cinéma Educateur by laïcist activist Gustave Cauvin in 1929, and the Union Française des Offices du Cinéma Educateur Laïque (UFOCEL) in 1933. Given the educational mission assigned to cinema in France in the 1930s,

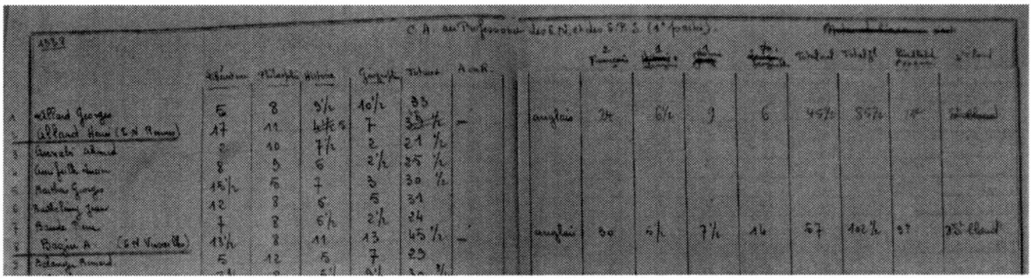

FIGURE 2.4: Bazin's grades at the selective entrance examination of the Ecole Normale Supérieure of Saint-Cloud, 1938 session (Archives nationales, Fontainebleau, France, versement 20000384 Art. 9)

it is very likely that Bazin was exposed to pedagogical documentary films during his school years. For instance, Paul-Emile Benuraud, a Rochefort-based elementary school teacher who created the Office d'Enseignement Cinématographique du Centre-Ouest, might well have provided the École normale in La Rochelle with films, as one of the 300 institutions in the Charentes and Poitou regions in the 1930s, until he was sacked by the Vichy regime.[13] Moreover, the École normale of Versailles purchased its first projector in 1919 from Gaumont and would rent pedagogical films from varied institutions including the Musée pédagogique in 1921 (a brochure found in the archives lists 269 titles of pedagogical films in geography, the majority of which focused on French landscapes), the Office cinématographique d'enseignement et d'éducation (a document indicates 180 films on geography) and the Touring-Club de France (fifty "pellicules-ciné" on French landscapes and the colonies were lent to the École normale of Versailles).[14] Lastly, Bazin was undoubtedly aware of Albert Kahn's amazing Archives de la Planète, since Catholic geographer Jean Brunhes, who was an outreach person at the archives, regularly delivered talks on geography to the young *normaliens* of Saint-Cloud until his death in 1930.[15]

The solid background Bazin obtained in geography, geology, and cartography between 1934 and 1941 helped establish the key problematic of his 1945 "Ontology of the Photographic Image": the preservation of an essence through an image in which man plays no role. In this respect, it should be stressed that Bazin was exposed to a particular type of "scientific" map, for Vidal de la Blache, along with the development of French cartography at the end of the nineteenth century, met the goals and the strategic needs of the French army by providing accurate and detailed cartographic descriptions of space, then referred to as *cartes d'état-major*. Maps consequently brought a significant contribution to the advent of the notion of objectivity in French visual culture, for maps constitute a type of image deprived of perspective, the "original sin of Western painting," as Bazin put it.[16] Moreover, Bazin's background in geography and geology made him understand that "the map is a visible inscription of an essence" as Louis Marin later put it, an assumption which echoes Bazin's conception of the work of art: "to save Being by means of appearances." Drawing on the *Logique de Port-Royal*, Marin points out that "we say without pretension or preparation that a portrait of Caesar is Caesar, and that a map of Italy is Italy."[17] Interestingly, Bazin also discusses the preservation of the essence of power through the portrait of the king: "Louis XIV did not have himself embalmed. He was content to survive in his portrait by Le Brun."[18] It is thus not surprising that Bazin later emphasized the intersection of maps and cinema, since both offer an accurate and objective

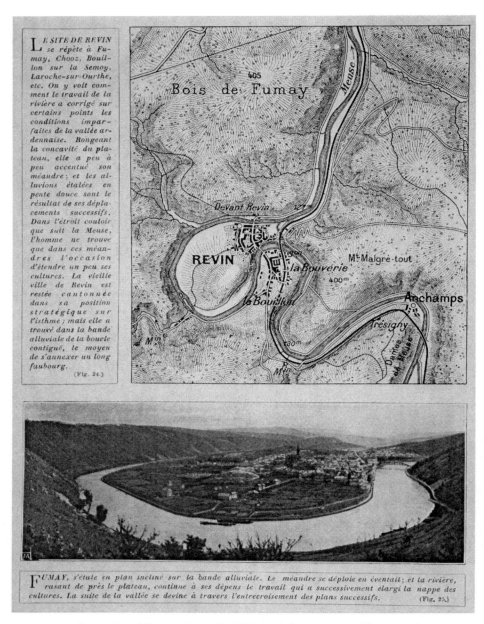

record of reality: the director is "an official witness, so to speak, along with the meteorologist
or geologist."[19]

Geography is palpable not only in Bazin's ontology but also in his conception of the
language of cinema. The objectivity of the *carte d'état-major* paved the way for a conception of
the photographic image whose ambiguity derives from depth of field and the tension between
immobility and movement, as exemplified in his analysis of George Marshall's death in Wyler's

The Little Foxes (1941) and the so-called "kitchen sequence" in Orson Welles' *The Magnificent Ambersons* (1942). He notes:

> The entire dramatic interest resides . . . in the film's immobility. . . . The entire scene turns around her, but her dreadful immobility only comes truly to the fore with Marshall's two exits from the frame, first in the foreground to the right and later in the background to the left. Rather than following his lateral movements, which would have been the natural tendency of any less intelligent observer, the camera remains imperturbably stationary. . . . Nothing could have heightened the dramatic impact of this scene more than the absolute immobility of the camera. The slightest movement, which is precisely what a lesser director would have taken to be the thing to do, would have lowered the dramatic voltage. Here the camera in no way substitutes for a typical viewer. The camera itself organizes the action, using the frame of the image and the mental coordinates of its dramatic geometry.[20]

Bazin comments on the sequence-shot from *The Magnificent Ambersons* in these terms:

> The scene charges itself like an electrical condenser as it progresses and must be kept carefully insulated against all parasitic contacts until a sufficient dramatic voltage has been reached, which produces the spark that all the action has been directed toward. Take, for instance, Welles' favorite scene in *The Magnificent Ambersons*: the one in the kitchen between Fanny and George and, later, Jack. It lasts almost the length of an entire reel of film. The camera remains immobile from start to finish. . . . Fanny's pain and jealousy burst out at the end like an awaited storm, but one whose moment of arrival and whose violence one could not exactly predict. The slightest camera movement, or a close-up to cue us in on the scene's evolution, would have broken this heavy spell which forces us to participate intimately in the action.[21]

In these two commentaries, Bazin develops an aesthetic of the potentiality of movement governed by three elements: the immobility of the actor, the immobility of the frame including the duration of the shot which defers the instant, and the movement of the *découpage*. The potentiality of movement helps inscribe reality's ontological priority over human meaning onto the plastics of the image, particularly in deep-focus shots, as the eyes of the spectator explore the space of the shot and wander from one object or character to another. Bazin's conception of the language of cinema has cartographic origins, for ambiguity and potential movement characterize both the films he praised and the maps he was familiar with.[22]

In this respect, it can be said that the question "what is cinema?" echoes another question: "what is geography?" Geography is the science of movements (erosion, rivers, seismic cataclysms, transportation, trade, migrations, etc.) which are represented on a motionless medium, maps. Moreover, the *cartes d'état-major* provide geographers with information that must be selected, processed, and organized in a structured commentary that has not been pregiven by the cartographer. Semiologist Jacques Bertin argues that the very absence of movement in maps is the necessary condition of their ambiguity, thus allowing the geographer to build on the combinations of the cartographic elements in order to analyze a given portion of space. By contrast, animated maps (in films or advertisements, for instance) make visible an intention of the cartographer in terms of presenting a theme or a problematic, since actual movement inscribes the presence of man in the plastics of the map and therefore undermines its fundamental ambiguity: "Though movement introduces another variable, this one is destructive [*écrasante*], for it mobilizes all perception and greatly limits the attention that we can give to the meaning of all the other variables."[23] In other words, maps lie at the crossroads of the ambiguity of the medium and the geographer's interpretation. To analyze a map means to combine the cartographic elements so as to excavate the dynamics of a given portion of space. Consequently, the absence of movement in maps, which is the necessary condition of their fundamental ambiguity, enlists the geographer's eye movements, as exemplified by Vidal's commentaries in his 1908 *La France: Tableau géographique*, a text which excavates and animates through words the potential movements inscribed in motionless maps and photographs.[24]

Thus cartography paved the way for Bazin's conception of the *language of cinema*. Though the specificity of the film medium is movement, Bazin translated the immobility inherent to maps to his conception of mise-en-scène; the common ground between maps and cinema does not pertain to the respective characteristics of their mediums, but to their aesthetics. By praising the resources of the immobility of the frame and the actor, and by insisting on the duration and the depth of field of the shot, Bazin devised the cinematic equivalent of the fundamental ambiguity of maps. In this regard, Bazin's aesthetic of immobility exacerbates the kinetic horizon of spectator expectation with regards to the instant of the actualization of movement. Both maps and Bazin's conception of mise-en-scène involve virtual movement whose interpretation lies on an internal montage.

Across the Fault Line of National Identity: The Geology of Universalism

In many respects, Bazin attached great importance to the concept of national identity, be it in terms of production, style, distribution, or reception. Reviewing international film festivals in the late 1940s, he discussed what he saw not only through the lens of the director's style and personality, but also in light of the country in which the films were made.[25] He acknowledged the importance of the national component when it came to awarding prizes at film festivals: "As, in the end, the prizes are going to nations, the selections are national and nobody can ignore that voting for a film furthers a country's prestige and fulfills national pride. This consideration should not be the initially determining factor: it could be a backup in a tie when deciding between two films whose qualities are roughly equal."[26] Bazin's position in terms of national identity needs to be contextualized in the crisis of the French film industry after the Liberation, caused by the flooding of the market with Hollywood films banned during the Occupation. He admired American cinema but pressed for French "quality."[27] In 1949, Bazin argues that Renoir is "the most national, the most ineradicable of our directors."[28] In 1952, he does not hesitate to claim that "in these times of crisis, cinematic patriotism is proper."[29] He emphasized the need to develop the French film industry in a national framework at the expense of what he called "the monstrous Tower of Babel of coproduction,"[30] which he saw as "an absurd, and possibly mortal peril for the quality of cinema"[31] since it inevitably created certain "geographic discordances."[32]

In addition to the context of the reconstruction of the French film industry, Bazin's interest in nation lies with one of the functions he assigns to cinema, which is to crystallize a collective instinct, shaping a "myth" for a given society, an assumption clearly influenced by André Malraux's "Sketch for a Psychology of the Cinema."[33] As early as 1947, Bazin notes for instance that the western genre embodies "the American national epic"[34] and the "constants of American civilization."[35] It is no surprise then that Bazin points out that distributors should take into account the cultural characteristics of the markets they target, as these undermine the very possibility of an audience to assimilate imported films which are shaped by a foreign idiosyncrasy. The paramount importance of the sociological context in which a film is conceived explains why Bazin is reluctant to assign legitimacy to remakes. The stucture of a given plot and mise-en-scène cannot be adapted to another milieu: "It is impossible to shoot a film dealing with a social issue localized in a time and place outside of its human and material context."[36] This stance is exemplified by the American version of Marcel Carné's *Daybreak* (1940): "*Le Jour se lève* is a tragedy at Aubervilliers. It cannot be the same thing in the suburbs of San Francisco."[37] Bazin thus showed skepticism toward transnational adaptations of literary works: "Alexandre Dumas reexamined and completed by the Italians is hardly any more respected than if it were by Hollywood."[38] Hence the numerous texts in which Bazin describes the challenges of cross-cultural reception: when a film is made in a foreign country, the spectator is exposed to a cultural context which does not necessarily intersect with that of the country in which the film is shown. According to Bazin, it is the director's responsibility to bridge the cultural gap by maintaining a balance between national values and universal moral ones.[39]

The quest for such a balance was palpable in Bazin's assessment of the representations of landscape in French cinema. He sharply criticized the French films of the 1940s because they missed an opportunity to represent the country's geographical diversity.[40] He reinforced his criticism in a 1949 article entitled "le *Tour de France* du cinéma," a text in which he condemned "the geographical anonymity of so many French films."[41] The standardized, abstract representation of French landscape casts a shadow on the founding myth of France as a country combining the diversity of regions in a united nation aspiring to universalism: French cinema "is far from having drawn everything out of this territory that we studied with pride in primary school, the variety and the harmony given to its natural design [*génie*]."[42] The idea that the nation is the product of a balance between diversity, unity, and universalism was a staple of the French intellectual landscape in the nineteenth and the first half of the twentieth century, forwarded by Vidal de la Blache who noted in his 1903 *Tableau*: "Between these opposite poles, France's nature has developed a richness in scale [*richesse de gamme*] that one does not find elsewhere. Through a continuous interference of causes—climatic, geologic, topographic—the Midi and the North have disappeared, intertwined and reappeared. . . . The overall impression is that of an average [*moyenne*], in which the seemingly disparate shades have blended into a series of gradual nuances."[43] To Vidal, France is a country whose identity is characterized by a balance establishing unity between regional differences: "All variety, all inequality, and most of all, all contrast, are motives for exchange, for relations and reciprocal insight."[44] In other words,

Vidal's geography stresses the importance of contact zones between varied milieux, giving rise to the common denominator: nation. Likewise, Bazin's conception of French national cinema is based on the idea that films cut across local differences and assimilate transnational influences in order to convey a sense of unity and universalism. Bazin praises Marcel Pagnol's films since their representation of Provence derives from the "intersection of France with the Mediterranean civilization."[45] Bazin was familiar with the Midi during his formative years; it was the subject of the written exam in geography during the 1938 term at Saint-Cloud: "The Two Aspects of the French *Midi*: The Oceanic South and the Mediterranean South from the Perspective of Climate, Vegetation and Rural Life including Agriculture and Housing."[46] Moreover, Bazin's analysis of the intersection of Provence with Mediterranean civilization was discussed at the same time in the works by Fernand Braudel, one of the prominent historians of the École des annales, greatly influenced by Vidal. Bazin's reading of Pagnol clearly echoes Vidal's assessment of the exchanges between varied milieux which gave rise to a balance integrating differences: "By bringing the Eastern Mediterranean and Western Europe into contact, the sea fulfills the role that would appear to belong to it in the realm of civilization as in the physical world, that of softening the contrasts, leveling [*combler*] inequalities."[47] Hence Bazin praises Pagnol for balancing the local and the universal, avoiding the pitfall of folklore and clichés: "Thanks to Pagnol, cinematic regionalism has not only captivated the French public, it has risen to the universal, it has dazzled the greatest American technical experts and conquered the world."[48] To Bazin, universal values are no less important than national ones, a credo which is best exemplified by the evolution of his reading of Renoir.

It can be argued that Bazin's approach to Renoir through the lens of the nation in the late 1940s was only a transitional step toward a more universalist interpretation of that auteur. In 1949, Renoir himself was clearly ahead of Bazin in this respect: "Of course, the best works will always be those that are attached to the homeland [*terroir*], but the world has become international and the great modern technical experts—like scholars—will be at home everywhere."[49] In the same year, Renoir also declared: "The scholar, like the artist, is now more than ever a specialist independent of national geography. . . . I do not mean to say that the best works are not those that remain intimately attached to the homeland, on the contrary. But that at the heart of it, this rather indispensable link is not incompatible with a more internationally minded conception and organization."[50] In 1951 Bazin, who had proclaimed that the director of *The Rules of the Game* is "the most national, the most ineradicable of our directors,"[51] had to admit that his previous analysis testified to a "nationalist prejudice,"[52] for his reading of Renoir through the lens of the nation had evolved toward a dialectics based on the mutual integration of the local and the universal: "Those who knew and loved him should feel reassured, for America has not devoured our Renoir. All the more indeed—but is this a misfortune?—he clarified French virtues, he stripped away [*dépouill*] the accidents in order to reduce them to the essential. . . . A sense of the universal, of the relativity of history and geography, situates and confirms his French identity."[53]

Bazin's viewing of *The River* (1951) marks a turning point in his reevaluation of Renoir's American period in that this time the nation appears clearly secondary with regards to the universal themes addressed by the film. Though Bazin concedes that "Renoir proclaimed his ties to his country many times, declaring himself, as a director, as integral a part of French civilization as the light of the Ile-de-France, Brie cheese and red wine," he concludes that "we have to submit ourselves to the evidence: Renoir is the most French of international directors" because his works are characterized by "his quest, by way of accident, to a universally human essence."[54] In the wake of Renoir's words, but also Vidal's conception of exchanges and integration of local differences into a whole, Bazin eventually agrees that films are the product of a "zone of intellectual and material exchange in which national divisions have become secondary."[55]

Bazin's so-called "nationalist prejudice" was shaped by the challenging situation of the French film industry after the Liberation, including the cultural and economic issues raised by the Blum-Byrnes agreement. Yet in cutting across the fault line of nation under the auspices of universal values in 1951 Bazin in fact was returning to the ideology of the École normale supérieure of Saint-Cloud, as exemplified by the subjects of the 1938 exams he sat for. Taking as a starting point a quote from William James, the exam in philosophy focused on the issue of the particular versus the universal, while the exam in history was on the creation of the Third Republic.[56] Moreover, Bazin's interest in a balanced approach to universalism and nation was discussed in the very first text he published in 1941, "L'enseignement primaire supérieur." Against the Vichy government which planned on dismantling the French educational system after the 1940 defeat, Bazin made a case for the mission assigned to elementary teachers, which lies at the crossroads of the local idiosyncrasy of the pupils living in the French regions and the universalism promoted by the Third Republic: "The teacher holds a unique and privileged place in the community. He has to assert himself as a factor of synthesis and continuity in local life by making the children aware of the resources within their own familiar horizons, even utilizing these resources as cultural material and thus establishing an organic and vibrant link between the earth, tradition, and man. But he must also bring a foreign, heterogenous element, as the introducer of a universal culture."[57] The conception of education that Bazin elaborates in this text would underwrite his criteria as a critic for establishing the quality of a given film: its capacity to cut across the fault line separating nation and universal moral values. Thus, employing the terminology of geography and geology, Bazin developed a broad approach to national cinema at the very moment the United Nations was born.

Topography, Geology, Evolution

An internationally renowned film critic, Bazin had numerous opportunities to put into practice his background in geography by analyzing the topography and the geology of film festivals. For instance, he established a link between the atmosphere of the Venice Biennale and the very location of the facility where the films were shown. When reviewing the 1954 Sao Paulo film festival, he goes on at length about the demography of Brazil and its impact on the city that hosts the festival, before discussing the films themselves.[58] As early as 1946, however, Bazin seemed to place an emphasis on the depth of the earth rather than its surface, that is, on geology rather than topography: "the geological cross-section made in cinema by the Festival was fascinating to those interested in knowing where cinematic art and industry are heading."[59] Under the topography of the festivals (daily anecdotes, gossip, political pressures on the jury) lie the geological tendencies in terms of themes, production, and distribution: "The official competition is the geography of cinema, but it is geology that controls geography."[60]

The opposition Bazin forms between the surface and the depth of Festivals provides only one instance of a sophisticated approach to cinema shaped by methods he learned in map analysis [*commentaire de cartes*] at the École normale supérieure. Those school exercises would consist in first describing the topography ("geography" in the quote above), then explaining topography by identifying the geological layers which lie underneath; lastly the candidates had to define the impact of systems of erosion on topography and geology, giving rise to the study of geomorphology. These three components of map analysis lay beneath Bazin's method of film analysis, as he examined form, content, and the evolution of style over time. To Bazin, therefore, analyzing a film consists in excavating three strata of interpretation and establishing relationships between these levels. First the topography of a given film must be described through the analysis of style and mise-en-scène; tellingly, Bazin sometimes employed a topographical word when referring to style ("The great and true *auteurs* conquer, in retrospect, these high *plateaus* of style").[61] This topography then needs to be explained by reference to two geological layers lying underneath: the sociological context in which the film was conceived, and its moral significance. Bazin routinely related this kind of topography and geology, as when in a 1947 text he invited the spectators going to ciné-clubs to excavate the "aesthetic geology of the film." This expression reveals that form and content should never be dissociated in analysis: "It is not art when the problems of form and content can be validly separated."[62] For Bazin, surface realism is not an end in itself, for reality includes a universal moral significance; conversely, content cannot be conceived without its stylistic embodiment. Bazin's integration of topography and geology is perhaps best exemplified in his 1948 reading of Marcel Carné's *Le Jour se lève*:

> But we will see that the commentary has attempted, through several formal observations, to dive into the subject by showing that the physical geography of the work would remain rigorously determined by an artistic geology, in which the "content" and the "form" are made totally clear. Like that of tragedy, the true necessity of this tale and its characters is purely metaphysical. The realism of the mise en scène, the characters, the plot, the set, the dialogue, is but a pretext, like the modern incarnation of an action that one would not know how to define outside of its contemporary appearances, but which essentially overtakes it. And yet this action is precisely valuable and convincing only in relation to its realism.[63]

Le Jour se lève raises a universal theme that cannot be reduced to its actualization in a given context: here, Bazin's analysis of Carné's film testifies to the primacy of the "metaphysical" geological layer over the sociological one. On the other hand, this close interdependence of form and content lies at the crux of reality's inherent ambiguity: no matter how important the metaphysical geology of a film, it cannot be dissociated from its formal topography, for symbolism (meaning) cannot precede realism (raw depiction).

The unity of topography and geology comes up even more insistently in his discussion of Orson Welles' *Citizen Kane* and *The Magnificent Ambersons*: "Analysis and reflection reveal, above all, a stylistic unity. Within the context of Welles' filmography, these two works constitute a vast aesthetic land mass whose geology and relief justify simultaneous study."[64] Geology and relief cannot be dissociated because *Kane* and *Ambersons* are the "cinematic equivalents of realistic novels in the tradition of, say, Balzac. On one level they appear to be powerful, critical testimonies on American society. But one must pass beyond this first level of significance, where one soon reaches, beneath these social deposits, the crystalline mass of moral significance."[65] This same year, he also wrote of another key film, *Paisà* (1946), that the significance of its socio-logical layer depends on its moral geological *massif*: "After trying to trace the geographical boundaries of this cinema, so penetrating in its portrayal of the social setting, so meticulous and perceptive in its choice of authentic and significant detail, it now remains for us to fathom its aesthetic geology."[66] This instinct to explore the topographical and excavate the geological layers of films characterizes Bazin's reading of Kurosawa in 1957: "Assuredly, and for a hundred reasons, *Ikiru* [1952] is a specifically Japanese film. But what is striking and asserts itself in one's mind about this work is the universal value of its message.... The internationality of *Ikiru* is not geographic but geologic."[67] The topography of filmic forms is thus to be read on the basis of a specific cultural context which does not, however, exert determinism. In positing that a film is not solely the product of a given cultural and sociological context, Bazin shows himself a stu-dent of Vidal's views on *possibilism*. In opposition to the determinism developed in Germany by Friedrich Ratzel, one of Vidal's masters, *possibilism* is the theory that the environment sets cer-tain constraints on or limitations to a given milieu, but culture is otherwise shaped by man's actions. In his *Tableau de la géographie de la France*, Vidal argues that "a region [*contrée*] is a reservoir [of latent energies] where nature has planted the dormant seeds, the use of which depends on man."[68] In his 1921 *Principles of Human Geography*, he states that "human affairs are fraught with contingency,"[69] thus attaching his approach to geography to an idealist stance of the sort that later influenced Bazin.

Topography and geology are two major components of map analysis, prerequisites for geomorphology, an approach to the evolution of a given landscape over time, based on the impact of erosion systems. From Bazin's perspective, erosion designates the combination of factors that influence filmmaking, whether in terms of production, distribution, technique, or style. Pointing out that sound technology "is no longer the aesthetic fault line that divides two radically different aspects of the seventh art" and that a "bridge can be thrown [*jeté*] over the fault of the 1930s," Bazin develops a conception of the evolution of filmmaking which is marked by stability and continuity: "Since the technical determinisms were practically elimi-nated, we must then look elsewhere for the signs and principles of the evolution of language: in new subjects and by consequence new styles necessary for their expression. In 1939 talking pictures had reached what geographers call the 'profile of equilibrium' [*profil d'équilibre*] of a river. That is to say a certain mathematically ideal curve, which is the result of sufficient ero-sion. Having reached its profile of equilibrium, the river flows without strain from its source to its mouth and stops widening its bed."[70] Drawing on the notion of the "equilibrium profile," discussed by Emmanuel de Martonne in his *Traité de géographie physique*, Bazin uses a hydro-graphic metaphor to designate the stylistic consistency that films maintain over a given pe-riod, attaining the classical stage of their evolution. He indirectly refers to the last sentence of Vidal's *Tableau géographique de la France*: "When a gust of wind violently shakes the surface of a very clear body of water, everything vacillates and mingles; but, after a while, the image at the bottom takes a new shape. An attentive study of what is fixed and permanent in the geo-graphical conditions of France must be or must become our guide, more than ever."[71] Bazin attaches great importance to the geological permanence of universal themes, whatever the "social deposits" under which they lie. While he notes that a new cycle of erosion modifies the topography of films due to the emergence of new national cinemas in 1952, the geological

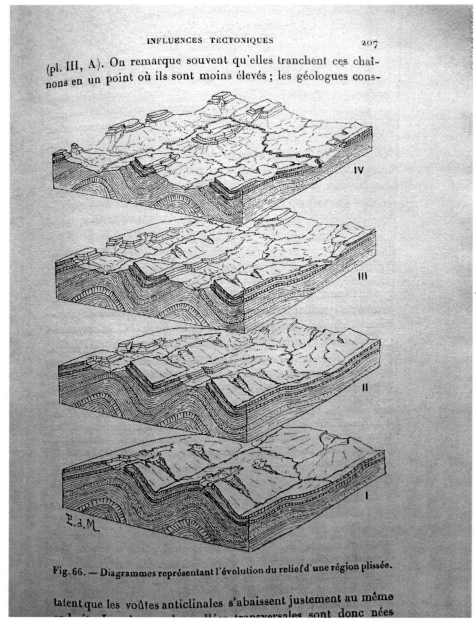

Fig. 66. — Diagrammes représentant l'évolution du relief d'une région plissée.

FIGURE 2.6: A prototype of evolution. Emmanuel de Martonne, *Abrégé de géographie physique*. Paris: Armand Colin, 1932 (courtesy Armand Colin Editeur)

substratum remains unchanged, since the permanence of universal themes cuts across the fault lines of nation: "It is not to the films considered individually so much as to their outline as a group that we owe the vague sentiment we feel of a profound movement, of tiny but powerful ruptures of equilibrium by creative forces. Something has moved in cinema that will slowly modify its topography. I am not necessarily saying that this is important or decisive, but enough has happened to initiate a cycle of erosion, and noticeably readjust its landscape"[72] [figure 2.6].

Conclusion

First and most important, the influence of his specific form of education between 1934 and 1941 enabled Bazin to gain skills in geography, geology, and cartography. He became familiar with cartography just as he was developing his views on the ontology of "images in which man plays no role." His obsession with the ambiguity of reality might be seen at play in the tension between the immobility of maps and the potentiality of movements across them, which are the object of every interpretation not delivered by the cartographer himself. Second, Paul Vidal de la Blache, the founding father of the French school of geography, clearly influenced Bazin by shaping his conception of cinema as a unity achieved through diversity. Bazin can thus be situated in the wake of a French philosophical backdrop which maintains a balance between scientific determinism and the autonomy of the mind. Lastly, his background in cartography also provided him with a methodology in terms of interpreting films by integrating the three key components of map analysis: topography (style), geology (sociological and moral layers), and geomorphology (the evolution of forms over time under the pressure of erosion).

Thus the French school of geography influenced Bazin in his ambition to address cinema by integrating its ontological, technical, stylistic, economic, and sociological aspects. Before the institutionalization of cinema studies, Bazin's approach to the seventh art was marked by a quest for both complexity and unity that Vidal posited in these terms: "What geography, in exchange for the help it has received from other sciences, can bring to the common treasury, is the capacity not to break apart what nature has assembled, and so to help us understand the correspondence and correlation of things, whether in the setting of the whole surface of the earth, or in the regional setting where things are localized. . . . Here there is, without any doubt, an intellectual benefit that can be extended to all uses of the mind."[73] In the wake of the French school of geography, Bazin called for an ecology of mind.

Notes

1. André Bazin, "La Reine Christine," *France observateur*, 249 (February 17, 1955).
2. Bazin, *Qu'est-ce que le cinéma?* trans. Tom Conley in *Cartographic Cinema* (Minneapolis: University of Minnesota Press, 2007), 6.
3. My corpus encompasses the Bazin archives located at the Archives départementales de la Charente Maritime for the 1934–1937 period, the Archives départementales des Yvelines for the 1937–1938 period, and the Archives nationales de France for the 1938–1941 period. My research is also indebted to the École normale supérieure Lettres et Sciences Humaines, Lyon, and to the Bazin archive of the Yale University Film Studies Program.
4. Dudley Andrew, *André Bazin* (New York: Oxford University Press, 1978), 65–68.
5. Archives départementales de la Charente Maritime, 1T 1958. On Bazin's formative years, see Andrew, *André Bazin*, 9–37. The economic crisis of the mid-1930s made the selective entrance examinations particularly competitive: only one in five applicants was admitted between 1934 and 1937; see Jean-Noël Luc and Alain Barbé, *Des Normaliens: Histoire de l'École normale supérieure de Saint-Cloud* (Paris: Presses de la fondation nationale des sciences politiques, 1982), 105.

6. "'Elève brillant, de beaucoup supérieur à ses camarades. Esprit littéraire et philosophique, aptes à des études supérieures. Candidat à une 4e année lettres avec succès escompté. Je ne serais pas étonné que M. Bazin devint dans la suite un professeur de premier plan. Mais la santé est à ménager.' La Rochelle, le 15 juillet 1937. Le directeur, M. Tarnier." Archives départementales de la Charente Maritime, 1T, 1958.

7. A letter written from Oscar Aurias, director of the ENS of Saint-Cloud, to the French Ministry of Education, April 4, 1938, indicates that "nos élèves . . . nous arrivent presque tous plus ou moins déprimés par une longue et pénible préparation . . ." Archives nationales de France, versement 200000384-art 2.

8. *Journal officiel de la République Française* (September 29, 1937); Archives départementales des Yvelines, 37T 373: "Organisation de la 4e année, programme, candidats (listes, notations, résultats) 1920–40."

9. The register of the library of the École normale de Versailles: between 1935 and 1938, shows they had purchased sixty-one maps of France, the majority of which were *cartes d'état-major*. This number does not include the maps purchased by the École Normale prior to 1935. Archives départementales des Yvelines, 37T 311, 37 T312, 37T 299.

10. Emmanuel de Martonne and André Cholley, *La France, interprétation géographique de la carte d'état-major à 1:80 000* (Paris: Librairie Armand Colin, 1934).

11. See the register of the "Procès verbal d'installation" of the faculty members at the ENS of Saint-Cloud, Archives nationales de France, versement 20020198, article 17.

12. Lucien Febvre, *A Geographical Introduction to History* (New York: Knopf, 1925).

13. See Raymond Borde and Charles Perrin, *Les Offices du 'cinéma éducateur' et la survivance du muet: 1925–40* (Lyon: Presses universitaires de Lyon, 1992), 31–32. See also "Le film-parabole dans les Offices du 'cinéma éducateur" en France dans l'entre-deux-guerres. Histoire d'un cinéma de propagande et étude d'un genre cinématographique.' Ph.D dissertation, University of Paris 3 Sorbonne-Nouvelle, 2009.

14. Archives départementales des Yvelines, Versailles: 37T 306; 37T 307.

15. The registers of the Archives de la Planète in Boulogne indicates that ten screenings of autochromes were organized for the *normaliens* between 1921 and 1931; see registers Z 1850, Z 1851, and Z 1852.

16. Bazin, "The Ontology of the Photographic Image" in *What is Cinéma?* vol. 1, trans. Hugh Gray (Berkeley: University of California Press, 1967), 12.

17. *Logique de Port-Royal* cited by Marin in "Les voies de la carte," *Cartes et figures de la Terre* (Paris: Centre Georges Pompidou, 1980), 47.

18. Bazin, "The Ontology of the Photographic Image," 10.

19. Bazin, "Cinema and Exploration," in *What Is Cinema?* vol. 1, 159.

20. Bazin, "William Wyler, the Jansenist of Mise en Scène," in *What Is Cinema?* trans. Timothy Barnard (Montreal: Caboose, 2009), 48–49. For an analysis of the relationship between cinema and immobility, see Ludovic Cortade, *Le cinéma de l'immobilité: Style, politique, réception* (Paris: Publications de la Sorbonne, 2008).

21. Bazin, *Orson Welles* (Los Angeles: Acrobat Books, 1991), 68–73.

22. Tom Conley introduced this assumption in his seminar "Cartography, Film and Literature" (Harvard University, 2005). See the introduction to his *Cartographic Cinema*.

23. Jacques Bertin, *Sémiologie graphique* (Paris/The Hague: Gauthier-Villars/Mouton, 1967), 42.

24. Didier Mendibil has shown that 78 percent of 245 photographs and 58 maps examined by Vidal have elicited comments testifying to ocular movements; "Paul Vidal de la Blache, le 'dresseur d'images.' Essai sur l'iconographie de *La France: Tableau géographique* (1908)," in Marie-Claire Robic, *Le "Tableau de la géographie de la France" de Paul Vidal de la Blache* (Paris: CTHS), 77–105.

25. See Bazin, "Cannes devient la capitale du cinéma: 23 nations sont représentées au festival international du film," *Parisien libéré*, 653 (September 19, 1946); Bazin, "Triomphe de la France à Bruxelles: Bilan d'un festival," *Ecran français*, 106 (July 8, 1947); Bazin, "A propos de l'échec américain au festival de Bruxelles," *Esprit* (September 1947).

26. Bazin, "Je voudrais bien vous y voir," *Cahiers du Cinéma*, 35 (May 1954).

27. See Bazin, "Il faut sauver le cinéma français: Notre production nationale ne doit pas être écrasée par l'Etat," *Parisien libéré*, 1039 (January 18, 1948); Bazin, "Il faut défendre le cinéma français" *Radio, Cinéma, Télévision*, 98 (December 2, 1951); Bazin, "Hier soir à Cannes, devant un parterre de vedettes, la France pour inaugurer le Festival a joué son atoût-maître: *Le Salaire de la peur*," *Parisien libéré*, 2672 (April 16, 1953); Bazin, "Au festival de Cannes, le cinéma brésilien nous réveille mais le cinéma suédois nous endort," *Parisien libéré*, 2674 (April 18, 1953).

28. Bazin, "Avant de partir pour les Indes tourner son prochain film, le metteur en scène de *La Grande Illusion* a retrouvé pour quelques heures son Paris," *Parisien libéré*, 1616 (November 23, 1949).

29. Bazin, "Les jeunes dans le cocotier," *France observateur*, 92 (February 14, 1952).

30. Bazin, "La Cage d'Or," *Parisien libéré*, 2255 (December 14, 1951).

31. Bazin, "Fille dangereuse," *Parisien libéré*, 2719 (June 11, 1953); see also "La Maison du silence," *Parisien libéré*, 2696 (May 15, 1953); "La Belle de Cadix," *Parisien libéré* 2893 (December 31, 1953).

32. Bazin, "L'ennemi public n.1," *Parisien libéré*, 2901 (January 9, 1954).

33. André Malraux, "Esquisse d'une psychologie du cinéma." *Œuvres complètes*, vol. 4 (Paris: Gallimard, bibliothèque de la Pléiade, 2004), 14.

34. Bazin, "La caravane héroïque," *Parisien libéré*, 844 (June 4, 1947).

35. Bazin, "Le mouvement des Ciné-Clubs en France depuis la Libération," *DOC Education populaire 48*, 7. See also "Le train du dernier retour. Retour de flamme!," *Parisien libéré*, 4004 (July 26, 1957); "Réalité et réalisme dans les films américains," *Education nationale*, 11 (March 14, 1957); "Le western reflète un moment de l'histoire américaine," *Radio, Cinéma, Télévision*, 43 (November 12, 1950); "La loi du fouet," *France observateur*, 168 (July 30, 1953); "Henry V," *Parisien libéré*, 933 (September 17, 1947); "L'homme d'Octobre," *Parisien libéré*, 1334 (December 29, 1948); "Evasion," *Parisien libéré*, 3302 (April 23, 1955); "La sorcière, film typiquement nordique," *Parisien libéré*, 1468 (June 3, 1949); "Suède," *Reflets économiques et commerciaux* (ESSEC) (Spring 1955); "Bienvenue Mr. Marshall," *Parisien libéré*, 2754 (July 22, 1953); "Conclusion de Venise: le cinéma s'endort," *Carrefour* (September 10, 1953); "La porte de l'enfer," *France observateur*, 216 (July 1, 1954); "Les Sept Samouraïs," *France observateur*, 291 (December 8, 1955); "Le Festival de Cannes: Awara," *France observateur*, 155 (April 30, 1953).

36. Bazin, "Le Journal d'une femme de chambre," *Ecran français*, 155 (June 15, 1948); "Le Journal d'une femme de chambre," *Parisien libéré*, 1161 (June 9, 1948). Bazin later acknowledged that he underestimated the film in "Le petit journal du cinéma," *Cahiers du Cinéma*, 62 (August 1956).

37. Bazin, "'M.' le Maudit," *Radio, Cinéma, Télévision*, 110 (February 24, 1952). See also "Lourdes et Hollywood: Le chant de Bernadette," *Parisien libéré*, 809 (April 23, 1947); "Les films des mousquetaires," *Parisien libéré*, 2492 (September 18, 1952); "Remade in USA," *Cahiers du Cinéma*, 11 (April 1952); "Désirs Humains. *La bête humaine* vue par Fritz Lang," *Parisien libéré*, 3369 (July 12, 1955). The exceptions that confirm Bazin's assessment of transnational adaptations can be found in: "Cyrano de Bergerac. M. de Bergerac n'est pas assassiné," *Parisien libéré*, 2229 (November 13, 1951); and "Coquelin nous voici!" *Cahiers du Cinéma*, 7 (December 1951).

38. Bazin, "Le fils de d'Artagnan: Bon sang ne peut mentir," *Parisien libéré*, 2105 (June 20, 1951).

39. Bazin, "Les Pieds plats: quand les dieux du dimanche jouent au base-ball," *Ecran français*, 201 (May 3, 1949); "Alice au pays des merveilles: une œuvre incertaine," *Ecran français*, 203 (May 17, 1949); "La Femme de l'année…," *Parisien libéré* 1608 (November 14, 1949); "Ville haute, ville basse," *Parisien libéré*, 2150 (August 11, 1951); "Comment l'esprit vient aux femmes," *Radio, Cinéma, Télévision*, 91 (October 14, 1951); "Un tramway nommé désir," *Parisien libéré*, 2353 (April 7, 1952); "Le roman de Genjis," *France observateur*, 104 (May 8, 1952); "La Putain respectueuse," *Cahiers du cinéma*, 16 (October 1952); "La P . . . respectueuse," *Parisien libéré*, 2515 (October 15, 1952); "La Putain respectueuse," *France observateur*, 127 (October 16, 1952); "La P . . . respectueuse," *Radio, Cinéma, Télévision*, 144 (October 19, 1952); "Cinéma et sociologie," *France observateur*, 150 (March 26, 1953); "Un si noble tueur," *Parisien libéré*, 2912 (January 22, 1954); "Une fille de la province," *Parisien libéré*, 3325 (May 20, 1955); "Sayonara Madame Butterfly 1951," *Radio, Cinéma, Télévision*, 430 (April 13, 1958); "Cannes: à défaut d'un bon festival, un bon palmarès," *France observateur*, 419 (May 22, 1958).

40. Bazin, "Le cinéma et l'art populaire," *L'Information universitaire* (June 25, 1944); "Bilan de la saison 43–44," *L'Information universitaire* (July 8, 1944); "Réflexions pour une veillée d'armes," *Poésie*, 44 (July–October, 1944).

41. Bazin, "Le Tour de France du cinéma," *Ecran français*, 209 (June 27, 1949).

42. Ibid.

43. Paul Vidal de la Blache, "La France: tableau géographique (1908)," in *Tableaux de la France*, ed. Jean-Pierre Rioux (Paris: Omnibus, 2006), 382–83.

44. Paul Vidal de la Blache, "Le principe de la géographie générale," in *Annales de géographie* (1896), 138.

45. Bazin, "Le Tour de France du cinéma." This problematic is also exemplified by Renoir's *Toni* and its foreword: "The action takes place in the French Midi, on the Mediterranean, just where nature, destroying the

spirit of Babel, knows so well how to bring about the fusion of races." Original: "L'action se passe dans le midi de la France, en pays latin, là où la nature, détruisant l'esprit de Babel, sait si bien opérer la fusion des races."

46. Archives départementales des Yvelines, 37T 373.

47. Paul Vidal de la Blache, "La France: Tableau géographique," 348.

48. Bazin, "Le Tour de France du cinéma."

49. Bazin, "Avant de partir pour les Indes tourner son prochain film, le metteur en scène de *La Grande Illusion* a retrouvé pour quelques heures son Paris," *Parisien libéré*, 1616 (November 23, 1949).

50. Bazin, "L'auteur de *La Grande Illusion* n'a pas perdu confiance dans la liberté de création," *Ecran français*, 230 (November 28, 1949).

51. Bazin, "Avant de partir pour les Indes tourner son prochain film, le metteur en scène de *La Grande Illusion* a retrouvé pour quelques heures son Paris."

52. Bazin, "Le Fleuve de Jean Renoir," *Parisien libéré*, 2262 (December 21, 1951).

53. Bazin, "Jean Renoir retrouvé," *Radio, Cinéma, Télévision*, 72 (June 3, 1951).

54. Bazin, "Le Fleuve: Jean Renoir, un réalisateur mystique," *France observateur*, 85 (December 27, 1951).

55. Bazin, "Jean Renoir: le cinéma sort de l'enfance. Il existe désormais un public pour la qualité," *Radio, Cinéma, Télévision*, 84 (August 26, 1951).

56. "Examine this remark by William James: 'No matter how you look at it, the monstrous primacy that is conferred to universal concepts cannot help but surprise. That the philosophers since Socrates should have contended as to which should most scorn the knowledge of the particular and should most adore knowledge of the general, is something which passes understanding. For, after all, must not the most honorable knowledge be the knowledge of the most valuable realities? And is there a valuable reality which is not concrete and individual? The universal is worthless aside from its ability to help us through reasoning to discover new truths about individual entities.'" The subject of the written exam in history read: "L'établissement du régime républicain en France des élections du 8 février 1871 à la fin de la crise boulangiste (élections du 22 septembre 1889)," Archives départementales des Yvelines, 37T 373.

57. Bazin, "L'enseignement primaire supérieur," *Rencontres*, Cerf (July 20, 1941), 69; the article is signed "André Basselin."

58. Bazin, "Pour un festival à trois dimensions," *Cahiers du Cinéma*, (May 1953); "Un festival sérieux: Sao-Paulo," *France observateur*, 198 (February 25, 1954); "A Sao Paulo, ville champignon de près de 3 millions d'habitants, le festival fait une grande place à la France," *Radio, Cinéma, Télévision*, 216 (March 7, 1954); "A Sao Paulo, festival de la gentillesse," *Parisien libéré*, 2936 (February 19, 1954).

59. Bazin, "The Cannes Festival of 1946," in *French Cinema of the Occupation and Resistance*, ed. François Truffaut, trans. Stanley Hochman (New York: Ungar, 1984), 136. See also "A Sao Paulo, festival de la gentillesse," *Parisien libéré*, 2936 (February 19, 1954); "Le Voyage à Punta del Este," *Cahiers du Cinéma*, 58 (April 1956); "Découpage/Il Montaggio," *Venti anni di cinema a Venezia, 1932–52*; "Pour un festival à trois dimensions," *Cahiers du Cinéma*, 23 (May 1953).

60. Bazin, "Découpage/Il Montaggio,"

61. Bazin, "A propos de Cannes," *Cahiers du Cinéma*, 22 (April 1953), 9.

62. Bazin, "Le film en filigrane: L'art et la manière," *Ecran français*, 127–28 (December 9, 1947).

63. "Marcel Carné, Le Jour se lève," *DOC 48*, 4 (January–February 1948), republished in *Le Cinéma français de la Libération à la Nouvelle Vague*, ed. François Truffaut (Paris: Editions d'l'Etoile, 1983), 101.

64. Bazin, *Orson Welles: A Critical View* (Los Angeles: Acrobat Books, 1978), 64.

65. Ibid, 65. See also Bazin, "Le découpage et son évolution," *L'Âge Nouveau*, 93 (July 1955), 58–59.

66. Bazin, "An Aesthetic of Reality: Cinematic Realism and the Italian School of the Liberation," in *What Is Cinema?* vol. 2, trans. Hugh Gray (Berkeley: University of California Press, 1971), 30. Bazin commented on Rossellini's *Europe 51* in similar geological terms: "But *Europe 51* has in a way passed beyond the social plane to flow into the zone of spiritual destiny." "Si Zampano a une âme . . .," in Guido Cincotti *La Strada: Un Film de Frederico Fellini* (Paris: Editions du Seuil, 1956), 117.

67. Bazin, "Vivre," *Cahiers du Cinéma*, 69 (March 1957), republished in *Le cinéma de la cruauté* (Paris: Flammarion, 1975), 222.

68. Paul Vidal de la Blache, *La France: Tableau géographique*, 329.

69. Paul Vidal de la Blache, *Principles of Human Geography*, trans. M. T. Bingham (New York: H. Holt and Company, 1926), 31. In his review of his German master Friedrich Ratzel's *Anthropogeographie*

(1882–1891), Vidal called into question the notion of determinism; see "La géographie politique d'après les écrits de M. Friedrich Ratzel," in *Annales de géographie*, VII (1898), 45.

70. "Découpage," *Venti anni di cinema a Venezia, 1932–52*, 363–66, 369.

71. Paul Vidal de la Blache, *La France: Tableau géographique*, 783.

72. Bazin, "La foi qui sauve: Cannes 1952," *Cahiers du Cinéma*, 13 (June 13, 1952).

73. Paul Vidal de la Blache, *Des caractères distinctifs de la géographie*, cited by G. J. Martin and P. E. James, *All Possible Worlds: A History of Geographical Ideas* (New York: John Wiley and Sons, 1993), 193.

3

Evolution and Event in
Qu'est-ce que le cinéma?

Tom Conley

In the previous chapter, Ludovic Cortade carefully reconstructs Bazin's formation in geography and its zones of contact with his film criticism. Cortade discerns how for the critic topography, a study of the physical forms of given milieux, is countered by geology, a science reaching into a layered history of the earth that includes, as Freud had famously noted in *Civilization and its Discontents* (1930), mental strata. In what follows I would like to see where geography and geology bear on Bazin's notion of *evolution* and their impact, correlatively, on that of the *event* of cinema. As a final note, I would like to suggest that where Bazin writes of evolution and event, he anticipates what, in strong political and aesthetic senses alike, Gilles Deleuze calls "stratigraphy." The aim is to see how Bazin might indeed be close in spirit to the great film-makers whom Deleuze eternized in the name of *stratigraphes*.[1] Attention will be drawn first to the ways that evolution figures in Bazin's own style or manner of writing in his landmark essay on film language. Then its relation with his work on the American Western will be taken up in order to correlate his work on space with his notion of the cinematic event.

At the beginning of "Théâtre et cinéma" (originally published in two issues of *Esprit*, June and July–August, 1951), explaining how cinema grows out of theater, Bazin makes an unsolicited appeal to embryology. The players in the *Boireau* and *Onésime* series, he observes, are less related to a primitive form of stage than to the very structure of the farce they move forward.[2] As cinematic actors they emerge or, better, they *evolve* into cinema from the preconditions of theater. The stage, he writes, "imposed restrictions of time and space that held it in a somewhat larval state of evolution."[3] Film becomes what it is when, in the matrix of theater, it undergoes metamorphosis prior to reaching an adult "stage" of development. "Cinema allows an elementary solution to be pushed to its ultimate consequences on which the stage had imposed restrictions of time and space that held it in a sort of larval state of evolution." [Le cinéma permet de pousser à ses ultimes conséquences une situation élémentaire à laquelle la scène imposait des restrictions de temps et d'espace qui la maintenait à un stade d'évolution en quelque sorte larvaire] (QQC, 133). A species of Mexican salamander, he adds, reproduces itself in its intermediate state before a hormone that is injected into it allows it to mature. He develops the metaphor further:

In the same way we know that the continuity of animal evolution presented incomprehensible gaps [*lacunes*] until biologists discovered the laws of pedomorphosis that taught them not only how to integrate embryonic forms of the individual into the evolution of species, but even to consider certain individuals, apparently adults, as beings blocked in their evolution. In this sense certain genres of theater are based on dramatic situations that were congenitally atrophied before the appearance of cinema. (QQC, 133)

Darwin and Julius Huxley (to whom reference is made) notwithstanding, Bazin compares the velocities of evolution among animals to two of the seven arts. Cinema is esteemed in a state of faster development (and a product emanating from a greater variety of forms that enable a greater degree of natural selection) where theater lags behind; injected into theater, a hormone (such as cinema) might cause it to develop from an amphibious to a developed state. In its stunningly "larval" condition—Bazin writes of silent comedy in France of the years 1910–1912—cinema can realize what theater could never imagine itself to become.

Less compelling than the elegance or the strategic virtue of the metaphor is the ostensive obsession with different types of evolution. Biological evolution, he reminds us, can be very slow, of *longue durée*, at the same time that a mutation can impose a rapid and sudden shift. Bazin develops the figure under the subsection titled "Un peu d'histoire" ("A little history"), a formula borrowed from the Michelin *Guide vert*, under whose rubric sketches of dates and events are appended to the descriptions of places and monuments. Evolution is suggested to bear on the nature of human history. Its slow and immutable process can undergo, as might humans in the environment on which they impose themselves, sudden metamorphoses. For the embryologist, history does not always evolve from a primitive state to one of maturity. Many incomplete, even ancestral elements of a finished being constitute its very nature; they allow it to change in any number of ways, and not always in the direction of the dubious perfection of "man": Bazin thus argues implicitly for a richly progressive *and* regressive, often haphazard character of the "evolution" of cinema. It is open-ended and, in today's idiolect, a work in process or a state of *becoming*.

"Évolution du langage cinématographique" is often taken to be a cornerstone of Bazin's film theory. Its promotion of deep focus and the long take that Renoir, Welles, and the Italian neorealists retrieve from silent cinema and craft in new ways explains much of what Bazin takes to be the timeless character of the seventh art. Crafted from three different pieces, the seventh chapter of the single-volume edition of *Qu'est-ce que le cinéma?* can be likened to a layered landscape in which the sight of various rifts and folds causes its creative force to come forward. When read in a Cartesian fashion, as a "tableau" or a "fable"—that is, when it is read in view of visual perspective—it reveals at its vanishing point a geological conceit explaining shifts and rifts of change.[4] Much as in the appeal to embryology in "Théâtre et cinéma," a line of demarcation is drawn to mark a continuity and a rupture in the evolution of film.

In 1939 the talkie had reached what geographers call the profile of equilibrium [*profil d'équilibre*] of a river, in other words, this ideal mathematical curve that is a resultant of sufficient erosion. Having reached its profile of equilibrium, the river flows effortlessly from its source to its mouth and no longer hollows out its basin. But if some geological movement intervenes to raise the peneplain, modifying the altitude of the source, the water continues to exert force, penetrating the adjacent terrain, sinking into it, hollowing and rounding it out [*l'eau de nouveau travaille, pénètre les terrains sous-jacents, s'enfonce, mine et creuse*]. Sometimes, where there are layers of limestone, a new relief is suddenly drawn on the plateau in almost invisible concavities, but it is complex and tortuous for as far as the path the water follows. (QQC, 71)[5]

Suddenly the form of the essay overtakes its content, indicating to the reader that, much like Montaigne in his *Essais*, we are "on the manner, not on the matter of expression" [sur la manière, non sur la matière du dire].[6] The modes of expression that Bazin calls "necessary and sufficient to the art of cinema since 1930" (QQC, 71) inspire him, it appears, to develop a metaphor of a measure fitting the aesthetic evolution of cinema. A style of thinking and writing, a *manière de penser* of his own or what Montaigne would call a "dictionnaire à part [lui],"[7] comes boldly forward where the idiolects of geology and geography serve the ends of a history of cinema. If the river's equilibrium undergoes sudden upheaval, it can be inferred that the upward thrust of the unspecified "geological movement" might be the volcano on whose edge Jean Renoir had said that he and his nation were dancing when he was filming *The Rules of the Game* (1939). The anticipation and the advent of the Second World War change the landscape. By a mutation decisive for the evolution of the seventh art, a state of near-eternity, a "classical" continuum, is upset by an event, however much it had been foreseen, whose aftereffects are far from being settled.

The geological figure recurs decisively at another site in the essay. Orson Welles is lionized for what he did in *Citizen Kane*, in 1941, "in a vast geological displacement of the foundations of cinema that almost everywhere confirms in some manner this revolution of language" [dans un vaste déplacement géologique des assises du cinema qui confirme un peu partout de quelque manière cette révolution du langage] (QQC, 76). Evolution is punctuated by revolution much as a river by a great geological event. To underscore the difference Bazin applies the distinction to Italian neorealism. Much as in Welles, the long take and deep focus its directors confer upon their films bring forward a compelling "sense of the ambiguity of the real" (QQC, 77). At the time of the essay's writing (1951) the *evolution* of the movement would have been at most eight years, from *Ossessione* (1943) through *Bicycle Thieves* (1948) to later examples, but more pertinently only two, given his mention only of *Paisà* (1946), *Germany Year Zero* (1948), and *Thieves*. By contrast, he remarks, America does not witness a shift in its evolution "through some *revolution* in the technique of editing" (QQC, 77; stress added). In their style the Italians are "slow" and less likely to make manifest great cinematic upheaval because they appeal to the shapes and forms of "primitive" (or "larval") cinema as it had been prior to many of its technological metamorphoses.

At the end of the article, in what would be in the recesses of its landscape, the Italians are shown reaching back and over the decade of the 1930s, to Murnau and Stroheim (along with Dreyer and Flaherty) to make clear and confirm "this evolution of language since 1940" (QQC, 78). The neorealists are like Renoir, implied to be geologists or stratigraphers who refuse appeal to montage; their creative gaze discerns the secrets of the world without shattering it into bits and pieces, "revealing the hidden sense of beings and of things without breaking their natural unity" (QQC, 78).[8] The jump over the decade that includes the war years provides a dialectical frame by which three decades are apposed in order to offer historical and aesthetic insight. Certain styles of 1920–1930, recovered in 1940–1950, become a foil to the efflorescence of sound cinema in the decade 1930–1940. When displaced into a later period, the manner and style among chosen directors of the late silent era foment a revolution, indeed a mutation that confirms the continuum of an evolution.[9]

To understand how Bazin's formulations figure in the graphic rhetoric of his argument for realism we must see how the metaphor of continuity and rupture at the center of the "Théâtre et cinéma" is anticipated at the beginning. Two figures, each of medieval facture, are keynote. One, based on cycles of forms, puts a "classical" moment at the top of an implied allegorical Wheel of Fortune, while the other depicts film moving horizontally, indeed geographically, along an "aesthetic path," in its search for form.[10] The latter is measured by signposts, while the compass of the former would be drawn by stations or degrees of a circle. In 1928, Bazin claims, silent film reaches its apogee. It is "supremely adapted to the 'exquisite discontent'" of silence that the sound tradition could only "toss back into chaos" (QQC, 63). The new technology is poised to be the deceptive sign of an "aesthetic revolution" (ibid.) that in the years 1928–1930 suddenly prompts a mutation.

To herald the fact that it does not, Bazin appeals to a typological view of history of the kind inherited from the medieval *Mirror of Human Salvation*. The "revolution" would be part of an ever-ongoing dialectical "evolution" by which an event in the Old Testament of silent film is found confirmed and realized in the New, that is, in sound films that take cognizance of the style and form of the earlier age.[11] The marvel of the invocation of figural realism belongs to a vision of discontinuity inhering in continuity. The temporal gist of the biblical typology that he uses to envisage a history of film that cannot end (or that will end with the end of Time) anticipates the geological and geographical figure at the center of the essay. The advent of sound is not "the aesthetic fault line that divides two radically different aspects of the seventh art" (QQC, 67). Silent cinema does not find its demise in the sound medium because the "veritable order [*plan*] of cleavage continues without rupture" (QQC, 67–68). A subjacent figure of earthly time, whose angstrom units might be millennia, conveys the idea of eternal continuity and of the sudden return of concealed strata of history. The peneplain of the years 1920–1930 pushes into that of 1940–1950, and then the profile of cinematic equilibrium, as it were, is thrown awry when human history intervenes. The year 1939 signals not only a classical balance of sound and image but also the signing of the Hitler-Stalin pact and Germany's invasion of Poland. It locates, too, the advent of directors who exploit the long take and deep focus to record the duration of the world in which events are shown in all of their ambiguity.

In its final state the essay on the evolution of film language resembles a landscape. Its arguments subtend the aesthetics of a gaze upon a world whose duration and consequence exceed the limits of human ken. It explains Bazin's affinities for the American Western whose geographies invite deep focus and the long take. Because of its rugged and rocky aspect, that delights the geologist's eyes, the western landscape indicates to its observers that they are utterly exterior to it and that their projective fantasy of living upon it is out of the question. The camera that records these spaces indeed becomes the "spectator and nothing but the spectator" (QQC, 146). Those who discern the geological evolution informing the world on which human dramas unfold are experiencing a sublime ambivalence about the frailty and gratuitousness of the human condition. Clearly the western features shot around Lone Pine, Monument Valley, or

Bryce Canyon remain the *prima materia* for Bazin's favorite filmmakers of the silent era. Like the gaze Bazin brings to the landscape, the American Western is stratigraphic.

To see why, we can juxtapose "L'Évolution du langage cinématographique" to his two major pieces on the American Western, "Évolution du western" (1955), which appeared in the same year as "Le Découpage et son évolution" (one of the three articles that Bazin conflated into "L'Évolution du langage cinématographique") and "Un western exemplaire: *Sept hommes à abattre*" (*Seven Men from Now*, 1956; published in *Cahiers du Cinéma*, August–September 1957). In both Bazin considers the *longue durée* of time and space in the Western from its inception and early years up to the middle 1950s. He begins with Thomas Ince, for Ince's style cannot be discounted when "forty years of cinematic evolution" are taken into consideration (QQC, 243).[12] From its inception the Western is the "bedrock" of American cinema, and for that reason any study of its transformations over time requires an archeological gaze.

To reinforce his view of the geology of the Western Bazin returns almost paradoxically to aesthetic principles borrowed from then fairly recent (and now classical) treatments of the evolution—if an oxymoron is allowed—of religious art.[13] For one of Bazin's masters, Henri Focillon, the evolution of Romanesque and Gothic cathedrals could be discerned in successive and sometimes mixed phases that move from an *experimental* moment in which a search for practical solutions to vexing problems are essayed; to a *classical* turn in which the problems are solved when different modes or styles of expression conjoin to produce a new and hybrid product; then, to a radiating [*rayonnant*] phase in which the elements are pared down, sometimes in filigree, to yield refined treatment of the classical form; finally, to a *baroque* stage where the elements are turned inward so that the monuments decline (as in a grammar) the history of their own development.[14]

Bazin's "primitives" of the silent Western are likened to the medieval miniatures from which patterns of stained glass tell sacred narratives. In the longer history they attest to the ground of the Western that finds its classical moment of perfection, like cinema in "L'Évolution du langage cinématographique," in 1939. In a sentence that echoes the metaphor of the river's course Bazin begins "Évolution du western" by asserting, "On the eve of the War the western had reached a clear degree of perfection. The year 1940 marks a plateau beyond which a new evolution fatally had to take place, an evolution that the four war years simply delayed, and then inflected nonetheless without determining it" (QQC, 239). A coy irony primes the essay where a "new" evolution—a contradiction insofar as it would rather be a revolution—is supposed to alter the eternity of the genre.

Thus the Chartres of the Western, the work of classical balance that solves all of the thematic and aesthetic problems the genre had confronted, is John Ford's *Stagecoach*. The masterpiece of 1939 reaches "a perfect equilibrium among the social myths, historical reference, psychological truth and the traditional themes of the western mise-en-scène" (QQC, 239). Ford's feature is symptomatic of a coincidence of history and evolution: history, because it responds to a growing nationalistic consciousness in America during the prewar years under Franklin D. Roosevelt; evolution, because it crystallizes what the Western had been doing over the twenty previous years. Ford was one of a group of directors who worked in both eras and earned their chevrons by making generally anonymous but finely crafted films owing their virtue to the presence of the silent style within the sound medium. The names enumerated—King Vidor, Michael Curtiz, Fritz Lang, William Wyler, Ford, George Marshall—belong to auteurs who worked in both eras. Aesthetic evolution buttresses that of geology: "without claiming to explain everything by the famous law of aesthetic ages" (QQC, 230), he advances that Ford's postwar features (*My Darling Clementine*, 1946; *Fort Apache*, 1948) are a "baroque embellishment" to the "classical" order of *Stagecoach*. Yet aesthetic history alone does not entirely account for the shift from perfection in 1940 to the problematic Western after 1945. A "more complex evolution" (QQC, 231) is required to account for why the genre saw the production of intellectual (in other words, baroque) avatars that play on the history and structure of its earlier forms. A "moral drama" owing to highly aestheticized camerawork defines Fred Zinnemann's *High Noon* (1950), while George Stevens' *Shane* (1953) mythifies the very myths that found the genre.

Nonetheless, he notes, as if anticipating Louis Althusser's theory of ideological reflection, these *surwesterns* ("superwesterns") affect only the "most excentric layer of Hollywood." Their producers wish to show that the "old Western" was an antique, indeed an obsolete form, if not deriving from a puerile past that had to be erased from memory. The new Western is pitched to bring the genre into the complexities of adulthood, with existential dilemma and ambivalence replacing scenarios built on battles of good versus evil. In the postwar years the character of Los Angeles is such that the "shockwaves" of the new Westerns are in fact superficial; they hardly affect the economic core of "ultracommercial" Westerns that a new youth watches on television. These granite-like *couches inférieures* [lower strata] (QQC, 234) that lay beneath the superwestern attest to the fact that "traditional" features were continuing to take root and burgeon without bearing new "intellectual or aesthetic alibis" (ibid.).

The argument takes a sharp turn when Bazin abandons the task of explaining the "evolution of the genre through the genre." He considers auteurs among its determining factors. In the late 1940s and early 1950s, a plethora of directors continued to make sturdy films built on prewar traditions. Hawks, in *Red River* (1948) and *The Big Sky*, (1952) is neither baroque nor decadent; Walsh, in *Saskatchewan* (1954), reaches back to American history, while in *Colorado Territory* (1949), *Pursued* (1947), and *Along the Great Divide* (1951) he moves the "B" level upward without engaging the rhetoric of the *film à thèse* that characterizes the new species. Along with Nicholas Ray's *Johnny Guitar* (1954) these features neither deviate from traditional themes nor do they replace "naïveté" with preciosity, cynicism or pomp. They enrich the genre from within itself thanks to their "psychological savor" (QQC, 236). "Traditionalist veterans," such as Walsh, have younger postwar counterparts in Anthony Mann, who recaptures "the lost secrets" of the genre in a new time, and in Robert Aldrich, who marries the classical style with a "novelistic" component that endows the film with renewed force.

The essay on Budd Boetticher's *Seven Men from Now* (1957) further confirms Bazin's hypotheses. A film that he saw in its original (undubbed) version in a small theater on the Champs Elysées in the "dead season," *Seven Men from Now* responds magnificently to the ideology of a necessary transformation in which the genre moves from a primitive condition to a so-called maturation into adulthood. Unlike *Shane* or *High Noon*, Boetticher's modest feature offers neither symbols, philosophical innuendo, nor even a penumbra of psychology: "nothing more than ultra-conventional characters in very well known roles, but an ingenious setting and especially a constant invention with respect to details that can renew the interest *of the settings and their actions*" (QQC, 246; stress added). There follows a close reading of the ever-slight deviations from the general *topoi*, which include: a plot that seems run-of-the-mill but contains unforeseen reversals; the care that the camera takes not to react overly rapidly to duels and shoot-outs; costumes that slightly jostle our sartorial expectations; absence of parody that would underline the "Westernness" of the Western; irony evinced in bodily movements and not in the dialogue; absence of overt estheticism or intellectual content. In sum, the film uses *style* to reinforce and broaden the scope of the inherited genre.

The slow speed of the evolution witnessed in the earlier article is suddenly felt where Bazin notes Randolph Scott's likeness to the exteriority of William S. Hart. Like the silent actor, his physiognomy "translates nothing because there is nothing to translate" (QQC, 246). The movie shows, he concludes, that the Western of 1957 is not "condemned to be justified by intellectualism or spectacle" (QQC, 247). Rather, *Seven Men from Now* "refines on the primitive structures of the Western while not meditating on or straying from them in order to gain on interests foreign to the essence of the genre" (ibid.) Most of all he finds in Boetticher's rocky décor a site of "setting and action," a presence of evolution obtained from geology. The director "knew how to make prodigious use of the landscape, of the varied matter of the earth, of the grain and the form of the rocks" (QQC, 246).[15]

The attention drawn to the physical and mental landscape bears on Bazin's broader sense of evolution. The "event" that Bazin experienced in his viewing of *Seven Men from Now* in isolation, in the "dead season" of cinema, is felt through the critic's uncommon sense of space, not only because he knows that it is essential to the genre but especially for the reason that it is crucial to any appreciation of the history of cinema. The emotional force that the film exudes "is born of the most abstract relations and of the most concrete beauty" (QQC, 245-46)—in other words, of Aristotelian action "taking place" in a décor that is absolutely indifferent to it. What he notes allusively in this article is developed to a far greater degree in "Théâtre et cinéma," in which he rewrites Henri Gouhier's maxim about theater and presence. Gouhier stated, "The stage welcomes all illusions, except that of presence," which Bazin rewrites as "the cinematographic image can be emptied of all reality, except one: that of space" [on peut vider l'image cinématographique de toute réalité, sauf d'une: celle de l'espace] (QQC, 162). The space in which the hero's pursuit of seven criminals literally *takes place* confirms more broadly that cinema is "essentially a dramaturgy of nature" to the extent that it cannot exist "without the construction of an open space replacing the universe instead of being included within it" (ibid.). This reflection comes on the heels of a remark apropos of Bresson's use of sounds that are "carefully chosen for their indifference to the action, which guarantees its truth" (ibid.): this applies in Boetticher's film to space that is at once indifferent to the action but that brings it forward so as to transform the story and its setting into what elsewhere in *Qu'est-ce que le cinéma?* Bazin calls an event.

When our apprehension of space comes forward through the immutable duration of the landscape, we realize what Bazin implies wherever he writes of the "event" of cinema. At the end of "L'Evolution du langage cinématographique" he rediscovers the great landscapes and seascapes that in *La Terra trema* (*The Earth Will Tremble*, 1948) Luchino Visconti shoots at the seaside village of Aci-Trezza. The "most aesthetic of the neorealists," Visconti crafts his epic film with *plans-séquence* "où le souci d'embrasser la totalité de l'événement se traduit par la profondeur de champ et d'interminables panoramiques" (QQC, 78) [where ambition to include the totality of the event is translated by the depth of field and endless panoramic shots]. Visconti's cinematic style is accounted for through mention of a totalizing effect. To what does it refer? To Visconti's keen sense of topography? To the difference between the location on-screen and what is off, in the movie theater? To a glimpse of totality within and through cinema *tout court*? Partial answers are found in the remarks that tie the essay on film language to those on the American Western.

In the final paragraph of "Évolution du western," Bazin affirms that the cinema of 1940–1950 is not limited to extending the films of the 1920s but in fact discovers in them "the secret of a realistic renewal of storytelling," [le secret d'une régénérescence réaliste du récit] (QQC, 80), which is endowed with a capacity "to integrate the real time of things, the *duration of the event* which classical editing insidiously replaced with an intellectual and abstract time" (ibid.).[16] The superwestern had purveyed intellectual and abstract—that is, thematic, allegorical, psychological—treatments of the genre to repress or eliminate it from memory. However, contrary to the directors of the superwestern, Boetticher and Mann use geology and topography to frame their narratives and not to carry an allegorical function. For Bazin it is especially Boetticher—perhaps because Mann occasionally infuses recent human history into his décors—who would find the duration of the event of the film itself in the landscape, in the meticulously slow pans, two-shots and deep-focus takes of riddled patterns of stone baked in sunlight, indeed décors that call into question the reasons why humans travel through them.[17] The duration of the event would have staunchly philosophical inflection that summons the very location and being of the human species in the world at large. In Boetticher's film, at stake is not just the tale of a sheriff's just vengeance in a hostile environment but more compellingly, in view of the spectator, what promotes our consciousness of our being in the world. Such is what Gilles Deleuze, who owes much to Bazin in his film theory, calls an *event*.

For Bazin the event of cinema finds explanation in what Deleuze makes of it in *Le Pli* (*The Fold*, an essay of 1988 on Leibniz and the baroque, conceived shortly after the work on cinema). Responding to the question he poses (as the title of the fifth chapter), "*Qu'est-ce qu'un événement?*" (what is an event?), Deleuze stages the apprehension and sensation of being in the world in a landscape, which could be that of the American Western of the 1950s—with the exception that here it is the Egyptian desert, the land of hieroglyphs, where Napoleon's soldiers, crossing a plain, file by the great pyramid. When they gaze upon it they realize all of a sudden that the monument has been looking at them over a very long duration of time. The soldiers find themselves in a "nexus" or "swarm" of "prehensions" that causes them to realize that they are "prehenders" being "prehended." As soon as they feel what they see, they see that they are being seen. The event that the Western conveys is a process of simultaneously conscious and unconscious subjectivation and objectivation. Through sensation and perception at once active and passive, one can move into the world and let the world enter the geography of one's body: a feeling of space and being is grasped, and so also an intimation of an open-ended totality of things.[18] To a strong degree the event takes place by virtue of the sensation of geological time that cuts through the perceiving subject. For Bazin its experience in cinema requires deep focus and a long take; it also demands, as he shows throughout his writings, a sense of the times and speed of geological and aesthetic evolution. They both belong to a greater "life of forms" that includes those of the earth's crust, the living organism, and also the seven arts.

By way of conclusion it can be said that in his frequent treatment of evolution Bazin resembles what Deleuze calls a "stratigrapher."[19] Faithful to the tenets of *Qu'est-ce que le cinéma?* Deleuze ranks the Italian postwar directors among the first and finest stratigraphers because they turn landscapes into events.[20] They look at the world in its layers, its *strata*, while at the same time they are *strategists* who use the longer history of the medium to craft new—but also very old—forms of film writing. They create the events of their cinema through landscapes that are the settings and subjects of their films. In a dialectical turn in the final paragraphs of "L'Evolution du langage cinématographique," Bazin sums up by recalling that in the silent era montage "evoked" what the director was seeking while in 1938 montage "described" what today, in 1953, the director "writes" with film (QQC, 80). Writing is precisely where Bazin, in his appreciation of the evolution of cinema, is at once the stratigrapher and a graphic strategist, a coequal of the filmmakers. It is hoped that reading Bazin as a "stratigrapher" in his usage of evolution will further open—*ouvrir*—his work and engage the events it creates through its appreciation of cinema.

Notes

1. Gilles Deleuze, *Cinema 2: The Time-Image*, trans. Hugh Tomlinson (Minneapolis: University of Minnesota Press, 1989), 244.

2. In the notes to his translation of this essay in *What Is Cinema?* (Montreal: Caboose, 2009), Timothy Barnard informs us: "Boireau and Onésime were the title characters of two popular comic film series in early French cinema. The pioneering *Boireau* films were produced by Pathé between 1906 and 1908 . . . and the *Onésime* films were produced by Gaumont between 1912 and 1914," 298.

3. André Bazin, "Théâtre et cinéma," in *Qu'est-ce que le cinéma?* (Paris: Editions du Cerf, 1975, 131. Further reference to this edition will be cited parenthetically as QQC. Where the wording and manner of the French command attention, citations are made in the original and are followed by translations that in all instances are mine. Translations of selected works from *Qu'est-ce que le cinéma?* can be found in *What Is Cinema?* vols. 1 and 2, trans. Hugh Gray (Berkeley: University of California Press, 1967 and 1971); and *What Is Cinema?* trans. Timothy Barnard (Montreal: Caboose, 2009).

4. Louis Marin applies this method of reading to La Fontaine and other classical authors in *Des pouvoirs de l'image* (Paris: Editions du Seuil, 1992), chapter 1. Elsewhere I have used a similar mode of reading in Conley, *The Self-Made Map: Cartographic Writing in Early Modern France* (Minneapolis: University of Minnesota Press, 1996), 296–97.

5. Elsewhere in this volume Ludovic Cortade translates a very similar quotation from "Découpage," one of the sources for "Evolution of the Language of Cinema"; see Cortade, p. 25 infra.

6. Michel de Montaigne, "Essais," in *Oeuvres complètes*, ed. Albert Thibaudet and Maurice Rat (Paris: Gallimard/Pléiade, 1962), 906.

7. Ibid., 1091.

8. The expression reaches back to the Romantic Age in which, as Jacques Rancière has shown via Nerval in respect to Godard, words are things and speak hidden or hieroglyphic languages. Even further, it recalls the hermetic geology of Gesner, Agricola, Münster, and other Renaissance polymaths who find signs of God's presence in the infinite variety of nature. See Jacques Rancière, *Film Fables* (Oxford: Berg, 2006), chapter seven. Original French version, 2001.

9. It can be asked, too, if Bazin follows Walter Friedlander's famous "grandfather law," postulated to show that in the age of Italian mannerism artists found creative force not by imitating their masters but their masters' masters, thus resolving oedipal conflicts that would inhere in direct imitation of paternal models. See *Mannerism and Anti-Mannerism in Italian Art* (New York: Columbia University Press, 1957 reprint).

10. In "Peinture et cinéma" (QQC, 187–92) he signals that montage "reconstitutes a horizontal temporal unity, *geographical in a way*," in contrast to the temporality of painting, which "is developed *geologically, in depth*" (QQC, 188; stress added). The connotation is similar here.

11. In *Early Netherlandish Painting* [2 vols.] (New York: Harper & Row, 1971 reprint), Erwin Panofsky builds much of his study of Northern art of the fourteenth and fifteenth centuries on that model. Erich Auerbach studies it against the background of modern history in *Scenes from the Drama of European Literature* (Minneapolis: University of Minnesota Press, 1984 reprint).

12. Elsewhere, in Bazin's treatment of the grounding myths that the Western deploys to stylize the historical facts it purports to reconstruct, in "Le Western ou le cinéma américain par excellence" (a preface to J. L. Rieupeyrout's book of a nearly eponymous title), Bazin reaches back to Tom Mix, William S. Hart, and Douglas Fairbanks Sr., ostensibly in order to complicate the hypothesis that the modern Western is a direct reflection of American history.

13. Oxymoron, partially because his treatment of Bresson's covertly religious cinema (WC 125–43) is stylistic, and because religion in Bazin cannot be dissociated from aesthetic ontology (a point that Philip Rosen makes infra.). And, too, because the great French works on medieval art, from Emile Mâle to Camille Enlart or Jean Bony to Louis Grodecki, are dedicated to iconography and, above all, to evolutions of form.

14. Henri Focillon, *Vie des formes* (Paris: Ernst Lenoux, 1934), translated as *The Life of Forms in Art*, sets the groundwork for Focillon's grand historical two volumes, *L'Art d'occident* (Paris: Armand Colin, 1938). Like Bazin, Focillon moves across disciplines in his descriptive treatment of the "life" of aesthetic forms. It can be surmised that Focillon's influence on Bazin's idea of evolution moves through the latter's relation with André Malraux's quasi-cinematic history of art. I once tried to sustain the correlation of Focillon and Malraux in "Intervalle et arrachement: Malraux, Henri Focillon et l'affinité de forme," *Revue des lettres modernes (série André Malraux)*, 4 (1979), 3–21.

15. Bazin does not mention that despite the aridity of the stony background in bright sun, the setting for much of the drama, the dénouement is countered by a diluvial nightscape at the very beginning of the film. The attention he draws to the arid world in fact makes the watery contrasts all the more striking.

16. Bazin uses *régénérescence* to convey a spirit of renewal. An uncommon word, found infrequently in dictionaries, *régénérescence* would be the ideal antonym of *dégénérescence* or degeneration. It may be that the term bears a chemical inflection in accord with the geological tone of his reading.

17. Boetticher no doubt belongs to a deeper archeology because the landscape is not the frame for narratives, as they tend to be in Mann's Westerns, based on Sophoclean tragedy in which the rocks and boulders that acquire an anthropomorphic presence constitute a mute choir that "observes" the events taking place.

18. The event has much to do with what Raymond Bellour draws from Daniel Stern, author of *The Present Moment in Psychotherapy and Everyday Life* (New York: Norton, 2004), in a comparative treatment of Deleuze and Bazin. See Bellour, *Corps du cinéma: hypnoses, émotions, animalités* (Paris: POL, 2009), chapter 6 and passim.

19. Gilles Deleuze, *Cinéma 2: L'Image-temps* (Paris: Editions du Seuil, 1985), 317–26.

20. At the outset of *Cinéma 2*, establishing a new classification of cinematic images, Deleuze builds on the concept of the *image-fait*, which Bazin coined in his study of *Paisà*, to show how in that film each shot is an event, is "a garment of reality anterior to meaning" (QQC, 282).

4

The Reality of Hallucination
in André Bazin

JEAN-FRANÇOIS CHEVRIER

Bazin, Reader of Breton, a Reader of Taine

"The Ontology of the Photographic Image" is generally considered the theoretical foundation of André Bazin's conception of realism.[1] But a brief citation—with neither quotation marks nor mention of its source—opens up a chink in the edifice. It appears toward the end of the essay. Bazin distinguishes "the existence of the photographed object"[2] from the painted picture, closed in on itself: sharing "in the existence of the model like a fingerprint, . . . photography plays a real part in natural creation rather than substituting for it." The brief citation occurs in the following paragraph, which deals with surrealist photography, and highlights the surrealists' preference for photography over painting to render their monsters credible:

> This is something that Surrealism foresaw when it turned to the gelatin of the photographic plate to create its visual teratology. The Surrealists' aesthetic goal was inseparable from the machine-like impact of the image on our minds. The logical distinction between the imaginary and the real was eliminated. Every image should be experienced as an object and every object as an image. Photography was thus a privileged technology for Surrealist practice because it produces an image which shares in the existence of nature: a photograph is true hallucination.[3]

Without saying so, Bazin adopts an expression put forth by Hippolyte Taine in 1857: "[External] perception is a *true hallucination*," as opposed to the common definition of hallucination as false perception.[4] This reversal could only have interested Breton who, in the wake of Rimbaud, contrasted "voluntary" hallucination to the norms of realism. In 1870, Taine clarified this expression in *De l'intelligence* (*On Intelligence*). From this book, Breton extracted the image of a hallucinated hand that apparently haunted him, since it appears at least three times in his writings. In 1924, in his *Manifeste du surréalisme*, he mentions "that pretty hand which, during the last pages of Taine's *L'Intelligence*, indulges in some curious misdeeds."[5] Hallucination is the *method* that offers a remedy for the disenchantment noted at the outset:

So strong is the belief in life, in what is most fragile in life—*real* life, I mean—that in the end this belief is lost.[6]

The surrealists used hallucination to rail against the state of things and the "realist" definition, in every sense of the term, of the everyday. The radical expression of this revolt on the fringes of surrealism was the "absolute idealism" advocated by Roger Gilbert-Lecomte:

> To write the poems of Rimbaud or Nerval, to paint the pictures of de Chirico, Masson or Sima, you need to have lived the big adventure, given a knife blow to the fake settings of the perceptible, know that forms are transformed, that the world vanishes in sleep, that hallucination does not differ from perception, and that you cannot contrast a state of health that would be the norm with other states known as pathological. Label: "absolute idealism." We must also believe that another experience of the real, besides the one given by our senses, is possible.[7]

"Absolute idealism" is only an expression. Nonetheless, it does sum up the corrosive power of the *scandal of hallucination* as "perception without object" (according to the classical definition of psychiatry).[8]

Taine founded his psychological theory on the primacy of sensation and the assimilation of image to sensation. It is precisely this assimilation that Sartre reproached him for in *The Imaginary* (*L'Imaginaire*, 1940), after having criticized the primacy of sensation in *Imagination: A Psychological Critique* (*L'Imagination*, 1936). Already in 1934, Maurice Merleau-Ponty had denounced a "psychology of perception loaded with philosophical presuppositions, which enter through the seemingly most innocent notions—sensation, mental image, recollection, understood as permanent beings . . ."[9] In *De l'intelligence*, Taine wrote:

> In order to establish that external perception, even when accurate, is an hallucination, it is sufficient to observe that its first phase is a sensation.—In fact, a sensation, and notably a tactile or visual sensation, engenders, by its presence alone, an internal phantom which appears an external object. Dreams, hypnotism, hallucinations strictly so-called, all subjective sensations are in evidence to this. . . . As soon as ever the sensation is present, the rest follows; the prologue entails the drama. The patient imagines that he feels in his mouth the melting pulp of an absent orange, or the cold pressure on his shoulder of a hand which is not there, that he sees a number of passers-by in an empty street, or hears clearly articulated sounds in his silent chamber.—. . . the objects we touch, see, or perceive by any one of our senses, are nothing more than semblances or phantoms precisely similar to those which arise in the mind of a hypnotized person, a dreamer, a person laboring under hallucinations, or afflicted by subjective sensations. The sensation being given, the phantom is produced: it is produced, then, whether the sensation be normal or abnormal; it is produced, then, in perception where there is nothing to distinguish it from the real object, just as in sickness where everything distinguishes it from the real object.[10]

The Taine citation in Bazin's text highlights the difference between surrealism and phenomenology.

Bazin also uncovers a question that was central in the psycho-physiological redefinition of the art of images in the nineteenth century: hallucination's place between perception and imagination. The idea of perception as true hallucination was thought convincing because the effectiveness of the camera obscura, confirmed and popularized by photography, appeared like the model of a mechanism for the formation of mental images.[11] For Baudelaire, the "government of imagination" was threatened simultaneously by painters who believe only in what they can see and touch—it always comes back to the question of belief—and by photography's popular success. In substituting itself for actual perception, hallucination was a corruption of realism. This is why the scandal of a "perception without object" seduced the surrealists. Taine's theory links this scandal to the "phantoms" that take shape in the brain, like images in the darkroom.

In 1866, when he was preparing *De l'intelligence*, Taine questioned Flaubert on the connections between hallucination, memory, and artistic imagination. Later, the psychiatrist Eugen Bleuler distinguished "in schizophrenics the four main characteristics of hallucinations: intensity, distinctness, projection, and reality value," adding that they "are entirely independent of each other, Each can vary within maximal limits without affecting the others."[12] These characteristics were already noted by Flaubert. But for him, pathological hallucination is essentially a "sickness of memory": "You feel images escaping from you like a hemorrhage."[13] In "artistic" hallucination, on the contrary, the joy of imitation comes from a "concentration of memory":

> So indisputably, for me, does memory play a part in hallucination, that the only way to imitate someone perfectly (to reproduce his voice and portray his gestures) is by great concentration of memory. To be a good mime, your memory must be of hallucinatory clarity—you must actually see those you imitate, be permeated by them.[14]

The joy of artistic creation, wrested from terror, stems from the hold of imitation over memory. Bazin's "mummy complex" is a variation of a theory that engages quite well with phantoms. The mummy is the permanent image of a being that perdures after death as a pure appearance. This confidence in the image was renewed in the nineteenth century, when photography arrived to produce a material equivalent of what Flaubert called "hallucinated" memory.

In 1866, the year of the Taine-Flaubert correspondence, Dr. Ambroise-Auguste Liébeault, a pioneer of research on hypnosis in Nancy, began accumulating cases, anecdotes, observations, and legends on the subject of hallucination. The records he compiled were contributions to an already abundant and repetitive psychiatric literature, which had grown since the beginning of the 1850s. Liébeault sees "the germs of hallucination" in the exercise of a "faculty of mental reproduction" which can become an "artistic advantage" when it is particularly developed, without necessarily leading to madness.[15] Liébeault calls *faculty of reproduction* that which Flaubert describes as a mimetic (mimic) concentration of memory. For Bazin, the mummy is a being of memory, animated by the cinematic mimic.

In *Phenomenology of Perception* (1945), published in the same year as "The Ontology of the Photographic Image," Maurice Merleau-Ponty related the "hallucinatory deception"—hallucination is not a perception but it passes as such—to an "essential function." Deception functions because perception itself supposes a presumption of reality, an antepredicative evidence, prior to judgment, prior to the critical distinction (which only occurs in order to dispel an ambiguity):

In so far as we believe what we see, we do so without any verification, and the mistake of the traditional theories of perception is to introduce into perception itself intellectual operations and a critical examination of the evidence of the senses, to which we in fact resort only when direct perception founders in ambiguity.[16]

Instead of enclosing hallucination in the realm of error, Merleau-Ponty sees in it the effect of a belonging to the "world," prior to the critical posture that distinguishes the true from the false.

To have hallucinations, and more generally to imagine, is to exploit this tolerance on the part of the antepredicative world, and our bewildering proximity to the whole of being in syncretic experience.[17]

Likewise for Bazin, filmic realism must include hallucination (and what it was for Flaubert and the surrealists); filmic realism can only be a reconciliation with the world if it integrates not just the "power of the false," as Deleuze said, but the experience that precedes the distinction of the true and the false.

However, what doesn't come to light with Merleau-Ponty is that hallucination is a field of mental operations: for the relation of addition/subtraction that defines human action in the world, it substitutes the affirmation of what isn't and the negation of what is. Like the mystical vision extracting itself from appearances, hallucination privileges psychic reality over the physical world. But it does not infer the existence of the supernatural. Before manifesting the positive characteristics identified by Bleuler, it represents the negation of perceptive actuality.[18] However, this negation works in the context that justifies a broadened demand for realism. In Mallarmé, who thinks *Nature* and not "absolute idealism," this negation is the condition for a poetic activity that celebrates the earthly *stay*, without claiming to add anything to the world.[19]

Ultimately, Bazin owes as much to Mallarmé as he does to Flaubert and to surrealism. To Mallarmé he owes the idea of the empty screen, which is the support for any projection and the condition of cinematic realism. Here the "mummy complex" is nearing its end. The image will not be a fixing of appearance for eternity—because there is no image. The truth of the screen favors a negative hallucination, one that does not produce an additional reality, but an empty actuality.[20] Bazin wrote about Robert Bresson's *Diary of a Country Priest* (*Journal d'un curé de campagne*, 1951):

Just as the blank page of Mallarmé and the silence of Rimbaud is language at the highest state, the screen, free of images and handed back to literature, is the triumph of cinematographic realism.[21]

The Ants of Neorealism, or Zavattini's Dream

My first question is the following: how can the idea of the hallucinatory gestures that emerged from the Flaubert/Taine correspondence explain the treatment of the everyday, as Bazin observed—and experienced—it in the cinema? Flaubert is the writer in whom realism, the everyday, and hallucination are fitted together, tied, and canceled in a meticulous mnemograph. So what about the Italian neorealism that Bazin saw? How did he look at it? In the same way I was drawn to a detail from "The Ontology of the Photographic Image," I am now going to examine a small descriptive distortion in the 1952 essay Bazin devoted to Vittorio De Sica's *Umberto D.* (1952).

Hallucination is a scandal, but this scandal has nothing exceptional about it; it is a daily occurrence. The word "scandal" derives from the Greek *skandalon* for snare or trap, and from the Latin *scandalum* for stumbling block. For the psychiatrists of the nineteenth century, when psychiatry was called *alienism*, hallucination was a phenomenon that could present two aspects: pathological or physiological. By *physiological*, they understood ordinary, everyday. Their favorite example was the daydreaming that occurs in states of half-sleep, called *hypnagogic*; the term was coined by the historian and wide-ranging author Alfred Maury, a friend of Flaubert and Taine, who studied the mechanism of dreams from his own experience (as would Freud, who cites him several times in *The Interpretation of Dreams*).[22] Just as a dream does, hypnagogic hallucination permits self-observation, at no risk, of the mechanisms of pathological hallucination and delirium. It is an intermediary zone and a bridge between normalcy and madness.

Hallucination was thus not only the characteristic symptom of madness (characteristic to the point that for a long time *hallucinated* was synonymous with *mad*); it was also a psycho-physiological phenomenon observable among the *facts* of daily life.

This notion of the *fact*, so important in Bazin's reflection on the art of filmic storytelling, owes as much to the novel (Stendhal) as to positivism (Taine, disciple of Comte). In his long essay from 1948, "An Aesthetic of Reality: Cinematic Realism and the Italian School of the Liberation," he discerns a new way of adapting the syntax of shots to the reality of facts.[23] Conventional syntax is logical; it links causes and effects, but facts oppose this presupposed continuity (founded on an abstract determinism) with a material discontinuity (concrete), on which is founded another continuity. I will consolidate his reasoning via three quotes (the first recalling the stone, or stumbling block, of *scandalum*).

1. The technique of Rossellini undoubtedly maintains an intelligible succession of events, but these do not mesh like a chain with the sprockets of a wheel. The mind has to leap from one event to the other as one leaps from stone to stone in crossing a river. It may happen that one's foot hesitates between two rocks, or that one misses one's footing and slips. The mind does likewise. Actually it is not of the essence of a stone to allow people to cross rivers without wetting their feet any more than the divisions of a melon exist to allow the head of the family to divide it equally. Facts are facts, our imagination makes use of them, but they do not exist inherently for this purpose.[24]

2. The unity of cinematic narrative in *Paisà* is not the "shot," an abstract view of a reality which is being analyzed, but the "fact." A fragment of concrete reality in itself multiple and full of ambiguity, whose meaning emerges only after the fact, thanks to other imposed facts between which the mind establishes certain relationships.[25]

3. But the nature of the "image-facts" is not only to maintain with the other image-facts the relationships invented by the mind. These are in a sense the centrifugal properties of the images—those which make the narrative possible. Each image being on its own just a fragment of reality existing before any meanings, the entire surface of the screen should manifest an equally concrete density.[26]

Bazin is looking for a materiality of the image. He is opposed not to editing [*montage*], but to its rhetorical use in a cinema of programmed emotion. In editing and its effects he is looking to uncover collage, from which editing materially derives. Unlike editing, collage, as an artistic process, presupposes heterogeneity of material. Now collage first appeared in poetry, in particular via Jules Laforgue (*Grande Complainte de la ville de Paris*, 1884), where heterogeneity focuses on the semantic fields and registers of language, and not on material elements. Bazin here applies to cinematic *photogénie* a principle of realism, true to collage, according to which the equality of the elements of concrete contiguity must be privileged over the hierarchy of compositional motifs (according to the tradition of painted theater). Collage is the democratic procedure that absorbs narrative discontinuity in an "equal, concrete density." I mean *democratic* in the sense used by Fernando Pessoa, alias Álvaro de Campos, in his great poem *Salut à Walt Whitman*:

> *Grande democrata epidérmico, contiguo a tudo em corpo et alma*/Great epidermic democrat, contiguous to all in body and soul.[27]

This line sums up, it seems to me, the egalitarian utopia that underpins the idea of realism inferred by Bazin from postwar Italian cinema.

In 1952 Bazin wrote about *Umberto D.* This was four years after his essay "The Italian School of the Liberation" which was written before neorealism had been defined. In those intervening four years the term emerged. In 1948, Bazin saw in *Paisà* "the equivalent on film of the American novel."[28] In 1952, neorealism exists: it is represented in its most exemplary manner by an Italian author, Cesare Zavattini, the screenwriter of Vittorio De Sica's *Bicycle Thieves* (1948).

In writing about *Umberto D.*, Bazin confidently resumes his argument from 1948:

> The narrative unit is not the episode, the event, the sudden turn of events, or the character of its protagonists; it is the succession of concrete instants of life, no one of which can be said to be more important than another, for their ontological equality destroys drama at its very basis.[29]

Bazin henceforth calls "ontological equality" that which in 1948 he had described in a more felicitous expression as "equally concrete density."[30] More than *Paisà* or *Bicycle Thieves*, which was neorealism's manifesto, *Umberto D.* is the film of everyday duration distinct from the dramatized time of the event. The two dramatic elements are Umberto D.'s expulsion by his landlady and the pregnancy of "the little maid," as Bazin calls her, who works in the boarding house. These are enormous, deeply moving events in the restricted lives of the two characters. One scene (beginning at 30'30") epitomizes for Bazin this intensive reduction of the dramatic range:

> One wonderful sequence—it will remain one of the high points of cinema[31]—is a perfect illustration of this approach to narrative and thus to direction: the scene in which the maid gets up. The camera confines itself to watching her doing her little chores: moving around the kitchen still half asleep, drowning the ants that have invaded

the sink, grinding the coffee. The cinema here is conceived as the exact opposite of that "art of ellipsis" to which we are much too ready to believe it devoted.[32]

This sequence is in fact exemplary, because it introduces the art of the micro-narrative into the dramatic genre, inaugurating what today is associated more with "experimental" cinema. In the duration of daily gestures, *Umberto D.* alters the thickness of the historical narrative. Bazin continues:

> Ellipsis is a narrative process; it is logical in nature and so it is abstract as well; it presupposes analysis and choice; it organizes the facts in accord with the general dramatic direction to which it forces them to submit. On the contrary, De Sica and Zavattini attempt to divide the event up into still smaller events and these into events smaller still, *to the limit of our sensitivity to duration.* Thus, the unit event in a classical film would be the scene "where the maid gets out of bed"; two or three brief shots would suffice to show this. De Sica replaces this narrative unit with a series of "smaller" events: she wakes up; she crosses the hall; she drowns the ants; and so on. But let us examine just one of these. We see how the grinding of the coffee is divided in turn into a series of independent moments: for example, when she shuts the door with the tip of her outstretched foot. As it goes in on her the camera follows the movement of her leg so that the image finally concentrates on her toes feeling the surface of the door.[33]

In fact, the description of the sequence is inexact. Bazin has conflated two scenes from the film. In the sequence he describes, the maid does not drown the ants in the sink. The ants appeared in an earlier sequence (beginning at 11'). What's more, they weren't in the sink but on the wall. The maid turned the faucet hose on them and then torched them with a burning newspaper [figures 4.1–4.2]. This inaccuracy is telling,[34] because the first scene occupies a key moment in the script: it is the moment when the film's two dramatic strands intersect. Umberto D. has just learned that he is being kicked out of the boarding house. He is seated in a corner, collapsed, when the maid, who got her dress wet when spraying the ants on the wall, asks him if he sees something. The old man is surprised; there is no spot on her dress, and in any case, water doesn't stain, but the maid is thinking of something else: she tells him she is pregnant. The second sequence in the kitchen—the one Bazin describes—contains a reminder of the first: the maid again turns the faucet hose on the wall, but her gesture is brief and we don't see what it applies to. It is a clever reminder, partaking in a very skillful art of storytelling. Astonishingly, Bazin was taken in by the process.[35]

The conflation of these two scenes is noteworthy if one thinks of the quasi-symbolic value of the detail of the ants in a text that speaks of a division/miniaturization of an event, pushed to the limits of perception ("to the limit of our sensitivity to duration"). The second scene is of great "psychological" subtlety: obsessed with her pregnancy, the maid nonetheless enjoys closing the door with her foot (without moving from her chair) while grinding the coffee [figures 4.3–4.4]. She is just as obsessed by the ants as she is by what has developed invisibly in her belly. Significantly, Bazin sees the ants in the cavity of the sink.

In another text on De Sica, also written in 1952, Bazin speaks of an "invisible subject":

FIGURES 4.1–4.2: *Umberto D.* (De Sica 1952)

These two sequences [Umberto's D.'s going to bed and the little servant awakening in the morning] undoubtedly constitute the ultimate in "performance" of a certain kind of cinema, at the level of what one would call "the invisible subject," by which I mean the subject entirely dissolved in the fact to which it has given rise; while when a film is taken from a story, the latter continues to *remain visible* like a skeleton without its muscles; one can always "tell" the story of the film.[36]

Bazin has obviously been taken in by this gradual absorption or interiorization of the plot in the filmic event. The organic metaphors are eloquent: the subject's invisibility lies in the slight flesh of the images, in the play of details that proliferate, like ants, in the body of the film. Recounting the sequence, Bazin himself grazes the limits of perception, and, in clearing this boundary, passes from the register of conscious to that of unconscious perception. This passage is carried out in the condensation and the distortion of the narrative detail. The reduction of the dramatic range—accentuated by the enclosed space of the kitchen, displayed for us by the camera—has shifted the dramatic interest from the manifest content to the latent, "invisible" content.

Neorealist cinema broke with the more or less codified norms of psychological dramatization. The kitchen scene depicts a behavior in keeping with the fact, which Bazin describes as

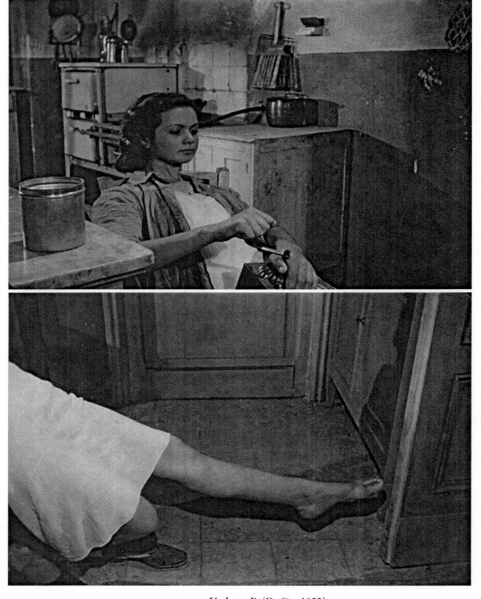

FIGURES 4.3–4.4: *Umberto D.* (De Sica 1952)

"multiple and full of ambiguity." This ambiguity partakes of both a psychological complexity and the language of the unconscious. Neorealism, as viewed in *Umberto D.* and as interpreted by Bazin, is operated by the unconscious.

It seems noteworthy to me that Bazin inserted into the second kitchen scene the image of the ants. During the 1920s, filmic *photogénie*, as it was celebrated by Jean Epstein in particular, was based on the hallucinatory and hypnotic power of the close-up,[37] whereas neorealism favored the sobriety of medium shots. But the image of the ants on a part of the wall is similar to a close-up in its effect of tightening and dislocating (un-boxing) the frame: in slavishly following the story, the camera is going to stumble on a blank surface, troubled by a tiny, living world. Since Dali and Buñuel's *Un chien andalou* (1929), the hallucinatory appearance of ants is a motif associated with surrealist cinema [figure 4.5]. A year later, Cocteau reemployed it in *Le Sang d'un poète* (*The Blood of a Poet*, 1930). Bazin defines neorealism, but he is *haunted* by surrealism, because realism is unable to dispel hallucination which, as Flaubert notes, follows a principle of mimic or mimetic restitution.

In 1967, Zavattini published excerpts from the diary he kept during the war, where we find these two notes:

> War seems more formidable when you aren't in the middle of one.
> Ants have overrun a wall in the kitchen; they march along in a way that reveals their certainty that I won't discover their nest, while in fact I'm already discovering it and. . .[38]

A small theater of cruelty works its way into the everyday of *Umberto D.* The procession and the massacre of the ants in wartime is an additional proof that the dramatic narrative interprets, condenses, and distorts a historical thickness, like memory and dream. The tiny, living world on the blank part of the wall also corresponds to the cases of milling and microscopic hallucinations described in a psychiatric literature (Gatian de Clérambault and Raoul Leroy) of which the surrealists were aware.[39]

We now need to contextualize the two sequences from *Umberto D.* that Bazin condensed in the history of the debate between Hollywood and neorealism. They propose a narrative mode that is neither that of the cinema of the 1920s nor that of Hollywood, but one that partially integrates them both. It was up to the critic Parker Tyler to have identified some of the recurrent themes of the Hollywood imaginary in *The Hollywood Hallucination* (1944). The second chapter of this book is entitled "Hollywood's Surrealist Eye." Parker Tyler was one of the editors of the magazine *View*, which encouraged the introduction of surrealism in the United States during its publication from September 1940 to March 1947. In 1969 he published *Underground Film: A Critical History*, which retraces the sloughing off of European experimental cinema in the context of North American counterculture.[40] *Umberto D.* thus reveals the hallucinatory component of the everyday as interpreted by neorealism, in response to Hollywood and to its underground alternative (which fought over the "expressionist" heritage of European cinema in Hollywood by transforming it).

Bazin saw in "the scene in which the maid gets up" the outline of a Zavattini project:

> Have I already said that it is Zavattini's dream to make a whole film out of ninety minutes in the life of a man to whom nothing happens? That is precisely what "neorealism"

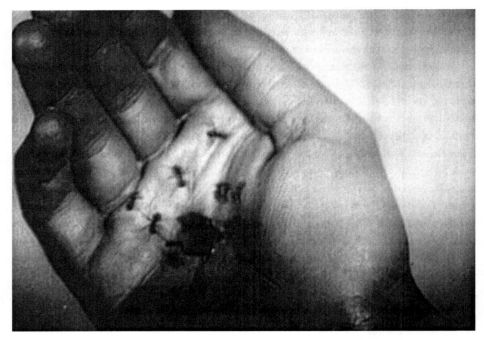

FIGURE 4.5: Surrealist ants (*Un Chien Andalou*, Buñuel 1929)

means for him. Two or three sequences in *Umberto D.* give us more than a glimpse of what such a film might be like; they are fragments of it that have already been shot.[41]

The next year, Zavattini himself wrote:

> With De Sica, we are preparing a film that will probably be called *Il tetto* [*The Roof*]. I don't yet know the structure it will take, but it will probably be the same kind of narrative as *Bicycle Thieves*. A simple story. Even simpler. At the time, we were criticized for doing a film where nothing happened. What a mistake! I think that too many things happened in *Bicycle Thieves*. We are looking for a story where you'll see only the daily life of a man: eating, drinking, working and struggling. All that will become a surprising sight, a lesson in courage.[42]

Zavattini's words are tinged with rage. What Bazin calls "Zavattini's dream" is really a heroic battle pitting the intelligence of matter and the unconscious versus a machine for programming emotions. The goal was to break film industry rhetoric and Hollywood propaganda. Bazin shared this battle, without however subscribing to the intellectual communist's militancy. Zavattini's dream is, he says, "to make cinema the asymptote of reality." This expression appears in the final lines of his essay on *Umberto D.*:

> De Sica and Zavattini are concerned to make cinema the asymptote of reality—but in order that it should ultimately be life itself that becomes spectacle, in order that life might in this perfect mirror be visible poetry. *As to itself, at last, cinema changes it.*[43]

Zavattini's dream is thus also, for Bazin, a Mallarmean dream, since the article's concluding expression reworks the first, famous line of the poem "Tombeau d'Edgar Poe," (1877) "Tel qu'en lui-même enfin l'éternité le change"/"As to Himself at last eternity changes him."[44] While this could be read as a facile, flattering nod to school learning, the allusion is more serious. It confirms that Bazin cares about linking up the fullness of cinema with a transcendence of the image, and that this transcendence works for him by passing the limit: in art, it is always a question of trying to pass limits, where realism carried to its height is an *apotheosis* of the real in the image. Bazin's "invisible subject" corresponds to the "book about nothing" of which Flaubert dreamt:

> What seems beautiful to me, what I should like to write, is a book about nothing, a book dependent on nothing external, which would be held together by the internal strength of its style, just as the earth, suspended in the void, depends on nothing external for its support: a book which would have almost no subject, or at least in which the subject would be almost invisible, if such a thing is possible.[45]

Flaubert expressed this dream when he wrote *Madame Bovary*, the great realist novel from the 1850s. Likewise, there is no pious imagery in the outline of the total film of an ordinary day. *Umberto D.* is perhaps the outline of a dream. But it is first and foremost a film-trap in which Bazin allowed himself to be ensnared. The little maid is not an immaculate saint. The ants of neorealism take part in a little theater of cruelty, and Bazin's errors participate in the work of the unconscious operating in the matter of the film. The ants that the little maid drowns and burns are the motif of an oneiric mechanism originating in hallucination. As viewed and recounted by Bazin, *Umberto D.* is one of those films that reveal how the unconscious expresses itself in the everyday, and in the dramatic imitation of ordinary gestures.[46]

Translated by Sally Shafto

Notes

1. "Ontologie de l'image photographique" stands as the opening essay in *Qu'est-ce que le cinéma?* (Paris: Le Cerf, 1975; 9–17). Its original version was published in 1945 in an anthology edited by Gaston Diehl, *Les Problèmes de la peinture* (Lyon: Éditions *Confluences*).

2. André Bazin, "The Ontology of the Photographic Image," in *What Is Cinema?* trans. by Timothy Barnard (Montreal: Caboose, 2009), 9.

3. Ibid., 9–10. The translator has slightly modified the end of the translation of this passage: for "une hallucination vraie" Barnard translates "a really existing hallucination." Bazin ends the paragraphs by observing: "This is proved by Surrealist painting's use of *trompe l'oeil* and its meticulous attention to detail" (10). In the first version of this essay, he clarifies: "In contrast to Cubism (whose abstract tendencies radically separate it from photography) Surrealism seeks by all means to obtain this credibility of the image that photography alone allows it to achieve." Trans. S. Shafto.

4. Hippolyte Taine, *Les Philosophes classiques du XIXe siècle en France*, quoted and glossed by Tony James in *Dream, Creativity and Madness in Nineteenth-Century France* (New York: Clarendon Press, 1995), 164–66.

5. André Breton, "Manifesto of Surrealism," in *Manifestoes of Surrealism*, trans. Richard Seaver and Helen R. Lane (Ann Arbor: University of Michigan Press, 1969), 5. Taine's hallucinated hand appeared nearly simultaneously in "Caractères de l'évolution moderne et de ce qui en particie," *Pas perdus* (Paris: NRF, 1924). Taine's hand makes a final, full-blown appearance in *Surrealism and Painting*: "I have already had occasion to refer, in another context, to the incident reported by Taine in connection with a most moving case of

progressive hallucinations where the reasoning faculties remained unimpaired. The story concerns a young man under strict dietary treatment for five days for some ailment, who from his bed followed the mysterious movements of a creature of his dreams, a supremely graceful creature who came and sat near him in the pose of the *thorn dancer*, resting an exquisite hand on the coverlet scarcely twelve inches from his eyes, and did not withdraw it when he at last summoned up the courage to grasp it tentatively . . ." Breton, *Surrealism and Painting*, trans. Simon Watson Taylor (New York: Harper & Row, 1972), 14. Translation lightly modified for accuracy.

6.   Breton, "Manifesto of Surrealism," 3.

7.   Roger Gilbert-Lecomte, "Ce que devrait être la peinture. Ce que sera Sima" (catalog of the first exhibition of the "Grand Jeu," 1929), republished in Œ*uvres complètes* vol. 1, ed. Marc Thivolet (Paris: Gallimard, 1974), 138.

8.   The idea that hallucination constitutes a "logical scandal" was put forth by Henri Ey. It corresponds to the phenomenon of "perception without object." The author of the monumental *Traité des hallucinations* observes that this classical definition of psychiatry "with its elliptical and contradictory wording summarizes well the paradox and enigma of Hallucination." H. Ey, *Traité des hallucinations* (Paris: Masson et Cie, 1973), 46.

9.   Maurice Merleau-Ponty, "The Nature of Perception," (1934), tr. by Forrest Williams in *Research in Phenomenology* X (1980), 11.

10. Hippolyte Taine, *On Intelligence*, vol. 2, book 2, ch. 1, trans. T. D. Hayes and revised with additions by the author (New York: H. Holt, 1884), 6–7. Original English text (London: Reeve and Co., 1871), Part II, Book 1, Chapter 1, 221.

11. This model asserted itself at the moment when the most recent research in the area of experimental psychophysiology, particularly in Germany, called into question a mechanical optic (impersonal, disembodied) deduced from the functioning of the camera obscura. For more on this topic, see Jonathan Crary, *Techniques of the Observer: On Vision and Modernity in the 19th Century* (Cambridge: MIT Press, 1990).

12. Eugen Bleuler, *Dementia praecox*, trans. J. Zinkin (New York: International Universities Press, [1911] 1950), 109.

13. Gustave Flaubert, "Letter to Hippolyte Taine, December 1, [1866]," in *The Letters of Gustave Flaubert 1857–80*, ed. and trans. Francis Steegmuller (Cambridge: The Belknap Press of Harvard University Press, 1982), 98.

14. Ibid.

15. Liébeault cites a list of famous individuals who enjoyed this benefit, from Michelangelo and Raphael to Balzac. According to Liébeault, Balzac reported that "if he imagined a penknife entering his flesh, he would feel the pain; and that in imagining the battle of Austerlitz, he saw the troops fight; he heard the rattle of the weapons, the gunfire, the scream of the wounded, etc." Similarly, a colleague, the English psychiatrist A. L. Wigan, "speaks of a painter who having his conceptions pose in front of him had only to copy them." *Sommeil provoqué et les états analogues* (Paris: Octave Douin, 1889), 94–95. First edition, *Du sommeil et des états analogues considérés surtout au point de vue de l'action du moral sur le physique* (Paris: Masson, 1866).

16. Merleau-Ponty, *Phenomenology of Perception*, trans. Colin Smith (New York: Humanities Press, 1962), 342.

17. Ibid, 343. Merleau-Ponty also asserts: "We succeed, therefore in accounting for hallucinatory deception only by removing apodeictic certainty from perception and full self-possession from perceptual consciousness." Ibid.

18. See André Green, "Le travail du négatif et l'hallucinatoire (l'hallucination négative)," *Le Travail du négatif* (Paris: Les Éditions de Minuit, 1993), 217–87. Green defines negative hallucination as "representation of the absence of representation."

19. Mallarmé deals with the theme of an earthly *stay* in "Bucolique," *Divagations* (1897); Œ*uvres complètes*, vol. 2, ed. Bertrand Marchal (Paris: Gallimard, "Bibliothèque de la Pléiade," 2003), 252–56. Translated by Barbara Johnson (Harvard University Press, 2007). Until recently, Mallarmé's reference to Nature was ignored in favor of an overinterpretation of his interest in the verbal and linguistic sign. According to Mallarmé, "Nature is, we add nothing to it . . ." but the poet can seize and arrange *relations of aspect and number*. See *La Musique et les lettres* (1895); Œ*uvres complètes* vol. 2, 67–68.

20. André Green clarifies: "It should also be noted that negative hallucination is not limited to non-perception but is completed by the unconsciousness of non-perception." ("Le travail du négatif et l'hallucinatoire," 261).

In the artistic realm, in particular in Mallarmé, the mechanism is on the contrary supported by a conscious intention (with the particular gratification that results from its operation). Here we encounter Flaubert's distinction between pathology and art, *vis à vis* positive hallucination.

21. Bazin, "*Le Journal d'un Curé de campagne* and the Stylistics of Robert Bresson," in *What Is Cinema?* vol. 1, 141. The emptied screen from a Bresson film corresponds to Mallarmé's poetics of the void insofar as it allows for the sudden appearance of words on the screen beyond or below the image. Bresson inscribes on the screen: at the end (in the beginning) was (is) the Word, represented by the sign of the cross. The Mallarmean void is here the place of the biblical representation of the incarnated Word.

22. In 1845, the *Annales médico-psychologiques* published Jules Baillarger's article "De l'influence de l'état inter-médiaire à la veille et au sommeil sur la production et la marche des hallucinations." In 1861, Maury collected his observations in *Le Sommeil et les rêves*, subtitled *Études psychologiques sur ces phénomènes et les divers états qui s'y rattachent, suivies de recherches sur le développement de l'instinct et de l'intelligence dans leurs rapports avec le phénomène du sommeil* (Paris: Didier et Cie, 1861; revised and expanded, 1878). A long chapter is devoted to "hypnagogic" hallucinations. For a biography of Maury's career and literary friendships, see Frank Paul Bowman, "Du romantisme au positivisme: Alfred Maury," *Romantisme*, 21–22 (1978), 35–43.

23. Bazin, "An Aesthetic of Reality: Cinematic Realism and the Italian School of the Liberation," in *What Is Cinema?* vol. 2 (Berkeley: University of California Press, 1971), 16–40.

24. Bazin, "An Aesthetic of Reality: Cinematic Realism and the Italian School of the Liberation," 36. This passage brings out the etymology of "scandal," the "stone of scandalum" just mentioned by the author, which is a "pierre d'achoppement," the stone that makes one stumble. [Translator's note].

25. Bazin, "An Aesthetic of Reality: Cinematic Realism and the Italian School of the Liberation," 37.

26. Ibid. Corrected here is a translating error or printing typo in the last sentence where "screen" (*l'ecran*) is given as "scene." [Translator's note].

27. Fernando Pessoa (Alvaro de Campos), *Salut à Walt Whitman*, in *Fernando Pessoa & Co.: Selected Poems*, ed. and trans. Richard Zenith (New York: Grove Press, 1998), 59. Symbolist poet Jules Laforgue was one of the first French poets to read and translate Whitman.

28. Bazin goes so far as to write: "The aesthetic of the Italian cinema, at least in its most elaborate manifestations and in the work of a director as conscious of his medium as Rossellini, is simply the equivalent on film of the American novel." Bazin, "An Aesthetic of Reality," 39.

29. Bazin, "*Umberto D*: A Great Work," in *What Is Cinema?* vol. 2, 81.

30. Bazin, "An Aesthetic of Reality: Cinematic Realism and the Italian School of the Liberation," 37. Original French: "égale densité concrète." *Qu'est-ce que le cinéma?* 282.

31. Hugh Gray, slightly mistranslates this phrase. Bazin calls this scene a high point of cinema ("l'un des sommets du cinéma"), which Gray inaccurately renders as: "one of the high points of the film." Translator's note.

32. Bazin, "*Umberto D*: A Great Work," 81.

33. Ibid. The italics in the quote indicate an emendation of the Gray translation. Instead of Gray's "to the extreme limits of our capacity to perceive them in time," the current translator prefers: "to the limit of our sensitivity for duration."

34. Hervé Joubert-Laurencin points out that Bazin in his first articles on *Umberto D.*, in May and June 1952 after Cannes, wrote only that the little maid "drives away the ants" (*Cahiers du cinéma*, June 1952). It was thus after the film's national release in October that he distorted the narrative by condensing the two scenes and placing the ants in the sink. Thus in the four months from Cannes to Paris, he reworked the film by writing about it.

35. The evocation of the ants in the second kitchen scene is a typical ellipsis: the maid's gesture of spraying a little water on the top of the wall is meaningful only because it refers back to the earlier scene.

36. Bazin, "A Note on *Umberto D*," in "De Sica: Metteur en Scène," in *What Is Cinema?* vol. 2, 76–77. The italics indicate an emendation of the Gray translation. Instead of "the latter continues to survive by itself," ("reste distincte") the current translator prefers: "remains visible."
    This essay is a chapter from the book on De Sica, published in Italian in 1953.

37. In 1921 Jean Epstein notably wrote in *Bonjour cinéma*: "I can never express how much I like the American close-ups. They are sharp. Suddenly, the screen displays a face and the drama, in a tête à tête, addresses me personally and swells to unforeseen intensities. Hypnosis. Today, tragedy is anatomical." J. Epstein, *Écrits sur le cinéma*, vol. 1, ed. Pierre Leprohon, (Paris: Seghers, 1974), 93.

38.   Cesare Zavattini, *Cinéparoles*, trans. Nino Frank (Paris: Denoël/Les Lettres Nouvelles, 1971), 290. Original Italian: *Straparole* (Milan, 1967). In the preface, Zavattini reports that his notes on the war years, included at the end of the volume, were previously unpublished.

39.   See Gaëtan Gatian de Clérambault, "Du diagnostic différentiel des délires de cause chloralique" (1909), in *Œuvres psychiatriques* (Paris: Frénésie Éditions, 1942); "Les Introuvables de la psychiatrie," 1987, 146–47. Raoul Leroy was a doctor first in the asylum of Evreux, then in the one of Ville-Évrard; in Saint-Dizier (Haute-Marne), he directed the Neuro-Psychiatric Center of the Second Army where André Breton served as an intern from July to November 1916. On Leroy, Breton, and Lilliputian hallucinations, see Alain Chevrier, "André Breton et la psychopathologie de son temps: deux exemples," *Mélusine*, 21 "Réalisme-surréalisme" (2001), 213–26.

40.   Parker Tyler was a regular contributor to Jonas Mekas' journal *Film Culture*. In 1947 he published *Magic and Myth of the Movies* (H. Holt & Co., 1947).

41.   Bazin, "*Umberto D*: A Great Work," 82.

42.   Cesare Zavattini, "Dieci anni dopo," in *Neorealismo ecc.*, ed. Mino Argentieri (Milan: Bompiani, 1979), 158. The French version is in *Les Lettres françaises*, 1954.

43.   Bazin, "*Umberto D.*: A Great Work," 82. The italics indicate an emendation of the Gray translation. Instead of Gray's "be the self into which film finally changes it," the current translator prefers: "as to itself at last cinema changes it," which better captures the Mallarmé reference

44.   Mallarmé, "Tombeau d'Edgar Poe," in *Collected Poems*, trans. Henry Weinfeld (Berkeley: University of California Press, 1994), 71.

45.   Flaubert, "Letter to Louise Colet, January 16, 1852," *The Letters of Gustave Flaubert 1830–57*, 154.

46.   It's possible that Bazin did not read much Freud, but in an amusing article on the frustrations of the film critic exposed to the seductions of the Cannes beaches, he writes: "This is when the critic understood that the cinema is a dream. Not as it is sometimes understood because of the illusory nature of the cinematic image, nor because spectators find themselves as if immersed in a passive daydream, nor even less because it makes possible all the fantasies of dreams, but more profoundly in the strictly Freudian sense, because it has done nothing more than "dramatize" the fulfillment of a desire." Bazin, "Cannes-Festival 47," *Esprit* (November 1947), 773–74.

5

Beyond the Image in Benjamin and Bazin

The Aura of the Event

MONICA DALL'ASTA

Was Bazin directly inspired by Walter Benjamin's "The Work of Art in the Age of Its Technological Reproducibility" in the elaboration of his uniquely influential theory of film? Did his ontologic conception of film as reproduction somehow occur to him while reading Benjamin's most famous writing?[1]

Answering this question would be of strategic importance in acknowledging what should appear to be quite obvious, if subterranean: the Benjaminian lineage in the French cultural tradition, since Bazin seems to be the missing link in an otherwise recognizable critical constellation, which includes André Malraux, Jean-Luc Godard, Guy Debord, and Serge Daney. The debt these authors owe Benjamin, mainly uncredited, marks their own assumption of his idea of critique as appropriation, where the practice of citation goes without the use of quotation marks.[2] As for Bazin, no evidence has been uncovered to date that he may have known the essay, but his elaboration of the theme of technological reproducibility shows so many points of convergence—as well as divergence—with Benjamin's theory, that doubt is inescapable.[3] At any rate, the hypothesis is not implausible, since the "The Work of Art" essay was for a long while only available in French, published in 1936 by the Institute for Social Research in its journal, which at the time was issued in Paris.[4] It was not until 1955 that a later German version of the essay (initially destined to appear in the Moscow-based journal *Das Wort*) was finally issued in Germany, while the first English translation did not come into being until 1968.[5] So in fact for more than twenty years the corpus of reflections to which Benjamin had attributed the most decisive value, in programmatic terms,[6] remained accessible only to Francophone readers. While certainly not intentional, this exclusively French destiny was also not entirely accidental on Benjamin's part, as publication in French was quite an unusual choice for the Institute journal—an exception that can only be explained by the author's explicit vow that the essay should chiefly address "the avant-garde of French intellectuals."[7]

Benjamin's desire to influence the French cultural debate can be linked to the political climate that had emerged in the country with the rise of the Popular Front. The exiled philosopher looked on the rhetoric of this period with a certain amount of skepticism, but also with the sense of urgency of an intellectual who wished to become, as he put it, "an engineer . . . of the proletarian revolution."[8] But despite its ambitions, the text failed completely to stimulate debate. The most notable exception to the general neglect was André Malraux's solitary tribute in his 1940 "Sketch for a Psychology of the Cinema,"[9] in anticipation of the much more important role Benjamin's theory of art would come to play in that author's aesthetic thought, first thoroughly exposed in *Le Musée Imaginaire* (1947).[10] In other words, and certainly not by chance, the single significant trace of the text's reception at the time of its publication just happens to be one of the most influential French essays on film of the period. Moreover, and again certainly not by chance, Malraux's "Sketch" is the only text referenced by Bazin in "Ontology of the Photographic Image."

Of course, to claim Bazin's knowledge of Benjamin's essay on the basis of his knowledge of Malraux's would be to argue from a false syllogism, but the coincidence can become our cue to compare the two authors' respective theories of technical reproduction. Whether or not Bazin did have a chance to read the essay is certainly less interesting from this perspective than recognizing how cogently his theory of ontological realism can be regarded as a coherent development of the problematic posed by Benjamin in his theses on reproducibility and exposability. There are moments in his theory when Bazin truly seems to engage in dialogue with some basic assumptions of the "The Work of Art" essay. Though there is no evidence that this may have been the actual case, a close and productive critical dialogue can easily be construed (or imagined) on the basis of textual comparison. Revealing this linkage is the aim of the present investigation: a retroactive attempt to accomplish what Benjamin wanted all along, establishing a legacy among "the avant-garde of French intellectuals."

At first, Bazin's theoretical attitude, with its insistence on concepts like authenticity and revelation, would seem to be at odds with Benjamin's central thesis, a sheer reversal of the notion according to which, as an outcome of reproduction, the filmwork is by its own nature devoid of any aura. Yet things are not so simple, for nowhere in his writings does Bazin allow the reader to indulge in an aestheticist view of the cinema; never are we allowed to think that the filmwork counts only insofar as it satisfies the requirements of art. Actually for Bazin the auratic value of a filmwork is inversely proportional to its value as art, for cinema's value derives from being imperceptible or transparent in front of the singularity—or aura—of what it reproduces: only then can the filmwork acquire a sort of indirect aura, obtained, Bazin writes, by "a transference of reality from the thing to its reproduction" (WC, 13–14). This is the core of his famous "poetics of transparency," according to which, to accomplish its revelatory mission, cinema as a technical-linguistic apparatus must step down to make room for reality, since in film "nature at last does more than imitate art: it imitates the artist" (WC, 15).

Now, what at first seemed to have been a complete reversal of Benjamin's invitation to appreciate film precisely on the basis of—and not despite—its lack of aura appears much more ambiguous in Bazin's theory. We could call it a reversal only if we could demonstrate that Benjamin's opposition between aura and reproducibility was reducible to a positive and a negative value; but this is not the case. One need only analyze the different ways in which these concepts are used in several of his essays to grasp their ambivalence. His peculiar dialectical method is characterized by a ceaseless oscillation and reversal of the terms involved in the opposition, explicitly defined as "dialectics at a standstill."[11] For Benjamin, aura and reproducibility are themselves *both* values, which can *eventually* become positive or negative depending on the circumstances in which they become operative: that is to say, they are *mobile* values, in a reciprocal relationship of inversion. The more the former falls, the more the latter rises.[12]

This question over Benjamin's attitude toward the loss of aura (is it positive or negative?) has been posed too simply. Just consider the many different formulations of the notion across various key essays. Two examples are particularly telling. The first concerns the shift from the negative role that aura is called to play in "The Work of Art" (when in section two it is equated with the oppressive authority of tradition) to the thoroughly positive function it acquires in section five of his last work, the decisive "Theses on the Philosophy of History" (when the "true picture of the past," as the collective gesture of quoting history typical of all revolutionary events, is described as the unreproducible image *par excellence*, which "flashes up at the instant when it can be recognized and is never seen again"). The second example of ambivalence is even more astounding since it shows up in the penultimate paragraph of "The Work of Art" essay itself, when Benjamin writes that in chemical laboratories the imperialistic war machine has developed processes by which "aura is abolished in a new way." By associating the destruction of aura with human annihilation Benjamin presents it as the least desirable event imaginable, yet he does so at the end of an essay that demonstrates precisely the opposite, the maximum desirability of the loss of aura in the frame of Marxist cultural politics.

The apparent contradiction revealed in this passage might represent a key to the interpretation of the essay as a whole, in that it provides a strong indication of what I would call a biopolitical conception of aura. The whole critique of the auratic image can productively be read as a vow that the desacralization of art would free human beings from subjugation to the principle of authority and promote a process of secular, collective apperception of the unrepeatability and singularity of each human life. In other words, the *immediate* obliteration of aura that occurs in the phenomenon of human annihilation finds its reversal in a form of *mediated* destruction whose object is the semblance of authenticity carried by the images through which power has always concealed the reality of its violence. This explains why Benjamin is so harsh in criticizing those exponents of French cinema who indulge in describing the film experience in terms of magic; though the only relevant name he mentions is that of Abel Gance, his critique fits the attitude of the so-called first avant-garde as a whole, including its concept of *photogénie*. According to Jean Epstein, for instance, *photogénie* is a "mystery" that reveals itself in the form of an ephemeral yet punctual aesthetic experience, corresponding to an experience of singularity.[13] A similar superimposition of *photogénie* and singularity can be found in Louis Delluc's observation that the most photogenic physiognomies are not necessarily the prettiest ones but can rather be found among uncommon and peculiar subjects, those endowed with a most specific aspect and personality.[14] Epstein would later elaborate on this notion in contending that film language, quite unlike verbal language, is bound to operate with elements that, inasmuch as they are concrete, are singular and unrepeatable by their very nature.[15]

This view of concrete *photogénie* is firmly opposed by Benjamin in section three of his essay as a mystification of the true power of the medium, which he describes as the principal agent of a new form of perception, whose "'sense of the universal equality of things' has increased to such a degree that it extracts it even from a unique object by means of reproduction." *Photogénie* paralyzes the audience in the contemplation of an image of singularity, without developing any critical sense of how that image was produced. The trap of *photogénie* is best

exposed in the French version of the essay, and particularly in the section in which the act of filming is equated to the kind of selection or filtering routinely used in factories, where "countless workers are subjected every day to countless mechanical tests. These tests take place automatically: those who prove inadequate undergo elimination."[16] In other words the "beautiful semblance" (section nine) that *photogénie* strives to reintroduce into the film experience risks becoming a new criterion for the selection of individuals, according visibility to the exhibition of just those subjects or physiognomies that best respond to the camera's elaboration of their appearance. Benjamin is careful to remark how this technically driven type of selection nonetheless depends on expert teams, as "the camera director in the studio occupies a place identical with that of the examiner during aptitude tests" (The Work of Art, note 10). The biopolitical aspects of *photogénie* as a form of artificial selection appear most vividly in the final version of the essay, in the famous footnote concerning the figures of the film star and the dictator. As the quintessential products of media competition, these figures actually exhibit a semblance of uniqueness that removes them to a separate, inaccessible universe, but which in fact is a mere result of the photogenic elaboration of their image, accomplished by specialized technicians.[17]

The real focus of the essay, then, is not the photographic rendering of the image, but rather montage, that is, not the process of reproduction as such, but the discursive handling of the images of things and people once (re)produced. To put it as clearly as possible, the examples of the film star and the dictator demonstrate that the process of image multiplication does not ensure per se that the spell of aura has been eliminated from the world of images;[18] this result can only be obtained through a *destructive* usage of montage, one that programmatically denies the illusion of wholeness and integrity, and aims instead to disaggregate and fragment the subjects of the reproduction into a multiplicity of perceptions. Benjamin's discourse here is more suggestive than analytical, for he does not discriminate between different styles of montage, for instance between Leni Riefenstahl's sophisticated construction of Hitler's staggering uniqueness in *Triumph of the Will* (1935), and, on the opposite side, Dziga Vertov's choral composition celebrating multiplicity and difference in *The Man with a Movie Camera* (1929). Yet Benjamin's belief is clear: the multiplication, disaggregation, and even actual explosion of perception—which reproducibility *allows* but which only proper montage *ensures*—is of the greatest importance in the process of social emancipation, because it can contribute to the development of a collective critical attitude, leading audiences to compare various images and viewpoints and thus relativizing the value of any single image. Shots come one after another as so many "positional views" on the object (The Work of Art, section 8), something that can transform the movie theater into a schoolroom for critical—and political—analysis.

Many of these motifs resonate intensely in Bazin's writings. From his essay on the Stalin myth in Soviet cinema to his critique of Hollywood editing as a form of visual illusionism, to his support for the use of nonprofessional actors in Italian neorealist cinema, Bazin demonstrates a drive to develop the possibilities and responsibilities of cinema as a social agent in a way that seems to pick up—and step up—Benjamin's project. Yet Bazin writes at a totally different moment, when the consequences of the greatest destruction of human aura that the world has ever known are under everybody's eyes.

What should cinema do with the devastation of war and its aftermath? We know Bazin's answer: it must bear witness to all this, expose it, broadcast its visibility; but it must do so as a genuine witness, so that the singularity of each thing that has been damaged is preserved in the indexical mode of cinematic signs. After all, an index points to something particular. This reappearance of the theme of singularity corresponds to a reformulation of the question of aura in the discourse on film. Yet Bazin does not claim the value of the filmwork to be based in a new aesthetics, as was the case with *photogénie*. On the contrary, he firmly refuses to attribute a cult value to the film image, for his appreciation of cinema takes place at the expense of the image; the image, he writes, should tend to "the most neutral kind of trasparency" (WCII, 57) in order to achieve "an added measure of reality" (WCII, 27; "plus de réalité"). The value of a film increases as its style diminishes, when cinema as a technological-linguistic apparatus makes room for "raising the limpidity of the event to a maximum, while keeping the index of refraction from the style to a minimum" (WCII, 57). And so, Bazin upholds a sort of reversed aesthetics, in which the value of a filmwork is inversely proportional to its aestheticizing tendencies. Clearly expressed in the pages on neorealism, this attitude is further developed in his reflections on the so-called cinema of cruelty, a critical category that would prove enormously influential to later generations of French film critics, up to and beyond Serge Daney.[19]

Bazin's distinct contribution to the concerns he shared with Benjamin comes most pointedly through the concept of *événement* (event), which he draws from contemporary existentialist philosophy. His insistence on the dimension of time reactivates the dialectic of aura and reproducibility. By preserving the physical trace of what it records and reproduces, cinema is literally for Bazin a technique that "embalms time" (WC, 14), a new social practice that completely transforms the phenomenology of memory.[20] What is preserved and transmitted in film reproductions is much more than simply images: it is, very exactly, the remnants of the past, the sensible residue of a singular, unrepeatable duration that was already passing by, never to return, at the time when it was being filmed.

Unlike any other of the visual arts, cinema, under certain conditions, can make the spectator aware of the original unrepeatability that rests at the core of reproducibility itself, encouraging the perception of the uniqueness of the events reproduced and then re-presented on the screen. However, this strong perceptual effect cannot be taken for granted, being the product of what, in Benjaminian terms, we might call the circumstances of exposure: the exposure of the film stock in the first place (that is, of the film as witness), but more importantly the exposure of the subjects reproduced, to which should be added the spectator's own exposure to the reproduction. Bazin aims to provide the spectator with critical tools to assess the witness-value implied in different filmworks.

The most important of these tools are the linked concepts of sequence-shot [*plan-séquence*] and forbidden montage [*montage interdit*]. Bazin's reversal of Benjamin's theses is so complete here that it is tempting to read it as an actual response. Yet this reversal is not a simple refusal, since Bazin evidently accepts the Benjaminian assumption that aura dissipates through the systematic fragmentation of the continuity of action in montage.[21] But whereas Benjamin in the "The Work of Art" essay did not distinguish between *découpage* and *montage*, in fact discussing the first in terms of the second,[22] Bazin situates this distinction exactly at the center of his critical discourse. First, he shows that the most truly deconstructive practice in filmmaking is represented not by montage, but by *découpage*, that is, by the breakdown of the profilmic scene into separate shots, as preconceived before the filming in view of the editing.[23] In fact, he argues that montage of the traditional (or classical) sort plays a *constructive*, rather than destructive role, for it generally works to *recompose* fragments, building a simulacrum of wholeness, or spatiotemporal coherence. Even more troubling, montage can create the illusion of a reality that never existed in front of the camera in the first place, a phantasmagoria that looks real but is nothing other than a concatenation of vapid images. In short, montage can be used to confound the audience's perception of the circumstances of exposure, thus subjecting them to the thrust of a highly directed discourse that does not appear to be one, insofar as it conceals itself under the immediate evidence of reproduction.

This is why the notion of *plan-séquence* is so crucial, for it refers to the one technique that, because of the dimension of time, can put the spectator in a condition to assess the authenticity of what is shown on the screen.[24] By adjusting the duration of the shot to the duration of the action reproduced, the long take puts the spectator in front not of an image, but an event such as it presented itself to the camera eye during the process of recording. As if to anticipate Deleuze's definition of the event as an "emission of singularities,"[25] Bazin makes clear that the uniqueness revealed in continuous filming is actually a function of multiplicity, since it depends on the interaction of various coexisting elements within the scene—as in the famous example of Nanook and the seal (WC, 50–51).

Moreover, and more importantly, duration—as a continuous modulation of multiplicity—allows us to witness not just the visible scene developing before the camera, but the invisible side of the event, the living presence of the look onto the scene from *behind* the image. Since the type and the degree of exposure of the subjects reproduced are determined from the perspective of this invisible sphere, we can sense its virtual exhibition in the duration of the shot and so assess the reciprocal positions of the filmed and the filming subjects in the there-and-then of reproduction. This would seem to reconstitute aura not in terms of aesthetics but rather in terms of ethics, and even in biopolitical terms, if it is true that a major effect of the sequence-shot is its ability to draw the invisible subjects who are in control of the reproduction into a relationship of visibility that can be tested and criticized by the viewer. In any case, the final addressee of this critique of exposure is the film spectator, who will have to gauge the degree of his or her own exposure. Bazin here has introduced a cinematic conscience, the awareness of the responsibilities of the medium in relation to what has aptly been called the historicity of the film image.[26] Thus Bazin's critical theory seems to reverse the thought of Benjamin only to reenact it on a different level, in a strange, delayed version of "dialectics at a standstill."

But there is still more. This vision of cinema does not entail, as is usually believed, a complete refusal of montage; instead it provides the context for a thorough reformulation or reinvention of its possibilities. Beyond the complementary destructive/constructive forms of classical editing, Bazin argues, modern cinema has disclosed the potential for what could be described as an expository deployment of montage—a revelatory, then critical practice that he endorses under the name "neo-montage," best represented today by the type of film one would ascribe to the found-footage genre.[27] Entirely composed of archival materials, films like *Paris 1900* (1947) or *La Course de taureaux* (*Bullfight*, 1951), both produced by Pierre Braunberger, are for Bazin demonstrations that montage can still be used not just to create a phantom of reality, but precisely to offer a more acute perception of the historicity, or witness-function, of film reproductions. Unlike both the continuity editing of Hollywood and Eisenstein's dialectical montage, this neo-montage aims not to generate a simulacrum of unity through the synthetic combination of disparate fragments, but on the contrary to bring out the singularity of each shot, as the record of "the sensible continuum out of which the celluloid makes a mold both spatial and temporal."[28] This is the opposite tack from the invisible deconstruction of recorded reality that classical *découpage* practices with a final synthesis in mind; instead, neo-montage achieves an openly visible analysis of its material, aiming to reveal the conditions of its original exposure.

Bazin's profound approval of *La Course de taureaux* (notwithstanding its violation of what, in the same essay, "Death Every Afternoon," he describes as the cinematographic taboo par excellence: the repetition of the unrepeatable, sacred event of death) may stem from the way its expository style of editing provides the spectator a critical approach to the images. The same, however, cannot be said of another film mentioned in the article, a newsreel of 1949, which he calls "a haunting documentary about the anti-Communist crackdown in Shanghai in which Red 'spies' were executed with a revolver on the public square. At each screening, at the flick of a switch, these men came to life again and then the jerk of the same bullet jolted their necks."[29] Discussing this document in opposition to *La Course de taureaux*, Bazin seems to indicate (though as usual in his subtly allusive style) that cinema's real taboo is not the "ontological ob-scenity" of certain images but the (ever more) frequent lack of proper expository context in which to situate them. The conscientious practice of this new kind of montage can provide a context that puts spectators in a position to gauge the images reproduced. Expository montage, familiar to students of found-footage films, has both "analytical" and "critical" potential, both of which Bazin's conceptual frame supports.[30] Indeed, in offering what is surely the first critical account of found-footage as a filmmaking practice, Bazin comes surprisingly close to the famous Benjaminian concept of a materialist historiography based on montage and citation.

Of course all this could never prove that Bazin actually read "The Work of Art"; nonethe-less, I hope to have provided a sufficient number of clues that lead to the idea that both theories are engendered from a single assumption: namely, that the only genuine truth that reproduc-ibility brings to light in its systematic destruction of the myth of art is that images are nothing more than images, and that if something like aura has ever been around, it will have to be found elsewhere, outside the filmwork, in the uniqueness of living experience.

Notes

1. This article is based on a much longer text containing additional bibliographic precision. See Monica Dall'Asta, "Benjamin/Bazin: dall'aura dell'immagine all'aura dell'evento," in *Benjamin, il cinema, i media*, ed. Roberto De Gaetano (Cosenza: Pellegrini, 2007), 187–231.
2. Examples range from Malraux's elaboration of a new method of historical knowledge of art based on the concept of reproduction—for more on this, see Dudley Andrew and Steven Ungar, *Popular Front Paris and the Poetics of Culture* (Cambridge: Harvard University Press, 2005), 370–78—to Serge Daney's reception of the Benjaminian notion of experience, mediated by Giorgio Agamben (particularly *Infancy and History: On the Destruction of Experience*, Verso, 2007), repeatedly quoted by Daney in *L'exercise à été profitable, Monsieur* (1993), up to Godard, whose *Histoire(s) du cinéma* (1988–1998) is a literal application on film of the histo-riographical method described by Benjamin in his *Theses on the Philosophy of History* (1940). See Monica Dall'Asta, "The (Im)possible History," in *Forever Godard*, ed. Michael Temple et al. (London: Black Dog, 2004), 350–63. As for Guy Debord, his concept of "situation" faces the consequences of what Benjamin called "exposability."
3. Dudley Andrew and Steven Ungar write that Benjamin "seems not to have directly inspired" the work of either Malraux or Bazin (*Popular Front Paris and the Poetics of Culture*, 370). Yet Andrew's own *André Bazin* (New York: Oxford University Press, 1978), depicts a voracious reader who would hardly have allowed Benjamin's essay on film to have escaped his attention.

4.   Walter Benjamin, "L'œuvre d'art à l'époque de sa réproduction mécanisée," *Zeitschrift für Sozialforschung* (May 1936), 40–68; now in *Écrits français*, ed. Jean-Maurice Monnoyer (Paris: Gallimard, 1991), 140–71. The French version was translated by Pierre Klossowski with the assistance of Benjamin himself, based on a previous unpublished German version, "Das Kunstwerk im Zeitalter seiner technischen Reproduzierbarkeit," in *Gesammelte Schriften*, vol. 7:1, ed. Rolf Tiedemann and Hermann Schweppenhäuser (Frankfurt am Main: Suhrkamp, 1989), 350–84; English translation: "The Work of Art in the Age of Its Technological Reproducibility (Second Version)," in *Selected Writings* vol. 3, 1935–1938, ed. Howard Eiland and Michael W. Jennings (Cambridge: Harvard University Press, 2002), 101–13.

5.   A third, significantly revised German version was completed by Benjamin (who hoped for Bertolt Brecht's help to get it published in the USSR in *Das Wort*, a Germanophone journal of literary criticism) in the spring of 1939. First published in *Schriften*, ed. Theodor Adorno and Gretel Adorno (Frankfurt am Main: Suhrkamp, 1955), this version was to become the basis for all subsequent foreign translations, including the one published by Hannah Arendt in her famous *Illuminations* anthology (New York: Harcourt, 1968), and translated by Harry Zohn as "The Work of Art in the Age of Mechanical Reproduction." A new English translation by Harry Zohn and Edmund Jephcott appears as "The Work of Art in the Age of Its Technological Reproducibility (Third Version)," in *Selected Writings* vol. 4, 1938–1940 (Cambridge: Harvard University Press, 2003), 251–83. For a close comparison of the different versions of the text see Miriam Hansen, "Room-for-Play: Benjamin's Gamble with Cinema," *October*, 109:1 (2004), 3–45; and Bruno Tackels, *L'œuvre d'art à l'époque de Walter Benjamin: Histoire d'aura* (Paris: L'Harmattan, 2000).

6.   Benjamin, letter to Werner Kraft, October 26, 1935: "Let me note that I have completed a programmatic essay in art theory. It is called 'The Work of Art in the Age of Mechanical Reproduction.'" *The Correspondence of Walter Benjamin, 1910–1940*, ed. and trans. Manfred R. Jacobson and Evelyn M. Jacobson (Chicago: University of Chicago Press, 1994), 517.

7.   Benjamin, Letter to Max Horkheimer, February 28, 1936: in Gesammelte Briefe vol V, 1935-1937, ed. Theodor W. Adorno (Frankfurt: Suhkamp Verlag, 1999), 252. "If this work is to have an informative value for the avant-garde of French intellectuals, its political position must not be obliterated."

8.   Benjamin, "The Author as Producer" [1934], in *Selected Writings* vol. 2, 1927–1934, ed. Michael W. Jennings et al. (Cambridge: Harvard University Press, 1999), 780. The Popular Front was in part launched in June 1935 by the Congress of Anti-Fascist Writers, chaired by André Gide and André Malraux, which Benjamin attended, but without intervening in the discussion. Benjamin's skepticism toward the Popular Front can be found in a letter to Fritz Lieb of July 9, 1937, in *Correspondence*, 542.

9.   André Malraux, "Esquisse d'une psychologie du cinéma," *Verve*, 8 (1940), 69–73. This entire journal appeared simultaneously in English, with Malraux's text titled "Outlines of a Psychology of the Cinema" translated by Stuart Gilbert. The reference to Benjamin's text appears only in the French edition, on page 71, the only footnote in the essay.

10. Malraux, *Le Musée Imaginaire* (Geneva: Skira, 1947). On Benjamin's possible influence on Malraux, see Rosalind Krauss, "Reinventing the Medium," *Critical Inquiry*, 25 (1999), 291; and Edson Rosa da Silva, "La rupture de l'aura et la métamorphose de l'art: Malraux, lecteur de Benjamin?" *La Revue des lettres modernes*, 10 (1999), 55–78.

11. Benjamin, *The Arcades Project*, ed. Rolf Tiedemann, trans. Howard Eiland and Kevin McLaughlin (Cambridge: Harvard University Press, 1999), 463. See also Susan Buck-Morss, *The Dialectics of Seeing: Walter Benjamin's Arcades Project* (Boston: MIT Press, 1991), 217–27.

12. Benjamin, "The Work of Art in the Age of Its Technological Reproducibility (Second Version)," 105–6.

13. Jean Epstein, "Magnification," in *French Film Theory and Criticism* vol. 1, 1907–1939, ed. Richard Abel (Princeton: Princeton University Press, 1988), 236. For *photogénie* as a "great mystery" see Epstein, "Bonjour cinéma" (1921), in *Écrits sur le cinéma* (Paris: Seghers, 1974), 37.

14. "If you aim for the *pretty*, you'll only get the *ugly* . . . [Yet] an individual, whether beautiful or ugly, will keep his or her expression which the camera will enhance." Louis Delluc, "Photogénie" (1920), in *Écrits cinématographiques* vol. 1 (Paris: Cinémathèque française, 1985), 35.

15. "To things and beings . . . cinema thus grants the greatest gift . . . in the highest guise: personality. . . . Every aspect of the world, elected to life by the cinema, is so elected only on condition that it has a personality of its own." Epstein, "On Certain Characteristics of *Photogénie*" (1924), in *French Film Theory and Criticism*, 317.

16. Benjamin, *Ecrits français*, 154; my translation. Original: "Le processus du travail, surtout depuis sa normalisation par le système de la chaîne, soumets tous les jours d'innombrables ouvriers à d'innombrables épreuves de tests mécanisés. Ces épreuves s'établissent automatiquement: est éliminé qui ne peut les soutenir." This point has been moved to note 10 in the English versions, losing its full formulation.

17. Benjamin, "The Work of Art in the Age of Its Technological Reproducibility (Third Version)," *Selected Writings* vol. 4, 277 (footnote 27): "Radio and film are changing not only the function of the professional actor but, equally, the function of those who, like the leaders, present themselves before these media.... This results in a new form of selection—selection before an apparatus—from which the star and the dictator emerge as victors."

18. Patrice Rollet contends that Benjamin was "less concerned with the [destiny of the] traditional aura ... than with this *aura of substitution* which denies the irremediable loss of the first." Rollet, "The Magician and the Surgeon: Film and Painting," in *The Visual Turn: Classical Film Theory and Art History*, ed. Angela Dalle Vacche (New Brunswick: Rutgers University Press, 2003), 40.

19. Bazin, *Le cinéma de la cruauté: de Buñuel à Hitchcock*, ed. François Truffaut (Paris: Flammarion, 1975); English translation, *The Cinema of Cruelty: From Buñuel to Hitchcock* (New York: Seaver Books, 1982).

20. The Bergsonian inspiration that spans Bazin's work represents an important common feature with Benjamin's late writings, though the essay on film is precisely the one which allows no room for the notion of duration. One could say that Bazin reinjects Bergson and duration into Benjamin's film theory.

21. Confirming my view is Jon Wagner who writes, "What is most significant is not the critical possibility of a formalist/realist synthesis, but whether that synthesis has in fact occurred. Benjamin, I think, predicts it, and Bazin, I believe, begins to accomplish it." Wagner, "Lost Aura: Benjamin, Bazin and the Realist Paradox," *Spectator*, 1 (1988), 65.

22. In the French version, these two terms are equivalent: "La nature illusioniste du film est une nature au second degré–résultat du découpage. Ce qui veut dire: *au studio l'équipement technique a si profondément pénétré la réalité que celle-ci n'apparaît dans le film dépouillée de l'outillage que grâce à une procédure particulière – à savoir l'angle de prise de vues par la caméra et le montage de cette prise avec d'autres du même ordre.*" Benjamin, *Ecrits français*, 160 (italics in original).

23. This key distinction is laid out in detail by Timothy Barnard in the endnotes to his translation of *What Is Cinema?* (Montreal: Caboose, 2009), 261–81.

24. See Diane Arnaud, infra, for a full discussion of the relation of the *plan-séquence* (sequence-shot) to *découpage*.

25. Gilles Deleuze, *The Logic of Sense* (New York: Columbia University Press, 1990), 60.

26. See Philip Rosen, *Change Mummified: Cinema, Historicity*, Theory (Minneapolis: University of Minnesota Press, 2001) 301–4.

27. Bazin, "Death Every Afternoon," in *Rites of Realism: Essays on Corporeal Cinema*, ed. Ivone Margulies, trans. Mark A. Cohen (Durham: Duke University Press, 2003), 27–28.

28. Ibid., 30.

29. Ibid., 30–31. For further discussion of this disturbing footage see Hervé Joubert-Laurencin, infra.

30. Nicole Brenez distinguishes the "critical" and "analytical" tendencies in found-footage cinema in "Montage intertextuel et formes contemporaines du remploi dans le cinéma expérimental," *Cinémas*, 1–2 (2002), 49–67. For a Bazinian analysis of recent found-footage films, see Dall'Asta "Benjamin/Bazin: dall'aura dell'immagine all'aura dell'evento."

6

Bazin as Modernist

COLIN MACCABE

For many in the '70s, Bazin was read not through the cinema but through the nets of Parisian theory. When I first wrote about Bazin, in *Screen* in the summer of 1974,[1] I treated him as a theoretically naïve empiricist, a kind of idiot of the family. In fact, what was idiotic was to construct an Althusserian straw man out of Bazin's commitment to the real. Bazin's elegant writing interrelated the variables of filmmaking—industry, art, technology—with a depth and sophistication that *Screen's* analyses desperately needed. Indeed, his understanding of these variables was what made his commitment to the real anything but a naïve empiricism, conjugating at the same time technology and sociology, author and audience. It was this multiple understanding of the real which was crucial to any developed theory or criticism of cinema. But this multiplicity was impossible to recognize for those seduced by that Parisian rereading of modernism which reduced the real to sexual difference.

It was only when I started preliminary work on my biography of Godard in the early '90s, after nearly a decade of producing films, that I recognized that Bazin was unsurpassed as a writer on cinema. Still, as Hegel remarked somewhere, if you're thinking something, then there's a high probability that a lot of other people are thinking it too, and when I began a process which might yet lead to the publication of a complete works it was a pleasant surprise, even fifteen years ago, to find how many people were beginning to read and reread the founder of *Cahiers du Cinéma*.

It is often said that a prophet is without honor in his own country but at that time I was surprised to find that *Cahiers* regarded the idea of an *oeuvres complètes* as a product of a pedantic university spirit, *un projet des cuistres*. However, I took some solace in the fact that Godard himself, when I sought his advice, felt that an academic complete works of Bazin replete with variants, sustained by detailed biographical and institutional readings, was worth the immense expenditure of effort. Godard's encouragement determined that the British Film Institute found some small pittance for a researcher to go back through the archives of the *Le Parisien libéré* and *Télérama* and dig out Bazin's short reviews of recently released films and his even shorter previews of films scheduled to appear on television. However, I was not persuaded that the game was worth the candle until all the papers had been collated and, dipping into them, I found to my slight surprise and complete delight that every review and preview, however short, brought the whole weight of Bazin's experience and thought about the cinema to bear in luminous sentence after luminous sentence. Here I must pay tribute to Dudley Andrew. If we look at the contemptibly dismissive attitude of the '70s, it was Dudley who saved our honor with a biography that still repays reading. When I began to look for collaborators in the early '90s, Dudley was the most enthusiastic, the most hardworking, the most generous of friends; he even provided a beautiful daughter to explore the dusty archives for the aforementioned pittance. "The Complete Works of Bazin" was jettisoned in 1998, another small consequence of New Labour's comprehensive destruction of the British Film Institute as a center for research and reflection on the cinema. However, I am more convinced than ever that the project must go forward despite some remaining skepticism.

Recently, Raymond Bellour wondered if the labor and difficulties entailed by a genuine scholarly edition were warranted for a writer who, in whatever regard he may be held, cannot be considered in the same breath as modernist writers of the first order, his example being Proust.[2] I would make two comments on that. The first is that the work to be contemplated is not really so terrifying. As recent work on Bazin has demonstrated—I am particularly thinking of such magisterial studies as Ludovic Cortade's on the subject of Bazin's geography lessons[3] —much of the biographical and scholarly work necessary for comprehensive annotation has already been accomplished. And although a putative editor might be daunted by the existence of as many as four variations of a single Bazin article, the fact is that all these variants are in print. One of the astonishing discoveries of the early '90s was that there were no "foul papers"; that Bazin had printed every word that he had ever written, and if, like a good journalist, he had sometimes printed them three or four times, the problem of variation is relatively limited. More important, this empty bottom drawer gave further force to my experience of dipping into the occasional journalism: Bazin was a writer who at every moment and on every occasion that he sat down to write brought with him the entire history and theory of the cinema in a continuous reflection; his writing and rewriting really does find its place with the great modernists.

If any skeptic has bothered to read my title "Bazin as Modernist," he or she could be incredulous on at least three counts. A theorist might complain that Bazin is famous as a realist and, from Lukacs' denunciation of modernism (as the degradation of bourgeois subjectivity no longer able to cope with a real which promises death to its own class) to Greenberg's celebration of an art which has left representation behind to follow form and function, all are agreed that modernism is to be opposed to a realism which it supersedes and displaces. A literary historian might be affronted by the simple chauvinist mistake which transposes a category that makes perfect sense in English—modernism is that moment which registers the fatal shock of the First World War in a series of closely linked works—Joyce's *Ulysses*, Eliot's *The Waste Land*, Woolf's *Mrs. Dalloway*—for which there is simply no equivalent in French, where modernism is allowed to stretch from Baudelaire to Valéry, a genealogy in which it would be more than bizarre to want to place Bazin. Finally, a more naïve reader might say that I have missed the point entirely and that Bazin's embrace of the cinema with its mass audience and its established genres was designed precisely to avoid the pitfalls of modernism. Certainly that is how Eric Rohmer and his disciples took it as they consciously elaborated a new classicism, Godard in the vanguard, in the yellow *Cahiers* of the '50s.

The third objection is the most easily dealt with because, of course, so many of the most important modernisms were classicisms. From Joyce's *Ulysses* to Broch's Virgil, from Eliot's

Dante to Pound's *Sextus Propertius*, modernism has sought in the classic a refuge from a tired and inane romanticism forever pounding its chest with its emphasis on subjectivity. Modernism searches everywhere—in language, in the body, in history—for that objectivity which will deliver us from the horrors of personality into the bliss of being. Modernism has, it is true, found this bliss a trifle difficult to disseminate. I refer here to what can be called the "Aunt Josephine" problem. When Joyce finished *Ulysses*, finished that long journey in which he had realized that the only way out of the paralysis of Dublin was the way in, he sent a copy to his mother's sister, Josephine Murray, arguably the person to whom he had been the closest for the longest time, certainly the only person with whom he was ever to discuss his most intimate problems. When his aunt sent back word that she could not make head or tail of the book, Joyce replied in a letter —ridiculous or tragic according to taste—in which he urged his aunt to go out and find a copy of Homer's *Odyssey* and, that read, his own book would become transparently readable.

If Bazin thought, as Godard certainly did, that they were the modernists who could escape this cruel fate, death spared him the impasses which were to confront both the New Wave and the more general project of a film criticism that would produce an improved cinema. By 1963, as *Les Carabiniers* played to empty cinemas in Paris, if it was not yet clear that the New Wave was in fact the Last Wave, it certainly was clear, to use Joubert-Laurencin's elegant formulation, that the Nouvelle Vague was in fact a Vague Nouvelle[4] and a *nouvelle* without an audience. This is the topic of Godard's *Le Mépris* (*Contempt*, 1963) where the misquotation from Bazin that prefaces the film has the merit of condensing Bazin's project in which criticism of the cinema will, through improved cinematic art, deliver a better world. It is that project of which *Le Mépris* recounts the last days as Aunt Josephine reappears in the guise of Brigitte Bardot, uninterested, unimpressed, contemptuous, while European cinema goes down before the energy of American Capital.

Bazin's project, which may seem merely quixotic to anybody under fifty, was in fact a well-thought-out response to the crushing defeat of the popular movements of the immediate post-war era. In those heady days, he would retreat to the Café Flore and from there endeavor to produce the criticism which would educate an audience to demand better films which would deliver a better world. But this strategy was dependent on critics continuing to play a small but vital economic role as films were released in two or three cinemas in capital cities and a film's economic success was, in small part, a function of its critical reception. This function disappeared in the summer of 1975 as Hollywood adopted the platform release in which a film opens in a thousand cinemas, now often two or three thousand, with saturation television advertising. For those who like their history simple and full of crude lessons, I am happy to remind you that the first film for which this strategy was adopted was Steven Spielberg's *Jaws*.

If Godard's career allows us to read cinema in the '60s as a rerunning of the modernist paradoxes of the audience, David Trotter's brilliant book *Cinema and Modernism* (2007) makes clear that we must read Bazin as part of the original reaction to the cinema as a technology and thus as part of that modernism defined by Joyce, Eliot, and Woolf. One of the immense merits of Trotter's book is to make clear that modernism is importantly defined by its reaction to cinema, as much as by its reaction to the First World War.

This recasting of modernism makes relations between cinema and literature central to both media in a way which is not reflected by the current rigid compartmentalization between literary criticism and film studies in universities. Trotter's book challenges the fundamental assumptions of twentieth-century literary criticism. Richards and Eliot promoted the university study of literature as a deliberate response to the threat posed by popular culture, of which cinema was the most dangerous element. On this account popular culture in general and cinema in particular encouraged imprecise and sloppy forms of feeling and thought which only the close reading of difficult texts could remedy.

For Richards and Eliot, cinema and literary modernism are constituted within completely different intellectual and aesthetic paradigms. So powerful was this ideology that for several generations it was able to ignore the uncomfortable fact that the leading modernists were deeply interested in, and influenced by, cinema. More recently, it is this interest and influence which has been the focus of two decades of literary scholarship. Emblematically one could point to Joyce's forming of a consortium of businessmen in Trieste to launch Dublin's first cinema, or to the magazine *Close-Up*, which in the late '20s and early '30s attempted consciously to conjugate modernist concerns and cinema. These two examples can be multiplied many times over.

If Trotter draws on and adds to this recent scholarship, he does so with a very different emphasis. The question of influence has been posed by most literary critics in terms of technique, preeminently the technique of Soviet montage. Trotter has two very different arguments against this widespread understanding of influence. Firstly, as a matter of historical fact, neither the films nor the writings of the great exponents of Soviet montage were available in the West when the great modernist texts (*Ulysses*, *The Waste Land*, *Hugh Selwyn Mauberley*) were published in the immediate aftermath of the Great War. But even if one were to grant that montage, as the fundamental procedure of all cinema, did crucially influence these texts, Trotter has a more important argument. The emphasis on technique has, for Trotter, obscured the influence of the cinema as medium. The crucial fact about this new medium, as Bazin argued so powerfully in "The Ontology of the Photographic Image," is that for the first time representation occurs without the intervention of human subjectivity. Trotter develops Bazin's argument in terms of the ways in which both modernist writing and early cinema investigate the possibilities of representation without human intervention.

This idea of a "degree zero" of representation had appeared in late nineteenth-century literature in guises as different as symbolist poetry and the naturalist novel before the Lumière brothers invented "the last machine."[5] Bazin himself had noticed this in an aside in which he claimed that the best way to understand the relations between twentieth-century literature and cinema was not in terms of influence or borrowing but as a "certain aesthetic convergence."[6] This convergence is the subject matter of Trotter's book, and he demonstrates brilliantly how cinema's impersonality, both in the moment of its representation of reality and in the moment of its projection to an audience, is central to worlds as different as Joyce's Dublin, Eliot's Wasteland, and that of Woolf's Mrs. Ramsay.

Trotter's book does much more than develop recent literary scholarship to produce readings of three modernist classics that emphasize the medium of cinema as central to their construction. His interest is in both the elements of Bazin's "convergence"—not simply how literature uses cinema to develop its notion of impersonality but how cinema promotes a modernist emphasis on reality. For this latter element, Trotter draws on the very considerable scholarly rediscovery of early cinema. However, he uses this better understanding of how film differentiates itself from literature to emphasize, particularly in the work of Chaplin and

Griffith, how film shares modernist literature's concern to break with conventional forms of representation in order to render a more complex reality. Eric Auerbach, at the end of his discussion of Woolf's *To The Lighthouse*, characterizes modernism's commitment to reality in the following terms: "What takes place here in Virginia Woolf's novel is precisely what was attempted everywhere in works of this kind (although not everywhere with the same insight and mastery)—that is, to put the emphasis on the random occurrence, to exploit it not in the service of a planned continuity of action but in itself. And in the process something new and elemental appeared: nothing less than the wealth of reality and depth of life in every moment to which we surrender ourselves without prejudice."[7]

Auerbach is writing in 1945 at a time when linking modernism to a deepened realism is not controversial. Developments in the '50s—one thinks of both Lukacs and Greenberg—began that polarizing of opinion that opposed modernism to realism; but it was in the classic works of Parisian theory that this opposition became absolute, as all realism according to Barthes' classic *S/Z* is simply an ideological operation to mask the only reality—sexual difference. The conceptual emphasis on the already instantiated, so evident in Foucault's "discourse," Althusser's "ideology," Derrida's "text," meant that this theory was unremittingly hostile to any notion of a reality which might have escaped the nets of language. If we were to consider the relation between language and reality, then there could be no question of mapping language onto reality because there was no way to get to that reality except in language. This view of language and reality as constituting two homogenous realms in which one had to choose between a false empiricism (reality determines language) and a true idealism (language determines reality) was heavily dependent on the hegemony of a Saussurean model. Language, understood here as the systematic *langue* which underpins any natural language, could only be analyzed internally without any reference to reality; indeed negative differences rather than positive identities constitute Saussure's object of study. However brilliant Saussure's analysis may be at solving the problem of the specification of the identities that linguistics studies, above all the definition of the phoneme, it is fundamentally misleading when we come to consider the relation between language and the real from a multitude of other perspectives. Most important, whatever our notion of meaning, which will always refer to other words, we also need a notion of reference—that is to say, the variety of practices within any particular discourse by which we encounter and analyze the real. These practices are not "outside" language but they are multiple and multiply contradictory—from Dr. Johnson kicking his stone and refuting Berkeley's "thus"; to the observations of an astrophysicist; to the camera and the multitude of ways in which the photographic image is used from the cinema theater to the police station.

For Bazin, in all great cinema there is a fundamental "gain" of reality, the ability to allow the spectator to explore reality further. This notion has little to do with empiricism because the reality that the camera grasps is not independent of that camera. If this is not evident in the more directly theoretical of Bazin's formulations, it is completely obvious when we look at his criticism. In the sequence of essays that constitute the first volume of *Qu'est-ce que le cinéma?* Bazin moves between documentary and fiction while trying to elaborate the criteria by which films develop the ontological possibilities of the image; *Kon-Tiki* (1950) is praised because despite its undeniable technical defects the camera participates in the reality and struggle of the voyage. Films about Stalin are dismissed because despite their extraordinary technical virtuosity, the contradictions of reality are extinguished from the screen as Stalin's omniscience renders everything from the battle of Stalingrad to a broken-down tractor transparently comprehensible.

Bazin famously took Welles and Rossellini as his great examples, but it is interesting how different these examples are. Welles' great advance for Bazin is formal and technological. He uses the new lenses available at the end of the '30s to produce a depth of field that leaves the spectator free to pick out significance in a more complex image. The complexity of Rossellini's image is achieved by an amalgam of fiction and reality. Most strikingly this comes in the use of nonprofessional actors; the streets of the towns and cities of *Paisà* (1946) are so vivid because the figures that inhabit them are not actors but the men, women, and children who are living through the dreadful realities of postwar Italy. Although Rossellini was to evolve through at least three different stages, culminating after 1962 with the historical films made for television, his methods did not change. The man who called cranes "vulgar and stupid" had no time for elaborately staged camera movements. What mattered to him was the interaction between camera and setting which allowed "reality" to appear; a key guarantee of this was the use of nonprofessional actors.

Perhaps the most remarkable example of this grasping of reality is Rossellini's use of the performance of the office clerk Jean-Marie Patte as the young French king in *La Prise du pouvoir par Louis XIV* (1966). Patte's striking performance was grounded in an astonishing difficulty. Patte, who had never acted before a camera, was incapable of learning his lines, which thus had to be written out for him on huge boards distributed around the set. Most directors might have blanched at this, but here exactly was the reality that Rossellini would never shy away from. Patte's anxiety and his inability to look his interlocutor in the face (since he is reading his lines from a board) are exploited to produce a king visibly using will to triumph over circumstance.

If we understand Bazin's realism not as a single relation between representation and reality but as a complicated series of relations between camera and setting, then it is evident that he is to be counted with the great modernists of the twentieth century. And his modernism belongs to a strain that adamantly avoids the simple division between elite and popular art that has increasingly marred recent critical discussion. It may be among Bazin's most important claims to supremacy as a critic that in his work the mainstream and the avant-garde coexist so easily. As Trotter's book shows, right at the center of the films of Griffith and Chaplin one finds an emphasis on the random occurrence, linking these works to the modernist masterpieces and to a joint political project of a democratization of life, a focus on what Auerbach called "the elementary things which men in general have in common."[8]

Of course at his death, Bazin was very largely identified with *Cahiers du Cinéma*, widely perceived both as right wing and anti-avant-garde. The full history of *Cahiers* and Bazin in the '50s has, I think, despite Antoine de Baecque's tireless efforts,[9] yet to be written. But just as there is absolutely no evidence of a change in Bazin's political commitment to the left, there was equally no change in his commitment to the full range not just of cinema but of the moving image in all its aspects. It is important to remember that it was Bazin who insisted that the first issues of *Cahiers du Cinéma* were of a journal devoted to both film and television and, perhaps even more tellingly, that Bazin was on the RTF's list of nuisance callers because of the frequency with which he bombarded this station with complaints about the accuracy of their natural history programs. There seems little doubt that when Bazin began the journal, it was not just television but also the full range of experimental cinema that he wished to cover. A strong indication of this can be found in the collections of opinions on the avant-garde that *Cahiers* published in 1952 and which took an extract from Hans Richter as its starting point. Bazin's own contribution stresses the importance of the avant-garde of 1925–1928, and his admiration for it, although he condemns its attempt to separate itself completely from commercial film-making, an attempt which contributed to its collapse. For Bazin an avant-garde must be linked to a mainstream; it cannot constitute itself as an entirely separate realm.

To claim Bazin as modernist today is as much to make a claim about modernism as about Bazin. There are many who assert that both are relics from the past, modernism a last desperate attempt by the Western tradition to cope with the realities of mass culture, Bazin hopelessly outdated by the technological revolution that is replacing analog with digital. It is true that computer-generated imagery puts into question Bazin's axiom that the photographic image is an automatic record of what has been placed before the camera. But then what is surprising is that in the twenty-seven years since CGI was first used in a feature film (*Tron*), audiences still seem to demand the guarantee of realism which Bazin analyzed as the great aesthetic promise of the cinema. If one regards the vast majority of contemporary films and indeed television, CGI is either relegated to the edge of the frame or is used for obvious special effects. Cinema continues to be the realistic medium that Bazin heralded. A recent telling example was Steve McQueen's remarkable film *Hunger* (2008). There can be no doubt that a great deal of the force of the film came from McQueen's decision to starve his lead actor, Michael Fassbinder, to the absolute limits of medical safety. No amount of makeup, camera angles, or digital effects could have brought home the devastating violence of a hunger strike as powerfully as the sight of a body wasting away before our eyes.

McQueen's training in film has taken place within, and thanks to, the new space of distribution and exhibition which has opened up over the last twenty years. For the development of digital technologies has led more and more artists like him to work in the moving image, while museums and galleries have become the venue where some of the most exciting uses of film can be viewed. An example of the new realities that such work can make available is found in Filipa César's 17-minute film *Rapport* (2007), shot during a three-day seminar where the principles of neurolinguistic programming were used to liberate psychic potential in a group of managers. This film makes clear, in a way which would be almost impossible in more conventional forms, how contemporary capital depends on harnessing individual narcissism to achieve corporate goals.

There can be no doubt that we have here a Bazinian "gain" in reality. From the technological point of view it is impossible to imagine this film without the mini-DV technology that was used to shoot it. The film gains its force from its ability to observe unobtrusively the participants over a long period of time [figures 6.1–6.2]. Older cameras did not have this ability: not only did they require frequent changes of magazines, and thus a crew of at least two, to service these changes, but the weight of the camera placed a severe physical limit on the amount of time that a shot could be held.

If from this aesthetic and technological perspective, César is following a direct line from Welles' use of new lenses in 1940, the site of exhibition and the financing of the film *Rapport* depends on new realities that Bazin could scarcely have imagined at his very early death. It is a common mistake to think that the credit crisis which began in July 2007 is something new. Marx's analysis of crisis as endemic to capitalism in *Capital* volume 3 has proved more and more

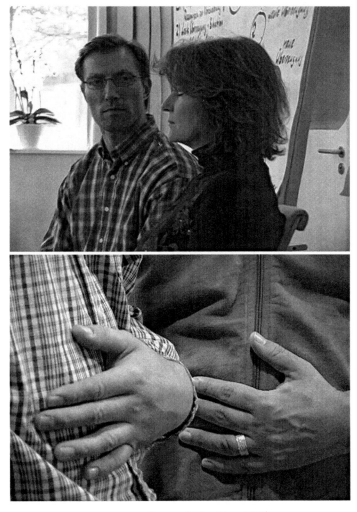

FIGURES 6.1–6.2: *Rapport* (Filipa César, 2007)

accurate since Reagan and Thatcher dismantled the social democratic settlement of the Second World War. For more than a decade now as value evaporated from currencies, commodities, equities, and stocks, the wealth managers of investment banks have advised their nervous high net worth clients that a wise spreading of risk counsels a 10 percent investment in art. One of the side effects of this investment advice together with the development of the new technologies is a new exhibition site for the cinema. You cannot see *Rapport* in a cinema but in a museum—in my case at Tate Modern.

How Bazin would have analyzed this development can only be guessed at, although it is remarkable to think that if he had lived to the age of his friends Alain Resnais and Chris Marker he would have had the opportunity to do so. What can be said is that these new developments—together with both the DVD market and the enormous growth of festivals as a form of exhibition—have given a new role to the Bazinian critic, now rebaptized as curator.

FIGURES 6.3–6.4: "The Hollow Men," Moscow (Chris Marker 2008)

FIGURES 6.3–6.4: (Continued)

Modernism was always a fundamentally utopian movement, a belief that the most developed forms of art could reach the most democratic audiences, and so in conclusion let us celebrate such a utopian moment. Early in 2008 the Garage Group in Moscow approached Chris Marker for a work that would be projected as a massive public video installation on top of the city's Mosenergo building, running twenty-four hours a day. Marker's choice was a single-screen version of his eight-screen installation *The Hollow Men* that had premiered in 2005 at the Museum of Modern Art in New York and which had been inspired by Eliot's poem of the same name [figures 6.3–6.4]. Thus modernist art illuminates contemporary reality.[10]

Notes

1. Colin MacCabe, "Realism and the Cinema: Notes on Some Brechtean Theses," Screen, 15:2 (Summer 1974), 7–27.
2. Raymond Bellour, "The Tense of the Shot (with Daniel Stern)," lecture delivered at Yale University, December 6, 2008.
3. See Cortade, ch. 2 *infra*.
4. This formulation is the title of an essay by Hervé Joubert-Laurencin, in *Nouvelle Vague, nouveaux rivages*, ed. J. Cleiric (Rennes: Presses Universitaires de Rennes, 2001).
5. Hollis Frampton, "For a Metahistory of Film," quoted in Ian Christie, *The Last Machine* (London: British Film Institute, 1994), 7.
6. André Bazin, "In Defense of Mixed Cinema," in *What Is Cinema?* vol. 1, trans. Hugh Gray (Berkeley: University of California Press, 1967), 63.
7. Erich Auerbach, *Mimesis: The Representation of Reality in Western Literature* (Princeton: Princeton University Press, 2003), 552.
8. Ibid.
9. Antoine de Baecque, *Cahiers du cinéma: histoire d'une revue* (Paris: Seuil, 1991).
10. MacCabe, "Moscow Memories," *Sight and Sound*, 19:2 (February 2009), 11.

7

Film and Plaster

The Mold of History

Jean-Michel Frodon

You have looked into the face of something that will be alive for all eternity, for your eternity and for mine!
—Maurice Blanchot, *Death Sentence*[1]

The essential purpose of this text is to fight a hopeless battle. It finds itself up against a force much greater than my own, the force of an *idée reçue*, an established formula which has been accepted and endlessly repeated. This formidable adversary is named "the ontology of cinema." I would say that outside of the most theoretical circles it is scarcely mentioned. And I would not bother to challenge this phrase were it only a matter for theorists. But the idea that comes with the expression "the ontology of cinema," that is to say its definition, carries other considerable consequences: in the very practice of filmmaking, in its pedagogy, in criticism, and in the realm of regulatory and political decisions, as well as the decisions of institutions such as museums, television networks, and so forth. Closer to home, at *Cahiers du Cinéma*, we need to ask what the *Cahiers* ("Notebooks") are about today, since, far less than at the time of the journal's creation, the word *cinéma* no longer goes without saying. And so this question is at the center of studying the effects of contemporary technical revolutions, in the realm of the production of images and sounds as well as in their circulation.

The expression "ontology of cinema" comes from André Bazin, and it is through him, through his own study of cinema, that I believe it legitimate to bring the expression back into question, even if the stakes now far exceed the exegesis of his theories, which we recently celebrated, with our admiration and gratitude intact, through the double anniversary of his birth in 1918 and death in 1958.

André Bazin and the "Essence of Cinema"

As all Bazin readers know, the word "ontology" is featured in the title of his lead essay in *What Is Cinema?*[2] but that word does not properly speaking apply specifically to cinema there, since the full title is "Ontologie de l'image photographique." The fact remains that the book's title

What Is Cinema? contains the hypothesis of a definition. The book itself also includes numerous references, explicit or implicit, to a supposed *essence du cinéma* or *nature du cinéma*. Moreover, Bazin called the first volume of *Qu'est-ce que le cinéma?*—the only volume of his great tetralogy he saw completed before his death—"Ontologie et langage." There is hardly a doubt then that Bazin himself had recourse to essentialist vocabulary and that he thought in such terms, at least at times. Yet I believe that ontology does not do justice to the genuine direction of his research; it is not what gives it coherence and pertinence, or keeps it so fertile today.

Upon Bazin's death, Eric Rohmer wrote in *Cahiers'* special issue dedicated to their founder that Bazin never ceased to ask "the big question" (what is cinema?), and that he had in fact "answered that question."[3] Rohmer strives to depict Bazin as a savant, the founder of a new science, who established the axiomatic basis of a new geometry through "a construction of the same order as Euclid's." However, if Bazin could indeed be said to have "answered the question," it is only in the sense that he himself indicates in the foreword to *Qu'est-ce que le cinéma?* where he writes, "This title is not so much the promise of an answer but rather a question that the author poses to himself throughout these pages"[4]—something he indeed pursued during his entire life as critic and theorist. If Bazin did in some sense "answer the question," it was not by establishing a body of doctrines that resolve it once and for all, but instead by constantly reopening and reformulating the question of cinema's uniqueness in its relation to human beings, nature, society, other arts, and other forms of expression. The multiplicity of his texts—their number as well as their heterogeneity—indicates the breadth of his sphere of interests and the diversity of his approaches, all playing a role in his manner of "answering the question."

André Bazin was only twenty-seven years old when in 1945 he published "The Ontology of the Photographic Image." The foundation of his definition in this text centers on the recording powers of the motion picture camera. But Bazin himself saw a need to bring it back into question, something signaled by the addition of a final sentence in the 1958 version, which did not appear in the original: "On the other hand, of course, cinema is also a language." [D'autre part le cinéma est un langage.][5] This sentence opens onto many other issues, but it is primarily intended to underline that what precedes it does not say everything; it is not the only cornerstone of his thought, or wasn't anymore in 1958.

Although the Bazin of "The Ontology of the Photographic Image" demonstrates an essentialist approach, this would not last long. In 1948, he published in *La Revue du cinéma* his great article "William Wyler ou le Janséniste de la mise en scène," where he writes:

> Cinema is not some sort of independent matter whose crystals must be isolated at all costs. It is, rather, matter in an aesthetic state, a form of narrative entertainment. Experience has already shown us that we must beware of equating cinema with a given aesthetic or, even worse, with who knows what kind of style, some sort of substantialised form that the filmmaker is obliged to use, at least as seasoning. A film's 'purity', or better yet, to my mind, its cinematic quotient should be calculated on a different basis from painting, theater, or the novel.[6]

This text was published in March 1948, two months after his first big article on Italian neorealism, "Cinematic Realism and the Italian School of the Liberation," in *Esprit* January

1948. These dates are important because of the idea, imposed later on, that neorealism could have been, for Bazin, the realization of the essence of cinema, an idea clearly contradicted by the sentence just cited: "Experience has already shown us that we must beware of equating cinema with a given aesthetic . . ."

A Fundamental Need

Working against an "ontological" approach, it is possible to understand Bazin's process as "anthropological," even very early on and, I believe, in a much more faithful and more operative fashion. As early as 1946, this conception takes shape with "The Myth of Total Cinema" published in *Critique* and later forming the second selection in *What Is Cinema?* Bazin talks about cinema as the fulfillment of a specific relationship between human beings, reality, and imagination, the same relationship that he himself described at the beginning of "The Ontology of the Photographic Image" as "one of human psychology's most fundamental needs."[7] A fundamental need does not refer to the essential nature of something but to a *relationship*. And it is this relation that then mobilizes all of Bazin's works. This "fundamental need" is made explicit in "The Myth of Total Cinema," particularly when he writes: "The concept men had of [cinema] existed so to speak fully armed in their minds . . . and what strikes us most of all is the obstinate resistance of matter to ideas."[8] Bazin thus develops the hypothesis that technology took a long time to allow the realization of this fundamental need which human beings had forever carried but which came about only at the end of the nineteenth century. That the *cinématographe* would come to fulfill an ancestral expectation, a "fundamental" one for humans, would explain for example why this invention spread around the world so quickly, welcomed everywhere with so much enthusiasm.

This approach allows us to think of cinema without essentializing it, without relying on an ontology that must inevitably undermine the evolution of techniques and social practices. It is supported by the appearance of practices that tried to respond to this "fundamental need" well before the invention of the *cinématographe*, indeed, given the logic of Bazin's hypothesis, ever since the dawn of humanity. We find a description of such practices in Georges Didi-Huberman's powerful study, *La Ressemblance par contact.*[9]

Though Didi-Huberman does not directly address cinema,[10] his entire book can be read as a narrative of the ways in which humanity has responded to this famous "fundamental need" from its beginning in the Paleolithic era, then more specifically in the West—namely, how humans constructed systems of representation without any break in continuity between what is shown and what does the showing. From the very outset, the issue was never about confusing signified and signifier but, on the contrary, about seeing in this *material transition* from the one to the other the chance to construct specific imaginary relations (quite different from those permitted by other representational procedures) thanks to the inscription of the real in its traces. From hand and footprints in rock caves to the myriad complex uses of the imprint by Marcel Duchamp, to whom the entire second half of the book is devoted, Didi-Huberman recounts a great adventure of material and spirit during which we encounter such heroes as Pliny the Elder, Canova, Donatello, and Rodin.

This narrative clarifies what is always at stake, though continuously reformulated—that is,. the construction of representational methods that retain some link with the material—through

the angle of certain imprinting techniques. Among these he focuses on a sector normally considered minor: plaster casting. Although Didi-Huberman does not discuss Bazin, anyone familiar
with him cannot read these evocative pages without thinking of the author of *What Is Cinema?*
on the subject of the death mask, the mummy, the Veil of Veronica or the Shroud of Turin. In
the same way, Didi-Huberman takes up, this time quite explicitly, Walter Benjamin's "The
Work of Art in the Age of Mechanical Reproduction," a text so frequently interpreted that it
has all but disappeared under a veil of simplistic paraphrases—and a text where cinema is directly at stake, even if this is not Didi-Huberman's particular angle.

Blaming the definition of art such as it was established in the Renaissance around
painting, he acknowledges that imprint techniques, and notably plaster casting, introduce a
certain wildness into art history ("ensauvage l'histoire de l'art," G. D-H.) in a way that echoes
Bazin's central idea of impure art, an idea infinitely more important and extensive than the
one area where he explicitly used this expression, film's relation to literature and theater. If
one takes up sculpture, rather than painting, the artistic field plays out the complexity of the
connections between real and artistic gesture,[11] the articulation of the mystery of creation
and the mystery of material processes; Didi-Huberman recovers this through an explicit and
theoretically justified anachronism regarding the mythological sources of the representational arts (according to the Greeks and then Pliny). Against the classical and still dominant
notion of artistic creation established by Vasari in the sixteenth century, he notes the legitimacy of a less noble but still active conception of the methods of representation, which pro-
claims the power of material traces in the formation of artworks. One could add to this the
research of David Hockney on classical painting[12] which also underscores how much the
intensive use of mechanical devices and particularly the camera obscura allowed the processes of mechanical reproduction to intervene in masterpieces very early on, such as processes of montage like those which the great sculptor Canova (1757–1822) was fond of
using, and others that Rodin pushed even further, especially with his assemblage of the
séquences enregistrées which comprise his sculpture *The Age of Bronze*. The convergences, explicit or subliminal, between Didi-Huberman's research and film theory, Bazinian theory in
particular, are legion. Thus we find the relation between aesthetic pursuit and the scientific
use of the image, notably in anatomy. Hence the pages (160–171) on Rodin's expansion of
working with plaster beyond its traditional capacities, to compose an unexpected connection
to palpable life, by giving movement, as informed by language, the possibility of another relationship with time. Here we intersect Deleuze's reflections on cinema which are equally
clear in the way the latter's ideas (following Bergson) on *l'intervalle*, the undifferentiated
interval, accord with what Didi-Huberman finds in Duchamp. In the same way, put quite
simply, it is logical to hear an echo of Duchamp's neologism "*l'inframince*" (as discussed by
Didi-Huberman) and the word *pellicule* (film, celluloid), or the fact that in English the word
for *moulage* is "casting."

In reading *La Ressemblance par contact* one continuously dwells on Bazin's intuitions
about the "fundamental need," as the book shows how often through the ages this need has
found ways to be sated. Cinema thus constitutes an especially accomplished and powerful
response to this need, because of its capacity to produce artifacts of representation that carry an
imprint of the world *in its four dimensions*, that of time being undoubtedly the most decisive,
and the one that escaped the techniques of transfer in prior centuries.

The Real and Belief

On the other hand, Didi-Huberman's research ultimately contradicts Bazin's affirmation that "cinema is an idealist phenomenon," an *idée pure* which calmly waited in some Platonic heaven for inventors and technicians to want to create devices so it could descend to man. Didi-Huberman's book supports the quite opposite notion that with whatever tools he possessed, mankind never stopped developing processes of world-representation. He has done so by carefully conjoining material traces, which verify the existence of the world while at the same time building a new link to the "imaginary" in complex relation with the unconscious, with the "real," and among humans. Contemporary research in neurobiology even aims to localize quite precisely the parts of the human brain that specifically correspond to this construction of a link between the real and the imaginary, neural zones where elements of the recording of information transmitted by the senses are associated with specific systems put together by the brain; all this occurs under the effects of inherited processes on the one hand and new developments that individuals are capable of on the other.[13] The famous "fundamental need" thus responds even to physiological dispositions that are quite specific and particular to humans.

If this need is defined as the construction of a certain relationship with the four dimensions, then the temporal dimension must be the most important since it represents something shared by all human beings: the fact of being destined for death *and the knowledge of that fact*. Rohmer hailed Bazin's phrase, "cinema is the achievement in time of photographic objectivity,"[14] as the culmination "in film theory of a Copernican revolution."[15] But it seems possible to extend what Bazin and Rohmer referred to as a solely photographic process to a group of infinitely older practices that have developed across centuries and even millennia.

This order of relationship with the world, with the four dimensions structuring techniques of imprinting, forms a "halfway point" between the response to the stimuli of the physical world according to the laws that govern it, and the production of representations or other manmade artifacts that try to overcome these laws. All this is part of a spiritual practice. Bazin was a practicing Christian, and he frequently addressed the relationship between cinema and religion, but it is also fair to consider that for him cinema might occupy a status comparable to that of religion: though it uses entirely different processes and effects, cinema, much like religion, rests upon belief, a belief that provides the means to live in this four-dimensional world where everyone's destiny is death.[16]

Does this mean that André Bazin could have been a mystic of cinema? That is what the ontological approach suggests. On the other hand, an anthropological perception does justice to the fact that while Bazin saw the uniqueness of cinema in the special relation that it maintains with reality, contrary to what is often claimed, he does not conceive of this connection as a stable one, established once and for all, but rather as a dynamic relationship with the mutations of the real world. Simply because, for him as for many—including the author of these lines—in the end, what is important is not cinema but rather the real world and those who live in it. As his biographer Dudley Andrew writes, "Bazin is no longer interested in a realistic cinematic art, but in reality itself,"[17] which is how Jean Renoir summed it up in his testimony at his friend's death by saying that he had been driven by "his immense love for everything that makes up the world in which we live."[18]

Demonstrating the priority that Bazin gives to the real world is decisive in understanding how André Bazin's work can be useful today, particularly in an age where technological developments are reputed by some to have destroyed these obsolete conceptions. Few film theorists were as open to technical advances as Bazin, who was also curious to understand how these innovations reformulated earlier configurations and conceptions. It is more than probable that the appearance of new media, of new ways to record and create images and sounds, to transmit them and to reach audiences, would have sparked Bazin's enthusiastic interest even more than the innovations of his time, principally television. Bazin never interpreted TV as an announcement of the death of cinema (as Rossellini did, for example), but rather as an emergence of other possibilities, and you can bet he would have watched the rapid development of digital technologies with the same curiosity. Contrary to what might be said elsewhere, these technologies far from invalidate his conception of cinema.

Of course analog recording techniques are well on their way to an accelerated disappearance. And of course the mode of belief [régime de croyance] established between films and their spectators is modified by the new technologies. If we limit Bazin's theories to the process of analog recording, there is no doubt that they would only pertain to the past. If on the other hand we recognize the decisive place of that "fundamental need" we have been discussing, it becomes clear that the ways one can respond to this need are numerous and susceptible to transformation through their specific processes, processes that make up the series of stages denoted by Didi-Huberman, from the negatives of hands in the Altamira caves to Duchamp's ready-mades (and he could have added others, such as monotype engraving).

Consequently, the issue becomes understanding how this foundational connection between the real and the imaginary manifests itself in given objects, thanks to devices of representation: what Bazin calls in the Wyler essay their "cinematic quotient."

Where Is Cinema?

In order to appreciate these constants and progressions, I must begin by proposing that the key transformations of the last twenty-five years do not concern cinema but rather the real world itself. While Bazin was writing on cinema, he was writing in a world where, at least in the West, there was an established distinction between reality and representation. Since then, the principal phenomenon has been a disappearance of this clear division in the real world itself (surely that division was always an excessive simplification). The development of new interactions between various levels of reality and unreality have made reality itself different, even if they have not made it actually disappear. In addition, these interactions have, as a matter of course, transformed cinema's relationship with reality, and on two levels at once: cinema as a technical, economic, and social practice is a stakeholder in this new world, while cinema simultaneously describes, deliberately or not, what happens in the world. This does not in any way eradicate the "fundamental need," founded on the necessity of a connection *and* a separation between the world and those who people it, the necessity of an inscription in space and time with one's own death on the horizon, without which there is no possible construction of oneself. And if cinema is the name of that which permits us to respond to this anthropological need to construct specific connections to place and time, the current question may now be less "what is cinema?" and instead "where is cinema?" or better put, "where is there cinema?"

The first answer to this question would be, still: in films. More films are made today than ever before in its history. All of these films use digital technologies to some extent, some are 100 percent digital, but many are the product of directors who are continuing the work of cinema according to various modalities, sometimes very innovative and other times quite classical. It is not a question of pretending that digital does not change anything important, since the transformations—in shooting, in postproduction and then in distribution (from DVD screening rooms to the internet)—are immense. It is about showing how much directors as diverse as Lynch, Varda, Weerasethakul, De Palma, Sokurov, Lars von Trier, Jia Zhang-ke, and Pedro Costa condition this construction of a cinematic relationship to the real with new tools, and reformulate the potentialities of the trace of the real in four dimensions using processes of digital coding.

But of course regarding the question "where is there cinema?" the answer is certainly not mechanical: it is in films. While many films involve a very weak "cinematic quotient," or even none at all, cinema (in the sense of the term given here) has now passed into works and productions of all kinds, some of which refer to it explicitly and others not at all. In museums and art galleries, on the stages of theaters, operas, and dances, in architecture and design, as well as in comic strips, the organization of characteristic forms of cinema never stops finding new relevance, to further fuel this desire.

Notes

1. This essay originally appeared in French in *Cahiers du Cinéma*, 644 (April 2009), where the author was editor in chief. The epigraph comes from Maurice Blanchot, *Death Sentence* (Barrytown, NY: Barrytown/Station Hill Press, 1998), 79. Original: "Vous avez vu face à face ce qui est vivant pour l'éternité, pour la vôtre et pour la mienne!" *L'Arrêt de mort* (Paris: Gallimard, 1948).

2. André Bazin, "The Ontology of the Photographic Image," in *What Is Cinema?* vol. 1, trans. Hugh Gray (Berkeley: University of California Press, 1967), 9–16.

3. Eric Rohmer, "La 'somme' d'André Bazin," *Cahiers du Cinéma*, 91 (January 1959); translated in Rohmer, *The Taste for Beauty* (Cambridge: Cambridge University Press, 1989), 93–105.

4. Bazin, *Qu'est-ce que le cinéma?* (Paris: Editions du Cerf, 1975), 7. Original: "Le titre de cette série *Qu'est-ce que le cinéma?* n'est pas tant la promesse d'une réponse que l'annonce d'une question que l'auteur se posera à lui-même tout au long de ces pages."

5. Bazin, "The Ontology of the Photographic Image," 16.

6. Bazin, "William Wyler, the Jansenist of Mise en Scène," in *What Is Cinema?*, trans. Timothy Barnard (Montreal: Caboose, 2009), 67. The final phrase of this translation differs from Barnard's since the author is citing Bazin's 1948 original and not the 1958 version Bazin slightly modified (translator's note).

7. Bazin, "Ontology of the Photographic Image," in *What Is Cinema?* trans. Timothy Barnard, 3. We use Barnard's translation here as it emphasizes the "fundamental need" (Gray's translation calls this "a basic psychological need in man").

8. Bazin, "The Myth of Total Cinema," in *What Is Cinema?* vol. 1, trans. Hugh Gray, 17.

9. Georges Didi-Huberman, *La Ressemblance par contact: Archéologie, anachronisme, et modernité de l'empreinte* (Paris: Minuit, 2008). This text elaborates material in *L'Empreinte*, the catalogue he edited for the Centre Georges Pompidou in 1997.

10. Didi-Huberman's sole film reference, and a minor one, is to *Anemic cinéma* by Marcel Duchamp, 1926.

11. Though the title of this text is a modest and affectionate homage to Rohmer's great work "Celluloid and Marble," it is important to note that in this series of five articles where Rohmer examines the relation between cinema and the other arts, which he published in *Cahiers* between February and December 1955, he does not focus on sculpture, despite the title.

12. David Hockney, *Secret Knowledge: Rediscovering the Lost Techniques of the Old Masters* (New York: Studio, 2006).

13. See Jean-Pierre Changeux, *Du vrai, du beau, du bien: Une nouvelle approche neuronale* (Paris: Odile Jacob, 2008).

14. Bazin, "The Ontology of the Photographic Image," in *What Is Cinema?* vol. 1, trans. Hugh Gray, 14. This translation is amended from Gray's "Cinema is objectivity in time."

15. Rohmer, "La 'somme' d'André Bazin," translated in *Taste for Beauty*, 97.

16. Such an assertion is not necessarily limiting, as it also demands a place for desire, for the erotic dimension of this particular relationship to real presence, though "sublimated" in the imprint. This necessarily brings us to examine the hypothesis of the "new intermediary" with another immense space of representation: dreams.

17. See Dudley Andrew, *André Bazin* (New York: Oxford University Press, 1978), 111.

18. Jean Renoir, "André Bazin, notre conscience," *France observateur* (November 20, 1958).

8

From Bazin to Deleuze

A Matter of Depth

Diane Arnaud

Gilles Deleuze's substantial references to André Bazin contributed to rehabilitating the critic's reputation after it had been relegated to near oblivion throughout the structuralist era. When Dudley Andrew comments on this eclipse, he makes it clear that Bazin's return in the mid-'80s came mostly from Deleuze's two *Cinéma* volumes, "which effectively squelched semiotics in favor of a philosophy of the image that looked to films as manifesting a form of thought."[1] If we listen to Jacques Rancière, Deleuze prolongs and echoes the modernist thinking of Bazin, taking into account the break between "the movement-image" and "the time-image" in relation to the historical break brought about by neorealism. Moreover, in his own, more professional undertaking, Deleuze would lay "a solid foundation" for "the correct intuitions and the theoretical approximations of occasional philosopher André Bazin, [*philosophe d'occasion*]."[2] This rehabilitation suggests that Bazin's theorizing needed to be somehow enhanced. Even for Hervé Joubert-Laurencin, always concerned with protecting Bazin's writings from the limitations of "bazinism," Gilles Deleuze "philosophically ransomed" Bazin's opinions on the *profondeur de champ* (depth of field).[3] Joubert-Laurencin expresses his surprise that Bazin's analytical postulates are nevertheless defended to excess in *The Time-Image* (1985). Contrary to the standard critical line, which from Mitry to Jean-Louis Comolli has rejected the "surplus of realism" that Bazin found in Welles' use of depth, Deleuze's commentary on Bazin is strikingly subtler. That is why I have chosen to focus on depth of field to explore Deleuze as a visionary reader of Bazin.

Taking into account several of Bazin's texts, most dating from 1948 to 1951, Deleuze gradually adds several factors to the Bazinian notion of depth of field that shed light on the significance of its scope for theory. Deleuze's cross-referencing leads him, on the one hand, to link depth of field to an "excess of theatricality" and the development of cinematographic intelligence, and, on the other hand, to understand the realist aesthetics of the sequence-shot [*plan-séquence*] through Bergson's "perception of change." Furthermore, this rejuvenated conception of depth helps Deleuze pass beyond the dead end of determinism without possibilism, of evolution without "stratigraphy," and so opens up new ways of opening Bazin. What results is the "vast geological displacement" traced in this anthology by Tom Conley. We might therefore state that Deleuze did not exactly "philosophically ransom" Bazin, but he did prolong his intuition, expressed as early as 1948, that "contiguity" and "*cristallographie*" stem from in-depth *découpage*.

Depth of Field, from Function of Reality to Excess of Theatricality

Before studying the connection between Bazin and Deleuze, as far as depth is concerned, we should address the philosopher's paradoxical attitude toward the critic. The first specific reference to Bazin's analyses in Deleuze's writings on the cinema is in fact the description of the pan-shot in *Le Crime de Monsieur Lange* (1936). According to François Truffaut's preface to Bazin's posthumous and incomplete work on Renoir, it is the last film on which Bazin wrote after having watching it on TV from his deathbed.[4] Deleuze's commentary, in the second chapter of *The Movement-Image* (1983), sounds like a thwarted connection inspired by Bazin, something above and beyond a chance encounter—a kind of renaissance. The connection, like the shot, involves a pure movement of emancipation: "It is always a great moment in the cinema, as for example in Renoir, when the camera leaves the character, and even turns its back on him, following its own movement at the end of which it will rediscover him."[5] This reference extols the camera's own movement, including a possible opposite direction in the framing which brings out a temporal perspective in the spatial expression of the mise-en-scène. In the same vein as the camera's movement in *Le crime de Monsieur Lange*, Deleuze's following of Bazin, after a slight shift, facilitates new connections. There is always, on the philosopher's behalf, the desire both to depart from and derive from Bazin with more or less bias.[6]

From the outset, Deleuze does not conceal his opposition to Bazin concerning depth of field, but here his cautious opposition inevitably undergoes modification. According to the wording in chapter four of *The Time-Image*, "The Crystals of Time," "We will be all the more hesitant to give [depth of field] the role intended by Bazin, namely of pure function of reality."[7] The philosopher goes against the idea of a single purpose for depth of field by calling for multiple functions, integrating the possibility of change or evolution "into the flow of the sequence-shot." More than a euphemism, in this hesitation there is potentially a need to reformulate, a will to deviate from the direct trajectory between the technical and the aesthetic aspects traced by "The Evolution of the Language of Cinema." Indeed, in the following chapter, "Peaks of Present and Sheets of Past," he declares: "Bazin's position was nevertheless complex: he showed that this gain of reality could be achieved through 'an excess of theatricality' [*surcroît de théâtralité*]," (Cinema 2, 108; 142). In a note, Deleuze rewords this idea of multiple functions in considering Wyler's depth of field as Bazin analyzed it in his two-part article "William Wyler, the Jansenist of Mise en Scène," published in *La Revue du cinéma* in 1948, and which he put at the end of the first volume of *Qu'est-ce que le cinéma?*, "Ontologie et langage"; this text, because of its insistence on theater, already indicated the development of the second volume on "Cinéma et les autres arts." Among numerous analyses, Deleuze identifies that of a long shot from *The Little Foxes* (1941) "where the fixed camera records the totality of the scene in depth, as in the theatre" and where the character is able to leave the cinematographic field before dying far at the back. He concludes from this that: "Cinema here produced an 'excess of theatricality' which will in the end strengthen the feeling of reality," (Cinema 2, 299, note 16; 142, note 15).

Deleuze's conclusion is of interest on several scores. Though there are approximations and inferences in this reading of the 1948 text on Wyler, his understanding is visionary. Indeed, among the several shots analyzed by Bazin, Deleuze chooses, without explicitly noting it, the long shot of murder by omission, which is technically out of focus. He could not overlook it insofar as Bazin pinpoints quite clearly that Gregg Toland, Wyler's cameraman, was instructed not to focus on the whole depth of the field of view, so that the spectator cannot clearly see that Marshall falls on the staircase and dies.[8] Deleuze's view of *profondeur de champ* excludes in fact any consideration of what is cinematographically in or out of focus in favor of a model of composition as found in pictorial perspective.[9]

This counterexample is actually justified in relationship to what is defended by Bazin in his article on Wyler. Although he is very attached to depth of focus in his historical study of *découpage*, especially in "Pour en finir avec la profondeur de champ" and in the later "Evolution of the Language of Cinema," here he is wary of technical dogma, as is clearly shown in the second part of his text, when he returns to the murder scene in *The Little Foxes* which does not systematically respect depth of focus. In the end, Bazin leaves aside the dogmatic nature of "in" or "out of" focus by accepting that perspective alone is enough to produce the same impact as a lack of focus (WCB, 64; RC, 58). What really matters is the effect of the mise-en-scène on the spectator: this technique creates attention and apprehension. We have to try to look over the shoulder of Bette Davis, who turns her back to Herbert Marshall, to see in the distance the conclusion of a drama where we can only half-see the main character (WCB, 49; RC, 41). The apprehension is aggravated by our desire to push aside the person who hides the action *"in order to see better"* (WCB, 62; RC, 58, emphasis added). Bazin in fact compares the murder scene in *The Little Foxes*, later cited by Deleuze, and the break-up scene in *The Best Years of Our Lives* (1946), despite their different uses of limited focus. Thanks to depth of field, the realistic effect shared by these films comes from the simultaneous mise-en-scène of two distinct actions: the primary dramatic action as such, and a sort of secondary action which is the shot itself over time (WCB, 64; RC 58-59).

Through his defense of realism, not just of subject matter but of visual aesthetics, the definitive effect of the shooting technique is weakened, even though the use of depth of field with simultaneous action—from 1938 to 1946, from Renoir to Wyler through Welles—remains associated with the spectator's ability to carry out the actual *découpage* (WCB, 55; RC, 46). As he says, "There is no one realism, but many realisms. Every era seeks its own, meaning the technology and aesthetic which can best record, hold onto and recreate whatever we wish to retain of reality," (WCB, 52; RC, 44). His defense of Wyler is based therefore on that director's style without style, a realism of neutrality, which takes care not to issue from any pre-set aesthetics and "to look like cinema." That is why Bazin, even in his 1958 readjustment, continues to support Wyler's work on behalf of aesthetics in the abstract. This *cinéma-écriture*,[10] while in no way distorting the theater, shows cinema in all its purity (WCB, 67-68; RC, 62). Already in 1948 he praises the fidelity which the single set and fixed camera brought to the adaptation of *The Little Foxes* from the play by Lillian Hellman. Of the emblematic shot of the murder, he writes: "Here we can see not only all the things which film can add to the resources of theatre but also that the greatest cinematic quotient can be obtained, paradoxically, with the minimum degree of mise en scène" (WCB, 49; RC 41).

Strikingly, Deleuze refers to this dual defense voiced in the 1948 article: the realist aesthetics of in-depth *découpage* extending to simultaneous mise-en-scène, and the purity of the cinematographic event in filmed theater. It is symptomatic therefore that the words "excess of theatricality," which Deleuze uses after commenting on the function of depth of field in Wyler's mise-en-scène, is an expression only formulated by Bazin in his article "Theater and Cinema." This text, written in 1949 and published in 1951, characterizes the successful cinematographic adaptation of *Les Parents terribles* (1948) by Jean Cocteau, underscoring the structure of the scene and its psychological corollaries: "The specific help given here by the cinema could only be described as an excess of theatricality."[11] In the same way that Deleuze opts to concentrate on a shot with little depth of focus, highlighting the idea that Bazin favored the aesthetic understanding of realism rather than technical dogma, Deleuze's reuse of the expression *surcroît de théâtralité* makes it easier to understand depth of field in connection with the *intelligence* of *cinéma impur*. The fact that Deleuze intuitively brings together Bazin's quotations on Wyler and Cocteau between 1948 and 1951 turns out to be particularly exact in light of the writing and evolution of those texts.

If one follows Bazin's route from 1945 to 1950 as described by Jean-Charles Tacchella (in an appendix to Andrew's biography), it is clear that in 1948 a variety of human and intellectual events bear on these aesthetic issues. Though Bazin was reluctant to meet filmmakers, he interviewed Wyler, Welles, and Cocteau.[12] The impact of *Les Parents terribles* also engendered one of the first defenses of filmed theater, as "theater transformed by black and white magic into pure cinema" in *L'Ecran français*.[13] Cocteau wrote a preface to Bazin's book on Welles in 1949, using notes taken the previous year. Thus in "Theater and Cinema" it is no surprise that the various developments of that year led to new thinking. Bazin considers *Les Parents terribles*, *Macbeth*, and *The Little Foxes* among the adaptations which have solved the dialectics of cinematographic realism and theatrical convention. Depth of field is one of film's options in ensuring the success of *théâtre cinématographique*, by involving the spectator's view. A function of vision is therefore more sought after than a function of reality. The spectator has a free choice among several possible *découpages*, with the feeling—in the background, so to speak—of being totally present at the event. The importance of depth of field in the films of Welles and Wyler compels the spectator, faced with the absence of arbitrary fragmentation, to make a choice, corresponding to the choice of the psychological viewpoint in Cocteau's works, which is "from the point of view . . . of an exceptionally perspicacious spectator placed in an all-seeing position,"(WCB, 178)[14] and which is "wedded here to the pure rhythm of attention."[15]

As laid out in another 1951 text, "In Defense of Mixed Cinema," these same features of fidelity and efficacy, the astonishingly perspicacious mobility of the camera, and the use of deep focus, are part of the "development of cinematographic intelligence."[16] Deleuze's interest in depth of field sheds light on its significance and complexity in Bazin's texts. Through the understanding of depth over time, the concept of realism changes.

Depth of Time, from Psychological Realism to Perception of Change

The philosopher's intelligence lies in seeing that Bazin's view of depth of field encompasses the concept of duration. It is therefore relevant to study Deleuze's references relating depth of field to the sequence-shot, since this connection grounds Bazin's psychological realism in Bergson's conception of flow and perception. Deleuze is one of the few who recognized that "Bazin was able to propose and resolve the problems of depth of field by inventing the notion of the 'sequence-shot'" (Cinema 2, 107; 140). Indeed, Bazin's work on Welles stretches depth of field *découpage* to its temporal limits, that is, the absorption of the concept of shot "in a *découpage* unit which might be called the sequence-shot."[17] This Bazin citation, referenced in chapter 5 of *The Time-Image*, links the intelligence of the cinematographic process to the intelligence of the spectator. Thus, the synthetic language resulting from depth of field *découpage* is more realistic and more "intellectual" than traditional, analytical *découpage*. Bazin develops its aesthetic implications: "In a way it forces the spectator to participate in the meaning of the film by distinguishing the implicit relations, which the *découpage* no longer displays on the screen like the pieces of a dismantled engine. Obliged to exercise his liberty and his intelligence, the spectator perceives the ontological ambivalence of reality directly, in the very structure of its appearances."[18] The static shot of George and Fanny in the kitchen in *The Magnificent Ambersons* (1942) is then discussed from this point of view. Though he does not specifically mention this extract, Deleuze complains that "Bazin has often analyzed this kitchen scene, but without making it dependent on the function of remembering which takes place (or tries to take place) in it" (Cinema 2, 299, note 18; 144, note 17).

Deleuze's commentary on Bazin's supposedly short-sighted view of Wellesian in-depth *découpage* is part of the that so-called philosophical ransom, which would disqualify the function of reality Bazin sees at work and instead promote the direct time-image. From the philosophical perspective of Bergson followed by Deleuze,[19] depth of field opens up memory to depth of time: "In this freeing of depth which now subordinates all other dimensions we should see not only the conquest of a continuum but the temporal nature of this continuum: it is a continuity of duration which means that the unbridled depth is of time and no longer of space" (Cinema 2, 108; 141-142).

By directing our reading of Bazin to something lacking, that is, the failure of "the function of recollection" in his analyses of the kitchen scene, at the same time Deleuze indicates their importance in the history of film criticism and theory.[20] Such pinpointing, which appears as a sort of reproach, summons a memory of the texts. Bazin's linking of *profondeur de champ* to *plan-séquence*, a concept he invents, occurs just before he again analyzes the kitchen scene, and leads him to explain "a surplus of abstraction" in the in-depth *découpage* on the basis of "a surplus of realism" (*surcroît de réalisme*).[21] This is the expression that Jean-Louis Comolli uses in his "Note sur la profondeur de champ" when he argues against it, on the basis that the image produced, discontinuous and composite, is less real.[22] According to Nicole Brenez, Deleuze diplaces these antithetical spatial visions of depth (Bazin's attachment to so-called continuity versus Comolli's vision of discontinuity) in order to solve it in temporal as well as spatial terms.[23] Nevertheless, she makes it clear that Deleuze's idea of an original substance joining all regions of time stems from Bazin's commentary on *Macbeth*, which conjures up "a prehistoric" and "equivocal universe," linked to "a prehistory of conscience at the birth of time and sin, when sky and earth, water and fire, good and evil, still aren't distinctly separate."[24] The concept of depth lies therefore within this temporal primordial background from which results "a surplus of realism," since there are various forms of realism: ontological realism (presence of the objects), dramatic realism (no separation between the actor and the décor), and most importantly psychological realism, "which brings the spectator back to the real conditions of perception, a perception which is never completely determined a priori."[25] Opposition to Bazin's *surcroît de réalisme* should be tempered if viewed in terms of perceptive attention over time.[26]

Thus Bergsonian thought opens up Bazin's thinking on depth of field, the sequence-shot, and psychological realism. Ludovic Cortade has pinpointed the influence of *Creative Evolution* (*L'Evolution créatrice*, 1907) as regards the ontological dimension of time, anchored for Bazin not so much in continuity as in the ambiguity of reality.[27] What is of greatest interest to us here is not the question of belief and doubt, but the condition of perception implying change over time. In his article "The Perception of Change," Bergson suggests going beyond our perception of things so as to then delve deeper, "to deepen and to extend it."[28] The philosopher sets the limits of our faculties of perception: "Ancillary to action, it isolates within reality as a whole that which is of interest to us; it shows us less the things themselves than that which we can draw from them."[29] It is through the arts that we develop another vision of reality, less narrow and action-driven.

For Bazin, undoubtedly echoing Bergson, natural perception works according to a cinematographic analytical *découpage* that subordinates reality to action. In his 1948 text on Wyler, he specifies that our eye continuously changes planes under the impetus of interest or intention, but that this mental and intellectual accommodation takes place a posteriori: "In any event, we are *free* to create our own mise en scène" (WCB, 54; RC, 45). In-depth perception of the sequence-shot fits into this theoretical framework as an artistic vision capable of preserving the ambiguity of reality by deepening and extending perception to encompass several possible systems of *découpage*. As Andrew says, such virtual liberty guarantees for the viewer "this free interplay between man and the objects in his perceptual field."[30] Such postulates are also to be found in a long passage in Bazin's first version of *Orson Welles*, written in 1949 and published in 1950. Once again, Bazin considers the mechanism of perception in reality. Virtual *découpage* carried out by attention, subsequent to involvement in an action, causes a loss of certain aspects of the object. As Bazin asserts, "The object is always able to remind me of its reality as an object (for instance if it's glass by cutting my hand) and thus to modify the planned action."[31] The freedom of the object is thus also in the hands and in the eyes of the subject, free to be distracted from action by reality itself which ceases to be a mere "tool." That is where the aesthetics and metaphysical involvement of depth of field intervenes: "It obliges the spectator to use his freedom of attention and at the same time makes him feel the ambivalence of reality. A scene like the kitchen scene in *The Magnificent Ambersons* becomes unbearable."[32] In his synthesized 1958 version, the one to which Deleuze refers, Bazin rewords this two-page passage in the paragraph mentioned above, which connects the "intelligence" of the spectator's liberated perception to the intellectual dimension of *découpage* in depth of field.

Deleuze, without realizing it, urges a genetic approach when referring to Bazin's analysis of the kitchen scene. If one looks at the omitted pages in the 1949 typescript available in the "Fonds Robert Lachenay" of Paris' Bibliothèque du Film (La Cinémathèque française), the metaphor of a boned chicken is developed to set an analytical mise-en-scène off against realistic *découpage*: "Instead of an analytical *mise en scène* which pulls reality to pieces like a chicken, Welles' *découpage* grasps the meaning of events while retaining its natural relationship with adjacent, contiguous reality."[33] Even if the impression of continuous and homogenous reality is important for Bazin,[34] his aesthetic defense of in-depth *découpage* is concerned with what potentially cuts and sections. For Ludovic Cortade, who refers to Bachelard's conception of duration, that ambiguity of the realism expressed by in-depth *découpage* relies on temporal discontinuity: the hesitation felt over time by the spectator.[35] Thus, because of depth, that "exceptionally perspicacious spectator placed in an all-seeing position" would find his perception freed more by contiguity than by continuity or by discontinuity. Depth would liberate the perception of change to operate in a stream of *correspondances*.

Depth as Correspondance, from Contiguity to Cristallographie

Deleuze's use of Bazin's texts on depth reveals a mode of continuity which also proceeds by contiguity in the structuring of images through the history of cinema. According to Rancière, inter alia, Deleuze's major inheritance from Bazin's work is to consider neorealism as a turning point in the evolution of cinema. It is a great contribution to the theorization of the difference between the movement-image and the time-image,[36] a split, a "crisis of action," due to the historical break of the world war between them. The study of Deleuze's reading of Bazin produces another form of articulation that links the two types of images to a common basis: the depth of field of the sequence-shot.

Deleuze, in the second chapter of *Cinéma 1*, clearly explains what, from a Bergsonian perspective, he means by unity of shot, and he proposes four types of unity of movement. The third type is a sequence-shot with Welles' or Renoir's depth of field marking a new concept of depth. Contrary to early cinema, where depth is designed as a superimposition of parallel slices each of which is self-sufficient, here depth engenders perpetual interaction among the different planes (Cinema 1, 26; 42). Such evolution already appeared in the history of painting from the sixteenth to the seventeenth centuries, according to Wölfflin's distinction between "plane and recession." It is through this prism that Deleuze examines "Pour en finir avec la profondeur de champ"[37]: "The cinema presents exactly the same evolution, as two very different aspects of depth of field which were analysed by Bazin," (Cinema 1, 221, note 25; 43, note 25). In chapter 4 of *Cinéma 2*, the new concept of depth is repeated and expanded, still associated with the pictorial model and the same references, that is, preferences: Wyler, Welles, Renoir. When Deleuze draws our attention to various passages in "The Evolution of the Language of Cinema," those passages come from "Pour en finir avec la profondeur de champ" which have been examined in *Cinema 1*. This "reprise" involves a pure movement of emancipation, as with the commentary on the long shot in *Le Crime de Monsieur Lange*. The very nature of depth of field understood as "depth of image," referring both to Bergson and Merleau-Ponty,[38] is to show time in itself. From this stems the first direct time-image linked to a function, memory, already present as opened up in the movement-image of the third kind. The transformation and conversion of the movement-image into time-image, through depth of field, operates by a kind of contiguity-continuity that integrates difference-discontinuity over and beyond any crisis. This brings us back to a modification of power in the Bergsonian idea of perception, where "the whole problem is to understand how the image becomes a different one because perception has taken care to see otherwise."[39]

One sees better with depth of field because it affects the theoretical power, the possibility "to see everything," that is the ambivalence of reality and the intelligence of cinema, so close to Bazin's heart. It is in fact the possibility of understanding the connections between and the modifications of dimensions over time: depth of the image "confirms unity of actor and decor, the total interdependence of everything real from the human to the mineral. In the representation of space it is a necessary modality of this realism which postulates a constant sensitivity to

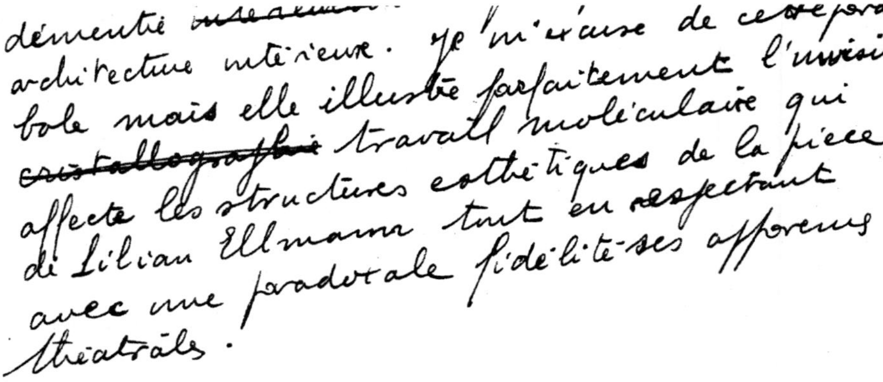

FIGURE 8.1: "Cristallographie" under Bazin's erasure in his Wyler manuscript

the world but which opens to a universe of analogies, of metaphors, or to use Baudelaire's term, in another, no less poetic sense, of correspondences."[40]

The connection between Deleuze and Bazin should be understood in such terms. Even beyond his use of Bergson,[41] Bazin opens the way for Deleuze's *image-cristal* thanks to his own rich metaphors. In the 1948 manuscript on Wyler, when he metaphorically compares the invisible stratification process of the sea shell—which can be seen only if broken—to the aesthetic structure of the mise-en-scène, Bazin introduces the visionary notion of "*cristallographie*" [figure 8.1].[42]

Notes

1. Dudley Andrew, "The Godfather Critic and *Cahiers du Cinéma* Founder André Bazin Still With Us After Fifty Years," *Film Comment* (November–December 2008), 42.

2. Jacques Rancière, *Film Fables*, tr. Emiliano Battista (Oxford: Berg, 2006), 108. The term *philosophe d'occasion* might better be rendered "amateur philosopher." The full original from *La Fable cinématographique* (Paris: Seuil, 2001), 145: "Aux intuitions justes et aux approximations théoriques du philosophe d'occasion qu'était André Bazin, Deleuze aurait donné leur fondement solide: la théorisation de la différence entre deux types d'images, l'image-mouvement et l'image-temps."

3. Hervé Joubert-Laurencin, "Tombeau d'André Bazin," *Imagens*, 8 (1988).

4. François Truffant, introduction to André Bazin, *Jean Renoir* (New York: Simon and Shuster, 1973), 8; French version, *Jean Renoir* (Paris: Ivrea, 2005), 10.

5. Gilles Deleuze, *Cinema 1: The Movement-Image*, trans. Hugh Tomlinson and Barbara Habberjam (Minneapolis: University of Minnesota Press, 1986), 23. *Cf.* Deleuze, *Cinéma 1*: L'Image-mouvement (Paris: Minuit, 1983), 38. This book will henceforth be cited parenthetically as Cinema 1, with its corresponding page in the original French immediately after.

6. Arnaud Macé, "L'image moins le monde: Gilles Deleuze hanté par André Bazin," in *Gilles Deleuze et les images*, ed. François Dosse and Jean-Michel Frodon (Paris: Cahiers du Cinéma, 2008), 45. According to Macé, Deleuze's reference to Bazin's concept of the *image-fait* denotes, if not definite ungratefulness, then at least a certain reluctance to recognize its specificity and importance as regards the *image-temps*.

7. Deleuze, *Cinema 2: The Time-Image*, trans., Hugh Tomlinson and Robert Galeta (Minneapolis: University of Minnesota Press, 1989), 85. *Cf.* Deleuze, *Cinéma 2*: L'Image-temps (Paris: Minuit, 1985), 113. Deleuze refers to Bazin's ideas on depth staging in Renoir's *The Rules of the Game* (1939). This book will henceforth be cited parenthetically as Cinema 2, with its corresponding page in the original French immediately after.

8. André Bazin, "William Wyler, the Jansenist of Mise en Scène," in *What Is Cinema?* trans. Timothy Barnard (Montreal: Caboose, 2009), 49. This article was originally published as "William Wyler, ou le janséniste de

la mise en scène," in *La Revue du cinéma* 10 (February 1948) and 11 (March 1948), and reprinted with slight modifications in *Qu'est-ce que le cinéma?* vol. 1 *Ontologie et langage* (Paris: Editions du Cerf, 1958). This article will henceforth be cited parenthetically as WCB, and its corresponding page in *La Revue du cinéma* as RC.

9. According to David Bordwell, the term *profondeur de champ* as used by French critics in the 1940s and '50s could already "presume depth staging, whether or not all planes are in focus," in Bordwell, *On the History of Film Style* (Cambridge: Harvard University Press, 1997), 56. Nevertheless, Bazin, as Deleuze should know, tends to mark the difference more clearly between deep focus and staging in depth when referring to depth of field.

10. Bazin, "William Wyler, ou le janséniste de la mise en scène," in *Qu'est-ce que le cinéma?* vol. 1, 173.

11. Bazin, "Théâtre et cinéma" [1951], in *Qu'est-ce que le cinéma?* (Paris: Editions du Cerf, 1985), 148. My translation. Original: "L'apport spécifique du cinéma ne se pourrait définir ici que par un surcroît de théâtralité." Hugh Gray's translation does not emphasize the term "surcroît de théâtralité" as reused by Deleuze: "The specific help given here by the cinema can only be described as an added measure of the theatrical." Bazin, "Theater and Cinema," in *What Is Cinema?* vol. 1, trans. Hugh Gray (Berkeley: University of California Press, 1967), 93. Barnard renders it far better: "Film's specific contribution can only be defined here as an increase in theatricality" (WCB, 179).

12. Jean-Charles Tacchella, "André Bazin from 1945 to 1950: The Time of Struggles and Consecration," in Dudley Andrew, *André Bazin* (New York: Columbia University Press, 1990 [2nd ed.]), 245–50.

13. Bazin, "*Les Parents terribles*: Du théâtre transformé par la magie blanche et noire en pur cinéma," *L'Ecran français*, 180 (December 1948).

14. Bazin, "Théâtre et cinéma," 146. Original: "d'un spectateur extraordinairement perspicace et mis en puissance de tout voir." This passage, oddly enough, is missing from Hugh Gray's translation mentioned above.

15. Bazin, "Theater and Cinema," in *What Is Cinema?* vol. 1, 91. Cf. Bazin, "Théâtre et cinéma," 144.

16. Bazin, "In Defense of Mixed Cinema," in *What Is Cinema?* vol. 1, 69. Cf. Bazin, "Pour un cinéma impur" [1951], in *Qu'est-ce que le cinéma?* 99.

17. Bazin, *Orson Welles* (Los Angeles: Acrobat Books, 1991), 78. Cf. Bazin, *Orson Welles* (Paris: Cahiers du Cinéma, 1998), 88. Bazin published a book on Welles originally in 1950 by Editions Chavane, before an updated text from his fuller 1958 work in progress was published in 1972, edited by André Labarthe. The 1998 French edition reproduces this 1972 expanded edition.

18. Bazin, *Orson Welles* [English], 80.

19. For further development on the *profondeur de temps*, see Alain Ménil, "Deleuze et le *bergsonisme du cinéma*," *Philosophie*, 47 (1994), 49.

20. See Andrew, *André Bazin*, 122. "Of Welles' kitchen scene in *The Magnificent Ambersons*, [Bazin] claims that the emerging dramatic forces are a product of the long take—that is, of the surging forward of hidden relationships within the block of time frozen before us."

21. Bazin, *Orson Welles* [English], 80.

22. Jean-Louis Comolli, "Note sur la profondeur de champ," *Cahiers du Cinéma*, Scénographie, Numéro Hors-Série (1980), 88–89. Reprinted in Comolli, *Cinéma contre spectacle* (Paris: Verdier, 2009).

23. Nicole Brenez, "L'être selon l'image: Orson Welles, *Citizen Kane*," in *De la figure en general et du corps en particulier* (Brussels: Deboeck, 1999), 210–11.

24. Bazin, *Orson Welles* [English], 80. Deleuze quotes this passage in *Cinema 2: The Time-Image*, 115–16 (English), 151 (French).

25. Bazin, *Orson Welles* [English], 80.

26. According to Jean-Louis Comolli, the effect of in-depth *découpage* is to make the image not more real but specifically less real, since the only reality shown is that of our vision.

27. Ludovic Cortade, *Le Cinéma de l'immobilité* (Paris: Publications de la Sorbonne, 2008), 63–71.

28. Henri Bergson, "La perception du changement" [1911], in *La Pensée et le mouvant* (Paris: PUF, 2003), 148. Original: "pour la creuser et l'élargir."

29. Ibid, 152. Original: "Auxiliaire de l'action, la perception isole, dans l'ensemble de la réalité, ce qui nous intéresse; elle nous montre moins les choses mêmes que le parti que nous pouvons en tirer."

30. Andrew, *André Bazin*, 128.

31. Bazin, *Orson Welles* (Paris: Chavane, 1950), 58. Original: "L'objet est constamment libre de me rappeler à sa réalité d'objet (par exemple, en me coupant la main, si c'est du verre) et par là-même, de modifier l'action prévue."

32. Ibid, 59. Original: "Elle [la profondeur de champ] contraint le spectateur à faire usage de sa liberté d'attention et lui fait du même coup sentir l'ambivalence de la réalité. Une scène comme celle de la cuisine dans les *Ambersons* finit par devenir intolérable."

33. Bazin, *Orson Welles* [1949], Typescript in the Fonds Lachenay, Bibliothèque du film, La Cinémathèque française, 63. Original: "Au lieu de la mise en scène analytique qui désosse l'action comme un poulet, le découpage de Welles saisit des événements sans doute chargés de sens mais sans que celui-ci soit totalement dégagé comme tel et débarrassé, pour les besoins de la cause, de ses rapports naturels avec des réalités contiguës." In Bazin, *Orson Welles* [1950], 60, "les réalités contiguës" replaces "des réalités contiguës." In relation to such a cutting of reality, the metaphor of the boned chicken could bring to mind David Lynch's *Chicken Kit*.

34. Bazin, *Orson Welles* [1958], 86. Original: "l'impression d'une réalité continue et homogène." We refer to the edited text in French because the English translation does not take into account the notion of continuity and homogeneity.

35. Ludovic Cortade, *Le Cinéma de l'immobilité* (Paris: Publications de la Sorbonne, 2008), 71.

36. Rancière, "D'une image à l'autre: Deleuze et les âges du cinéma," 145–46.

37. Bazin, "Pour en finir avec la profondeur de champ," *Cahiers du Cinéma*, 1 (1951), 22–23.

38. Deleuze, *Cinema 2: The Time-Image*, 298, note 14. *Cf. Cinéma 2: L'Image-temps*, 142, note 13. Deleuze links Bergson and Merleau-Ponty, who both show how distance (*Matière et Mémoire*) and depth (*Phénoménologie de la perception*) are temporal dimensions.

39. Alain Ménil, "Deleuze et *le bergsonisme du cinéma*," *Philosophie*, 47 (1994), 37. Original: "Tout le problème est de comprendre comment l'image devient une image autre, parce que la perception se montre attentive à voir autrement."

40. Bazin, *Jean Renoir* (New York: Simon and Shuster, 1973), 90. French original (Paris: Ivrea, 2005), 83–84.

41. Bazin, "Un film bergsonien: *Le Mystère Picasso*," *Cahiers du Cinéma*, 60 (1956). Translated in Bert Cardullo and A. Piette, *Bazin at Work* (New York: Routledge, 1997).

42. Bazin, "William Wyler ou le janséniste de la mise en scène," Manuscript in the Fonds Lachenay, of the Bibliothèque du film, La Cinémathèque française (Paris). One can see in comparing the later with this earliest extant version that *travail moléculaire* replaces *cristallographie*, which is crossed out in the following passage: "Je m'excuse de cette parabole mais elle illustre parfaitement l'invisible ~~cristallographie~~ travail moléculaire qui affecte les structures esthétiques de la pièce de Lilian Ellman [*sic*] tout en respectant avec une paradoxale fidélité les apparences théâtrales." *Cf.* La Revue du cinéma 10, 45.

9

Deconstruction *avant la lettre*

Jacques Derrida Before André Bazin

Louis-Georges Schwartz

Tout fleurira au bord d'une tombe désaffectée.
—Jacques Derrida, *La Vérité en peinture*[1]

Reverse Philology

If, ordinarily, philology studies the historical development of language by reading rhetorical transformations chronologically, perhaps one can imagine a reverse philology that would analyze earlier literature in terms of what was written afterward, using an apparent similarity of signifiers to grant a later text permission to guide a reading of an earlier one. Reverse philology, were it legitimate, might show latent conceptual complexes becoming manifest by pointing at literary history from behind. To claim that the writings of Jacques Derrida had an influence on those of André Bazin would be an impossible twist. Bazin died in 1958, four years before Derrida's first important publication.

And yet Bazin and Derrida made consonant use of words, or signifiers, related to "being" [*être*]. Although only Derrida is conventionally read as a critic of classical ontology, they both rejected the Aristotelian tradition in which being and nonbeing are mutually exclusive categories, rewriting the opposites as poles of a spectrum. Without having read Derrida, Bazin can be misunderstood as a naïve realist, a phenomenologist, or a semiotician of the index, as his conventional Anglophone exegetes have done. Without having read Bazin, the ontological dimension of Derrida's writings can easily be overlooked and taken as simply beyond ontology, reducing "~~being~~" and "hauntology" to terms outside the philosophical tradition to which they refer.

To write that Derrida influenced Bazin means in part that motion picture technology affected the history of thought. Classical film theory had a strong tendency to deconstruct its own philosophical premises, but most theorists organized their works so as to restrain and disguise the need to rethink their own assumptions. Bazin, however, used film to invent a new concept of "being" in the language available to him. He allows his thoughts about photographic images to condition his assumptions about ontology. His writing can guide the reader through an implicit but unrestrained deconstruction of the concept "being." Derrida's early work explicitly deconstructed ~~being~~ and confronts readers with Bazin's thought remade into what it already was.

From the perspective that reverse philology affords me, it appears as if something has passed between writings by Derrida and Bazin, something that has changed and yet become more explicitly itself in the transition. That a revised concept of being might have been transmitted from one to the other fascinates all the more since that revised concept is so different from what the conventional readings of Bazin assume, as if some *Nachträglichtkeit* in philosophical culture has allowed it to arrive without anyone noticing that it had ever been there in the first place.

Perhaps this passage can be named by the Derridean neologism "teleiopoesis," a term that plays off the etymology of "poetry" to mean, roughly, an act of imaginative making, performed with and sent to others, differing from itself in transmission.[2] Teleiopoesis can occur locally and through identifiable acts of speaking and listening, reading and writing, or it can take more diffuse passages.

Of Photography

I will begin my readings with two essays, each written early in the careers of their respective authors: "The Ontology of the Photographic Image" (first published in 1945) and Derrida's "Différance" (1968), each readable as a rhetorical flower bordering the figure of the tomb. In the early paragraphs of each essay, we find the scene of a grave that encrypts an original concept of being.

Bazin's title, "Ontologie de l'image photographique," names the branch of philosophy that studies being. It functions as a generic marker, reminding the reader of other ontologies and asking to be understood as one of them. From the beginning of the twentieth century through the 1950s, "ontology" was a term in a struggle within continental philosophy over where philosophy should begin. Edmund Husserl argued that philosophy must begin by establishing a theory of knowledge, or an epistemology, since any claim whatsoever assumes knowledge.[3] Martin Heidegger countered that a first philosophy could only be an ontology since any knowledge assumes existence.[4] For Emmanuel Levinas, philosophy, which is always spoken or written, assumes a relationship to another and therefore must start with ethics.[5] Within that debate, certain conventions had been established, for example that of starting with the division of philosophy claimed as first philosophy to the exclusion of all other philosophical and extra-philosophical concerns, such as the problems of psychology, anthropology, biology, or any other science.

Are we to understand Bazin's title as referring to an analysis of the photographic image according to the categories of a preestablished theory of being that the essay will presuppose, or are we to understand that the essay will present a new or revised ontology whose categories would be established according to the figure of the photographic image?

Bazin's conventional exegetes have read the title in the former manner, but I want to read the title in the latter. Strictly speaking, the second reading is impossible, for "being" ought not to be thinkable on the basis of a particular existent. Nonetheless, the typography of the current French edition of the 1958 revision of the ontology essay, the best-known version, suggests the second reading.[6] The title is printed on two lines with the break between "Ontologie" and "de," a line break that could be translated with a colon as in "Ontology: Of the Photographic Image," suggesting that the photographic image would provide an ontology or be immanent to the ontology elaborated in the essay.[7]

A Potential Psychoanalysis

The essay's "body" begins:

> *Une psychanalyse des arts plastics pourrait considérer la pratique de l'embaumement comme fait fondamental dans leur genése. A l'origine de la peinture et de la sculpture, elle trou-verait le "complexe" de la momie.*
> If the plastic arts were put under psychoanalysis, the practice of embalming the dead might turn out to be a fundamental factor in their creation. The process might reveal that at the origin of painting and sculpture there lies a mummy complex.[8]

Bazin wrote these first two sentences in the conditional. *Pourrait* is the conditional form of the verb *pouvoir*, to be able to, and *trouverait* of *trouver*, to find. These two sentences and their mode set up the premises for the rest of the essay. Bazin's later claim that the invention of photography was "the most important event in the history of the plastic arts" only makes sense in light of the potential "mummy complex" introduced at the beginning. The article elaborates its entire argument within the state of virtual being indicated by this conditional, a massive "perhaps."

The conditional is already a way of talking about being otherwise than as full, present, and the opposite of nonbeing. Late in his career, in *Specters of Marx*, Derrida writes:

> Wherever deconstruction is at stake, it would be a matter of linking an *affirmation . . . if there is any*, to the experience of the impossible, which can only be a radical experience of the *perhaps*.[9]

By affirming survival beyond death in the conditional, the grammatical mode of the perhaps, the essay chooses the route of deconstruction, not naïve realism, phenomenology, or the semiotics of the index.

The alert reader will notice that in addition to writing in the conditional, Bazin violates the generic norms of ontological and phenomenological writing by potentially putting the plastic arts under psychoanalysis, a specific science. One expects such writings to start by bracketing off anything other than the problem of being or our apprehension of being. If ontology provides a first philosophy, it must be prior to any psychology, because psychology already implies knowledge of being since it assumes that a psychological entity exists. In the beginnings of modern phenomenology, Husserl and Heidegger both exclude the psychological from their respective ontological and epistemological investigations. The "Ontology" essay derives a theory of being from existents rather than generating a philosophy from certainties.

What would this psychoanalysis of the plastic arts be? It would certainly differ from Freudian psychoanalysis. The mummy complex that it may reveal has no direct relation to sexuality, nor could one construe this complex as a version, or inversion, of the death drive, which aims at inertia and not survival. If Bazin has been read as a phenomenologist, perhaps the truth of such a reading can be found not only in his attention to cinematic perception, but also in his analysis of the photographic image as a relationship between humans and death. Heidegger organized much of *Being and Time* around such a relationship and one might fantasize that Bazin's psychoanalysis might be part of the small tradition of *Daseinsanalyse*.[10] I am not arguing that Bazin was a Heideggerian, their analyses of the human relation to death being so different, but I do want to point out that from the beginning, Bazin's essay takes up a major theme of modern continental philosophy: human finitude.

Bazin calls embalming "a" [*un*] possible factor in their genesis. The indefinite article indicates the existence of other factors, and that the mummy is not a simple fact, but a compound. Like Freud's psychoanalysis, Bazin's posits a complex, divided origin for symptoms.

Graves and Images

The word mummy in the second sentence directs readers to Egypt:

> The religion of ancient Egypt, aimed against death, saw survival as depending on the continued existence [*pérennité*] of the corporeal body. Thus by providing a defense against the passage of time it satisfied a basic psychological need in man, for death is but the victory of time. To preserve, artificially, his bodily appearance is to snatch it from the flow of time, to stow it away neatly, so to speak, in the hold of life. It was natural, therefore, to keep up appearances in the face of the reality of death by preserving flesh and bone. The first Egyptian statue, then, was a mummy, tanned and petrified in sodium.[11]

Bazin here defines the human experience of death as an agonistic relationship to time. On the outer wall of this crypt, Bazin inscribes a difference between the survival of the one who has died and the continued existence of his or her body, "*la pérennité matérielle du corps*."[12] The *Trésor de la langue française* defines *pérennité* as "durability," "permanence," or "perpetuity," and notes that the word is used particularly to describe the continuity of a thing or a species across a series of individuals or organisms.[13] And so *pérennité* does not exactly mean continuous physical endurance. The flower at the edge of the grave that Bazin will soon describe is not quite a perennial, as Anglophone gardeners call individual plants that last many seasons. What flowers here is a corpse that endures through generations of human individuals, a life that exceeds the individual. Here the undead condition of the one who was alive and the mummy exert a pressure on the rhetorical level of the text, displacing the binary oppositions, or philosophemes, of life and death, individual and species, producing the figure of paradox in Bazin's sentence and setting up the more elaborate paradox in the group of sentences.

Bazin's French does not create a firm opposition between appearance and reality. Anglophone readers have understood that appearances are kept up in the face of the reality of death, that survival is an illusion and that death is real. For French readers, however, the passage is much more ambiguous, as the Egyptians preserve the appearance of the dead one through the medium of his very mortal remains. In the French, reality and appearance are brought very close together, almost conflated.

Bazin calls the mummy—the preservation of appearance in the medium of reality—the first statue. The mummy is already a plastic art, already an image, already somehow an aesthetic production. This short sentence shows us that what interests Bazin is not the index, whatever both his supporters and detractors claim. The mummy as an image ontologically connected to its model, the mummy *is* its model in flesh and bone. It prefigures the photograph of which Bazin will write that it *is* its model.[14] Index describes neither mummy nor photograph. The word never appears in the essay for an index may be caused or inscribed by what it expresses, but is an entity different from what it expresses. The mummy and the one who might survive are one being. Bazin treats them as simulacra, ontologically connected entities without a simple origin.[15] The paradox about the birth of art grows into a scene at the edge of a grave, in an embalming tent, a site which encourages him to write what his language cannot express, a radical impossibility.

> Pyramids and labyrinthine corridors offered no certain guarantee against *ultimate pillage*. Other forms of insurance were therefore sought. So, near the *sarcophagus*, alongside the corn that was to feed the dead, the Egyptians placed *terra cotta statuettes, as substitute mummies which might replace the bodies if these were destroyed*.[16]

Now, the mummy has been put in its sarcophagus. The mummy is not the bare corpse; as a treated, embalmed corpse it is not a simple entity, but one with parts. Furthermore, the sarcophagus contains the mummy while bearing its image on its surface, already reduplicating it. From the outset, Bazin's mummy has been a figure of difference linked to that which survives the living being. It is not the same as the living being, but its "appearance." It enables survival by virtue of a modicum of difference. In the sarcophagus, the mummy figures the possibility of spatial difference, its elements separating in a volume.

Next to this figure of potential spatial difference, we find terra-cotta statues— not the statuary jars in which the organs of the dead were preserved but replicas of the mummy, "substitutes" for it, guarding against its possible destruction. The statues constitute a reserve, and the tomb becomes the site of an economy. If the mummy is a figure of spatial difference, the statuettes are figures of the possibility of temporal deferral. They are there just in case. If the mummy is despoiled they will come into play. Thus they constitute a potential or conditional signifying chain.

What do we find in the household of the Egyptian dead? A combination of difference and deferral, a staging of *différance*, an origin of *différance*. We find a figure for Derrida's necessary neographism combining difference and deferral. In his eponymous essay, Derrida writes that *différance* refers to the possibility of nonidentity in general as well as to the possibility of difference in time and space or "the becoming-space of time and the becoming-time of space."[17]

In elaborating *différance*, Derrida must address its ontological status. Said aloud, the word is indistinguishable in French from *différence* and while the *a* can be seen, the play between the *a* and the *e* cannot. Thus *différance* has a rather problematic mode of appearance, not quite that

of a word, which normally gives itself to hearing and sight. Since it entails the potential of time
and space and hence the potential of presence, the *a* of *différance* cannot "become present,
manifest," it cannot be shown, necessarily being prior to any manifestation. When Derrida
writes "*différance* is," he crosses out the verb to be, writing "~~être~~" *sous rature*, because *différance*
falls between being and nonbeing, in the excluded middle separating the terms of conventional
philosphemes.

Derrida, like Bazin, writes the excluded middle between being and nonbeing in a tomb,
as if he and Bazin were visiting the same graveyard. Derrida describes the *a* he has substituted
for the *e* of *différence* as a pyramid, referring to the capital letter's shape. He continues:

> The *a* of *différance* thus is not heard; it remains silent, secret and discrete as a tomb:
> *oikesis*. And thereby lets us anticipate the delineation of a site, the familial residence and
> tomb of the proper in which is produced by *différance* the *economy of death*. This
> stone—provided one knows how to decipher its inscription—is not far from an-
> nouncing the death of the tyrant.[18]

Both tombs bury the proper by haunting us with an ontology in which being can be attenuated
and shared, so that the boundaries between classically delimited entities become permeable.
The tyrant whose death the grave from "Différance" almost announces, refers both to Creon in
Hegel's treatment of Antigone and to the classical concept of being.[19] The "tomb of the proper
in which is produced by différance the economy of death," could be a description of the sarcophagus and the statuettes in Bazin's crypt.

The ancient tomb seeks to restore the presence of the dead by providing a differing body
to ensure his or her survival, even to the extent of laying a store of statuettes in reserve, to provide a body if the sarcophagus should be destroyed. The reserve itself, however, temporalizes
and economizes the relation to an impossible presence, since to provide for the destruction of
the sarcophagus is to acknowledge the possibility of destruction for each and all of the substitute bodies.

Sartre's Photograph of Pierre

Bazin goes on to develop a psychological history of painting as torn between spiritual expression and the desire to create an illusionist version of the world we see, culminating in the invention of photography.

> This production by automatic means has radically affected our psychology of the image.
> The objective nature of photography confers on it a quality of credibility absent from all
> other picture-making. In spite of any objections our critical spirit may offer, we are
> forced to accept as real the existence of the object represented, actually *re*-presented, set
> before us, that is to say, in time and space. Photography enjoys a certain advantage in
> virtue of this transference of reality from the thing to its reproduction.[20]

Here we find *différance* at work in photography. The French encourages a straightforward
reading: "l'objet représenté, effectivement re-présenté." The repetition of *représenté*, spaced out

by a hyphen prompts us to reread the first iteration as the combined denotation of its parts and the object thus posited as capable of multiple presences. This would be impossible under the classical philosopheme of presence wherein presence is not detachable from the entity to which one ascribes it. Something is either here or there. In order to make sense of this, we have to imagine using the verb "to be" in a nonclassical, deconstructed sense.

Bazin continues:

> A very faithful drawing may actually tell us more about the model but despite the promptings of our critical intelligence it will never have the irrational power of the photograph to bear away our faith.
>
> Besides, painting is after all, an inferior way of making likenesses, an *ersatz* of the process of reproduction. Only a photograph can give us the kind of image of the object capable of satisfying the deep need man has to substitute for it something more than a mere approximation, a kind of decal or transfer. The photographic image is the object itself, the object free of the conditions of time and space that govern it. No matter how fuzzy, distorted or discolored, no matter how lacking in documentary value the image may be, it shares, by virtue of the very process of its becoming, the being of the model of which it is the reproduction; it *is* the model.[21]

Bazin cannot be any clearer on this point: "Elle *est* le modèle." However, as Noël Carroll notes, the sentence makes no sense.[22] For if we insist, with Aristotle, that "it is impossible for the same attribute at once to belong and not belong to the same thing and in the same relation" (*Metaphysics*, 1005b), then we cannot accept the ontological identity of photograph and model because we can easily imagine a situation where the model is destroyed but the photograph survives. In that case we would have to say that the model both does and doesn't exist. The Aristotelian solution adopted by most of Bazin's readers posits the photograph and the model as different entities and reads Bazin's assertion of ontological identity as imprecise or hyperbolic. I see things otherwise. I read the sentence not only as a statement about the being of photography, but a new concept of being, a step beyond existential thought.

In the introduction to the current edition of *What Is Cinema?*[23] Dudley Andrew draws attention to the philological connections between this page of the "Ontology" essay and Sartre's meditation on the photograph in *L'Imaginaire* (*The Imaginary*, 1940). The care in his philological work is stunning. He has analyzed Bazin's copy of the book, mapped out which pages are cut and which aren't, interpreted Bazin's underlinings and read typed notes on key passages. Andrew traces Bazin's claim that the photograph is its model to Sartre's descriptions of looking at a photo: "I envision Pierre in his physical individuality. It [the photo] acts upon us—almost—like Pierre in person. I say 'This is a portrait of Pierre' or, more briefly, 'This is Pierre.'"[24]

While the formulations are very close, Bazin's formulation is much bolder. As in any ontology worthy of the name, the essay asks us to use the verb "to be" and to conceive of existence in new ways. Bazin outstrips Sartre, and "The Ontology of the Photographic Image" opens up onto its future in French philosophy. Sartre writes "almost" but Bazin does not. Without that "almost," the meaning of the word "is" changes in Bazin.

Where Bazin is non-Aristotelian, in *L'Imaginaire* Sartre writes being and nonbeing as mutually exclusive categories. On this point Sartre is absolutely classical. *Being and Nothingness*

(1943) names two categories that can only be related as contradicting one another. "Man," as Sartre calls us, brings the two together in the self-nihilation that makes our future projects possible. This is where existentialism begins. But Bazin has outstripped existentialism.

In sum, for Sartre the photograph is not Pierre, but rather something that makes us conscious of Pierre in a particular way. The photograph is the false Pierre, because it does not share Pierre's being. It only acts on us as if it does. A corollary of Sartre's ontology of the excluded middle, the photograph manifests Pierre only as absence. But for Bazin, the photograph *is* its model. The verb *être*, to be, here indicates ontological identity, a being that is shared by the image and its object. And this shared being amounts to the originality of Bazin's essay. Bazin's use of the photograph contradicts Sartre's. In the second paragraph of the section from which Andrew's citations of Sartre's are taken, Sartre describes himself turning to the photograph to supplement the details of a vague mental image of Pierre. Later, when he introduces the analogon, the details of the photograph become part of our imaginative synthesis. That synthesis has a kind of existence, but it *isn't* Pierre.

As we have seen, Bazin asserts that "a very faithful drawing may actually tell us more about the model but despite the promptings of our critical intelligence it will never have the irrational power of the photograph to bear away our faith."[25] What is important to Bazin is precisely not the way the features of an image provide material for a synthesis of what it shows, but its shared being with its object. Bazin will say that photographs preserve their objects "enshrouded as it were in an instant, as the bodies of insects are preserved intact, out of the distant past, in amber."[26] Here we find another concordance, another trace of teleiopoesis between Bazin and Derrida. Late in his career, in an essay entitled "Typewriter Ribbon," Derrida refers to the discovery of "a prodigious archive . . . in Pacardy . . . [where] layers of fauna and flora were found, protected in amber . . . an insect surprised by death, in the instant . . . at which it was sucking the blood of another insect."[27]

Derrida uses the figure of insects in amber for a problem similar to Bazin's: how events might be archived. However, in Derrida's essay the figure specifies a definable event in the life of the insects so that the punctual moment may be captured. Both preservations in amber, Bazin's and Derrida's, figure *différance* by concretizing the becoming space of time. In each, the past becomes spaced out in and as fossilized tree sap. In Bazin, beings from the past are preserved in space; in Derrida an event is preserved, a *jouissance*. Tracing the figure of this amber archive in reverse perhaps reveals an ontological complex at the origin of Derrida's *écriture* influencing Bazin's discovery of a new mode of being in the photographic image, *avant la lettre*.

Notes

1. Derrida, *La Vérité en peinture* (Paris: Flammarion, 1978), 94. Translation: "Everything will flower at the edge of a deconsecrated tomb." Derrida, *Truth in Painting* (Chicago: University of Chicago Press, 1987), 81–82.
2. For Derrida's notion of teleiopoesis see *The Poltics of Friendship* (New York: Verso, 2005), 32 and *passim*.
3. Edmund Husserl, "Prolegomena to Pure Logic," in *Logical Investigations*.
4. See the first chapters of Martin Heidegger, *Being and Time: A Translation of Sein und Zeit*, trans. Joan Stambaugh (Albany: State University of New York Press, 1996). Original publication date, 1929.
5. Emmanuel Levinas, "Is Ontology Fundamental?" in *Emmanuel Levinas: Basic Philosophical Writings*. ed. Adrian T. Peperzak, Simon Critchley and Robert Bernasconi (Bloomington: Indiana University Press, 1996).
6. Paris: Editions du Cerf, 1958.

7. For a brilliant analysis of the colon and immanence in the context of a reading of an essay by Gilles Deleuze, see Giorgio Agamben's essay "Absolute Immanence," in *Potentialities*, trans. Daniel Heller-Roazen (Stanford: Stanford University Press, 1999).

8. André Bazin, "Ontologie de l'image photographique," in *Qu'est-ce que le cinéma?* (Paris: Editions du Cerf, 1975), 9. *Cf.* Bazin, "The Ontology of the Photographic Image," in *What Is Cinema?* vol. I (Berkeley: University of California Press, 1967), 9.

9. Jacques Derrida, *Specters of Marx: The State of the Debt, the Work of Mourning, & the New International*, trans. Peggy Kamuf (New York: Routledge, 1994), 35.

10. See *Being-in-the-World: Selected Papers of Ludwig Binswanger*, trans. Jacob Needleman (New York: Basic Books, 1963).

11. Bazin, "The Ontology of the Photographic Image," 9. The use of Egyptian antiquity as the figural ground for ideas of the primordial in both Bazin and Derrida will have to be worked out in relation to French colonialism and orientalism elsewhere.

12. Hugh Gray translates this as "continued existence" in *What Is Cinema?* vol. 1, 9. While Gray's translation conveys part of Bazin's meaning in clear English, it loses Bazin's rhetoric.

13. *Le trésor de la langue française informatisé* [electronic resource], conception et réalization Jacques Deinde (Paris: CNRS, 2002).

14. Bazin offers his readers a series of such prefigurations of the photograph. In addition to the mummy, the series includes the Shroud of Turin, the Veil of Veronica, death masks, and molds. Scholars often understand this series as a set of metaphors, but perhaps it can more usefully be understood as a group of examples of pre-photographic and pre-cinematic technologies. See Frodon, infra.

15. This is why the advent of the digital does not consign the "Ontology" essay to irrelevancy.

16. Bazin, "The Ontology of the Photographic Image," in *What Is Cinema?* vol. 1, 9. My emphasis.

17. Derrida, "*Différance*," in *Margins of Philosophy*, trans. Alan Bass (Chicago: University of Chicago Press, 1982), 8.

18. Ibid., 4.

19. See Alan Bass' translator's footnote 2 in "*Différance*," p. 4.

20. Bazin, "The Ontology of the Photographic Image," 13–14.

21. Ibid., 14.

22. See Noel Carroll, *Philosophical Problems of Classical Film Theory* (Princeton, NJ: Princeton University Press, 1988).

23. Berkeley: University of California Press, 2004.

24. Jean-Paul Sartre, *The Imaginary: A Phenomenological Psychology of the Imagination* (New York: Routledge, 2004), 23. See also Dudley Andrew, "The Ontology of a Fetish," *Film Quarterly*, 61:4 (Summer 2008), 62–67.

25. Bazin, "The Ontology of the Photographic Image," 14.

26. Ibid.

27. Jacques Derrida, *Without Alibi*, trans. Peggy Kamuf (Stanford, CA: Stanford University Press, 2000), 130.

PART TWO

Aesthetics

10

Belief in Bazin

Philip Rosen

Bazin's use of the French word *croyance*, commonly translated as "belief," raises questions about the most influential appropriations of his thought in the English-speaking world, which have mainly been based on the publication of selections from *Qu'est-ce que le cinéma?* translated by Hugh Gray in 1967 and 1971.[1] At crucial points, Gray renders *croyance* as "faith" rather than "belief."[2] Clearly, there are many contexts in which "belief" and "faith" are interchangeable terms, as are *la croyance* and *le foi* in French. But leaving aside etymological discussion, it seems connotatively easier to tilt "faith" toward a religious attitude. Of course, "belief" can apply to religious commitment. Yet it can signify more epistemological generality and less subjective valance.

By historical coincidence, such translation decisions complemented other impulses in Anglo-American film theory. The English-language Bazin appeared at a moment when structuralist and poststructuralist semiotics, as well as ideological analysis, challenged direct appeals to the real as well as to realist aesthetics, no matter how sophisticated. Bazin became the target of sustained critiques, initiated by contemporaneous French theoretical polemics.[3] In the Anglo-American context, however, these critiques did not have the element of a revolt against the father. They functioned instead to construct an "other" against which to define a "self," where that other insisted on a primordial cinematic realism in opposition to the new paradigm based on cinema as signifying process. Since close semiotic analysis of textual systems was the new order, Bazin's commitment to realism surely compromised his insights into stylistic systems. And since the cinematic apparatus was now understood as ideological, Bazin's ontology was described as naïvely mistaken, essentialist, and idealist. Such labels coalesced with the suspicion that his theories are grounded in a religious outlook, for Bazin's interest in a certain strain of liberal Catholic thought (e.g., Emmanuel Mounier, Teilhard de Chardin) was well-known.

Gray's translation of *croyance* as "faith" inadvertently abetted such critiques of Bazin, including the view that some of his key ideas are undergirded by religious conceptions. This is not necessarily or completely wrong. But rendering *croyance* as "faith" does prejudge and override possible ambivalences and ironies in some of Bazin's explicit and implicit references to religion and religious concepts.[4]

To illustrate: suppose we were to retranslate "faith" in two much-noted Bazinian sentences. In one, the famous opposition that sets up the dialectic of the evolution of the language of cinema would then be between "directors who *believe* in the image and those who *believe* in reality," ["*croient*" in Bazin; "put their faith in" for Gray] (WC1, 24; QQC, 64). Perhaps this does not seem like an enormous difference. But Bazin himself occasionally used variations on this formula that seem to support a more neutral or secularized connotation. For example, here is a literal translation of a passage from a 1952 *Esprit* essay on Renoir: "I call expressionist all aesthetics which . . . place more confidence [*confiance*] in cinematographic artifices—that is, what is generally understood as 'cinema'—than in the reality to which they are applied."[5]

Gray reinforced his rendering by other translation decisions. For example, another term important in certain of Bazin's key essays is "fidelity" [*fidélité*] and related forms of the word. There is no English cognate for the French adjectival form *fidèle*, which Bazin sometimes uses in the context of accurate depiction or translation. Gray's solution is to translate *fidèle* as "faithful," as when we speak of a faithful pictorial rendering. By itself, this is certainly reasonable. But with *croyance* already translated as "faith," it encourages a possible connotation by repeating the same root term, a repetition not present in Bazin's original language. Consider this retranslation: "*The most exact* [*le plus fidèle* in Bazin; "a very faithful" in Gray] drawing may actually tell us more about the model, but despite the promptings of our critical intelligence it will never have the irrational power of the photograph to bear away our *belief*" ["*croyance*" in Bazin; "faith" in Gray, thus repeating "faith" in the same sentence, while Bazin uses two terms] (WC1, 14; QQC, 14).

With such nuance as a prelude, let us rethink belief in Bazin's theory. A possible starting point is a 1951 essay that seems to deal precisely with a relation between religious belief and cinema, "Cinema and Theology."[6] It begins by identifying three types of films manifesting cinema's interest in God throughout film history: spectacles portraying the Acts of the Apostles and the lives of early Christian martyrs; hagiographies of the saints, depicting their miracles; and the priest's or nun's story. Most of the article deals with the third, most recent category, and the focus narrows further. Bazin concentrates on a few French films, especially *Dieu a besoin des hommes* (*God Needs Man*, 1950), which he compares to *La Symphonie pastorale* (1946). Both are adaptations from novels directed by Jean Delannoy and scripted by Jean Aurenche (with Pierre Bost for *Dieu a besoin des hommes*). Perhaps, then, the opening of "Cinema and Theology" is simply a rhetorical ploy leading to consideration of a then-current cycle of adaptations of novels about clerics in ambiguous moral situations.

Perhaps. But the particular and the general are not easily separated in Bazin. Even articles on individual films often refer to his theoretical concerns and to his view of cinema history. Given the original English-language receptions of Bazin, it may seem surprising that one such concern in "Cinema and Theology" is adaptation. The essay pays serious attention to the relation of these films to their literary sources. This connects it with some of Bazin's most important writing, as does its year of publication.

Throughout 1951 and 1952, one of Bazin's major concerns was arguing that contemporary adaptation from literary sources did not necessarily undermine but actually could advance the specific aesthetic virtues of cinema. There was the remarkable two-part essay "Théâtre et cinéma" (1951) and major articles dealing with novelistic adaptation, especially "*Le Journal d'un curé de campagne* et la stylistique de Robert Bresson" and "Pour un cinéma impur" (1952).

These last two share common references with "Cinema and Theology," including Bresson and the screenwriters there discussed.[7] In addition, Bazin invoked the same films in several later articles also concerned with adaptation, such as his 1954 *Esprit* piece on René Clément's *M. Ripois* (1954). There he calls novelistic adaptation "the problem [which] dominates the esthetic evolution of postwar French cinema." Indeed, for Bazin, Bresson was as important to postwar adaptation as Renoir was to prewar realism. He consistently treated *Diary of a Country Priest* (*Journal d'un curé de campagne*, 1951) not only as the most important of the third category of religious films identified in "Cinema and Theology" but also as a landmark adaptation and a key accomplishment in postwar cinema.[8]

But what does adaptation have to do with belief? The short answer is that, for Bazin, cinema is a matter of realism, and cinematic realism is a matter of *croyance*, that is, belief. Thus, in Bazin's writings, if a certain regime of literary adaptation occupied a leading position in a phase of the evolution of cinema, it necessarily involved an evolution in the configuration of belief.

This requires elaboration. The reference that throws its shadow on belief throughout Bazin's writings is "The Ontology of the Photographic Image." Eric Rohmer long ago asserted that the premises for Bazin's entire logic are in this essay.[9] It has recently come in for renewed appreciation, though perhaps leading in a different direction than it once did, as our digital era reconsiders the status of photographic and cinematic images from a new historical perspective. This text does not claim that a photograph or film image provides a guaranteed duplication or semblance of the real. This is clear in a passage I retranslated above: "The most exact drawing may actually tell us more about the model, but despite the promptings of our critical intelligence it will never have the irrational power of the photograph to bear away our belief." Here the special character of cinema is not reducible to a technologically determined objectivity but derives also from a drive of human subjectivity having to do, precisely, with belief. The "Ontology" essay treats photography and cinema as historically privileged media for this drive, but a crucial aspect of this subjectivity is something irrational. The distinctive cultural and aesthetic role of photographic and cinematic technologies resides in their relation to this irrationality. In addition, as the phrase "our critical intelligence" suggests, even for cinema, an objective, complete reproduction of reality remains an impossibility. It is thus a short step from this sentence to Bazin's "*myth* of total cinema," which underpins his perspective on cinema aesthetics.[10] The problem for a subject driven to believe in the reality of an image is the gap between film and reality. The two can never completely fuse; hence, the irrational characteristics of the drive necessary for belief in the reality conveyed by an image. Bazin's conception of realism entails a special sensitivity to the objective gap between film and reality, the consequence of which is that any realism demands aesthetic decisions. These remain in constant confrontation with the subjective drive to overcome the inevitable insufficiency of cinematic representation.[11] Bazin's shorthand term for this drive in the "Ontology" essay is "psychology," whose noted figure is the "mummy complex." This figure begins the essay, and later he calls cinema "change mummified," in Gray's wonderfully suggestive, if not literal, rendering.[12] In Gray's translation, the allusion to psychoanalysis in the term "mummy complex" is an isolated instance; however, in the original French, there are additional psychoanalytic references. Shortly after describing the realistic appeal of the photograph as irrational, Bazin explicitly characterizes that power as stemming from the depths of the unconscious.[13] And when he responds to Malraux about photography and art history, Bazin associates the psychological obsession to reproduce the world with the term "desire," which is also missing in Gray's translation.[14] It may seem forced, but it is useful to point out that,

like desire in psychoanalytic theory, the mummy complex and consequently the myth of total cinema pursue an impossibly perfect mental mirage, in the form of a duplication-in-identity of objective existents. Furthermore, like desire in psychoanalysis, the mummy complex derives from a wish
to sustain the existence and power of the subject. That is, artistic representation originates in a need
to counter knowledge of the inevitable dissolution of the subject (death), by material preservation
against decay associated with the passage of time. This projection of subjectivity into objective
materiality is a kind of antimaterialist desire at the origin of cultural representation, articulated socially in religious practices but exceeding them. This is why moments such as Bazin's notorious
praise for *Bicycle Thieves* (1948)—"plus de cinéma" (QQC, 309)—seem to me aimed at describing
the target of a fundamental desire to believe in the reality of the image, rather than an objective fact.
While this desire exists before cinema, it is something to which cinema appeals in new and special
ways. How a film configures an impossible belief involves the aesthetics of cinema.

From this angle, Bazin's evaluations of films and his accounts of film history are grounded
not only in what a film shows of the real world but also in *how* it shows it, its "language" or
aesthetics. Bazin repeatedly insisted that cinema must select from the world, for the image is
framed, projected on a flat service, restricted in color range, limited in time, and so forth;
hence, his close and influential attention to "the language of cinema"—film style as well as narrative strategies. If cinema embodies limitations and the abstraction of real time and space
along with the objects and beings that exist in them, then how one goes about abstracting
things expresses an attitude toward reality.

This means a film manifests a stance toward how humans take stances toward reality.
Using a psychoanalytic term, we could say that cinematic aesthetics becomes a *prop* for a transaction with the real in the face of an inadequacy of representation or lack that threatens the
subject. Serge Daney could compare Bazinian realism to the theory of fetishism. (And of course
a fetish was a religious object before it became a psychoanalytic analogy). Mannoni's account of
fetishism presents itself precisely as an account of *croyance*. Mannoni's remark "there are many
ways to believe and not believe"[15] might be a motto for Bazin's accounts of films.

This still leaves another question. Given the irrational elements described here, what is it
about cinema that makes it and its "language" the special prop of this desire, this will to believe?
Despite recent critiques of this approach, I continue to think that Peter Wollen fastened on a
linchpin of Bazin's conception of the special attraction for belief in photography and cinema
when he compared Bazin's account of photography and cinema to the semiotic concept of
indexicality, derived from Peirce.[16] The presence of the object at the origin of the production of
the image by an inhuman machine makes the image seem a trace of the actual object. This—not
its appearance—gives the photograph a radically more intense appeal to the drive to believe
than any previous forms of image; cinema adds to photography the trace of duration.[17] There is
nothing irrational in recognizing that a certain technology produces an indexical representation in this sense. But for Bazin a spectator's knowledge of how a photographic or film image
was produced intersects with investments of a different nature. The subjective desire of the
mummy complex finds the object-centered indexical image as a privileged target. It finds a medium it can believe in more than others.

There are religious allusions in the "Ontology" essay, but in themselves they do not demonstrate that Bazin's theory of realism derives from a model of religious belief. Yet as a key prop
for belief, indexicality does lead beyond what is directly perceived in the image, namely to the

phantom of an absolutely secure, everlasting subject, which is figured as the defeat of death. Perhaps, then, cinema is like religion, at least in soliciting a similarly profound investment in something everlasting, which means something beyond the sensible, beyond the worldly constraints of space and time. This may explain Bazin's sly remark about religious films depicting miracles: "The cinema is in itself already a kind of miracle . . ."[18] But Bazin actually opposes cinematic belief to any direct symbolization or display of spiritual transcendence. There is a serious joke in "Cinema and Theology" concerning films about priests: given the spectacular spiritual iconography of Catholicism, it might be an advantage for the makers of a Catholic film to have a Protestant sensibility.[19]

A paradox of cinematic realism is that the mummy complex, whose desire for the everlasting should be so consonant with transcendence and the spiritual, draws us back to the concrete world. Photography and cinema can feed the desire and irrational belief in the reality of the image because they are defined by a material connection between image and physical world. Belief attracted by and to indexicality can lead toward engagement with whatever in concrete reality overflows any symbolic, transcendent meaning. In pursuit of its own overweening desire, the subject is engaged by its own physical limits. In that case, cinema enables a model transaction between the world and its apprehension, between the inhuman and human, between the physical and value, between object and subject. Thus the indexical relation can become a kind of ideal figure or standard for such relationships.

Now let us focus on the question of belief and adaptation. Bazin's writings on adaptation are informed by an indexical ideal echoing that of the "Ontology" essay. His most important treatise on adaptation as such is surely "Pour un cinéma impur" (Gray blunts Bazin's *anti*-essentialist polemic by rendering "*cinéma impur*" as "mixed cinema").[20] Bazin here complains that adherents of montage theory reduce authentic cinema to something like an aesthetics of the cinematic apparatus as such. But for Bazin, the cinematic apparatus is inseparable from a relation to something *exterior* to its technology. In the "Ontology" essay, this exteriority amounts to the worldly entities registered by the camera. The very nature of cinema, then, is precisely *not* to be something in and for itself, but to be constituted in relation to something outside itself. This would mean that cinema history and even cinematic specificity *necessarily include the non-cinematic*. This definitional inclusion of the non-cinematic within the cinematic also pervades Bazin's account of adaptation. Literature and theater are not foreign excrescences polluting and obscuring pure cinema, he argues, but are part and parcel of cinema's social and economic history—which includes motivations for adaptation. Here the exterior "object" which is to be filmed is the literary text. This perspective finds its most extreme case in novelistic adaptation: what if the preexistent entity being filmed is not an object but a prose fiction?

We should note that Bazin's writings on adaptation are engaged in a triple project, at the very least: first, the polemic against purist theory; second, an intervention in postwar film culture, for which, he repeatedly asserts, adaptations are central; third, ideas about the history of cinema. In relation to this last, he employs the term "avant-garde" in several articles in the early 1950s, which often include references to films discussed in "Cinema and Theology."

A succinct explication appears in "L'Avant-garde nouvelle," written around 1949 for the Biarritz festival of *films maudits*, and republished in *Cahiers* in 1952. Thinking of filmmakers associated with the historic avant-gardes of the 1920s as well as a text by Hans Richter, Bazin comments that this avant-garde wished to advance cinema by working on the purely cinematic, to the exclusion of both subject matter and the utilitarian, mass, commercial aspects of cinema. Yet, he argues, nothing followed from it, and most of its filmmakers have stopped making films. But, he reasons, a true avant-garde is precisely a movement in advance of something; something which should follow and occupy the terrain where it has led. By this criterion, the 1920s avant-garde failed. A counterexample is Jean Renoir, who innovates but neither deemphasizes subject matter nor deplores commerce. Something always follows, even from his films that are not at first commercially successful. Renoir is a model of the true "avant-garde" because he participates in and affects the historical development of cinema.

Thus, Bazin is arguing that cinema does not exist as an a priori concept separate from economic and social contexts, and apart from audiences and the subject matters which concern them. An avant-garde leads the development of cinema as it actually exists. Here Bazin implicitly defines his own ambitions as a writer: it is the job of the critic to recognize this kind of avant-garde when it appears, which means recognizing the place of films and filmmakers that lead cinema history, rather than praising purely cinematic or isolated projects.[21]

This approach is most fully elaborated in "Pour un cinéma impur." There he asserts that new developments in cinema had previously stemmed from the following chain: technical changes entailed new forms appropriate to those means, and themes appropriate to those forms; hence, for example, Soviet montage and Hollywood classicism. But by the late 1930s, technical innovation stabilized. Consequently, cinema had entered "the age of the scenario," which entailed "a reversal of the relationship between matter and form."[22] In this historical phase, cinema would progress through subtle inventiveness within the existing pool of forms rather than formal innovation—until some future technological shift would again destabilize cinematic form. Dudley Andrew, who long ago emphasized this essay, suggests that "Pour un cinéma impur" could be called "the evolution of the content of cinema."[23] For Bazin, in the postwar period, form (or style) could only refresh itself by responding to developments in the matter [le fond], the material filmed, with all the resources cinema had already developed. For a variety of reasons, including both culture and commerce, literary adaptation became a leading element of le fond.

Now, Bazin's concern for adaptation as a crucial source of the postwar avant-garde converges with his ideas about belief in cinema. He holds that in the best postwar adaptations, cinematic respect for the preexistent world finds a corollary in a particularly intense drive to respect the preexistent literary source. His term for this level of respect is "fidelity." However, it is not self-evident that his account of cinematic realism could simply be transferred to an account of fidelity. A novel is not an object, which could be preserved like the physical bodies assumed in the "Ontology" essay. Transposing a narrative from written language to cinema obviously changes the technical means of presenting it, so literal preservation of a novel in a film is impossible. Bazin's solution is that fidelity must take into account the *differences* between the cinema and written texts, so that a filmmaker may then compensate for these differences by aesthetic means. In Bazin's magisterial essay on *Diary of a Country Priest*, he praises Bresson's explicit ambition of absolute fidelity to the source text, in the face of Bernanos' hyperboles impossible to duplicate on screen. Nevertheless, according to Bazin, there is an equivalent in "the ellipses and litotes of Robert Bresson's editing [*découpage*]." This leads to a general principle: "The more important and decisive the literary qualities of the work, the more the adaptation disturbs its equilibrium, the more it needs a creative talent to reconstruct it on a new equilibrium not indeed identical with, but equivalent to, the old one."[24] Now, this equivalence cannot claim the kind of objective identity proposed to a subject by the camera's indexical, existential connection to a physical object or person. But over and above the material level, fidelity may instead aim at the *aesthetic* ("the literary qualities"), precisely because it must be achieved in and through the differences, the gap, between source text and film.

This suggests parallels with the "Ontology" essay's obsessive subjective drive for timeless preservation of the physical. What strikes Bazin about postwar adaptation is the intensification of a drive for another kind of preservation, that of the letter of the literary text. Just as total cinema is not achievable, neither is total adaptation. In both cases, filmic depiction has an extreme aim (perfect duplication), and in both cases that depiction necessarily falls objectively short of its aim. The gap between filmic depiction and the preexistent is filled in by subjectivity, not only that of the audience but also that which emerges in a dialectic of aesthetic choices associated with the auteur. In the essays on ontology and on adaptation, the question becomes whether a film's aesthetic choices are mandated by the value of respect, as opposed to imposing its mastery over the object of depiction. In adaptation the aesthetic of the novel becomes the object of respect: "In short, to adapt is no longer to betray but to respect" [Adapter, enfin, n'est plus trahir, mais respecter.][25]

Perhaps, then, it is not surprising that indexicality as an ideal hovers in the background of descriptions of fidelity. There are, for example, analogies between fidelity and the camera, but they sometimes refer to the gap between image and reality and, obliquely, to the dialectics of subjectivity underlying the ontology. For example, here is a passage from the "Impure Cinema" article, as Gray renders it:

> In order to attain this high level of aesthetic fidelity, it is essential that the cinematographic form of expression make progress comparable to that in the field of optics. The distance separating *Hamlet* from the *film d'art* is as great as that separating the complexities of the modern lens from the primitive condenser of the magic lantern. Its imposing complexity has no other purpose than to compensate for the distortions, the aberrations, the diffractions, for which the glass is responsible—that is to say, to render the *camera obscura* as objective as possible. The transition from a theatrical work to the screen demands, on the aesthetic level, a scientific knowledge . . . comparable to that of a camera operator in his photographic rendering.[26]

Even more explicit is Bazin's characterization of Bresson's aesthetic attitude. Here is my literalistic rendering: "Bresson treats the novel as he does his characters. It is a brute fact, a given reality which one must in no way attempt to adapt to the situation, to inflect it according to such and such a momentary requirement of meaning; but on the contrary, one must attempt to confirm it in its being."[27] This could apply to one of Bazin's descriptions of Stroheim's gaze at the world, or of neorealism.

Of course, there should be a distinction between indexicality as a figure or ideal for fidelity in adaptation, and indexicality as the technical imprinting of a trace that supports (props) the drive to believe in the ontology of the image. While adaptation must deal with material objects (it is cinema, after all), Bresson's fidelity must be to the *aesthetic* of the novel. Nevertheless, on this level, Bazin uses the same level of rhetoric that he notoriously deployed in the "Ontology" essay, overriding the difference between image and object: "It is hardly enough to say of this work . . . that it is in essence true [*fidèle*] to the original because, first of all, it *is* the novel . . ."[28]

How can one believe an adaptation *is* the novel? Such an assertion harks back to the irrational components of the "Ontology" essay—the mummy complex, the obsession and sub-jective drive to capture and preserve the real against the passage of time in spite, or because, of the gap between representation and reality. Recall that for Bazin, cinematic aesthetics is a stance toward the real, and toward how one may take stances toward the real. This makes aesthetics an expression of subjectivity facing that which is materially other to itself, objectivity. But if fidelity concerns a film's relation to the aesthetic of the novel, this means that the pursuit of the source text in adaptation is a pursuit not just of objectivity, but of subjectivity.

In a lovely little 1952 article, "Faut-il croire en Hitchcock?," Bazin claims that directors such as Welles and Wyler show that cinema is not the addition of mise-en- scène to the scenario, as one imagines the way it works in theater. In these cineastes "there is only writing and style as in the novel." He goes on to say, "Today the avant-garde is no longer in depth of field and long shots, but in sound and uses of new freedom of style, in order to push back the frontiers of ci-nema."[29] Bazin excludes Hitchcock from this avant-garde. His is a mastery of established tech-niques applied to the scenario which contributes nothing new to this freedom.

There are many articles where Bazin attributes to a postwar avant-garde the freedom and flexibility he associates with the novel. We might understand this comparison as follows. In apprehending a novel, including even the subjectivities of characters, we are routed through a prior subjectivity, that of the author. This prior subjectivity is manifest in the very materials of written literature, the language and style of the text. In the postwar period, Bazin claims, cine-matic language and style had evolved a freedom and flexibility comparable to that of novelistic language. This makes a new level of fidelity available; however, that fidelity does not consist in a confining and slavish literal imitation but is associated with additional freedom for the creating subject.

Bresson's film represents Bernanos' novel—including its style and language—to the spec-tator, but it does so through Bresson's own style and aesthetic, or "language of cinema." There-fore, Bresson's subjectivity is simultaneously made available to us, thanks to his drive to preserve Bernanos' aesthetics —that is, subjectivity—as first encountered in *the latter's* language. In this sense, it is not only the novelistic representation of reality but also the existence and being of subjectivity itself that the postwar avant-garde cinema can engage and embody, with the sup-pleness of the novel.[30]

An account of subjectivity was always at the heart of Bazin's ontology of cinema. If the indexical characteristics of cinema propose a new promise to the subject for dealing with the threat time poses to its own existence, this led Bazin to an underlying issue: how can this sub-ject be reconciled with its own material existence in the real, without distorting the real by imposing its own reassuring abstractions or conventions on the latter? He saw unprecedented benefits in the interaction between "psychology" and aesthetics in cinema, as modes of experi-encing and apprehending the world. This also included subjectivity's own place in the world. But the subtle aesthetic developments Bazin saw in postwar adaptation took this further. True, the "evolution of the content of cinema" must always begin from the material world, but postwar adaptation meant it mobilized subjectivity itself as an object of depiction. The ultimate consequence of fidelity in adaptation is to evince belief in the possibilities of subjectivity itself, subjectivity characterized by belief and also by the potential for freedom.

In the early 1950s, on top of his thesis that a primary component of subjectivity in relation to cinema is the drive to believe, Bazin played with the idea that belief itself had become an historically central object of depiction. For example, in an important 1952 essay, "Les deux époques de Jean Renoir," Bazin once again positions adaptation at the leading edge of cinema, alongside films dealing with religion. These become an avant-garde content: "The greatest novelty of the recent history of cinema is the appearance of worthy treatments of religious subject matter." He names *Miracle in Milan* (1951) and (again) *Diary of a Country Priest* as the most significant examples of this "paradoxical avant-garde," while mentioning (again) Delannoy and *Dieu a besoin des hommes*.[31]

These films lead us back to "Cinema and Theology." It may be that Bazin thinks his third type of religious film, the story of a priest or nun experiencing doubt, is an advance not simply because it is about religion as such, but because it is concerned with writing subjectivity, and in particular with depicting belief and its failures. He claims of *La Symphonie pastorale*, "This is not to say that the movie has no religious significance, but only that this significance does not imply any a priori ideas, not even the idea of God; the only thing implied is *belief* in God."[32] These films do not only embody subjectivity confronted with an alien, worldly exteriority as in the "Ontology" essay; they bracket the transcendent so as to thematize belief within the world. They take on the problem of representing and interrogating subjectivity in its search for security in belief, in a medium slanted toward belief in its constitutive realism.

This kind of project overlaps with that of perfectionist adaptation, for the only way to believe in the absolute fidelity of an adaptation is through believing in its depiction of a subjectivity, through the auteur's encounter with the aesthetics of the literary source. That a line of postwar French adaptations of novels had as their subject religion and belief could not have escaped the attention of someone who thought cinema a matter of realism, with its realism grounded in belief.

Giorgio Agamben defines religion as "that which removes things, places, animals, or people from common use and transfers them to a separate sphere. . . . Every separation has a religious core."[33] In Bazin, cinema is constituted by separations: between reality and film, concrete and abstract, psychology and aesthetics, material and spiritual, time-filled and timeless—and (most of all) objectivity and subjectivity. But Bazin is also a dialectician, and dialectics mitigates the force of these separations. In Bazin, not one of these terms is reducible to its contrary, but each is mutually constitutive of its contrary. On Agamben's definition, this makes Bazin's relation to religion ambivalent. For Bazin, cinema had a special, necessary task. It both brought the objective world to subjectivity, and subjectivity to the world. But as it evolved, it could bring subjectivity face to face with itself. This could happen solely through a leap of *croyance*.[34,35]

Notes

1.   All citations noted as "QQC" are from André Bazin, *Qu'est-ce que le cinéma?* (Paris: Editions du Cerf-Corlet, 2007). All citations noted as WC1 are from André Bazin, *What Is Cinema?* vol. 1, trans. Hugh Gray (Berkeley: University of California Press, 1967 [rev. 2004]). For another significant example regarding *fidèle* translated as "faithful," compare QQC, 127 and WC1, 143.

2. This essay was composed before the appearance of a new annotated translation of selections from *Qu'est-ce que le cinéma?* also entitled *What Is Cinema?* trans. Timothy Barnard (Montreal: Caboose, 2009). All citations from it will be cited as WCB. Barnard does sometimes translate *croyance* in a terminology of "belief" instead of "faith," but is not consistent. He renders the first passage "The most faithful drawing can give us more information about the model, but it will never, no matter what our critical faculties tell us, possess the irrational power of photography, in which we believe without reservation" (WCB, 8). From my perspective this is an improvement, but the first clause still tilts *fidèle* toward Gray's connotative emphasis. In the next passage, however, Barnard produces the same terminology as Gray: "those filmmakers who put their faith in the image and those who put their faith in reality" (WCB, 88).

3. I will find it necessary to say some things about this and some other choices made by Gray. But this should not detract from the invaluable service he performed by transmitting so many major texts by one of the major thinkers and critics in the history of cinema.

4. A major exception in the 1970s was Dudley Andrew, *André Bazin* (New York: Oxford University Press, 1978).

5. See, e.g., Andrew, 44, 65–67.

6. "J'appelle expressioniste toute esthéthique qui, dans cette conjoncture, fait plus de confiance aux artifices cinématographiques—c'es-à-dire à ce qu'on entend généralement par 'cinéma'—qu'à la réalité à laquelle ils s'appliquent." Bazin, "Les deux époques de Jean Renoir," *Esprit*, 20 (March 1952), 501.

7. André Bazin, "Cinema and Theology," in *Bazin at Work: Major Essays and Reviews from the Forties and Fifties*, ed. Bert Cardullo, trans. Alain Piette and Bert Cardullo (New York: Routledge, 1997), 61–72. This article was originally published as "Cinéma et théologie," in *Esprit*, 19 (February 1951), 237–45.

8. Bazin, "*Le Journal d'un curé de campagne* and the Stylistics of Robert Bresson," in *What Is Cinema?* vol. 1, 143; "*Le Journal d'un curé de campagne* et la stylistique de Robert Bresson," in QQC, 127. *Qu'est-ce que le cinéma?* vol. 2 ("Cinéma et les autres arts") includes the major texts on adaptation named in this paragraph, as do Gray's and Barnard's translations.

9. See Bazin, "Des romans et des films: *M. Ripois* avec ou sans nemesis," *Esprit* 217–218 (August–September 1954), 313–14.

10. Eric Rohmer, "La 'Somme' d'André Bazin," *Cahiers du Cinéma*, 91 (January 1959), 37–38.

11. Bazin, "The Myth of Total Cinema," in WC, 17–22; WCB, 13–20; "Le mythe du cinéma total," in QQC, 19–24.

12. For a full elaboration of these points see Philip Rosen, "History of Image, Image of History: Subject and Ontology in Bazin," in *Rites of Realism: Essays on Corporeal Cinema*, ed. Ivone Margulies (Durham, NC: Duke University Press, 2003); and in a fuller version in Rosen, *Change Mummified: Cinema, Historicity, Theory* (Minneapolis: University of Minnesota Press, 2001), chapters 1, 3.

13. In the French, Bazin puts *complexe* in scare quotes (QQC, 9), which indicates the care with which he designates his transfer of psychoanalytic terminology. This nicety is not in Gray (WC, 17) while Barnard puts "mummy complex" in scare quotes (WCB, 3). On the definition of cinema, Bazin's exact wording is "comme la momie du changement." (QQC, 14). On psychology and aesthetics in Bazin's ontology, *cf.* Dudley Andrew, "Foreword to the 2004 Edition," in *What Is Cinema?* vol. 1, trans. Hugh Gray, xiv–xv.

14. The important and complex French passage is: "L'objectif seul nous donne de l'objet une image capable de 'défouler,' du fond de notre inconscient, ce besoin de substituer à l'objet mieux qu'un décalque approximatif: cet object lui-même, mais libéré des contingences temporelles" (QQC, 14). Barnard's rendering makes more of its purport available: "Only the photographic lens gives us an image of the object that is capable of relieving, out of the depths of our unconscious, our need to substitute for the object something more than an approximation. That something is the object itself, but liberated from its temporal contingencies" (WCB, 8). Compare WC1, 14.

15. Bazin, "Ontologie de l'image photographique," in *Qu'est-ce que le cinéma?* 11: "un désir tout psychologique..."

16. Serge Daney, "The Screen of Fantasy (Bazin and Animals)," in *Rites of Realism: Essays on Corporeal Cinema*, 34–35; O. Mannoni, *Clefs pour l'imaginaire; ou, l'autre scène* (Paris: Editions du Seuil, 1969), 24. See also Boaz Hagin, "Examples in Theory: Interpassive Illustrations and Celluloid Fetishism," *Cinema Journal*, 48:1 (2008), esp. 8–13.

17. Peter Wollen, *Signs and Meanings in the Cinema* (Bloomington: Indiana University Press, rev. 1973), 124ff. For important critiques of reading Bazin through the concept and/or terminology of indexicality, see Daniel Morgan, "Rethinking Bazin: Ontology and Realist Aesthetics," *Critical Inquiry*, 32 (2006), 441–81; Tom

Gunning, "Moving Away from the Index," *Differences* 18:1 (2007), 29–52, and, especially on Bazin and the photograph, Gunning, "What's the Point of an Index? Or Faking Photographs," in *Still Moving*, ed. Karen Beckman and Jean Ma (Durham: Duke University Press, 2008). There is no space here to engage these articles with the seriousness they deserve. But to give some very general, perhaps cryptic indications: in my view, Morgan reframes Bazin in interesting and important ways; however, I do not think his reading gives proper weight to what Bazin calls "psychology" in the "Ontology" essay, that is, the place of subjectivity. This de-emphasis is important to his argument against a reading through the concept of indexicality. I find Gunning's investigations on the appeal of the image to be subtle and brilliant. Yet he is careful to say he is not completely excluding indexicality from his rethinking of that appeal, and I am not yet convinced that his points about Bazin constitute so great a departure from a reading that emphasizes indexicality.

18. Roland Barthes also highlighted the irrational appeal of the photograph, emphasizing that a photograph seems to be irrefutable evidence of the prior existence of an object, but to different conclusions than Bazin. Roland Barthes, *Le Chambre Claire*, (Paris: Gaillimard, 1980).

19. Bazin, "Cinema and Theology," in *Bazin at Work*, 61. Original: "le cinéma tient déjà en lui-même du miracle . . ." "Cinéma et théologie," in *Qu'est-ce que le cinéma*, 238.

20. Bazin, "Cinema and Theology," 61; "Cinéma et théologie," 240.

21. Barnard correctly literalizes the title: "For an Impure Cinema: In Defense of Adaptation."

22. Bazin, "L'avant-garde nouvelle," *Cahiers du Cinéma*, 10 (March 1952), 16–17.

23. Bazin, "In Defense of Mixed Cinema," in *What Is Cinema?* vol. 1, 74. Original: "l'âge du scénario; entendons: d'un renversement du rapppport entre le fond et la forme." Bazin, "Pour un cinéma impur: Défense de l'adaptation," in *Qu'est-ce que le cinéma?* 105.

24. Andrew, *André Bazin*, 177. More generally, see Andrew's discussion of this essay and adaptation in relation to Bazin's account of the evolution of the language of cinema, pages 177–87. In recent work, about which I only learned after writing this paper, Andrew has returned to the question of adaptation in Bazin, and he also relates it to "Ontology of the Photographic Image." Our views were developed independently. See Dudley Andrew, chapter 4 of *What Cinema Is! Bazin's Quest and its Charge* (Wiley-Blackwell, 2010); see also Andrew, "Bazin Phase 2: Die unreine Existenz des Kinos," *Montage A/V*, 18:1 (2009).

25. Bazin, "In Defense of Mixed Cinema," in *What Is Cinema?* vol. 1, 68; "Pour un cinéma impur," in *Qu'est-ce que le cinéma?* 97, for both sentences.

26. Bazin, "In Defense of Mixed Cinema," 68; "Pour un cinéma impur," 99.

27. Bazin, "In Defense of Mixed Cinema," 69. Original: "Il y a aussi loin du Film d'Art à *Hamlet* [the film of Laurence Olivier] que du primitif condensateur de la lanterne magique au jeu complex de lentilles d'un objectif moderne: son imposante complication n'a pourtant d'autre objet que de compenser les déformations, les aberrations, les diffractions, les reflets dont le verre est responsable, c'est-à-dire de rendre la chambre noire aussi *objective* que possible. Le passage d'une oeuvre théâtrale à l'écran requérait sur le plan esthéthique une science de la fidélité comparable à celle de l'opérateur dans le rendu photographique."
Cf. "For an Impure Cinema," in WCB, 131: "The distance between the *film d'art* and *Hamlet* is as great as that between the primitive condenser lens of the magic lantern and the complex range of lenses in modern cinema. The impressive intricacy of this fidelity, however, has as its only goal to compensate for the distortions, aberrations, distractions and reflections for which the lens is responsible; that is to say, to make the camera as objective as possible."

28. My translation. Original: "Bresson traite le roman comme ses personnages. Il est un fait brut, une réalité donné qu'il ne faut point essayer d'adapter à la situation, d'infléchir selon telle ou telle exigence momentanée du sens, mais au contraire confirmer dans son être" (QQC, 118–19). Here is Gray: "Bresson treats the novel as he does his characters. It is a cold, hard fact, a reality to be accepted as it stands. One must not attempt to adapt it to the situation at hand, or manipulate it to fit some passing need for an explanation; on the contrary, it is something to be taken absolutely as it stands" (WC, 136). I find Barnard to be more precise (WCB, 151), but he translates *être* as "essence" rather than "being."

29. My translation. Original: "Il est presque insuffisant de la dire par essence 'fidèle' à l'original, puisque d'abord elle *est* le roman" (QQC, 127). Compare WC, 143 and WCB, 159. I prefer Barnard, but both translate *fidèle* as "faithful."

30. Bazin, "Faut-il croire en Hitchcock?" *France observateur*, 88 (January 1, 1952), 24.

31. See Andrew, "Foreword to the 2004 Edition," on adaptation and the consciousness of the writer.

32. My translation. Original: "La plus grande nouveauté de l'histoire récente du cinéma est l'apparition d'un traitement valable des sujets religieux." Bazin, "Les deux époques de Jean Renoir," *Esprit*, 20 (March 1952), 501.

33. Bazin, "Cinema and Theology," in *Bazin at Work*, 64. This is Bert Cardullo's translation, except he also renders *croyance* as "faith," which I have once again changed to "belief." Original: "Non qu'il n'ait une valeur et une signification religieuse, mais celle-ci ne suppose aucune donnée à priori, pas même Dieu; seulement la *croyance* en Dieu."

34. Giorgio Agamben, *Profanations*, trans. Jeff Fort (New York: Zone Books, 2007), 74.

35. Research for this paper was carried out at the Yale Film Studies Center. I am grateful for the encouragement to use the Bazin archive and to the helpful staff. Some passages of this essay are derived from my article, "Bazin et la 'croyance,'" in *CinémAction* 134 (2010), numéro spécial, "Croyances et le sacré," edited by Agnès DeVictor and Kristian Feigelson.

11

The World in Its Own Image
The Myth of Total Cinema

Tom Gunning

Most of us can remember a time when displaying a sympathy for, or even a particular interest in, the ideas of André Bazin encountered the objection that he was an "idealist." The term was seldom used to open a serious discussion of the philosophical context of Bazin's thought—such as his relation to either the Hegelian or the Platonic tradition—but instead to label his writings as politically retrograde or naïve, a bit like the use of the terms "terrorist" or "socialist" in American politics. In the '60s and '70s the term "idealist" was politically charged and a great many positions or approaches that could hardly be seen as adhering to either the German or Hellenic idealist traditions—such as phenomenology—were nonetheless denounced as idealist. I remember being told that investigating early cinema was politically suspect, since "the search for origins is an idealist project," a claim that might have given pause to the author of *The Origin of the Family, Private Property and the State*. It likewise might seem odd that a film theorist like Bazin who advocated a cinematic style based in a direct relation to reality rather than in images that convey authorial intention or communicate unequivocal significance would be understood as an idealist. Insofar as idealism has been understood as an aesthetic movement, it has generally been contrasted with realist modes.

Bazin's relation to idealism poses an issue as complicated as defining the term itself and has a specific context in '60s French Marxism which I could not fully explicate here. While I oppose using the term as a shibboleth designed to prevent us from taking Bazin seriously, I do not deny that Bazin may himself have seen his view of cinema as related to idealism. He claimed at least once (in his essay "In Defense of Rossellini") that he was not a philosopher and carrying on a consistent philosophic discourse was not the primary aim of his criticism, however fundamental we may find his theoretical texts.[1] Nor am I going to attempt a philosophical discussion here of Bazin's relation to idealism. However I may flirt with it, I, like Bazin, do not consider myself a philosopher, even if some of my best friends are. Indeed, I have argued elsewhere that attempting to rework Bazin's insights into philosophical terms, as in Peter Wollen's highly influential interpretation of Bazin's analysis of the ontology of the photographic image in terms of Peirce's concept of the index, entails ignoring important aspects of Bazin's position, even if it illuminates others.[2] My goal remains modest: to investigate Bazin's own account of the origins of motion pictures, his essay "The Myth of Total Cinema," which, in its claim that cinema existed first as an idea, may appear to constitute an argument for an idealist approach to cinema.[3] But if there is an ideal described in this essay, it remains rooted in Bazin's claim that cinema's vocation lies in its relation to realism. Defining that realism remains the elusive task of any reading of Bazin. If we avoid explaining "total cinema" as simply indicating Bazin's idealist project—a nearly metaphysical match between cinema and reality—the term becomes surprisingly complex. The myth of total cinema may seem to describe film as a simple duplication of the world in all its sensual qualities, but a myth always exceeds a concept, and Bazin's essay examines one of the traditional tasks of myth, a tale of origin. Further, this essay draws me as a film historian, since it stands as Bazin's principal discussion of early cinema. As such, "The Myth of Total Cinema" not only challenges traditional (and even subsequent) historiography but also highlights the fault line in Bazin's realism: its relation to illusion and deceit.

Bazin perhaps comes closest to a confession of a more or less Platonic idealism when in this essay he states seemingly straightforwardly, "The cinema is an idealist phenomenon. The concept men had of it existed so to speak fully armed in their minds, as if in some platonic heaven . . ." (WC, 17). But Bazin's use of "idealist" in this first paragraph of the essay, far from being straightforward, initiates a complex rhetorical inversion. Rather than simply an essay in either film theory (its main reception in discussions of Bazin thus far) or film history (possibly an equally important context, if less explored), the essay originally appeared in 1946 as a book review of the first volume of Georges Sadoul's monumental history of international cinema, *Histoire générale du cinéma: L'invention du cinéma*, published that same year.[4] Sadoul not only offered the first scholarly multivolume history of the cinema, but since the 1930s and his early association with the surrealists, he had been the more or less official spokesman on cinema for the French Communist Party. Thus Bazin opens his review with an ironic claim:

> Paradoxically enough, the impression left on the reader by Georges Sadoul's admirable book on the origins of the cinema is of a reversal [*inversion*], in spite of the author's Marxist views, of the relations between an economic and technical evolution and the imagination of those carrying on the search [*chercheurs*]. The way things happened seems to call for a reversal of the historical order of causality, which goes from the economic infrastructure to the ideological superstructure, and for us to consider the basic technical discoveries as fortunate accidents but essentially second in importance to the preconceived ideas [*l'idée préalable*] of the inventors. (WC, 17)

In other words, Bazin doesn't simply describe the cinema as an idealist phenomenon, a product of the imagination more than of economic and technical circumstances. He claims, somewhat perversely, to derive this view directly from Sadoul's text, rather than from his own philosophical predispositions. He introduces this claim as both a surprise and a reversal, coming as it does from a reading of a bona fide Marxist historian. Indeed, Bazin assumes the canonical Marxist causality of deriving the cultural superstructure from a materialist base as the norm, a norm he claims that Sadoul's account seems to reverse. Carefully read, Bazin offers in this essay a highly ironic approach to Sadoul's book rather than simply offering a naïve idealist theory of the cinema.

Recent historiography of early cinema clarifies the complex nature of Bazin's reading of Sadoul, as Sadoul's highly empirical history of the invention of the cinema has been criticized by revisionists as inherently teleological, presenting successive devices as stages in an inter-locked series of inventions that seem to move inevitably toward the achievement of continuous projected motion pictures.[5] Rather than this coherent narrative of technical progress, the revisionist historians have proposed new and broader models of the materialist base of cinema's invention (as in Michael Chanan's provocatively named and too rarely cited *The Dream That Kicks*), or placed within a broader conception of the modernization and disciplining of perception (as in the work of Jonathan Crary), or supplemented by more detailed and less teleological accounts of what is sometimes called the archaeology of the cinema (as in the research of Charles Musser, Laurent Mannoni, and Deac Rossell).[6] All these approaches draw directly or indirectly on the historical methods of dialectical materialism. But Bazin does not offer this sort of revision of Sadoul's history, correcting or deepening its research or questioning its teleology. Rather than objecting to Sadoul's method, Bazin claims to be drawing out what he sees as the implications of his account. He finds in Sadoul's history of the invention of the cinema less a description of scientific and technological progress than evidence of an obsessive fascination with achieving a complex and "total" mimesis of the world. It is this mimetic vocation of cinema that functions like an ideal, arguably in Sadoul's history, and certainly in Bazin's understanding of cinema's origin.

In spite of his claim simply to be following Sadoul in his discovery of the idealist basis of the cinema, Bazin most certainly performs a deliberate act of what Harold Bloom might call a misreading, an appropriation and rerouting of Sadoul's account. Bazin's claim that neither science, technology, nor economics determined the invention of the cinema cannot be taken seriously as historiography (and indeed the revision of Sadoul's accounts in recent decades, rather than following Bazin's denigration of these factors, has instead deepened research into them). Bazin's approach dives under historiography to find the place where theory and history intertwine. From Sadoul's chronology of the invention of cinema, Bazin abstracts (and here lies what could be described as his idealist move) and formulates what he considers a more primary motivation, which he does describe as "an idea" (WC, 18). Cinema's actual technological development appears as a delay in the materialization of the already articulated idea (". . . we must here explain, on the other hand, how it was the invention took so long to emerge . . ." [WC, 19]). If Bazin describes this delay in the invention of the cinema as "a disturbing phenomenon" (ibid.) this is because he finds the idea fully articulated in the imagination of cinema's inventors, and merely marking time until its material embodiment is actually achieved. But what was it that the inventor envisioned: animated photographs? The analysis of motion? An extension of the magic lantern? Rather than these technical goals, Bazin claims they are pursuing an idea. This idea constitutes the cornerstone of Bazin's myth of cinema: "In their imaginations they saw the cinema as a total and complete representation of reality; they saw in a trice [*d'emblée*] the reconstruction of a perfect illusion of the outside world in sound, color, and relief" (WC, 20).

While Bazin's account of this "guiding myth" of the invention of cinema minimizes the sort of historical contextualization that has marked the revisionary history of early cinema offered in the last decades, it is both subtle and prescient of the more recent archeology of cinema. The post-Brighton scholars dealing with the invention of cinema have emphasized the history of projection to a degree Bazin does not (whether Musser's extensive history of "screen practice," or Mannoni's exploration of the centuries of the "grand art of light and shadow," especially of the magic lantern), but Bazin's discussions of the role of stereoscopy and of Villiers de l'Isle-Adam's novel *Tomorrow's Eve* (*L'Eve future*, 1886) anticipate themes crucial to later scholars. Rather than offering more fine-grained research into the predecessors of film, Bazin's conception of cinema's origins takes a different tack, more synthetic than teleological. For Bazin, the *idée fixe* that drives the invention of cinema depends on fusing technical aspects that many histories of cinema tend to investigate separately. While most histories of the emergence of projected moving images focus primarily on the achievement of moving photographic images, Bazin not only adds in the factors of sound, color, and relief but also makes the totality of these the goal and the motivation for cinema's invention: "There was not a single inventor who did not try to combine sound and relief with animation of the image" (WC, 20).

Thus, Bazin's description of cinema's origin resembles the period in which he was writing (even anticipating the full scope of his career after this specific essay), the postwar era in which color processes and 3D (or other immersive effects such as Cinerama or Cinemascope) seemed poised to become the norms of cinema, rather than isolated special effects. As another salvo in his struggle against the canonization of silent cinema as a lost golden age, Bazin's account of the invention of the cinema posits decades of film history as a delay reluctantly endured in the realization of an ideal already fully glimpsed at the point of origin and on the verge of genuine realization as he wrote. Bazin brings his essay's rhetoric of reversal to a climax as he charts film's technological development not simply as a linear progression, but as actually circling back to fulfill the original ideal: "Every new development added to the cinema must paradoxically, take it nearer and nearer to it origins. In short, cinema has not yet been invented!" (WC, 21). Twisting back on itself, film history not only finds its future in its past, but film's technological development also fulfills expectations inherent in cinema's original promise. Bazin's essay both opens and concludes with a radical gesture of rhetorical inversion whereby ultimately history becomes subsumed under theory.

Rather than practicing revisionist historiography, "The Myth of Total Cinema" discovers in cinema's origins a theory of its essence. Bazin shrewdly placed this essay right after "The Ontology of the Photographic Image" to open *Qu'est-ce que le cinéma?* Taken together, these two essays form the basis of a theoretical argument for the priority of realism in the cinema, although one could argue that his stylistic arguments for realism as a mode of film practice contained in "The Evolution of the Language of Cinema" and the essays on neorealism give this theoretical position its ultimate justification. Studies of Bazin so far give the "Ontology" essay more attention than "The Myth." This is understandable, since it is the more theoretically argued piece. That essay's discussion of the ontology of the photograph, and of cinema as an extension of photography, has primarily been read, following Peter Wollen, as based in the indexicality of the photograph (although Bazin never uses this Peircean term). While I do not question the relevance of this interpretation, elsewhere I have questioned whether the index supplies a complete understanding of Bazin's claim for the nature of photographic ontology.[7] Whatever the outcome of this debate, it is striking that nothing in "The Myth of Total Cinema" seems dependent on indexicality or even necessarily on photography, as is made clear by Bazin's frequent reference in the essay to the painted or drawn animations of Reynaud's *Pantomimes lumineuses* (which are not even photographic).[8]

Bazin's essay emphasizes that Reynaud, along with Edison and even the Lumière brothers, had envisioned cinema as fully endowed with those aspects of realistic reproduction which would be specifically excised from the canonized image of silent cinema (precisely those aspects whose absence Rudolph Arnheim at the end of the silent era had stressed—and valorized—as essential to film's role as art rather than mechanical reproduction: sound, relief, color).[9] Bazin's *idée fixe* of total cinema extends beyond "mechanical reproduction" and signals a desire for an ideal which we recognize as his central theoretical claim about cinematic realism: "namely an integral realism, a recreation of the world in its own image, an image unburdened by the freedom of interpretation of the artist or the irreversibility of time."[10] The myth of cinema's origin does not primarily concern artistic expression, as the theorists of cinema in the '20s (articulating the achievements of that decade's filmmakers) would claim. Rather, at the point of its invention cinema pursued not only the possibility of a complete mimetic presentation of the world but also the creation of an image beyond the manipulations and interpretations of artists, not a particular artist's image of the world, but the "world in its own image."

We find here the paradoxes that recur in Bazin's description of the cinema, which could be dismissed as unresolved contradictions, or as yet to be articulated complexities, but which I see as challenges not only to an ongoing reading of Bazin but also to our continued speculation on the nature of cinema and related media. Bazin locates the origins of cinema less in the progressive achievement of a scientific and industrial research project than in the obsessions of a handful of inventors. This may at first seem to posit a psychological basis for the origin of the cinema, close perhaps to what he describes in the "Ontology" essay as a "basic psychological need in man" to overcome death and time.[11] (Philip Rosen, in his discussion of Bazin's "mummy complex" emphasizes the important role obsession plays in Bazin).[12] But does Bazin's myth of total cinema simply historicize a metapsychology of the anxious subject reassured by cinematic illusion? Before linking Bazin's myth of the origin of cinema with the metapsychology of ideological illusion described by apparatus theory, one must stress certain differences. For Baudry, Metz, and other '70s theorists, the "cinema-effect" shored up the spectator's imaginary investment in a coherent subject. Bazin's myth moves beyond the subject, envisioning an image of the world not dependent on the expressive role of artistic subjectivity. Bazin may root the origin of the cinema in the obsession of its inventors, but the significance of this ideal cannot be reduced to subjective investment. Rather than subjectivity, Bazin's total cinema strives to achieve "the world in its own image." This unique image seeks precisely to overcome the distinction between subjectivity and objectivity, and even between materialism and idealism.[13]

In "The Ontology of the Photographic Image," Bazin makes a distinction that has troubled me for years "between true realism, the need that is to give significant expression to the world both concretely and its essence, and the pseudorealism of a deception aimed at fooling the eye (and for that matter the mind); a pseudorealism content in other words with illusory appearances."[14] Bazin stresses that realistic traditions in art combine these two tendencies, so we should not view them as mutually exclusive. But the opposition between them must bear on his myth of origins. Did the obsession with total cinema that haunted its inventors exceed pseudorealism, and in what manner does it attain what he calls true realism? The most likely answer would be that total cinema can partake of both aspects and that the challenge of cinema as an art form lies neither in expressing individual subjectivity nor in simply reproducing the traits of movement, color, sound and relief as components of illusion, but rather in presenting the world in its own image, a task that must be more elusive than it might first appear. As one of the most subtle (and crucially flexible and dialectical) critics of style, Bazin is dedicated to tracing the pursuit of this image through the interrelation of narrative structures and visual strategies.

While defining the nature of "the world in its own image" may demand reading and digesting Bazin's full corpus, I believe that his attempt to read Sadoul's history backward provides the best clue to emerging from this maze, especially his enigmatic claim that cinema has not yet been invented. Tracing the figure of total cinema involves not only a process of historical research but also an engagement with the future, so that the question, what is cinema? never becomes simply, what was cinema? but always asks, what will cinema be? If Bazin's differentiation of a true realism from a pseudorealism constitutes more than a platitude, his comments on the "deception aimed at fooling the eye" might provide at least a negative way (in the sense of the *via negativa* of theologians defining God by describing what He is not) to grasping the nature of a true realism. According to Bazin, pseudorealism aims simply at "duplicating the world outside"; purely "psychological," it satisfies an appetite for illusion, and illusory techniques such as perspective constitute its means.

It would be difficult to separate total cinema from this appetite for illusion, an appetite that Bazin seems to understand as ongoing, never thoroughly satisfied. The history of total cinema, then, seems not simply to chart a progressive course or realization of an initial vision (or a Platonic ideal), but rather to project a dialectical process in which achieving the ideal of the "world in its image" involves sublating the processes of illusion, absorbing its techniques, yet also transcending them. Thus Bazin's ideal of total cinema might ultimately resemble Hegel more than Plato since it reveals itself in the unfolding of the history of film as one stage sublates rather than abolishes the preceding one, a history that has not yet reached its end.

The specter of pseudorealism raises the crucial issue of how Bazin's theory of total cinema relates to the current fascination with immersive media, both as an ongoing technology and a historical tradition. Recent historical investigation of immersion (such as the fine work of Oliver Grau and Alison Griffiths) broadens the prehistory of cinema beyond the rather narrow track of the representation of motion which most archaeologies of the cinema have privileged, opening it to such traditions as the panorama as a predecessor and expanded cinema as a descendent.[15] But from the panorama to virtual reality and other computer-generated environmental systems, the emphasis (at least in critical analysis) tends to be on sensation and physical effects. While Bazin never directly states this, I believe that it was precisely the stimulation (and simulation) of sensation that Bazin associated with pseudorealism, with trompe l'oeil, with that aspect of the image that he opposed to his ideal of realism and designated as a trick, an illusion—a deceit.[16] I think a full reading of Bazin makes it clear that cinematic realism uses the devices of total cinema in the service of creating an image of the world—beyond individual expression, communication of information, or the representation of a single viewpoint, beyond, in essence, the simple trick of fooling the eye. However, if Bazin might warn against techniques of simulation, this essay makes clear that the total illusion that the cinema aspires to goes beyond any mere trick and offers something new. I believe that the novelty that Bazin finds in the myth underlying the invention of cinema consists less in the word "cinema" than in the modifier "total." For Bazin, unlike most historians of technologies, the invention of cinema lies not in any particular technical aspect of the cinema—such as the photographic analysis of motion; the mechanical achievement of the synthesis of motion; the systems of projection; or the devising of a flexible continuous base, each of which has its own history and inventors—but rather in the ideal of their totality, their integration into a whole (each of these elements taken singularly poses simply a technical problem to be solved). In true gestalt fashion this whole equals more than the sum of its parts, and it is the total pattern that drives the invention of cinema.

This totality should not be understood as a crowning synthesis—neither a *gesamtkunst-werk*, nor a technological system. If we take seriously Bazin's differentiation of a true and a pseudoreality, total cinema offers more than a complex process of duplication. Bazin calls this something more: "the world in its own image." I read this phrase as equivalent to the phenomenological concept (used by both Merleau-Ponty and Heidegger) of the worldhood of the world. The worldhood of the world forms the ultimate referent of the myth of total cinema. Thus total cinema does not posit a Hegelian universal totality but rather the phenomenological image of the world as bounded by a horizon, and it is in the nature of a horizon to be expanded. The decades that have passed since Bazin's book review essay demonstrate the acuity of his grasp of the future as implied in his reading of the past. I firmly believe Bazin would view the ongoing development of new media not as the end of cinema but as a stage in its continuing invention. Rather than immersion, I believe the appropriate term for a Bazinian understanding of contemporary media would be "expanded cinema," to reappropriate a term from the '60s. Far from an outmoded idealist conservative, it may be that Bazin himself has not yet been invented.

Notes

1. André Bazin, "In Defense of Rossellini," in *What Is Cinema?* vol. 2 (Berkeley: University of California Press, 1971), 99.
2. Tom Gunning, "What's the Point of an Index? Or Faking Photographs," in *Still/Moving: Between Cinema and Photography*, ed. Karen Beckman and Jean Ma (Durham, NC: Duke University Press, 2008), 23–40.
3. Bazin, "The Myth of Total Cinema" in *What Is Cinema?* vol. 1 (Berkeley: University of California Press, 1967), 17–22. Further references to this article will be cited parenthetically as WC.
4. The essay was originally published in *Critique*, 6 (November 1946).
5. Among the revisionists, along with Charles Musser and myself, see André Gaudreault, *Cinéma et attraction: Pour une nouvelle histoire du cinématographe* (Paris: CNRS, 2008); see also "Les *vues cinématographiques* selon Georges Méliès, ou: comment Mitry et Sadoul avaient peut-être raison d'avoir tort (même si c'est surtout Deslandes qu'il faut lire et relire)," in *Georges Méliès, l'illusionniste fin de siècle?*, dir. Jacques Malthête et Michel Marie (Paris: Presses de la Sorbonne Nouvelle/Colloque de Cerisy, 1997), 111–31.
6. Works that should be cited here are Michael Chanan, *The Dream that Kicks: the Prehistory and Early Years of Cinema in Britain* (New York: Routledge, 1996); Jonathan Crary, *Techniques of the Observer: On Vision and Modernity in the Nineteenth Century* (Cambridge: MIT Press, 1990); Laurent Mannoni, *The Great Art of Light and Shadow: Archaeology of the Cinema* (Exeter: University of Exeter Press, 2000); Charles Musser, *Before the Nickelodeon: Edwin S. Porter and the Edison Manufacturing Company* (Berkeley: University of California Press, 1991); Musser, *The Emergence of Cinema: the American Screen to 1907* (New York: Scribner, 1990); Deac Rossell, *Living Pictures: The Origins of the Movies* (Albany, NY: SUNY Press, 1998); and Gunning, *D.W. Griffith and the Origins of American Narrative Film: The Early Years at Biograph* (Urbana: University of Illinois Press, 1991). Since this revisionary project was sparked by the 1978 FIAF colloquium at Brighton, England, these scholars are sometimes referred to as "post-Brighton."
7. Gunning, "What's the Point of an Index? Or Faking Photographs."
8. Gunning, "Moving Away from the Index: Cinema and the Impression of Reality," *differences*, 18:1 (Spring 2007), 29–52.
9. Rudolph Arnheim, *Film as Art* (Berkeley: University of California Press, 1966).
10. Bazin, "The Myth of Total Cinema," 22. Mary Ann Doane has drawn attention to the aspect of this quote that I leave untouched here, the significance of the "irreversibility of time." Although I do not follow her suggestion (its possible relation to indexicality), I do find it extremely provocative that Bazin, while he maintains the importance of the unity of space and time in the creation of a realist image in cinema, nonetheless

does not seem to think time must remain irreversible. However, I take this less as a reference to the literal of reversal of time (as in the cinematic effect of reverse motion) than as a reference to cinema's ability to replay a past moment so as to fix or capture the flow of time, snatching it out of its ephemerality.

11.   Bazin. "The Ontology of the Photographic Image," in *What Is Cinema?* vol. 1, 9.

12.   Philip Rosen, *Change Mummified: Cinema, Historicity, Theory* (Minneapolis: University of Minnesota Press, 2001), especially 10–14.

13.   Rosen acknowledges this ambition to overcome the subject/object split, (see ibid., 12), but denies its possibility, seeing all phenomenology as simply limited by subjective investment.

14.   Bazin, "The Ontology of the Photographic Image," 12.

15.   Oliver Grau, *Virtual Art: From Illusion to Immersion* (Cambridge, MA: MIT Press, 2003); Allison Griffiths, *Shivers down your Spine: Cinema, Museums, and the Immersive View* (New York: Columbia University Press, 2008). In contrast, C. W. Ceram's classic work *Archeology of the Cinema* (New York: Harcourt, Brace & World, 1965) limits itself to tracing the history of the moving image.

16.   Bazin's discussion of the *truc* (trick) in cinema is typically dialectical and complex; cinema cannot do without tricks, he claims, but must acknowledge their subordination to reality. See Bazin, "The Virtues and Limitations of Montage," in *What Is Cinema?* vol. 1, 43–47.

12

The Afterlife of Superimposition

Daniel Morgan

One of the most famous oppositions in film history sets Lumière against Méliès, or rather documentary against fantasy, the two great traditions of cinema they engendered. Almost equally famous, especially since Jean-Luc Godard's films and writings of the late 1960s, is the objection that this opposition is false: "But today, what do we see when we watch their films? We see Méliès filming the reception of the King of Yugoslavia by the President of the Republic. A newsreel, in other words. And at the same time we find Lumière filming a family card game in the *Bouvard et Pécuchet* manner. In other words, fiction."[1] Where Méliès shows the reality of colonial exploitation in *A Trip to the Moon* (1902), Lumière films the fantasies of the bourgeoisie. It may be surprising to hear a similar position being articulated almost twenty years before Godard; it is even more surprising to hear it through the voice of André Bazin. His version goes as follows: "The opposition that some like to see between a cinema inclined toward the almost documentary representation of reality and a cinema inclined, through reliance on technique, toward escape from reality into fantasy and the world of dreams, is essentially forced. . . . The one is inconceivable without the other."[2]

It is not by accident that Bazin comes to this formulation in his curious essay, "The Life and Death of Superimposition." Unlike Godard, Bazin is not interested in accusing Lumière of filming an ideological fantasy, but rather, as is so often the case, in the intersection of ontology and style in cinema. Bazin argues that treating the traditions of Lumière and Méliès as codependent allows us to see why, despite its fundamentally realist orientation, cinema has historically been attuned to the fantastic: it has to do with the pleasure resulting from the combination of the "unbelievable nature" of the things we see in a film and "the irresistible realism of the photographic image" (BW, 73).[3] Superimposition is a technique—historically, it has been one of the most important—for producing this effect. Bazin's essay comes at a moment where he thinks its role may be changing.

I don't intend in this essay to provide a history or theory of superimposition—about the relation of in-camera effects to lab work, for example—or even a detailed analysis of key films. I have two reasons for focusing on Bazin's short article. The first involves the way the essay on superimposition illuminates the complex arrangement of ideas of technique, style, and medium in Bazin's work, and places them within a historical approach. My sense is that it is in such seemingly minor essays—on superimposition, on Cinemascope, on the films of the day—that we find Bazin's best work in thinking through the implications and significance of his own theoretical commitments.[4] The second has to do with what, following the title of Bazin's essay, we might call superimposition's afterlife, and, in particular, with the way superimposition is picked up by Godard in his monumental late video project *Histoire(s) du cinéma* (1988–1998). Despite very real and deep differences between them, Godard appropriates Bazin's critical vocabulary even as he turns to an older set of techniques. Looking at Bazin and Godard through this lens will shed light on the ambitions of both, as well as their relations to one another.

In this context, the essay on superimposition provides a rare example of a through-line in French film practice and criticism that stretches from the 1920s to the present. If the occasion for the essay, the chance for Bazin to announce the death of superimposition, is a set of then-current American films—*Tom, Dick and Harry* (1941), *Our Town* (1940), and *Here Comes Mr. Jordan* (1941)—he draws on two larger cinematic contexts. One is an engagement with post-WWI Swedish cinema, and its use of traditional superimposition to generate the appearance of the supernatural. This tradition forms the background to his analysis of the more recent films. The other context, while only implicit, is nonetheless central to the essay. The topic of superimposition is, for Bazin, an occasion for one of his sustained attempts to criticize and undo the influence of the "pure cinema" movement in 1920s France: the cinema embodied by (among others) Epstein, Delluc, and Dulac.[5] That movement held superimposition to be a privileged technique, a cinema-specific device that transforms our apprehension of the world. In Dulac's words, "Superimposition is thinking, the inner life . . ."[6] Rather than a way to represent mental states on screen, Dulac suggests that superimposition itself constitutes cinematic thought: the act of bringing two layers of images together is in itself a way of thinking in and with cinema.

Bazin's essay, however, is overtly concerned with a more familiar use of superimposition. He treats it as a one of the central ways of presenting the fantastic—dreams, the unconscious, ghosts—in a cinema that strives to be realist, and argues that two contemporary developments provide insight into this topic. The first is a turn to purely psychological means for depicting the fantastic, moments where viewers, rather than being directly shown something, are asked to infer its presence from the actions of characters. The second is a new technique, dunning, that allows a three-dimensional incorporation of fantastic elements; rather than being placed, as it were, on top of the image, superimpositions can be fully integrated into the everyday. With these developments, Bazin thinks that traditional two-layer superimposition is now unable to contribute to a genuine effect of the supernatural. Realist cinema that aims to incorporate the fantastic has developed new techniques, and so it requires a corresponding shift in the formal strategies of the films that use them.

But why is Bazin interested in films that use superimposition? After all, according to standard accounts of his critical enterprise, which consider him committed to the idea of a realism faithful to the visual appearance of the world, he shouldn't be interested in this topic. Superimposition does not lend itself to those styles he describes as "putting faith in reality," but inclines instead toward an emphasis on the image as such. If one of the central claims of this interpretation is that Bazin's ideal cinema uses technique to erase the appearance of artifice,[7] here he seems to be explicitly considering the realistic possibilities of a cinema that not only uses but flaunts an artificial technique. And he does so not by rejecting or rethinking the terms of an older way of thinking about superimposition but by accepting the earlier account at face value—that, in Ricciotto Canudo's description from 1926, superimposition "permits . . . the extraordinary and striking faculty of representing immateriality"—and then testing whether the technique now achieves its goals.[8] So what's the logic at work behind this essay? How can we square his interest in superimposition with what we know about his broader theoretical and historical commitments?

Making sense of Bazin's discussion of superimposition requires that we rethink some basic aspects of his account of cinema. In particular, we will have to take a less familiar look at his understanding of the ontology of cinema, and how it relates to stylistic possibilities. The topic begins with "The Ontology of the Photographic Image," where Bazin claims that a change in the history of art arrives with photography: "for the first time, between the originating object and its reproduction there intervenes only the instrumentality of a nonliving agent." Because the photographer has no control over the formation of the image, "we are forced to accept as real the existence of the object reproduced, actually re-presented." Generally, this position has been understood as putting forward an understanding of photography—and therefore of cinema as well—as based on an indexical relation between an image and the object it is of.[9] But something else is going on here: a photograph, Bazin asserts, has a closer tie to reality than does a sign. There is, in his words, a "transfer of reality from the thing to its reproduction." Bazin works through several ways to articulate this peculiar claim, eventually settling on terms like "identity" or "equivalence" to describe the relation between image and object in photographic media. The full force of his argument comes in one of the most famous passages from the "Ontology" essay:

> The photographic image is the object itself, the object freed [*libéré*] from temporal contingencies. No matter how fuzzy, distorted, or discolored, no matter how lacking in documentary value the image may be, it proceeds, by virtue of its genesis, from the ontology of the model; it *is* the model [*elle est le modèle*].[10]

As I have argued elsewhere,[11] we have to take Bazin's denial of an ontological distinction between image and object seriously. If the familiar postulate of indexicality is here—the photograph is formed by a causal process that depends for its effect not on criteria of resemblance but on the process of production—it is inadequate to Bazin's full position. When he says, "it *is* the model," he has moved away from the realm of the indexical. No one would say that a footprint is a foot, or that a bullet-hole is a bullet, despite the causal, nonsubjective relation between them.

This way of formulating Bazin's argument raises an obvious question: what does it mean for an object in a photograph to be identical (ontologically, not just visually) to the object photographed? Much as Bazin tries, he finds himself unable to resolve this problem, resorting throughout his work to a range of metaphors to describe the relation between image and object, a partial list of which includes mummy, mold, death mask, mirror, equivalent, substitute, and asymptote.[12] Each metaphor captures something important about what a photograph is but nonetheless fails in some way.[13] We might describe the implication of this practice as the "metaphor rule": for each essay, the task of exegesis is to figure out what goes right and what goes wrong with the metaphors Bazin uses to describe the ontology of the photographic image, and why, in light of the particular films or problems he is discussing, Bazin is drawn to them. Despite the differences between them, what is common to most is that they suggest an ontology of the photographic image that is more robust than indexical signs.

The difficulty with this account of Bazin's arguments has to do with the fact that it does not quite fit our familiar understanding of what a photograph is. I think this lack of fit reveals something important, namely that photography has almost no role in his account of cinema. Because the argument of the "Ontology" essay suggests a progression of the arts based on technological development, and because this essay is placed at the beginning of Bazin's works, it has been easy to think that his conception of cinema is built on an understanding of photography: cinema is photography plus duration. This is, it seems to me, a basic, if understandable error, one that mistakes the rhetorical presentation of an argument for its content. (I'm tempted to describe such a mistake as a form of "photographic determinism," an assumption of the primacy of the prior medium.) Rather than deriving cinema from photography, Bazin, when read carefully, turns out to be doing the reverse: he begins with an understanding of cinema, and then, since he knows that cinema is comprised of individual frames and therefore that it must have a photographic base, extracts an account of photography from it.[14] Bazin lacks an independent account of the earlier medium: photography is just cinema minus duration. As a result, he has a poor understanding of how photography actually affects us, since he persistently describes it in ways that better fit the experience of cinema; in Barthesian terms, he replaces the temporality of the "that was then" that ordinarily attends photographs with the "this is now" of cinema. My sense is that to best understand what Bazin thinks about the ontology of cinema it is necessary to stay away from the topic of photography. Photography functions as a rhetorical device he employs at a certain moment in his theoretical framework, nothing more—cinema itself is his primary concern.

The immediate benefit of reading the "Ontology" essay in this way is that the need to think of Bazin as arguing for a direct realism bound to reproduce the appearance of the world disappears. It is true that he specifies a relation between style and ontology: what a photograph is, and what objects in a photograph are, determines the stylistic possibilities for what a realist film should be like. But rather than a logic of entailment, in which we read style off ontology, Bazin holds that while realism may be oriented by the ontology of the photographic image, it is not determined by it, and so remains open to a range of styles and genres. As he notes, "There is no one realism, but many realisms."[15]

The deep idea that makes such an account possible is not one commonly associated with Bazin. It is that a film, to be realist, only has to respond to, or take into account *in some way*, the ontology of the photographic image: it has to acknowledge it. What form this acknowledgment takes is open to the individual films to achieve. This model of realism leaves film rooted in its ontology but also open to the aesthetic variety of films that Bazin wants to call realist. After all, he will talk about realism not only in the films of Welles, Renoir, Murnau, and Dreyer but also in those of Bresson, Olivier, even Eisenstein. These films exhibit quite different styles, going beyond a simple correspondence between film and reality. Bazin's critical project is to show how each style, in its own way, works to acknowledge the ontology of the photographic image.

Taking all of this together, the implication is that for Bazin, style and ontology cannot be treated independently of one another. There is a tendency to understand Bazin as subscribing to a two-stage account of cinema: he secures an ontology that then leads to, opens up, or furnishes the ground for stylistic exploration. But this relation is a two-way street. Bazin's repeated recourse to metaphors to describe the ontology of cinema suggests that his understanding of precisely what that ontology amounts to changes, or is inflected, in response to the subject at hand. Style and ontology, then, are best understood as relational concepts within Bazin's thought, a tension that ensures a productive dynamic at the heart of his discussions of films.[16] Rather than a codified set of beliefs, Bazin provides a flexible model; rather than a doctrine, he articulates a method.

It is only by holding in mind this account of the relation between style and medium that we can understand Bazin's essay on superimposition. In treating some of the different uses to which superimposition has been put, Bazin aims at a larger target (one that interested him deeply): the question of how, in a medium that trades in the physical or visible world, filmmakers can successfully (accurately? realistically?) represent nonphysical events, whether they be supernatural or psychological. Bazin sees two ways to resolve this problem.

The first involves one of the strategies he saw in certain American films, where the viewer is asked to infer the presence of the supernatural from the physical world shown on screen. An example of this would be the treatment of the rabbit in *Harvey* (1950), or the way characters betray unconscious motivations in *Tom, Dick and Harry*. This tendency must have seemed especially congenial to Bazin, as it follows in rough outline what he elsewhere describes as the "phenomenology of sainthood": the inability to give physical or visual proof of the presence of grace or divinity. The most powerful version of this position is in his essay on Bresson's *Diary of a Country Priest* (*Journal d'un curé de campagne*, 1951), where Bazin draws attention to the final image of the film, a white background on which a black cross appears, which he describes as "awkwardly drawn" rather than photographed. He writes of this image: "the screen, free of images . . . is the triumph of cinematographic realism."[17] While there might seem to be a paradox here—how could it be that the very absence of physical reality is in fact a triumph of realism?—Bazin is in fact being quite careful. One of his recurrent critical axioms is that genuinely religious cinema will not, or cannot, show spiritual grace or transcendence on film. Grace does not have a recognizable physical manifestation. Thus, because film is indelibly connected to the physical world, the spiritual reality Bresson is interested in simply cannot be shown: to do otherwise would be to betray the tenets of his faith. Bresson's solution, as Bazin sees it, is to show the priest's state of grace by *negating* the photographic dimension of the image.

There is, however, a type of film that doesn't follow this model: this is the ghost or fantasy film so popular in Swedish cinema. It is in these films that superimpositions are prominently found.[18] When Sjöström or Stiller used superimpositions to reveal the supernatural within the world of the film—the appearance of death in *The Phantom Chariot* (1921) or the ghost of a murdered lover in *Sir Arne's Treasure* (1919) [figure 12.1]—these beings were overlaid on the world photographed by the camera. Traditional superimposition thus worked to bring two very different realities—one natural, one supernatural—into the same space, into the same world.

It is certainly the case that Bazin does not exactly like these films, but he does not object to them on the grounds that they are misguided to *try* to represent the supernatural. Instead, much as he tries to articulate the terms of a "historico-materialist cinema" in his essay on Stalin and Soviet cinema, he is prepared to entertain the possibility of something like a "spectral

FIGURE 12.1: *Sir Arne's Treasure* (1919)

realism." The problem, for him, has to do with the subsequent development of cinematic technique. If the superimpositions of Sjöström and Stiller seemed exemplary at one time, new techniques demand a new perspective. Now, Bazin argues, these techniques appear as clichés: "Superimposition on screen signals: 'Attention: unreal world, imaginary characters'; it doesn't portray in any way what hallucinations or dreams are really like, or, for that matter, how a ghost would look" (BW, 74). To defend the earlier films as cinematic models, Bazin thinks, is to succumb to the false idea that superimposition alone guarantees a *compelling* presentation of the supernatural. He writes, "One might have thought that the process that had helped so many films to achieve the status of masterpiece, had once and for all gained its patent of nobility and credibility" (BW, 75). The error of this way of thinking lies in the belief that there could be a "once and for all."

Bazin draws particular attention to the kind of innovation at work in a scene from Sam Wood's adaptation of Thornton Wilder's play, *Our Town*. Emily Webb, in a coma and imagining that she is dead, sees herself in front of her mother, and tries (and fails) to enter the conversation. But then, Bazin notes, "when the ghost happens to walk around the table, we begin to feel strangely ill at ease: something abnormal is occurring and we can't quite figure it out" (BW, 75). Our uneasiness results from the fact that a ghost is, for the first time, being "true to itself": able to fully inhabit the three-dimensional world of the diegesis. The new technique employed in *Our Town* goes beyond the traditional form of superimposition that we are used to, which simply juxtaposed two distinct levels of images, and this allows Bazin to develop a larger principle: "There is no reason why a ghost should not occupy an exact place in space" (BW, 76). Bazin sees here a new form for producing the pleasure that results from the interaction of the unbelievable and the implicit reality of the world on the screen.

Bazin's analysis of the historical changes in the use of superimposition is part of a relatively unappreciated aspect of his work, namely his account of the historical development of cinematic styles. He is often taken to hold that there is an ideal realist style—the "equilibrium profile" he describes in "The Evolution of the Language of Cinema"—one that, once achieved, ought to exist in a kind of static state.[19] In fact, he holds a firm belief that all styles are historically contingent, that cinema (even realist cinema) is continually being transformed in response to its circumstances. Rather than advocating a single kind of realist cinema (based on a long-take, deep-space aesthetic), he sees danger when filmmakers cling to or fetishize specific techniques. Each realist style will be superseded by subsequent developments both within and outside of cinema. The basic feature of Bazin's account of realism is to treat it not as a doctrine but as a way of understanding the interaction between style and medium.

Bazin claims that *Our Town* deals a fatal blow to traditional superimposition, and so requires a new development in style, because it shows new (and, he thinks, better) ways for achieving the same goals, innovations that make it impossible any longer to see the older techniques as aesthetically and psychologically compelling. From this perspective, "Superimposition can, in all logic, only suggest the fantastic in a conventional way; it lacks the ability actually to evoke the supernatural" (BW, 76). Because that kind of superimposition cannot integrate the two levels of reality, its vitality as a practice comes to an end; as the title of the essay puts it, the technique dies. Of course, Bazin does not mean that filmmakers stopped using superimpositions altogether, or that he expected they would. His account is more Hegelian: superimposition simply ceases to be of importance to cinema. It may live on in various forms, but its status as a vital part of cinema is over.

The question I want to explore for the rest of this essay is this: Does traditional superimposition—at least on the terms through which Bazin understands it—have an afterlife? The answer to this question lies in Jean-Luc Godard's *Histoire(s) du cinéma*, a four-and-a-half-hour video essay composed of a montage of photographs, film clips, images of paintings, music, and texts. *Histoire(s) du cinéma* is many things: a thesis on the interrelation (actual and potential) between the history of cinema and the history of the twentieth century; an account of the powers of a medium; an argument about the historical centrality of the New Wave; and so on. It is also—and this is less easily recognized—a sustained defense of superimposition as an aesthetic and analytic technique. If a 1943 film like *Our Town* incorporates the ambitions of traditional superimposition while developing new techniques, Godard explicitly returns in 1998 to the older technique. Throughout the episodes of *Histoire(s) du cinéma*, Godard employs two-and three-layered video-based superimpositions as the centerpiece to his own historiographic practice. Thus, we find him, baton in hand, "conducting" a dance from *Adieu Philippine* (1962); or, in another episode, using multiple layers of images (and references) to demonstrate the workings of montage [figure 12.2]; or, most controversially, after showing George Stevens' footage of Ravensbrück, fusing Elizabeth Taylor in *A Place in the Sun* (1951) with the Magdalene from Giotto's *Noli me tangere* as a way to work through the relation of cinema, art, and the horrors of the Second World War. In each case, superimposition enables Godard to do his historical and film-historical work.

Godard's most sustained defense of the power of superimposition comes in a sequence that deals with another filmmaker: the "Introduction to the Method of Alfred Hitchcock," one

FIGURE 12.2: *Histoire(s) du cinéma* (1997)

of the central sequences in episode 4A. The sequence begins with Hitchcock's own voice telling us about his practice while Godard recites the following lines:

> We've forgotten why Joan Fontaine leans over the edge of the cliff, and what it was that Joel McCrea was going to do in Holland. We don't remember why Montgomery Clift was maintaining eternal silence, or why Janet Leigh stopped at the Bates motel, or why Teresa Wright still loves Uncle Charlie. We've forgotten what it was that Henry Fonda wasn't entirely guilty of, and why exactly the American government had hired Ingrid Bergman.
>
> But, we remember a handbag. But, we remember a bus in the desert. But, we remember a glass of milk, the sails of a windmill, a hairbrush. But, we remember a row of bottles, a pair of spectacles, a sheet of music, a bunch of keys. Because through them and with them, Alfred Hitchcock succeeded where Alexander, Julius Caesar, Hitler, and Napoleon had all failed. By taking control of the universe.

The images we see during this speech are all clips from Hitchcock's films, many of them showing the moments referred to by Godard (though rarely in synchronization with the voice-over).

There is a consensus that something important goes on in the sequence. Jacques Rancière, for example, has claimed that Godard's treatment of Hitchcock exemplifies his overall approach to the history of cinema. He argues that Godard strips the clips he uses of their original narrative context so as to more easily (and more completely) embed them into his own world, a process that results in a kind of aesthetic formalism predicated on the "pure sensory presence" of isolated details.[20] Before we can judge the terms of this criticism, however, we need to get clear on what the sequence itself does. It is a mistake to read it as one of unambiguous adulation or admiration,[21] for if Godard creates a tribute to the power of Hitchcock's films, he also attempts to undo that power. Implicitly diagnosing himself as having fallen under the spell of Hitchcock, Godard seeks to cure himself (and us): call it a case of remembering, repeating, and working through. A talking cure of sorts.

The complexity of Godard's engagement with Hitchcock in this sequence will allow us to see why the charges Rancière makes against Godard's aesthetic misconstrue the nature of the ambitions of *Histoire(s) du cinéma*, while at the same time helping to show the depth of Godard's relationship to Bazin. Both of these projects turn on Godard's rethinking of the powers, limits, and (hence) possibilities of superimposition.

The sequence is structured around a basic claim. Godard repeatedly asserts that the power of Hitchcock's cinema is in the way we forget his films' plots: why Joan Fontaine cannot trust Cary Grant, why Janet Leigh stopped at the Bates Motel, or why Montgomery Clift keeps silent (actually, Hitchcock and Truffaut forgot this one, too). Instead, we remember details, individual moments from the films: the privileged objects and images that pervade Hitchcock's work. (Again, this is the charge Rancière levels against Godard: that he removes the original narrative context of clips in order to place them into his own *Histoire*.) In achieving this result, Hitchcock takes control over the universe: he succeeds where "Alexander, Julius Caesar, Hitler, and Napoleon had all failed."

The first thing to recognize about the sequence is that the claims Godard is making are patently absurd. *Of course* we remember the plots of Hitchcock's films: we remember that Marion Crane stole $40,000 from her employer, and that she got off the main highway because of the rain; we remember that Ingrid Bergman is being sent to disrupt a hidden Nazi spy ring in Argentina; we remember that Joan Fontaine is worried because her husband, Cary Grant, may be trying to kill her. Even if we somehow didn't remember these narrative facts, Godard's highlight reel reminds us: Marion driving in the downpour from *Psycho* (1960); the uranium spilling out of the bottle in *Notorious* (1946); the lighter in the gutter from *Strangers on a Train* (1951); the strangely lit glass of milk from *Suspicion* (1941). These are not random images but narratively charged moments.

Godard is certainly defining his own practice in relation to Hitchcock in this sequence, but he is doing so through opposition rather than emulation. What's going on is an issue of method, of critique. At various moments, Godard includes aural recordings of Hitchcock discussing his own cinematic method. Each time Hitchcock asserts something about his cinema, however, Godard's montage undercuts it. Take Hitchcock's central claim: "The public aren't aware of what we call montage, or in other words the cutting of one image to another. They go by so rapidly, so that they [the public] are absorbed by the content that they look at on the screen." If Hitchcock argues that the public are drawn into the stories being told, absorbed into the narratives, Godard has been saying that what we remember in Hitchcock's films is precisely *not* their narrative: "we have forgotten [*on a oublié*] . . ." It is instead the privileged moments, the instances of cinematic detail that remain in our mind. This is a cinephilic approach to Hitchcock's films that, by offering alternate modes of appreciation, undermines the claim to narrative omnipotence. (Godard's claim might actually be more subtle: when watching the film, we are absorbed into the narrative; it's only afterward, when we try to remember, that we forget this.) These issues come to a head when Hitchcock states that the public's absorption with narrative content leads to their ignorance of the practice of montage. Again Godard works against him, this time by including parts of the shower sequence from *Psycho*, certainly one of the most recognizable acts of montage in the history of cinema. When Hitchcock claims that the public doesn't notice the images—literally, the frames—as they go by, Godard produces a precise counterpoint. Right as Hitchcock says these words, Godard inserts a shot from *Vertigo* (1958), with Kim Novak—as Judy remade, or made over, as Madeleine—reaching around James Stewart. The shot is slowed down, advanced frame by frame. If we had never noticed the passing of images, we certainly do now.

We can now understand why Godard makes an argument for the importance of details. In his view, Hitchcock's form of control depends on an unthinking absorption into the narrative of the film: the audience is caught up by the stories, moved along, manipulated. At several points in the sequence, Godard is at pains to link Hitchcock's practice to a kind of seriality: the idea that, as Hitchcock puts it, "one picture comes up after another." We see an iconography of seriality in the fireworks from *To Catch a Thief* (1955) that accompany this phrase, as the images come one after another, moving forward in an inevitable progression; they link the idea of seriality to the power of narrative. It's also present in the rows of bottles in the wine cellar from *Notorious*, and in the notes of music on the score from *The Man Who Knew Too Much* (1956). Against seriality, Godard employs the resources of cinephilia, and its fetishistic emphasis on detail over and against the plot of the film. Thus, rather than a straightforward declaration of principle or method against the self-evidence of our memory of these films—the way Rancière understands the sequence—Godard's attention to freestanding details constitutes a calculated attack on a specific target, a way of undoing the centrality of narrative. By offering an alternate mode of appreciation, he undoes Hitchcock's claim for narrative omnipotence.

These moments of subversion secure the distance from the power of Hitchcock's narrative drive necessary to allow Godard to set out an aesthetic of simultaneity and disjunction for his own ends. The central technique Godard uses in this project is superimposition. This is most visible in a superimposition that runs throughout the sequence: the image of Hitchcock's face (and hand) that appears over the clips, a construction that positions the authorial figure in control of—hence responsible for—the world he creates. I think we can understand this image as an announcement of Godard's own intentions, as he will solicit two very different kinds of superimpositions from within Hitchcock's work. The first opens the sequence (and we tend to forget that it is a superimposition): this is the reflection in Marion Crane's rearview mirror as she anxiously checks to see whether the police officer is still following her [figure 12.3]. On Godard's line of thinking, it is a quintessentially Hitchcockian superimposition: wholly subordinated to the narrative, thoroughly narrativized, it loses visibility as an act of montage and is seamlessly incorporated into the diegesis. By contrast, the other superimposition—taken from *The Wrong Man* (1956) and used as the final shot of the sequence—is given a very different role. In the shots leading up to it, Godard quickly alternates—another favorite device in *Histoire(s) du cinéma*—between the spectral image of Hitchcock and a shot of Kim Novak walking amidst the redwoods in *Vertigo*.[22] In between these images, he inserts the following intertitles, "The only one, with Dreyer, who knew how to film a miracle," before introducing the clip from *The Wrong Man*, where Manny, in despair at not being able to clear his name, prays to the image of Christ on the wall. Cutting to a close-up of his face, Hitchcock begins a superimposition: we see a man walk from the background into close-up, his features

FIGURE 12.3: *Psycho* (1960)

superimposed over Manny's. This is the "right man," the man whose arrest will prove Manny's innocence.

Why does Godard call this a miracle? With the comparison to Dreyer, it is safe to assume that Godard is thinking about *Ordet* (1955), when Johannes raises Inger from the dead. But what happens in *The Wrong Man* isn't supernatural: a habitual criminal commits another crime and is caught. Where's the miracle?

It is precisely here that Godard draws on a Bazinian framework, not in his use of a religiously inflected vocabulary—that's another topic—but in his appraisal of Hitchcock. Bazin, as is well-known, did not much like Hitchcock, although he trusted the taste and judgment of his younger friends and colleagues sufficiently to acknowledge that he was probably missing something. What bothered him had to do with narrative: "It is not merely a way of telling a story, but a kind of a priori vision of the universe, a predestination of the world for certain dramatic conventions."[23] As Bazin saw it, Hitchcock made narrative into a metaphysical condition of his films: nothing lies outside narrative, there is no space for free action—in short, a kind of metaphysical determinism. Godard sounds a similar theme in his early writings, talking about "the sense of a machine grinding inexorably on" in a 1957 review of *The Wrong Man*.[24] But where Bazin looks to Hitchcock's dark humor as a counterweight within the metaphysics of narrative, Godard thinks something more drastic is necessary. The force of Hitchcock's narrative is of sufficient power that only a miracle—something from outside normal possibilities—can break it.[25] The superimposition in *The Wrong Man* is a miracle precisely because it breaks the metaphysical conditions that define the world of the film: Manny is allowed to go free despite having been caught up in the inexorable narrative machine. This miracle is as genuine, given the nature of the Hitchcockian universe, as Johannes raising Inger from the dead in *Ordet*.

Hitchcock creates a miracle, then, and it is one that is enacted through superimposition. When he acknowledges, at the level of form, that Manny might be innocent—that identity has not been proven—the dramatic arc of the film shifts. Indeed, it is as though the precondition for the narrative shift is the revelation of the other man to the audience.

But Godard is not content with Hitchcock's own superimposition. There are in fact three layers to the superimposition: two from *The Wrong Man*, and a third showing Hitchcock himself [figure 12.4]. It's this third layer that allows Godard to mark a difference with Hitchcock's use of the technique. When Hitchcock employs superimposition to create a miracle, it is still under his control: everything remains within the context of the larger narrative structure.[26] Manny may be proven innocent, but guilt does not disappear from the world: it transfers to the new man, and, most heartbreakingly, to Rosa (his wife), who blames herself for doubting him.[27] When Godard introduces the superimposition of Hitchcock himself, however, he breaks the diegetic frame: we are presented with a juxtaposition—in Godard's terms, a *rapprochement*—of elements both in and out of the world of the film.

At this point, we can see in Godard's use of superimposition the logic Bazin originally objected to when he looked back at Swedish cinema. Because traditional superimpositions are unable to integrate the two levels of reality, they deal a blow to diegetic coherence. But it's precisely this break in diegesis that Godard wants. Where Hitchcock seeks to narrativize superimposition, and Bazin wants it to be integrated into the world, Godard uses it to create what he calls, quoting Pierre Reverdy, an image: "[The image] cannot be born from a comparison but from a juxtaposition of two more or less distant realities. The more the relationship between the two juxtaposed realities is distant and true, the stronger the image will be."[28] When Godard sets out here the possibility of simultaneous, disjunctive montage, he is, in a sense, taking up the terms of Bazin's criticism while reversing the judgment.

This reversal is motivated by a deeper shift in their approaches to problems of technique and medium. Where Bazin treats superimposition primarily in line with his concerns over cinematic

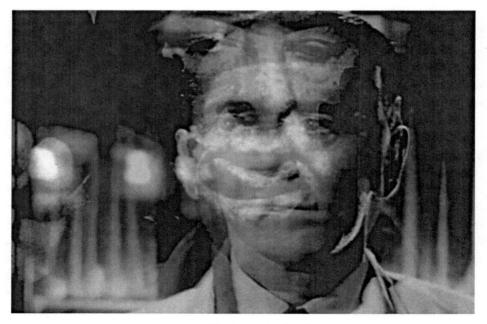

FIGURE 12.4: *The Wrong Man* (1956)

ontology, Godard displaces it onto historiographic concerns: how—and on what terms—two very different parts of film history (or history itself) can be brought together. In a key moment from episode 2A, for example, Godard superimposes Julie Delpy reading Baudelaire's *Le Voyage* over Turner's painting *Peace (Burial at Sea)* [figure 12.5], and then over Laughton's *Night of the Hunter* (1955). It's not just a matter of the stunning compositions Godard produces, or the fantastic affinities he makes—though these are the preconditions for the historiographic concerns that emerge.[29] In bringing these elements together, Godard specifies the terms of cinema's emergence out of the nineteenth century ("Cinema is a nineteenth century matter that was resolved in the twentieth," he says). Rather than the scientific and technological line exemplified by photography, however, Godard suggests that cinema draws on a painterly tradition centering on the creation of images. Baudelaire's poem, with its invocation of the imagination, the fantasy of travel across various lands, stands as the *ur*-text behind this work. It is the work of Godard's superimpositions to establish affinities between layers of images—and the traditions of painting, literature, and cinema they represent here—affinities which are thereby held up to an audience for judgment.

If the affinities generated by superimposition create the conditions for the possibility of historiographic montage, they do not ensure its success; nothing in the technique can serve as a guarantee. And that's fine. Godard is not Hitchcock; he is not interested in using superimposition to sustain the power of diegesis, to secure his power over viewers. The connections Godard draws—between Baudelaire and Turner, between Baudelaire and Laughton—are only, and can only be, conditional, possible, contingent. The task is then to judge the significance in the contingency of the declared affinities, to determine the scope and validity of the historical arguments.

FIGURE 12.5: *Histoire(s) du cinéma, 2A* (1998)

In a sense, Godard returns to Dulac's claim that superimposition is the intelligence of cinema, going back to the tradition that Bazin disdained and ignored. But it's a return that comes in light of the subsequent history of cinema. Superimposition did in fact die; so, Godard thinks, did cinema. In its wake, Godard resurrects superimposition in his videographic practice not *as* cinema but for cinema, in order to reveal and understand something about the medium and its history. Superimposition may have an afterlife; it's just that, within the line of thinking that moves from Dulac to Bazin to Godard, it's not in the world of cinema anymore.

Notes

1. Jean-Luc Godard, "Speech delivered at the Cinémathèque Française on the occasion of the Louis Lumière Retrospective in January 1966: Thanks to Henri Langlois," in *Godard on Godard*, ed. Tom Milne (New York: Viking, 1972), 235.

2. André Bazin, "The Life and Death of Superimposition," in *Bazin at Work: Major Essays and Reviews from the Forties and Fifties*, trans. Alain Piette and Bert Cardullo (London: Routledge, 1997), 73. Henceforth cited parenthetically as BW.

3. Stanley Cavell makes a similar point in *The World Viewed* (Cambridge: Harvard University Press, 1979), 16–17.

4. It is worth noting, however, that "Vie et mort de la surimpression" is in fact the third essay in the original French publication of *Qu'est-ce que le cinéma?* placed right after the more celebrated "The Ontology of the Photographic Image" and "The Myth of Total Cinema."

5. The most explicit version of this criticism is his essay "In Defense of Mixed Cinema," in *What Is Cinema?* vol. 1, trans. Hugh Gray (Berkeley: University of California Press, 1967), 53–75.

6. Germaine Dulac, "The Expressive Techniques of the Cinema," in *French Film Theory and Criticism, 1907–1939: Volume I, 1907–1929*, ed. Richard Abel (Princeton: Princeton University Press, 1988), 311.

7. As Bazin puts it in a review of De Sica's *Bicycle Thieves* (1948): "No more actors, no more story, no more sets, which is to say that in the perfect aesthetic illusion of reality there is no more cinema." Bazin, "Bicycle Thief," in *What Is Cinema?* vol. 2, trans. Hugh Gray (Berkeley: University of California Press, 1971), 60.

8. Ricciotto Canudo, "Reflections on the Seventh Art," in *French Film Theory and Criticism*, 301.

9. The classic statements of this position are Peter Wollen, *Signs and Meaning in the Cinema* (London: BFI, 1998), 79–106; and Philip Rosen, *Change Mummified: Cinema, Historicity, Theory* (Minneapolis: University of Minnesota Press, 2001), 3–41.

10. Bazin, "The Ontology of the Photographic Image," in *What Is Cinema?* vol. 1, 13–14. I have modified Hugh Gray's translation slightly.

11. See Daniel Morgan, "Rethinking Bazin: Ontology and Realist Aesthetics," *Critical Inquiry*, 32 (Spring 2006), 443–81.

12. At times, Bazin makes this into a method: "I apologize for proceeding by way of metaphor, but I am not a philosopher and I cannot convey my meaning any more directly." Bazin, "In Defense of Rossellini," in *What Is Cinema?* vol. 2, 99.

13. Bazin's hesitancy and experimentation at this crucial point in his argument should not be read as an evasion of the problems inherent in the model of ontological identity. His metaphors represent a series of attempts at understanding the peculiar ability of photographs to give us more than a representation, however direct and unmediated. Indeed, we might treat Bazin's situation as a practical example of what Stanley Cavell calls photography's ability to generate a condition of "ontological restlessness," (Cavell, *The World Viewed*, 17).

14. In this context, it is noteworthy not only that photography appears with remarkable infrequency in his writings but also that "The Myth of Total Cinema," which immediately follows the "Ontology" essay, is explicit in its attempt to ground the realism of cinema on non-technological grounds.

15. Bazin, "William Wyler, the Jansenist of Mise en Scène," in *What Is Cinema?* trans. Timothy Barnard (Montreal: Caboose, 2009), 52.

16. It is precisely this relationality that allows us to see how Bazin might be extended to newer media: what matters is less the terms of a particular account of a medium than the way the medium is itself brought into play with respect to the specific works being constructed in and with it.

17. Bazin, "*Le Journal d'un curé de campagne* and the Stylistics of Robert Bresson," in *What Is Cinema?* vol. 1, 141.

18. Bazin remarks elsewhere that Nordic filmmakers made ghost films like Americans made Westerns: as a basic way to demonstrate competence; see Bazin, "La Sorcière: Film typique du cinéma nordique," *Le Parisien libéré*, 1468 (June 3, 1949).

19. See Ludovic Cortade, infra, for more on the importance of this figure in Bazin.

20. See Jacques Rancière, "Godard, Hitchcock, and the Cinematographic Image," in *For Ever Godard*, eds. Michael Temple, James S. Williams, and Michael Witt (London: Black Dog Publishing, 2004), 224. He makes this argument across several additional works: "The Saint and the Heiress: À propos of Godard's *Histoire(s) du cinéma*," trans. T. S. Murphy, *Discourse*, 24:1 (2002), 113–19; *Film Fables, trans. Emiliano Battista* (Oxford: Berg, 2006), 171–88; and "Sentence, Image, History," in *The Future of the Image*, trans. Gregory Elliot (London: Verso, 2007), 33–68.

21. Since when, we might wonder, is being compared to Hitler a good thing?

22. The sequence in *Vertigo* itself contains an implicit superimposition, mapping Carlotta's life onto Madeleine's in the discussion of the time line drawn on the cross section of the tree.

23. Bazin, "*The Man Who Knew Too Much*—1956," in *The Cinema of Cruelty: From Buñuel to Hitchcock*, ed. François Truffaut and trans. Sabine d'Estrée (New York: Seaver Books, 1982), 166.

24. Godard, "*The Wrong Man*," in *Godard on Godard*, 49.

25. It is in that same early article that Godard first describes the moment he will show in *Histoire(s) du cinéma* as a "miracle" (ibid., 53). It's curious that Bazin does not invoke the miraculous in his review of the film; see Bazin, "Le faux coupable," *France Observateur*, 366 (May 16, 1957).

26. As Godard puts it in the review from 1957, "With each shot, each transition, each composition, Hitchcock does the only thing possible for the rather paradoxical but compelling reason that he could do anything he liked."

27. Godard's analysis here follows the terms of Eric Rohmer and Claude Chabrol, *Hitchcock, the First Forty-Four Films*, trans. Stanley Hochman (New York: F. Ungar, 1979). Rick Warner draws attention to Godard's affinity with this work in his essay, "Difficult Work in a Popular Medium: Godard on Hitchcock's Method," *Critical Quarterly*, 51:3 (Fall 2009).

28. Or, as he puts it in 4B, quoting Bresson, "Bring together things that have never been brought together and did not seem predisposed to be so." [Rapprocher les choses qui n'ont encore jamais été rapprochées et ne semblaient pas disposées à l'être.]

29. Cf. Richard Neer, "Godard Counts," *Critical Inquiry*, 34:1 (Autumn 2007), 135–71.

13

The Difference of Cinema in the System of the Arts

Angela Dalle Vacche

We no longer believe in the ontological identity of model and portrait, but we recognise that the latter helps us to remember the former and thus to rescue it from a second death, spiritual this time. The production of images has even dispensed with any notion of anthropocentric usefulness.
—André Bazin, *"The Ontology of the Photographic Image,"* 1945[1]

For André Bazin, the cinema may be a minor, popular, industrial art,[2] but the unique ontology of its medium puts it on a different plane from all the arts that precede and follow it. Despite cinema's radical difference, Bazin wrote about its relationship to the traditional arts, since this new medium could not help but engage in a sustained dialogue with previous means of representation. Although more research needs to be done on music and dance, in *What Is Cinema?* literature and theater emerge, in the end, as Bazin's privileged interlocutors for the cinema. At the same time, Bazin's overview of the older arts in dialogue with the cinema is flexible enough so that it never becomes systematic or prescriptive to the point of excluding recent developments, such as digital media, from pursuing new kinds of conversations with film.

Cinema's ontology encouraged Bazin to ignore all the standard modernist models. Gotthold Lessing, for instance, argued for aesthetic specificity and for the strictly segregated tasks of poetry and painting, privileging the former. And Richard Wagner urged a return to a primitive fusion through the use of many media under a single dramaturgical impulse.[3] Like a cultural anthropologist, Bazin pushes the arts well outside the library and the museum into the unstable world of existence. Thus, he can study the arts' interaction with film in the context of living cultures and changing societies. Cinema's ontology is characterized by three fundamental features: an anti-anthropocentric vocation, a cosmological search, and symbiotic encounters. These features come from its photographic base, but also from its nineteenth-century heritage. Bazin envisions film as a turn-of-the-century invention with a double-sided aesthetic allegiance: to realism on one hand, and to movement on the other. Given the nineteenth century's emphasis on likeness and anecdote,[4] cinema detaches its own achievement of realism from the painter's brush, thanks to the automatic, nonhuman mechanics of photography. Thus the camera is revolutionary because it can record traces of the world without the human hand. Before becoming a photographer, Henri Cartier-Bresson was trained as a painter and his framings bear witness to his pictorial eye. Yet nobody can say he used his hand to paint a photograph.

Bazin, although influenced by Maurice Merleau-Ponty's phenomenology, clearly holds views different from the philosopher. The latter felt that painting was the art form most suited to the philosophical enterprise.[5] Bazin, however, ranked film and theater way above painting in his scheme, because they offer a mise-en-scène of objects on stage or on screen, by manipulating real space and real time. Painting, particularly after all the experiments of the nineteenth century, may approach a certain realism but it is constitutionally static, whereas theater and film deploy internal and external temporalities. As the child of photography, cinematography adds the invisible fourth dimension of time to a rejection of the human hand. At the most basic level, thanks to chemistry and physics, nature takes over the creative role of the artist.

Anti-Anthropocentric Vocation

With the "Ontology" essay, Bazin resituates photography and, implicitly, the cinema, under the umbrella of the three-dimensional plastic minor arts or quasi-automatically produced images. Considering cinema's humble origin, Bazin's position is sensitive to the decorative and minor arts of Art Nouveau where a mixture of abstract and figurative patterns prevails within automatic processes. A product of the British Arts and Crafts movement, Owen Jones' *The Grammar of Ornament* (1856),[6] argues that the key question facing designers was how to find a language for aestheticizing machine-made objects, rather than using machines to copy visual forms evolved from manual skills. Such mindless creativity points to Bazin's interest in photography as a proto-surrealist form of automatic writing with light. For him, light's non-differentiating impact on objects is utterly distinct from the self-consciousness of the painter's manual virtuosity. The crucial implication of this nonmanual, and therefore anti-anthropocentric, understanding of the camera is that, instead of man-made interpretive representations such as objects or images, photographs belong to a completely different league. As fuzzy as they may be, photographs are molds, tracings of their material sources. From the marriage of energy and matter, a photograph is a new child in the order of natural creation, even before being part of the psychology of relics and souvenirs that Bazin famously dubs our "mummy complex."[7]

Bazin remarks that a spiritual death is even worse than a physical one when he explains the Egyptians' practice of mummification. If we dig deeper into Egyptology, we discover that, in addition to the preservation of the body, crucial components for achieving afterlife in ancient Egypt invole the mummy's particular position inside the pyramid, the latter's labyrinth planned in relation to the sun, the moon, and the stars, and the pyramid's limestone used as a lens-like source of light refraction[8] In short, besides the embalming process and the laying of statuettes around the mummy, the construction of the pyramid itself included the architectural and optical components of a huge prism. The latter was a proto-cinematic apparatus whose cosmological power was more important than its illusionistic efficiency on a hypothetical audience. As a machine for a spiritual resurrection, the Egyptian pyramid—in contrast to Plato's cave—may be Bazin's empowering architectural reference to set in motion the photographic mummy toward modern cinema's electrification of shadowy traces.

Besides the ancient craft of mummification, Bazin was also interested in the minor art of death masks because of their analogical status in relation to the photographic process. As a kind of masking through which we peer through the world's surface, the screen is characterized by an outward-bound, centrifugal force, that links cinema to life and, consequently, to a realist ontology. Bazin specifically opposes cinema's frame to that of painting where a centripetal pull slants the viewer's gaze toward the center of the canvas. Since cinema spins out of itself into the cosmos, the screen amounts to a mobile framing beyond which people and things may drop out of sight, into the off-screen. The screen's two sides are unlike the wings of the stage that keep the performance from bumping into the cardboard and nails holding up the scene. Everything on a limited stage can be controlled, whereas the screen opens onto what is beyond itself, alert to whatever is going on during the shooting, whether planned or unplanned. The blurry border between screen and off-screen contributes to cinema's anti-anthropocentric status because material contingencies of the world compete with human control.

Interestingly, anti-anthropocentrism engages a special relation with architecture, since the anthropocentric ideal is based on Leonardo's famous drawing of Vitruvian Man (1487) inspired by Vitruvius, a Roman architect and the author of *De Architectura* [figure 13.1]. Architecture, just like cinema, is supposed to be an industrial medium, with a democratic or collectivist potential in contrast to the elitism of painting. In his collection *Qu'est-ce que le cinéma?* Bazin limits himself to an understanding of architectural space as a subspecies of theatrical space. In fact, both spaces are defined by limits and barriers whose definition depends on the presence of human performance. But Bazin's meager interest in architecture may be due to his anti-anthropocentric view of cinema. Considering that the primitive hut was the first form of shelter, any architectural construct that does not relate to human use is a failure, in clear contrast to painting where, for instance, the lonely objects of still life contribute to a low genre. And this is why Bazin devotes a whole essay to painting and cinema, but not to architecture. Painting can focus intensely on objects, and it does so in ways comparable to how architecture addresses human presence. Without the anthropocentric element, architecture becomes sculpture, a special kind of object in and of itself.

In contrast to the anthropocentric nature of theatrical space, the screen is an alien, inorganic being that, free of gravity, depends only on light, while its psychological impact comes from absolute size, internal use of scale, and the mobile framings of editing or camera work. It is as if there were an irrational ontological leap from the human stage to the nonhuman screen. Only in cinema can impossible ways of seeing—such a bird's-eye view—become possible. This is why Bazin readily links cinema to Icarus' notorious but self-destructive dream of flying.[9] The cinema and aviation are both anti-anthropocentric enterprises, in that the camera and the airplane free us from the downward pull of the earth. They enable us to engage in a nonhuman kind of motion aspiring to the exploration of the rest of a universe beyond what we normally could know. Despite Icarus' and the camera's ability to fly like a bird, Bazin's realism is grounded enough not to forget the unbridgeable gap between cinema and life. This is perhaps why Bazin uses the term "gravity" over and over again to summarize the purpose of entire films. Just as his handling of old and new genres in the history of film follows a Darwinian scheme, so Bazin's sense of the cinema is Newtonian. He reserves "heaven" for a Platonic ideal which he cites, though never fully embraces, in "The Myth of Total Cinema."

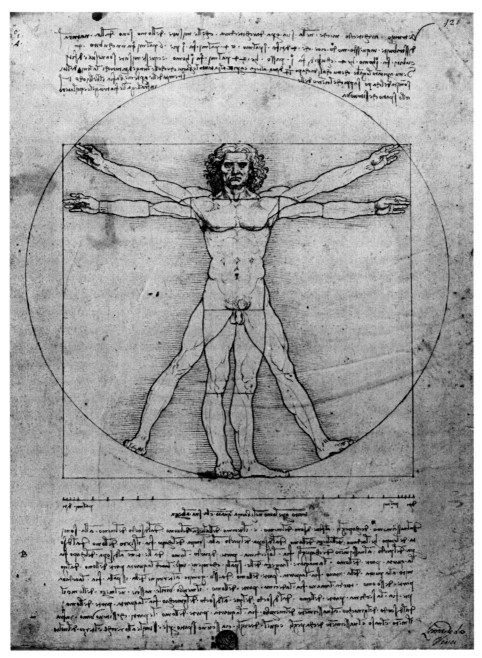

FIGURE 13.1: *Vitruvian Man* (Leonardo da Vinci, ca.1487)

Photo: Alinari/Art Resource

In contrast to cinema's fluctuating boundary, traditional theater needs footlights—as small as they may be—to separate the performers from the audience. In the theater, the audience attends to the primacy of the words spoken by performers in their own roles, here and now. However, in the movie theater the spectator's body is absent from the traces of bodies on screen. Like footprints left in the sand, these traces prove that these bodies were once there, in front of the camera at the moment of filming. Yet, during the projection, despite their lifelike motions, they are absent except for the shadows on the screen, which, in turn, derive from the traces left on the film stock. Put another way, the death mask imprinted on the film stock comes to life twenty-four frames per second. As philosopher Stanley Cavell stresses, in contrast to the stage-play and the mood of the audience, films go on mechanically. They unroll with total indifference to their spectators who are, in any case, invisible in front of the screen.[10] In writing about film, Virginia Woolf argued that "unlike theatre, cinema shows what life looks like when we are not there to see it." The idea that "for one party to be present, the other must be absent,"[11] suggests that the film spectator is a sort of living dead, and the allegedly "living" images of the cinema are a form of death-at-work. One could say that, as a result of this ontological circularity between absence and presence, life and death, motion and stillness, the cinema exists in the modality of the future anterior, the most circular of tenses in which the present moment of film projection constantly surfaces and disappears between what will be the next frame and what was the last one.[12]

To say that the spectator's present tense comes and goes from one flickering frame to the next, does not mean, however, that the category of anti-anthropocentrism involves the removal of the human figure from the screen. Rather, this term describes the body's displacement from the center of the world, where Leonardo lodged his Vitruvian man as the source of the proportions of Renaissance city planning. This literally humanized unit of measure served as an impossible ideal of beauty, because it was mathematically embedded in an abstract grid of lines from the window of Renaissance perspective. For Bazin, the screen of cinema, despite the medium's realist vocation, is more a mirror than a window on the world.

When in "Theater and Cinema—Part Two" Bazin counters the window metaphor with that of the mirror, he takes us back to the camera obscura which functioned with a mirror placed within it. Bazin mentioned this device first in the "Ontology" essay, identifying it negatively with Leonardo da Vinci.[13] In fact, Leonardo, attached as he was to the painter's manual skills, felt that his camera obscura was an inferior gadget. This was because the internal mirror allowed only for a mindless interception of the world outside. Privileging the mirror, Bazin accomplishes what Eric Rohmer called his Copernican revolution.[14] Just as the astronomer reversed the hierarchy between the earth and the sun, so Bazin reverses the hierarchy between man and the world, since cinema introduces an anti-anthropocentrism that diminishes the human control operating in the traditional arts.

Copernicus argued that the sun, instead of the earth, is at the center of our universe. Similarly, Bazin implies that objects, sets, nature, animals, nonprofessional actors, children, and real locations steal the show in film. In a section of the essay called "Behind the Décor," he mentions such things as a banging door, a leaf in the wind, and waves beating on the shore to indicate the object-based and nonhuman qualities of cinematic space as compared to that operating in theater. Addressing Jean Cocteau's 1948 adaptation of his play *Les Parents terribles* (1938), Bazin argues that the flame of drama depends as much on the architectural layout of the apartment as it does on the actors' performances, since on the screen—unlike on the stage in this case—a door left ajar can be more significant than a character lying on a bed, delivering a monologue.[15]

Two more sets of metaphors establish Bazin's sense of cinema's relation to the nonhuman. He distinguishes the dazzling, ornate chandelier of the legitimate theater from the "little flashlight of the usher" which, in French movie houses, leads us to our seats and "to the night of our waking dream."[16] In contrast to the public decorations that adorn theaters, the cinema engages our curiosity to see into the dark areas of life, to uncover what is otherwise private or invisible. This metaphor of the flashlight morphs into two other technologies of vision later in "Theater and Cinema" when Bazin writes:

> The camera puts at the disposal of the director all the resources of the telescope and the microscope. The last strand of a rope about to snap or an entire army making an assault on a hill are within our reach. Dramatic causes and effects have no longer material limits to the eye of the camera.[17]

The telescope and the microscope serve an anti-anthropocentric mission, as they situate human experience in a context whose scale is nonhuman, either incredibly small or unbelievably massive. Neither the microscope nor the telescope allows for the graded proportions negotiating distance with proximity that the window of Renaissance humanism demands. Integral to the Copernican revolution, the telescope and the microscope share the use of the anamorphic convex lens, while they both emerged from the seventeenth century's Northern European scientific acumen. Flemish and Dutch art can be said to have developed in a non-anthropocentric, Keplerian direction because, at least for a while, this visual culture was unaware of Alberti's concave and centripetal space.[18]

Considering that the camera's convex lens is a progenitor of both the wide angle and deep focus in cinematography, one wonders whether the anti-anthropocentric streak of Bazin's film theory accounts for his admiration of Orson Welles' acrobatic long takes and trompe l'oeil, hyper-realist visuals. Likewise the outward-bound convex lens is important for Jean Renoir's panoramic, but also internal and impartial view of a range of human behaviors. Must we conclude that Bazin is not a self-oriented humanist in the Albertian sense? Without a doubt, he was advocating a new kind of humanism, one in touch with the problems of postwar Europe which the Renaissance model could not solve. Just as his philosophy of Personalism stood out as an alternative to both utilitarian individualism and to mass collectivism, so Bazin felt that the cinema had a crucial building role to play in the development of a new kind of community of social persons after the horrors of the Holocaust and Hiroshima.[19]

Cosmological Search and Symbiotic Encounters

One of the most intriguing statements Bazin makes in the "Ontology" essay is that a photograph is comparable to a snowflake or a flower.[20] Given his strong scientific background,[21] these analogies were chosen, I believe, because they exemplify two natural weaves of space and time. Snowflakes and flowers are the products of unique events, just as each photograph is unique because it corresponds to a specific moment in time. Apparently, like snowflakes, children, and photographic shots, no two pyramids are alike either, each being produced at a specific moment and position. Thus we may think of the pyramid as both the tomb and the womb for the birth of a new child.[22] According to Sanford Kwinter's *Architectures of Time* the "physics" of the contingent event has only been understood in modernity:

> Each [snowflake] is different because the crystal maintains its sensitivity both to time and its complex milieu. Its morphogenetic principle is active and always incomplete . . .

the snowflake interacts with other processes, across both space and time; [in contrast to an ice-cube, a system operating in an unreal time], [the snowflake] . . . belongs to a dynamical, fluvial world.[23]

With flowers and snowflakes, the flavor of Bazin's aesthetic system begins to approximate a cosmology of little things which belong to a dynamic unpredictable temporal realm outside of human history. Furthermore, Bazin signals his interest in a natural history of cross-media adaptation when he writes: "The film of a painting is an aesthetic symbiosis of screen and painting, as is the lichen of the algae or mushroom."[24] Bazin's vocabulary here is crucial: the lichen is the paramount example of organic or inter-medial symbiosis. This means that two or more minuscule creatures living together are more successful within their partnership than they would have been if they were living on their own. Cinema is a symbiotic medium, in the sense that it mediates between the human and the nonhuman, art and nature, and by doing so, it enhances both sides, as long as the two are willing to accept each other and celebrate their ontological differences.

Left to itself, painting displays a self-centered "vanity." Bazin draws this term from Blaise Pascal's *Pensées* CV: "How vain a thing is painting . . ."[25] Worse, it turns out that "perspective was the original sin of Western painting . . . redeemed from sin by Niépce and Lumière."[26] This analogy undoubtedly echoes the essay "Re-faire la Renaissance," which his nonconformist Catholic mentor, Emmanuel Mounier, published in the October 1932 issue of *Esprit*. Here the spokesperson of the so-called Personalist movement[27] condemned bourgeois individualism for its solipsistic and technocratic aspects. In Mounier's footsteps, Bazin compared Renaissance perspective to an overly easy psychological addiction. Perspective's illusory sense of mastery over space in depth led to a facile pseudo-realism which inhibited the visual arts' development toward a genuine realism—one still based on a psychological leap of faith into the image but also open to a more phenomenological approach.[28] In fact, for Bazin true realism may include, but does not end, with three-dimensional optical illusion, because its broader purpose is not to fabricate a believable reality but to disclose the mysteries and epiphanies of lived experience.

In associating Renaissance perspective with original sin, Bazin may seem to contemplate a return to the prelapsarian aesthetics of the Early Middle Ages, where a dialectical marriage or balance between spiritual and scientific values may be found. On the contrary, I would argue that the history of vision, rather than nostalgia, is behind Bazin's choice of the Romanesque style.[29] The latter's optical and haptic features anticipate a comparable mix of abstraction and figuration in art nouveau and surrealism, and also in the realist ontology of the cinema.[30] In his essay "Les Eglises romanes de Saintonge," published posthumously in *Cahiers du Cinéma*, Bazin acknowledges that the medieval era involved terror, ferocious religious wars, and a general sense of desperation. Yet the Romanesque churches of Saintonge stand out, not because of art history per se, but because, through them, architecture intertwined itself with this location's natural geography in an uncanny symbiosis.[31] Bazin was completely taken by this region's search for new models of coexistence between human and nonhuman elements. In Saintonge, the codependency of architecture and vegetation had kept these modest churches from decaying into utter ruins. The churches look as if they have generated some form of experimental architecture, with unruly vegetation intertwining with the cracks of the walls, along Roman arches, and around sculptures. In a word, these churches appealed to Bazin because they were living social facts, not monuments. Bazin's article was the preparatory work before shooting a film about contemporary Saintonge, not an art historical documentary.

More specifically, Saintonge stood out as an example of dialectical reconciliation between material form and spiritual content through the churches' Romanesque sculptures. Bazin discusses this kind of façade-relief in ways that echo his writings on how anonymous and small events were beloved by the Italian neorealist filmmakers: "The Saintongean sculptor shies away from major dramatic topics [*grands sujets dramatiques*], he is an observer of daily life, addressing secular life and sacred themes with the same realism."[32] In short, Bazin chooses early medieval art, because it openly calls attention to the symbiosis of concrete and abstract elements. Meanwhile, this paradoxical union thrives on its popular, even childlike appeal, while its openly instructional and narrative functions are less deceptive and misleading than the sleek combination of infinity and telos in the vanishing point of Renaissance perspective.

In line with his search for a popular art that is rooted in real time and space, but which can also offer a wealth of societal introspection and critical self-awareness, Bazin not surprisingly ranks theater and literature at the highest level of his aesthetic system. Theater and literature are the two art forms which, when intersecting film on the screen, best convey the same combination of abstract thought and material grounding that he appreciated in Romanesque sculpture. The statuary of Saintonge is the inspiration for a true kind of realism that would start with material existence as a matter of fact, in order to glimpse the forever elusive and changing essence of being. By referring to a specific sculptural group discussed by art historian Monsieur le Chanoine Tonnelier and called *Combat des Vertus et des Vices*,[33] Bazin lingers on the "simultaneously vividly realistic and highly spiritual"[34] Romanesque style. In other words, the Romanesque is a hybrid form oscillating between depth and flatness, while, in *Combat des Vertus et des Vices,* this mixture is most recognizable through folds of dress on top of one-dimensional arms and legs. Thus, in contrast to the fully three-dimensional Gothic style so heavily involved in transcendence, apocalypse, and death, Bazin praised the naïve, curvy, Romanesque style, with massive walls, rounded domes, tongues sticking out, long beards, floating figures, and childlike expressions of wonder and delight.

For Bazin the art of the Early Middle Ages, like the cinema, is both realist and abstract. On one hand, as an embodied form of perception or a source of optical and haptic effects, the camera is a sort of moving form of thought or a chisel sculpting into the void—bringing concrete, yet absent objects out in a plastic, but also mental sense, to the extent of making them present through an abstract edge. By virtue of their projected weight on the screen, moving images are ontologically realist, because they literally flaunt metaphysical presence to the fullest. However, it is especially when objects in film overstretch themselves in a pompous allegorical fashion that they degenerate into rigid symbols or boring clichés. Bazin was distrustful of symbolism, because rigid ideals would prevail too much over concrete and ever-shifting realities.

Conclusion: Objects, Objectivity, *Objectif*

In the footsteps of Bazin's ontogenetic insights about film's dialogue with other arts, some directors and some periods of filmmaking manage to make objects strangely heavy and abstract, concrete and elusive, poignant yet silent and intriguing. Thus, they avoid the pitfalls of an all too grounded one-dimensional symbolism pushing a monolithic thesis above the complexities of lived experience. Well after his death, Bazin's writings make us look with unprecedented attention at Godard's cars and guns, at the Italian diva film's cigarettes and roses, and at Hitchcock's doorknobs and telephones. All these objects are dangerously heavy and predictable and yet, despite the banality of their use and the frequency of their presence, they appear to be multifaceted and kinetic in a mysterious sense. As such, they are comparable to a shorthand for a genre, a signature, or a style. This is probably the case because these things are so profoundly steeped in the fabric of daily life that their metonymic or metaphoric valence is only one of many facets of their presence.

For Bazin, photography assigns a new, equalizing, and thus democratic value to all things. This is due to the camera's indifferent gaze, where it is easy for the lens, or *objectif*, to displace a human being from the center and make a person appear as an object like any other included in the field of vision. Thus, the human element becomes "Other" on the screen. Only through filmmaking can we glimpse this sense of Otherness about what a human is. In a word, cinema is looking at the world from the other side of the screen which, in true mindless, mirror-like fashion, does return to us all its reflections, by placing everything on the very same level of importance. So equalizing and merciless is the eye of cinema that, on one hand, it can rejuvenate perception and show the world off with childlike energy. On the other, this very same eye can be cold and matter-of-fact in surveying the cruelties and mediocrities of human nature.

Why, then, does Bazin use the word "ontology" next to "photography" instead of deploying the well-known category of "medium specificity" used by his professional colleagues writing in France during the '50s? That Bazin's way of thinking was both solitary and innovative can be inferred from Jean Leirens in *Le Cinéma et le temps* (1954). There, Leirens juxtaposes Claude Mauriac's *L'Amour du cinéma* (1954), a text with an emphasis on medium specificity, to the philosopher Gabriel Marcel's notion of "ontological exigency."[35] Involved in Emmanuel Mounier's Personalist circles, and in debates with Paul Ricoeur, Jean-Paul Sartre, Jean Wahl, and Emmanuel Levinas, Marcel argued that the nature of being was and would continue to be an unsolvable puzzle, precisely because the human experience is part of a larger cosmological realm that mankind will never be able to master to the very end. It is this margin of the unknown that photography and the cinema explore and expose in ways no other medium, craft, digital imaging, or art form can even begin to match.[36]

The aesthetic and cosmological implications of Bazin's anti-anthropocentric system of the arts are neither mystical nor idealistic, but secular and scientific. His dialectical approach marries science and spirituality to produce cinema, its child. Such an approach is radically ethical, urging us to consider films as living entities, parallel yet asymptotic to our lives. For films are the imprint of the material culture of their times, while they also contain thought. Thus, they are as worthy of respect and care as animals have become since the discovery of the genome. Just like all living beings, films are subject to damage and decay; even though they are living records of people and things which were there, films are nonhuman because they are made of celluloid and light, matter and energy. They are by definition "The Other," or "The Double." In the end, as surrogate beings suspended in a sort of embalmed state, films might offer us ideas for more symbiotic and ethically constructive relations between those who are in power and at the center, and those who are in the margins, but capable, nevertheless, of finding their voices as shadows in motion.

Notes

1. André Bazin, "The Ontology of the Photographic Image," in *What Is Cinema?* trans. Timothy Barnard (Montreal: Caboose, 2009), 4. Emphasis mine. Other references to *What Is Cinema?* vol. 1 will rely instead on the edition translated by Hugh Gray (Berkeley: University of California Press, 1967). Original: "On ne croit plus à l'identité ontologique du modèle et du portrait, mais on admet que celui-ci nous aide à nous souvenir de celui-là, et donc à le sauver d'une seconde mort spirituelle. La fabrication de l'image s'est même libérée de tout utilitarisme anthropocentrique." *Qu'est-ce que le cinéma?* (Paris: Editions du Cerf, 1975), 10.

2. Bazin, "In Defense of Mixed Cinema," in *What Is Cinema?* vol. 1, trans. Hugh Gray (Berkeley: University of California Press, 2005), 58. On various systems of the arts across centuries, see James Monaco, *How to Read a Film: Movies, Media and Beyond* (New York: Oxford University Press, 2009), 22–67.

3. On medium specificity, see Gotthold Ephraim Lessing, *Laocoon: An Essay on the Limits of Painting and Poetry*, trans. Ellen Frothingham (Boston: Robert Brothers, 1874); on the concepts of *gesamtkunstwerk* and medium specificity, see Marshall Cohen, "Primitivism, Modernism, and Dance Theory," in Roger Copeland and Marshall Cohen, *What is Dance?* (New York: Oxford University Press, 1983), 161–77; on primitive modernism and fusion, see Richard Wagner, "From the Art-Work of the Future," in Copeland and Cohen, *What Is Dance?* 191–96; on medium specificity, see also Noel Carroll, *Theorizing the Moving Image* (New York: Cambridge University Press, 1996), 3–74.

4. Bazin, "Theater and Cinema—Part Two," in *What Is Cinema?* vol. 1, 119.

5. Michael B. Smith, ed., *The Merleau-Ponty Aesthetics Reader: Philosophy and Painting* (Evanston: Northwestern University Press, 1993).

6. Owen Jones, *The Grammar of Ornament* (London: Day and Sons, 1856).

7. Bazin, "The Ontology of the Photographic Image," in *What Is Cinema?* vol. 1, 13–14. Also useful is Katherine Thomson-Jones, *Aesthetics and Film* (London: Continuum, 2008), 16–39.

8. On these issues, see Thomas McEvilley, *The Shape of Ancient Thought* (New York: Allworth Press, 2002); Vivian Davies and Renée Friedman, *Egypt* (London: British Museum, 1998): "It was the hope of every Egyptian to be reborn after death, to attain an afterlife with the sun-god Ra and be resurrected with each sunrise, and to join with Osiris in the cyclical regeneration of nature and plant life with the receding Nile flood," 54.

9. Bazin, "The Myth of Total Cinema," in *What Is Cinema?* vol. 1, 22.

10. Stanley Cavell, "Audience, Actor, Star," in *The World Viewed: Reflections on the Ontology of Film* (New York: Viking Press, 1971); republished in Leo Braudy and Marshall Cohen, eds., *Film Theory and Criticism: Introductory Readings*, 5th ed. (New York: Oxford University Press, 1999), 335.

11. Virginia Woolf as cited by David Trotter, *Cinema and Modernism* (Oxford: Blackwell, 2007), 168.

12. On the future anterior and the aesthetics of the cinema in relation to psychoanalysis and phenomenology, see Domietta Torlasco, *The Time of the Crime: Phenomenology, Psychoanalysis, and Italian Film* (Stanford: Stanford University Press, 2008). See also Hervé Joubert-Laurencin, infra.

13. On Leonardo and the camera obscura, see Jonathan Friday, "Photography and the Representation of Vision," *Journal of Aesthetics and Art Criticism*, 59:4 (2001), 356.

14. On Bazin's Copernican Revolution, see Eric Rohmer, "André Bazin's Summa," *The Taste for Beauty* (New York: Cambridge University Press, 1989), 97.

15. Bazin, "Theater and Cinema—Part One," in *What Is Cinema?* vol. 1, 91; "Theater and Cinema—Part Two," in *What Is Cinema?* vol. 1, 102.

16. Bazin, "Theater and Cinema—Part Two," in *What Is Cinema?* vol. 1, 107.

17. Ibid., 103.

18. Edward G. Rustow, *The Microscope in the Dutch Republic: The Shaping of Discovery* (Cambridge: Cambridge University Press, 1996).

19. Sarah Wilson, "Paris Post-War: In Search of the Absolute," in *Paris Post War: Art and Existentialism 1945–55*, ed. Frances Morris (London: Tate Gallery, 1993), 25–53.

20. Bazin, "The Ontology of the Photographic Image," in *What Is Cinema?* vol. 1, 13.

21. Hugh Gray, "Introduction," in *What Is Cinema?* vol. 1, 1.

22. Mark Lehner, *The Complete Pyramids* (London: Thames and Hudson, 1997).

23. Sanford Kwinter, *Architectures of Time: Toward a Theory of the Event in Modernist Culture* (Cambridge, MA: MIT Press, 2001), 27–28.

24.   Bazin, "Painting and Cinema," in *What Is Cinema?* 168.

25.   Bazin, "The Ontology of The Photographic Image," 12.

26.   Ibid.

27.   Eileen Cantin, *Mounier: A Personalist View of History* (New York: Paulist Press, 1973).

28.   Bazin, "The Ontology of the Photographic Image," 15.

29.   Bazin, "Les Eglises romanes de Saintonge: Projet de film d'André Bazin," *Cahiers du Cinéma*, 100 (October 1959), 24. My colleague Ludovic Cortade tells me that Bazin was likely to be familiar with Louis Réau, *L'Art religieux du moyen-Age: La sculpture* (Paris: Fernand Nathan, 1946).

30.   The Romanesque style was also one of the fundamental topics of Alois Riegl and Walter Benjamin. On Riegl, Benjamin, and Bazin, see *The Visual Turn: Classical Film Theory and Art History*, ed. Angela Dalle Vacche (New Brunswick, NJ: Rutgers University Press, 2002), 1–32.

31.   Simon Hodgkinson has been working on the impact of the Saintonge churches on Bazin's ideas about aesthetics and cinema. See his "Rapt in Plastic: Word and Image in the Criticism of André Bazin," M.Phil thesis, History and Theory of Art, Kent University, 1999.

32.   Bazin, "Les Eglises romanes de Saintonge," 12.

33.   A photograph of *Combat des Vertus et des Vices* is published on page 58 of Bazin's article.

34.   André Bazin, "The Ontology of the Photographic Image," 12.

35.   Jean Leirens, *Le Cinéma et le temps* (Paris: Editions du Cerf, 1954), 96, 110; Claude Mauriac, *L'Amour du cinéma* (Paris: Albin Michel, 1954); Claude Mauriac, *Petite littérature du cinéma* (Paris: Editions du Cerf, 1957); Gabriel Marcel, *Position et approaches concretes du mystère ontologique* (Louvain: E. Nauwelaerts, 1949).

36.   Gabriel Marcel interacted with Bazin on one known occasion, for a twenty-minute radio program called Tribune de Paris, February 9, 1948, where the subject of the debate was: "Must art be renewed? The Art of cinema, its evolution and its influence on the other arts."

14

Malraux, Bazin, and the Gesture of Picasso

Dudley Andrew

Although the first of Bazin's dozen articles on the topic of film and painting were penned in the last weeks before 1950, he had been ruminating about comparative aesthetics from the beginning of his career as a critic. That career is usually said to originate with "The Ontology of the Photographic Image." It is often forgotten that this most famous essay appeared in an immense anthology published in 1945, called *Problèmes de la peinture*, edited by art historian Gaston Diehl, and alongside entries by Matisse, Dufy, and Rouault. More important, Bazin's first footnote is to André Malraux's "Sketch for a Psychology of the Cinema," which he had read in the luxury art journal *Verve* in 1940. This was Malraux's fourth installment in *Verve* of a psychology and world history of art, an outline for the popular volumes he would begin to publish in 1947. Bazin idolized this charismatic author and hero during the Resistance years, joining a Malraux study group in 1942 at the Maison de Culture near the Sorbonne, the same place where he founded his first ciné-club. When the war ended, and just as *Problèmes de la peinture* finally came out, Bazin raced to the Max Linder Theater to watch *Espoir*, the film Malraux had put together in 1939 but, except for a couple private screenings, could not exhibit until the war was over. You can imagine the pressure the young Bazin must have felt in reviewing it, especially since it was commissioned by *Poésie*, a journal read by the French intelligentsia; indeed Malraux read the review there and replied personally to Bazin a few months later, praising his acuity.

As far as I know, the two men never interacted again. On the one hand, in the immediate postwar, Malraux was surely too busy with the roller coaster of Gaullist politics to even go to the cinema, let alone worry about its developments. On the other hand, his orientation, it has become increasingly clear to me, diverges sharply from Bazin's and always did, though the latter may not have immediately recognized this. In fact, these men ought to have been in steady contact from 1948 when both retreated to the world of the arts in part because the increasingly ideological wars occasioned by Stalin's reaction to the Marshall Plan spoiled hopes for a renewed European culture. Both fell victim to the ire of the Communist Party as the cold war settled in, and both had serious bouts of illness (Bazin's far worse) requiring convalescence during 1950. In a sanatorium, Bazin thought deeply about literary adaptation and about films on art, publishing a series of major essays from 1951 to 1953 that he would subsequently group together to form the bulk of "Cinéma et les autres arts," the second volume of *Qu'est-ce que le cinéma?* Malraux, for his part, had already brought out the three volumes of *Le Musée Imaginaire* by 1950, but he profited from his months in recovery to put together the definitive Pléiade edition of *Les Voix du silence*, instantly a bestseller in 1951.

Malraux should have been in touch with Bazin when in 1951 the latter reported that the film on art ("*le film sur l'art*," which is not at all the same as "*le film d'art*") had "snowballed since the war . . . becoming the most important development in the past twenty years in the history of documentary, maybe in the history of cinema itself."[1] How could the author of *Museum Without Walls* neglect this popular format of dissemination and criticism? Yet he ignored it completely. Don't films on art, like books on art, bring painting to the masses through a technology that permits convenient comparisons of examples brought next to one another on the same scale? Malraux should at least have understood the film on art to be a parallel commercial enterprise to the one he promoted, whereby paintings and sculptures could migrate from museums to ordinary homes in the form of art books. Postwar improvements in the technology of photo-duplication had made books like *Les Voix du silence* possible, bringing about a reformation in the sociology of aesthetics comparable to the reformation in religion resulting from Gutenberg's Bible, though of a lower order, of course. Painting has been taken from museum curators and put in the hands of the faithful, under the guidance of the written commentaries of art historians. Do not films on art participate in just this project, their voice-over commentaries and tracking cameras guiding the audience to comprehend the achievement of the great creators? Malraux seemed not to care.

It is only fair to pose the same question to Bazin. Why was he not drawn to mention Malraux's illustrated history and psychology of art when writing on films that take on this subject? Perhaps he entertained such a prospect, only to realize that their attitudes about art, and certainly about cinema, were deeply opposed. Let's begin with Malraux's insistence that art be attached to the sacred. Douglas Smith points out that while Malraux may have operated within the problematic of desacralization laid out by Benjamin, he did not think that the photographic reproduction of great works of art dissipates the aura surrounding originals.[2] Like replicas of religious icons, well-produced art books and magazines such as *Verve* keep the public physically in touch with the timeless universality of painting, with its immensity and destiny. Maurice Blanchot said as much when he reviewed *Les Voix du silence*.[3]

From his archive of hundreds of photographs, Malraux had built a museum without walls, located in the universal ether that each human being floats within while contemplating the triumph of art, whether standing in front of an original or looking at its photographic reproduction. Photographs in fact increase the chances for the common viewer to partake in the drama of artistic effort and triumph since they suggest the lines that can be traced connecting the projects of artworks to each other. For instance, through photographs of paintings (sometimes just parts of paintings), Malraux links the theological motifs of religious art in the Renaissance to the quest of painters after the French Revolution where religion might seem absent (from Raphael to Ingres, for example, or from Leonardo to Pierre-Auguste Renoir, or from Del Pionbo to Van Gogh via Delacroix and Cézanne[4]). In this way he makes a theology of art itself, painting in our day having become its own raison d'être, indeed humankind's raison d'être. In its heroic, modernist phase, where artists serve as the creators of value as such, questing figures like Van Gogh or Picasso (easily his favorites) rightly stand out in the public imagination. They incarnate the myth of creation, its torture and doubt, its fluidity and confidence, and, above all, its transcendence. Why did he not attend to the films being made of these and other artists?

Although Bazin may have agreed that a certain spiritual quantity can be transferred from original artwork by photographic calque to film, Malraux's heroic view must have seemed outmoded, precluding the more down-to-earth humanism that Bazin found in Jean Renoir, in neorealism, and in the modern cinema in general, whose prophet he had become. True, Malraux had once stood alongside Eisenstein, Trotsky, Breton, and other leaders in the advanced guard of the struggles over politics and culture. He had fought in Spain, while putting together *Espoir*, the most daring film to have been made in prewar France, and he had once been the voice for new political relations (socialism) and new artistic enterprises (cinema foremost among them). Yet after the war he stood beside de Gaulle and scarcely kept up with cinema. Instead he levitated above the scorched earth of Europe. As Blanchot immediately divined, his *Musée Imaginaire* is a zone protected from history.

And so Bazin must have been disappointed that Malraux pulled back from cinema (and from socialism) on the postwar cultural battlefield. For not only did Malraux fail to recruit films on art for the liberal democratic campaign of his art books, but the role he accords cinema in those books is the typical one that Bazin was out to overturn. Malraux treats cinema the way he treats lithography in the nineteenth century; these invented technologies afford new sites for artists to exercise their drive to create. Malraux insisted that cinema's raw appetite for visible reality—precisely what Bazin found revolutionary about the medium—must be overcome through powerful composition and robust montage. *Potemkin* (1925) remained his touchstone, for its formal audacity and political potency. But *Potemkin* was a quarter century old in 1950 and Malraux was out of touch with the modern cinema.

Malraux must have deemed the genre of "*le film sur l'art*" servile, while in Bazin's view its hybridity brought it right up to date as a subgenre of the "film essay" that Alexandre Astruc had claimed was ushering in the era of a *nouvelle avant-garde*.[5] Neither pure cinema nor pure painting, this genre seemed capable of altering both forms. In his first review of such a film, the 1949 *Rubens*, Bazin wrote that anyone genuinely schooled in art history (he could have had Malraux in mind) "might find such [a film] superfluous or sacrilegious," but he believed the filmmakers had devised "properly cinematographic means to produce a penetrating critical look at paintings." He was struck by the way they isolated and then rotated on its axis a section from a vast Rubens canvas, in order to show the circular design of the entire picture. Drawing a conclusion that taps into Sartrean phenomenology, he writes that Rubens "clearly shows the existence of virtual movement, a space of suspended rotation lodged in the immobility of the painting." This virtuality "awaits its imaginary deliverance via the sensibility of someone standing before the canvas and contemplating it."[6] Thus the film operates both on the painting and on the spectator by forcing an aesthetic conjunction that tells us something about painting, about cinema, and about spectatorship. "Who can complain of this?" he innocently asks, preempting the scoffs he knew would come from art scholars.

Bazin was able to cut to the heart of the aesthetic problem of filming Rubens because he had recently advised Alain Resnais on his first major film, *Van Gogh* (1948). Resnais often helped Bazin with his outreach activities at *Travail et Culture*, and he had shown him the 16mm version of his project. Bazin argued that it should be redone in 35mm, and he may have been instrumental in putting Resnais in touch with his eventual producer, Gaston Diehl, the same art historian who had published Bazin's "Ontology" essay in *Problèmes de la peinture*.[7] Like

Rubens, Van Gogh is made up largely of details rather than of entire canvases. Resnais' camera is first and foremost deictic: "here, look at this," it says, in proposing a view of some startling reality.[8] But what reality does Van Gogh—the painter and the film—confront us with? Certainly not with historical reality, for Resnais uses but does not focus on biography. This is no pedagogical effort to show us the great man's birthplace or photographs of his family or reproductions of his letters to Theo. Nor does Resnais give us a slideshow of the paintings conveniently organized to maximize their effect. Rather he has constituted, Bazin says, "a work to the second degree with its own interest and its own autonomy."[9] Leaping to the idea he would elaborate two years later in "Painting and Cinema," Bazin insists that every painting finds its ontology within a hermetically sealed frame, and that this is a necessarily "interior" ontology. Cinema, on the other hand, only appears to have a frame; in fact what we see on screen is limited as by a mask, a rectangular keyhole through which we strive to look at what is beyond our limited range. The moving camera and successive camera setups elaborate an extensive space quite at odds with that of painting.[10] By letting his camera rove across Van Gogh's oeuvre, as though it were spread out in front of him, Resnais explores an already constituted aesthetic space.

And so Resnais' project (supported by Bazin) differs fundamentally from Malraux's, despite the fact that both trace a narrative through the details of artworks. Who can forget the image of Malraux standing magisterially above his scores of photos of artworks, ready to move them around as in a puzzle until they might provide a totalized image of Human Creation? Malraux wanted the covers of *Les Voix du silence* to frame the locus of the absolute; he took each artwork to be closed in upon its own timeless existence, while serving as a fragment of the larger picture of man's artistic quest. In contrast, if Resnais lays out Van Gogh's paintings on the floor, it is to remove their frames and let them meld into a single extensive territory that his camera can meander across. [figures 14.1–14.3] Bazin might say that in this, as in his later

FIGURES 14.1–14.3: Resnais' *découpage* (*Van Gogh*, 1948)

documentaries, Resnais is concerned not with the *frame* but with *framing*, which is a quest to explore a world beyond the self, indeed beyond the human. Blanchot thought that Malraux had built his "Musée Imaginaire" in the heavens. If so, Resnais gives earthlings a view of it through the panning telescope of his camera. This way he brings paintings out of the imaginary and down to earth.

Resnais' *Van Gogh*, like other films on art, could have demonstrated to Bazin how different was his entire conception of cinema from Malraux's. True, the latter had praised Bazin lavishly for his subtle understanding of the techniques of *Espoir*, particularly ellipsis and rapprochement (metaphor), but in fact Bazin finds both techniques highly literary and counter to cinema's natural proclivities which are, respectively, continuity and contiguity. Bazin's cinema offers humans a look at the world stretching out in time and space beyond what they normally are able to see. Films that cut off extension to control and intensify meaning—films like *Espoir*, for instance—give up this technological prowess; cinema may thus join the arts, just as Malraux wanted, but Bazin held out for something additional. He wanted something different for cinema, and something different from it.

There is a reason Bazin dedicated but a single essay to photography; its finality (its preterit tense) like its definitive framing, were the concern of others—of Malraux, for instance. Of all cinema's attributes, nothing mattered more to Bazin than its ongoingness, its registration of time flowing. Malraux might bring the majesty and absoluteness of art to a mass audience through the agency of photographs; Bazin would bring them films that displayed paintings and painters in the process of becoming the myths by which we know them. Of Resnais' *Van Gogh* he wrote that we literally enter into "the world of Van Gogh" through the keyhole of the cinema. Nothing outside the paintings appears in the film, and the paintings, their frames removed, interact and meld.[11]

Despite being in black and white, Resnais' *Van Gogh* absorbs the spectator, sucking him through the frame, as opposed to Vincent Minelli's biopic, *Lust for Life* (1956) which puts the painter on stage, theatricalizing his achievement [figure 14.4]. In Minelli's theater of art, Bazin lamented, everything is visible except what we care about, Van Gogh's creativity.[12] Resnais' humble camera "understood far better how to let us edge up to this adventure of the soul," in comparison with "Minelli's impotence to enter into the mystery of artistic creation."[13] Minelli was blocked at the outset from getting inside Van Gogh because he chose Cinemascope, a format whose dimensions mimic those of the stage where the dimensions of Van Gogh's paintings can never quite "square" with those of the screen. Resnais' screen coincides with the imaginary

FIGURES 14.4: Kirk Douglas as Van Gogh (*Lust for Life*, Minnelli, 1955)

space of the paintings, rendering the interior of artistic creation "sensible." When you see a painting attached to the wall, it's like "a cork floating on water," Bazin says in a fugitive article, since the wall is attached to the house which belongs on a street which runs through a city, which is situated in a region, and so forth. But if you bring the camera up to the frame of the painting, then let the frame disappear by passing into the painting's space, a new sort of documentation is at work, and a new artwork can emerge "at the second degree."[14]

Joining sections of paintings in ways Van Gogh himself would never have imagined, the film discloses new potentials in canvases that may have become too familiar. Starting with Van Gogh's remark, "I always feel like a traveler who is going somewhere, going to a destination,"[15] Resnais tracks that artist's movements and preoccupations from Holland to Paris to the Midi, interspersing self-portraits that make the stages of his increasingly grim *vie spirituelle* into a geography of the soul. "The director has treated the whole of the artists' output as one large painting [a landscape or cityscape] over which the camera has wandered freely. . . . From the 'rue d'Arles' we climb through the window of Van Gogh's house and go right up to the bed with the red eiderdown." Often tracking seamlessly or dissolving from an area of one picture to another area of a different picture, he sometimes zooms in to a detail or gives us a continuity cut, *un raccord*. Bazin was amused that Resnais "has even risked a reverse shot of an old Dutch peasant woman entering her house" [figures 14.5–14.6]. He has made a sort of animated film about Van Gogh's travails, using him as cartoonist, except that, unlike animation cells, each painting exists beyond the film, carefully guarded in a museum. "What may seem symbolic and abstract takes on the solid reality of a piece of ore," Bazin says, whereas the drawings that go into cartoons are used up by the films for which they were designed. We call them "transparencies." Van Gogh's paintings are anything but transparent.

Bazin denigrated standard films in the genre as mere pedagogical conveniences, suites of photographic reproductions, nothing more than slide shows with commentary, rather like Malraux's art books.[16] Douglas Smith in fact finds Resnais' *Van Gogh* and particularly his next film, *Guernica* (1950), to operate as does the *Musée Imaginaire*, with montage (aided by voice-over) articulating a heroic story of artistic creation. Bazin would disagree. The photographic reproductions in art books *refer to* artistic achievements, while cinema, in the hands of someone like Resnais, *animates* Van Gogh's painted world. Malraux uses a *montage* of photos, whereas Resnais edits in classical *continuity*, the film acting as a scroll that unfurls a tale of continuous creation, arrested only when the artist put an end to it with a bullet through his heart. This film is literally immersed within the painted world it both moves through and sets in motion.

For Bazin and Malraux alike, technological reproduction widens the circle radiating from the *tremblement* caused by the artist's original creative gesture. That gesture, or rather its product, is visible in photographs of artworks, whose stasis replicates the timelessness of what they picture; art books stand as records of past creation. But Bazin, who was allergic to museums, preferred the life (the animation) of cinema to the propriety of photographs. Resnais' *Van Gogh* moved him not as a reproduction of great art but as a productive gesture in its own right, made out of the stuff of art. After all, a film purporting to be "on art" should make us feel the creativity that we value in art. This attitude he shares with his contemporary Merleau-Ponty, whose essay on Cézanne came out when Bazin was in contact with the philosopher.[17] Merleau-Ponty and Bazin want us to "return painting to the painter's living work rather than enshrine the completed or abandoned artwork as a fetish of capital exchange," whether in museum or art

FIGURES 14.5–14.6: *Van Gogh* (Resnais, 1948)

book.[18] Resnais moved in this direction with *Van Gogh* by de-framing the art and exploring it laterally as a territory replete with relations and anecdotes. Yet this too constitutes a retrospective homage to creativity, compromised by the explanatory voice that insists on a particular evolution of the artist's vision and concerns.

To get at painting itself—rather than at paintings—should be the goal of any truly ambitious film on art. And in fact Merleau-Ponty was sure he had seen just such an attempt. In one

of his most important aesthetic statements, "Indirect Discourse and the Voices of Silence"—
itself an elaborate reaction in 1952 to Malraux's *Voix du silence*—he recalls being profoundly
struck by a 1946 film about one of his favorite painters:

> A camera once recorded the work of Matisse in slow motion. The impression was
> prodigious, so much so that Matisse himself was moved, they say. That same brush that,
> seen with the naked eye, leaped from one act to another, was seen to meditate in a
> solemn, expanded time—the imminence of a world's reaction—to try ten possible
> movements, dance in front of the canvas, brush it lightly several times, and crash down
> finally like a lightning stroke upon the one line necessary. Of course, there is something
> artificial in this analysis. And Matisse would be wrong if, putting his faith in the film, he
> believed that he really chose between all possible lines that day and, like the God of
> Leibniz, solved an immense problem of maximum and minimum. He was not a
> demiurge; he was a human being. He did not have in his mind's eye all the gestures
> possible, and in making his choice he did not have to eliminate all but one. It is slow
> motion which enumerates the possibilities. Matisse, set within a human's time and
> vision, looked at the still open whole of his work in progress and brought his brush
> toward the line which called for it in order that the painting might finally be that which
> it was in the process of becoming. By a simple gesture he resolved the problem which in
> retrospect seemed to imply an infinite number of data (as the hand in the iron filings,
> according to Bergson, achieves in a single stroke the arrangement which will make a
> place for it). Everything happened in the human world of perception and gesture; and
> the camera gives us a fascinating version of the event only by making us believe that the
> painter's hand operated in the physical world where an infinity of options is possible.
> And yet, Matisse's hand did hesitate. Consequently there was a choice, and the chosen
> line was chosen in such a way as to observe, scattered out over the painting, a score of
> conditions which were unformulated and even informulable for anyone but Matisse,
> since they were only defined and imposed by the intention of executing that *particular
> painting which did not yet exist*.[19]

Merleau-Ponty may well have learned of this 1946 film by François Campaux from Bazin
who mentions it while developing his notion of the "sketch" in his famous essay on the aesthetics of neorealism. Writing in *Esprit* in January 1948, where Merleau-Ponty surely picked up
his vocabulary, Bazin declared that in recent Italian films "the camera must be ready to move as
to remain still [but] . . . without the god-like character that the Hollywood camera crane has
bestowed on them." This human camera, he also says, exhibits a certain dynamism like "the
movement of a hand drawing a sketch, leaving a space here, filling in there, here sketching round
the subject and there bringing it into relief. I am thinking of the slow motion in the documentary on Matisse which allows us to observe, beneath the continuous and uniform arabesques of
the stroke, the varying hesitations of the artist's hand."[20] This passage, written years before Merleau-Ponty's reference to the same film, comes just a page after Bazin reminds us that "Van
Gogh repainted the same picture ten times, very quickly, while Cézanne would return to a
painting time and again over the years. Certain genres call for speed, for work done in the heat
of the moment." Here Bazin finds himself ahead of a genre he is cheering on, a genre he will see

come into its own, for the film on art will indeed learn to represent creativity "in the heat of the moment." And Bazin would be there to measure its progress when in 1956 Henri-Georges Clouzot teamed up with the most celebrated creator of the century to deliver *The Picasso Mystery* (*Le Mystère Picasso*, 1956).

Bazin, I contend, had developed ideas about cinema parallel to Merleau-Ponty's general aesthetic of active and embodied gesture; indeed Bazin's writings in *Esprit* may have encouraged the philosopher to explicitly counter Malraux's (and Sartre's) ideas of art as enshrined achievements. Amédée Ayfre helps draw this line of thought when he cites both Bazin and Merleau-Ponty in "Neo-Realism and Phenomenology," a long article that appeared in *Cahiers du Cinéma* in November 1952, a few months after Merleau-Ponty's "Indirect Language and the Voices of Silence" had come out in *Les Temps modernes*.[21]

Another linking figure, more important in my view, is Fernand Deligny, the educator and psychiatrist who in the 1960s would befriend Felix Guattari and influence Gilles Deleuze. From 1947 to 1949, Deligny worked as a specialist for disturbed children at the offices of *Travail et Culture* at 5, rue Beaux Arts, alongside Bazin and Chris Marker.[22] All three had met in 1946 when Deligny, a regional director of *Travail et Culture* north of Paris, screened Nicolaï Ekk's *The Road to Life* (1931). Marker would review in *Esprit* Deligny's book *Vagabonds effectives* (1947), a paean to unadaptable adolescents and teachers, modeled on Rimbaud and—pertinent for us—on Van Gogh. Deligny was moved to assemble an imaginary dialogue between Van Gogh's letters and Antonin Artaud's book on Van Gogh's suicide when Artaud died in 1948.[23] This occurred just as Marker's friend Resnais was bringing to a close his film on the artist. There must have been innumerable discussions among these men since Bazin had found Deligny an apartment in his own building on rue Cardinal Lemoine. Did they know about, or had they seen, Artaud's final sketches from the asylum? This would have been primary material for Deligny's project, which went under a rubric he may well have picked up from Merleau-Ponty: "A language other than Speech."

Deligny admitted that his own particular brand of cinephilia could be summed up by this sentence of Malraux's in his correspondence with Bazin: "What interests me in cinema is its way of linking man to the world (as a cosmos) in a manner other than language."[24] When he came to shoot a film himself, which he did throughout the '60s aided by Chris Marker, Deligny gave it a title on which we should meditate: *Le Moindre Geste* (*The Slightest Gesture*, 1971). He believed pre-linguistic or extra-linguistic expressions form the primary data by which to understand children, especially autistic ones. He shared Bazin's fascination with children and with animals, a fascination at once moral and philosophical. For both men language, which names everything it touches, may let us forget that human beings act and react in a world that is only partly human. The child's gestures, hesitations, instincts, and screams are there to be comprehended; and cinema is an instrument of both expression and comprehension. Living in daily contact with Deligny, Bazin must have discussed with him Merleau-Ponty's *Sens et nonsense* when it appeared in 1948, and he must have read closely Merleau-Ponty's great essay of 1951, "The Child's Relations with Others"[25] (for at the time the philosopher held the chair of child psychology at the Sorbonne).

Late in 1955 Deligny published, "La caméra, outil pédagogique," where he maintains that, far better than written language to which adults are addicted, the camera can respond to and grasp the gesture of the adolescent as it forms a response to circumstances he feels within and without.[26] The cinema can give us access to the world of the adolescent through his or her gestures and it can do so at the moment of their coming into whatever significance those gestures take on. Is this not precisely how Bazin valued *The Picasso Mystery* when it took the Jury prize at Cannes four months after Deligny's essay appeared?

Bazin's magnificent article on "A Bergsonian Film" announces that the genre of the film on art has leaped to a higher plateau, for Clouzot and Picasso both recognized from the start the hybrid nature of the work they were coproducing. This time no framed paintings preexist the film like pieces of ore, no objects in oil on canvas that the film explores. This time we are not presented with the space of the canvas but with its temporality, as it fills up, is filled in, then reduced, reformed, and reworked in a palpable rhythm. This is the rhythm of Picasso's unpredictable creativity as it breathes life into a form for the camera to absorb. "This marks the second revolution in films about art," Bazin says, after Resnais had achieved the first revolution. Where Resnais' camera roamed freely across a wide aesthetic space laid out as already completed, Clouzot superimposes his own *cadrage* on the borders Picasso works within. With nowhere to go, the camera looks deep into the frame as a site of "vertical" movement, tunneling into time as paintings appear (and "'appears' is the right word," says Bazin[27]) during the course of the shooting and the projection. Picasso himself considered this work a palimpsest to "be able to show the paintings underneath the paintings" (BW, 213), a kind of mystic writing pad constituting the painter's "*image-temps*" [figures 14.7–14.8]. Bazin mimes one of Bergson's formulations: "Free forms in their nascent state . . . are evidence that freedom lies in duration" (BW, 214). Then Bazin anticipates Deleuze when he concludes, "Only film could make us see duration itself" (BW, 213).

Bazin doesn't shy away from the eerie consequences of this Bergsonian film, "a work that exists in time, that has its own duration, its own life, and sometimes—as at the end of the film—a death that precedes the extinction of the artist" (BW, 212). *The Picasso Mystery* leaves us with nothing to hold onto: no canvas, no image, merely the roll of 35mm film that we can project again . . . or today, the DVD that sits on our shelf ready to be inserted for another eighty minutes of life and death.

By refusing to provide a final canvas, Clouzot and Picasso assumed, at least for this project, the priority of painting over "the painting," a priority approved of by Bazin and Deligny. *The Picasso Mystery* lets us recognize that any canvas in a museum is only the more-or-less arbitrary arrested development of a continual process, the final "vertical section" of a creative flow coming out of the depths of time. Many vertical sections pass onto the film, each a kind of "cell" for the animation that brings these to life as a process.

In articulating the revolutionary novelty of *The Picasso Mystery*, Bazin opposes its use of "vertical sections" of temporal progression to the horizontal layout of sketches or of affiliated paintings that standard films in the genre utilize to imply artistic development. The latter he likens to cards in a game of solitaire. The filmmaker lays them out until they are all used up in the apotheosis of the final image or canvas. This is exactly how books of an artist's sketches have given us insight into the "ontogenesis" of a work. *The Picasso Mystery* gets beyond such gross approximations of the discontinuous to the temporal realism of continuous vision. By implying that Picasso's drawings and overdrawings might as well be animation cells, Bazin would have us take them all at once stacked vertically like a deck of cards, not spread out on the table. Watching the film is tantamount to flipping through the cards, each of which is a "section," or what Deleuze would call, following Bergson, a "sheet of the past" in the memory volume.

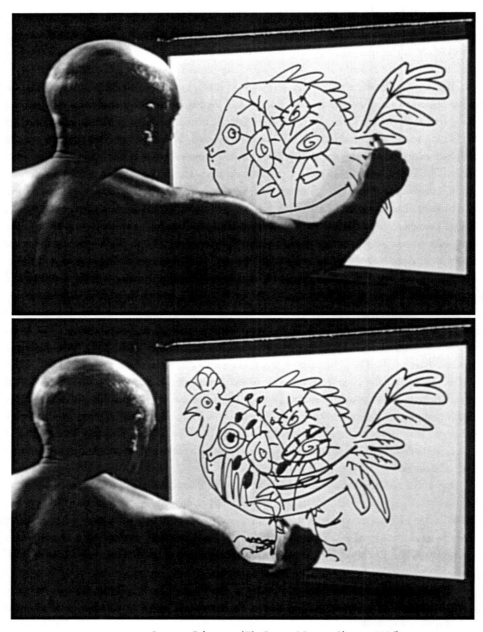

FIGURES 14.7–14.8: Screen as Palimpsest (*The Picasso Mystery*, Clouzot, 1956)

Bazin's attention to the genre of the film on art discloses the nature of both media and adds to his unflagging quest to understand *Qu'est-ce que le cinéma*? For, unique though it may be as an exercise, *The Picasso Mystery* displays something about the screen that Bazin could apply to the cinema *in toto*, as a way to get around the classical view such as the one Malraux sketched in 1940. Recall that for Malraux the art of cinema was born with the practice of editing where mechanically recorded pictures, of no importance in themselves except as "identity cards," submit to abstract design: "The means of reproduction in the cinema is the moving photograph, but its means of expression is a sequence of planes. . . . Thereafter it was able to select the 'shot' and coordinate significant 'shots': by selectivity to make up for its silence."[28] We have seen how in his books on art Malraux spread out his shots like "identity cards" in a mosaic pattern, selecting the most vivid to be placed alongside one another. He thought of the gaps between them as spatial ellipses, which trigger effects of "rapprochement" in the inquiring viewer. Bazin has now taken this idea of "planes" much further, calling on Bergson's notion of the vertical image of consciousness as memory. Each *plan*, or shot, exists as one moment in the totality of the image flow constituting the film. And the screen, which for Malraux, Arnheim, and Eisenstein is a flat surface on which to lay out and juxtapose views, becomes for Bazin a cone, extending into the volume formed by the added dimensions of deep space and of time. What else do we mean when we praise a film as being "deep"? For Bazin the world is large and continuous, while human perspective comes in disjointed planes; those who understand this best—Renoir, Rossellini, Bresson, and now Clouzot and Picasso—accept both perspective *and* continuity. Above all they accept the gap between them, which is the gap between subjectivity and objectivity, a gap across which the spark of creativity leaps in every production worthy of the name "art-film."

Notes

1. André Bazin, "Le Film d'art: est-il un documentaire comme les autres?" *Radio, Cinéma, Télévision*, 75 (June 24, 1951).
2. Douglas Smith, "Moving pictures: The Art Documentaries of Alain Resnais and Henri-Georges Clouzot in Theoretical Context (Benjamin, Malraux and Bazin)" in *Studies in European Cinema*, 1:3 (November 2004).
3. Maurice Blanchot, "Time, Art, and the Museum," in *Malraux: a Collection of Critical Essays*, ed. R.W.B. Lewis, trans. Ben Archer (Englewood Cliffs: Prentice-Hall, 1964). Originally published as "La Musée, l'Art, et le Temps," *Critique*, 43–44 (December 1950–January 1951).
4. André Malraux, *Les Voix du silence* (Paris: Gallimard, 1951), 576–79.
5. Alexandre Astruc, "The Birth of a New Avant-Garde: *La Caméra-Stylo*," in *French New Wave, Critical Landmarks*, ed. Peter Graham with G. Vincendeau (London: B.F.I, Palgrave, 2009). Originally published in *Ecran français*, March 1948.
6. Bazin, "Quand Rubens et Van Gogh font du cinéma," *Parisien libéré*, 1474 (June 6, 1949).
7. Bazin was with Resnais when it premiered at the Venice festival in August 1948.
8. James R. Cisneros, "Imaginary of the End, End of the Imaginary: Bazin and Malraux on the Limits of Painting and Photography," *Cinémas* (Spring 2003), 149–69.
9. Bazin, "L'Espace dans la peinture et le cinema," *Arts*, 210 (April 5, 1949).
10. Ibid.
11. Bazin, "Sur les films de peinture: Réponse à Bourniquel," *Esprit*, 161 (November 1949).
12. Bazin, "*La Vie passion de Vincent Van Gogh*: La Peinture à l'huile," *Parisien libéré*, 3855 (February 1, 1957).
13. Original: "avait su beaucoup mieux nous faire approcher cette aventure de l'âme," in comparison with, "l'impuissance de Minelli à nous faire entrer dans le mystère de la création artistique." My translation.
14. Bazin,"Le film d'art: est-il un documentaire comme les autres?"
15. Original: "Il me semble toujours d'être un voyageur qui va quelque part et à une destination." My translation.
16. Bazin, "L'art à télévision: Une émission qui perd sur tous les . . . tableaux," *Radio, Cinéma, Télévision*, 458 (October 26, 1958).
17. Maurice Merleau-Ponty, "Cezanne's Doubt" in *Sense and Non-sense* (Evanston, IL: Northwestern University Press, 1948), appearing originally in 1945.
18. Galen Johnson, "Structures and Painting: Indirect Language and the Voices of Silence," in *The Merleau-Ponty Aesthetics Reader* (Evanston, IL: Northwestern University Press, 1993), 24.

19. Merleau-Ponty, "Indirect Language and the Voices of Silence," in *Signs*, trans. R.C. McCleary (Evanston: Northwestern University Press, 1964), 45–46.

20. Bazin, "An Aesthetic of Reality: Cinematic Realism and the Italian School of the Liberation," in *What Is Cinema?* vol. 2, trans. Hugh Gray (Berkeley: University of California Press, 1971), 33. Originally published as "Le Réalisme cinématographique et l'école italienne de la Libération," *Esprit* (January 1948).

21. Amédée Ayfre, "Néoréalisme et phénoménologie," *Cahiers du Cinéma*, 17 (November 1952), translated in *Cahiers du Cinéma, the 1950s*, ed. J. Hillier (Cambridge, MA: Harvard University Press, 1985).

22. See the appendix "Chronologie" in Fernand Deligny, *Oeuvres*, ed. Sanra Alvarez de Toledo (Paris: Editions l'Arachnéen, 2007), 1822–23.

23. Deligny, *Oeuvres*, 158 and 213.

24. Deligny reads this sentence on camera in "A propos d'un film à faire" (1989). This text is reprinted in "Ce qui ne se voit pas," *Cahiers du Cinéma* (February 1990).

25. Merleau-Ponty "The Child's Relation with Others," in *The Primacy of Perception*, ed. James Edie (Evanston, IL: Northwestern University Press, 1964), 96–155; originally published as "Les Relations avec autrui chez l'enfant" (Paris: Centre de Documentation Universitaire, 1951).

26. Fernand Deligny, "La Caméra: outil pédagogique," *Vers l'éducation nouvelle*, 97 (October–November 1955).

27. Bazin, "A Bergsonian Film: *The Picasso Mystery*," in *Bazin at Work*, ed. Bert Cardullo (New York: Routledge, 1997), 211. Hereafter cited parenthetically as BW.

28. André Malraux, "Sketch for a Psychology of the Moving Pictures," in *Reflections on Art*, ed. Susanne Langer (Baltimore, MD: Johns Hopkins University Press, 1958), 320.

15

Incoherent Spasms and the Dignity of Signs

Bazin's Bresson

NOA STEIMATSKY

Bresson is naturally drawn to the most sensual aspects of the face which, to the extent that no acting is involved, is simply a privileged imprint of existence, the most legible trace of the soul. Nothing about these faces eludes the dignity of the sign. . . . What we see, rather, is closer to painful concentration, to the incoherent spasms of a reptile moulting or an animal dropping its young.
—ANDRÉ BAZIN, *"Diary of a Country Priest and the Robert Bresson Style"*[1]

But how *are* signs born of such agonizing, "incoherent spasms"? How is the carnal imprint made "legible"? Bazin's discussion circles around cinema's semiotizing process; its paradigm is the human face. What he struggles to describe, we shall see, is a more elemental "dialectic" of the image than the workings of *découpage* or of montage syntax, narrative or poetic; yet it is predicated on a reconsideration of the passage of the image into language. This is not the seemingly dismissive afterthought—those famous last words—of "The Ontology of the Photographic Image," where language appears as an addendum to the absolute identity of nature's imprint but a more advanced exploration of their imbrication that the above citation from Bazin's great essay on Robert Bresson's *Diary of a Country Priest (Journal d'un curé de campagne*, 1951) suggests.[2] A revision of the ontological realism raised in the earlier writings seems here underway, decisively breaking with the medium specificity into which such an "ontology" might slip, and preparing for a more nuanced conception of a dialectic of the image as it emerges from mute visual presence into signification. In this argument the face—the supreme visual entity so heralded in 1920s film theory and practice—is in fact set *against* the pure opticality which Bazin associates with the first cinematic avant-gardes. Sound, voice, language infuse a literary and theatrical but also philosophical charge into the human countenance which now emerges as measure for the dialectic of *imprint* and *text*, of *image* and *sign* in the cinema. Working through Bresson's film, Bazin defines a systemic negation, self-alienation, what I will also call a reticence of the image.[3] The face—turned outside-in, as it were—assumes this dialectic, emerging as a medium through which Bazin projects a new, postclassical cinematic avant-garde.

Echoed here is Alexandre Astruc's call, three years earlier, for "The Birth of a New Avant-Garde: *La Camera-Stylo*," that was to be taken up in the more ambitious reaches of the New Wave.[4] Bazin's own search, in this as in other essays, for a new cinematic consciousness of his time—bound up with a conception of temporality, and of historicity as applied both to the postwar, and to sound cinema's postclassical condition—can be seen as a brilliant elaboration of Astruc's manifesto. This dimension of Bazin's essay thus exceeds a critical account of adaptation, or of a *stylistique* of one particular filmmaker. In this it is more profound than the essay's ostensible conclusion, famously cited by Truffaut in his manifesto against the *cinéma du papà*: "After Robert Bresson, Aurenche and Bost are merely the Viollet-Le-Duc of film adaptation" (WCB, 159). In fact, Bazin's most radical insights peak early in his essay, interlaced with his struggle to describe a *dialectique*—the term recurs—which is, in effect, a *semiological* consciousness at work in the cinematic image. His insights, or premonitions, suggest a consideration of the rhetoric of the image, with a view toward increasing its flexibility as a sign. This semiotic dimension precedes, in principle, the syntactic considerations of montage. Even as the cinematic image is molded of matter as raw and as weighty as flesh, as layered and as overdetermined as the human countenance, an internal dialectic, effecting alienation-within-ontological-identity, yields the possibility of a cinematic *écriture* not unlike that envisioned by Astruc, and more elaborately defined.[5]

Rereading Bazin's essay in this light one is struck by the repeated emphasis on the face as anchor of a dialectical potentiality of the image. Bazin considers how the physique, and the work, of actor and character are registered even as they are contained by the filmmaker's restraining, withholding technique. It is as if, knowing cinema's powers to exploit the rich potentiality of the human figure, Bresson progressed, paradoxically, by limiting, opposing, or attacking it—like some autoimmunological condition. The way in which the self-confining, reticent constitution of the image is poised between the cinematic face and our look is suggested immediately with Bazin's observation of how—in perverse contrast to the concrete, "violently visual" presence of even minor characters in Bernanos' novel—Bresson's adaptation

> . . . is constantly removing them from our view. In place of the novel's concrete power to evoke, the film gives us the constant poverty of an image which hides from view by virtue of the simple fact that it does not develop. (WCB, 141)

Bazin reports how circumstances of the production of *Diary of a Country Priest* forced Bresson to cut out about one third of the film for his final print: a harsh but crucial intervention that will not in and of itself account for his style but that amplifies, firstly, the assertive role of ellipses and litotes that, paradoxically, take the place of Bernanos' textual hyperbole.[6] These figures of reticence are nowhere more potent than when they assault the face, immediately effecting a negative conception of actor, character, and agency, and by implication causality. But how is this worked into the constitution of the image?

Importantly, what Bresson will come to dub "model"—deprived of expressive plenitude, neutral or passive as the term suggests—is not "absorbed" in the film but sustained as one among the elements that make up the work's dialectical machinery (or "mechanism" will be Bazin's term) of consciousness.[7] Such sustained heterogeneity of elements is of a kind with what we find in Bazin's conception of the literary text in adaptation. Here just as in other essays he makes clear that the source text is not to be diffused or "digested" in the film but palpably retain its own existence: that its *literariness* should persist even as it has migrated into a different medium, and even as it may seem to obstruct the machinery of cinema.[8] Source materials, antecedent to the film, enter it in unintegrated form, willfully interfering with the pure-image-in-movement, with the sense of absorption and transparent flow. The resulting "impure cinema" thus evolves in a "dialectic of concrete and abstract" (WCB, 145), which does not hang exclusively on the syntactic and symbolic juxtapositions of montage but can be identified at more primal junctures: the subjugation of even underdeveloped, resilient materials of image or of sound that maintain their prior identity, to the internal dialectics of the shot or segment. We find a close precedent in Astruc's sense of the *caméra-stylo*:

> [Every film] is the site of passage of an implacable logic that works from its one end to the other, or better still of a dialectic. This idea, these significations, to which the silent cinema tried to give rise through symbolic association, we take to exist *in the image itself*, in the unrolling of the film, in each gesture of its characters, in each of their words, in these camera movements that link objects to each other and persons to objects.[9]

Even an actor's gesture, as selected, enframed, reframed by camera movement, as traced in the "unrolling of the film," should be taken as an instance of that dialectical range of relations—already present within the shot—an internal multiplicity that evinces inner tensions, propelling the primal indexical reference to another order: the altered visuality and temporality of cinema.

Alongside such *dialectique*, by which Bazin describes the relationship of parts—the heterogeneous "realist" orders, none of whose founding identities is dissolved in the film—is his term *dépaysement* (QQC, 112) that describes the relationship of the image (shot or part thereof, including sound) to its founding imprint. *Dépaysement* suggests dissociation, defamiliarization, displacement: the disorientation of an exile torn from native land. Bazin follows this up with yet another and more celebrated metaphor: the "grain of sand" (WCB, 145) that grips the mechanism, interfering with the hypothetically transparent, communicative flow of the work. While preparing his case (the following year) "for an impure cinema," this latter metaphor also engages a metonymic figuration of the camera's mechanical and optical functions. Following its logic through, we surmise that already in the basic cinematographic process, those are foreign elements (of the external, profilmic world) that enter the apparatus to partake, by interference, in the constitution of the film. Might not one also associate with this principle of interference the very shadows obstructing the passage of light through camera and then projector, themselves obstructive, negative entities that define the filmic image?

The internal tension of mutually interfering registers, first observed in *Les Dames du Bois de Boulogne* (1945), already suggested to Bazin the ways in which Bresson's flipping of concrete and abstract, opacity and transparency, image and signification, expounds a new cinematic conception prompted by the advent of sound. In that earlier Bresson film, concrete natural sounds—rain, a waterfall, a horse's trot—were propelled as intrusive, indifferent (and in that sense "realist") elements that disturb the script's hermetic neoclassical order of dramatic and verbal artifice, and that resist absorption by conventional, transparent verisimilitude of action or character development. The evident amplification (in the postproduction mixing stage) of sound elements in juxtaposition with post-sync dialogue was to emerge, in fact, as a hallmark of Bresson's method, radicalized in later years. Not only would he consistently avoid direct sound but (as editors and actors would report) even at the recording studio Bresson would also prevent the "meeting" of the actor with her own face, the synthesis of voice, and language, with image.[10] Rather than have her speak out her lines in front of the projected sequence, Bresson would record the actor's voicing of discrete phrases over numerous (at times fifty or more) sound takes and would then further fragment these into parts, later joining words from different takes to recompose dialogue and then lip-match it where necessary. Increasingly, even such simulated matching was of less concern since dialogue would often unfold over scenes in which characters were turned or turning away, or whose faces were otherwise deframed, relegated to off-screen space. Any sense of synthesis of image and language through expressive performance is drained in such a practice, which doubles up the already "automatic" principle of the model's performance. It amplifies the process of *dépaysement*, the self-alienation at work within the shot, among and within its parts: actor/model, performance, image, speech are all fragmented, displaced, defamiliarized, turned against themselves (as it were) in their transmutation from the world and into the film work. The imprints of sound and image are thus grasped as materials at once raw, primal, and resistant, unpliable. They interfere with—even as they ostensibly partake in—the communicative functions of the film, its narrative, discursive, and poetic functions. The work of the actor's face is, likewise, torn, displaced yet sustained as primary material. Even in advance of the juxtapositions of montage and, theoretically, even in advance of particular choices of framing and pacing, any sense of fictional verisimilitude and spatiotemporal flow cracks under the emphatic solidity, the static, unpliable, "undeveloping" impression (or imprint) of the face, as it becomes its own image.

But how to unpack the totality of human presence in the cinema into distinct elements—how can we know the dancer from the dance? Even without hindsight of Bresson's subsequent work, and even in view of an early film that might still be said to incorporate some accented, expressive devices (as in the use of music, lighting, and instances of framing and movement), Bazin diagnoses already in *Diary of a Country Priest* a refusal of psychological realism which interferes with the transparent cohesion of the image. He observes how the radical leveling of different functions of the voice, diegetic or not, affects the relation of image and language, and profoundly alters the sense of the image as such. This is the basis for his intriguing discussion of the face with which we began:

> What we are required to read in the actors' faces is not at all the momentary reflection
> of what they are saying but the essence of being, the mask of destiny. This is why this
> "poorly acted" film makes us feel the absolute necessity of its faces, the obsession of an
> oneiric recollection. The most typical image in this sense is that of Chantal in the
> confessional, dressed in black and withdrawn in shadow. The actress Ladmiral shows us
> only a grey mask, hovering between night and light, rough like a wax seal.
>
> Like Dreyer, Bresson is naturally drawn to the most sensual aspects of the face
> which, to the extent that no acting is involved, is simply a privileged imprint of

existence, the most legible trace of the soul. Nothing about these faces eludes the dignity of the sign. They reveal to us not a psychology but an existential physiognomy. . . . Their features do not change: their inner conflicts and stages of battle with the Angel are not plainly conveyed by their appearance. What we see, rather, is closer to painful concentration, to the incoherent spasms of a reptile moulting or an animal dropping its young. When we speak of Bresson stripping his characters bare, we mean it literally. (WCB, 148–49)[11]

This difficult, powerful passage suggests that cinematographic contingency (as understood in the "Ontology" essay), registered in the fleeting nuance of expression and gesture, is turned over entirely, in Bresson's work, to the absolute "dignity of the sign." What might have been imprinted on film is turned over to an order of images that renders it permanent, necessary, legible (thus "dignified"). Namely, Bazin no longer conceives of the image here as an objective imprint; nor is it a representation of whatever motivating forces, or causes, might underlie such objects—say, those shifting "inner conflicts" that might affect the actor's face. These are not the signs of character psychology or intention captured thereon, but something more permanent, approached in a crystallizing process of reduction. Bresson's faces thus come into being in a painful negation, a withdrawal of the model's original plenitude or flow (as "person"), and by assuming the mask of the filmic image. This metamorphosis is not a lucid formal process or a sublimating abstraction, but a spasmodic self-alienation by which the subject splits, sheds, gives off part of itself in the most intensified realization of its being, but which is also its own annihilation—hence the metaphors of birthing and molting, as if nothing less than large muscular contractions or a flaying of the skin, a disgorging, inside-out spasmodic convulsion would yield "interiority." Inner being is "stripped bare" as physiognomic disarticulation, giving birth to the cinematic face by engaging the body and, more importantly the *film's* body, its cinematic system, the image as a whole. All this is achieved, paradoxically, from within the withdrawn, ascetic disposition of Bresson's models. Perhaps it is this paradox that prompts Bazin's observation that Bresson's faces command and haunt us like an "oneiric recollection"—ghosts from the past that return to possess the viewer in the different time, and place, of the film's projection.

Just as Bresson's use of post-synchronization disintegrates the actor's performance—paring off, like an onion, his or her very being—so the dialectical *dépaysement* of the (facial) image undoes the causal, referential chains that cinema readily draws between character, motivation, gesture or action, between identity and optical surface, between inside and out. This breakdown of the passage from motivating source (object) to reference opens up a new order of signification. The productive dialectic between the face's visuality and its textuality surpasses the mute index and achieves consciousness—not as what we would call "signified," and certainly not as direct reference, but as a cumulative, and deferred, temporal effect of the film.[12]

In its original *Cahiers du Cinéma* publication, this difficult area of Bazin's essay is illustrated with a production still [figure 15.1]: Claude Laydu's profile in close-up, eyes lowered, occupies the left side of the frame, his illuminated countenance set against the darkness of the confessional wherein Nicole Ladmiral's head, facing forth and looking down at him, is situated slightly higher and more receded in center frame, her complexion grayer by comparison. Both profile and frontal faces appear somewhat disembodied (even more so in the still as published than in the actual film as shot) since the left side of the frame slices off Laydu's hair, while the

« ...J'avais devant moi maintenant un visage étrange, défiguré non par la peur mais par une panique
plus profonde, plus intérieure... A ce moment il s'est passé une chose singulière... Tandis que je fixais
ce trou d'ombre où, même en plein jour, il m'est difficile de reconnaître un visage, celui de
Mademoiselle Chantal a commencé d'apparaître peu à peu, par degrés. L'image se tenait là sous mes
yeux dans une sorte d'instabilité merveilleuse, et je restais immobile comme si le moindre geste
eut dû l'effacer ». Georges Bernanos, « Le Journal d'un Curé de Campagne », page 166.

FIGURE 15.1: from *Cahiers du Cinéma* 3 (June 1951)

girl's clothes and hair blend into the enveloping darkness, leaving her face to float therein. And
so, under this production still, runs the caption drawn from Bernanos' novel:

> ... I had before me now a strange face, disfigured not by fear but by a more profound,
> more internal panic. ... At that moment a peculiar thing happened. ... While I was
> staring into that hole of shadows where, even in broad daylight, I can barely recognize a
> face, that of Mademoiselle Chantal began to appear, bit by bit, by degrees. The image
> was suspended there, under my gaze, in a sort of marvelous instability, and I stayed
> immobile for fear that the slightest gesture would have effaced it.[13]

Considered alongside the particular choice of still, and placed close by Bazin's complex discussion, this quasi-Proustian passage evokes, indeed, some sense of tense reciprocity of concrete
and abstract, substantiality and apparition in the play of light and dark, movement and stillness, visibility and withdrawal. Yet when we turn to Bernanos' original passage we find that it
does not really correspond to the blocking of figures and faces in this image: the fact of Chantal
being on her knees is emphasized twice over in the novel, while in the still she looks from an
upper and almost hieratic frontal view—in blatant reversal of the conventional positioning of
persons in a confession—at the priest who, in lowered profile, seems not to be looking outward
at all (again, this runs against Bernanos' description) but appears engrossed in contemplation.
We might consider, in any case, that a first-person narrator is not likely to describe directly his
own spatial disposition but let it (if at all) only be inferred. The juxtaposition, in the still, of

frontal and profile, looking and listening, address and withdrawal, might have suggested to Bazin the gray wax seal or mask—the static, blatant presentness of Chantal—a mode of the face that flips over to (and is in a sense interiorized by) the marked *linearity* of the profile that articulates the "writerly" world of priest/narrator/journal-keeper.[14] This is the dialectic of mute carnal imprint and textual, readable sign.

If we now follow Bazin's thesis on the continued autonomy, the *presence*, of the novel in Bresson's adaptation—which so radically foregrounds its own linear textuality in both verbal delivery style as in the punctuation of actual scenes of writing—we might conjecture that even as he is "living" or "acting" the scene remembered and described in his diary, the priest, looking downward, appears to be *listening*, rather than *seeing* it (this against Bernanos' emphasis on the intensity, the primacy of the look in this encounter). Moreover, it is as if, even as he listens, the priest is *already* engaged in the writing down of the event. One might see connoted here—and amplified by Chantal's almost androgynous face and enigmatic expression hovering over the writer—the pictorial trope of the angel dictating to the Evangelist.[15] The scene as focalized through the production still, wherein the human countenance would seem to command our view emerges, then, simultaneously as a scene of writing: its textuality overhauling its resplendent visuality. Indeed its very temporality—conflating the pastness of the "event," the distinct (second) pastness of its diary-writing, and the complex sense of their colliding *presentness* in the cinematic image—is, in its profound multiplicity and self-division, *anachronistic*. Its colliding temporalities, its constitution as a scene of writing that intrudes upon the salience of faces, and its overall textual emergence, render it a dialectical image indeed.[16]

Bazin's sense of a dialectic inflecting the constitution of the cinematic image—an image that ruptures under the pressure of language, and in a synesthetic slippage from seeing to reading, from visuality to textuality—may be informed, as well, by Bazin's reading of Bernanos. In the selected passage from the novel the experience of seeing is in fact (as Bazin had earlier observed) most vivid. Yet one notes that it too is already inflected by a sense of reticence, for Chantal's face is said to emerge as a miraculous apparition in the confessional's "hole of shadows"—an almost infernal space by this epithet, an area not normally available to sight and where the face-to-face should be elided. In fact, what seems conveyed in the Bernanos passage cited by Bazin is an image *in process of* transformation: a face in the process of effacement, just as its meaning, its fundamental identity, emerges in the priest's understanding. Without indulging in ekphrastic elaboration of physiognomic and expressive features or gestures, the passage describes Chantal's face *as if it were already an image*, but an inherently unstable one, suspended between visibility and effacement and before which, therefore, the priest must himself remain immobile, since it appears almost as an apparition, an ephemeral projection. Such disposition of the immobile viewer before an intensely temporalized image as described by Bernanos would surely connote for someone like Bazin the experience of a spectator transfixed in the movie theater. Its defining feature by his account is its reticence, its withdrawal, the negative features bound up with its productive (if convulsive) contraction *as* sign. This is not the mythical plenitude of the solid imprint, nor strictly an experience fully contained in the spatial, formal dimension of the visual. Rather, it is an image born into consciousness and language; compounding temporalities and thereby representational strata, it is capable of delivering us *elsewhere*, quite exceeding the singular instance of its material formation and its referential dimensions.[17]

Bazin is defining, then, a dialectic of brute, mute visuality of the face and its own negation in the face's textuality: its readability, and writability. This, in his terms, is the simultaneous, continued interference of

> two kinds of pure reality. On the one hand, as we have seen, the actors' faces are stripped of all expressive interpretation and reduced to their epidermis, surrounded by a nature free of artifice. On the other hand lies what we would have to describe as the reality of the writing. (WCB, 151)

The reduced "epidermis" of uncoded, raw material equivalent to the cinematographic support of the image undergoes finally, in Bazin's interpretation of Bresson, a quasi-allegorical trajectory in the particular case of *Diary of a Country Priest*, since the image recedes, with the film's unfolding, before a different "reality" of signs: the Letter, the Word, the Cross. *En abîme*, we witness it within the very sequence with which we have been concerned, whose decisive instant, triggered by the priest's demand, is surely the passage by camera movement from Chantal's face, eventually isolated in close-up, down through the darkness enveloping her body, to her illuminated hand at her pocket, from which she produces a letter. Might we not see this movement through darkness as figuring the passage, explored herewith, from imprint to sign, from the Face to the Letter, embedded in the work of cinema? And is not such passage, navigating between the visible and the invisible in the emergence of identity, intimated in our very concept of *character* and its etymological layering: at once the agency of an inscription and its result?

Georges Didi-Huberman dwells on such duality in cult images as they articulate divine character: the contact-imprint of the face of God is bound up with its necessary withdrawal, or indeed effacement, that would yield the aura. Yet the aura becomes independent of visual plenitude and (as Benjamin emphasized), predicated on distance or withdrawal from view.[18] Though Bresson would appear, temperamentally, quite removed from ritualistic investment in cult images, for Bazin, of course, such objects as the mummy, the death mask, or the Shroud of Turin have already served as privileged figures for the photographic/cinematographic image's claim to identity and presence—themselves independent of mimetic values. With the lesson of Bressonian reticence, however, such "ontological" basis no longer suffices for a discussion of cinema, as the image is self-alienated, trespasses identity (and mimesis), and is set in a productive dialectic with its other: the pure sign, the mark of absence. The sign does not index some individual, singular interiority behind the mutable face, does not articulate the contingent, indexical immediacy of the imprint but rather, Bazin will conclude, points toward an altogether different, more permanent identity, perched beyond absence, opening onto an order of signs always mediated, always deferred.[19]

But Bazin is no structuralist semiotician, and his reading of the transfiguration of the image into sign unfolds as a theology: the radical exteriorizing of meaning that defeats the visible in mystical darkness–or light. At the conclusion of such movement "the image could have said nothing more" (WCB, 156); its last visible trace is the simple black cross on the white screen: the bare, iconoclastic sign that remains after the Deposition of the body, and after the Assumption of its image. Born, like a mythological being, of the convulsive, brute matter of the world, and emerging into the "dignity of signs"—if only to be consumed and negated by such theophanic light of meaning—the image, one surmises, would yet traverse a historical destiny before satisfying Bazin's continued question, What Is Cinema?

Notes

1. I am using Timothy Barnard's translation of André Bazin's "*Diary of a Country Priest* and the Robert Bresson Style," in *What Is Cinema?* (Montreal: Caboose, 2009), 139–59; in this instance, 148–49. It will henceforth be cited as WCB. However, where Barnard's translation departs from Bazin's terminology on concepts that recur in my discussion, I have taken the liberty to alter them. Bazin's essay originally appeared as "*Le Journal d'un curé de campagne* et la stylistique de Robert Bresson," *Cahiers du Cinéma*, 3 (June 1951), 7–21; it was reprinted with some revisions in *Qu'est-ce que le cinéma?* (Paris: Editions du Cerf, 1975), 107–27. It will henceforth be cited parenthetically as QQC. I have also consulted Hugh Gray's translation in *What Is Cinema?* vol. 1 (Berkeley: University of California Press, 1967), 125–43.

2. See Dudley Andrew's discussion of the essay and the startling, belated addition of its freestanding, closing statement, in his "Foreward to the 2004 Edition," of *What Is Cinema?* vol. 1, trans. Hugh Gray, xiv.

3. I discuss the reticence of the image, with autistic perception as my model and Bresson as a privileged instance, in my essay "Of the Face, In Reticence," in *A Museum without Walls? Film, Art, New Media*, ed. Angela Dalle Vacche (Palgrave/MacMillan, forthcoming).

4. Alexandre Astruc, "Naissance d'une nouvelle avant-garde, la caméra-stylo," *Écran français*, 144 (March 30, 1948), translated in *The New Wave: Critical Landmarks*, ed. Peter Graham and Ginette Vincendeau (London: BFI, 2009). See Bazin's use of this concept e.g., "Découverte du cinéma: Défense de L'avant-garde" *Écran français*, 182 (December 21, 1948); "A la recherche d'une nouvelle avant-garde," *Almanach du théâtre et du cinéma* (1950), 146–52; "L'avant-garde nouvelle," *Cahiers du Cinéma*, 10 (March 1952), 16–17.

5. Bazin attends to such "conflict at the very heart of identification" as the privileged zone of consciousness that theatricality may affect in "Theater and Cinema—Part Two," in *What Is Cinema?* vol. 1, trans. Hugh Gray, 113.

6. In this formulation I am drawing also on Bazin's "Pour un cinéma impur" of 1952, where he observes how Bresson converts Bernanos' "violence of the text. The real equivalent of the hyperbole of Bernanos lay in the ellipsis and litotes of Robert Bresson's editing." Bazin, "In Defense of Mixed Cinema," in *What Is Cinema?* vol. 1, trans. Hugh Gray, 68. I have not verified if the reputed cut of some forty-five minutes of the film took place in the script or editing stage; I depend rather on Bazin's report.

7. Bresson's epithet "model" for actor was formulated later, though Bazin himself intimates something of it already here, through the vocal monotone of delivery and reduced psychological expressivity of the face. In a review of *A Man Escaped* (*Un Condamné au mort s'est échappé*, 1956), Bazin may have suggested the notion of "modeling" to Bresson, who would associate it with his experience as painter: ". . . he literally drains his actors to the point of emptying them of all expressive will. Then he shapes them [*les modèle*] as he wants and extracts from them their extraordinary melody beyond any simulacra of performance and acting." Bazin, "*Un condamné à mort s'est échappé*," *Education nationale*, 32 (November 22, 1956). Editor's translation.

8. The most significant among these being perhaps "L'Adaptation ou le cinéma comme digeste," *Esprit*, 146 (July 1948), 32–40, translated in *Film Adaptation*, ed. James Naremore (New Brunswick, NJ: Rutgers University Press, 2000), and "Pour un cinéma impur" (1952). On this subject see Dudley Andrew, "Private Scribblings: The Crux in the Margins around *Diary of a Country Priest*," in *Film in the Aura of Art* (Princeton, NJ: Princeton University Press, 1986), 112–30. On related issues see also Ivone Margulies, *infra*.

9. Astruc, "Naissance d'une nouvelle avant-garde, la caméra-stylo." My translation and emphasis.

10. Concerning post-sync in his later productions, see accounts by Bresson's crew in *Il caso e la necessità: il cinema di Robert Bresson*, ed. Giovenni Spagnoletti and Sergio Toffetti (Turin: Lindau, 1998). Included are remarks by Jacques Kébadian, assistant director on *Au hasard, Balthazar*, and *Mouchette*, 157–59; Jean-François Naudon, assistant editor on *Lancelot du lac* and editor of *L'Argent*, 169–74; and Dominique Sanda, who plays the protagonist of *Une Femme douce*, 179–84.

11. Among my few adjustments to Barnard's translation, here is the reinsertion of Bazin's words, translating "l'obsession d'un souvenir onirique"; these are in the original *Cahiers* version of the essay, but not in its reprint in *Qu'est-ce que le cinéma?*

12. Bazin describes Bresson's film as an obverse reflection of Dreyer's: the *Diary*, he says, is like a silent film with spoken titles (WCB, 153) while *The Passion of Joan of Arc* (1928) was already, virtually, a talkie—so Bazin will observe in "*La Passion de Jeanne d'Arc*: Ames et visages," *Radio, Cinéma, Télévision*, 112 (March 9, 1952), 3. In the Bresson essay Bazin performs his own graphic-editorial gesture in having a production still from *Diary*, discussed in detail below, mirror on the facing page a still from Dreyer's *Joan of Arc*.

13. Bazin, "*Le Journal d'un curé de campagne* et la stylistique de Robert Bresson," *Cahiers du Cinéma*, 3 (June 1951), 14; caption to the production still. My translation, based in part on that of Pamela Morris in Georges Bernanos, *The Diary of a Country Priest* (New York: MacMillan, 1937), 133–34. The ellipses are Bazin's, in his meticulous "edit" of Bernanos' original, *cf. Journal d'un curé de campagne*, 1936, rpt. (Plon, 1961), 141–42.

14. On the opposed connotations of the still frontal face versus the active profile view (as in the frontal address of a saint versus the profile of a kneeling donor), see Meyer Schapiro, *Words and Pictures: On the Literal and the Symbolic in the Illustration of a Text* (The Hague and Paris: Mouton, 1973), esp. 37–49.

15. See Jean Bourdichon's folio of *St. Matthew Writing* in *The Great Hours commissioned of Anne of Brittany* (1503–1508, at the Bibliothèque nationale). See also Caravaggio's several renderings (1602) of *St. Matthew and the Angel* at San Luigi dei Francesi (Rome).

16. Though he would not have been familiar with Walter Benjamin's concept from the unfinished *Arcades Project*, Bazin's use of *dialectique* in an essay deeply engaged with image and language could send us in this direction. See Dall'Asta *infra*. On Benjamin's concept, see Eli Friedlander, "The Measure of the Contingent: Walter Benjamin's Dialectical Image," *Boundary 2*, 35:3 (2008), 1–26; On the cinematic sense of visual memory and the temporality of the journal form, see P. Adams Sitney, "The Rhetoric of Robert Bresson" (1975) and "Cinematography vs. the Cinema: Bresson's Figures" (1989), reprinted in *Robert Bresson*, ed. James Quandt (Toronto: Cinematheque Ontario Monographs no. 2, 1998), 117–43, 145–63 respectively.

17. The suspension of the face between visuality and textuality is echoed again in a Bernanos passage omitted in Bazin's quotation: the priest considers the supreme *semiotic* condition of the face in light of the disfiguration of the "mask of agony" that he had heard physicians attribute to their suffering patients, which he weighs vis-à-vis Chantal's spiritual "panic."

18. On "imprint" as primal image-matrix, carrying both ritualistic and juridical functions and underlying facial resemblance that precedes representational mediations, see Georges Didi-Huberman, *Devant le temps: Histoire de l'art et anachronisme des images* (Paris: Minuit, 2000), especially "L'Image-matrice: Histoire de l'art et généalogie de la ressemblance," 59–83, and the exhibition catalog *L'Empreinte* (Paris: Centre Georges Pompidou, 1997). Jean-Michel Frodon, "Cinema and Plaster," *infra*. references this work in detail. For Didi-Huberman's analysis of *character* see his *Confronting Images: Questioning the Ends of a Certain History of Art*, trans. John Goodman (University Park: Pennsylvania State University Press, 2005), 191–92. "For the 'true' *portrait*—true through its contact, a truth not apparent through its appearances—required the implementation of its *withdrawal*, according to a dialectic that Walter Benjamin doubtless would have called the 'aura.'"

19. Bresson's transformation of narrative action from accident into necessity has a parallel in Bazin's interpretation of the metamorphosis of cinematographic contingency into the "dignity of signs."

16

Animals

An Adventure in Bazin's Ontology

SEUNG-HOON JEONG

Bazin once attempted to bring a parrot from Brazil to France. As it was contraband in his psittacosis-phobic country, this animal lover's anxiety continued all through his trans-Atlantic journey until an unexpected happy ending; the customs official paid no attention to his pet, "*Coco est français.*"[1] This lovely anecdote is entitled "De la difficulté d'être coco" ("About the difficulty of being Coco") and not 'of *bringing*' Coco, that is, it is about Coco's *becoming* French, a socio-ontological shift from a potential terrorist carrying a virus to a legitimate family member [figure 16.1]. It is no surprise that Bazin instinctively detected animals on screen since his attitude toward film seems inseparable from his attitude toward animals. Why not trace his reviews of animal films—whether fiction, semi-fiction, or documentary—so as to see how the animal appears to him as man's ontological other. Animals can nudge us to rethink his core cinematic vision.

Though few in number, certain of his film reviews are noteworthy in relation to the Coco story. Bazin wrote twice on Gianni Franciolini's *Hello Elephant* (1952), a fantasy-neorealist film, rather like De Sica's *Miracle in Milan* (1951) to which he compares it. *Hello Elephant* concerns a poor teacher forced to abandon a baby elephant that he received from an Indian prince.[2] Remarkable is a scene present only in the script (which Bazin had obtained), in which the elephant runs through the streets to rejoin the teacher marching in a strike for higher salaries; this climax was, Bazin assumes, either never shot or censored. The elephant, a pure gift from the prince, is rejected by the community, only to return as both invader and ally of the minority within the community. Like a "white elephant in your room,"[3] the society must decide whether this gift, either hospitable or hostile, and in any case unwanted and difficult to dispose of, should be authorized or ostracized. The animal thus stands for a deprived class or abandoned individual. Bazin recognized such solidarity between alienated men and animals elsewhere, most memorably in another De Sica film, *Umberto D.* (1952): "The cinema has rarely gone such a long way toward making us aware of what it is to be a man. (And also, for that matter, of what it is to be a dog.)"[4]

In the fiction films just mentioned Bazin writes about animals in the context of social ontology; but when he turns to semi-fictional or semi-documentary films featuring animals, it

CAHIERS DU CINÉMA

91 · ANDRÉ BAZIN · 91

FIGURE 16.1: André, Janine, and Coco

is cinema's aesthetic ontology they help him uncover. The famous question they inevitably raise concerns spatial unity in genres that are at once real and imaginary. In Albert Lamorisse's *White Mane* (*Crin Blanc*, 1953), "Crin Blanc is at one and the same time a real horse that grazes on the salty grass of the Camargue and a dream horse swimming eternally at the side of little

Folco."[5] The ploy of using several horses for one horse-character is permitted in a film operating as a real-imaginary chiasmus. Prefiguring the psychoanalytic principle of fetishist disavowal, Bazin writes: "If the film is to fulfill itself aesthetically we need to believe in the reality of what is happening while knowing it to be tricked."[6] What matters is neither the diegetic representation of the animal nor its real existence as such, but the dialectic between diegetic representation and nondiegetic enunciation (on the director's side), and between a belief in the imaginary and an understanding of the illusion (on the viewer's side).

Why animals, then? Because in trying to anthropomorphize animals, Bazin notices the most muscular use of montage effects, finding that this process shatters cinema's natural realism. Montage elicits the illusion of animals' humanized actions and builds a symbolism of human animals when it forcibly joins shots of widely varying kinds. Too often only the manipulation of screen effects matters when spatial and temporal continuity is sacrificed. Hence Bazin's famous prohibition against montage: "When the essence of a scene demands the simultaneous presence of two or more factors in the action, montage is ruled out."[7] The genuine suspense in Harry Watt's *Where No Vultures Fly* (1951) emerges with parents, child, and lioness all in the same full shot. The same holds true for Nanook's seal hunt and Chaplin's lion's cage.[8]

However, this aesthetic credo does not rule out all types of cutting. If montage "tricks the film" by deceiving the spectator, *découpage*—the script or planning for spatiotemporal unity— "films the trick" by allowing the spectator to invest belief over knowledge, as the aforementioned principle: "I know, but all the same (I believe in this illusion as real)." Conversely, montage versus *découpage* opposes the illusion that exists only on screen and the illusion that sends us back to reality. Hervé Joubert-Laurencin rephrases this opposition as manipulation versus prestidigitation, manufacture versus artisanship.[9] Regarding *La Course de taureaux* (*Bullfight*, 1951), Bazin sees the editor's artistic fingers as fulfilling "both the physical verisimilitude of *découpage* and its logical malleability."

> The linkage of two bulls in a single movement does not symbolize the bulls' strength; it surreptitiously replaces the photo of the nonexistent bull we believe we are seeing. The editor makes sense of her editing just as the director of his découpage, based solely on this kind of realism.[10]

Likewise, he approves of *The Great Adventure* (1953) which achieves "a true aesthetic of animal films" by linking shots that have been carefully thought out according to the actual locations and movements of foxes and otters. To capture their presence, the director simply exercised enormous patience instead of controlling or directing the creatures; they were "no longer tamed but familiarized."[11] It is not montage but *découpage* that respects and preserves the ontological otherness and the presence of animals. Thus Bazin's ontology of the photographic image evolves into the ontology of cinematic *découpage*.[12]

Such ontological realism enables an animal documentary to become a semi-fiction that claims to represent genuine emotions within an animal family or community. In this regard, Bazin's substantial article on the Disney film *Perri* (1957) involves a more complex dialectics of documentary and fiction.[13] First, as a documentary of a real squirrel's life, it follows the shift just mentioned from willful montage to carefully observant *découpage*, and thus contributes to the evolution "from comic animation films based on burlesque synchronism to sentimental realism and its [virtual] animation."[14] Second, *Perri's* realism is paradoxically based on the logic of simulacrum, because "natural Disney" recopies "animated Disney" who only searches in nature for what resembles his drawings. For Disney, "It is not the cinema that attributes human behavior to animals, but rather the animals themselves acting before the camera according to predeterminations that preside over a dramatic sequence."[15] Third, this simulation of animation by nature mingles with actual animated sequences in some scenes. "The animated characters are not introduced or inserted into the photographic background alongside the real characters; they *become* real or return to the drawing, along with a back-and-forth that supposes a reciprocity and ambiguity integral to this universe."[16] Now the animal appears like an amalgam not only of the real and imaginary, documentary and fiction, but also of actual and animated documentaries, which is the same as actual and animated fictions.

In other words, the ontological other within the *filmed* diegesis becomes an ontological hybrid at the level of the *filming* enunciation; the animal penetrates different modes of the cinematic image and joins together their differences. Because of its hybrid identity, this potential of "becoming" seems to enable the animal film to reach an ideal of anthropomorphism far beyond the kind of clichéd illusions that it easily achieves through montage. Bazin points out, for instance, not just an objective shot of genuine drama in nature (a beaver and a squirrel on the tree in the same shot) but also the squirrel's subjective shot (we see the beaver climbing up the tree with the squirrel's tail in the foreground, indicating his position at the place of the camera). This "*découpage* in depth" amounts to the "free indirect discourse" that Pasolini and Deleuze would postulate in shots of this sort. As an effect, the human spectator can be inside an animal's consciousness.[17]

At this point *La Course de taureaux* draws our attention again; its apparently objective shots cause highly subjective reactions in spectators because of the repetitive staging of its "metaphysical kernel: death." Like the sexual act (which Bazin reminds us is called "the little death"), death is "the absolute negation of objective time, the qualitative instant in its purest form."[18] Clearly, both Eros and Thanatos bring us face to face with our other; in this film man experiences death indirectly as an ontological shift via an encounter with an animal. This is reinforced when we witness the death of the bull, who mutates before our eyes into the same ontological state to which we ourselves are inevitably heading. What counts in Braunberger's *La Course de taureaux* is not the kind of sympathetic becoming-other operating in semi-fictional films, but the sheer encounter with an antagonistic other and furthermore with the indifferent environment out of which it appears and into which all living beings will dissolve. Taking the torero's position, we the audience are invited into, and then immersed within, this arena as ontological battleground. Spectatorship turns from fetishism into participation.

Not coincidentally, some documentaries of adventure are shot by directors who are the subjects within the (diegetic) surroundings that they film. A couple of these semi-documentary films suggest that their director is repositioned as character. Flaherty's *Louisiana Story* (1948) fascinated Bazin not only because "an alligator catches a heron" but also because of "the silence of an invisibly populated marsh." In the first case, two oppositional others are pictured in an objective shot; in the second, the director's subjective involvement is implied in the spatial whole, where two ontological others, the human and the animal multitude, coexist.[19] The former encourages the aesthetic ontology of visible *découpage*; the latter leads to an existential ontology open to the invisible and the unpredictable. Although this film, no less than a Disney story, depicts a child's reunion with his animal friend, Bazin sees something more profound in Flaherty, whose "cinema [reveals] the glory of nature and of the men who wrestle with it like Jacob with the Angel."[20] This angel is precisely an invisible ontological other. When Bazin cleverly mocks *Naked Amazon* (1954) for being "a bit too clothed," these clothes are nothing other than an overbearing design.[21] Scenes such as an anaconda attacking a blonde woman or her struggle against ferocious crocodiles lose their potential horror effect because they are so patently preplanned that the film crew can be felt hovering nearby, ready to intervene. In this sensationalist semi-romantic documentary, animal otherness becomes a target for (abusive) visual exploitation.

An exemplary case from Bazin's perspective is Jacques-Yves Cousteau's and Louis Malle's *The Silent World* (1956). This genuine documentary of the deep sea includes three types of shots that Bazin carefully distinguishes: (1) an objective two-shot of a shark attacking a whale, the latter being a fellow mammal with which the spectator may feel sympathy; (2) self-reflexive shots of the shooting equipment and of the cameraman who is the subject of filmic enunciation descending into the closed diegetic space of the ocean; and (3) subjective shots of the sea as a whole, in effect the Real as the matrix of life that includes invisible others:

> . . . mysterious and invisible nebulae of plankton reflect in the echo of the radar. Out of this life form we are merely one more grain abandoned with others upon the ocean beach. Man, say biologists, is a marine animal who carries the sea in his interior. Nothing surprising, therefore, that diving should give him without doubt the latent feeling of a return to origins.[22]

As the animal here takes the molecular form of plankton, this "return to origins" can be viewed as "becoming-animal" in the Deleuzian sense of "becoming multiple, imperceptible, clandestine" until reaching the ontological "plane of immanence." This becoming-other in (3) goes beyond identifying with a visible entity or unified organism as in (1); it deterritorializes our subjectivity into a fundamental intersubjectivity or a-subjectivity that has always already been roiling within us. But this encounter with, or incorporation into, the Real can be experienced by the audience only through the persistent filming subject on the verge of losing his life. So (2) actually indicates the focus of Bazin's ultimate question: What Is Cinema?

Reviewing several related adventure films, Bazin pursues his own critical adventure beyond animals, but as though driven by them. He repudiated *Scott of the Antarctic* (1948), a studio work, because it is futile "to imitate the inimitable, to reconstruct that which of its very nature can only occur once, namely risk, adventure, death."[23] Its deceptive montage deprives Scott's unique adventure of its spatiotemporal aura. Knowing that it was shot not in the Antarctic but rather the Alps must frustrate the viewer's investment of belief, in a way that does not occur in *White Mane* and *Course de taureaux* where knowing the trick does not break our belief in the real.

Bazin's comparison between *Greenland* (1949) and *Kon-Tiki* (1950) is crucial in this regard: one is constructed via a perfect montage of disparate shots, while the other shows "almost nothing"[24] but does so in spatiotemporal continuity; the first looks like "the exhaustive and ideal testimony, the automatic copy, of the event," while the other can only be "the partial testimony [which] out of necessity represents its object only very weakly."[25] However,

Greenland's glossy appearance betrays such fastidious preparation that the excitement of a genuine encounter with the landscape (and any serious risk) is undercut; whereas, *Kon-Tiki* is unpredictable from beginning to end, as Thor Heyerdahl's amateur filmmaking is integral to an adventure that truly reenacts the hypothetic migration of ancient Peruvians to Polynesia. Far from grooming nature to play the background in a drama of human heroism, the 16mm camera serves as objective witness to danger in a way that is inseparable from the cameraman's (and spectator's) subjective participation in it. At the limit, recording this voyage is so difficult that "the cinema," Daney says, "becomes a reality and then annuls itself, becomes itself the impossible."[26] For Bazin, in this sense, "*Kon-Tiki* is the most beautiful of films, but it doesn't exist."

> How much more moving is this flotsam, snatched from the tempest, than would have been the faultless and complete report offered by an organized film, for it remains true that this film is not made up only of what we see—its faults are equally witness to its authenticity. The missing documents are the negative imprints of the expedition—its inscription chiseled deep.[27]

The screen shows only "the remains of an unfinished creation about which one hardly dares to dream." And yet it is "in the insufficiency of its form" that the cinema preserves "the subjective authenticity, the moral quality of adventure."[28] We invest our belief not merely in what is present but in what is absent. Bazinian indexicality can thus be readdressed. The cinematic image is not simply the trace of fullness, but "the imperfect, always already punctured trace of an ambiguous world."[29] It is an index not just of a "gain in reality," but of a "loss of reality"; an index of what should have been represented but couldn't be. An index of its own failure, let's call it a "para-index," indicating the absence of something beside it, something beyond its visualization. No longer an index-record of the visible, *Kon-Tiki* shows the operation of the para-index indicating the invisible [figure 16.2]. When Bazin says that the cameramen of *Annapurna* (1953) look like "mummies," his metaphor does not refer to their fixed presence, but rather to the unrepresentable experience of an avalanche that snatched their camera away, the experience of the Real that made their faces frozen in trauma.[30] Nevertheless, only through failed indexicality can the film still lead us to what is missing. So, regarding these cameramen and others who cannot deliver the goods, we should "excuse them for having returned" from the Real without jumping into death.[31]

So, where, after all, is the animal? Bazin permits us to understand that it appears on the threshold between the seen and the unseen, between positive and negative imprints, between subjectivity and nothingness.

> When an exciting moment arrives, say a whale hurling itself at the raft, the footage is so short that you have to process it ten times over in the optical printer before you can even spot what is happening.... The image is almost illegible.... This marvelous film exists all in all only in the form of a wreck.[32]

"Blowing up" this photographic image à la Antonioni would only confirm the "para-indexicality" that indicates the "para-ontological" state of the animal. The whale is part of the sea, apparent without appearing, like the "phasmid," that stick insect Georges Didi-Huberman

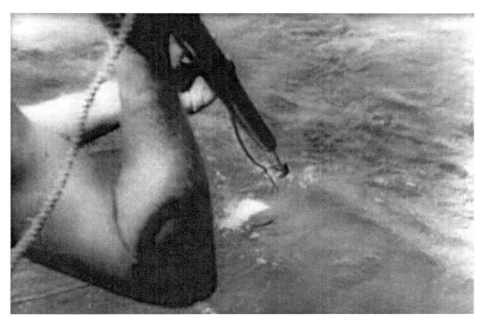

FIGURE 16.2: Invisible animal (*Kon-Tiki*, 1952)

describes whose body perfectly resembles twigs or leaves so as to incorporate rather than imitate its environment.[33] Bazin was drawn to the indifferent Real and observed forms that come out of and return to it, like the invisible plankton. He grows lyrical in characterizing "sharks, giant sea breams, flying fishes, and whales [which] . . . in a cool place in the shadow of the balsa floor . . . never broke this pact of Eden."[34] And yet, the giant basking killer whale is formidable: "A stroke of its tail and we would go down with the camera to the bottom of 6,000 or 7,000 meters."[35] This animal as phasmid, whose etymology implies "phantasm" and "apparition," can in a trice mutate into a dangerous beast, sweeping us into the abyss that effaces all ontological boundaries.

We can now rewrite Bazin. First, he would rule out montage, not just in the depiction of the phenomenological copresence of two visible objects, but also in the representation of the ontological copresence of a filming subject and an invisible object. Second, he would insist that heterogeneity lies not only in the visual field, but more fundamentally on the boundary between visible reality and the invisible Real. Indeed, "that obscure object" that fascinates him is nothing but the Lacanian *objet a* that lurks below the Real and suddenly attacks, thwarting the subject's mise-en-scène and drawing him into the mise en abyme of sublime depth and more sublime death. Daney reads Bazin through this Lacanian lens: "Whoever passes through the screen and meets reality on the other side has gone beyond *jouissance*. . . . The screen, the skin, the celluloid, the surface of the pan, exposed to the fire of the real and on which is going to be inscribed— metaphorically and figuratively—everything that could burst them."[36] He compares this flimsy screen to the Derridean "hymen," the virgin's membrane, which when ripped institutes marriage, the fusion of two others; thus, sexual orgasm stands as the little death of one's unity. Daney pursues the analogy: "The trip switch is therefore the death of the filmmaker. . . . You have to go to the point of dying for your images."[37] The greatest *jouissance* would come not from the death of an animal or a man within a film, but from that of the "man with a movie camera." Yet since "the representation of a real death"—whether of the bull or the bullfighter—is the "obscenity of the cinematic image,"[38] Bazin not only stood ready to accept cinema's failure to capture the ultimately invisible animal but he also gladly accepted the failed representation of the director's potential death as at the ontological core of cinema. In sum, the entirety of Bazin's reflections on animals could well be titled "De la difficulté d'être cinéma."[39]

Notes

1. André Bazin, "De la difficulté d'être Coco," *Cahiers du Cinéma*, 91 (January 1959), 57.
2. Bazin, *"Bonjour, Eléphant!" France observateur*, 186 (December 3, 1953), and *"Bonjour, Eléphant!*: On a souvent besoin d'un plus gros que soi," *Parisien libéré*, 2866 (December 1, 1953).
3. Werner Herzog used this phrase in *Grizzly Man*; see Seung-hoon Jeong and Dudley Andrew, "Grizzly Ghost: Herzog, Bazin, and the Cinematic Animal," *Screen*, Spring 2008.
4. Bazin, "De Sica: Metteur en Scène," in *What Is Cinema?* vol. 2, trans. Hugh Gray (Berkeley: University of California Press, 1971), 78.
5. Bazin, "The Virtues and Limitations of Montage," in *What Is Cinema?* trans. Hugh Gray (Berkeley: University of California Press, 1967), 47.
6. Ibid, 48. *Cf.* "Montage interdit," *Qu'est-ce que le cinéma?* (Paris: Cerf, 1981) 56.
7. Ibid, 50. *Cf.* "Montage interdit," 59.
8. Serge Daney captures a paradox of Bazin's law: "A cinema seeking continuity and transparency at all costs is identical to a cinema that dreams of filming discontinuity and difference as such." Daney, "The Screen of Fantasy: Bazin and Animals," in *Rites of Realism: Essays on Corporeal Cinema*, ed. Ivone Margulies (Duke University Press, 2003), 33.
9. Hervé Joubert-Laurencin, "Une lettre en souffrance: Post-scriptum à 'Montage interdit' d'André Bazin," in *La Lettre volante: quatre essais sur le cinéma d'animation* (Paris: Presses de la Sorbonne nouvelle, 1997), 15–34.
10. Bazin, "Death Every Afternoon," in *Rites of Realism*, 28. See also Ivone Margulies infra.
11. Bazin, *"La Grande aventure," France observateur*, 269 (July 7, 1955), 30.
12. The fullest discussion of this term can be found in the notes Timothy Barnard appended to his translation of *What Is Cinema?* (Montreal, Caboose: 2009), 261–81. See also Diane Arnaud, infra, and Monica Dall'Asta, infra.
13. Bazin, *"Les Aventures de Perri*: Walter Disney romancier et poète de la nature," *Parisien libéré*, 4234 (April 22, 1958); Bazin, *"Les périls de Perri," Cahiers du Cinéma*, 83 (May 1958), 50–53.
14. Bazin, *"Les périls de Perri,"* 52.
15. Ibid.
16. Ibid., 53.
17. Ibid., 52.
18. Bazin, "Death Every Afternoon," 30, c.f. "Mort tous les après-midi," 64–65. See also H. Joubert-Laurencin, infra.
19. Bazin, "Un grand film: *Louisiana Story," Parisien libéré*, 1595 (October 29, 1949).
20. Bazin, *"Louisiana Story* aura été la dernière histoire de R. Flaherty," *Parisien libéré*, 2135 (July 25, 1951).
21. Bazin, *"L'Amazone nue*: un peu 'habillée,'" *Parisien libéré*, 3331 (May 28, 1955).
22. Bazin, "Le Monde du silence," in *Qu'est-ce que le cinéma?* 36.
23. Bazin, "Mort du documentaire reconsitué: *L'Aventure sans retour," France observateur*, 106 (May 22, 1952). See also Bazin, *"L'Aventure sans retour*: Glace sans Esquimaux," *Parisien libéré*, 2389 (May 20, 1952).
24. Bazin, *"Kon-Tiki et Groenland*: Poésie et aventure," *Parisien libéré*, 2371 (April 28, 1952).
25. Bazin, "Le *Kon-Tiki* ou grandeur et servitudes du reportage filmé," *France observateur*, 103 (April 30, 1952), 24.
26. Daney, "The Screen of Fantasy (Bazin and Animals)," 37.

27. Bazin, "*Annapurna*," *France observateur*, 154 (April 23, 1953), 23.

28. Bazin, "Le *Kon-Tiki* ou grandeur et servitudes du reportage filmé," 24.

29. Joubert-Laurencin, "André Bazin et le documentaire, ou *Excusons-les d'en être revenu*," in *Les Écrans documentaires* (Paris: L'Université de Paris-Diderot. 1997), 2.

30. Bazin, "*Annapurna*," 23.

31. Bazin, "Avec *Naufragé volontaire* et *Forêt sacré* le reportage filmé devient une aventure spirituelle," *Radio, Cinéma, Télévision*, 275 (April 24, 1955).

32. Bazin, "Le *Kon-Tiki* ou grandeur et servitudes du reportage filmé," 23.

33. Georges Didi-Huberman, "Le Paradoxe du phasme," in *Phasmes: essais sur l'apparition* (Paris: Minuit. 1998), 15–20.

34. Bazin, "Le *Kon-Tiki* ou grandeur et servitudes du reportage filmé," 23.

35. Bazin, "*Kon-Tiki* et *Groenland*: Poésie et aventure."

36. Daney, "The Screen of Fantasy (Bazin and Animals)," 34–35.

37. Ibid., 37.

38. Bazin, "Death Every Afternoon," 30.

39. An earlier, longer version of this essay appeared in *Senses of Cinema* 51 (2009). Thanks to Dudley Andrew for editing this definitive version.

17

Bazin's Exquisite Corpses

Ivone Margulies

When Bazin outlines Jean Gabin's destiny (an inevitable death fulfilled in each of his characters), or when he describes how even prior to his death Humphrey Bogart resembled a corpse in reprieve, or when he speaks of Chaplin's aging body and his myth's parallel evolution, or in his analyses of Stalin icons in Soviet cinema, we can see that his texts resemble a macabre party where guests in various degrees of decomposition, or with different and even competing claims to liveliness and uniqueness, commingle.[1]

Spreading across several published pieces, Bazin's cine-mythographies trail certain films and stars along two incompatible horizons: the actors' contingent lives and the stars' immutable fates. Bazin's stress on the notion of an embodied destiny gives these narratives about actors, historical figures, and celebrities an existential dimension. At the same time, his critical exercises replicate cinema's power to create afterlives that hover between past and present incarnations.

Crowded with simulacra, Bazin's articles on referential genres such as historical and reenactment films rehearse, in their proliferation of doubles, the problem at the heart of his ontology: that in embalming a lived duration, an image may indeed have a life of its own, tainting the singularity of a moment, of an identity. Each of his articles occasions thoughts about cinema's specific share in a preservational process and about the medium's ability to form a gelled imprint of a changeable existence. And especially when writing on actual stars, whether alive, aging, or dead, he is compelled to puzzle over cinema's ontological perversion, its animistic and resurrecting function. These essays persistently converge on the moment when an image, "a hallucination that is also a fact,"[2] stands freakishly side by side with a living body. This collocation, traceable to Bazin's affinity for surrealism,[3] evinces as well a reluctance to tame cinema's spectrality, to reduce its multiple, coexisting temporalities.

I attend to the force field of such circulating images by looking at Bazin's texts on Chaplin, on Stalin's myth in the cinema, on Luis Procuna, a bullfighter who reenacts his own life events to fill in gaps left by newsreel footage, and on death. Each of the four sections of this essay—Charlie versus Chaplin; Charlie versus Hitler, Bazin versus Stalin, and Torero/Necrophagy—tracks Bazin's attempt to secure cinema's alliance with the ephemeral, the faulty, and the contingent.

Bazin's Chapliniana: Charlie versus Chaplin

Chaplin's relation to his star image was marked by constant attempts to break his aesthetic contract with the audience, to offer them something else besides the little tramp's brand of pathos. As an exorcism, Chaplin once even filmed the tramp drowning, though he never added it to the final edit of *City Lights* (1931).[4] Bazin's discussion of Chaplin is thus attuned to the filmmaker's own agonistic relation to his myth, a critical replay of Chaplin's persona's evolution.[5]

Bazin tracks Charlie's avatars in "Landru—Verdoux—Charlot," his longest essay on Chaplin. He starts by comparing Verdoux to his matrix, the wife-assassin Landru, but soon moves to closer doubles. He typically compresses one film into others, a character into another. He firmly rebuts the contention that the film's weakness lies in its hesitation between a realist depiction and a Charlie film: "Realism here would be a mere illusion. If Charlie persists as a superimposition in Verdoux, it is because Verdoux is Charlie."[6]

His interpretation of Charlie's significance as a tramp is packed with Charlies who are constantly fleeing from the police, and who confirm a "vague culpability" in each awkward, leg-lifted flight. It is this parade of Charlies that Bazin sees coming to rest on Verdoux's final image:[figure 23.2]:

> When he marches towards the guillotine in his shirtsleeves in between the henchmen, the audience cannot fail to see it—they are going to guillotine Charlie. That is his revenge, paradoxical but terrible. Society commits in its turn the greatest of cinematographic crimes, the one it did not dare do from the time that the little man precipitately fled from the police clubs. Charlie is finally a martyr.[7]

In "Mask and Celluloid," a section from "Landru—Verdoux—Charlot," Bazin rephrases his notion of photography as a mold that exposes reality. His essays replicate a collapsible pattern of revelations whose variations are intended only to enhance the curtain-pulling drama: Verdoux is Charlie, Charlie is Chaplin. At the end of *The Great Dictator* (1940), "Charlie advances towards the close-up's proscenium and speaks. . . ."[8] [figure 17.1] Bazin refers to Chaplin's speech, but it is mainly the scene's visual and tactile properties he values: "A strange metamorphosis takes place: for the first time we feel something or someone behind Charlie, a sort of terrible secret which the photographic chemistry, despite the author's will, reveals . . ."[9] More explicitly, "The transition from orthochromatic stock to panchromatic should itself alone have brought on a veritable morphological disorder, more serious perhaps than even the introduction of the spoken word: acknowledging and revealing that the actor was aging, it ate away at the character."[10] Five years later he would remark that with panchromatic stock, "The arrival of gray [*l'apparition du gris*] undermined the very essence of the myth."[11]

All of Bazin's work on Chaplin is about a body constructed and ravaged by cinema. Interweaving the man's ephemeral destiny with his filmic corpus, and frequently using foreboding qualifiers, Bazin associates cinema with existential time; the unavoidable malaise affecting the film skin can only be recognized in human, mortal terms. Aging is essential in Bazin's fascination with seeing time, and cinema, work over bodies. His remarks on *The Great Dictator* ascribe to this newly nuanced film-stock a decanting effect, whereby the mustache floats, black and

FIGURE 17.1: *The Great Dictator* (1940)

young as ever, above the pasty flesh. Still, in this "close-up proscenium" the wrinkles are Chaplin's alone. When he turns to write on *Limelight*, this tale of a face climaxes in a pendulum-like paragraph:

> What is at first baffling in *Limelight* is the complete removal of Chaplin's "make up."
> Most certainly, Chaplin was not absent from his last films, and his transient or secret
> presence at Charlie's side even played an essential role in giving new effectiveness to the
> myth. Moreover, with the advent of panchromatic stock, Charlie's mask no longer
> adhered properly to Chaplin's face. Or, we could say it adhered so well that we discerned
> under the painted plaster the nearly imperceptible wrinkles and the pathetic facial
> vibrations. . . . And since *City Lights* Charlie had already become the chrysalis of
> Chaplin. With *The Great Dictator*, no doubt remained, and the final close up showed us
> the dramatic moulting of the mask to reveal his face. Without this dissociation Monsieur
> Verdoux may not have been possible . . . whatever it is, we had up to this point two
> substantial points of reference: Charlie's mask and Chaplin's face.[12]

Both mask and face are constructs in a reversible mise en abyme. Chaplin's discomfort with his own mythical skin excites Bazin's existential thrust, sparking in his writings a pattern of continual emergence. His fondness is finally for images of becoming, a plasticity which Chaplin himself illustrates in the post-facial surgery scene from *A King in New York* (1957).[13] Arriving in the United States, King Shadov is prompted by a young starlet to have plastic surgery. The vapid, redone face is shocking by being most unlike Chaplin. In a brief scene Shadov tries out his new mask in the mirror and old recognizable tics erupt out of the tightly stretched surface.

This suite of guises bursting out confirms his body as a host, possessed by various Charlies [figure 17.2].

In the essays above, Chaplin and Charlie shuffle within a circumscribed circle of close relatives and filmic personas. "To be or not to be" becomes a more complex question in cinema once Bazin crosses real with fictional characters, contemporary historical beings with imaginary ones. To heighten the intrigue, why not introduce some new mustachioed characters?

The Great Mustache Robbery: Charlie versus Hitler

Let me begin with Chaplin running after his mustache. Bazin famously defines *The Great Dictator* as a matter of justice: "First phase: Hitler takes Charlot's mustache. Second round: Charlot takes his mustache back. Meanwhile, however, it is no longer only a Charlot mustache but it has become a Hitler mustache. By taking it back, Charlot takes out a mortgage on Hitler's own existence, which he could dispose of as he likes."[14]

Bazin's essay "Pastiche or Postiche or Nothingness over a Mustache" is more than a blow-by-blow analysis of Chaplin's reclamation of his trapezoidal signature. As the critic analyzes Chaplin's engagement with topical history, he cleverly extols the consequences of this dispute between two mythical beings—one imaginary, the other real.

Confrontation between unlike beings is crucial to Bazin's conception of cinematic realism. As Serge Daney has shown, Bazin's examples for the interdiction of montage—man and animal framed together in a long shot—are not meant to represent the integrity of reality, but to create a temporal and spatial expansion, to provide the best possible stage for the emergence of the Real. Rather than split the screen, Bazin is much more invested in showing "the

FIGURE 17.2: *A King in New York* (1957)

split occurring in it."[15] The heterogeneity of man and animal becomes as striking as their mutual risk. The permanent possibility of death (in a bullfight, in the cage in which Chaplin meets a lion) presents Bazin with occasions to stress contingency as the central quality of cinema and realism.[16]

But death is not the sole instance chosen to dramatize a categorical impasse, the manner in which representation and reality can split up in full view. Other examples bearing the mark of heterogeneous realities, that of the filmmaking process and the filmed event, remind one of cinema's essential link with the ephemeral, material, world: as large as the bridge over the River Kwai (about to be blown up in David Lean's 1957 film) or as minor as the wig of a king about to be deposed, it is those pro-filmic elements most imbued with transience that are selected to evince cinema's close association with a lived and finite duration. For instance, when he states in his review of *La Marseillaise* (1938) that "Louis XVI is hindered by the fact that his wig is askew,"[17] this remark on yet another hair appendage, grants to both king and actor an extra measure of contingency. The hairpiece falling off from Louis'—and Pierre Renoir's—head, or migrating like a black butterfly from Charlie to Hynkel, is a charged supplement, a sign of concrete theatricality—for Bazin, the real.[18]

Bazin puts this supplement to good use in his indictment of dictator images. Only a mustache in flight can do justice to a true interpretation of imposture. In "Pastiche or Postiche or Nothingness over a Mustache," his most Sartrean essay, Bazin subscribes to the same idea as Lubitsch's *To Be or Not to Be* (1942) when he reads Chaplin's clowning in *The Great Dictator* as an assemblage of floating attributes, available for the taking:[19]

> For what is Hynkel but Hitler reduced to his essence and deprived of his existence? Hynkel does not exist. He is a puppet, a marionette in which we recognize Hitler by his mustache, by his size, by the color of his hair, by his speeches, by his sentimentality, by his cruelty, by his rages, by his madness, but also as an empty and senseless amalgamation, deprived of all existential justification.[20]

In "The Ontology of a Fetish," Dudley Andrew insightfully explains Bazin's "Ontology of the Photographic Image" essay as a creative appropriation of Sartre's *The Imaginary*. In a typed page found inside a copy of Sartre's book—once owned by Bazin—we find the following reflections on photography's dual reference: "a bizarre angle suffices to grab the eye in this way, on its form, before the eye can escape toward the reality that it aims at."[21] Andrew's article also points to a connection particularly germane to my argument, regarding Bazin's fondness for seeing both the material and figurative sides of cinema and cinematic beings.[22] Sartre illustrates how a Maurice Chevalier impersonator selects and rearranges recognizable signs: the straw hat, the fat protruded lower lip. He observes that while a portrait might resemble the model perfectly, in the impersonator's case the "material of the imitation is a human body. It is rigid, it resists. [Franconay], the impersonator, is small stout and brunette, a woman who is imitating a man. The object produced by means of her body is a feeble form that can always be interpreted in two distinct ways. I am always free to see Maurice Chevalier as an image or a small woman who is making faces."[23] Sartre admits that the most pleasant moments ensue from the instability of the proposed synthesis. The result of impersonation, this "hybrid state, neither fully perception nor fully image,"[24] is of endless interest to Bazin, whose aesthetics privilege the joining of irreconcilable image registers.

Note for instance Bazin's critical pirouette to subsume even *The Great Dictator*'s most unsuccessful hybrids under the coherence of a premeditated attack. In a 1948 essay, Bazin's verdict on the film is: "Badly constructed, heteroclyte and heterogeneous."[25] In an earlier essay he admits the sole fortuitous personality transfusion occurs during the globe dance scene because there Hynkel is most like Charlie. Calibrating differences and similarities in his analysis, he comes to this zero-sum equation: "It was necessary for Hynkel to behave no less like Charlot than Hitler, that he become at once as much one as the other—to be nothing."[26]

Bazin confronts the stupefying resilience of myths by way of a most crowded route, full of mustachioed characters, each pointing to a new relationship between existence and ideality, between historical contingency and what Bazin rightly perceives as a new historical product—that of the mediatic dictator. "Mythical power: Hitler's mustache was a real one!" he concludes, grounding his use of the prop in historical consequence.

In this textual analysis qua-masquerade, Bazin's aesthetics are aligned to his humanist ethics. Nonetheless, if the unstable synthesis of impersonation appeals to Bazin it is because the actor's literal presence, his resistant, rigid body, provides a glimpse into cinema's human, material dimension. Bazin renders homage to Chaplin through one of these hybrids: meshing flesh and celluloid, he makes cinema partake in the fading star's finitude. The same qualifier, "rigid," gains an entirely different valence when applied to the erection of Stalin's monument in cinema.

Bazin versus Stalin

The "thingness" that threatens to void Hynkel of any justification, the nothingness that hovers around the objectification of beings, is central to Bazin's ontology of cinema: it constitutes the negative pole in an evaluation system that constantly privileges the incomplete, the faulty, those gaps that invite a subjective investment in the cinematic image, as Serge Daney and Philip Rosen have argued.[27] This problematic is at the center of Bazin's extended bout with Stalinist cinema.[28]

Replicating Chaplin's and Lubitsch's poke at contemporary authoritarianism, "The Stalin Myth in Soviet Cinema," written in 1950, is Bazin's most daring cine-mythography. The essay comes in the wake of a growing rigidity in the French left cultural establishment, which was trying to corner Bazin into a formalist camp.[29] His clarity about the deification of Stalin is compounded by his aesthetic integrity and analytical suppleness, as well as passion for signs of threatened life in cinema. All this he brings into a sustained reflection on films about historical figures and celebrities.

Bazin puzzles out the phenomenon he sees as unique to contemporary Soviet cinema: its depiction of Stalin while the statesman is still alive. He carefully distinguishes the Stalin films from all other kinds of biographical and historical reconstitution according to one main criterion: the relation of the represented lives to the objective course of history. It is the timeless dimension of either History (à la Stalin) or of celebrities that most complicates the correlation between cinema and lives. Stars who have already achieved a legendary status can be represented, since they are measured against an unchanging essence.[30]

Circling around the question of mythical and historical representation, Bazin's text inevitably brushes against the hero's biography, a genre in ascendance within socialist realism. As positive counterexamples to Stalin's statuary films, he advances *Peter the Great* (1937, 1939) and *Chapayev* (1934), films that present "men who serve History. . . . [in] groping toward an infallible historical consciousness" (SM, 33). *Chapayev*, a great socialist realist hit, is praised by Bazin for its portrayals of this real hero's failures: "Even his most obviously heroic actions, are undercut without diminishing the psychological level at all" (SM, 33). Although Bazin identifies the commissar as the official voice of Party objectivity, he could not be privy to the intense behind-the-scenes work done to rewrite history, to square biography with myth. According to Evgeny Dobrenko, when the film was shown to Chapayev's family and his comrades-in-arms, "they declared that nothing in the film really happened like that and . . . having been given [their] views, [Stalin] replied with the sacramental phrase: 'They're lying, like eyewitnesses.'" "Similitude" became one of the main problems in socialist realist biographical films because it posed limits on historical myth.[31]

The kernel of the dispute, different for Stalin and Bazin, lies in the value bestowed on living. In a perceptive twist on Bazin's words, Ian Christie states that "cinema provided Stalin with the 'living' image of his otherwise mummified state."[32] Bazin accurately describes the issue faced by Stalin as he tried to erase the "blemishes" from his version of history—from recantations to the physical elimination of eyewitnesses, from trials to his incredibly involved participation in the rewriting of films and characters: "as soon as a man is said to have participated in History . . . a part of his biography is irremediably 'historicized.' . . . You cannot reduce a man to nothing but History without in turn compromising that History by the subjective presence of the individual" (SM, 37).

The physical elimination of "dissidents" went in tandem with the need to maintain the coherence of this immutable history embodied in a waxlike Stalin. "According to the Soviet 'Stalinist' Communist perspective, no one can 'become' a traitor. That would imply that he wasn't always a traitor" (SM, 37). Becoming, or images of becoming, are, in short, forbidden.

What Bazin objects to are the political effects of this mythical representation, its interface with a totalitarian system: "To make Stalin the principal hero and determiner of a real historic event while he is still alive implies that from now on he is invulnerable to any weakness, that the meaning of his life has already and definitely been attained, and that he could never subsequently make a mistake or commit treason" (SM, 36). In the examples discussed—*The Vow* (1946), *The Battle of Stalingrad* (1949–1950), and *The Third Blow* (1948)—the Stalin figures do not evolve.

At the essay's end Bazin advances the idea that if Stalin achieves a truly ontological quality in his cinematic portrayals, it is because the image is by nature "other" than normal propaganda, "seeming completely superimposable with reality. . .The cinema is in its essence as incontestable as Nature and History." (SM 39). He recognizes the extra pull of referential genres in lending credibility to any fiction, stating that a "cinematic reconstitution of Stalin, is enough to define forever his place and meaning in the world—enough to fix his essence irrevocably" (SM, 39). This concluding paragraph, in an otherwise damning and prescient account of Stalinist cinema's symbiosis with historical reality, has a puzzling quality, for cinema is here definitely complicit in the production and reproduction of essences.

Bazin's thoughts on cinema's power to multiply the images of stars and deadly dictators in order to endow them with a life of their own is not inconsistent with his ontology, his perception of the photographed object's freedom "from temporal contingencies," "its position outside (historical) time altogether."[33] And yet the recognition that the representation of history manifest in

Stalinist cinema is "a hypertrophy of a condition that pervades all cinema"[34] creates a real impasse in Bazin's ontological theory. Hence the cut-and-dried quality of the essay's ending. The contradictions between the actual existent and his transcendental image do not deserve, in Stalin's case, to enter Bazin's dialectics, to be "resolved" through his "beloved paradoxes."[35]

To sum up, let's compare the treatment of the Chaplin myth with that of Stalin.[36] Bazin treats the circuitry of Chaplin personas as a flux, implying an evolving cine-corpus. Chaplin's body and face function, like celluloid, as reminders of a frail humanity. More than any of his other essays, "The Stalin Myth," establishes Bazin's contempt for any cinema that forecloses the objective contingencies of history. To Stalin's myth Bazin can only oppose the few newsreel images of Stalin at the Red Square and at the Yalta conference because "they record reality, remaining therefore fundamentally ambiguous."[37] If this phrase, representing Bazin's mandate for cinema, has an impotent ring in the context of Stalinist cinema, it finds a new life in his texts on death.

Torero/Necrophagy

In *The Emergence of Cinematic Time*, Mary Ann Doane accounts for the complex relation cinema entertains with contingency by detailing the progressive transformations of cinema toward a narrative and a temporal logic autonomous from the external reality it so easily records and archives. She finds in the execution film, an early subgenre of the *actualité*, the heightening of these dilemmas: how to preserve the sense of actually being there, how to get rid of "dead time," of uneventful time. In *Execution of Czolgosz, with Panorama of Auburn Prison* (1901), it is the pan outside the prison that guarantees the effect of contiguity between cameraman and an unfilmable, reconstructed execution. In *Electrocuting an Elephant* (1903), it is an ellipsis that demarcates significant from insignificant moments, death from the nonevent of tying the elephant up.[38] We find in Bazin's critical evaluations a range of related emphases—on copresence, on ellipsis—used to maintain tension between the open-ended ambiguity of reality and signification. Doane's bold assertion that "the contingent and death" are similar "in being often situated as that which is inassimilable to meaning"[39] helps explain Bazin's convoluted rulings on the representation of death in cinema: he either hails it as a unique event of moral import or co-opts it as one more contingent moment; but death remains, in his work, the intractable sign of the real.

Bazin's first argument against cinema's potential to replicate and thereby defile the uniqueness of death relies on facts. "We do not die twice"[40] is Bazin's conclusive explanation for why the uncanny that so obsesses him—the passage from animate to inanimate, from subject to object—has to be left off screen. The second point he makes recovers as ritual the threatening replay of cinema: "the representation on screen of a bull being put to death . . . magnifies the quality of the original moment through the contrast of its repetition. It confers on it an additional solemnity."[41] This supplemental solemnity, a semantic slow motion, postpones the ultimate "cut," reclaiming its sublimity for cinema.

Bazin keeps the relation between the frozen finality of record and the changeable flow of reality in constant textual abeyance: his ciné-mythographies introduce a continual flux of competing doubles, and even when he gestures toward sorting them out, their status in limbo provokes attention. Not surprisingly, in their structure his statements parallel the perceptual uncanny and its animate/inanimate oscillations: change mummified.

His essay "The Life and Death of Superimposition" confirms his fascination with cinema's trafficking in simulacra in a seemingly technical remark. He states that "the reciprocal transparency of superimposition doesn't permit us to say whether the ghost is behind or in front of the objects or whether in fact the objects themselves become spectral to the degree that they share space with the ghost."[42] The problematic representation of afterlives leads him to ponder the credible cohabitation of heterogeneous elements. The eventual contamination of objects and specters is finally what interests Bazin most about cinematic lives and bodies. For him the undecided status of cinema's images is most alive once his object—the actor's (or animal's) body—is bracketed between life and death.[43]

Given his reiterated claims to impose limits in representing death, we may ask what kind of being, besides a ghost, gets a moral permit to live again and again on screen? I propose my own personal hobbyhorse, reenactment films, as the likeliest candidate for a Bazinian discussion. As a genre, reenactment raises anew the question of the present and presence in cinema, establishing alternate priorities for realism. Although reenactment films are often propped on a topical interest event, their reconstructed temporality is far from immediate. Restaging would seem therefore to magnify the paradoxes Bazin is fond of. The question of age, for instance: if we define reenactment as a person acting out events of her past, the time elapsed between fact and re-presentation cannot betray the passage of time. In this form of performative representation, the split between past and present, between representation and reference, is nonetheless continually reiterated and kept alive. Reenactment brings into the picture a foreign body, a changed, and transformative presence. Always at odds with the present that it references, this body is an active and disturbing *revenant*.

And yet Bazin wrote little on reenactment, and when he did he ignored the genre's most taunting limit—death.[44] In his reviews of Zavattini's segment of *L'amore in città* called *Love of a Mother* (1953), he revisits the neorealist practice of using nonprofessionals, though with a twist: what would happen if by an incredible coincidence, rather than using someone from the street that looked the part, one chose the actual Caterina to play Caterina? This is "an idea of a poet, not a realist," he says,[45] pointing out that this casting choice has little to do with either resemblance or acting skills. "We know," he states, that "the assassin doesn't necessarily look like a killer. But we have to note that reality here goes beyond the prudence of art. Not because the evidence in its brutal reality renders art derisory, but on the contrary because being given this scenario (real or not) no interpretation and no mise-en-scène could better show its value."[46] His choice of a criminal metaphor alerts us, inadvertently, to the link, implicit in all of Zavattini's rhetoric, between reenactment and atonement. In this film, codirected with Maselli, Caterina is tried for abandoning her son and absolved before reenacting this tale of error and penance.

In "The Stalin Myth," Bazin remarks briefly on Marcel Cerdan who plays himself in *The Man with the Clay Hands* (*L'Homme aux mains d'argile*, 1949) and *Fame and the Devil* (*Al diavolo la celebrità*, 1949). He claims that the actual boxer's presence is entirely dispensable and that his employment in the film only highlights in extremis "the identification of the man Cerdan with his myth" (SM, 32). We can ascribe his disinterest in this "phenomenon" to his general disregard for the exemplary arc of the biopic, and, most of all, to his contempt for the scripted principle at work in this mostly contrived film genre.

The missed opportunity with Cerdan is nevertheless illuminating if only regarding the sports film Bazin wrote the most on—bullfighting. One may not play oneself dying, and this temporal and corporeal limit should be enough to define the reverse interest of replaying one's life oneself. The sports biopic—*The Greatest* (1977), *The Bob Mathias Story* (1954), *Endurance* (1999)—is one of the most frequent reenactment subgenres. While the narratives invariably replicate the performer's record of struggle and accomplishment, sports reenactments foreground the question of literalness: how can the acting appear through one's routine work? In the sports film, the strain between routine and drama needs to be articulated through visible signs, bodily marks. Expertise has to be cloaked in exertion, the physical effort needs to be dramatized, coming closer to pain and risk of death.

Opening the Bazin archive at Yale University, I was hoping to find that Bazin had written more on reenactment. And indeed I came across the following page from *Radio, Cinéma, Télévision*, a page that seems to speak to me alone. It consists of two adjoining columns by Bazin. One is called "Toro," a review of Carlos Velo's *Torero (Bullfighter*, 1956), in which the famous Mexican matador Luis Procuna plays himself; to its left sits an article called "Information ou nécrophagie," where Bazin writes on a television program[47] [figure 17.3].

First the bullfighting: typically whenever Bazin writes on bullfight films he establishes a hierarchy based on the protagonist's actual risk. There are compilations like *La Course de taureaux* (*Bullfight*, 1951) and fiction films. Some films are played by actors and by real bullfighters as stand-ins in the arena, while others insert documentary images of actual bullfights to stand just for the perilous moments. In *Tarde de Toro* (*Afternoon of the Bulls*, 1956), three fictional toreros are played, both inside and outside of the arena, by three celebrity bullfighters: Ortega, Bienvenida, and Enrique Vera. Although Bazin discounts the film for still being a scripted, staged, and choreographed fiction, in his review he praises its mise-en-scène of integral realism,

FIGURE 17.3: A revealing conjunction in *Radio-Cinéma-Télévision*

since "as soon as the camera gets close, the corrida scenes are actually interpreted by matadors that risk their lives and really kill the bull."[48]

We may ask what makes *Torero*, the film on Procuna, so extraordinary? For Bazin the film's originality does not rest in Procuna playing himself: "The Mexican producer Barbachano Ponce had been a newsreel director and had an archive of footage featuring a number of famous bullfights, as well as images of the torero's wedding. Because of his initial notoriety, images of Procuna were available, and the director had only to recreate some private scenes and film new bullfights with multiple cameras." Filmed in a newsreel style, these images are, he hastens to add, "indiscernible from the documentary ones."[49]

Something else clinches this review as critical to understanding Bazin's thoughts on life and death in the cinema—its placement on the page side by side with "Information or Necrophagy." This article on a different topic curiously complements his enthusiastic appreciation of Luis Procuna's biopic. In "Information or Necrophagy" Bazin addresses the ethical issue raised by a TV program as to whether images representing men's deaths, especially accidental, should be made public.[50] Bazin regrets having to say so, but feels these images should be censored. He explains his compunction: "After having offered us a fabulous underwater outing in the mode of *The Silent World* . . . the camera casually approaches, as if out of an unplanned but refined curiosity, the remains of a plane recently fallen at sea: the pilot is at his post, drowned, the eyes half open."[51] The almost accidental discovery of this corpse, combined with the association of the hallucinating color footage in these underwater documentaries is, he avers, shocking.

In "La mort à l'écran" ("Death on the Screen") Bazin makes no reference whatsoever to bullfighting, foregrounding instead the details of the public executions in Shanghai, calling attention to cinema's "scandal," its "ability to see death as a moment identical to others while it is the only one of our acts that by its very essence cannot re-start." "The screen can," he says, "make us watch this monstrous and unthinkable phenomenon: to re-die."[52]

His *corrida* film reviews, on the other hand, rarely skip a mention of danger and risk, as Bazin seems in fact to scan the screen anxious for that instance of radical discontinuity he so obsessively wants and dreads to see. "Death Every Afternoon," published in *Qu'est-ce que le cinéma?*, combines Bazin's review of Braunberger's film *La Course de taureaux* with "La Mort à l'écran," thus effectively linking his attraction to spectacles of death, both in suspense and as replayed.

In "Toro" he remarks in passing: "In the film on Manolete . . . an actor played him but in the arena it was the poor bullfighter, and his death was his real death."[53] But what particularly commends the film to Bazin is the possibility, afforded by reenactment, of extending the life that will be at risk in the bullfighting scenes. Imbued with the contingency so cherished by the critic, this seamless combination of reenacted and newsreel footage protracts an endangered life, constituting therefore Bazin's perfect biographical film. This biopic's promised suspension of death, filmed mainly in documentary newsreel, is undoubtedly a more satisfying spectacle than Marcel Cerdan's safe, scripted, and stilted act.

Bazin's enthusiastic reception of the Procuna film becomes even more understandable once it is read side by side with the following paragraph, which concludes "Information or Necrophagy": "The death of a soldier, that of a bullfighter or of a race-car driver, has a meaning even if debatable. From the start the document addresses us through the equivocal horror of our senses. But there are no exquisite corpses!"[54]

Bazin's objection to the camera's chancing upon a corpse is prefaced by his own half-guilty perception of an aesthetic equality between corpses and underwater life. He then qualifies the various deaths according to the dead man's willingness to consciously risk his life. Here, as in so many of Bazin's writings, the last phrase condenses in a pithy statement the main terms with which the entire essay grapples—the ethical versus the aesthetic weights of this document. But it is the surrealist reference in his final sentence that impels us to see these two essays as a superimpression forming a composite, an exquisite corpse. On one side, the *Torero* review relishes any extra footage extending the threat to Procuna's filmic life; on the other, Bazin asserts his fascination with chance through an exclamatory denegation, as he playfully literalizes the exquisite corpses, the cherished cinema bodies he describes.

Notes

1. Andre Bazin, "The Destiny of Jean Gabin," in *What Is Cinema?* vol. 2, trans. Hugh Gray (Berkeley: University of California Press, 1971), 176–78; "Mort d'Humphrey Bogart," in *Qu'est-ce que le cinéma?* vol. 3 (Paris: Editions du Cerf, 1960), 83–88.

2. Bazin, "The Ontology of the Photographic Image," in *What Is Cinema?* vol. 1, trans. Hugh Gray (Berkeley: University of California Press, 1967), 16.

3. See Adam Lowenstein, "The Surrealism of the Photographic Image: Bazin, Barthes, and the Digital *Sweet Hereafter*," *Cinema Journal*, 46:3 (2007), 54–82.

4. Noël Simsolo, "Chaplin et ses images," in *Chaplin aujourd'hui*, ed. Joel Magny and Noël Simsolo (Paris: Cahiers du Cinéma, 2003), 30.

5. See Charles Maland, *Chaplin and American Culture: The Evolution of a Star Image* (Princeton, NJ: Princeton University Press, 1989). See also Rochelle Fack *infra*.

6. Bazin, "Landru—Verdoux—Charlot," *Education Populaire*, Doc 48, 6, n.p. This lengthy essay is the matrix of several other essays, for instance "Charlie Chaplin," in *What Is Cinema?* vol. 1, 144–53, and "The Myth of Monsieur Verdoux," in *What Is Cinema?* vol. 2, 102–23. When they correspond completely, I refer to the English version; in this case, "The Myth of M. Verdoux," 105.

7. Bazin, "Monsieur Verdoux: Le Martyre de Charlot," *Le Parisien libéré*, 1035 (January 14, 1948), 2. See also "Monsieur Verdoux, or Charlot Martyred," *L'Ecran français*, 131 (December 1947) and translated in *Essays on Chaplin*, ed. and trans. Jean Bodon (New Haven, CT: University of New Haven Press, 1985), 31.

8. Bazin, "Landru—Verdoux—Charlot," n.p.

9. Ibid. A compressed variation of this paragraph appears in "The Myth of Monsieur Verdoux," 110–11.

10. Bazin, "The Myth of Monsieur Verdoux," 120.

11. Bazin, "If Charlot Hadn't Died," in *Essays on Chaplin*, 51–52.

12. Ibid.

13. Interestingly, Bazin's reviews of *A King in New York* do not mention Chaplin's facial changes.

14. Bazin, "Pastiche or Postiche or Nothingness over a Mustache," in *Essays on Chaplin*, 16–17.

15. Serge Daney, "The Screen of Fantasy (Bazin and Animals)," in *Rites of Realism: Essays on Corporeal Cinema*, ed. Ivone Margulies, trans. Mark A. Cohen (Durham, NC: Duke University Press, 2003), 33.

16. Andre Bazin, "Death Every Afternoon," in *Rites of Realism: Essays on Corporeal Cinema*, trans. Mark A. Cohen, 29. "Mort tous les après-midi," in *Qu'est-ce que le cinéma?* vol. 1, combines the article of the same name that he wrote for *Cahiers du Cinéma* in 1951 with "La Mort à l'écran," published in *Esprit*, 159 (September 1949). On the interrelation of cinema, contingency, and death, see Mary Ann Doane, *The Emergence of Cinematic Time: Modernity, Contingency, The Archive* (Cambridge: Harvard University Press, 2002), 140–71. Bazin's acute interest in the potential coincidence of death and cinema is apparent in his review of *Gide*: "Allegret understood this well since he does not edit out the last second of the shot in which Gide abruptly looks at the camera and lets a plaintive cry escape: 'Cut!'" Bazin, "André Gide," *France observateur*, 96 (March 13, 1952), 24. On the protraction of a cinematic death, see Margulies, "Delaying the Cut: The Space of Performance in Wenders' *Lightning Over Water*," *Screen*, 34:1 (Spring 1993), 54–68.

17. Bazin, *Jean Renoir*, ed. François Truffaut, trans. W. W. Halsey II and William H. Simon (New York: Simon and Schuster, 1971–1973), 67.

18. In "Bodies too Much," in *Rites of Realism: Essays on Corporeal Cinema* I have insisted on the privilege given by Bazin to pro-filmic contingencies in the production of the cinematic image. This is a key notion in Philip Rosen's *Change Mummified: Cinema, Historicity, Theory* (Minneapolis: University of Minnesota Press, 2001), and in Serge Daney's "The Screen of Fantasy." Recent texts have taken this aspect of Bazin's realism in exciting new directions: see Seung-Hoon Jeong and Dudley Andrew, "Grizzly Ghost: Herzog, Bazin and the Cinematic Animal," *Screen*, 49:1 (Spring 2008), 1–12; see also Rosalind Galt, "'It's So Cold in Alaska': Evoking Exploration Between Bazin and *The Forbidden Quest*," *Discourse*, 28:1 (2006), 53–71.

19. In Lubitsch's *To Be or Not to Be*, the conceit of a theatrical troupe facilitates the acting out of real Nazis by actors. The film's clever move from Hitler to fictional Nazis shifts the question from authenticity to phoniness.

20. André Bazin, "Pastiche or Postiche or Nothingness over a Mustache," 17.

21. Dudley Andrew, "The Ontology of a Fetish," *Film Quarterly* 61:4 (Summer 2008), 64. Adam Lowenstein has convincingly argued that Bazin's turn to the surrealists' understanding of photography as factual hallucination at the end of "The Ontology of Photographic Image" essay is a response to Sartre's attempt to keep the processes of perception and imagination separate; Lowenstein, "The Surrealism of the Photographic Image," 56–57.

22. Andrew, "The Ontology of a Fetish," 62.

23. Jean-Paul Sartre, *The Imaginary: A Phenomenological Psychology of the Imagination* (London, Routledge, [1940] 2004), 25–26.

24. Ibid., 29.

25. Bazin, "The Myth of M. Verdoux," 110.

26. Bazin, "Pastiche or Postiche or Nothingness over a Mustache," 19.

27. See Daney, "The Screen of Fantasy," and Rosen, *Change Mummified*, 13–31. See also Rosen, "History of the Image, Image of History: Subject and Ontology in Bazin," in *Rites of Realism*, 56–58. Rosen's essay first appeared in *Wide Angle* 9:4 (Winter 1987–88) 7–34. an issue edited by Dudley Andrew.

28. Rosen develops a cogent argument for the centrality of time in Bazin's ontology and his sense of the betrayal of history in Stalinist films; Rosen, *Change Mummified*, 33–35. Bazin, "The Stalin Myth in Soviet Cinema." See note 30 for full citation.

29. Dudley Andrew, *André Bazin* (New York: Columbia University Press, 1990), 137–44. See also Antoine de Baecque, "Georges Sadoul, *Les Lettres françaises* et le cinéma Stalinien en France," in *La cinéphilie: Invention d'un regard, histoire d'une culture 1944–1968* (Paris: Fayard, 2003), 84–88.

30. Bazin, "The Stalin Myth in Soviet Cinema," trans. Georgia Gurrieri in *Movies and Methods*, II (Berkeley CA: University of California Press, 1985), 32. This essay will henceforth be cited parenthetically as SM.

31. Evgeny Dobrenko, "Creation Myth and Myth Creation in Stalinist Cinema," *Studies in Russian and Soviet Cinema*, 1:3 (Intellect Ltd., 2007), 248.

32. Ian Christie, "Canons and Careers: The Director in Soviet Cinema," in *Stalinism and Soviet Cinema*, eds. Richard Taylor and Derek Spring (London: Routledge, 1993), 166.

33. Daniel Morgan, "Rethinking Bazin: Ontology and Realist Aesthetics," *Critical Inquiry*, 32 (Spring 2006), 452.

34. Rosen, "History of the Image, Image of History," 62.

35. Ibid., 60–61.

36. Myth is not necessarily a negative construct in Bazin as proven by his take on the Western, Gabin, and Bogart. Rosen, *Change Mummified*, 33; "History of the Image," 60.

37. Rosen, *Change Mummified*, 31.

38. Doane, *The Emergence of Cinematic Time*, 140–152.

39. Ibid., 145.

40. Bazin, "Death Every Afternoon," 30.

41. Ibid., 31.

42. Bazin, "The Life and Death of Superimposition," in *Bazin at Work*, 76. See also Daniel Morgan, *infra*.

43. For an enlightening analysis of Bazin's affinity for notions of becoming and the conjunction—afterlife, animal and man, see Seung-hoon Jeong and Dudley Andrew, "Grizzly Ghost: Herzog, Bazin and the Cinematic Animal."

44. See my analysis of Antonioni's episode *Attempted Suicide* in Margulies, "Exemplary Bodies: Reenactment in *Love in the City, Sons, Close Up*," in *Rites of Realism*, 225–30.

45. Bazin, "L'amour à la ville," in *Qu'est-ce que le cinéma?* vol. 4 (Paris: Editions du Cerf, 1962), 148.

46. Ibid, 149. Cf.*Cahiers du Cinéma*, 69 (March 1957), 46.

47. Bazin, "Toro: Une révolution dans le réalisme," and "Information ou nécrophagie," *Radio, Cinéma, Télévision*, 408 (November 10, 1957).

48. Bazin, "Après-midi de taureaux: 90 minutes de vérité," *Parisien libéré*, 3780 (November 5, 1956).

49. Bazin, "Toro: Une révolution dans le réalisme."

50. Bazin, "Information ou nécrophagie."

51. Ibid.

52. Bazin, "La Mort à l'écran," *Esprit*, 159 (September 1949), 442–43. See also Hervé Joubert-Laurencin, *infra*.

53. Bazin, "Toro: Une révolution dans le réalisme."

54. Bazin, "Information ou nécrophagie."

18

Rewriting the Image

Two Effects of the Future-Perfect in André Bazin

Hervé Joubert-Laurencin

But we sense the glare of the studio lights on Burgess Meredith's rosebushes. . . . Still there is a melancholy pleasure in re-encountering Renoir, even in such an unsuccessful effort. . . . His American works are still "Renoir films," as characteristic as his French films, but this time characteristic in their failures (actes manqués).
— André Bazin, *Ecran Français, June 15, 1948, reprinted in Jean Renoir, p 94.*

Every bungled action (acte manqué) is a successful, even well-phrased, discourse.
— Jacques Lacan, *"Fonction et champ de la parole et du langage" in Ecrits1, 147*

Under the title *La Réécriture sur image* (rewriting the image), I aim to describe processes of redoubling in the writings of André Bazin. This description falls under a more general theoretical hypothesis that I will not develop here, but that I can state in one sentence: the future perfect is the tense of cinema. Roland Barthes dreamt of associating the perfect tense with photography: a photo always says, according to him: "it was"; in the cinema, I would argue that this becomes: "it will have been." To this idea, let us add a corollary: whenever you write about cinema, you are always already in the act of rewriting.

Rewriting the Image as a Form of the Future Perfect

The film already existed. Once described, it is already both irreparably dead, transformed into the past, and always incomparably alive, constantly evolving, stretched towards the future in anticipation of a new screening which will overthrow what was written about it.

Film images make two demands on a writer. In the first place, what the writer can say is by definition inexact in relation to what took place, or more precisely, what didn't take place. The semiological period of film studies was useful in that it scientifically determined the limits of any science of describing films: it proved that it is impossible to transform a complex phenomenon consisting, according to Christian Metz's scheme, of five materials of expression, that is, a *film,* into a single one, that is, the written *page.* But the categories of the linguist Louis Hjemslev do not explain everything. As a science of signs, the semiology of film implies a common ground between the film spectator and the one who writes about it, an idea which critics like Bazin, without having theorized it, challenge through their very practice. At the moment of writing about a film, once the logic of the film is abandoned, the logic of life returns. After that moment, events are settled, and what occurred cannot be undone. Writing does not possess this superior faculty that belongs to cinema: to make what happened not to have happened. In the *Nicomachean Ethics,* Aristotle has Agathon say: "Of this one thing is even god deprived, to make what has been done not to have happened."[1] Nevertheless, every film editor can do this, by choosing one take—one possible world—over another, thus constructing *what is* in dynamic opposition to *what isn't.* This is why, if we apply Giorgio Agamben's idea of "de-creation" to the cinema, we can consider editing as an act of contingency.[2] Writing about a film is, on the contrary, tied to the necessary.[3] For this reason it can never completely describe the sensorial experience of watching, even when it comes to a single shot.

Secondly, whatever a rewriting of the image is able to awaken and enliven with the help of stylistic devices (in Bazin, mainly through countless extended metaphors) appears stillborn compared to the power of expectation and revitalization at every new screening, which will always be richer than that unique mental screening frozen by writing. Here we find the famous problem known as "interminable (film) analysis." Effectively, when you write about cinema, the film will have been there irremediably ahead of you. And the more you overshoot it, the greater will be its lead on you.

Bazin surely knew this. He knew his limits. He knew that his was a gesture of repetition. This is why, paradoxically, he occasionally manages to escape the circle of repetition of the same, the vicious circle that threatens all film critics. This is why he was often considered the greatest of them, yet why at the same time he seemed so humble. His humility was not a matter of his faith or physical weakness, nor was he considered great because he was an ineffable genius: he appeared both humble and of peerless authority because he had touched on the force of de-creation particular to his art, rewriting the image, for criticism is inversely proportional to cinema's force, which is made up of retakes and redoublings, of paradoxes and inversions, of salubrious hiccups that are far more significant than the moralisms of the critical judgment. The humility of his writing contains more potential than the positions of power tied to established theories, or to the good taste of a period. (The very notion of de-creation, according to Giorgio Agamben, consists in distinguishing potentiality from power).

Without knowing it, Bazin was talking about this very thing when he invented a superb phrase for describing the human sciences; in characterizing Pierre-Dominique Gaisseau's film, *Forêt sacrée (Sacred Forest,* 1954) he wrote: "Knowledge sacrifices the sacred to its sacrilege."[4] Toward the end of the film, after months of discussion and acclimatization, the ethnologists filming this risky adventure are given about 100 ritual incisions on the shoulder blade in order to be initiated into the Tomas, the tribe they are observing, with, at first sight, the spectacular goal of penetrating their "sacred forest." But the film stops there; we learn nothing more about the mysteries of this forest that they took such trouble to penetrate. The Westerners leave scarified and depressed, not because they feel that they have sacrificed themselves for science, but because they feel a noble and terrible remorse for having upset the social order (thus, a laudable scientific feeling is expressed at the end of this little-known film). The fetish-priest who, out of friendship, initiated them, will have some explaining to do to his community. The conclusion of this apologue is that the scientist's initiation went for nothing. He loses on both counts; for only in this way, according to the film's moral and Bazin's admiration, can he manage properly to carry on his work.

In what follows, I describe two jolts, two hiccups during which Bazin, by virtue of letting go (it is possible in both cases that he doesn't realize what he is discovering, but also that he has complete command of his subject), manages to curb the temporal fatality of repetition involved in rewriting the image and to turn it around with full evocative potential. Thus his criticism functions not with its own force but by riding the force of what he encounters.

The first jolt comes in his encounter with Orson Welles, when he clearly sees what is in the process of happening in film history and invents the concept of the sequence-shot [*plan-séquence*]. The second time, he sees what is about to happen next: he blinks his eyes before what can only be described as unlikely jump-cuts.

Sequence-shot

It was in the archives of the Cinémathèque Française that I first noticed an actual instance of rewriting by Bazin. The recently acquired Lachenay collection contains three major manuscripts that allow us to register the progress of Bazin's thinking and manner of writing. One of them is a handwritten manuscript and a typescript, both complete, for his book on Orson Welles, published by Chavane in 1950. I have always preferred this first Welles book to the subsequent version that Bazin expanded but also dismembered at the end of his life, and that André Labarthe posthumously published in 1972.[5]

A line-by-line comparison of the three texts leading to Bazin's first book permits this observation: he invented the expression *plan-séquence* ("sequence-shot," with the hyphen) in 1949, while studying the films of Orson Welles. This is an indisputable fact, but nonetheless impossible to verify without recourse to the archives, given the present editorial state of his oeuvre. This is not a new discovery. Gilles Deleuze already clearly stated in *The Time-Image*: "Bazin was able to propose and resolve the problems by inventing the notion of 'sequence-shot.'"[6] I must assume that Deleuze had closely read the 1950 book. He restores the quote marks that Bazin himself suppressed—as the archives indicate—between the stage of the hand-written manuscript and that of the typescript:

> We clearly see that the "classical" sequence made up of a series of shots analyzing the action according to the consciousness that the filmmaker wants to make us aware of is resolved here in a single and unique shot. Just as easily, when needed, Welles' découpage in depth of field works toward the disappearance of the notion of shot in a unity of découpage that one might call the "sequence-shot."[7]

Modesty or timidity? In any case the quote marks around "sequence," then "sequence-shot" disappear once the text is typed.

Now for a second rewriting in the literal sense: when Bazin changes the structure of his book in 1958, he uses the expression that we can suppose had, after eight years, passed into the everyday language of cinephiles and film critics, putting it before the aforementioned paragraph that signals its lexical invention. For this reason, the 1958 iteration of the term makes no sense, and above all becomes invisible as such, at least as Bazin's invention and expression, his *mot d'auteur*. In the second edition (Editions du Cerf, 1972), André Labarthe drives the point home by providing a header to the passage that Bazin added in 1958: "The Intuition of the Sequence-Shot," a passage that retrospectively attributes Bazin's own invention to the filmmaker: "One may imagine that the intuition of the sequence-shot, this new unit in film semantics and syntax, grew out of the vision of a director accustomed to placing the actor within the décor."[8] This attribution is undoubtedly reasonable because it is indeed a question of describing Welles' new stylistics, but does it express an unhealthy modesty on Bazin's part or the tranquil assurance of an inventor sure of himself? The response is "neither of the two," if we can somehow get outside the usual power game.

The tiny scriptural detail (two poorly typed quotation marks, subsequently crossed out by hand) is only the beginning of the question of rewriting. The complete historical record goes as follows:

1. It is indeed Welles who in *Citizen Kane* (1941) invents a kind of shot that became his hallmark. If "every shot of a sufficiently marked duration and that integrally contains the development of an action" can be considered a sequence-shot, then *Citizen Kane* includes "28 shots" of this sort "of at least 50 seconds, representing 43 minutes of screening."[9] Interestingly, the analysis by Thomas-Berthomé—a modern study that is difficult to contest since it benefits from all sorts of techniques and post-Bazinian methods of investigation (access to prints, video-cassettes, DVDs, a half century of theoretical literature)—reaches the same conclusions more often than might have been expected.

2. The sequence-shot does not exist. If it is a reality, it is only a discursive one, and not a practice. (It may be crucial to write words about *Citizen Kane*, but it is pointless to try to reshoot it in the laboratory). Perhaps as an "effective discourse," since it is "nicely turned," the sequence-shot is no more than a Freudian slip, as Lacan suggests in my epigraph.[10] This lexical invention is a Bazinian invention. It is an invention *tout court*, something that is productive, and not a mere classification. The shot is opposed by definition to the sequence: Bazin's expression must be understood as a paradox, an initial hypothesis.

Chronologically, Bazin notes the arrival of a new kind of editing, including effects of "editing within the shot" (to use Eisenstein's words). He sees in the two Ws (Welles and Wyler) the first signs of what after his death will be called the modernity of cinema. He subtly notes their antithetical uses and even varied usages within each filmmaker's corpus. In his great 1948 text "William Wyler ou le jansénisme/te de la mise en scène,"[11] he already describes by extension what he is going to call the following year the "sequence-shot": "Even découpage, as the aesthetic of the relationship between shots, is drastically reduced: shot and scene tend to become one."[12]

But he hasn't yet formulated the neologism. In his polished, superb text in the first issue of *Cahiers du Cinéma* (April 1951), "Pour en finir avec la profondeur de champ" (of which unfortunately too little remains in "The Evolution of the Language of Cinema," his after the fact cut-and-paste job for *What Is Cinema?*), Bazin talks routinely about "the depth-of-field sequence-shot of the modern director."[13] Marking the dialectical progress in the history of film language and a sign of its modernity, the sequence-shot thus signals not a renunciation of editing, but its integration from within.

The core of the sequence-shot is best understood in his fine essay, "La technique de *Citizen Kane*," published in *Les Temps modernes* in February 1947. The article contains the usual condemnations of what became loosely known as "Hollywood's transparent editing" after Bazin's death. In several instances he describes this "legendary supple and transparent cinema," ridiculing it and opposing it to Welles' "verbal alchemy."[14] What Bazin generally calls "analytical cutting" is here called, in an original, even unique way, "découpage-editing." Finally, in a simple phrase that seems fundamental to me today in light of my subject, he explains that "this cutting which I would call analytical, tends never to show two things on screen at the same time."[15] I conclude that what Bazin liked in Welles' original style was precisely the appearance of two things at once, and if possible two things very different from each other. Here again he defends radical contiguity against a fraudulent continuity, as he would in the animal films in his essay "Montage Interdit" ("Editing Prohibited").[16] In fact, on the next page we come upon the astounding analysis of the scene of Susan's suicide in *Citizen Kane*. It's true that Bazin praises its depth of field construction without knowing that the shot had been faked using a matte technique (running the same portion of the film stock twice through the film gate: as Zbigniew Rybczynski would do to the nth degree in his film *Tango* in 1980), that produced a sharpness which would otherwise have been technically impossible, and including a middle blurry zone where Kane's wife murmurs in a half-coma between the giant glass of water in the front plane and the door in the background. Still, this does not prevent his text from seeing everything, understanding everything, and feeling everything, to the extent of articulating it, at least for those who know how to read Bazin, those, that is, who stop trying to catch him out. But what does Bazin really talk about? Not about depth of field in the style of Wyler, nor about some automatic supplement of reality, but about an "image stretched between two poles."[17] Bazin's interest goes to polarization and intensity. His concluding remark is classic: "Then the dramatic overload of the image suddenly dissipates as Welles changes shots."[18]

For Bazin, realism is not a moralizing touchstone [*point d'arrivée*] for judging good cinema; it is a point of departure that finds a sinuous trajectory, different in each film, each experience, sometimes each shot. Here, an economy of the variable intensity of the theatrical stage is at stake: neither false nor true, neither open nor closed, what is really at stake, we could say with Bruno Tackels, is Welles' work as stage-writer.[19] In fact, the ultimate explanation for the invention of the sequence-shot (and ultimate proof of Bazin's seriousness) occurred in 1948 at Venice: Bazin the journalist interviews Welles and presents him with his analysis of the shot of Susan's poisoning. To which the *orso gentile*, Welles, answers: "I didn't have a preliminary *découpage*. I invent my *découpage* on the set. The walls were movable, which enabled me to place the camera where I wanted at any given moment."[20] Bazin wrote his book on the heels of this ideal encounter. His lexical invention is thus only the written form, the rewriting of an invention that Welles, inventor of forms, "writer in cinema" as Bazin says, had already written on his film set.

Readers of Deleuze know the fundamental importance of Bazin's lessons for the invention of his philosophy of cinema: very early in *Cinema 1*, while describing Gilbert Simondon's notion of the difference between mold and modulation in the technical object, Deleuze acknowledges an essential passage in Bazin.[21] Perhaps this precise passage from "Theater and Cinema" is what offered Deleuze his notion of "image-movement" which is nothing other than the shot defined by its intensive multiplicity. Then, immediately after, Deleuze discusses the sequence-shot according to Mitry, keeping in mind Rohmer and Chabrol's view in their book on Hitchcock,[22] before providing his own explanation of "what is cinema" with his famous sally on the false match as the dimension of the Open. This is his final word concerning the definition of the shot as unity, and hence concerning the definition of cinema.

The false match will in fact be my second jolt: but I prefer to call the two false matches I am going to talk about—and that Bazin sees without seeing—"improbable jump-cuts."

Two Improbable Jump Cuts

A jump cut is the removal of several frames from the middle of a shot. It may be invisible to the eye or it may provoke a visual change. In Godard's *Breathless* (*A bout de souffle*, 1960), it becomes intentional and definitely visible. But that film was shot in summer 1959, not long after Bazin's death.

And before? Ten years earlier, in 1949, Bazin wrote one of his most beautiful articles on eroticism and death—on the way cinema can bring them together—after having seen and reseen a shocking newsreel image of summary executions in the middle of a Shanghai street. A few years later, in 1953, he reviewed a French film for children, Albert Lamorisse's *White Mane* (*Crin blanc*, 1953), and again raised an eyebrow on what is virtually another hard-core image. After the 1949 snuff movie, we now have a sequence "of a child being beaten": the young boy in the film is dragged by a galloping white horse that finally settles down, slows its pace, stops, and turns its head toward him before becoming his friend. It is an S & M script, where a child is tortured with a horse and rope, as in some perverse spaghetti Western from the 1970s.

Some time ago I pinpointed a curiosity in Bazin's appropriation of *White Mane*: the famous moment where he refers to a change of shot (a cut) which he believes failed and which he discusses to justify one of the rare dictums of his critical career (the "editing prohibited" dictum). Bazin claims peremptorily that the shot/reverse-shot between the horse and the child at the moment when, at last calmed down, they look at one another, should have been replaced by a pan [figures 18.1–18.2]. In this way the spectator could have willingly believed in hindsight that the child had indeed gone through hell in the film just to become a man-horse, as in some new myth (which the closing shot will signify, according to Bazin's careful reading). Later on, a moralizing Serge Daney would abuse Bazin by suggesting that as a Christian he wanted the scene to be given in single-shot continuity the better to revel in the story's cruelty. (In fact, Daney here projects himself into Bazin).[23] What is staggering is that this is not some indifferent moment in the film's narrative and symbolic economy; it is truly the integral center, its fold, the moment when the myth of "the child-animal" arises from the backdrop of a documentary about the Camargue region of France. And in this exact spot, a moment before the match-cut condemned by Bazin, a technical false match occurs, a slightly unconventional linking cut along the axis between the camera and the child on the ground, visible only by repeated viewings on tape or DVD, or at an editing table. I am convinced that this is what Bazin's eye saw, this tiny visual disturbance. Technically, we're speaking of something that is the opposite of a jump cut, since it concerns two nearly identical shots following one another, but the result is the same: the effect of a quasi-invisible visual jump [figures 18.3–18.4]. Still, neither Lamorisse nor *Crin blanc* revolutionized film grammar [*l'écriture du cinéma*] in the postwar period. However,

FIGURES 18.1–18.2: Dubious shot/reverse-shot (*White Mane*, 1954)

the film is utterly of its time, 1953. Consider John Ford's *The Searchers*, which Jean-Louis Leu-trat sees as the origin of the modern false match, related to the broken line characteristic of Navajo rugs. Ford's film dates from 1956 while Rossellini's *Voyage to Italy*, which Alain Bergala associates with what he calls the "ontological false match," is from 1954.[24] Intentional or not, the little visible-invisible cut that divides *White Mane* in two is clearly present already in 1953, and it is indeed around this that Bazin constructs a complete theory, one that he finally recanted

FIGURES 18.3–18.4: Incongruous cut on axis (*White Mane*, 1954)

in 1958 when he recognized with horror the total success of "editing prohibited" in *Perri*, a quite dishonest Walt Disney production, a film set in the savagery of wild nature, but where any possibility of some sudden emergence of the real by an involuntary mismatch had been strictly ruled out.[25]

Double blindness. A first blindness was theorized by Bazin himself: strictly speaking, "editing prohibited" is a stylistic dictum that Bazin formulated in relation to one case, but whose consequence would lead to the worst in Disney and elsewhere. Second blindness: Bazin misses the false match in a shot right nearby the case he had noticed, and so he misses the effect of its meaning which we can now understand to be structurally and historically crucial.

My little analytical experimentation on double blindness contributes to a double view: proper rewriting of the image consists in stumbling where there is a fault, by hiccupping on the story's (and history's) own hiccup.

Long after having spotted Bazin's acute awareness of the false match in *White Mane*, I noticed that the newsreel that he mentions in 1949, which gave rise to his bold concept of "ontological pornography," was available on the Internet, called "In [*sic*] Streets of Shanghai." We see five prisoners, hands tied behind their backs, pushed onto a crowded square and executed one after the other with a bullet to the back of the neck. A moment later they are lying in their own blood.

Describing this sacred horror in a brilliant, Bergsonian philosophical demonstration, Bazin insists precisely on the abnormal series of redoublings that this abnormal spectacle of death produces in the image. "To change the metaphor, death is to duration as a sexual moment is to love in general, the ultimate experience of a kind of coitus with time."[26] Here, as in the following sentence, and even more explicitly in his article on the filmed bullfight that brings up the theme again several years later,[27] orgasm is taken as the annihilation of consciousness, impossible to define in its own moment, only by its prelude and its aftermath, and consequently comparable to death in the sense of "the absolute zero of time," its "point of sudden arrival." For Malraux, death transforms life into destiny; this is also true for Sartrian existentialism, whose watchword, magnificently quoted by Bazin in the second issue of the *Cahiers du Cinéma*, was: "death will only be afterwards."[28] Spinning Bazin's metaphor, if Bergsonian duration is coitus, death is its orgasm. But even more, orgasm in the sexual act can be neither shown nor seen as it is, just as a living being cannot see his death since he is only declared living at the moment when he discovers he is mortal, at the moment of his death. There again cinema rewrites; if death snatches lived life from under our eyes each time we rewatch these poor men dying in the newsreel, then indeed Bazin is right, it deserves the name porno (we "see them re-die" he writes, which is more exact and more philosophico-filmic than "to again see them die"). Thus in Bazin the snuff movie is pornographic not by moral judgment, but by a philosophical logic particular to his epoch, close to that of his contemporaries Klossowski, Bataille, and Blanchot.

Then Bazin points to the most painful detail: "the gesture of the policeman who had to make two attempts with his jammed revolver."[29] Once again we have the *White Mane* effect: by dint of looking repeatedly at this newsreel fragment, "In Streets of Shanghai"—though my modern experience at home on YouTube[30] is not like Bazin's at each film screening—I see how this briefest of episodes unrolls, a policeman's monstrous gesture of firing without killing at first, before he clears his jammed gun in order to start over: an almost invisible jump cut, but one which you can never forget once you've seen it, as it shortens the atrocious suspense! Undoubtedly, the policeman took too long in reloading his pistol for the accelerated editing style that is characteristic of newsreels from the period, with its vulgar voiceover commentary. Once again, Bazin was not able to discern as we can today this tiny visual jump, barely perceptible at a public theater screening; yet once again we can suppose that he subliminally sensed it, and devised around this precise, and historically dense stumbling block, a consistent theory.

In short, Bazin saw all that was going to happen in the discussion and use of this image. More exactly, he may have "seen nothing," like Duras' and Resnais' character in Hiroshima, but he wrote it all. He wrote it before *Breathless*; before Resnais' feature-length films; before America would feel the repercussions of the assassination of J.F.K., when history itself stammered.[31] For the Shanghai scene repeated itself in Vietnam, when a policeman killed a prisoner in the middle of the street and was photographed and filmed. The cinema took possession of this event. Today this repetition of horror can be seen on YouTube without any technical glitch and without waiting: it occurs in the Peter Davis film from 1974, *Hearts and Minds*.[32] This sequence would inspire Pasolini in *Salo, or the 120 Days of Sodom* (1975). According to his screenwriter Sergio Citti this was practically Pasolini's only personal contribution to a script that had been completely reworked before he took an interest in it.[33] The scene in *Salo*, falsely Sadian, rests on a Pierre Klossowski premise: it concerns the pretense of killing a young boy, the winner of the best-ass competition, the future star of hard-core, the best of the slaves elevated to the top class in the society of the spectacle. . . but the gun is empty, so his death can be repeated as often as you like. "Dead without a requiem, the eternal dead-again of the cinema,"[34] says Bazin about the filmed bullfights and the bloody newsreels from Shanghai, the snuff movies of their day.

Let me close: Bazin was the last innocent scholar, coming just before scholars arrive who "know," like Jean-Luc Godard, to stick with the example of the jump cut, since Godard is famous for being "the first" to make conscious use of it, albeit less spectacularly. In this matter he stands as a scholar who "knows," while Bazin's knowledge—his way of seeing without seeing—has "sacrificed the sacred to its sacrilege."

To Cause a Stammer Is a Creative Act

As an epilogue let me explain that the idea of the second "é" in my title ("*réécriture*") came to me on second thought (this instead of "*récriture*" which exists as proper French, and which would normally be my preference as it seems less awkward).[35] Rereading this text one day, I phonetically heard "*arrêt sur image*" (freeze-frame) in the phrase "*ré-écriture sur image*" (re-writing the image). Apparently, this wouldn't suit me since I envisioned "re-writing the image" as part of a dynamic filmic discourse, a resurgence rather than a stopping or a fixing, and I remain affectively loyal to the moral condemnation of the freeze-frame so often used at the end of films, expressed by my dearly missed friend Jean-Claude Biette in his article, "Malédiction du photogramme" ("The Curse of the Film Frame").[36] But the internal hiatus of this *réécriture* suits the meaning of the word and makes me think of Bazin's famous stutter which, incidentally, would constitute a real psycho-physiological explanation of the doubled form of his thought. "*Réécriture sur image*" is historically opposed to "*arrêt sur image*" if one considers this to be the central gesture of film, that is to say the "scientific discourse" of my own academic generation, rather than Bazin's discourse. Bazin lived before the era of the epistemological analysis of film, though he should henceforth, in good logic, follow it. Returning to Bazin is not to revert to a bygone state, but to overtake the frame's forward drive with the vehicle of writing, so as to once again capture what by definition must escape it.

Moral: as a film spectator, we have every right to not want to stop images; but if we choose to, whether we possess a Blue-Ray, HD-DVD or a simple DVD player, or even an old VCR, the fact is that in reality there is no *arrêt sur image*, no way of stopping images, except through writing.

Second moral: rewriting the image consists of going backward in order to go forward. Returning to Bazin is to turn around toward him, looking backward. But scientifically as well as in literary terms, it is to move forward.

"As if language became animal."[37]

Notes

1. Aristotle, *Nicomachean Ethics*, ed. and trans. Roger Crisp (New York: Cambridge University Press, 2000), 105.

2. For more on this topic, see Hervé Joubert-Laurencin, "Montage leur beau souci: Cassavetes, Pasolini, McLaren," in *Cinéma: Acte et présence*, ed. Michel Bouvier, Michel Larouche and Lucie Roy (Quebec: Nota Bene, 1999), 175–86. Giorgio Agamben put forward the idea of "de-creation" in Gilles Deleuze and Giorgio Agamben, *Bartleby: La formula della creazione* (Macerata: Ed. Quodlibet, 1994). English translations: "Bartleby Writes No More: Ethics for the Freedom Not To Be," trans. John Shepley, *New Observations*, 75 (April 1–May 14, 1990), 8–11. See also Agamben, "Bartleby, or On Contingency," in *Potentialities: Collected Essays in Philosophy*, trans. Daniel Heller-Roazen (Stanford: Stanford University Press, 1999), 243–71.

3. "Necessary" here means to not be able to not be, while "contingent" is the ability to not be. The two other of Leibniz's four modalities described in his *Elements of Natural Law* are the "possible" (to be able to be) and the "impossible" (to not to be able to be). Agamben takes up Leibniz in "Bartleby," ibid.

4. André Bazin, "*Forêt sacrée*," *France observateur*, 256 (April 7, 1955). Unless otherwise noted, translations are by Sally Shafto.

5. Bazin, *Orson Welles*, preface by André S. Labarthe (Paris: Le Cerf, 1972); in English, *Orson Welles: A Critical View*, trans. Jonathan Rosenbaum (London: Elm Tree Books, 1978).

6. Gilles Deleuze, *Cinema 2: The Time Image* trans. Hugh Tomlinson (Minneapolis: University of Minnesota Press, 1989), 107. Here and passim we restore the hyphen to "sequence-shot" that this and other English translations excise to render "plan-séquence," which appears with hyphen throughout Bazin's French versions. In her history of the term "sequence-shot," Elena Dagrada confirms this point: "The expression *sequence-shot* emerged in France around 1950, when André Bazin, in the process of composing the first edition of his monograph on Orson Welles, and in order to fully seize the language and style of the great director, felt the need to coin a new expression. He subsequently used it in several important essays, notably in the second edition of his book on the American filmmaker, written in 1958, shortly before his death." From: *Enciclopedia del cinema*, ed. Istituto della Enciclopedia italiana (Milan, 2004), 427, entry "Piano-sequenza."

7. André Bazin, handwritten, unpaginated manuscript of the book, *Orson Welles* (Paris: Chavane, 1950) in the Bifi-Bibliothèque du film, Cinémathèque Française, Paris, cote LACHENAY-B3. The fifty-six-page manuscript is followed by a typescript of sixty-six pages, annotated by hand. The quoted passage is located on page fifty-five of the typescript and corresponds to page fifty-four of the Chavane edition. The quote marks around *séquence* have been crossed out by hand and those around *plan-séquence* were not used in the typescript.

8. Bazin, *Orson Welles: A Critical View*, 67.

9. François Thomas and Jean-Pierre Berthomé, *Citizen Kane* (Paris: Flammarion, 1992), 172.

10. Jacques Lacan, *Ecrits I* [1966] (Paris: Points Seuil, 1970), 147.

11. The title varies, depending on the edition of the article ("Le janséniste" or "Le jansénisme"): different manuscripts for it are also found in the Lachenay Collection in the Bifi of the Cinémathèque Française.

12. Bazin, "William Wyler, the Jansenist of Mise en Scène," in *What Is Cinema?* trans. Timothy Barnard (Montreal: Caboose, 2009), 59.

13. *Cahiers du Cinéma*, 1 (April 1951), 23; *Qu'est-ce que le cinéma?* (1975), 74. Original: "le plan-séquence en profondeur de champ du metteur en scène moderne." Hugh Gray's translation in *What Is Cinema?* misapprehends the key term: "the sequence of shots 'in depth' of the contemporary director." Timothy Barnard's new translation of *What Is Cinema?* (Montreal: Caboose, 2009) also misses the force of the original: "modern filmmakers who use long takes and depth of field," 100. Barnard however includes an extensive note on the term *découpage* and on the issue of "continuity" central to the current essay.

14. Bazin's expression, "alchimie du verbe," would be immediately recognizable to a French reader as an echo of Rimbaud's fourth chapter of *A Season in Hell*, "l'alchimie du verbe." "Verbal alchemy" here replaces the existing

translation, "alchemy of modern cinematic language," used in "The Technique of *Citizen Kane*," in *Bazin at Work: Major Essays and Reviews from the Forties and Fifties*, trans. Bert Cardullo (New York: Routledge, 1998), 237. Note by Sally Shafto.

15. Bazin, "The Technique of *Citizen Kane*," 233. French original: "La technique de *Citizen Kane*," *Les Temps modernes*, 17 (February 1947), 946.

16. We rely here on Barnard's rendition of what Hugh Gray calls "The Virtues and Limitations of Montage," Barnard lays out the key distinctions among the terms editing, *découpage*, and montage in the endnotes of his translation of *What Is Cinema?*

17. Bazin, "The Technique of *Citizen Kane*," 234. The author here points out the euphonic homonymy between the words *pole* and *épaule* (shoulder) in Bazin's description of an "image stretched between two poles" and Kane's *coups d'épaule*, untranslatable into English. Note by Sally Shafto.

18. Ibid.

19. "Stage-writer" is a concept developed by Bruno Tackels in a series of books on contemporary theatrical experiences: *Ecrivains de plateau 1: Les Castellucci*, 2005; 2: *François Tanguy et le théâtre du Radeau*, 2005; 3: *Anatoli Vassiliev*, 2006; 4: *Rodrigo García*, 2007 (Besançon: Solitaires intempestifs).

20. Orson Welles, "Les secrets d'Orson Welles. Entretien exclusif par André Bazin et [Jean-Charles] Tacchella," *Ecran français*, 169 (September 21, 1948). In a poem, Pier Paolo Pasolini nicknamed Welles "orso gentile" (amiable bear).

21. Gilles Deleuze, *Cinema 1: The Movement-Image* (Minneapolis: University of Minnesota Press, 1987), 24.

22. Deleuze on Mitry's reaction to the "sequence-shot" is found on page 25 of *Cinema 1*. He and Mitry have in mind two fundamental pages of Eric Rohmer and Claude Chabrol, *Hitchcock, the First Forty-four Films*, trans. Stanley Hochman (New York: Ungar, 1979), 95–96.

23. Serge Daney. "The Screen of Fantasy (Bazin and Animals)," in *Rites of Realism*, ed. Ivone Margulies, trans. Mark A. Cohen (Durham, NC: Duke University Press, 2003). 32–41. Originally published as "L'écran du fantasme," *Cahiers du Cinéma*, 236–37 (March–April 1972), 31–40; a modified version of this text, "L'écran du fantasme (Bazin et les bêtes)," was published in *La rampe. Cahier critique 1970–1982* (Paris: Cahiers du Cinéma/Gallimard, 1983), 34–42.

24. Jean-Louis Leutrat, *John Ford: La prisonnière du désert: Une tapisserie Navajo* (Paris: Adam Biro, 1990), 46 and *passim*. Alain Bergala, *Voyage en Italie* (Crisnée: Yellow Now, 1990), 20, 49–50 and *passim*.

25. Bazin, "Les périls de Perri," *Cahiers du Cinéma*, 83 (May 1958), 50–53. For more details, see Hervé Joubert-Laurencin, *La lettre volante: Quatre essais sur le cinéma d'animation* (Paris: Presses de la Sorbonne nouvelle, 1997), 1–34, 79–82.

26. Bazin, "La mort à l'écran," *Esprit* (September 1949), 442. This article is partially reworked in "Death Every Afternoon," in *Rites of Realism*. However, this particular passage is not retained there.

27. Bazin, "Mort tous les après-midi.," *Cahiers du Cinéma*, 7 (December 1951). Republished in Bazin, *Le cinéma français de la Libération à la Nouvelle Vague (1945–1958)*, ed. Jean Narboni (Paris: Cahiers du Cinéma, 1983), 249–52; trans. in *Rites of Realism*.

28. See Bazin, "A Saint Becomes a Saint Only After the Fact (*Heaven over the Marshes*)," in *Bazin at Work: Major Essays and Reviews from the Forties and Fifties*, 205–9. Original: "Un saint ne l'est qu'après," *Cahiers du Cinéma*, 2 (May 1951). Bazin's title echoes Jean-Paul Sartre, *L'existentialisme est un humanisme* (Paris: Nagel, 1946) [1970, p. 22]: "Man as imagined by Existentialism . . . is first of all nothing. He will be something only after the fact."

29. Bazin, "Death Every Afternoon," in *Rites of Realism*, 31.

30. Available at http://www.youtube.com/watch?v=Oy3J-tnIIQk.

31. See Jean-Baptiste Thoret, *26 secondes: L'Amérique éclaboussée. L'assassinat de JFK et le cinéma américain* (Pertuis: Rouge profond, 2003). Bernard Benoliel offers the following commentary on this work, which concerns the reinvention of the paradox of cinema as a trace that records reality: "Does the assassination film inaugurate the era of 'a crisis of the visible'? What really fascinates in the Zapruder super-8 film? Its possibility to have seen the event and its incapacity to render it intelligible to us, its value as a film-witness and its state as a blind film." Bernard Benoliel, "L'expérience interdite: À propos et à partir d'un livre, *26 secondes: L'Amérique éclaboussée*," *Cinéma 07* (Paris: Léo Scheer, Spring 2004), 113–21; quotation p. 118.

32. See the trailer for *Hearts and Minds* on YouTube: http://www.youtube.com/watch?v=QcE6CdR60NY.

33. Joubert-Laurencin, *Pasolini: Portrait du poète en cinéaste* (Paris: Cahiers du Cinéma, 1995), 289–90. See too Pier Paolo Pasolini's own comment on this topic ("Interview with Gideon Bachmann and Donata Gallo,"

Filmcritica, 256 (August 1975); republished in Pasolini's complete works, vol. 8, *Per il cinema* (Milan: Mondadori, collection "i Meridiani," 2001), 3028: "It's a solution that I added myself to the film: pretending to kill the victim but in reality not killing him at all: to press a pistol on his temple, pull the trigger and to fire blanks; *the return to life [becomes] a perverse variant; it becomes the rite of a consummated death.*" Emphasis mine.

34.　Bazin, "Death Every Afternoon," 31.

35.　Translator's note: The author's original title in French is: "La Réécriture sur image: Deux effets de futur antérieur dans l'écriture d'André Bazin." By hyphenating "ré-écriture" later in this paragraph the author draws attention to his simulation of a stammer in his title. Difficult to imitate in English, we can only hyphenate the corresponding term: "re-writing" but without the possibility of hinting at an extra syllable the way the French does.

36.　Jean-Claude Biette, *Poétique des auteurs* (Paris: Cahiers du Cinéma, 1988), 128–30. Originally published in *Cahiers du Cinéma*, 379 (January 1986).

37.　The full citation with which I close: "To cause language itself to stammer, in the depths of style, is a creative process that penetrates great works. As if language became animal." Gilles Deleuze, "Re-présentation de Masoch," *Libération* (May 18, 1989), trans. Daniel W. Smith and Michael A. Greco in *Essays Critical and Clinical*, (Minneapolis: University of Minnesota Press, 1997), 73.

PART THREE

Historical Moment

19

The Eloquent Image
The Postwar Mission of Film and Criticism

PHILIP WATTS

At the very end of his life and in an article published posthumously, André Bazin took stock of his role as a professional film critic.[1] His appraisal was not entirely positive. "The main satisfaction that my profession gives me," he wrote, "comes from its near-futility. To write film criticism is more or less the equivalent of spitting from a bridge" (CF, 298). Few people read film criticism; reviews have little bearing on a film's success at the box office, especially in the face of mass marketing, and the exchange between critics and filmmakers is nearly nonexistent. This, writes Bazin, is as it should be. For the pleasure derived from being a film critic can be found not in having power over the commercial fate of a film, nor even in influencing filmmakers, but in helping to "extend" in the spectator the "shock of the work of art" (CF, 309). The task of the critic is not to bring to the reader "an objective truth" (CF, 308) but rather to engage the spectator, to help formulate judgment, to convince the spectator about the value of the filmic work of art. This is why, Bazin tells us, he always preferred the debates of the ciné-clubs to the articles he had to write to earn a living, for it was in these debates that he was reminded how a film exists within a web of arguments, of conversations, of deliberations and discussions about the status of movies, about the ways in which films function in society, and about the relation of cinema to the world. Film criticism is an extension of the aesthetic experience by other means, and Bazin insists that it cannot exist without the "intelligence" and "sensitivity" of the spectator. For Bazin, film criticism is part of a rhetorical practice. This helps to explain why even the briefest of his articles is constructed according to a rigorous argumentative logic, and why, throughout his writing career, he readily borrowed from an anachronistic rhetorical terminology to describe and defend the postwar cinematographic avant-garde.

Even while he advocated for an impure cinema, Bazin relied upon a descriptive terminology taken from the registers of classical eloquence. Terms such as "simplicity," "sobriety," "austerity," "clarity," "rigor," "purity"—a whole battery of qualifiers that come straight out of a rhetorical tradition—are scattered throughout Bazin's writings and constitute one of the foundations of his aesthetic theory. These terms are most visibly at work in the 1948 article "William Wyler, the Jansenist of Mise en Scène." The term "Jansenist" here is surely playful,[2] yet it bears a serious referent as a key term to Bazin's *art poétique*. What Bazin sees in the director of

The Little Foxes (1941) and *The Best Years of Our Lives* (1946) is an unrelenting stylist, dedicated to simplifying and purifying the image. This "styleless style" that Bazin finds in Wyler's films, his "asceticism," "spareness," and "neutrality," all conform to a rhetorical ideal whose goal was to reduce cinematographic language to its simplest forms and to transform the scenes and settings of the film into what Bazin calls a dramatic site "as impersonal as the antechambers of classical tragedies" (WCB, 47). Bazin was turning Wyler into a new Racine and Bette Davis into an American Phèdre.

The Wyler example is hardly an exception. In a 1944 article on Jean Grémillion, Bazin speaks of his "cinematographic virtuosity," which results in the "extraordinary erasure of his technique" (CF, 196). In an essay written two years later on René Clément, Bazin criticizes the "luxurious" images of Henri Alekan but praises Clément for his "tact" and his "simplicity" (CF, 146), and the "extreme sobriety" of his film *Au-delà des grilles* (*The Walls of Malapaga*, 1948) (CF, 151). About Robert Bresson, Bazin writes approvingly of the director's effort to create an "increasingly impoverished image" (WC1, 127), of a style that achieves "the most rigorous form of aesthetic abstraction while avoiding expressionism" (WC1, 132). As Bazin sees it, in filming *Les Dames du bois de Boulogne* (1944) Bresson engaged in the same stylistic rigor that characterizes the classical theater of that other Jansenist, Jean Racine.

This defense of stylistic austerity is at the center of Bazin's advocacy of Italian neorealism. What Bazin sees in De Sica's films is not a crude realism, but a long, drawn-out work that is the very opposite of improvisation: "De Sica's film took a long time to prepare, and everything was as minutely planned as for a studio superproduction" (WC2, 57). But the result of all this labor is the very opposite of a Hollywood spectacle. It is what Bazin calls "supreme naturalness," the result of "an ever-present although invisible system of aesthetics" (WC2, 58). Likewise, in his defense of Rossellini, Bazin writes, "To have regard for reality does not mean that what one does in fact is to pile up appearances. On the contrary, it means that one strips the appearances of all that is not essential, in order to get at the totality in its simplicity" (WC2, 101). Bazin makes explicit the equivalence he is drawing between Italian neorealism and classical eloquence:

> Rossellini . . . seems to strip [his film] down further each time, to stylize it with a painful but nonetheless unrelenting rigor, in short to return to a classicism of dramatic expression in acting as well as in mise en scène. . . . A film like this is the very opposite of a realistic one "drawn from life": it is the equivalent of austere and terse writing, which is so stripped of ornament that it sometimes verges on the ascetic. At this point, neorealism returns full circle to classical abstraction and its generalizing quality. (*Bazin at Work*, 138–39)

Bazin's classicism became an easy target for film critics and theorists in the 1960s and 1970s who, in their rush to define the image as an ideological form, often misunderstood his writings as a defense of transparent realism. But Bazin quite clearly understood film and criticism to be discourses in the contentious cultural field of the postwar period. To explain how film has moved beyond the narrative model of 1930s, he adopts a whole battery of terms that come out of an archaic rhetorical system (developed in the tribunals of seventeenth century France) whose goal was to persuade the audience through rhetorical simplicity stripped of ornament.[3] This form of eloquence came to so totally dominate the French educational system that Bazin certainly internalized it during his studies at the *lycée* and the *École normale supérieure* at Saint-Cloud. A more direct source for Bazin may have been André Gide, whom Bazin cites in the Wyler article and who, in the 1920s and 1930s, argued for the necessary ties between modernism and stylistic asceticism. To cite just one example, in fragments published in the *Nouvelle revue française* in 1935, Gide wrote that the most subtle and highest form of art is an art that remains undetected [qui ne se laisse pas d'abord reconnaître]. Only this stylistic asceticism, only this refusal of what Gide calls "mannerism" could allow the writer to open the modern work of art to multiple characters, to the proliferation of forms and the complexity of reality. For Gide, and for Bazin as well, stylistic purity allowed art to move toward the impurity of the world. Gide ends his 1935 fragment by quoting Pascal's famous maxim: "la vraie éloquence se moque de l'éloquence."[4]

Gide and Bazin were both fascinated by this Jansenist philosopher, an advocate of the *simple naturel*, whose defining characteristic was never to draw attention to itself.[5] In the final version of his celebrated essay "The Ontology of the Photographic Image," Bazin quotes Pascal's famous condemnation of the vanity of art that encourages us to see the painting rather than the thing represented in the painting. Photography and cinema allow us to overcome Pascal's objection. "Henceforth," writes Bazin, "Pascal's condemnation of painting is itself rendered vain since the photograph allows us on the one hand to admire in reproduction something our eyes alone could not have taught us to love, and on the other, to admire the painting as a thing in itself whose relation to something in nature has ceased to be the justification for its existence" (WC1, 16).[6] There is a dual program here: the self-referentiality of modern painting but also the declaration that in its mechanical reproduction of the world, photography has fulfilled the rhetorical ideal advocated by Pascal. My contention, then, is that Bazin's theory of cinema, and of realism in particular, did not entail the elimination of art or of the image or of the cinematographic apparatus, as critics such as Peter Wollen have maintained.[7] Rather, what Bazin calls realism depends upon the understanding of images as engaged in a rhetorical system in which stylistic restraint and the elimination of ornamentation "aims in essence at creating the illusion of reality" (WC2, 26).

So there is a stubborn coincidence in Bazin's writings between ontological realism and eloquence, all the more so in that Bazin sets up his postwar avant-garde against a form of filmmaking that he labels "baroque." In "Ontology of the Photographic Image," Bazin opposes cinema to what he calls the "tortured immobility of Baroque art" (WC1, 11).[8] "Baroque" remains, at best, an ambiguous term in Bazin's essays, often equated with falsity, illusion, and trickery. Even in his defense of Orson Welles—a "baroque" director if ever there was one—Bazin declares that *Citizen Kane* (1941) is Welles' baroque work and that *The Magnificient Ambersons* (1942) its "classical" counterpart, and that, all things considered, the second film is probably the greater of the two.[9] What is more, Bazin inscribes this classical/baroque opposition within a cold war aesthetic geography. For Bazin, William Wyler the "Jansenist" embodies a new "liberal and democratic" cinema coming from Hollywood, while Eisenstein is compared to Tintoretto, the Venetian master of baroque illusion (WC1 12). At a time when film was increasingly mobilized in the competitions of the cold war, Bazin turned to an aesthetic that, he believed, allowed the audience to free itself from the illusions and mystifications of partisan cinema.

Why place Bazin in this aesthetic and rhetorical *longue durée*? And why prefer rhetorical or cinematographic "clarity" if it is nothing more than another illusion, just like the baroque? Some might tie Bazin's aesthetic vocabulary to his schooling in a national system where reading Pascal was unavoidable and where these rhetorical ideals not only reigned supreme but were understood as embodying a national spirit. Certainly, when Bazin declares that "le français n'a pas le génie baroque," as he does in a paragraph on Max Ophuls, we might conclude that for all their originality, his essays reproduce a dominant national aesthetic and ideological system (CF, 37). But this type of interpretation, in which a thinker is understood as an instance of his times, does not prove very productive.

Rather, let me propose that Bazin's anachronistic Atticism is closely linked to the way he thought about the politics of cinema. There is no doubt that for Bazin, stylistic restraint is crucial in that it allows cinema and the spectator to encounter the world more directly. But a rhetorical understanding of cinema is also essential to Bazin's understanding of film as a popular art intimately tied to the politics and to the history of the contemporary world.

To be sure, in defending Atticism as an ideal for approaching cinema, Bazin is transferring onto film some of the symbolic prestige that French culture has traditionally invested in classical literature and philosophy. His defense of cinema is also a defense of what in 1943 he called "snobbism"—a "militant form of taste" in the aesthetic wars he was waging (CF, 292). And he isn't alone. Postwar French film criticism is saturated with references to cinema as a classical art: Eric Rohmer's argument that cinema should rely on stylistic purity, simplicity, and clarity as a way of reproducing the beauty of the world, Jacques Rivette's fascination with Corneille's tragic theater, Godard's claim that the Hollywood director Anthony Mann is the Virgil of modern times—all these declarations are attempts to bestow the prestige of the classical tradition on the movies.[10] At stake in such writings, and in Bazin's work in particular, is an attempt to upend aesthetic hierarchies. To be sure, "popular art" and "popular culture" are contested terms in the postwar years. For many on the left, using the phrase "popular culture" was key to recognizing forms of art and of cultural production associated with French peasants and workers that had been devalued and ignored by the dominant cultural institutions of France, from the Académie française to the national education system. For others, notably Louis Aragon, the term already smacked of elitism: to define an object as belonging to "popular culture," as opposed to defining it as art, was to devalue the work and to ask it to occupy the lowest rung of an aesthetic and social hierarchy.[11] For Aragon, this designation reified the very division between elite and working-class cultures that it claimed to contest.

Bazin's response to this debate is to bring together a vocabulary that is usually tied to the most serious philosophical and aesthetic subjects with the most popular art form of his times. Bazin had no interest in defending the purity of cinema as an art, nor defending some hierarchy of arts or of cinematographic genres. Opening Bazin's corpus involves reading seriously his essays on minor forms, on television, on musical comedies, on the Western, on everything that lies outside the purview of art cinema. What is more, when Bazin speaks of the purity of the image, it is most often when his gaze has been struck by the most common of objects, by the banal moments of everyday experience. What does Bazin see when he watches a film? The plot, to a certain extent, characters, actors, camera movement, to be sure, but also, invariably, the most trivial of things. Bazin's essays are a vast inventory of insignificant moments that constitute modern cinema: a wet sidewalk, the gesture of a child, the door of a restaurant, a ping-pong ball, the sound of a horse's hooves on the pavement, the squeak of a windshield wiper, the pox marks on an actor's face, the lapping of waves against a wooden rowboat, a maid closing a door with her foot. Bazin's entire system of eloquence is at the service of the most ordinary of objects and of revealing what he calls the "ontological equality" (WC2, 81) that inhabits the space of cinema. Both through its defense of film as a popular art and through this focus on the commonplace, Bazin's turn to rhetoric participates in what we might call, following Jacques Rancière, a reversal of aesthetic hierarchies.[12]

For Walter Benjamin, cinema was a democratic art because, for the first time, anything and anyone—common people in a crowd as well princes and movie stars—could be represented on the screen. For Bazin, cinema is a democratic art not just by virtue of its mass appeal but because it provides the occasion for an encounter between an archaic and prestigious rhetorical system and the commonness, disorder, and equality of everyday people and everyday things. In the classical rhetorical tradition, the simple style was reserved for the highest subjects, for philosophical and metaphysical truths. In Bazin's writing, films—those, of course, that he liked—put their eloquence at the service of all people and of all things. And if terms such as "simplicity," "purity," and "spareness" seem to show up with greater frequency when Bazin is speaking of realism it is because realism was the aesthetic of the ordinary. To borrow the language of aesthetic prestige was to close the gap between an "elite" and a "popular" cinema, reasserting film's role in our understanding of the common.[13]

If I have insisted so much on the function of rhetoric in Bazin's attempt to think visually, it is because cinema, for Bazin, was always intimately tied to pedagogy, to debates, to a sense of sharing a common space, and to what Dudley Andrew has called "the battle to attain community."[14] It is in this sense also that cinema is a rhetorical object for Bazin: it binds us to others: to friends, to rivals, to strangers, to all those who share a gaze, a narrative, and a world, even if only for a moment. For Bazin, as for Stanley Cavell in *The World Viewed*, it is in conversation and debate that we begin to understand a film, and it is in debates around a film that we begin to understand the world that surrounds us.[15] Cinema, for Bazin, was a social activity and screenings were intimately tied to discussion, debates, articles, correspondence, an endless deployment of moments of exchange and of persuasion.

This was brought home to me when I consulted the André Bazin archives that Dudley Andrew and Hervé Joubert-Laurencin have assembled. Within this treasure of articles I found several that Bazin had written on how to present and discuss a film with an audience, written as reflections on his active participation in *Travail et Culture*, a movement founded in September 1944 to coordinate educational activities around popular culture in postwar France.[16] The texts are precious pedagogical instruments, reminding us how Bazin's defense and promotion of cinema is always tied to more general conversations about the role films play in our being and working together. The purpose of ciné-club screenings is evident to him: the audience, especially the "popular" audience, is there to see a film, not to hear a lecture, and this raises specific "pedagogical" problems. No matter how well-prepared the presenters may be, Bazin tells us, they must never get in the way of the film. The goal of the presentation is to "educate the spectator" in the history of cinema, while being careful to minimize the introduction so that the spectator will receive the film "with its full force" [*de plein fouet*].[17] It is after the film, during the debate, that the real discussion takes place. At this point, Bazin calls upon what he terms his "general law" of ciné-club debates. He would write that the "debater," the leader of the discussions, must guide them with "open authority" [*autorité ouverte*] and "directed freedom" [*liberté dirigée*]. "The problem is that one must leave the audience with the illusion of critical freedom, while at the same time protecting the room against the bores and the obviously superfluous digressions."[18] In addition, the deft teacher should give the public the feeling of "critical freedom," that is, the freedom to judge the film. The art of the presenter is *not* to impose a particular way of seeing but to "respect the life of the debate" and to "provoke the opinions of the public."[19] The goal of the presentation is to make itself invisible.

Bazin's description of the ciné-club debate is uncannily similar to his descriptions of the realist image—its rhetorical efficacy resides in its ability to give a sense of interpretative freedom to the spectator. If William Wyler's films are "liberal and democratic," it is because he has adopted a style that, Bazin feels, encourages the critical freedom of the spectator. And if Bazin, somewhat improbably, calls Orson Welles a realist, it is because *Citizen Kane* allows for an uncertainty in interpretation that encourages the spectator "to exercise at least a minimum of personal choice" in interpreting the film (WC1, 36). Likewise, the rhetorical and pedagogical model that Bazin deploys in his description of a post-film debate is one in which eloquence carries the spectators toward truth, as if they had discovered it on their own. For Bazin, cinema is always tied to an argumentative network, it is always involved in the business of persuasion, in public debates, critical essays, conversations. But the key remains the active engagement of the spectator in the construction of meaning and judgment. A "liberal and democratic" cinema is a cinema that frees the spectator's thought, whose images encourage the spectator not to be distracted during the viewing, but rather to judge, to interpret, and to formulate hypotheses.

Bazin's views here are of a piece with the stated mission of *L'Ecran français*, a journal born of the Resistance and one of the most eclectic and richest film journals in postwar France, until it was absorbed by *Les Lettres françaises* in 1953.[20] In a July 1945 editorial, the editors declare that "our journal will be a combat publication. Our role is to convince and persuade. It is necessary that everything be set up so that quickly, thanks to cinema, the French spirit and French culture may once again shine [*rayonner*] not only in France, but throughout the world . . . The cinematographic art is the only internal means of expression that allows people [*les peuples*] to understand one another and to come together."[21] The critic as rhetorician, the need to defend and rebuild the French cinematographic industry, and cinema as an international language of fraternity and perhaps of Revolution; these are the stated goals of *L'Ecran français* in its early years. As years passed, however, and as the cold war took hold, all three of these goals became increasingly polemical, as the writers at *L'Ecran français* understood their mission to be not just a defense of French cinema but an incessant constant critique of Hollywood. Indeed, reading the issues from the last years of *L'Ecran français*, one is struck by the almost ceaseless demystification of Hollywood films. Typical of this strategy is the January 1952 article by Georges Sadoul on the Howard Hawks production, *The Thing From Another World* (1951). In their polar police station, Sadoul tells us, the "American occupiers" are divided into two camps that debate what to do with this creature they have found: the scientists who want to study it, and the military, whose "Führer" "takes out his revolver as soon as he hears the word 'culture.'" The military wins out, and the captain "electrocutes" the Thing—just as Americans electrocute their "blacks," Sadoul helpfully reminds his audience. *The Thing* is not just a sci-fi thriller, but what Sadoul calls an "avant-garde," announcing the onslaught of Hollywood science-fiction films in France, as well as the introduction of a violent American culture, armed with a nuclear arsenal and bent on "terrorizing" the world.[22]

It seems to me that Bazin's pedagogy of the image is constructed, at least in part, against this compulsion to demystify. For demystification—the uncovering of an economic or psychic reality behind a representational illusion—is precisely the mode of interpretation that gives full hermeneutic power to the licensed critic. Bazin's restoration to the spectator of even a semblance of interpretive freedom—what he called "directed freedom"—is the very opposite of this impulse. Demystification presumes that spectators have no interpretive aptitude, that left on their own they are necessarily duped by the image on the screen. Symptomatically, two of Bazin's most famous articles indulge in this type of exercise, only to turn it back against the experts: "The Entomology of the Pin-Up Girl," published in *L'Ecran français* in 1946 and "The Stalin Myth in Soviet Cinema," published in *Esprit* in 1950. Both show that demystifiers can always be demystified themselves. Well aware of cinema's role in the polemics of the cold war, Bazin's pedagogy of the image consistently argues for the spectator's freedom of interpretation, upending the hierarchy of critic above spectator. In the depths of the cold war, filled with critics who understood their role as that of uncovering the ideological mystifications at work in the moving image, Bazin's conception of his labor lay elsewhere. For a debate to succeed and for films to play a positive role in the polis, Bazin tells us, one needs more than the competence of the presenter and the interpretative authority of the critic. One needs the *lumière*, the light, the intelligence of the audience.

Bazin's notion of the eloquent image and its role in culture was ratified and sustained by the terrible history of his times, specifically, the discovery of the mass murders of the Second World War. For his defense of a simplified cinematographic style responds in fact to the use of films as evidence at the Nuremberg trials.

True, his championing of the image's potent power of credibility, this combination of technical realism and a rhetoric of visual austerity, clearly predates the Nuremberg trials. Bazin had begun to come to these conclusions sometime in late 1943, and formulated his theory in an article published in the spring of 1944.[23] At the same time, the immediate postwar years initiated what art historian Georges Didi-Huberman has called "a period of *visual evidence*, or *visual proof*," the moment when photographic and filmic documents of the Nazi death camps were used both as definitive proof against the accused Nazis standing trial in Nuremberg for war crimes and crimes against humanity, and as part of a pedagogical mission instituted by the Allied forces to reveal the truth of the horrors of the Nazi regime to the populations of Western Europe.[24] According to American legal scholar Lawrence Douglas, the American prosecutors at the Nuremberg trials, and in particular Robert H. Jackson, wanted to "establish incredible events by credible evidence" and bring "irrefutable" proof of these crimes without precedent, proof that would keep the memory of these events alive, proof that would defuse any skepticism about the extent of the horror; proof, Jackson believed, that images alone could provide.[25] The French historian Christian Delage has made it clear that the films taken at the concentration camps, and shown at the Nuremberg trials starting in November 1945, were the keystone to the prosecution's argument, and that they were given the same status as testimony and as other objective physical traces.[26] Indeed, they may have superseded oral testimony as the leading form of evidence delivered by the prosecution. At the Nuremberg trials, films were shown as one of the last pieces of evidence and by all accounts, it was the projection of the film

Nazi Concentration Camps (1945)—a documentary made by Allied forces—that sealed the fate of the Nazi criminals at their trials. Upon seeing *Nazi Concentration Camps*, the French journalist Madeleine Jacob, who was reporting on the trials for *L'Ecran français*, spoke of the "hallucinating testimony of the screen," and concluded: "I sincerely believe that at the moment when [the accused] left the docket they realized that the efforts of their lawyers . . . were now in vain."[27]

Even in this context, however, the credibility of the images was not a foregone conclusion. For the filmmakers who documented the opening of the camps, the evidence they wanted to provide was inseparable from a specific rhetoric of the image. These filmmakers were particularly concerned about filming in a way that would help to establish the visual and irrefutable proof of what they saw. For Sidney Bernstein, a filmmaker who had worked with Alfred Hitchcock and who was with the British army at Bergen-Belsen, the problem was precisely to maintain the power of credibility of images that would be used to educate a German populace, which, the Allies worried, might greet these images of the destruction of the European Jews with skepticism and disbelief. Bernstein and his crew decided to make films that would, to the greatest extent possible, avoid montage, use the long take and adopt extended depth of field in order to situate figures both in the foreground and the background. In scenes where town notables or soldiers are watching corpses piled in ditches, Bernstein and his crew wanted to prove by a long panorama shot and minimal voice-over commentary that witnesses were present at that moment so that no one could contest the truth of the image. This question of technique was made all the more significant by the fact that the Soviet film documenting Nazi crimes apparently relied heavily upon voice-over commentary and the dramatic juxtaposition of images, and when it was shown in Nuremberg in February 1946, it was considered less convincing to prosecutors and spectators alike.[28]

To what extent was Bazin's pedagogy of the image a response to the trials at Nuremberg? One would be hard-pressed to claim that Bazin is directly responding to prosecutorial strategies or to the use of film as juridical evidence. In his film criticism, Bazin never refers to the Nuremberg trials, and only rarely evokes the newsreels about the death camps that showed in movie houses throughout Europe starting in October 1945.[29] I have found only two articles referring to films about the concentrations camps. The first, published in *Cahiers du Cinéma* in 1952, discusses two films from Eastern Europe.[30] The second was his 1956 article praising Alain Resnais' *Night and Fog* (1955) where Bazin wrote that he was at first hesitant to see Resnais' film given that, "we saw, ten years ago, so many horrible documents that have never left our memories" (CF, 262). Still, in spite of this limited number of references, the images of concentration camps seem to have stayed with Bazin throughout his writings, not so much as a traumatic memory, but rather, in his attempt to tie cinema to a model of persuasion, debate, and credibility.

In his article on William Wyler, Bazin cites Wyler's stunning declaration that working in the Armed Forces—as Wyler, Frank Capra, and George Stevens had done—affected their later feature films. He notes that Stevens "is not the same man for having seen the corpses at Dachau." How could they not hold to an "ethic of realism" and bring across "some of the horror, some of the shocking truths," which they had witnessed during the war (WCB, 50–51). This "ethic of realism" for Bazin took the form of a commitment to a cinema of "austerity," "rigor," and "simplicity." For him, the film-viewing experience always consists of an initial "shock"—the word reappears throughout his essays—which the critic and spectator must then attempt to negotiate, to understand, to translate as best they can. This "ethic of realism" also meant that this negotiation with cinema must always be tied to deliberation, to our encounter with others, and to the ways in which we live together.

Notes

1. André Bazin, "Réflexions sur la critique," *Cinéma 58*, 32 (December 1958). Republished in *Le cinéma française de la Libération à la Nouvelle Vague* (Paris: Cahiers du Cinéma, 1983). This collection is henceforth cited parenthetically as CF. Parenthetical citations marked WCB refer to the Timothy Barnard translation of *What is Cinema?* (Montreal: Caboose, 2009), while those marked WC refer to the U. of Calif. Press volumes.

2. See Bazin's article from the 1955 Cannes film festival in which he compares the life of the film critic at Cannes to that of a monk in a monastery. Bazin "Du festival considéré comme un ordre," in *Qu'est-ce que le cinéma?* vol. 3: *Cinéma et sociologie* (Paris: Cerf, 1959). The article was originally published in *Cahiers du cinéma*, June 1955.

3. Marc Fumaroli, "Baroque et classicisme: L'Imago primi saeculi societatis jesu (1640) et se adversaries," in *Questionnement du baroque*, ed. Alphonse Vermeylen (Brussels: Editions Nauwelaerts, 1986), 110. For an analysis of how this "simple style" has historically been tied to ethics see Michel Foucault, *The Hermeneutics of the Subject: Lectures at the Collège de France 1981–1982*, trans. Graham Burchell (New York: Picador, 2005), 400–401.

4. André Gide, "Feuillets," in *Nouvelle revue française*, 24 (November 1935), 717–20. Translation: "True eloquence scoffs at eloquence."

5. Pierre Force, "Un Discours à pratiquer," in *Critique*, 615–16, 526–42. According to Force, Pascal does not condemn rhetoric, he simply inscribes himself in an Atticist tradition in which the transparency of language is a rhetorical ideal.

6. This quote is not in the 1945 version of the "Ontology" essay and Bazin may have added it in 1958 as a response to Eric Rohmer's June 1951 article titled "Vanité que la Peinture," which proclaimed that cinema was a classical art that would overcome the failings of the avant-garde because only cinema fulfilled the classical (and Pascalian) mission of revealing the beauty of nature. Cinematic realism is precisely the art that will "bathe our eyes in the pure light of classicism." Eric Rohmer, "Such Vanity is Painting" in *The Taste for Beauty*, trans. Carol Volk (London: Cambridge University Press, 1990).

7. Peter Wollen stakes his interpretation of Bazin on claims that for Bazin the cinematic image is a sign corresponding to what C. S. Peirce had called an "index." This leads Wollen to conclude, erroneously in my opinion, that for Bazin cinematography is "pre-cultural" and that Bazin is advocating a "radical purity" leading to cinema's annihilation. *Signs and Meaning in Cinema* (Bloomington: Indiana University Press, 1972), 131.

8. In the early version of this article, Bazin had even spoken of a "baroque heresy." See André Bazin, "Ontologie de l'image photographique," in *Les Problèmes de la peinture*, ed. Gaston Diehl (Paris: Confluences, 1945), 411.

9. André Bazin, *Orson Welles: A Critical View* (Venice, CA: Acrobat Books, 1992), 59.

10. On the relation between spareness and narrative theory in postwar French cinema and theater, see Ivone Margulies, "Refocusing French Spare Drama Around 1948" in *L'Età del Cinema: Criteri e modelli di periodizzazione*, XIV International Film Studies Conference, ed. Leonardo Quaresima and Valentina Re (Udine, Italy: Summer 2008).

11. On the debates around popular culture and the founding of *Travail et Culture* see, for instance, the document "Travail et Culture" presented by Robert Aimé and Maurice Delarue. This document is kept in the library of the Institut national de la jeunesse et de l'éducation populaire and was prepared, as best I can tell, in 1984. Call number: BR ASS6 TRA. My thanks to Sam Dilorio for bringing this document to my attention. See also Dudley Andrew and Steven Ungar, *Popular Front Paris and the Poetics of Culture* (Cambridge, MA: Harvard University Press, 2005).

12. Jacques Rancière, *La Parole muette* (Paris: Hachette, 1998).

13. André Bazin, "Pas de fossé entre un 'cinéma de l'élite' et un 'cinéma populaire,'" *Radio, Cinéma, Télévision*, 120 and 124, May 4 and June 1, 1952.

14. Dudley Andrew, *André Bazin* (New York: Oxford University Press, 1978), 7.

15. "It is the nature of these [movie-going] experiences to be lined with fragments of conversations and responses of friends I have gone to movies with . . . The events associated with movies are those of companionship or lack of companionship: the audience of a book is essentially solitary, one soul at a time; the audience of music and theatre is essentially larger than your immediate acquaintance—a gathering of the city." Stanley Cavell, *The World Viewed: Reflections on the Ontology of Film* (Cambridge: Harvard University Press, 1979), 9–10.

16. See Dudley Andrew, *André Bazin*, 85–96.

17. André Bazin, "Comment présenter et discuter un film!" *Ciné-Club*, April 1954.

18. Original: "Le problème étant de laisser la salle ne fût-ce qu'une illusion de liberté critique, tout en lui assurant un minimum de sécurité contre les raseurs et les digressions nettement superflues." André Bazin, "Comment présenter et discuter un film!"

19. See also André Bazin, "Conseils aux animateurs de Ciné-Club: Comment on prépare les débats au Ciné-Club d'Annecy," *Education populaire*, December 7, 1948.

20. Olivier Barrot, *L'Ecran français 1943–1953: Histoire d'un journal d'une époque* (Paris: Les Editeurs français réunis, 1979). See also Dudley Andrew, "Bazin Before *Cahiers*," *Cinéaste*, 12, 1 (1982), 12–16.

21. *L'Ecran français*, 1 (July 4, 1945), 2. The founding *comité de patronage* of *L'Ecran français* was made up of critics, intellectuals and members of the film profession, all more or less associated with the Resistance, including Georges Altman, Marie Bell, Albert Camus, Louis Daquin, Jean Grémillon, Henri Langlois, André Malraux, Pablo Picasso, Francis Poulenc, Georges Sadoul, and Jean-Paul Sartre.

22. Georges Sadoul, "*La Chose*: Le grand méchant navet qui tue," *L'Ecran français*, 342 (January 30, 1952), 9.

23. Bazin, "On Realism," in *French Cinema of the Occupation and the Resistance: The Birth of a Critical Aesthetic*, trans. Stanley Hochman (New York: Ungar Publishing, 1981). For Bazin's influence on Roger Leenhardt's theory of "primordial realism," see Dudley Andrew, *André Bazin*, 30–32.

24. Georges Didi-Huberman, *Images In Spite of All*, trans. Shane B. Lillis (Chicago: University of Chicago Press, 2008), 68.

25. Lawrence Douglas, *The Memory of Judgment* (New Haven: Yale University Press, 2001), 18.

26. Christian Delage, "L'image comme preuve: l'expérience du procès de Nuremberg," in *Vingtième Siècle. Revue d'histoire*, 72 (October–December 2001), 63–78.

27. Madeleine Jacob, "Les accusés de Nuremberg devant la preuve de leurs crimes," *L'Ecran français*, 26 (December 26, 1945), 10 [my translation]. Note the proximity of Jacob's phrase "*l'hallucinant témoignage de l'écran*" to Bazin's own phrase "*une hallucination vraie*" used to describe photography in the "Ontology of the Photographic Image," also from 1945.

28. See Delage, 71–74. See also Vincent Lowy, *L'histoire infilmable: Le génocide juif à l'écran* (Paris: L'Harmattan, 2001), 48.

29. Sylvie Lindeperg, *Clio de 5 à 7* (Paris: CNRS, 2000).

30. Bazin, "Le Ghetto Concentrationnaire," *Cahiers du cinéma*, 9 (February 1952).

20

Bazin in Combat

Antoine de Baecque

This essay draws in part from collections of correspondence—always an archetypal "historicizing" source that can replace published texts, with their traps and their "left-unsaids"—in a context of controversies (intellectual, political, cultural) that call for a reconstitution of the topography of the Bazinian battlefield, where he chose to intervene in the furious written conflicts [*guerres de papier*] of the time. These exchanges have been slowly pieced together, even though there is not, strictly speaking, a "Bazin archive" from which we can pull his correspondence and documents. The thousands of texts published by André Bazin make up a world still partially unexplored. His correspondence itself was, for a long time, notable only in its absence. Out of this absence and through sheer force of scholarly will, a mosaic has gradually appeared that can be *super*imposed on Bazin's texts, or rather seen beneath his texts, that is, "*under*imposed."

We have worked on letters and documents from various archives that are private, scattered, and assembled any way possible. Now the outline of a provisional Bazin archive is beginning to take shape, aided by the François Truffaut collections, partially on deposit at the BiFi and available for consultation; as well as the Georges Sadoul and Robert Lachenay papers, also at the BiFi, and Janine Bazin's materials conserved by André S. Labarthe.

With the help of these shards of correspondence, I would like to propose a counterportrait, quite different from the image of the agreeable Bazin who drew the praise of all his contemporaries, friends, and adversaries alike. The "Bazinian iconology," to use Hervé Joubert-Laurencin's fine expression, has made him out to be a sort of "secular saint" capable of understanding—and even liking—those who objected to him, not to mention the films that fell outside his critical vision. This mythical hagiography begins with the homage that François Truffaut put together in the ninety-first issue of *Cahiers du Cinéma*, January 1959, scarcely one month after his death. Truffaut painted a sensitive portrait of a "kind of saint in velvet cap," who "lived with total purity in a world that was itself purified through its contact with him." His morality, based on concrete actions, was defined by Truffaut, the privileged witness, in this way: "He was the one who destroyed the ridiculous rift that separated the cinema of the critic and that of the filmmaker. I blushed with pride if in the course of a discussion he happened to show his approval of me, but I felt an even keener pleasure when he would contradict me. He was the 'Just Man' that you liked to be judged by, and a father to me. Even his reprimands were precious, for they were proof of an affectionate correction that I had been deprived of as a child."[1]

This image of tolerance, this depiction of a "strict but so very human" Bazin, given as a dot-to-dot portrait, an "Ariadne's thread" to use Renoir's image,[2] prevents us from seeing one of Bazin's historical roles during the postwar decade by hiding his dissenters under a veil of fraternity. Bazin certainly played the role of standard bearer and figurehead, but he was just as much a part of the critical disputes; he relished this war on paper, and was not averse to helping deliver a verbal rabbit punch or a stylistic uppercut himself, although his physical restraint (and his fragility was a known fact.

Thus it is a portrait of a full-blooded Bazin that I want to sketch, breaking from the classic depiction of the saint heralded as the charismatic center of a cinephilic community brought together under him. This new portrait stems from a disconcerting report—like a police report: Bazin apprehended numerous times by patrols in untimely fights and brawls, Bazin the recidivist, Bazin public enemy number one—indicating his presence in every scuffle over cinema from 1946 to 1955: the controversy surrounding *Citizen Kane*, the war with Louis Daquin in *Ecran français*, the Stalin crisis and his dispute with Georges Sadoul, the Hitchcock affair, heated tensions caused by Truffaut's publication of "A Certain Tendency of the French Cinema," the feud over neo-formalism with anti-Communist undertones, and his second dispute with Sadoul and the Young Turks in 1955. In this critical landscape, which catches fire as quickly as a jungle in the throes of a cinephilic and ideological guerilla war, Bazin is omnipresent. Naturally he is there first to calm things down, to prevent ad hominem attacks and blunders, to put out the fires. But he is never the last one to play with matches. A portrait of Bazin as pyromaniac fireman.

My first approach concerns the psychology of the individual, a critical characterology. Bazin is a good, generous, tolerant, and deeply human man. All testimonies concur. But at the same time, they indicate an impulsive, vindictive, tense, anxious man, who takes up his pen to incite verbal violence, if I dare say so. The evidence lies in certain forgotten echoes. For instance there is a letter, dated October 30, 1951, that suddenly burst into a fit of anger; it was written by the critic, at the height of his established legitimacy, to a young Robert Lachenay, friend of François Truffaut, while the latter was rotting away in a military prison. It should be mentioned that Lachenay, a twenty-year-old cinephile, had provoked Bazin's ire with a fairly cheeky note at a time when he should have been helping Truffaut rather than complaining as he does here: "I am beginning to have had enough of Truffaut's affairs, of Truffaut's friends, and of Truffaut himself. For ten years he has used my room as a sewer and a changing room."[3] Lachenay is justifying his delay in sending a package to his friend in prison. But Bazin responds: "If you have had enough of Truffaut's friends, believe me that I have had enough of the service of those whom he has the foolishness to call his friends. Truffaut wrote me three times to ask for work [for them] and I had the weakness to take him up on it. I suppose that you might have scorned this inappropriate kindness but at least it proves that in the midst of all of his problems Truffaut cared about you. Let me say that towards Truffaut I think you are a bastard, and towards me, an oaf."[4]

This eruption in the autumn of 1951 exhibits a different personality, one that our love of that other one—the saintly Bazin—has covered up, and even suffocated, erased: Bazin the stammerer, anxious, hot-tempered, on edge. It corresponds to the description that Henri

Langlois gives of him—Langlois was never impressed by Bazin in his lifetime, and did not like him much—that of a nervous man in public, ill at ease with others, often heckled by his audience, particularly young people and students: "At the ciné-club in the Cité Universitaire," writes Langlois in notes on his lectures in 1949, "I once saw Renoir cornered, for example. It's a question of authority; you have to know how to trap the students. We must remove Bazin from the lectures at the Cinémathèque and the history of film courses, for example, because he too was boxed in at the Cité Universitaire."[5] This echoes Bazin's first trauma, his failure at the key oral exam of his life, something he himself announced with these words in a letter from 1941: "A catastrophe has struck me. I was washed out at the oral of the professoriat. More precisely they failed me because I stuttered in my extended explication of a text."[6]

The "catastrophe" of his oral language is, in a certain sense, formative: Bazin forges his reputation by writing through adversity, indeed he triumphs by writing, often so direct that it can be scathing, despite an orality that remains uncertain, confused, stuttering. I mean to paint a portrait of a man who fights with his pen to compensate for an absence of natural charisma: Bazin's stutter produces a polemicist; for him combat is necessary, functioning as the revenge of writing on his lack of eloquence. Jean-Claude Brialy, in his memoirs, *Le Ruisseau des singes*, (2000), also draws a little-known but revealing sketch of this aggressive temperament: "I did not see André Bazin with the gang of young Turks, except at *Cahiers du Cinéma*. I remember a very nervous man, a bit slouched over, with a hollow face, a large forehead, a pale complexion, and light, fevered eyes. Extremely generous, full of humor, he had an honesty and a rigor that was only equaled by his passion for cinema. In his enthusiasm as well as his indignation, he turned back into an aggressive adolescent, giving no quarter, always convinced of his opinions."[7] Bazin is portrayed here as a Dostoevskian figure, fueling his cinematic passion like the young Russians did their plots, furbishing weapons, sharpening arguments.

So André Bazin's office at *Travail et Culture* is not just a rallying point or a school for cinephiles: it is also a fortress from which literary arrows fly, critical projectiles for piercing retaliations. We know that the Parisian release of Welles' *Citizen Kane*, at the Marbeuf on July 10, 1946, was the site of the first great critical debate of the postwar period, setting up a climate of polemical efflorescence that shaped the French filmgoing world for a decade. First Sartre attacks *Citizen Kane*, for fairly bad reasons and with fairly bad arguments. Since it is an American film, the Communist Party falls in behind him in the nascent cold war atmosphere. It is Bazin who retaliates, in issue 17 of *Temps Modernes*, early 1947.[8] Fully cognizant of the stakes at hand, he adamantly establishes the artistic and cinematic nature of *Citizen Kane* by comparing the film to many major benchmarks of artistic thought, whereas Sartre had denigrated the film as a substitute for a novel, an ersatz of outdated literature. Bazin deploys two strategies. First, he cites prestigious literary references, like Joyce and Dos Passos, to situate Welles' film prominently within the history of American literary forms, forms that Sartre appreciated so much himself. Thus Bazin skillfully steps into his opponent's terrain the better to counter him. Second, he demonstrates the film's style to be more than mere free play; neither formalist nor aesthetic, it corresponds to the auteur's cinematic, even philosophical project. "The deliberate aim here is complete realism, a way of considering reality as if it were homogenous and indivisible, as if it had the same density at all coordinates on the screen,"[9] writes Bazin, who claims "integral realism" as a category in the history of forms. This controversy is all the more delicate as it pits Bazin against Sartre, one of his key references and admired models. This will be a constant in Bazin's combats: he does not go after distant or abhorred adversaries, but rather after those who are close to him, relations, often friends; he almost fights himself.

This is the case in March 1949 versus the Communist filmmaker Louis Daquin, not a friend of Bazin's, but someone whom he respects. In *Ecran français*—an intense polemical setting at this time, with the cold war becoming a given in French literary culture, since the journal brought together personalities from very different, even contradictory sides: Communists, Catholics, socialists, Gaullists, *hussards*—Daquin attacks "film analysis," and therefore Bazin as well. About the new trends in criticism, he writes, "It may happen that there could be a disagreement among individuals of different generations . . . But what can I do in front of the total incomprehension and indifference with which I greet this technico-aesthetico-philosophic language, evidently so dear to certain young critics, which cannot avoid offending certain cineastes."[10] Daquin states that without a subject, there can be no film; the subject alone gives genuine, "positive value" to creation, with no connection to "fictive and suspect" values that come from "aestheticism" or from a formalism designed to "disguise the emptiness and sterility of the only works tolerated today, by a bourgeoisie trying in vain to restrain its decadence and by a capitalism determined to destroy all that strives for the advent of a free and happy humanity."[11]

Bazin has no choice but to respond to Daquin's attack, given his leadership status among the young critics. He does so in *Ecran français*, March 29, 1949, in a formally measured tone, being gentle with "our friend Daquin," but unyielding in his ideas and opinions. "We are indeed a few who believe that analysis, let us even say formal analysis, holds an especially urgent significance nowadays because of the crisis of subject matter. Even insofar as cinema has, for the most part, exhausted its characteristic themes, now it has to conquer both sides of the road that it has cleared between the general fields of novelistic and dramatic literature. It is not irrelevant that Jean Renoir's characters learned to leave the shot in a certain manner, and that Orson Welles' camera replaced analytical montage with virtual cutting in a single shot thanks to its depth of field."[12] Bazin responds to Daquin's blunt "socialist-realist" irritation by focusing on form, shifting the terrain to discuss mise-en-scène with his usual profundity.

The polemic with the Communists took a new turn a few months later, in the summer of 1950, when Bazin, in his famous article "The Stalin Myth in Soviet Cinema," strikes out at the cinematic figure of the *Petit père des peuples*, and at the cult of personality in the Stalin films that transform it, comparing him to "Tarzan des studios hollywoodiens."[13] Such a provocation was deliberately meant to inflict damage, just for the sake of combat. This article engendered a fundamental "Stalin crisis in French criticism,"[14] where everyone had to take a stance in relation to Soviet cinema and the PCF. At this crucial moment—paradoxical in the eyes of history because it proved him right in a striking manner—Bazin found himself isolated, sometimes even abandoned by some of his "friends," who preferred to tout their fidelity to the progressive, Communist cause by praising Soviet cinema, even its most Stalinist examples.

Combat is even more bitter when the combatant fights alone, but this battle, violent though it was, proved essential in forging the personality and reputation of Bazin the critic. We see this in a letter that Georges Sadoul, the authority on Communist criticism and a contributor to *Les Lettres françaises*, addressed to Bazin, protesting the betrayal of their friendship, after he discovered Bazin's literary fire-ship.

The Argus [a periodical compilation of criticism] sent me a clipping from the issue of *Esprit* where you condemn me. You talk of "slander" and "practices of forgery" on my account. My intention is not to demand that you correct yourself, I am writing this because of the sincere friendship that I have for you, and which, I fear, has not entirely withstood the shock of your article "The Stalin Myth." Truly, knowing me as you do, did you believe that I would sit back without reacting, very forcefully, to your article? In the second part of your argument, you specify that neither *Esprit*, nor *Parisien libéré* "ever asked for an explanation of my opinions on films. Sadoul knows this very well." You know as well as I do that the various journals with which I collaborate have never asked for explanations of the films that I defend or the articles that I write. But because you know I am a Communist, you must have known that it would be impossible for me to avoid vehemently expressing my disagreement with "The Stalin Myth." I was not in Paris when your article fell into my hands. It made me angry, and all the more so because I have held you in such high regard. And because I never imagined that at a time in which war has become a horrific daily reality in Korea, I would see you write lines that place you in a camp far from the defenders of peace and liberty. I do not believe—and I don't think that you believe either—that film should be an art free of all immediate contingencies. Specifically regarding "The Stalin Myth," you adopted *Parisien libéré*'s Gaullist point of view. This deeply pains and disappoints me. Because I know that you are not a devotee of "Grand Charles," as you say. So, I deplore it all the more that your views coincide—or seem to have coincided—with his, and those of André Malraux. And rereading your articles does not manage to convince me otherwise.[15]

What Sadoul most obviously reproaches in Bazin, what hurt him the most, was the latter's premeditation. The fact that Bazin would have knowingly waved the red cape of "The Stalin Myth" in front of the Communist in order to provoke him, shock him, make him come off his hinges. A totally different Bazin appears here, no longer the saint but the agitator, marching in the front lines, looking for a fight, forcing his arguments and choosing his images, both ironic and spiteful, so as to bring his adversary out into the open where he can better argue with him.

This strategy ultimately links Bazin to the main polemicist of the era, François Truffaut, the direct successor of his blistering criticism, who readily uses this aggressive strategy to provoke, and sometimes insult, in order to wear down the filmmakers of the *qualité française*. In a sense Bazin found in Truffaut, his protégé and spiritual son, a better combatant than himself. Bazin recognized this quickly, and he undoubtedly appreciated Truffaut for it, though the passing of the torch forced Bazin to reposition himself in the sphere of critical combat, for Bazin was formerly the one who provoked controversy, especially with the Communists; now he would channel, direct, placate, still in charge of the combat but leading it from a different angle.

This *different* combat began as soon as Bazin read the first version of Truffaut's article entitled "Le temps du mépris," in December 1952, a rough draft of what would be published more than one year later in *Cahiers du Cinéma* (January 1954) under the famous title "Une certaine tendance du cinéma français" ("A Certain Tendency of the French Cinema"). This time Bazin's role in combat consists in supervising Truffaut, making him amend and rewrite the article to render it not less aggressive but more fine-tuned, so as to deliver blows that carry more weight and are better supported [*plus porteurs et mieux portés*]. Through this back-and-forth dialogue between teacher and pupil, the text became sharper. Thus, Bazin passed his combat on to the aggressive Truffaut, who was able to say things that, of course, the elder could not and would not say. During this year of dialogue and reworking "A Certain Tendency of the French Cinema," it were as if they went into battle tied together, or as if Truffaut were a young boxer being coached by his somewhat inhibited and weakened elder, the latter binding his hands, making him less wild and chaotic, more stinging with his blows.

Bazin then reorients Truffaut once the text appears in January 1954 and its devastating effects are felt throughout French cinema and criticism. He turns to the struggle against what he calls "neo-formalism," the generation of young Turks who storm his own revue, the *Cahiers du Cinéma*, in the aftermath of Truffaut. Here again, Bazin is in combat, but as a strategist and conciliator, for he understands what is at stake in this fight between two cinephilic clans: he knows not to favor an outburst within his own journal, which would undoubtedly bring about his its demise, but must remain firm in his positions, especially when up against the political and formalist drifting of his juniors. Bazin explains his position very clearly and lucidly to Sadoul—with whom he had reconciled—after Sadoul reproached him in a letter from early October 1955 for giving space in *Cahiers du Cinéma* to a young anti-Communist and right-wing critic—a formalist and lampoonist, a "McCarthyite" and propagandist. Bazin's position was that of "lookout," which is another way to be in combat, or at least aware of the combat of others, above the melee; sympathetic, but ready for the aftershock and prepared to emphatically whistle the end of hostilities. Bazin passed from combat to "combat referee," a position unique to this era of the cold war when there was a balance of terror.

He wrote to Sadoul on October 10, 1955:

> I have the feeling that your letter was, more than anything, an excuse to express a deeper and more vague concern, linked to the importance that a certain group has achieved at *Cahiers*, and the spirit that animates it. This spirit seems to be doubly distressing to you: in its aesthetic significance and in the political undertones that you suspect it of, given certain indications. This letter is meant to be as friendly as a conversation, so I am going to be extremely frank. Against all evidence I will not argue that my young friend Truffaut is a "leftist" writer, which is also not the case—far from it—for Rivette or Schérer [Eric Rohmer]. I will even admit to you that for one or another of them, a certain taste for impertinence—a result of their age and biographical history—makes them muse somewhat resentfully upon what we call, in a very vague sense, right-wing literature. God knows we don't encourage them, but what can we do! You have to know how to distinguish in terms of talent and competence, what's essential and what's secondary. If I thought that one of our usual collaborators had directly or insidiously made a remark or asserted, even outside of *Cahiers*, something akin to a fascist or ultra-reactionary aesthetic, I promise that Jacques [Doniol-Valcroze] and I would react. But I assure you that the issue is not at all political; even if a juvenile penchant for provocation and polemics sometimes gives rise to confusion, the question is entirely aesthetic. Our "Hitchcocko-Hawksians"—to use the epithet that you happily created—represent above all a generation of cinema fanatics for whom partiality is not in any way equal to erudition, and we think, Jacques and I, that such erudition simply deserves to be heard, despite a certain insolence. If I had to characterize it, I would readily call it

"neo-formalism," as its principles are very different from those of traditional formalism, which were mostly plastic. They integrate the style of the script to a great extent, and they postulate the continuity of genius among auteurs. Their positions seem to me, as you well know, very debatable, and I have been preparing a substantial refutation for a long time. But these positions lean, I believe first and foremost, on a real talent for writing, a passionate love of cinema, the ardor of youth, and an extremely laudable competence. You could reproach us now for giving them such a central place in the *Cahiers*. You would, alas, be right. But the main reason for it is the unremitting pros-elytic activity of our young-Turks, who flood us with more articles than, for example, Pierre Kast or Claude Roy do. Not to mention that we owe to their zeal some of the best elements of our content, especially the interviews.[16]

Bazin is again in combat, but here he is leading a very unusual combat against the defenders of what he calls "neo-formalism," a style that he clearly appreciates from a certain point of view—he does not hide this from Sadoul—but he also knows that he does not belong in its camp. The "you would, alas, be right," conceded to Sadoul at the end of the letter, says it all perfectly: Bazin is in combat in the sense that he knows he has to resist this trend of young criticism—those whom he calls "young-Turks" and Sadoul calls "Hitchcocko-Hawksians,"[17] two expressions that will pass into posterity—very delicately. He must somehow circumvent it just as he wel-comes it, channel it while preventing it, and stimulate it at the same time as he controls it, since these "young-Turks" are the vital force of his own journal, which would surely wither away quickly otherwise. One could say that it is a "constructive combat." In my opinion, this dialectic defines quite precisely the combatant that Bazin became over the years, particularly his rela-tionship with the young Turks: he prefers to discuss, converse, and understand what is against him rather than radically and frontally challenge it. This demonstrates a method of control and mastery, bulding up a "contradictory comprehension," a *maieutic* that shows his singularity as a critic.

So let's listen as Bazin "combats" the young Turks—the neo-formalists—in an essential text where he takes up Sadoul's term for himself, "Comment peut-on être hitchcocko-hawks-ien?" ("How Can One Be Hitchcocko-Hawksian?"): "Though the '*politique des auteurs*' seems to me to have driven its supporters to more than one particular error, it also seems that its gen-erally fruitful overall outcome justifies its existence against its detractors. It's a rare thing when the arguments that I have most often heard condemning them could convince me in all sin-cerity to go over to their side."[18] This combat of concession—"we do not agree, but this very disagreement fascinates and convinces me"—is quite typical of Bazin's thought process. But while the young critics of the future New Wave are rallying around Hitchcock, Bazin prefers to defend Huston, reserving a long and laudatory review of *The Red Badge of Courage* (1951) for *Cahiers*. Even if he recognizes the formal superiority of Hitchcock's cinema over that of Huston, he does not see *The Red Badge of Courage* or even *African Queen* (1951) as lesser works than *Rope* (1948) or *Strangers on a Train* (1951), "Because in the end subject matter also counts for something!"[19] Bazin revives and clarifies this heartfelt cry, at once radical and well-considered, in "Comment peut-on être hitchcocko-hawksien?" "I personally deplore," he says, "like many others, the ideological sterility of Hollywood, its increasing hesitance to deal freely with 'serious topics,' [*grands sujets*] and this is also what made me disappointed in *Scarface*

[1932] and *Only Angels Have Wings* [1939]. But I am grateful to the young admirers of *The Big Sky* [1952] and *Monkey Business* [1952] for detecting, with such passionate eyes, what the formal intelligence of Hawks' mise-en-scène hides in simple intelligence, despite the clear idiocy of the scriptwriters. And if they are wrong to not see or to want to ignore this idiocy, we at least would still prefer this bias in *Cahiers* rather than its opposite."[20]

The "we" used here effectively explains Bazin's final combat strategy: the critic has reached the point of being himself *and* his adversary, defending his own ideas *and* those of his opponent, since there is and always will be an opponent. By vehemently defending "subject matter," Bazin is echoing the tone of Daquin, who had been the aggressor five years earlier in *Ecran français*. Paradoxically, Bazin approaches the question by taking up all of the positions available in the critical combat zone. This is not opportunism or contradiction, but an "all-encompassing" and "comprehensive" style of fighting. Attacked as a formalist, he attacks the neo-formalists in turn.

We can read in Bazin—through the position he occupies and through his texts, more than any other critic of the era—this contradiction between his willingness to defend a marked point of view and his desire at the same time to legitimize and accept that of the someone else, and not just his own. Bazin not only agreed with himself, he was in agreement with his opponent; he knowingly placed himself in this extremely critical position. We have already noted how much Bazin accepted and indicated his own shifts and contradictions (even regarding the same film as time went by, for example *Europe 51* [1952] or *Casque d'or* [1952], first not well-liked, then defended and admired). It must also be emphasized how much Bazin sympathized with his opponents, to the point of making their arguments and points of view his own, all the while maintaining his original arguments and positions. This is *denial as method* [*dénégation comme système*]; illustrated, for instance, by an article on Chaplin and *Limelight* (1952): "Given a level of artistic creativity, and certainly when faced with evidence of genius, a contrary attitude is necessarily more rewarding. Instead of thinking of removing so-called faults from a work, it is wiser, rather, to be favorably predisposed to them, and to treat them as qualities, whose secret we have not so far been able to fathom. This is, I agree, an absurd critical attitude if one has doubts about the object of one's criticism; it requires a gamble."[21]

This "gamble" consists of simultaneously holding both contradictory points of view: being both himself and the other. Which goes to show—and I am concluding on this vision of the strange, singular and superb combatant named Bazin—that the combat, little by little, was integrated by this man within himself.

Notes

1. François Truffaut, "It was Good to be Alive," in *The 400 Blows*, ed. David Denby (New York: Grove, 1969), 190. Originally published in *Cahiers du Cinéma*, 91 (January 1959).
2. Jean Renoir, *Cahiers du Cinéma*, 91 (January 1959).
3. Bibliothèque du Film/Cinémathèque française, collection Robert Lachenay (B2).
4. Ibid.
5. Laurent Mannoni, *Histoire de la cinémathèque française* (Paris: Gallimard, 2006), 218.
6. Dudley Andrew, *André Bazin* (New York: Oxford University Press: 1978), 46.
7. Jean-Claude Brialy, *Le Ruisseau des singes: Autobiographie* (Paris: Robert Laffont, 2000), 96.
8. Cf. A. Bazin, "The Technique of *Citizen Kane*," in *Bazin at Work*, ed. Bert Cardullo (New York: Routledge, 1997).

9. Ibid. 235.

10. Louis Daquin, "Remarques déplacées," *Ecran français* (March 8, 1949).

11. Ibid.

12. Bazin, "André Bazin et Pierre Kast répondent à Louis Daquin: Entretien sur une tour d'ivoire," *Ecran français*, 197 (March 29, 1949).

13. Bazin, "The Stalin Myth in Soviet Cinema," in *Movies and Methods*, vol. 2, ed. Bill Nichols (Berkeley: University of California Press, 1985), 29–40. *Cf.* Bazin, "Le cinéma soviétique et le mythe de Staline," *Esprit*, 170 (August 1950).

14. Antoine de Baecque, "Georges Sadoul, les *Lettres françaises* et le cinéma stalinien en France," in *La Cinéphilie: Invention d'un regard, histoire d'une culture 1944–1968*, (Paris: Editions Pluriel, 2005), 63–96.

15. Laurent Marie, *Le Cinéma est à nous: Le PCF et le cinéma français de la Libération à nos jours* (Paris: L'Harmattan, 2005), 123–24.

16. Antoine de Baecque, *La Cinéphilie: Invention d'un regard, histoire d'une culture 1944–1968*, *op. cit.* 183–84.

17. The genesis of this expression, "Hitchcocko-Hawksian," at least in published form, in fact comes from an early article by Jacques Doniol-Valcroze, in *France observateur*, December 1954.

18. Bazin, "Comment peut-on être hitchcocko-hawksien?," *Cahiers du Cinéma*, 44 (February 1955).

19. Bazin, "De l'ambiguïté: *The Red Badge of Courage*," *Cahiers du Cinéma*, 27 (October 1953). Translated here by Liam Andrew.

20. Bazin, "Comment peut-on être hitchcocko-hawksien?"

21. Bazin, "The Grandeur of *Limelight*," in *What Is Cinema?* vol. 2, trans. Hugh Gray (Berkeley: University of California Press, 1971), 130.

21

Bazin the Censor?

Marc Vernet

A Complex Political and Legal Situation

In Bazin's era, cinematic censorship revolved around two complications that started to loom large at the end of the Second World War. The first complication: the comanagement of cinema in France by the government and the film profession. This situation resulted in the creation of the CNC (Centre National Cinématographique), a government entity autonomous of any Ministry (before Malraux, of course, cinema had been linked to various ministries: Information, Commerce and Industry, Fine Arts, etc.). Second complication: the seesaw of censorship between the national and the municipal levels, since statutorily, the mayor of a city has the right to police his domain; this includes all sorts of spectacles, along with their attendant security issues (the so-called public order [*ordre public*]). Whenever national surveillance appears to weaken, allowing the distribution of films that might incite some fringe of the municipal electorate, the mayor may believe he has the right to intervene under pretense of the police powers conferred on him. After several crises and numerous false steps, this issue would lead to the 1960–1961 reform of the 1945 arrangement: effectively Malraux—recognizing the ministerial exercise of censorship to be dangerous—lowered the guard at the national level; this provoked a wave of censorship at the local level. These two complications gave rise to others that together shook everything up: the relationship between the government and city mayors (for power), between Paris and the provinces (for morals), between the majority and the opposition (for reinforcing and undermining these respectively). In the midst of this, the film profession had to try to pull chestnuts out of the fire (with Autant-Lara in the lead, a man accustomed to turning the machinery of censorship administration to his advantage).

As we know, censorship always incubates on its own; a "Voltairian" country such as France flatly refuses the term "censorship." Censors speak of *contrôle* and *classement*, and never directly of *censure*. Nor do they ever actively censor, instead limiting themselves to an opinion or recommendation, and then handing responsibility over to the producer or director who can choose whether to follow it or not so as to obtain the notorious certificate, which is not even technically a "censor's" certificate. In order to smooth over political responsibility in the case of a certificate's refusal (this refusal must be publicly backed up and accorded the force of law under the jurisdiction of a political leader), the censors put into place a commission, that is, a censorship group, but under the rubric of "inspection" or "classification" and consisting of a large body representing all the entities presumed to be involved in the political as well as professional side. The profession would delegate the delicate task of any negative judgment to representatives of the audience.

In the postwar era, all this resulted in the formation of the "state-profession parity commission" (forty-one members according to Bazin himself, who seemed to include the deputies, among whom are those from the ciné-clubs and from criticism, as stakeholders in the profession). This commission comprised a representative from each putatively pertinent ministry (the Interior, Foreign Affairs, National Education) and from every related entity (the profession, generally appointed representatives from criticism and ciné-clubs, who would then bring on board someone to represent families). Censorship rests on two major official bases: good morals (what can be shown or implied in the movie theater) and public order (preventing demonstrations on the streets outside the theater).

Cinema as a Major Political Tool

What we have to remember is that in the middle of the '50s, cinema, as a mass medium, was still a political tool in the broad sense, falling under the same heading as the journalistic press and radio. Television was still mainly a technological curiosity, a luxury that had not yet found its way into every home (Bazin watched television, and films on TV; one of his final articles on censorship deals precisely with the question of censorship on television as it relates to young audiences).[1] And yet, compared to these two "rivals" (newspapers and radio), cinema benefited from an asset considered both unique and formidable: the image in movement. This confers it with a particularly emotional power, whether beneficial or harmful. Bazin believed in this power, believed in its reversibility, and thought it his duty to participate in channeling it in the direction of the good and the beautiful, and against its possible perversion. This is still the era of Catholic parish screening rooms, and of ciné-clubs run by Communist sympathizers and laymen. Recall that in the middle of the 1950s the Communist party still assumed its message could be heard via cinema, whether it be *Bel Ami* (1954) by Louis Daquin, made in Soviet-controlled Austria and East Germany, or Paul Carpita's *Le Rendez-vous des quais* (1953–1955), made illegally in Marseilles. In the case of Marcel Pagliero's *Un homme marche dans la ville* (*A Man Walks in the City*, 1950) the party thought it had to defend itself, outlawing it in Communist municipalities in the major French seaports (Sadoul would later issue his mea culpa for having successfully prosecuted this case). From this point of view, Carpita's *Rendez-vous des quais* can be seen as an attempted recovery of the Pagliero film, a kind of censorship by substitution, a reformed film correcting "the poor image" given by Pagliero of the ports and the dockers.

Bazin's Involvement

Surely it is for all of these reasons that André Bazin agreed to become a member of the *Commission de Contrôle*, between 1953 and 1957, along with his friend Jacques Doniol-Valcroze. Their presence can be verified in the commission's screening files, which include all the films that sought to obtain a censor's certificate, a notice with or without certain restrictions to minors

and to particular districts of the French Empire. In several of Bazin's articles he explicitly refers to the Commission's work, breaking the code of confidentiality.

We can consider the French censorship system to be in crisis starting in 1953, leading, after several aborted plans, to those reforms of 1960–1961 which had been greatly advanced by Bazin's analyses and reflections. The reasons for this crisis are numerous.

–The cold war climate that took hold in France in 1947, and the last serious attempts by the Communist party to return to power in the 1953–1955 period.
–The dismemberment of France's colonial empire and the end of the Indochina War, at the same time as the onset of the war in Algeria, following the independence of Tunisia and Morocco.
–The difficult winding down of the wartime economy (still felt in the consumer and housing markets—the winter of '54 and Abbé Pierre's famous "uprising of kindness"), and therefore a sort of détente among producers about representing poverty.

Here and there, starting in 1953, these elements can be found in the articles that Bazin devoted to censorship and its deployment, whether from a Communist or anti-Communist standpoint; just note the titles of his articles on Resnais' *Les Statues meurent aussi* (*Statues Also Die*, 1953) and Yves Allégret's *Méfiez-vous fillettes* (*Look Out Girls*, 1957): respectively "Encore la censure: les films meurent aussi" ("Censorship Once More: Films Die Too") and "Les fillettes doivent-elles se méfier des censeurs?"("Do the Girls Have to Look Out for the Censors?").[2]

Why did Bazin take part in this *Commission de Contrôle*? Because as noted, it comprised representatives from the profession and the public, and therefore critics. Bazin was the most distinguished of critics and so found himself in this position of responsibility. We could then say prima facie that Bazin always defends three things: criticism (it must be practiced, it must stay vigilant and take responsibility for itself), youth (they have to be protected, yet encouraged to love cinema), and cinema itself (which must remain an art of very high standards, even while taking risks). *Criticism*, because he believes that it must fully play its role in the French system, including in the commission. This legal role must not be abandoned (more practically, the commission is also the ideal place for viewing films before their release in theaters).

Youth, because cinema has the power to influence minds; this was a recognized and noble objective after World War II, and one of the principles behind the foundation of the Institute of Filmology, since cinema had served too many questionable causes during the war.

Lastly, *cinema*, because censorship can put pressure on producers who too readily aim at easy profits without thinking of the importance of art. His last two articles devoted to censorship ("Les fillettes doivent-elles se méfier des censeurs?" July 1957, and "Censeurs, sachez censurer," December 1957) were supported by the aggressive position of François Truffaut, and are clearly centered on producers' lack of willingness to organize themselves, whether to manage self-censorship or to resist the blows of the censors when the issue seems to merit it.

The Independence of Bazin

For those who have read articles on cinema in the '50s or taken an interest in censorship problems in France, it is impossible not to be astonished by the absolute and nearly immediate position taken by Bazin. While everyone is in the midst of uproar, denunciation, and a call to basic principles and sentiments (for varied but always noble and indisputable reasons—which is to say, reasons that are quite disputable, though masked by their partisanship), Bazin respects complexity. His analyses, whether for or against his own views, stand at the crossroads of various perspectives—comparing points of view. He is able to maintain an uncompromising equilibrium that owes everything to his subtlety of intelligence, to his carefully laid out style of criticism, and perhaps foremost to the honesty of his remarks and the exactitude of his information. Bazin is one of the rare scrupulous writers that I have read on cinematic censorship, even in his journalism, where he writes with incontestable rigor. Only Alain Resnais is his equal in discussing censorship and appropriate responses to it. This is why Bazin seldom sparks controversy regarding censorship. He does not intervene except when the debate seems skewed, the controversy useless or poorly engaged; in short, when public opinion seems to be centered on biased ideas. He wanted not to be a "righter of wrongs," so much as a "righter of debates," since for him, from the start, the question of censorship is always an open one, always up in the air, always difficult, always complex, and his interventions aim to emphasize just that: things are even more complicated than whatever is said, and discussion can not validly proceed unless we take all of the (numerous) overlapping aspects into consideration. If censorship exists, if it ought to exist for cinema, this is never self-evident; for censorship comes neither from nature nor from right [*droit*].

The Address to the Politicians, Then to the Professionals

Looking at the dozen articles between 1950 and 1957 where Bazin used the word "censor" or "censorship" in the title, one notes both an evolution and a re-echoing of positions. An evolution, because the first two instances (1950 and 1953) portray Bazin as relatively unassuming and opposed to censorship. But starting in 1954 and up to the end, he clearly becomes more engaged in a double-combat, both criticizing and defending the French system of censorship.[3]

As for echoes, these can be heard, for example, between "Les films changent, la censure demeure" (*Cahiers du Cinéma* 19, January 1953) and "Encore la censure: les films meurent aussi" (*France observateur*, January 17, 1957), as well between his article called "Voyage au bout de la nuit" (*Le Parisien libéré*, March 8, 1954) devoted to *La neige était sale* (*The Snow was Black*, adapted from Simenon, 1952), and the review of *Méfiez-vous fillettes*, which Bazin deems, like the one just mentioned, overly dark. But note the accuracy of the title of his first article on the topic, coming out in *Le Parisien libéré* of November 13, 1950, and remaining a constant reference point for his position: "Censure et censures au cinéma." According to him, if we continue to talk about censorship, then we must talk about all of the various gears and levels where the interests of the French administration and cinematic production intersect.

Though the series of articles starts in 1950 with a condemnation of censorship ("a disgraceful constraint"),[4] by 1957 producers are invited to clean up their own act and take charge; they know all the facts, so they may as well challenge the reigning system.[5] This evolution also pertains to the scope of these articles' publication: at first he writes within the framework of *Le Parisien libéré* (large print, not much space) while toward the end he has moved to *France observateur* (very small print, nearly the entire page). These two journals are privileged due to their periodicity, the first being daily and the other weekly, since questions of censorship are current events—though for Bazin this topic should not call for haste—and they will not wait for the following month. This confirms Bazin's double attitude regarding censorship, at once reflective and interventionist.

More precisely, in 1950 Bazin opened his file on censorship with a clearly negative prejudice, but straight away (this is very Bazin) it is corrected, or more exactly, relativized, with precisions and necessary distinctions. Censorship on the national level is a guarantee for the producer and the spectator because it saps strength from the more discreet and thus more efficient local censors. Though he does not say it here, we see that Bazin understood and was familiar with the American system,[6] in a much more detailed sense than many of his contemporaries and successors. In short, Bazin knows that in terms of cinema, one censorship always hides another. He therefore explicitly points to municipal Communist censorship, especially in the major French port cities, in reference to *Un Homme marche dans la ville*, an example he would bring up again later for good reason. At the end of this initial censorship article, Bazin notes that one should not "attack the censorship of films one likes while blocking the distribution of those one doesn't like."[7] This is a position and an argument that will remain constant throughout his analysis of the censorship phenomenon.

Beyond Good Conscience: A Respect for Complexity

The 1953 *Cahiers du Cinéma* article "Les films changent, la censure demeure," may seem quite dialectical but, all told, it comes off rather "black and white," both against the restriction of freedom of expression and for the still-living protagonists in the judicial affair. His final argument may be taken to be quasi "pro-life": it is a grievous decision not to allow a film to be born (this had to do with Antonioni's episode in *Sans amour* [1953], censored because of a rather sensational J3 case[8] which, citing the breakdown of morals among postwar youth, declared that the French state should not permit the exportation to Italy of footage shot in France).

The least one can say is that Bazin's position, while unchanging, at least stands as nuanced. He shows a concern for modernizing the gears of the complex and ambiguous mechanism of censorship; he takes care to dismiss back-to-back the declared adversaries of the day, the Communists and the anti-Communists; and he offers an undisguised defense of the moral code system of the Catholic Church.[9]

Political censorship forms one of the more difficult areas of the topic. Sometimes Bazin seems to justify it,[10] and sometimes he condemns it.[11] Looking closely, we see that there is a pacifist side to Bazin (he hates the quarrels between left and right caused by cinema in the name of the cold war), and so he disapproves of warmongering movies. He thus finds that political censorship can be justified. But then he condemns it (the case of the Resnais film) when it is Franco-French, linked to the personal or localized interests of politicos who operate from behind a mask. He would quite like to see censorship disappear, and wants the public to judge for itself (always a temptation in his articles; look at the text on the Allégret film that, according to him, does not deserve so much attention and publicity), but at the same time he recognizes that censorship gives birth to pre-censorship, which kills creativity; but creativity is killed only by cowardly producers who ought to have the courage of their craft.[12] Here he explicitly revives a position maintained by François Truffaut on the cowards of the film profession.

In reality, the pro-censorship Bazin defends four things: peace (he does not appreciate fire-starters), youth (like everyone else), but also, and not so paradoxically after all, cinema both as work [*oeuvre*] and as risk. He attacks hypocrisy and the lowering moral standards (to him morals and "darkness" go hand in hand with a useless kind of despair that cinema should not exist to promote). Finally, in questioning his fellow critics at *L'Humanité* and *Figaro*, he defends an idea of criticism based on its responsibility to provide honest and unbiased information, while upholding a vision of the profundity of cinema toward ends as unpartisan as possible. As for censors, producers, and critics: in the end Bazin invites them all to sweep up their own porches before attacking their neighbors.

In 1960, Henri Mercillon published three feature articles in *Le Monde* on the French censorship system—its domains, its dysfunctions, and prospects for its reform.[13] These articles mark the first big turning point on the subject since the Liberation; in the first article, Mercillon revives nearly word for word the analyses and arguments laid out by Bazin over the course of his final years. He came up with the following formula which could very well sum up one of the overarching aspects of Bazin's perspective: when it comes to the censorship of cinema in France, we find a happy marriage of vice, hypocrisy, and *tartufferie*.

Notes

1. André Bazin, "Censeurs, sachez censurer," *Radio, Cinéma, Télévision*, 411 (December 1, 1957).
2. Bazin, "Encore la censure: les films meurent aussi,"*France observateur*, 349 (January 17, 1957); and Bazin, "Les fillettes doivent-elles se méfier des censeurs?" *France observateur*, 374 (July 11, 1957).
3. For more on this topic, see Antoine de Baecque, infra.
4. Bazin, "Censure et censures au cinéma," *Le Parisien libéré*, 1918 (November 13, 1950).
5. Bazin, "Les fillettes doivent-elles se méfier des censeurs?" and "Encore la censure: Les films meurent aussi," see note #2.
6. The Production Code is indeed a system defined and maintained by the profession (to protect its sectors of the market), and not a state-or religious-based system. It is the profession (and not some administrative authority) that self-regulates nationally and internationally to avoid the backlash of local censors (thus treating a country of exportation to be one such local censor).
7. Bazin, "Censure et censures au cinéma."
8. A J3 refers to a juvenile delinquent in postwar France, preceding the "blousons noirs" of the '60s. The J3 actually designates the postwar ration ticket category for French of late adolescent age.
9. Bazin, "Le Vatican, l'Humanité et la censure," *France observateur*, 302 (February 23, 1956).
10. Ibid.
11. He condemns it in the article on *Les Statues meurent aussi*, ridiculing the minister who declared at the opening of the Cannes Festival that he was going to abolish censorship—*Le Parisien libéré* May 26, 1955 ("Première bonne nouvelle: le ministre déclare souhaiter la disparition de la censure . . .").
12. Bazin, "Les fillettes doivent-elles se méfier des censeurs?" *France observateur*, 374 (July 11, 1957).
13. Henri Mercillon, "La réforme du contrôle des films," *Le Monde*, April 6, 7, and 8, 1960.

22

Waves of Crisis in French Cinema

JEREMI SZANIAWSKI

Cultural mutations are always slower than economic ones.
—JEAN VIARD

Concern with the good standing and health of French cinema is omnipresent in the writings of André Bazin. The question of national cinema, reinforced by legislative acts and by festivals, stands at the core of many of his reflections. Bazin constantly monitors this health, and when he senses some danger or imbalance, he resorts to, albeit cautiously, the term "crisis": crisis of the subject, crisis of form, crisis of the integrity of film and of freedom of expression,[1] crisis of distribution and, last but not least, crisis of production. Often, if not always, this notion of crisis has economic underpinnings, of which Bazin is acutely aware. If some of his mathematical considerations may seem slightly naïve (and would most certainly no longer apply), it is nonetheless fascinating to see how—especially in a series of articles published in 1956—they support his call for an in-depth renewal of French cinema. He seeks alternatives in film form and in screenwriting to reduce the budgets of films so as to address the threat of a "Malthusian" cinematic production, as Bazin himself calls it. In so doing, he summons the New Wave without ever naming it.

Before taking stock of the crucial articles from of 1956–1957, written shortly before his death and the advent of the New Wave, let us go back to retrace the notion of cinematic crisis in Bazin, looking at early articles when his thought and rhetoric about this subject were taking shape.

In a May 1946 article entitled "Crise du cinéma français: *Scarface* et le film de gangster," published in *Esprit*, Bazin introduces for the first time the notion of economic crisis in the French cinema. Without going into detail, he establishes a two-edged relationship between foreign markets and the notion of competition:

The films that have come out in the last two months have hardly drawn much attention. With the issue of quotas having yet to be settled, American distributors limit themselves to reissuing old reels. New films are therefore almost exclusively French. Paradoxically, two years after the Liberation, the audience finds itself in a situation more or less analogous to that of the Occupation, quasi-autarchy. This partial suppression of competition can have its advantages—the quality of the French productions from 1940–44 proves it—on the condition that it does not last too long and most of all that the industry can take advantage of this respite. Alas, this does not seem to be the case for our cinema industry. We cannot keep up without the importation of new equipment, nor without the exportation of products (films) that can't be profitable on the national market alone. A film costing, on average, 20 million francs can no longer amortize itself within the French circuit of distribution. Yet people announce, here and there, film projects that are absolutely incompatible with a minimum of artistic standards and yet are getting underway in these bewildering economic conditions. Perhaps the few millions gained allows the producer to balance his budget. The complexity and gravity of the problems posed currently by the French film industry demands a precise and consequential policy, one that the government seems fairly unable to conceive and undertake. All the while the French cinema is slowly dying in studios equipped at the flea market, where technicians—by the way, among the finest in the world—bustle with the diabolical agility of handymen.[2]

Bazin's tone is rather somber; let's isolate in particular the low budgets and the cheaply equipped studios that he speaks of. It will soon become clear how the New Wave would solve this; by going out on the street, they would liberate themselves from the unnecessary costs and contingencies of working on sets resembling an antique shop's back room. Bazin's position on budgets would evolve over the years.

In 1948, he strikes at a slightly different issue, this time in *Le Parisien libéré*. Using his title as an alarm, ("Il faut sauver le Cinéma français: Notre production nationale ne doit pas être écrasée par l'Etat"), he deplores the gradual saturation of production and distribution, with double-bill practices largely to blame:

> From 1936 to 1938 French cinema lived under the regime of the commercial agreement of May 6, 1936, which fixed the contingent quota of American films imported each year to 188. If these 188 films from Hollywood could cohabitate each year on the French screens with 110 or 120 national films, it is because most theaters functioned on the basis of the double bill. The same number of cinemas could absorb twice as many films.
>
> The suppression of the double bill in 1941 was a necessary policy approved by the whole profession. For this practice had been nefarious from the artistic standpoint (one does not sell double bills the way one sells *double-crème*) as well as from the economic side: the box office of each screening venue had to be shared by two films. . . . In other words: if all the films distributed were shown in all cinemas, there would be room for half the films circulating in 1938.

> . . . 300 films saturated the French market before the war, 150 suffice to do so today. Why? Because the coefficient of the ticket price, that is to say, of the box office, did not follow the price of film production.

In fact, it's all there! The absolute numbers mean nothing! 188 American films in 1938 could cohabitate with 110 French films. They did less that year than do 100 American films today in relation to the 48 poor French films, authorized by the Washington agreements.[3]

Bazin then analyzes closely the economics of films: if, in 1938, a film cost around 3 million francs, the average cost had grown ten times to 30 million in 1947. But ticket prices did not follow suit: from 6 francs in 1938, these had increased to 25 francs in 1947, a coefficient of about four, not ten. Bazin "envisages" several solutions to this problem: bring in three times as many viewers, reduce the cost of production by three, make one-third the number of films, or eliminate two-thirds of the foreign films. None of these solutions, Bazin continues, is either realistic or even desirable (some are outright absurd). The sacrifice, he notes, must come neither from the spectator nor from the producer but from the government. In his eyes, the concept of subvention is germane since French cinema, held in custody by the Washington agreements, pays a heavy tribute and only earns one-sixth of what the French State gets through the same means. This is what Bazin has in mind when he says that the cinema must not be "crushed" by the government.

Change would not be long in coming . . . later in 1948 a law was voted to help production and to deregulate the price of tickets. The problem, at least for a while, was taken care of, and the following decade would be a particularly prosperous one for French cinema, with national production rising steadily, and amortizing itself.

The next time Bazin senses a crisis would be in 1951 and would concern filmmaking more than economics. This time he puts the word in brackets. In "De la forme et du fond ou la 'crise' du cinéma,"[4] he lays down some pragmatic bases for thinking about the debilitating self-censorship of the current cinema. Mainly he denounces the need producers feel to try to please a wide audience. For instance, one finds far more anticlericalism in the French novel than in the cinema. In spite of private ownership, says Bazin, French cinema behaves in the straitjacketed manner of State Radio. Rather than seeing the cause of this ill in financial considerations, Bazin blames the spirit of the time and the cold war political conjuncture for leading producers into this timorous attitude.

Five years later, in 1956, come Bazin's most eloquent and important reflections on the economic crisis of the French cinema, the first one appearing in *Le Parisien libéré*,[5] occasioned by a proposed half-year suspension of national film production. Just as the producers were preparing for this hiatus, the Economic Council gathered to examine a report by a certain René Richard on the crisis of French cinema. The situation announced itself as quite dramatic, but was it really? Apparently not: 125 to 135 films made in 1956 in France, contrasted with the 110 from 1955, indicate a healthy or even impressive growth (10%). "But if the number of films remains stable until 1955," Bazin notes, "their average cost has doubled between 1952 and 1955, mostly because of technical improvements (color, CinemaScope, etc.), and of the luxury of certain co-productions." The upshot: French investment in films had almost tripled (from 5 billion in 1952 to nearly 13 billion in 1956).

Bazin asks the—arithmetically and logically—obvious question: can these additional billions in production be amortized in exhibition? Clearly not . . . an answer that results in the idea to suspend production activity for six months. The oxymoron of "fallow production" is even more paradoxical given the fact that the economy is thriving, the profession blessed with full employment, and no other sign of austerity is in sight. Bazin, however, speaks of a "crisis of prosperity" (which is preferable, he notes, to economic depression). He then proposes an alternative: "In order to avoid the crisis, without resorting to dramatic measures . . . [why not] diminish the investment for next year, i.e., the average cost of films, by renouncing certain unnecessarily expensive productions."

Bazin's other proposals are familiar: accelerating the circulation of films, deregulating ticket prices ("at least above certain prices"), and limiting foreign competition ("at least for those [countries] that do not accept reciprocity"). Or anther possible alternative: "to increase the producer's share of the subvention law so as to allow the investment of this capital into exploitation." Despite all these suggestions, Bazin concludes by signaling that it is too early to speak of a genuine crisis in French cinema. The industry must tread carefully but should not panic.

This short programmatic article is one in a series on the topic published around the same time. Just the day before (October 24, 1956) he wrote similar things in *Carrefour*, and used the same examples. With insouciance he defuses the alarmist atmosphere: "One never sees a merchant claim *urbi et orbi* that his business is excellent. It is better, when a difficulty shows up, to play at Cassandra. . . . Let's not forget that this threat of crisis is the ransom paid for a particularly brilliant situation." After all, if overproduction is not desirable from an economic standpoint, it does not have "exclusively negative aspects." Through the "full employment" it creates, it can indeed offer "the French cinema its maximum of artistic chances, by giving work to filmmakers who would otherwise sit on the sidelines. . . . Who knows if, this year, Bresson or Rouquier would have otherwise made their films."[6]

This article from *Carrefour*, more stimulating than the one from *Le Parisien libéré*, discretely introduces a fundamental issue: "We should also take renewal into account . . . for the global vitality of French cinema: the cinema of technicians, including young operators, who can at last enjoy legitimate promotions." But, of course, it would cause mayhem to form a great deal of new talent on the eve of the collapse of the system. The true malady remains the surplus of investment and the excessive weight of coproductions. The solution, Bazin believes, "is not to make fewer films, but to make them with less money." While ten years earlier Bazin deplored shoestring budgets, in 1956 he champions them. It goes without saying, however, that the situation of 1956 is not that of 1946, technology having evolved to the point that it has started to allow for shooting outside the studios, on the streets. But Bazin hasn't yet reached this point in his thinking. He suggests the rationalization of work schedules to optimize the availability of studios, including shooting on all soundstages at once. Returning to recurrent if minor concerns, he denounces the cost of film processing and the price of . . . furniture rental.

At the end of the *Carrefour* article, Bazin touches the heart of the matter, using one of those biological metaphors of which he was so fond. Noting that one can attribute the crisis to definite factors (the appearance of TV in the United States and overproduction in France), he nonetheless refuses to consider them fundamental causes of the problem but rather symptoms of a more serious illness: "The potential crisis only bursts out as given pathological factors attack an organism already weakened and virtually sick. If TV, for instance, has shaken Hollywood, it is because cinema did not interest the American public sufficiently. . . . One must go to the bottom of the problem, which is, more or less, something of a direct artistic order. One must invent the genre of films, which, in 1956, will be capable of reviving the audience's interest in the cinema, and not trust old formulas which aren't successful any longer. Today as tomorrow, ideas will always be the cheapest commodity."

A few weeks later, in *Radio, Cinéma, Télévision*, Bazin publishes a two-part article entitled "Y a-t-il une crise du cinéma français?" Its subtitles are evocative and can serve to summarize his thought: "Too Many Films?"; "A Crisis Psychosis"; "Twice as Much Money Spent"; "Revenue Isn't Following Up"; "Not Enough Exclusive Runs?"; "Regulation of the Policy of Exclusivity?"; "Increase of the Price of Tickets?" His final subtitle reprises his conclusion in *Carrefour*: "Only Quality Pays."[7]

Bazin's rhetoric is solid, underlining the need to revise the form and the content of French cinema, the latter flirting, *perhaps*, with disaster. He speaks of the "ossifying corporatism" of French cinema, "reticent toward youth"[8] What is needed is a lighter and more flexible cinema, made by younger technicians, for lower budgets ("It is better to make films for less money than fewer films"), and which, through new forms and renewed subjects, would reinvigorate moviegoing habits. If this is not a definition of the New Wave, it resembles it very strongly.

Along similar lines, in a final point this artcle calls for a return to black and white—which will in fact come to dominate the most remarkable films from 1958 to 1963: "Everything leads one to believe that the new techniques (color and Cinemascope) have reached saturation level and that we are going toward an equilibrium where black and white films of classical conception will find a larger place than in 1955. It is therefore absolutely not retrograde to revert to them."

One last, highly pertinent article published in *France observateur* ("Situation économique du cinéma français") is dated February 10, 1957, and responds to a New Year's Day report from the Centre National du Cinéma which claims that French cinema is doing splendidly. But if optimism is now justified, following the alarming noises of the last trimester of 1956, Bazin reminds his readers of the need for caution in order to avoid a new crisis of overproduction. The latter would be "the opposite of that of 1947," with the shortage that took place that year. In the first part of the article, Bazin offers a fairly detailed summary of the indicators of good health of French cinema, but he finishes on a pessimistic note about its human implications.

> The increasing number of films does not seem, alas, to give much chance to young filmmakers. If it is true indeed that the French cinema is on the verge of producing too many films, the producers seem to care less and less to take risks on a market nearing saturation, and prefer to hold on to proven recipes and to work only with experienced directors. Of course, it would be absurd to complain about the quality of the production of 1956, but it has not revealed or confirmed any new element (save for Boisrond and Vadim, but in the most "commercial" movies). There is therefore an annoying contradiction between the optimism of the numbers and their [pessimistic] consequences for the renewal of artistic personnel. Speaking of which, we would like to be able to discuss, on the basis of such clear documents, the functioning for a year now of the "quality subvention." The careful silence that the commission in its charge has been surrounding itself with was justified during the delicate period of adjustment. This stage is behind us now, and one day an assessment will have to be made.[9]

Bazin thus concludes with the official version remembered by film history: the New Wave was a reaction, first and foremost, to the tradition of quality guarded by experienced but aging technicians and filmmakers, the *cinéma de papa*. But Bazin stresses the economic aspect at the core of this situation, which is too often neglected. And indeed one can see the contrast between Truffaut's excessive "Une certaine tendance du cinéma français" (1954) and the measured, structured, and multilayered arguments in Bazin's articles of 1956–1957.

Compared to the usual accounts of the climate on the eve of the New Wave—of aesthetic staleness and good economic health—Bazin reminds us that neither may have been entirely accurate. But this potential crisis could not be identified by simply looking at the numbers: 411 million tickets sold in 1957—the peak before the gradual descent. The New Wave was a genuine alternative to an unpleasant undertow, inevitable in view of the decline of the big budget productions, which Bazin, the visionary film critic, had foreseen with the remarkable clarity and insight that characterize his oeuvre as a whole.

Notes

1. Bazin has written some fascinating pages on the notion of censorship, official and officious. See the contribution of Marc Vernet, infra.

2. André Bazin, "Crise du cinéma français: *Scarface* et le film de gangster," *Esprit*, 122 (May 1946).

3. Bazin, "Il faut sauver le Cinéma français: Notre production nationale ne doit pas être écrasée par l'Etat/La crise du cinéma français: Responsabilités françaises," *Le Parisien libéré*, 1039 (January 18, 1948), 1–2.

4. Bazin, "De la forme et du fond ou la 'crise' du cinéma," *Almanach du théâtre et du cinéma*, 1951.

5. Bazin, "Crise du cinéma français?" *Le Parisien libéré*, 3771 (October 25, 1956).

6. Bazin, "Cinéma français: demain la crise?" *Carrefour*, 632 (October 24, 1956).

7. Bazin, "Y a-t-il une crise du cinéma français? (suite de notre précédent numéro)," *Radio, Cinéma, Télévision*, 356 (November 11, 1956). This is the second part of a two-part article; the first part is in the preceding issue of *Radio, Cinéma, Télévision*, November 4, 1956.

8. Ibid.

9. Bazin, "Situation économique du cinéma français," *France observateur*, 352 (February 7, 1957).

23

Bazin's Chaplin Myth and the Corrosive Lettrists

Rochelle Fack

In Bazin's criticism, Chaplin's work holds a special place, in the sense that his defense of Chaplin's talking films rests upon a premise that can be unsettling. It consists of determining the links that tie the characters in Chaplin's talking films to the myth of Charlot. Charlot, the silent film character, acts as the seamark, the reference point that structures Bazin's criticism.

Beyond the connections between the Chaplin characters endowed with speech and the myth of Charlot, who never spoke, there is another troubling element in Bazin's admiration for the former. He begins his critique by prioritizing the image in relation to sound, more precisely the body in relation to speech.

There seems then to be a kind of paradox, as he defends the sound films without immediately going after Chaplin's approach to sound, dialogue, or music; instead he explores the scenographic, pictorial, visual, and technical evolution of the image, including the fluctuations of the actor's presence in the shot. However, in observing this effacement of myth, we should not hastily conclude that Bazin does not attach importance to speech. In attempting to shed light on the role that Bazin gives to speech in the deterioration, then dissolution of the myth of Charlot, let me introduce the theory of Isidore Isou, founder of lettrism and author of the *Introduction to a New Poetry and a New Music*. This text is relatively contemporaneous with Bazin's writings on Chaplin, as it dates from 1947 and was followed up in 1952 with *Précisions sur ma poésie et moi* [*Details about My Poetry and Myself*]. Bazin's texts directly concerning Chaplin's films were written between 1945 and 1957, and those about other films in which we find reference to Chaplin, between 1946 and 1954.

First and foremost, I must clarify that the links between Isidore Isou and André Bazin are indeed indirect, as there is no way to establish that they ever met, or read, one another.[1] What connection they may have is through the medium of Charles Chaplin. The anecdote is well-known: after the failure of *Monsieur Verdoux* (1947), Chaplin decided to accompany the release of *Limelight* (1952), particularly in Europe. The Paris premiere took place at the Comédie Française, an event Bazin talks about at length in the opening of his article "The Grandeur of *Limelight*." After the screening, Chaplin gave a press conference at the Ritz, where a splinter group of young lettrists (led by Guy Debord, along with Serge Berna, Jean-Louis Brau and Gil

Wolman) distributed a violent tract aimed at Chaplin under the title "FINI LES PIEDS PLATS" ("NO MORE FLAT FEET"). It ended on these words:

> Go to bed, you budding fascist. Make lots of money. Mingle with high society (bravo for the groveling before little Elizabeth). Die soon, we can guarantee you a first-class funeral.
>
> The footlights have melted the makeup of the supposedly brilliant mime. All we can see now is a lugubrious and mercenary old man.
>
> Go home Mister Chaplin.[2]

Isou (along with Gabriel Pomerand and Maurice Lemaître) reacted in *Combat* (November 1, 1952), officially distancing themselves from this tract and from Debord. Thus, the affair was at the heart of the split between the "old guard" lettrists and the younger ones and seemingly unrelated to Bazin, concerned as it is with internal quarrels. Its relevance stems first from the fact that Chaplin seems to be the pretext for a famous schism. And, second, while Debord's attack is not especially surprising, the position taken by Isou certainly is. Why did Isou—agitator, extremist, so assertive in his actions, writings, and declarations—want to spare Chaplin?

I found my answer to Isou's position not in Chaplin the director, in Chaplin the actor, or in the character of Charlot. I found it rather in the Chaplin that Bazin renders as an evolving construction, an artistic phenomenon, and a myth that is converted into something else through a distinctive use of speech. This explanation, seen in the light of Isou's theories, clarifies what Bazin takes to be the basis of the erosion of the notion of myth.

With "Pastiche or Postiche, or Nothingness Over a Mustache" (*Esprit*, 1945), Bazin addresses this radical shift in Chaplin's filmmaking, though without closely tying it to his transition from silent to talking pictures. In the film that announces this transition, *The Great Dictator* (1940), Bazin writes of Chaplin's physical and plastic metamorphosis, motivated by revenge for the theft of a mustache. And when he says that he does not find all the transformations of Charlot into Hynkel equally successful, it is the sound (the speech on the soapbox) that does not completely convince him—since Hitler had already caricatured himself in an incomparable fashion—while it is the image (the dance with the globe) that he finds sublime.

In his later articles, when he looks at the technical progress of cinema and its impact on Chaplin the actor, he returns several times not to the advent of talking pictures but to the image and even its emulsion. In "The Myth of Monsieur Verdoux," he focuses on the finale of *The Great Dictator* (*La Revue du cinéma*, 1948):

> The transition from orthochromatic stock to panchromatic should itself alone have brought on a veritable morphological disorder, more serious perhaps than even the introduction of the spoken word: acknowledging and revealing that the actor was aging, it ate away at the character.[3]

This transition, from orthochromatic to panchromatic stock, refines and sharpens the image. Bazin even comes back to it in 1957, in an article on *Limelight*, entitled "If Chaplin Hadn't Died": "Moreover, with the advent of panchromatic stock, Charlot's mask no longer adhered properly to Chaplin's face. Or, we could say it adhered so well that we discerned under the painted plaster the nearly imperceptible wrinkles and the pathetic facial vibrations. Perhaps more than sound, it was the end of the pure black-and-white cinema that determined Charlot's evolution."[4]

The image removes the blotches and soot from Charlot's profile; it clarifies it, stitches its contours, chisels it. But despite this observation, with which we cannot help but agree, there remains the problem of understanding why Bazin emphasizes the physical transformation of Charlot/Chaplin in order to explain the degradation, then the loss of myth. Or rather, in this degradation of myth, how do we understand what role he leaves, indirectly, to speech? It is in addressing the influence of the talking picture on the notion of myth that Isou seems enlightening.

In his *Introduction to a New Poetry and a New Music*, Isou builds an evolution of the history of poetry, in order to extract clearly defined laws from the development of poetic creation. His analysis reveals what he terms two "hypostases" in poetic creation, the first being the amplic phase [*l'hypostase amplique*], the second, the chiseling phase [*l'hypostase ciselante*].

Amplique refers to poetry that begins from nothing, and which, as its name indicates, undergoes a process of amplification, heightening language and its forms, absorbing everything around it in its unlimited expansion (other artistic disciplines, all possible spaces, climates, states, audiences).

> The amplic phase constitutes an art at its most pregnant stage. It arises with the first artistic tendencies. It maintains the mark of free existence, without any competition. The question of originality does not yet come up, as all of it is original. *None of its content wears the mask of someone else.* Each creation tends to acquire Herculean forms. Spaces are extended, and the possibilities available are enormous.[5]

Such is the amplified phase, where everything is original and where nothing exists as reprise, continuation, prolongation, or critique.

There ultimately comes a point when this trajectory is inverted, and the *amplique* gives way to what Isou names the *ciselant*:

> In time, expressions pile up on one another. The free part diminishes, and artists have to work with reduced volumes. When these spaces are rendered completely diminished, having been colonized, the phase is switched. Suddenly with the appearance of a personality who understands immediately, or else gradually in successive stages, art enters its opposite zone. Huge totalities are replaced by little fragments, worked over in detail with the artist's meticulous care. The work of art no longer counts, so much as the material that is in the process of becoming the work. An art's value lies not in its extensiveness, but in the particularity of its forms, its minimalism, its subtle embroidery. Thick lines have been replaced by tiny skillful crenellations. Such art is a refinement.[6]

Here we see a reversion to a hypostasis where that which was expanding is reduced, worn thin, at risk. Isou lingers here, on this reduction, this pruning, which annihilates the heart of creation itself.

In the pathway through Chaplin's works that Bazin clears, we have the same double distinction of *amplique/ciselant*, even if it is of course not presented in these terms. Because the text deals with silent Charlots, I will start with the 1948 "Introduction à une symbolique de Charlot,"[7] even though it doesn't represent Bazin's first writing on Chaplin. He approaches

Chaplin's silent films through a multifaceted description of Charlot's character, composed of a series of features that are typical of him, and a range of symptomatic attitudes. Together they paint a portrait of the character that is not exhaustive, but a summation of situations, of relationships (to objects, to time), of movements (kicking, racing), and of styles, moral or popular (the myth, the sacred), which break the text open into a series of components that constitute, when aggregated, the myth of Charlot. There is an accumulation of various clichés of the vagabond, a combination of behaviors that are unique to him, and a repertoire of his most emblematic attitudes and reactions. Bazin gives us a spectral vision of the character, who is presented as an expanding force, and seems dedicated to spread out and store up adventures [figure 23.1]. In this way of depicting a divided and agglomerated portrait of Charlot, Bazin is describing an *amplique* character. The notion of amplitude is specifically described elsewhere, on another level, in this text: "But what distinguishes Charlie from the insect is the speed with which he returns from his condition of spatial dissolution within the cosmos to a state of instant readiness for action."[8] Thus the idea of amplitude is made apparent through an image that puts the character on a completely different scale. Bazin also describes this in another configuration: that of Charlot's connection to the movie theater, the public and its laughter: "At that moment the hall was no longer filled with the original laughter but with a series of echoes, a second wave of laughter, reflected off the minds of the spectators as if from the invisible walls of an abyss."[9] Bazin extends the amplitude of the myth of Charlot to factors outside of the film, to the present, to the audience's laughter.

With *The Great Dictator*, a collapse of the myth begins, for in the notion of the "transformation of being," the amplitude of the myth is reduced; it is no longer spread by film reels, skits, and adventures, but is actually transferred from one being to another, and is thus a less extensive

FIGURE 23.1: Charlot's *amplique* phase

movement. But it is with *Verdoux* that we find the *amplique/ciselant* inversion. Bazin first contrasts Verdoux to Charlot (according to women, money, career, relationship with work, social affiliation, the respect that they engender): "Charlie is essentially a socially unadapted person; Verdoux is superadapted."[10] He then concludes by converting one into the other, joining together what he tried to present as wholly separate. Thus Verdoux, approaching the guillotine, is none other than Charlot. It is not the character contrasted with Charlot who will be executed, but the one who he becomes again, at this moment, Charlot himself. The text concludes as follows: "This same road to nowhere, always taken from film to film by the little fellow with the cane, which some see as the road of the wandering Jew while others prefer to identify it with the road of hope—now we know where it ends. It ends as a path across a prison yard in the morning mist, through which we sense the ridiculous shape of a guillotine"[11] [figure 23.2].

Although Bazin still finds Charlot's myth active in *Limelight*, he no longer sees it in what to him is the disappointing next film, *A King in New York* (1957). He concludes his review this way: "Chaplin is still Chaplin, but now he is just Chaplin"[12] [figure 17.2].

As mentioned at the outset, the axis of myth brings Bazin to a defense of Chaplin's talking pictures, not as a direct result of his observations on speech, but on the contrary, by an analysis of the evolution of the image, which directly impacts the body of the actor who played Charlot. It would however be too quick to say that speech and sound drove the myth of films away, since myth is, by definition, a narration, an original story passed along by oral tradition. It is thus hard to see why the arrival of speech would have broken that which is transferred by speech. This seems contradictory at first glance.

Isou defined *amplique* poetry as a poetry of orality, as primary, when everything had yet to be made. *Amplique* poetry then grew by talking, breathing, declaiming, and singing. *Ciselante* poetry, on the other hand, must go from speech to the page:

FIGURE 23.2: *Monsieur Verdoux* (1947)

Until Baudelaire, poetry was understood publicly by its comprehension on the first reading, and this is why it was an *oral art*. Though the book may have served to retain and perpetuate it, in the amplic phase, the poem does not come alive [*prégnant*] except during *public reading*. In the chiseling phase, however, verse is only assimilated after persistent meditation, and it gains its meaning on the page. From Mallarmé to the Dadaists, poets added typographic novelties to books that had no oral significance.[13]

From this assertion, we could propose the hypothesis that for Bazin, what drives away the myth of Charlot in Chaplin's talkies is not just the talking. Bazin carefully implies this, while not lingering specifically on it. What spoils the myth, what breaks it up, and according to him, gradually kills it, is instead the role of speech in the mouths of the characters that Chaplin portrays (Hynkel, the little barber, Verdoux, Calvero, Shadoy). Their use of speech is confessional, in the sense that all of the films' dialogues are built to reach the moment of confession—in general the final one—for these characters, and for Chaplin himself behind them. What kills the myth is not the speech that grants the character a power of expression that he did not have before (when he did not have it, the words of others relayed it). . . . In taking the character for his word, often in head-on shots, before what are effectively the jurors of an assembly [figure 23.3], or of a tribunal, or those that comprise the audience of the show, Chaplin forces his characters to confess, their speech taking on the weight of a legal consignation . . . and this in the time of the film, the life of its author, and for all eternity. Such depositions through confession cut into—fatally *chisel*—the eternal characteristic that belongs to myth. Bazin notes this in "The Grandeur of *Limelight*" and he thus grasps that what pervades Chaplin's films is the relentlessly incommunicable nature of all confession: for a confession is not transmitted from voice to voice, from mouth to mouth, as from mouth to ear like a myth; rather it must be

FIGURE 23.3: Charlot's myth chiseled (*Monsieur Verdoux*)

pronounced by the one who experienced it. Bazin's reflections on the disappearance of myth in Chaplin's cinema thus hinge less on the sense of the myth that Charlot represents (the small man of the people, the poor man, the individualist, the roamer, or the wandering Jew). . . . He is less attached to the idea of the myth of Charlot than to the nature of all myth; to know how it is transmitted, dispersed, spread. The intervention [*prise de parole*] of the confession blocks not the symbol that the character Charlot stands for, as one might at first imagine; rather it blocks the orality inherent in myth.

Lastly, while Bazin and Isou may share a vision of the notion of creation, they wrote in diametrically opposed fashions. Isou's 1947 manifesto looks forward, since he announces a break with all that precedes him and puts forth an agenda, that of lettrism, based on what he declares poetic writing to be. Bazin, on the other hand, looks at a film that has just come out, or returns to one years later, even eighteen years after its release.[14] His writing is thus backward-looking.

Despite this opposition, their analyses converge; the oral tradition—what UNESCO calls "spiritual patrimony"—cannot support the urgent need to confide to everyone, in one's own name, for this is the very definition of public confession; this can only occur once, cannot be revived by those who hear it, and is not transmittable. For similar reasons, Isou dates the death of poetry, the finale of its *ciselante* stage, to surrealist writing. According to him, the surrealists definitively desiccated words through their desire to invest in them dreams and the unconscious.

I conclude by noting that while Bazin comes up with a conception of the evolution of creation that Isou expresses in the programmatic form of the manifesto, Bazin's elegance and his style exempt him from having recourse to the declarations, exclamations, and grandiosity that define the manifesto, as powerful as these may be.

Notes

1. Bazin would have heard about Isou from Eric Rohmer who published (under the name Maurice Scherer) a highly interesting article about Isou in *Cahiers du cinéma* in March 1952.
2. Jean-Michel Mension, *The Tribe*, trans. Donald Nicholson-Smith (San Francisco: City Lights Books, 2001), 117. Original: "Allez vous coucher, fasciste larvé, gagnez beaucoup d'argent, soyez mondain (très réussi votre plat ventre devant la petite Elisabeth), mourez vite, nous vous ferons des obsèques de première classe. Les feux de la rampe ont fait fondre le fard du soi-disant mime génial, et l'on ne voit plus qu'un vieillard sinistre et intéressé. Go Home, mister Chaplin."
3. André Bazin. "The Myth of Monsieur Verdoux," in *What Is Cinema?* vol. 2, trans. Hugh Gray (Berkeley: University of California Press, 1971), 120.
4. Bazin, "If Charlot Hadn't Died," *Essays on Chaplin*. trans. Jean Bodon (New Haven, CT: University of New Haven Press, 1985), 51–52.
5. Isidore Isou, *Introduction à une nouvelle poesie et à une nouvelle musique* (Paris: Gallimard, 1947). Original: "L'hypostase amplique est le moment plein d'un art. Elle apparaît avec les premières tendances artistiques. Elle garde l'empreinte des existences libres, sans rivalités. On ne pose pas encore un problème d'originalité, tout étant origine l. Aucune matière ne porte le masque de quelqu'un. Chaque création tend à acquérir des formes cyclopiques. Les espaces sont étendus, les possibilités mises à disposition sont énormes," 89.
6. Ibid. Original: "Avec le temps, les émissions s'ajoutent aux émissions. La portion libre baisse, on travaille sur des volumes diminués. Quand les espaces se sont totalement amoindris, étant colonisés, l'hypostase est changée. Brusquement, par l'apparition d'une personnalité qui comprend tout à coup ou lentement, par des formations successives, l'art entre dans le contraire.

Les massivités ont été remplacées par de petits morceaux, sur lesquels le détail artistique s'exercera minutieusement. Il ne compte plus l'ouvrage, mais le matériel qui devient l'ouvrage même. La valeur n'est plus dans l'immensité mais dans la spécialité des formes, des exiguïtés, des dentelles nuancées. Les grandes lignes ont été remplacées par des crénelures minuscules, mais habiles. L'art est un raffinement," 90.

7. This text is translated under the reduced title "Charlie Chaplin" in Bazin, *What Is Cinema?* vol. 1 (Berkeley: University of California Press, 1967).

8. Ibid., 149.

9. Ibid., 147.

10. Bazin, "The Myth of Monsieur Verdoux." in *What Is Cinema?* vol. 2, 106.

11. Ibid., 109.

12. Bazin, "A King in New York," in *Essays on Chaplin*, 66.

13. Isou, *Introduction à une nouvelle poesie et une nouvelle musique*. Original: "Jusqu'à Baudelaire, on lisait la poésie publiquement par sa compréhension à première lecture et c'est pourquoi elle était un art oral. Si le livre servait à retenir et à perpétuer, dans l'amplique, le poème ne devenait prégnant qu'à la lecture en commun. Dans le ciselant, le vers est assimilé après une persévérante méditation et il gagne son sens dans la page. De Mallarmé aux Dadaïste, on avait ajouté aux livres des innovations typographiques qui n'avaient aucun sens oral," 92.

14. Bazin, "Le temps rend justice aux Temps moderne," *Arts* (October 13, 1954), translated as "Time Validates *Modern Times*" in *Essays on Chaplin*, 5–10.

24

Radical Ambitions in Postwar French Documentary

STEVEN UNGAR

André Bazin's writings on documentary modes of reportage, exploration/travelogue, and art film are integral to the vision of cinema he theorized as an imaginative treatment of reality that simulates conditions under which experience seemingly speaks of its own accord.[1] The new Bazin archive lists approximately 100 texts—about 4 percent of his total output—that contain significant mention of documentaries. Between 1944 and 1958, these texts appeared mainly in the form of reviews of films by Robert Flaherty, Walter Ruttmann, Georges Rouquier, Léon Poirier, Georges Franju, Nicole Védrès, Henri-Georges Clouzot, Thor Heyerdahl, Jacques-Yves Cousteau, Jean Rouch, Alain Resnais, and Chris Marker.

Documentary practices are a primary object of analysis throughout the first ten chapters of *Qu'est-ce que le cinéma?* Commenting on Jean Thevenot's study of exploration films, Bazin welcomes the return to authenticity modeled on Robert Flaherty's *Nanook of the North* (1922) and Léon Poirier's *La Croisère noire* (*The Black Cruise*, 1926) in place of the trumped up exoticism that dominated many exploration and ethnographic films shot between the wars.[2] Reviewing Jacques-Yves Cousteau's *Le Monde du silence* (*The World of Silence*, 1956), he links technique and moral concerns in the kind of documentary that cheats (*tricher*) "for the sake of insight without however fooling its spectator" (QC, 40). Cheating in the above instance may mean nothing more than acknowledging cinema's reliance on imagination and technology to convey a strong sense of the real world. At the same time, Bazin's choice of term displays the importance he ascribes to all aspects of filmmaking in conjunction with choice and value in the real world.

From one review to the next, Bazin engages documentaries that explore the expressive potential of cinema beyond exposition and reportage. In particular, he explores what the mobilization of specific techniques implies for film's unique ability to disclose significant meaning— from a minor detail to a life-changing insight—as a lesson from which the spectator learns something new about the real world. This dual concern with the expressive and epistemological potential of documentary achieves a distinct breakthrough in articles Bazin writes between 1956 and 1958 on documentaries by Marker, Resnais, Rouch, and others within or near what Richard Roud would refer to in 1962 as Left Bank Cinema.[3] These articles are of special interest because they promote a considered reception of documentaries linking the emergence of the

French New Wave following Bazin's death to a cinematic avant-garde as far back as 1930. In addition, they contribute to an understanding of postwar experimentation with short subject forms influenced by a trajectory from photo-essay toward the essay film.

When Bazin first describes Chris Marker's *Lettre de Sibérie* (*Letter from Siberia*, 1956) as a cinematic reportage on past and present realities of the "vast, distant, and unknown territory" known as Siberia, he seems to align it with travelogue and exploration films, casting Marker as an image hunter in search of the exotic[4] [figure 24.1]. At the same time, Bazin is attentive to Marker's radical ambitions that subsume the cinematic material of the image to a primacy of the spoken word [*la parole*] and a central idea that structures the entire film. In this instance, the voice of Georges Rouquier that speaks the commentary starting with the film's opening sentence—"I am writing to you from a distant country"—announces an epistolary format that personalizes the filmmaker as a vocal presence. The fact that the sentence cites the title of a text by the writer Henri Michaux increases its evocative density.[5]

Bazin asserts that Marker's "radical ambitions" (Bazin's expression) in *Lettre de Sibérie* mobilize an absolutely new notion of horizontal editing in which "the image refers neither to what precedes or follows it, but instead laterally, so to speak, to what [is] being said."[6] Unlike earlier models of montage that produced meaning along the vertical axis of the filmstrip passing through the projector, meaning in Marker's film occurs as a relation between word and image ("from ear to eye") on the model of visual and sound tracks within individual frames. Effects of this horizontal editing are evident in a brief sequence-shot in Yakutsk—capital of what is now the Sakha Republic—seen three times in succession, each time with a different commentary [figure 24.1]. The commentaries start with: "For example, Yakutsk, capital of the Soviet Socialist Republic of the same name, is a modern city"; followed by, "Or perhaps, Yakutsk, with

FIGURE 24.1: One take for three shots. (*Letter from Siberia*)

a sinister reputation, is a gloomy city"; and finally by, "Or simply, Yakutsk, where the modern houses are slowly gaining on the gloomy older neighborhoods."[7]

Bazin reads Marker's intent in this exercise as showing the capacity of words to destabilize the seemingly fixed meaning of images and so to promote a more dynamic process of signification in which the role of words is no longer secondary.[8] And this to the point of creating an essay documented by film in which the term "essay" has the same meaning—"historical and political as well as written by a poet"—as in literature. In addition, Bazin openly associates horizontal editing with the notion of "a documented point of view" that filmmaker Jean Vigo had coined when introducing his 1929 film *A Propos de Nice*.[9]

Bazin reiterates his sense of this reconfiguration of word and image in an article for *Le Parisien libéré* in which he includes Marker among a generation of writers for whom the time of the image does not entail sacrificing the powers and virtues of language that remain the privileged expression of intelligence:

> This means that for Chris Marker the commentary of a film is not what is added to images chosen and edited beforehand, but is close to the primary, fundamental element that nonetheless acquires meaning and efficiency only with reference to the images that accompany it. Deprived of its soundtrack, *Lettre de Sibérie* has no meaning in a narrow sense, with the text alone nothing more than a fireworks of gratuitous ideas. If some spectators find this radically new conception of "the documentary" unsettling, it is because cinema has accustomed us more to the comfort of the eye than to intellectual attention.[10]

Bazin's take on the innovative nature of Marker's short subject extends to a third article in which he characterizes it as a documentary on the political reality of Siberia inflected by human geography. The reference here invokes the work of Jean Brunhes, a professor at the Collège de France whose *La Géographie humaine* (1910) had reputedly inspired Luis Buñuel to characterize his pseudo-documentary, *Las Hurdes* (*Land Without Bread*, 1932), as "a cinematic essay in human geography."[11] Echoing his earlier reference to Vigo, Bazin adds that "cinema" is secondary to "essay" when understood in a literary context, as in the assertion that Camus wrote essays.[12]

This article contains Bazin's strongest formulation concerning Marker's efforts to subsume the image to the word as the film's primary material linked to the expression of a central idea:

> *Lettre de Sibérie* is above all a film made of ideas (ideas stemming naturally from knowledge and lived experience), but ALSO—and here is where cinema enters the picture—of ideas articulated on the basis of documentary images. If the text in the film proves nothing without the images, it is no longer simply commentary. Instead it maintains a dialectical and *lateral* rapport with them, leading to an absolutely new notion of editing: no longer from one image to another and along the length of the filmstrip, but so to speak lateral, as a consequence and reflection of the idea's impact on the image.[13]

The emphasis Bazin places on ideas in this new dialectic of lateral editing responds to Alexandre Astruc's 1948 call for a cinematic avant-garde capable of expressing thought with a complexity rivaling that of the novel and the essay. To this end, Astruc advocates a cinema of the *caméra-stylo* (camera-pen) that will "gradually break free from the tyranny of what is visual, from the image for its own sake . . . in order to become a means of writing just as flexible and subtle as a written language."[14] And while Bazin never invokes the term "avant-garde" expressly with reference to Marker, the inflection of his practice via Astruc positions the phenomenon of lateral editing in *Lettre de Sibérie* as an extension of the human geography of Buñuel's *Las Hurdes* and Vigo's goal in "Toward a Social Cinema" to make films that address social issues and move the spectator emotionally.

A second antecedent for Bazin's remarks on horizontal editing is a 1940 text, "The Film Essay," in which the experimental filmmaker Hans Richter writes of an innovative practice that would replace the presentation of beautiful vistas with efforts "to find a representation for intellectual content," "to find images for moral concepts," and strive "to make visible the invisible world of concepts, thoughts, and ideas," so that viewers would become "involved emotionally and intellectually."[15] Richter's formulation approximates a synthesis before the fact by setting the dual emphasis on intellectual content and moral value that Bazin's cinematic realism would uphold in line with the intellectual and emotional involvement of the spectator Vigo had sought to promote in his 1930 call for a social cinema.

Five years before the articles on *Lettre de Sibérie*, Bazin had characterized Georges Franju's *Hôtel des Invalides* (1951) as a pacifist film whose reportage extends from the objective content of the National War Museum in Paris to "its subjective and moral content, in other words, a glorification of the military class as maintained in the hearts of the museum guides and wounded veterans who were servants of its cult."[16] Franju expresses his point of view in two lapidary assertions—"legend has it heroes" and "war has its victims" set, respectively, against images of Napoleon and a crippled veteran—that the rest of the film sustains through an ironic interplay of word and image.[17] A similar moment opens Resnais' and Marker's documentary short, *Les Statues meurent aussi* (*Statues Also Die*, 1953), whose very first words—"When men die, they enter history. When statues die, they enter the realm of art"—are heard in voice-over on a black screen.[18] In both instances, the dislocation of visual primacy by the rhetorical force of language is a provocation that promotes critique.

A closer antecedent of the horizontal editing Bazin identifies in *Lettre de Sibérie* is *Paris 1900*, a 1947 feature by Nicole Védrès that remains a key reference for the questions about documentary that Marker, Resnais, and others would raise over the following decade. Védrès was a writer whose training as an archivist likely inspired her 1945 compilation of still photos from Cinémathèque Française collections.[19] Two years later, she used archival photographs and early newsreels to make *Paris 1900*, which the French Film Critics Circle awarded the 1947 Prix Louis Delluc. In 1950, Védrès completed *La Vie commence demain* (*Life Begins Tomorrow*), a feature-length film whose antinuclear bomb stance included dialogues between a "man of the present" (Jean-Pierre Aumont) and a "man of the future" (André S. Labarthe) as well as appearances by Jean-Paul Sartre, Pablo Picasso, André Gide, Jean Rostand, Daniel Lagache, and Le Corbusier.[20]

Writing in the September 30, 1947, issue of *L'Écran Français*, Bazin lauds Védrès' intelligence in the choices she made in material sources and in editing.[21] Six months later, Bazin repeats the term when he asserts that the spectator is "not bored for an instant by this album of quaint and disconcerting images by Nicole Védrès whose intelligent documentary, filled with both humor and seriousness, is excellently narrated by Claude Dauphin."[22] Nearly fifty years later, Marker echoes Bazin when he invokes his debts to Védrès during the early postwar period in a text drafted for the program of the Cinémathèque Française's 1998 retrospective of his films:

> In two films, Nicole taught me that cinema was not incompatible with intelligence.... The challenge is not at all to intelligence in itself, but instead to the idea, fairly uncommon at the time, that intelligence could serve as the basis or raw material that commentary and editing take on in order to extract from it the object we refer to as film.[23]

From 1947 to 1958, and from Vigo and Védrès to Marker, we thus come full circle by means of a chronology that positions Bazin within a brief history of avant-garde documentary from interwar to early postwar France for which the newly available dossier of his complete writings provides unprecedented access.

A second set of questions Bazin raises with reference to documentary concerns the extent to which the radical ambitions he identifies in *Lettre de Sibérie* extend from formal innovation toward heightened awareness of societies in transition during a decade marked by cold war politics and the decline of colonialism. To restate the point somewhat differently, one might ask how documentaries whose ambitions concerning film form attract Bazin's attention also solicit his sense of political transition in conjunction with cultural difference. Building on Bazin's assertion in a 1953 essay published under the aegis of the activist *Peuple et culture* group, I want to explore briefly how documentaries by Marker, Resnais, and Jean Rouch convey abstract ideas about the world they present to spectators in concrete form.[24]

In *Les Maîtres fous* (1955), Rouch positions himself between the sect of the Haoukas (new gods) whom he had filmed in the Gold Coast (later Ghana) and the film's initial spectators in France. Statements displayed in writing at the very start of the film instruct spectators to consider the violence of certain sequences as a solution to the problem of readaptation that also shows how certain Africans view "our" European civilization.[25] Seconds later, another statement asserts that the filmed rituals disclose how at least some Africans see the British and French during a period of colonial decline. Both statements reflexively frame the film that follows without excluding the narrator himself.[26]

Bazin displays his attentiveness to the geopolitical context of *Les Maîtres fous* when he writes that Rouch had recorded the survival of a traditional practice and the birth of a cult whose spirits embody political and social power—the governor, the doctor, the locomotive driver—on a scale with the experiences of Africans under colonial rule. Significantly, Bazin ends his article by describing Rouch's project as an extension of what Resnais and Marker had sought to accomplish in *Les Statues meurent aussi*:

> Chris Marker and Alain Resnais had wanted to show us how statues of black art die. Rouch's film provides us with the logical complement by revealing to us how gods are also born. For if there is something worse than the death of a civilization, it is the reflection that it conveys to us of our civilization in the delirium of its death throes.[27]

The passage points to reflexive elements in both documentaries that disclose how Europeans might see themselves from the perspective of colonial subjects. Invoking the key term he would soon use with reference to *Lettre de Sibérie*, Bazin contrasts his negative judgment of exotic spectacle in exploration films by Enrico Gras with Rouch's ability to fashion "true images" that balance the force of images and a commentary whose objectivity infused with an intellectual passion moves *Les Maîtres fous* beyond reportage from filmed ethnography to history and political sociology.[28]

In a similar transition during the final ten minutes of *Les Statues meurent aussi*, educational reportage yields to denunciation whose intense mobilization of word and image led government censors to ban the orignal thirty-minute version of the film from commercial release in 1953. Here is a passage from minute twenty-three that may have riled government censors:

> We are the Martians of Africa. We arrive from our planet, with our ways of seeing, our white magic, and our machines. We cure the black man of his sicknesses, that is for sure. He catches our sicknesses, that is also for sure. Whether he wins or loses by the exchange, his art fails in all cases to survive.[29]

Much like Rouch in *Les Maîtres fous*, Marker asserts the intractable differences that led native peoples of occupied territories in sub-Saharan Africa to see the Europeans as invaders from outer space.[30] Bazin validates this assertion when he writes in April 1954 that censorship of the film upheld by three French ministries had seemingly made this pamphlet film into a taboo.[31] He also laments the fact that when French national television scheduled a broadcast of *Les Statues meurent aussi* the day it won the Prix Jean Vigo, the airing was dropped after the announcer stated that the film had failed to receive authorization for commercial release. Bazin concludes that because the required certificate did not formally apply to television, the film had been subjected to extraordinary surveillance, "as though some statues needed to be killed."[32] Perhaps, as in the following passage, it was Marker's use of the pronoun "we" that government censors found unacceptable:

> We want to see in [these objects] suffering, serenity, or humor when we understand nothing at all. Colonizers of the world, we want everything to speak to us: animals, the dead, statues. And those statues are silent. They have mouths and do not speak. They have eyes and do not see.[33]

Finally, Bazin's 1956 remarks on *Dimanche à Pékin* recapitulate his perspective on documentary short subjects whose commentary confers onto them a singular *PRÉSENCE* (Bazin's emphasis), absent in conventional reportages. He argues that what is at stake in Marker's film is less an absolute refusal of the picturesque than a recasting of a cultural encounter whose implications are also political: "In this period of passionate and unilateral politics, Chris Marker's thoughtful gaze onto millions of human beings whose existence or inexistence depends in no way whatsoever on our preferences reveals a pathos to which conventional travelogues fail to accustom us."[34]

In line with his remarks on *Les Maîtres fous* and *Les Statues meurent aussi*, Bazin qualifies the voice-over commentary in *Dimanche à Pékin* as embodying a refusal of the gaze that Western travelers cast onto an Asia whose identity they seek to appropriate. Marker dismantles this unilateral gaze by exposing within it the force of conventional projections of a "primitive"

China or Asia. Bazin's remarks on these three documentaries engage difference without making it either irreducible (and thus inaccessible) or overly familiar through categories and assumptions imposed from the outside. His attentiveness to efforts taken by Marker, Resnais, and Rouch to undermine conventions of the exotic matches his appreciation of their formal innovation; on both fronts he hailed the difference these documentaries promoted during a decade marked by the cold war and the decline of colonialism.

Notes

1. Dudley Andrew, *André Bazin* (New York: Oxford University Press, 1978), 113.

2. André Bazin, "Cinema and Exploration," in *What Is Cinema?* vol. 1, 155. (Original: *Qu'est-ce que le cinéma*, 27).

3. Roud coined the designation in "Left Bank Cinema," *Sight & Sound*, 32:1 (1962–1963), 24–27; and "Left Bank Cinema Revisited," *Sight and Sound* 46:3 (Summer 1977), 143–45. See also Claire Clouzot's broader take in *Le Cinéma français depuis la nouvelle vague* (Paris: Nathan, 1972), 46–80. François Niney refers to a postwar French school of notable [*beaux*] documentaries by Franju, Painlevé, Marker, Jean Cayrol, and Varda in *Le Documentaire et ses faux-semblants* (Paris: Klincksieck, 2009), 118. On the conjuncture of documentary and short subjects [*courts métrages*] in early postwar France, see Dominique Blüher and François Thomas, eds. *Le Court Métrage en France de 1945 à 1968: De l'âge d'or aux contrebandiers* (Rennes: Presses Université de Rennes, 2005).

4. See Pierre Leprohon, *L'Exotisme et le cinéma: les "chasseurs d'images" à la conquête du monde* (Paris: J. Susse, 1945). As I complete this article, the *New Yorker* is running Ian Frazier's two-part "Travels in Siberia" (August 3 and 10–17, 2009).

5. Chris Marker, "*Lettre de Sibérie*," in *Commentaires* (Paris: Seuil, 1961), 47. Georges Rouquier is best known for directing a pair of documentaries, *Farrebique* (1946) and *Biquefarre* (1983), that chronicle rural life in an isolated area of southern France. First published in 1937, "Je vous écris d'un pays lointain" is reprinted in Henri Michaux, *Oeuvres completes* (Paris: Gallimard "Bibliothèque de la Pléïade," 1998), vol. 1, 590–93.

6. Bazin, "*Lettre de Sibérie*," in *Le Cinéma français de la liberation à la nouvelle vague (1945–1958)*, ed. Jean Narboni (Paris: Cahiers du Cinéma, 1983), 180. First published in *France observateur*, 443 (October 30, 1958).

7. Marker, "*Lettre de Sibérie*," 63.

8. See Carol Armstrong's introductory remarks on the verbal framing of photographs in nineteenth-century illustrated books in *Scenes in a Library: Reading the Photograph in the Book, 1843–1875* (Cambridge, MA: MIT Press, 1998); see also John Tagg, *The Disciplinary Frame: Photographic Truths and the Capture of Meaning* (Minneapolis: University of Minnesota Press, 2009).

9. Bazin, "*Lettre de Sibérie*," in *Le Cinéma français de la liberation à la nouvelle vague (1945–1958)*, 180. See Jean Vigo, "Toward a Social Cinema," in *French Film Theory and Criticism, 1907–1939*, v. II ed. Richard Abel (Princeton, NJ: Princeton University Press, 1988), 60–63. Even before his articles on *Lettre de Sibérie*, Bazin already invoked Vigo's "documented point of view" as a precedent for Marker's *Dimanche à Pékin (Sunday in Peking*, 1956), which he describes as a synthesis of reportage, critique, story, and poetry for which the term "documentary" seems inadequate.

10. Bazin, "*Lettre de Sibérie*," *Le Parisien Libéré*, 4399 (November 3, 1958).

11. Nicole Brenez, *Cinémas d'avant-garde* (Paris: Cahiers du Cinéma, 2006), 44. See also Jeffrey Ruoff, "An Ethnographic Surrealist Film: Louis Buñuel's *Land Without Bread*," in *Visual Anthropology Review*, 14:1 (Spring–Summer 1998).

12. Bazin, "Deux Documentaires 'hors série,'" *Radio, Cinéma, Télévision*, 461 (November 16, 1958).

13. Ibid.

14. Alexandre Astruc, "The Birth of a New Avant-Garde: *La Caméra-stylo*," in *The French New Wave: Critical Landmarks*, revised edition, ed. Peter Graham and Ginette Vincendeau (London: BFI/Palgrave, 2009), 32. First published in *L'Ecran français*, 144 (March 30, 1948).

15. Hans Richter, "Der Essayfilm: Eine Neue Form des Dokumentarfilms," cited in English in Timothy Corrigan, "'The Forgotten Image Between Two Shots': Photos, Photograms, and the Essayistic," in *Still Moving: Between Cinema and Photography*, ed. Karen Beckman and Jean Ma (Durham, NC: Duke University Press,

2008), 44. This essay is discussed in Laura Rascaroli, *The Personal Camera: Subjective Cinema and the Essay-Film* (London: Wallflower, 2009). Her book provides a history of the essay-film, including a chapter on Chris Marker.

16. Bazin, "Georges Franju, *Hôtel des Invalides*," in Narboni, ed., 177. First published in *France observateur* (October 4, 1952).

17. The phrases in the original French—"la légende a ses héros" and "la guerre a ses victimes"—appear in *L'Avant-Scène Cinéma*, 38 (1964), 46. See also Kate Ince, *Georges Franju* (New York: Manchester University Press, 2005), 27–29.

18. "Quand les hommes meurent, ils entrent dans l'histoire. Quand les statues meurent, elles entrent dans l'art" (Marker, "*Les Statues meurent aussi*," in *Commentaires*, 13).

19. Nicole Védrès, *Images du cinéma français* (Paris: Chêne, 1945).

20. On the U.S. reception of the film, see Bosley Crowther, "THE SCREEN: TWO IMPORTS ARRIVE; 'Life Begins Tomorrow' From France is the New Feature at 55th St. Playhouse" (*New York Times*, November 18, 1952).

21. Bazin, "Nicole Védrès, *Paris 1900*,'" in Narboni, 168.

22. Bazin, "*Paris 1900*," *L'Écran français* (March 3, 1948), 2. The crew included a young assistant editor named Alain Resnais who soon completed the first of his short subject documentary "visits" to artists. Georges Sadoul agrees with Bazin that the essence of *Paris 1900* is montage, praising her as well for seeing beyond the bric-a-brac picturesque and conveying the historical reality of the period in decline toward World War I, almost with "the depth or complexity of the best historical novelist" ("Le Temps retrouvé: *Paris 1900*, de Nicole Védrès," in *Chroniques du Cinéma*, vol. 1 (Paris: Union Générale d'Éditions, 1979), 81–84. First published in *Les Lettres françaises*, 199 (March 11, 1948). Védrès assumes an openly feminist stance in "Petite Lettre à André Bazin sur un sujet intraitable," *Cahiers du Cinéma*, 30 (Christmas 1953), 27–28.

23. Marker, *Programme de la Cinémathèque Française*, January–February 1998, 5.

24. Bazin, "Le Langage de notre temps," *Regards neufs sur le cinéma*, ed. Jacques Chevalier (Paris: Seuil, 1953), 21.

25. *Les Maîtres fous*, in *Jean Rouch*, set of four DVDs (Paris: Editions Montparnasse "Le Geste Cinématographique," 2005).

26. Daniel Morgan studies how the basic construction of Rouch's films positions him to negotiate and work through the difficulty of bridging the gap between the audience of his films and the worlds his films show; "The Pause of the World," *Three Documentary Filmmakers*, ed. William Rothman (Albany, NY: SUNY Press, 2009), 139–56.

27. Bazin, "Jean Rouch, '*Les Maîtres fous*,'" in Narboni, 185–86. First published in *France observateur*, 389 (October 24, 1957).

28. Bazin, "Jean Rouch," 187.

29. Marker, "*Les Statues meurent aussi*," 21

30. A passage in Sembène Ousmane's 1956 novel, *Le Docker noir*, inverts this image when a character states that "For the [white] European, a well-dressed black man is one who adapts to their existence. As if the black man were coming from another planet" (*Le Docker noir* [Paris: Présence Africaine, 1973], 189).

31. Bazin, "Les Statues meurent deux fois: Le Prix Vigo," *France observateur*, 195 (February 4, 1954), 22.

32. Ibid., 23.

33. Marker, "*Les Statues meurent aussi*," 15. In a January 1948 letter written in Algeria at the end of a trip to North Africa, Bazin uses similar terms in referring to the Arabian [*sic*] world as so totally unassimilable, "absolutely another spiritual universe" that it was best to leave alone (cited in Andrew, *André Bazin*, 94).

34. Bazin, "*Dimanche à Pékin*, Grand Prix du court métrage," *France observateur*, 343 (December 6, 1956), 11.

Bazin on the Margins of the Seventh Art

Grant Wiedenfeld

André Bazin is known primarily as an advocate of realism, yet his admiration for animation, abstract film, and the essay-documentary belies a deeper mission: to advocate for cinema's variety. Analyzing his criticism of films by the likes of Norman McLaren, Jean Mitry, and Chris Marker, we find a Bazin who shepherds filmmakers in marginal genres *away* from realistic representation. This unexpected perspective clarifies the social motive behind Bazin's realist advocacy—the "popular vocation of cinema." Bazin redefines "avant-garde" filmmaking in relation to this populist aim and relegates elitist works, such as hard-core surrealist films, to a decadent *flanc-garde*.

Animation and Abstraction

Bazin draws some sharp boundaries between painting and cinema in "The Ontology of the Photographic Image" when he writes: "So, photography is clearly the most important event in the history of plastic arts. Simultaneously a liberation and a fulfillment, it has freed Western painting, once and for all, from its obsession with realism and allowed it to recover its aesthetic autonomy."[1] He would seem to segregate the arts, leaving abstraction to painting and reserving realistic representation for photography and cinema. Yet Bazin is content when a minor cinematic genre trespasses into the territory of the plastic arts, as in the case of Norman McLaren [figure 25.1]. When 3D first appeared, Bazin gives special attention to McLaren's hand-painted abstract films:[2]

> . . . in his small Canadian laboratory he is bringing about a poetic and brilliant revolution in the field of animation. I hardly get at this last aspect of his experiments by describing them as *abstract painting in motion and in 3D*. Years ago, Fernand Léger made *Ballet Mécanique* [1924] by transposing his painting practice into black and white photography of real objects. Today, 3D and color would offer him new tools that are completely pictorial although unimaginable in any format outside of 3D cinema: the painter can now create moving forms in space.[3]

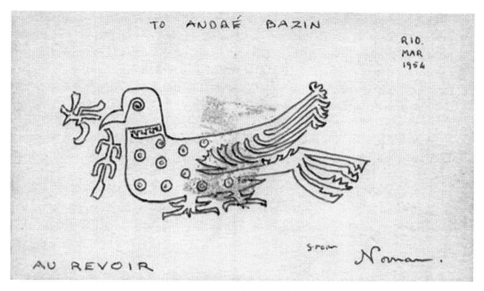

FIGURE 25.1: Norman McLaren's postcard to Bazin (Florent Bazin collection)

Whereas in other contexts Bazin vilifies the '20s avant-garde for its elitism, here he exemplifies what film, starting with *Ballet Mécanique*, can achieve as painting. McLaren's 3D experiments open a new dimension of space for the artist; film also affords painting the fourth dimension of time, as Bazin argues in his review of Henri-Georges Clouzot's *The Picasso Mystery* (*Le Mystère Picasso*, 1956). Bazin dubs Picasso's performance "A Bergsonian Film" because painting becomes truly gestural, that is, paint*ing*, not something already done and paint*ed*:

> What Clouzot at last reveals is the painting itself, i.e., a work that exists in time, that has its own duration, its own life, and sometimes—as at the end of the film—a death that precedes the extinction of the artist.... [O]nly film ... could realize the passage from the gross approximations of the discontinuous to the temporal realism of a continuous vision; only film could make us see duration itself.[4]

That is, only film can reveal Picasso's genius, which happens through duration. "It is a germination, a budding; form engenders form without ever justifying its existence. That *The Picasso Mystery* reminds us of McLaren is therefore not surprising.... [H]ere is a kind of animated film or painting that owes nothing to the image in itself."[5] In effect, Bazin implies that in a minor nonfiction genre, cinema can beat painting at its own game.

However, on the main stage of the feature film, Bazin gives little support to animation. He finds no painterly innovation in Walt Disney, who is hindered by the problem of realism. In his article "Animated Film Lives Again" Bazin defines animation as anything created frame by frame, from puppets to scratch films to Norman McLaren's puppeteering of real actors in *Neighbours* (1952). He tells the story of animation's renewal in 1956 as a consequence of, and a reaction to, Disney's success. Bazin describes Walt Disney's genius as more industrial than artistic:

The extraordinary complexity of work necessary for his animation's technical perfection demands a veritable factory and a *proportional market*. It is not a question of underestimating the genius and the merits of Disney, but one is forced to acknowledge that the logic of his system and his style had led him, and with him all animation, to an impasse: realism. This is so true that Disney understood it himself and set out to produce documentaries and films with actors.[6]

Since its massive scale naturally led Disney's productions in a realist and crowd-pleasing direction, Bazin saw competing animators turn toward artisanal modes of creation:

> . . . the animated film, beginning with the cartoon, should reject the rubbery realism of the American style and invent its own stylization and conventions. In so freeing itself from the bulky equipment necessary for realism, animated film could again become artisanal and thereby rediscover the inventiveness and variety of individual creation.[7]

Thus Bazin seems neither for nor against animation in principle. Everything depends on the specific genres under consideration, and genres can be classified according to the degree that they aim (whether properly or improperly) at realism. Bazin reviews Jean Mitry's abstract (but filmed) *Images for Debussy* (1951) to reinforce his conception of animation as unsuited for realist representation. Mitry's aesthetic exhibits clear traces of late '20s "pure cinema," which is better appreciated now that mainstream cinema has moved away from those techniques. Bazin criticizes the first half of the film for its "semi-realism" reminiscent of Kirsanoff's *Brumes d'automne (Autumn Mists*, 1929). He then praises the latter half, a rhythmic montage composed from filmed sequences of water. Mitry achieves through editing what Oskar Fischinger, Len Lye and McLaren did with paint; Bazin even notes that one sequence reminds him of *Fantasia* (1940). Yet Mitry's abstraction surpasses the animated film because its water sequences discover the fundamental rhythms of reality:

> The revelation of this rhythmic nature of matter contributes the most to emptying it of its realism, expressing a sort of first, abstract principle in relation to which material reality can only be second. The reflections affirm themselves first and foremost as rhythm. In relation to this essence, water is but an accident. As with the image of the sky in water, the relationship between the idea and object finds itself inverted. The sensible world is but a reflection and epiphenomenon of an essential musicality.[8]

This comment reveals the complex nature of Bazin's realism. His "Real" is Platonist in that its essence is abstract, with matter only secondary, that is, idea and mere appearance; yet Bazin is entirely modern in that this essence, rhythm, is fundamentally temporal. He does not appreciate Mitry's abstraction as pure sensation, but as the revelation of a deeper essence. His review of Jean Painlevé's scientific documentaries reinforces this perspective: "At the farthest reaches of interested and practical research, where the most absolute proscription against aesthetic intention as such reigns, cinematic beauty unfolds like a supernatural grace."[9] Only the modern invention of film could bring out the general essence of things from particular images; here Bazin recognizes the value of abstract filmmaking in a marginal context.

Documentary

As Bazin segregated animation from the feature narrative, he also differentiated documentary. This distinction is made evident in his advice for amateur filmmakers, and further supported by his reviews of Chris Marker's essay-documentary. Bazin discouraged amateurs from making fiction films. In his 1950 article "A la recherche d'une nouvelle avant-garde," he discounts the 16mm format as an amateur option, arguing that without expensive equipment like camera tracks and lights, the results are unrefined; and if one invests in such equipment, one ought to shoot in 35mm. "Amateurs with neither money, training nor actors are better off turning to so-called minor subjects for which their means are well suited. I'm talking about various types of documentary where camera mobility and a sound judgment of what to shoot are the essential thing."[10] Jean Rouch offers a perfect example, whose early 16mm ethnographic films surpassed a bevy of artsy short films at the 1949 Biarritz festival, and even stand up against big budget documentaries on Africa. *Les maîtres fous* (1955) gained Bazin's admiration: "I ask who, alone with his wife, discovered and filmed in 16mm an event where the spirit of man burns us like a flame. I ask who is making real cinema?"[11]

Bazin praises Chris Marker for inventing the essay-documentary, a form that deviates from realist depiction because it privileges text over image. He describes Marker's *Lettre de Sibérie* (*Letter From Siberia*, 1958) as "an essay documented by the film . . . an essay that is both historical and political as well as written by a poet."[12] By organizing the film around the voice-over instead of the image, the filmmaker liberates documentary technique: "Chris Marker doesn't limit himself to using documentary footage filmed on site, but all film material that is apropos: still documents, naturally (engravings, photos, etc.), and also animation—not hesitating, by the way, just like McLaren, to say the most serious things in the most silly manner (the mammoth sequence)."[13] Bazin is probably referring to Norman McLaren's 1936 film *Hell Unlimited*, a didactic indictment of the interwar military-industrial complex that employs crude animation. It might surprise us to see the author of "The Ontology of the Photographic Image" champion Chris Marker for having developed a new kind of documentary that privileges text over image. If we are to understand Bazin as a consistent, systematic thinker, we must conclude that he had different criteria for genres outside of fiction film. He does not describe Marker as an avant-garde pioneer for mainstream cinema but rather an essayist who has no pretensions that threaten the realist feature film's future. If Marker's new type of documentary poses any threat, it would be a threat to the traditional literary essay as the premiere medium for intellectual discourse. Here on the fringes of the seventh art we see what drives Bazin beyond his realist convictions—a desire for cinema to become the premiere cultural medium.

Two Avant-Gardes: Pioneers and Deserters

The '20s avant-garde might represent the antithesis of Renoir or Italian neorealism (Bazin's ideal), so his harsh criticism of the period should not surprise anyone. And yet, Bazin's argument against the 1920s avant-garde is not focused on its artificiality or lack of spiritual potency—that is, on aesthetic grounds. The main problem with the '20s avant-garde was its rejection of what Bazin calls "the popular vocation of cinema."[14] Pursuing a military conceit, he characterizes '20s avant-garde filmmakers as deserters who should have been pioneers, that is, scouts for a larger force. The role of the avant-garde is to take on new subjects and develop new forms of expression that ultimately strengthen popular cinema, a process like percolation. Bazin lists the crucial avant-garde directors: Méliès, Griffith, Stroheim, Bresson, and Renoir, down-playing the importance of Buñuel, Dulac, and Richter. He calls the latter a "*flanc-garde*," instead of an avant-garde, owing to their indifference to cinema's popular audience in favor of fine art's elitist circles.[15] Bazin does not accept the satellite model of a purist mode circling above pop-ular production. He specifically reproves thinking of cinema's popular vocation as a commercial constraint on film art, and admonishes purist decadence: "It is an intellectualist and idealist conception of art to distinguish a priori its techniques and inspiration from its economic and social context." The foremost artists should keep their focus on a popular audience and not retreat into an ivory tower.

Bazin proposes the short film as the proper area for innovation. He defines the purpose of short films as twofold: "to constitute a valid element of the cinema spectacle, and to serve as a workshop for young filmmakers."[16] Shorts can serve as *hors d'oeuvres* to the feature film and meanwhile fulfill an "experimental vocation."[17] He points to Vigo's experiments in *À propos de Nice* (1930) as a stepping stone to *L'Atalante* (1934). Within this avant-garde model, it is the job of the critic to distinguish among more esoteric experiments those innovations that the public may potentially accommodate. "It is not scandalous, insolent or particularly juve-nile to think that good criticism in the Middle Ages would have instructed knights to be of their time."[18] This chivalrous metaphor implies an artist's responsibility to the public at large. The nature of film as a mass medium requires this ethic, whether one produces features or short subjects.

Conclusion

Bazin recognized innovation in many minor genres, and he promoted short film production that would foster an expansion of the medium. Exploring his reviews within minor genres refracts his realist arguments for the popular feature like a prism, differentiating its sociological and aesthetic components from a general aspiration for the medium.

From the unavoidable sociological perspective, Bazin had no doubt that realism is best suited for the center stage. He ultimately believed that "while all the traditional arts have evolved from the Renaissance toward forms of expression reserved for a narrow elite of the financially privileged, cinema is congenitally destined for the world's masses."[19] Critics need to attend to the full gamut of films, but they should not let rarefied aesthetic concerns divert their attention from the cultural role cinema is destined to play in the mass society of the twentieth century. If the avant-garde has any importance, it should finally "advance" the level of popular cinema.

Notes

1. André Bazin, "The Ontology of the Photographic Image," in *What Is Cinema?* vol. 1, trans. Hugh Gray (Berkeley: University of California Press, 1967), 16.

2. Bazin had high hopes for 3D films unlike his *Cahiers* colleagues, Rohmer and Rivette, who preferred Cinema-scope because they believed that 3D distorted space and demanded a less classical mise-en-scène. Cf. Maurice Schérer [Eric Rohmer], "Vertus cardinales du Cinémascope," and Jacques Rivette, "L'Age des metteurs en scène,"

Cahiers du Cinéma, 31 (January 1954). Bazin embraced both formats because they equally participate in the myth of total cinema. Bazin, "La révolution par le relief n'a pas eu lieu," *Radio, Cinéma, Télévision*, 324 (April 1, 1956). All translations are mine unless otherwise noted.

3. Bazin, "Un nouveau stade du cinéma en relief: Le relief en équations," *Radio, Cinéma, Télévision*, 131 (July 20, 1952).

4. Bazin, "A Bergsonian Film: *The Picasso Mystery*," in *Bazin at Work*, trans. Alain Piette and Bert Cardullo (New York: Routledge, 1997), 212. Originally published as "Un film Bergsonien: *Le Mystère Picasso*," *Cahiers du Cinéma*, 60 (June 1956). Also see Dudley Andrew, infra.

5. Ibid., 215.

6. Bazin, "Le Cinéma d'animation revit," *Parisien libéré*, 3662 (June 19, 1956). My emphasis. Bazin declared that *Fantasia* was like "having too many cream-filled pastries." Bazin, "J'ai vu 'Fantasia,'" *Parisien libéré*, 608 (July 28, 1946).

7. Bazin, "Le cinéma d'animation revit."

8. Bazin, "L'Eau danse," *Cahiers du Cinéma*, 7 (December 1951), 58–59.

9. Bazin, "On Jean Painlevé," in *What Is Cinema?* trans. Timothy Barnard (Montreal: Caboose, 2009), 21. The original text was entitled "Beauté du hasard: le film scientifique," *Ecran français*, 121 (October 21, 1947).

10. Bazin, "À la recherche d'une nouvelle avant-garde," *Almanach du théâtre et du cinéma* (1950), 148.

11. Bazin, "Les maîtres fous," *France observateur*, 389 (October 24, 1957).

12. Bazin, "Chris Marker: *Lettre de Sibérie*," *France observateur*, 443 (October 30, 1958). My emphasis. See Steven Ungar, infra.

13. Ibid.

14. Bazin, "Découverte du cinéma: Défense de l'avant-garde," *Ecran français*, 182 (December 21, 1948). Elsewhere, Bazin makes of the '20s avant-garde a historical artifact, arguing that the need for innovation of visual forms died with the coming of sound. "The era of grand discoveries was closed," he declared. Bazin, "De la forme et du fond; ou, la 'Crise' du cinéma," *Almanach du théâtre et du cinema* (1951), 171. For more discussion on the necessity of the popular vocation of cinema, see Jeremi Szaniawski, infra.

15. Bazin, "A la recherche d'une nouvelle avant-garde," 150. Other critics like Rohmer dubbed it an "*arrière-garde*."

16. Bazin, "La longue misère du court-métrage," *Arts*, 500 (January 26, 1955).

17. Bazin, "L'affaire du court métrage," *France observateur*, 247 (February 3, 1955).

18. Bazin, "A la recherche d'une nouvelle avant-garde," 152.

19. Bazin, "Découverte du cinéma: Défense de l'avant-garde."

26

Television and the Auteur in the Late '50s

MICHAEL CRAMER

André Bazin's writings on television, which span from September 1952 until his death in November 1958, can be divided into two periods. The first, ending in September 1955 with his article "L'avenir esthétique de la télévision," finds him primarily concerned with the properties of this new medium (if indeed it is a medium), how it can be differentiated from cinema, and what new aesthetic and social possibilities it offers.[1] In the second, beginning with an article on Cinemascope and television published in December 1955 and concluding with a posthumously published interview with Marcel Moussy in December 1958, he turns to the question of what television means for filmmakers and the art of cinema.[2] During this period he repeatedly addresses the relationship between the two media in terms of how television, both as plastic medium and mode of production and dissemination, might affect film practice, and how established filmmakers might best take advantage of television. These questions move from the level of theory to that of practice when, in 1958, two of Bazin's preferred auteurs (and his personal friends) Jean Renoir and Roberto Rossellini, began work on films for television. In starting to formulate an aesthetics of television—always in its relationship to cinema—Bazin could test his ideas against the TV films of these two great directors, though primarily on the conceptual level, since he did not live to see what they produced for the small screen, work, it turns out, that both affirms and challenges his ideas about how filmmakers should engage with the new medium.

Bazin was quick to enumerate the four attributes of television he found fundamental to its uniqueness and potential, covering its aesthetic and social possibilities: its potential for live broadcast or "*reportage en direct*," its creation of a sense of intimacy with the viewer, the small size and lower quality of the image in comparison to cinema, and its potential as a means for the diffusion of culture. Bazin sees the liveness of *reportage en direct* as bestowing a hitherto nonexistent kind of temporality and presence upon the image. Just as photography created a new kind of image through mechanical and automatic reproduction, so does live broadcast create a new kind of automatic presence: "Television brings forth a new notion of presence, free of all visible human content and ultimately nothing other than the presence of the spectacle to itself."[3] While the live image is temporally copresent with the viewer in such a way that the filmed image can never be, it is also impossible to preserve. Whereas the filmed image is capable of mummifying change, the live TV image reproduces change as it occurs:

> A television travelling shot never passes over the same point twice. There are not identical framings, but rather leaves that can be laid on top of one another. We love the image that we will never see more than once.[4]

Finally, like the deep focus image in cinema, the live image gives the viewer a greater sense of participation in the work. In reference to Stellio Lorenzi's *La visite au Musée Rodin*, Bazin writes, "The bumpy travelling shots of the Orticon camera, the hesitant framings, the simple and brutal illumination of the floodlights, the slight hesitations in montage allow us to participate in the creation of the program."[5] We are copresent with the image as it comes into being, our subjectivity providing the condition for its very creation.

Central to the psychology of television is the sense of intimacy that Bazin believes is an effect of the liveness of the image, its small scale, and its site in the home:

> . . . I will not venture to define [the psychology of television], but there is at least one unquestionable given, namely the sense of intimacy experienced by the television viewer in relation to the characters who appear on his screen. This intimacy can even become troubling, at times implying reciprocity [*et jusqu'à impliquer la réciprocité*].[6]

In short, "intimacy is the privileged style of television."[7] As a result, effective television mise-en-scène should rely more on the actor than the setting and make ample use of close-ups. The intimacy of the television image likewise changes the status of the spectator in relation to the image:

> In its very nature, the cinema is not intimate, for it addresses itself to a collectivity of spectators, even if this collectivity remains one of individuals and does not create a community as in the case of the theater. Cinematic intimacy . . . is indeed monstrous, for it is almost "spatial."[8]

Television, meanwhile, is more human in its dimensions, less like the monstrous giants of the big screen and more like a guest welcomed into the home: it "penetrates each day into our living room, not to violate our intimacy but rather to integrate itself into it and enrich it."[9] Television programs most effectively draw upon this capacity for intimacy when making use of what Bazin calls "témoignage humain." Just as the photographic image gives us something of the object photographed, so does the television image of the human figure give us something of the human being himself: "Each time that a human being who merits being known enters into the field of the television camera, the image becomes more dense and something of that man is given to us."[10]

On a more banal level, but of equal importance to the filmmaker, are the small size and relatively low quality of the television image, which bring about certain limitations and virtues. For filmmakers working for television, the limited scale and low image quality may indeed become virtues, dictating an aesthetic that is different from, but not inferior to that of the big screen:

Television is condemned to simplicity: humility should be the primary virtue of a television director. While he should certainly not lack imagination, his mise en scène should strive for sparseness and efficacy.[11]

Insurmountable technical limits thus become central in dictating the aesthetic of the medium, or at least the one that Bazin would like to see emerge.

Finally, the mechanical arts and television above all "are as wonderful a means for the diffusion of culture as they are for entertainment."[12] Their efficacy as such draws upon their capacity for intimacy and liveness. In terms of the first, it brings the viewer into close contact with others, creating a space of conversation. In perhaps his most elegant statement about television's capacity to strengthen the connection between human beings, Bazin declares, "Before being a spectacle, television is a conversation."[13] This capacity will become central in Bazin's consideration of Rossellini's television work. As for liveness and copresence, Bazin finds it best exploited in scientific films, particularly those of Jean Painlevé:

Painlevé's great merit is not only to have resolved the contradiction between art and science, but to have, on the other hand, established an aesthetic and a poetic of cinema based on its scientific value. On television, this aesthetic could not be based on anything other than the scientific advantages of live broadcast.[14]

The live image permits us to observe natural phenomena as they occur, allowing them to unfold in a shared temporal frame while allowing us to experience them in a perceptually novel way.[15]

As Bazin begins to consider what sort of relationship or exchange does or should exist between cinema and television, and between those who direct films and those who make television programs, these four qualities and potentialities of this medium and its image serve as points of reference. What, he asks in "La télévision et la relance du cinéma," might lessons learned from television have to contribute to cinema, and how might film directors exploit its capabilities, either on the big or the small screen? He repeatedly laments that any consideration of this question on the part of filmmakers working for the cinema seems to be blocked by a number of factors, above all the conviction that television's technical and psychological attributes make it nothing more than a pale imitation of cinema. This conviction seems to stem from the disappointing experience of having seen films originally made for theaters rebroadcast on television, to which Hollywood has responded with further technical improvements.[16] From this point of view, television would seem to be a hopelessly inferior imitation of the cinema, condemned to marginality by its technical limitations. Even more potentially fatal is television's inability to reproduce the same kind of psychological conditions brought about by cinema:

The film [viewed in the cinema] is a "système de rêve," an imaginary microcosm of which the gravitational pull, independent of its artistic quality, acts more powerfully upon the imagination than the spectacles of pure television.[17]

When viewed as a medium intended to duplicate the experience of cinema, television appears a pathetic ersatz, and therefore, as Bazin puts it in the title of one of his articles, "a degeneration [*déchéance*] for filmmakers."[18] This attitude, however, seems to be more pronounced in France than in the United States. While many prominent American filmmakers have worked for television, French television directors seem only to move in the opposite direction, holding cinema to be their ultimate goal.

Bazin, of course, sees such a dismissive attitude as lamentable and mistaken, given the fact that American filmmakers have been able to parlay the apparent limitations of the television medium into aesthetic virtues. Here, Bazin moves beyond the aforementioned four qualities of television to consider how the rapidity of production and low budgets characteristic of television productions may themselves become aesthetic virtues or spurs to experimentation:

> The rapidity of execution of television films and the relative smallness of their budgets need not be negative constraints. On the contrary, through them the director can paradoxically find a greater liberty in his work and an inspiration that "real cinema" has often lost.[19]

These new liberties and possibilities need not be limited to small screen work, but may also be imported into the cinema, injecting it with the youthfulness and spontaneity of the new medium: "It is not only the artistic future of television, but also perhaps that of cinema, that may find new sap and vitality through this grafting of a young and almost still wild branch."[20]

As though in response to Bazin's call for European filmmakers to try their hand at television, Jean Renoir and Roberto Rossellini began work on television projects in 1958. Renoir's *The Testament of Doctor Cordelier* (1959) is shot on film but intended for television broadcast, while Rossellini's series, titled *J'ai fait un beau voyage* (1958) in its French version, mixes filmed material shot during Rossellini's sojourn in India with TV interviews and commentary by the director. Bazin spoke to both directors about their move to television in an interview and published two short articles on their projects at the end of October, only weeks before his death.[21] Repeating the sentiment voiced in some of his previous comments about television, Bazin attributes the two directors' willingness to venture into television to their contempt for convention and expectations. Renoir's move to television, for instance, is explained as an expression of

> ... the taste for renewal and experimentation that has always pushed Renoir to take new risks in respect to both his subjects and his technique. Even more, perhaps, it is that deep humility of an artist before his art that permits him to seize every opportunity to work from the moment that he begins to take pleasure in it, without concern for compromising his "standing" as a highly respected director.[22]

Humility, a key concept for Bazin, is thus located in the "humble" and technically impoverished medium of television, and in the artist who would turn to such a medium without reservation. Rossellini's decision to turn to television, meanwhile, is ascribed to his "spirit of initiative and adventure, his professional non-conformism. . . ."[23] The filmmaker who chooses to work in television is thus, his age notwithstanding, a sort of youthful rebel, contemptuous of the prejudices that keep others from venturing into unknown artistic territory.

Renoir's *Cordelier* provides an exemplary case of television's limitations and modes of production being used as the basis for a work on film. While the film was not broadcast live, Renoir's production methods aimed to capture the sense of liveness and spontaneity characteristic of television:

> This production will be filmed, but in the spirit of television, that is to say in a style drawing as closely as possible to live broadcast. The exteriors, shot in Versailles, will be filmed "on the sly," without passers-by being aware of it and with multiple cameras.[24]

Furthermore, Renoir's decision to adhere to the quick pace of filming for television conforms to Bazin's suggestion that the time limitations imposed on television should be used to aesthetic ends.[25] In his interview with Bazin, Renoir argues that the imposition of limitations and the corresponding lack of flexibility that they bring about constitute a kind of return to the early artisanal days of cinema.[26] The limitations and new aesthetic opportunities of television thus not only reinject new ideas and a new vitality into cinema, but do so by returning cinema production to a stage more reminiscent of its youth: the new is attained by looking backward, while this looking backward itself emerges only thanks to a new technology.

While Renoir's embrace of television aesthetics and production models in his filmmaking leads him to exploit the qualities of liveness and spontaneity identified by Bazin as essential aesthetic qualities of television, Rossellini's *J'ai fait un beau voyage* draws upon the medium's capacity for intimacy, especially in the form of "témoignage humain" and its efficacy as a mode for the dissemination of culture and knowledge. According to Bazin—who again, it must be reiterated, never saw the finished product—Rossellini's work will be "a series of ten programs centering on a series of particular aspects of the Indian problems to which the author will bring his personal account [*témoignage*] and his personal point of view."[27] We might say that Rossellini's program, at least in Bazin's conception, joins the quality of witnessing or "témoignage" that marked his war trilogy with the new kind of personal "témoignage" offered by television:

> These films, commented upon by their author, will be in a sense brief chapters of *India 58* [the feature film shot by Rossellini in India], bringing us Rossellini's personal testimony on contemporary India, in documentary form, but essentially in the same spirit of human knowledge [*conaissance humaine*] as *Germany Year Zero* [1948].[28]

The dynamics of exchange between television and cinema thus work in two directions: in one direction, filmmakers can bring to works shot on film the aesthetics and production methods of television, grafting onto the cinematic work its capacity for liveness and spontaneity (as in the case of Renoir). On the other, they may turn away from film production in favor of television, seeking its promise of a more intimate human relationship with the viewer and its usefulness in conveying "témoignages humains" and as a mode of cultural dissemination (as in the case of Rossellini).

Projecting forward from Bazin's on-the-spot writings about television, one can trace two legacies that he prophesied. On one hand, and in the cinema, we find the French New Wave, with its embrace of quick, improvisational shooting carried out with a minimal budget (and à la Renoir, often "on the sly"), manifesting the youthful energy that Bazin associates with television production. Granted, these films cannot be called "live" in the sense they would be if they were true TV broadcasts, but there can be little doubt that the sense of liveness and spontaneity sought by the filmmakers of the New Wave draws upon the same source of inspiration that Renoir and Bazin see as flowing from television. These same films, of course, are deeply influenced by Rossellini's works of the 1950s which, as Jacques Rivette argues, also adopt the "direct" aesthetic of television.[29] On the other hand, and on television, we find the later films of Rossellini, who found in the fast-paced, low-budget modes of production offered by television both an opportunity to work more prolifically than ever before and a kind of production procedure entirely befitting his preference for spontaneity and on-the-set improvisation. Rossellini's historical and pedagogical films represent furthermore the most ambitious attempt to enlist television (and the kind of audiences that it provides) in a large-scale project of cultural dissemination and education. Some of the qualities of television that Bazin saw as offering the greatest potential for filmmakers, however, would never be truly explored: both the New Wave filmmakers and Rossellini, even in his television productions, shot on celluloid, and made little effort toward exploiting the unique temporality of the "direct" so highly valued by Bazin. We might conclude that Bazin's call for a closer relationship between cinema and television ended with somewhat lopsided results: while there can be little doubt that his hopes that television would offer a source of inspiration and inject a new sense of vitality into the cinema were fulfilled both in the film works of the New Wave and in the television works of Rossellini, the examples of prominent filmmakers working in truly televisual forms (i.e., ones that would draw upon all four of the qualities that Bazin sees as defining the medium) and abandoning the film medium altogether, are all but nonexistent.

Notes

1. André Bazin, "L'avenir esthétique de la télévision," *Réforme*, September 17, 1955.

2. Bazin, "Le cinémascope va-t-il assurer le succès du style télévision au cinéma?" *Radio, Cinéma, Télévision*, 311 (December 31, 1955); André Bazin and Marcel Moussy, "Propos sur la télévision," *Cahiers du Cinéma*, 90 (December 1958), 21–25.

3. Bazin, "Un reportage sur l'éternité: La visite au Musée Rodin," *Radio, Cinéma, Télévision*, 148 (November 16, 1952).

4. Ibid.

5. Ibid.

6. Bazin, "L'avenir esthétique de la télévision."

7. Ibid.

8. Bazin and Moussy, "Propos sur la télévision."

9. Bazin, "L'avenir esthétique de la télévision"

10. Ibid.

11. Ibid.

12. Bazin, "La télévision moyen de culture," *France observateur*, 297 (January 19, 1956), 14.

13. Ibid.

14. Ibid.

15. Ibid.

16. "La télévision et la relance du cinéma," *France observateur*, 311 (April 26, 1956), 14.

17. Ibid.

18. "La Télévision est-elle une déchéance pour les cinéastes?...," *Radio, Cinéma, Télévision*, 387 (June 15, 1957), 3.

19. Ibid.

20. Ibid.

21. Bazin, "Cinéma et Télévision: Un entretien d'André Bazin avec Jean Renoir et Roberto Rossellini," *France observateur*, 442 (October 23, 1958), 16–18; "Deux recrues de choix pour la Télévision: Renoir et Rossellini," *Parisien Libéré*, 4388 (October 21, 1958); "Deux grands cinéastes vont faire leur débuts à la T.V.," *Radio, Cinéma, Télévision*, 458 (October 26, 1958).

22. Bazin, "Deux grands cinéastes vont faire leurs débuts à la T.V."

23. Ibid.

24. Bazin, "Deux recrues de choix pour la Télévision: Renoir et Rossellini"

25. Bazin, "Deux grands cinéastes vont faire leurs débuts à la T.V."

26. Bazin, "Cinéma et Télévision: Un entretien d'André Bazin avec Jean Renoir et Roberto Rossellini."

27. Bazin, "Deux recrues de choix pour la Télévision: Renoir et Rossellini"

28. Bazin, "Deux grands cinéastes vont faire leurs débuts à la T.V."

29. Jacques Rivette, "Lettre sur Rossellini," *Cahiers du Cinéma*, 46 (April 1955).

27

André Bazin's Bad Taste

JAMES TWEEDIE

Although he is best and justly known in film studies as the most insightful theorist of cinematic realism and as a dogged advocate for this mode of filmmaking, André Bazin's daily exercises in criticism—almost 2,600 reviews and essays in total—are far livelier and less dogmatic than the stiff caricature that appears in anthologies and schematic accounts of his work. Biographical accounts show Bazin at work in the dynamic atmosphere of postwar Paris, where he was central to the burgeoning *ciné-club* movement—involved in the establishment of new journals, notably *Cahiers du Cinéma*—and where he espoused leftist pedagogical causes. In the '50s he became the surrogate father of François Truffaut and the spiritual "godfather" of the French New Wave. He wrote on a slew of cultural phenomena and social topics with the agility of a journalist, yet he maintained a consistent tone throughout.

Any attempt to situate Bazin within the enormously rich milieu of his time must inevitably begin by revising and extending the version of Bazin preserved in his quasi-official and most directly traceable legacy: the venerable selection of essays titled *Qu'est-ce que le cinéma?*, a foundational and canonical text that is now half a century old in French and four decades old in its partial English version. Because of its stature and its provocative, all-promising title— surely a multivolume text called *What Is Cinema?* must try to answer its titular question— readers have sought a relatively direct presentation of Bazin's theory of cinema. In practice this means that Bazin is best known for the essays that, in their sweeping rhetoric and magisterial tone, most resemble a theory, those he grouped under "Ontologie et langage" (volume 1), "Cinéma et les autres arts" (volume 2) and "Néoréalisme" (volume 4).

Now the third volume, "Cinéma et sociologie," offers a repository of a different form of criticism altogether, with forays into such questions as eroticism, contemporary mythology, and popular genres. In fact, writing for daily and weekly outlets, Bazin's writing necessarily dealt with current issues, fashions, and events, like the festivals he regularly attended around Europe. Demonstrating an obvious fascination with science and technology, he reported in detail on Cinemascope, Cinerama, and television. He penned numerous articles on what today we would call trash television and cult cinema. This other Bazin seems very much a contemporary and kindred spirit of the Roland Barthes of *Mythologies* (1957) and a precursor of the kind of scholarship usually categorized under the broad rubric of cultural studies. There is the Bazin, for example, who writes—in an almost offhand manner, in an essay otherwise devoted to adaptation—"the cultural interest of radio . . . is that it allows modern man to live in an environment of sound comparable to the warm atmosphere created by central heating." He suggests that "radio has created an atmospheric culture that is as omnipresent as humidity in the air."[1] And he adds that he arrived at these conclusions during the course of his daily routine, which involved, of course, writing while simultaneously listening to the sultry sounds of the radio. Based on the everyday experience of culture, these observations are a prescient, if fledgling, attempt to theorize the now pervasive phenomenon of ambient media.

There is also the Bazin who published consistently on television and *télécinéma*, including one essay in a 1954 issue of *Cahiers du Cinéma* that developed "A Contribution to the Erotology of Television." That essay discusses the odd position of intimacy made possible by this new medium, suggesting that even otherwise aloof figures can be subjected to an erotic gaze in the comfort of the spectator's home. He writes, "Dare I take the extreme example of the coronation of the queen of England? I would not have the bad taste, of that you can be sure, to say that it suggests any impure thoughts, but in the end there is a very sublime eroticism in the myth of the princess of which popular tales are the evidence."[2] He goes on to suggest that "television allows us to live for a few hours in a position of intimacy with the queen, and I do mean intimacy," as we are confronted with unsuspected details like the enormity of the crown compressing her hair or the young woman's resemblance to the deceased king.

Despite Bazin's tepid denial of impure thoughts, or, rather, because of the invitation to enjoy his own guilty pleasures, we are tempted to reconsider the unique possibilities of a medium that transports minimized images into the home and in the process transforms our awe into intimacy, even when the figures flashing across the screen are supposed to be larger than life—the way they would appear at the cinema. He suggests that the erotics of television are defined by a dialectical relationship between the individual fantasies of the spectator confronted with the directness and presence of the figure on screen and the censorship imposed by the institution of the family. The mediatrix in this dialectic is the figure of the *speakerine* (the on-screen presenter of programs in French broadcasting) who reconciles the "indecent" address to the individual psyche and the constraints of "family consumption."[3] In both its public and private dimensions, television operates on a different register than does cinema, and in several dozen articles on the small screen, Bazin defines the particularity of its appeal—its liveness, its perceived intimacy—and chronicles its construction of an unprecedented mass audience. Bazin's copious writings on television and other forms of mass culture illustrate just how grotesquely some accounts have distorted a body of work that remains more playful and agile than stiff and doctrinaire.

Given the breadth of his work and his many fascinations, it would be impossible to pigeonhole Bazin as a theorist of one single manner of filmmaking without committing a category mistake. Too often we look for Bazin's theory of cinema in the manner of a visitor to a college campus who says, "I see the library and the dormitories and the football stadium and the classrooms, but where is the university?" In Bazin's case we can search for the answer to his famous question by consulting a handful of obviously theoretical essays, most of them longer, sustained apologies for a realist cinema. Yet for over a decade and half as a film critic, Bazin watched attentively and wrote seriously on a huge variety of films, and on topics with only a remote connection to film aesthetics. The archive compiled by Dudley Andrew and Hervé Joubert-Laurencin includes hundreds of reviews and essays that display a familiarity and enthrallment with popular cinema and media that rarely surface in the standard narratives of Bazin's career.[4] In essence, two approaches to film operate concurrently in the work of André Bazin: one is overtly marked as theory in a handful of magisterial essays, developed in relation to Welles, Renoir, and Italian neorealism; the other has no coherent identity at all, as it lies scattered in occasional pieces about individual films.

Viewed in its totality, Bazin's writing is remarkable not only for its theoretical and aesthetic insight but also for its frequent "lapses" into bad taste, with the term "taste" alluding to two crucial tendencies in his work. First of all, he was determined to expand the definition of cinema to include both popular entertainment and what would be called "art cinema," challenging the social insinuations of taste that Pierre Bourdieu would later identify as policing the border between art and spectacle. In the struggle to structure the field of cultural production, Bazin championed a cinema without "distinction." Second, his bad taste highlights an irreverence that colors so many of his essays, including not only that account of his private (if televisually mediated) encounter with the young queen but also a frequently impious attitude toward his own, supposedly higher theoretical calling.

Such irreverence helps reconnect Bazin to the social and cinematic revolutions occurring around him in France in the 1950s. Remember that although Truffaut famously dedicates *The 400 Blows* (*Les quatre cents coups*, 1959) to Bazin's memory [figure 27.1], Godard just as famously dedicates *Breathless* (*À bout de souffle*, 1960) to a B-movie factory, Monogram Pictures [figure 27.2]; these two gestures write the first draft of a bifurcated history of the New Wave— at once inheritor of neorealism's high-minded documentary ethic, and purveyor of a defiantly popularized low cult. Bazin helps us revisit both lines of that history and explore connections between them. Over time, a Bazinian aesthetic has become the hallmark for a particular mode of highbrow art cinema, but Bazin's writing on cinema also ventured (on alternate days or even within the same paragraph) into the depths of the most appalling and intriguing bad taste; in those moments he develops a conception of cinema rooted in the relatively unconstrained and undecided French culture that thrived in the years after the war and just before the economic miracle of the 1950s and 1960s.

Although much of Bazin's work reflects a fascination with the role of mass media in the shaping of public culture, his sociologically inflected writing coexists with an aesthetic and philosophical mode of criticism usually considered its diametric opposite. In the brief interludes between his sweeping accounts of the centuries-long prehistory of cinematic realism and his reviews of contemporary Hollywood and French film, Bazin passes effortlessly between a critical discourse attentive to the demands of the rapidly changing present and a more theoretical approach focused on an ideal form of the medium over the *longue durée*. On the most banal level for a professional critic, he provides a catalog of films worth seeing or avoiding; but he also examines the financial health of the local entertainment industry, indicates which stars are popular among the younger generation of audiences, and describes the implications of that worship of screen idols for French culture at any given moment. These are relentlessly practical and quotidian concerns, and they result inevitably in the simplification of a chaotic subject to a streamlined model that measures social effects in the relatively crude terms of box office returns and media saturation. In "The Language of Our Time," a 1954 essay published as the

FIGURE 27.1: *The 400 Blows* (1959)

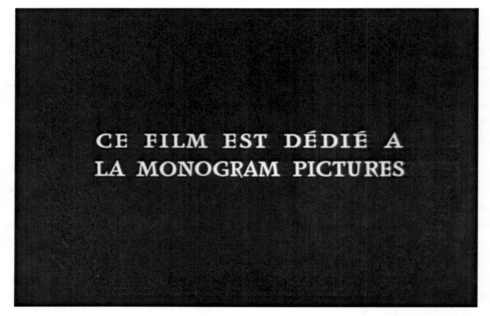

FIGURE 27.2: *Breathless* (1960)

"Introduction" to *Regards neufs sur le cinéma*, he asserts that "the importance of cinema in modern life no longer needs to be demonstrated. One need only recall some figures: each day tens of millions of people enter one of 100,000 dark rooms where the rites of this new 'religion' of shadows are celebrated."[5]

He later argues that popular culture in the modern age is defined not by any mode of representation, not by the style of the storyteller or the hand of the craftsman, but by the geographic expanse and number of people reached by the work of art. The form of the art object or film must be relegated to the margins of such an inquiry, as it focuses instead on the brute fact of ticket sales and the relationship between cinema and other technologies—the car, the telephone, the typewriter—effecting piecemeal the unification of the globe. Although Bazin always considered cinema a privileged art form, he was acutely aware of the inescapable fact that all film industries develop in a web of technological and economic forces and that "nearly all films are in one manner or another implicit forms of propaganda."[6] Although propaganda of this kind is "not always systematic and calculated, responding to a specific rallying cry," it does communicate the "diffuse expression of a way of life, a moral system, a subtle confirmation of the values of a regime or a civilization."[7] Yet he also emphasizes the inherent limits of a deterministic model based on assumptions about the overweening power of institutions and the passivity and homogeneity of audiences. In the same essay, Bazin describes the humbling experience of showing the same film in theaters and film clubs around France and North Africa, where he discovered that each audience "already saw something different from what they were shown."[8] The Bazin who experimented with this admittedly unscientific mode of reception study was as interested in the divergent experiences of the spectators as he was in the intricate or crude manipulation of form designed to produce a particular response.

Bazin, the voracious consumer of film and television who wrote frequently about the erotics of mass media, was also fascinated by the salacious and sensational, and he frequently bracketed his intellectual interest in aesthetics in order to pursue a sociological agenda that prioritized questions at the margins of acceptable discourse rather than pious philosophical rumination. In his regular reviews and in the manifesto-like tone of "The Language of Our Time," Bazin foreshadows the development of cultural studies and reception theory, and he lays out an agenda for a sociological study of cinema attentive to the standardizing influence of propaganda, the constitutive and enduring diversity of audiences, and the particularity of desire.

In dramatic contrast to these studies of pop culture, his essays on the ontology and evolution of cinema are characterized by an attempt to think through immensely complex systems while acknowledging the impossibility of arriving at a satisfactory model. His frequent allusions to geology, hydrology, biology, and zoology suggest that cinema is a system in a state of flux, with various technological and social forces affecting the production of a film, and even more variables operative in front of the camera, from the whims of the actors to the vicissitudes of light and weather.[9] His keyword—"reality"—refers to this natural condition of complexity within which the most ambitious films trace provisional and tentative diagrams or maps. "Total cinema" is another term for a hypothetical, boundless medium adequate to challenge the representation of reality in all its specificity. At odds with many more practically oriented conceptions of realism—including, for example, the essentially pedagogical mode of socialist realism—Bazin's writing valorizes a mode of filmmaking that, as Daniel Morgan and others have noted, is maddeningly difficult to identify and enumerate in concrete terms.[10] Bazin's idea of realism is notable as much for its capaciousness and flexibility as for its definitional precision.

In one of his most suggestive formulations, the concluding passage of an essay on *Umberto D.* (1952), Bazin argues that film follows an asymptote to reality,[11] cinema drawing ever more closely to the axis of reality, though the two never merge except in some ideal state where cinema and reality meet in infinity. I read the figure of the asymptote as a provocation rather than a convenient metaphor. If taken seriously, this view suggests a number of resonances that would link Bazin's writing on cinematic realism to the work of Alain Badiou, beyond their idealism and likely Platonism.[12] The foundational premise of Badiou's system of thought is modernity's "laicization" of the infinite; he argues that the modern revolution in mathematics initiated by set theory should serve as a model for contemporary philosophy and art criticism. His ambition, one shared by his favored artists, is to categorize and analyze manifestations of infinity, to contemplate and manipulate what would otherwise be dismissed as incalculable, and therefore inaccessible to systems of thought. Set theory for the first time encourages the analysis of infinity rather than an awestruck resignation or fear of the sublime. The Bazin of "The Ontology of the Photographic Image" and "The Evolution of the Language of Cinema" becomes a philosophically inclined theorist, whose fundamental axioms assert that reality is another name for a condition of flux, which an ideal form of cinema would be capable of bracketing off and momentarily presenting as the infinite to spectators who always experience it otherwise.

Bazin's suggestion that film follows an asymptote to reality is usually taken as an admonition that film can never be entirely consonant with reality, that there must always be a gap between the representation and the world it purports to document. But his writing is often energized by an idealist conception of film that emerges when the slightest detail transforms a mediocre picture into a glimpse of utopia. These moments gesture toward whatever remains uncountable and unknowable inside and outside the image, to a reality that "superabounds."[13] Bazin writes that even cinema, the most sensitive recording medium yet invented, "cannot make reality entirely its own because reality must inevitably elude it at some point."[14] His realism is defined not only through aesthetics and mode of production; it is founded on an awareness that the cinematic image is a fragment of an abundance that eludes the capacity of any medium to capture and contain it. Film can enclose that infinite expanse momentarily in a frame whose closest physical analogies he saw as the window and the mirror—Bazin cycles through these familiar comparisons, seemingly unsatisfied with all of them—but whose closest conceptual analog may be the provisional brackets of a mathematical set formed under specific conditions, a grouping that captures the contingent, the uncontainable, and the uncountable.

This way of thinking about Bazin also allows us to reconcile the seemingly traditionalist bent of his Catholicism and the insistently modernist aesthetic advocated in his most famous essays. For Bazin the engagement with an infinite reality can lead either to familiar theological territory where the complexity of this system of thought is ultimately absorbed into an all-encompassing god or nature; or it can confront the inherent multiplicity of the modern world under construction throughout the century of cinema and especially in the post-World War II moment when Bazin was at the height of his influence as a critic and teacher. In the moments when he is most concerned with the infinite nature of reality and the myth of total cinema, Bazin displays his most archaic and his most modern sensibility.

In the context of this overarching philosophy of cinema, Bazin's essays on popular movies are surprising not only because they are less often anthologized and read and therefore less familiar; they are also among the most revealing documents he produced, because if he really did believe in the evolution of the language of cinema and the inexorable advance toward total cinema, if he believed that the history of the arts was tending in a particular direction over the course of hundreds of years, then the stakes of this "defection" are even greater.

The "Cinéma et sociologie" volume of *Qu'est-ce que le cinéma?* stands as a catalog of those acts of betrayal. It begins with an idiosyncratic account of the peculiar rituals of the film festival, a favorite topic, and continues with a series of observations about films that draw him away from an aesthetic mode and into what we would probably call cultural studies today. The evolution of the medium, the ontology of the image: none of these touchstones surfaces here. Instead he explores the radically different terrain of mundane commercial culture where popular stars exert their gravitational pull and audiences encounter the limited range of identities on display and for sale on the streets of postwar France. Bazin's concern shifts from the horizon of total cinema to circumscribed conditions of the present. If total cinema imagines an idealized medium adequate to the complexity of reality itself, then sociology is the discipline concerned above all with the world as it is. It is a mode of thinking that derives its power from the capacity to categorize and enumerate the key elements of an insistently material world rather than some mathematically possible, totalized universe. If a Bazinian conception of realism begins with the premise that cinema must acknowledge the infinite reality that the camera can only bracket for a moment, a sociology of cinema is concerned with what can be rendered visible, quantified, and translated into knowledge in a ruthlessly constrained world.

Bazin's interest in sociology coincides with one of the heydays of French sociology, a flourishing of the discipline that at once produced and was nurtured by the overlapping and massive polling projects initiated by organizations like the National Institute of Statistics and Economic Studies (INSEE). Bourdieu's *Distinction* (1979), while published two decades after *Qu'est-ce que le cinéma?*, relies extensively on a series of surveys gathered in 1963 and again in 1967–1968; moreover, his account of the changing social function of film reflects changes in the public attitude toward cinema in France, a transformation of the medium's social status made possible by *Cahiers* critics like Truffaut, and through the educational and critical work of a far more ambivalent Bazin.

Bourdieu maintains that certain modes of film reception—including "gratuitous" knowledge of the names of directors—are associated with intellectuals determined to augment their cultural capital.[15] Other communities, usually less educated and socially powerful, are more concerned with the entertainment value of the medium and with stars.[16] For the young generation of critics and directors who energized French New Wave cinema at its outset, Truffaut foremost among them, film deserved to be elevated into the ethereal realm of high art. Their assaults on the film establishment were the power-play of a dominated class fragment, in Bourdieu's formulation. Bazin's annual accounts of film festival culture often take the form of satires of these ascendant cineastes and the somber atmosphere of their screenings.

While Bazin pokes fun at the high seriousness and affectation of his younger colleagues at *Cahiers*, much of his criticism grapples with the elusive notion of "authenticity," the key last word of his essay on the figure of the mass-produced, marketed, and distributed pin-up girl.[17] Here Bazin is concerned with the demise of the Hays Office and its enforced code of morality and the liberation of American cinema from the "phoniness" of Hollywood in the 1930s. Yet the implications of the term "authentic" lead us as far as possible from the multiplicity and ambiguity imagined as the ultimate ambition of the medium in his writing on realist cinema. If reality is by definition impossible to capture in any mode of representation, including cinema, an authentic film would attempt to establish a precise correspondence between the fictional universe exhibited on screen and a society understood through its own categories, including those derived from cinema itself. The unwavering ideal of reality is no longer an underlying premise in these essays concerned instead with a certain period in French history when cinema itself and the cult of the image were becoming the lodestar of a society undergoing a series of revolutionary transformations. An authentic cinema must be concerned with the finite society of today.

However, in other moments, Bazin holds a different version of sociology, one that complements his more abstract and philosophical conceptions of cinema. Among the many modes of sociology in postwar France, the one most akin to Bazin's views and the one developed with film most conspicuously in mind is the work of Edgar Morin, which Bazin reviewed favorably.[18] After his early forays into surrealism, movie stars, and the dynamics of mass communication, Morin undertook his six-volume elaboration of the theory and method titled *La pensée complexe*.[19] For both Bazin and Morin, cinema lies at the origin of the social scientific and philosophical study of complexity, and for Bazin the sociology of cinema was another means of approaching a reality characterized by both the openness of its ideal form and the limitations of actual political and cultural structures.

In a short 1949 essay published in *Les Cahiers pédagogiques*, Bazin suggests that cinema is a potentially revolutionary medium precisely because it can eliminate the practical and conceptual divide between art and entertainment, the elites and the masses, or philosophy and society. He asks whether previous, large-scale efforts to expand free public education and to end illiteracy have achieved their more profound goal of democratizing culture, especially in the light of recent historical events and the debasement of popular media. He writes, "To pose the question in the aftermath of fascism, at the time of the atomic bomb and of *Samedi-Soir* [a popular tabloid] is already to have the answer."[20] Mass education and literacy have not altered the relationship between the masses and the arts, which "have continued the evolution they have engaged in since the Renaissance." These remain the province of "a privileged elite, if not of money, then at least of culture."[21] And so, Bazin advocates a universal education in cinema to counteract the residual elitism of other art forms. Only then would the "real artistic leisure" of cinema realize its potential as a dialectical resolution of the lingering discrepancy between elite and mass culture.[22] "Art cinema" represents for Bazin a betrayal of this universalizing and democratizing aspiration, because cinema itself fuses art and spectacle in a way that challenges the very division between the elite and the popular, along with their attendant implications of good and bad taste.

Over the course of his career, Bazin's relatively untroubled movement between these seemingly different conceptions of cinema is one of the keys to understanding his relationship to the increasingly capitalist and Americanized culture in Western Europe of the 1950s, and to the New Waves that emerged just after his death, realizing his ideal of cinema without distinction. In the universe of economic miracles and radical social transformation, did cinema track the asymptote of reality or vice versa?[23] That oscillating relationship between cinema and reality becomes one of the major concerns of filmmakers in the late 1950s, and Bazin identified one of the best illustrations of this phenomenon in Fellini's *Nights of Cabiria* (*Le notti di Cabiria*, 1957), a paradigmatic film that undertakes a "voyage to the end of neorealism."[24]

Cabiria has always been taken to be both a romantic drawn to melodramatic stories and a hard-headed and practical analyst of her precarious situation. In the key scene when Oscar proposes to Cabiria, he promises to deliver her from a life of daily scrimping and scrounging, to transport her from a universe where fantasy is possible only on the silver screen into an actually existing dreamworld where happy endings actually come true. In the proposal sequence, we see the corners of Cabiria's mouth twitch into a smile and a frown, elation and heartbreak. The line traced by Giulietta Masina's lips suggests that in Italy of the late 1950s, it is no longer possible to envision a cinema that approaches ever closer to reality. Faced with the endless deferral of her desire—Oscar pledges that their moment of happiness will arrive tomorrow and tomorrow and tomorrow—Cabiria is tempted by the welcome if remote possibility of fulfillment, though she also remains suspicious. And as her lips purse into a barely perceptible smile and fall just as rapidly into a faint grimace, Cabiria not only measures the merits and intentions of her suitor and wavers in her commitment to a solitary but secure future; she also imagines the kind of world—or is it the kind of film?—she inhabits [figures 27.3–27.4]. As these expressions dance across her face, she seems to be asking herself if she is currently playing a role in a neorealist picture—in which case Oscar will throw her in a river and steal her money—or the kind of melodrama that she has previously indulged in only as a screen fantasy and resisted in her own materialist calculations. Her everyday life has been characterized by denial in anticipation of the day when she would be delivered into another kind of film. And she wonders, as Oscar expresses his love, whether that day has at long last arrived. When Bazin calls *Nights of Cabiria* "a voyage to the end of neorealism," he departs from his previous conceptions of realism because a cinema that truly follows an asymptote to reality would be a cinema without end. The end of neorealism is written on the face of Cabiria in this scene, because that necessary and empowering gap between cinema and reality no longer exists as her expression oscillates between fascination and mistrust.

Like Cabiria, we could wait until tomorrow for total cinema to arrive, but in the meantime another conception of the image has assumed a position of dominance. The end of neorealism is marked not by the end of cinema but the ubiquity of another way of seeing and representing the world, by the dissemination of images and the reconstruction of reality as the mirror of cinema. If the Platonic ideal of cinema is conceived along very clear axes, those most fundamental lines are erased and redrawn in the radically rebuilt world of Italy's economic miracle. At the end of his essay on *Umberto D.*, Bazin writes that "de Sica and Zavattini are concerned to make cinema the asymptote of reality—but in order that it should ultimately be life itself that becomes spectacle, in order that life might in this perfect mirror be visible poetry, be the self into which film finally changes it."[25] In this passage, we see Bazin struggling to discover the precise rhetoric for whatever is supposed to endure after the demise of reality: "life," "poetry," and "the self" are some of the candidates for this new term for art, this linguistic equivalent of cinema's *pensée complexe*. But he also acknowledges here that film transforms the self even in the moments when it adheres most tenaciously to reality. So that even in this, one of his most direct theoretical statements of cinematic realism, Bazin wanders across the same increasingly porous border between the world and its image.

The French New Wave is also a historical moment characterized by the oscillation between various conceptions of cinema, and the shocking transitions between them visible in *Nights of Cabiria* and in Bazin's writings. *Breathless* exists on the verge of these two universes, and its rough editing yokes them violently together.[26] Consider, for example, the scene where Belmondo's Michel Poiccard—the often cartoonish gangster whose actions and words are borrowed from his B-movie idols—pulls off a casual robbery in the restroom of a café. As Belmondo flings open the door to exit, Godard uses a bizarre and uncategorizable transition,

FIGURES 27.3-27.4: Flickering expressions in *The Nights of Cabiria* (1957)

at once jump cut and match on action, to link an environment and plotline that can only exist in movies to the actual Parisian sidewalks that a studio film can never reproduce. Is this transition between the haunts of a hoodlum and the quintessential Bazinian realist environment supposed to be jagged or smooth? I would suggest that Bazin's own career and the early history of the New Wave provide the best answers to that question. The gangster, another frequent topic in Bazin's writing, suddenly finds himself in a long tracking shot in a location that exposes him to all the vagaries of light and of urban space and of human behavior. Michel is the same aggressively artificial character as always, but here he and Patricia occupy a terrain defined primarily by its variability, by the interested bystanders who glance back at the camera or the light that wends its way through flickering leaves or the history accumulated on the surface of the buildings or even the weather itself [figures 27.5–27.6]. These are recycled characters from a

FIGURES 27.5–27.6: Glances from beyond the film (*Breathless*)

Dillingeresque B-movie or a Bogart film noir—a tough guy and his moll—who repeatedly pass through portals into another conception of cinema and space, marked above all by flux and variability.

  Bazin is not only a theorist of that latter universe but also one of the key chroniclers of a historical moment when that neorealist ambition of the immediate postwar era slowly morphed into the world that, to a large extent, remains with us today. In his moving eulogy for Humphrey Bogart, Bazin writes that Bogart was one of the most emblematic stars of the transition from the war to the new society in emergence in the late 1950s.[27] He argues that Bogart's very public physical decay, displayed on screen for all to see in *The African Queen* (1951), also marked the demise of a historical era. Bazin was acutely aware of the historical specificity of this period, this postwar moment of apparent opportunity, this age of openness heralded at its outset by the neorealist films that formed the foundation of his ontology of cinema, and punctuated at its end by films like *Nights of Cabiria*. Bazin would die twenty-two months after Bogart, but his career also bridged these distinct periods in film history. To open Bazin is to revisit those unprecedented and unequalled moments in film history and perhaps reopen our own era in film studies.

  One possible response to this version of Bazin is to notice how different it looks from canonical accounts of his theory but also how familiar it appears within the context of film studies today. Haven't I suggested that Bazin is actually like various luminaries of contemporary philosophy, sociology, and cultural studies, in other words that Bazin is intellectually acceptable once again because he was concerned about the same topics that concern us, that he's actually one of us? Maybe the Bazin who talks about the ontology of the photographic image and who makes absolutist claims about cinema remains somewhat "contaminated" by an idealist bent, but there's another, gentler, quirkier Bazin who would feel at home in today's seminar rooms and disciplinary conferences. For Bazin emerges from the reopening of his work as a radically alien figure precisely because he operated within the rarefied realms of aesthetics and philosophy, as well as the very mundane world of pin-up posters, radio broadcasts, and television. We need to understand and insist upon the radical otherness of Bazin and his historical moment, because he emerged within a constellation that remains inaccessible within the discipline of film studies today. He remained at once a philosopher and a sociologist of cinema and therefore one of the few critics capable of engaging with the medium in all its chaotic, coarse, and beautiful complexity.

Notes

1. Bazin, "Adaptation, or the Cinema as Digest," trans. Alain Piette and Bert Cardullo, *Bazin at Work: Major Essays and Reviews from the Forties and Fifties*, ed. (New York, Routledge, 1997), 44.

2. Bazin, "Pour contribuer à une érotologie de la télévision," *Cahiers du Cinéma*, 42 (December 1954), 74.

3. Ibid., 76.

4. See http://bazin.commons.yale.edu.

5. Bazin, "Le langage de notre temps," in *Regards neufs sur le cinéma*, ed. Jacques Chevalier, Collection "Peuple et Culture," 8 (Paris: Editions du Seuil, 1954), 5.

6. Ibid., 17.

7. Ibid.

8. Ibid., 16.

9. Dudley Andrew's biography of Bazin lists a number of formative intellectual influences, including Bergson, who instilled in Bazin "a deep feeling for the integral unity of a universe in flux" and compelled him to

develop a theory of cinema attuned to that permanent condition of change. See Andrew, *André Bazin* (New York: Oxford University Press, 1978), 21.

10. Daniel Morgan, "Rethinking Bazin: Ontology and Realist Aesthetics," *Critical Inquiry*, 32 (Spring 2006), 451–52.

11. Bazin, "*Umberto D*: A Great Work," in *What Is Cinema?* vol. 2, trans. Hugh Gray (Berkeley: University of California Press, 1971), 82.

12. Bazin more than once suggests that cinema was a fully formed idea before the materiality of the medium was even discovered and put to practical use. See also Prakash Younger, "What is Cinephilosophy," *Offscreen*, 13:2, http://www.offscreen.com/biblio/pages/essays/what_is_cinephilosophy/P1/.

13. Bazin, "The Evolution of the Language of Cinema," in *What Is Cinema?* vol. 1, trans., Hugh Gray (Berkeley: University of California Press, 1967), 27.

14. Ibid., 29.

15. Pierre Bourdieu, *Distinction: A Social Critique of the Judgement of Taste*, trans. Richard Nice (Cambridge, MA: Harvard University Press, 1987), 26.

16. Ibid., 26–27.

17. Bazin, "The Entomology of the Pin-Up Girl," in *What Is Cinema?* vol. 2, 162.

18. Dudley Andrew, "Edgar Morin," in *The Routledge Companion to Philosophy and Film*, ed. Paisley Livingston and C. Plantinga (New York: Routledge, 2009).

19. In his *Introduction à la pensée complexe* (Paris: Editions Seuil, 2005), Morin summarizes and continues the movement toward a theory of complex systems that had occupied him throughout his career and especially in his multivolume work, *La Méthode*.

20. Bazin, "École, culture et cinéma," *Cahiers pédagogiques* (June 1949), 240. On *Samedi Soir*, see *Time*, Feb.9, 1948.

21. Ibid., 241.

22. Ibid.

23. See Angelo Restivo, *The Cinema of Economic Miracles: Visuality and Modernization in the Italian Art Film* (Durham, NC: Duke University Press, 2002).

24. Bazin, "*Cabiria*: The Voyage to the End of Neorealism," in *What Is Cinema?* vol. 2, 83.

25. "*Umberto D*: A Great Work," 82.

26. Dudley Andrew argues that Belmondo's direct eye contact with the audience references the way Giulietta Masina's eyes look up at the camera in the last shot of *Nights of Cabiria*. It was in March 1960, while working on the script of *Breathless*, that Godard said he learned from Bazin how to watch the Fellini film. See *Godard on Godard*, trans. Tom Milne (New York: Viking, 1972).

27. Bazin, "Mort d'Humphrey Bogart," *Cahiers du Cinéma*, 68 (February 1957), 2–8.

PART FOUR

Worldwide Influence

28

Montage Under Suspicion

Bazin's Russo-Soviet Reception

John MacKay

To Naum Kleiman

The critical and theoretical work of André Bazin made itself felt in a significant way in the Soviet Union in the mid-1960s and has been important to Russian-language film writing ever since, particularly after the publication of one of his essays on Jean Renoir in a 1972 volume on that filmmaker, and a translation, also from 1972, of over 300 pages worth of selections from the four volumes of *Qu'est-ce que le cinéma?*, an edition that has become a bibliographical rarity.[1] "The Evolution of the Language of the Cinema" had already appeared in Russian translation in 1965 (in the journal *Problems of Film Dramaturgy*),[2] and to be sure, critics and scholars with knowledge of the French language had had access to Bazin's writings even earlier. Since the fall of the Soviet Union in 1991, the major journal *Kinovedcheskie Zapiski* [*Film Studies Notes*] has presented at least seven Bazin articles previously unavailable in Russian, and provided the site (in 1993) for seven papers by important Russian film scholars on the French critic's theoretical legacy.[3]

For convenience's sake, we might parse the phases of Bazin's Russo-Soviet itinerary into three periods: the initial late cold war reception, lasting from the mid-1960s through the mid-1980s, and the object of most of my attention in this brief paper; then, a short transitional phase overlapping with perestroika and the collapse of the USSR itself, lasting until around 1993; and the post-Soviet period proper, which has already seen a neoliberal "Yeltsin" moment and a neo-authoritarian "Putin" moment, and which is still unfolding in both predictable and unpredictable ways.

It was doubtless all too inevitable that the central problems raised by Bazin for his earliest Soviet readers would involve his critique of Soviet montage aesthetics, even if, at this initial stage, the philosophical, ethical, and political implications of that critique were left largely unaddressed. Indeed, it would be only a slight exaggeration (though a provocative one!) to claim that the Russo-Soviet response to Bazin amounts to an extended critical exegesis of certain passages from "The Evolution of the Language of the Cinema," passages by now deeply inscribed in the *chrestomathie* of film studies in Russia as elsewhere. It was in that essay, of course, that Bazin wrote that montage (in its early Soviet conceptualization) involves

... the creation of a sense or meaning not objectively contained in the images themselves but derived exclusively from their juxtaposition. The well-known experiment of [Lev]

Kuleshov with the shot of [actor Ivan] Mozzhukhin in which a smile was seen to change its significance according to the image that preceded it, sums up perfectly the properties of montage.

Montage as used by Kuleshov, [Sergei] Eisenstein, or [Abel] Gance did not show us the event; it alluded to it. Undoubtedly they derived at least the greater part of the constituent elements from the reality they were describing but the final significance of the film was found to reside in the ordering of these elements much more than in their objective content. The substance of the narrative, whatever the realism of the individual image, is born essentially from these relationships—Mozzhukhin plus dead child equals pity—that is to say, an abstract result, none of the concrete elements of which are to be found in the premises; maidens plus apple trees in bloom equal hope. . .[4]

Later on in the same essay:

In analyzing reality, montage presupposes of its very nature the unity of meaning of the dramatic event. Some other form of analysis is undoubtedly possible, but then it would be another film. In short, montage by its very nature rules out ambiguity of expression. Kuleshov's experiment proves this *per absurdum* in giving on each occasion a precise meaning to the expression on a face, the ambiguity of which alone makes the three successively exclusive expressions possible. [. . .]

Jean Renoir [by contrast] uncovered the secret of a film form that would permit everything to be said without chopping the world up into little fragments, that would reveal the hidden meanings in people and things without disturbing the unity natural to them.[5]

Now, if in the first phase of Bazin's Russian reception, the political dimensions of Bazin's montage critique were largely (if not completely)[6] passed by in silence, these returned with a vengeance during the second. The first article translated from a foreign language to appear in *Film Studies Notes* (in its very first issue in 1988) was Bazin's "The Stalin Myth in Soviet Cinema" of 1950.[7] Unfortunately, I have no sense of the actual response of Russian film scholars or the public to the article, apart from what can be gleaned from the brief introduction, which praises Bazin's analysis not only of the myth-building carried out by films like Mikhail Chiaureli's *The Vow* (1946) or Vladimir Petrov's *The Defense of Tsaritsyn* (1949), but also his speculations on the historical and ideological preconditions that might have led to those films' strange ossification of time and history in the "person" of Stalin. This self-consciously anti-Soviet moment also coincided with a renewed appreciation of Bazin as a metaphysical and even religious thinker, and I'll return to those motifs later.

The third or contemporary phase, dilating as I write, is the least mappable, but has so far been characterized less by an interest in Bazin as a "realist," or as a historian of film style, and more as an incomparably fertile thinker about specific issues in cinema studies (from mise-en-scène to the remake), and as a critic-philosopher of reality and representation as such. In the latter role, he has been considered alongside such figures as Husserl, Heidegger, Benjamin, and Deleuze—all of whom also, of course, confidently entered into Russian philosophical debates only after 1991.

But let me return now to the '60s and '70s, when the French critic first presented fascinating challenges to Russian film scholars throughout the "Thaw" (Khrushchev) and "stagnation" (Brezhnev) periods. He was a realist—a good thing!—and a highly learned and perceptive one, but not a socialist realist; his taste ranged globally, and had a strong populist leaning (quite good things in the Soviet '60s), if he also occasionally evinced excessive enthusiasm for classical Hollywood (i.e., American) cinema. Beyond ideology, there were problems of critically connecting with the archive of films that Bazin so brilliantly discussed and historicized in terms of style. As the great Eisenstein scholar Naum Kleiman indicated (in a conversation with Bernard Eisenschitz about postwar film history):

> The accents were distributed differently for us than in France. For you, there was a natural transition from neorealism to the New Wave, as mediated by André Bazin. We didn't have this experience; we never saw the best neorealist films. We didn't see a single work by Rossellini between *Rome Open City* [1945] and *General Della Rovera* [1959]. As far as de Sica goes, we watched *Bicycle Thieves* [1948], and then—*The Roof* [1956]. When you miss the parts, you lose the whole.[8]

On the other hand, as regards Bazin's earlier points of reference, there *was* a Soviet version of Jean Renoir which arose during the Popular Front period (1936–1938). In the pages of the important official journal *Iskusstvo Kino* [*The Art of Cinema*] in 1938, Georgii Alexandrovich Avenarius, years later the author of a major work on Chaplin, published a two-part article on Renoir with the programmatic title "From the Avant-Garde to the Popular Front," summarizing Renoir's career to 1938, and narrating the director's passage from the "organizational chaos and conceptual decadence" of the avant-garde to realism.[9] (And we might recall, in this light, Bazin's later comment that the strength of a 1920s Renoir work like *The Little Match Girl* [1928] resided in the "intrusion of Renoir's realism into the themes and techniques of the avant-garde.")[10] Later that year in the same journal, director Ilya Trauberg praised the realist antiromanticism of *La Marseillaise* (1938), its authentic portrayal of "the people" as "central protagonist," and its clear contemporary relevance to the antifascist struggle. Yet Trauberg also complained, in a distinctly non-Bazinian spirit, that the "absence of a single line of action breaks the spectator's attention," and that Renoir seemed not to understand that "the people and its leaders . . . [are] a single unity."[11]

Thus, problems of archive, and problems emerging from the confrontation of countertraditions of interpretation. Important though these factors were, however, it seems clear that Bazin's attitude toward montage presented the decisive challenge to Soviet scholars. To be sure, his critique was mounted from a recognizably realist (if not, again, a socialist realist) position. Yet as the new generation of film scholars in the USSR in the '60s knew only too well, montage aesthetics had been savagely criticized long before, indeed from the early 1930s onward, from an avowedly realist standpoint. (And it is important to recall, in this connection, that Georg Lukács was among those recruited in the late 1930s to provide theoretical armature for an anti-montage "realism," as evidenced in the famous Brecht-Lukács debates and elsewhere.)[12] The 1960s, too, were the moment when the first tentative scholarly recovery of the experimental work of the 1920s, with its roots in montage and collage aesthetics and frequent antirealist animus, was underway: I'm thinking of the Aleksandr Rodchenko exhibit in Moscow in

1961, Selim Khan-Magomedov's pioneering 1964 writings on constructivism, the first serious investigations into the legacy of avant-garde stage director and theorist Vsevolod Meyerhold, and the publication of Dziga Vertov's writings in 1966.[13] And the history of previous attacks upon montage, attacks carried out in an infinitely more militant spirit than Bazin's, could not but have generated ambivalence in the minds of Soviet film scholars encountering the French theorist in the 1960s.

They would have recalled articles like (to take but one example) the 1940's "Notes on Film Newsreel" by the important director and cameraman Rafail Borisovich Gikov, again published in *The Art of Cinema*. Here Gikov argues in favor of those documentary films that "have at their foundation concrete facts . . . but that preserve the real linkage binding those elements of reality," and against films—he names Vertov's *Man with a Movie Camera* (1929) first and foremost, followed by Mikhail Kaufman's *In Spring* (1929)—that are

> not tied to any concrete fact or event, and are conceived and carried out only on the basis of the author's ideas and notions about this or that phenomenon . . . setting themselves the task of creating a generalized image of certain phenomena . . . through the free linkage of various elements of reality.

This Vertov approach, as he terms it, "destroys the real connection of elements that make up a concrete fact, [thereby] destroying the truthfulness . . . of the film."[14]

Thus, to absorb Bazin into this context required a delicate theoretical operation, to which the blunt conceptual instruments of official Soviet aesthetics were not especially well suited. At the same time, of course, Bazin's writing offered a welcome occasion for film scholars working in the post-Stalin era to consider the fraught and overdetermined topic of montage afresh, with a brilliant foreign interlocutor to boot. And we are fortunate that Bazin enticed many of the finest film scholars of the period to engage with his work, including Kirill Razlogov, Vladimir Sokolov, and the aforementioned Naum Kleiman.

To offer a summary conclusion in advance: it is my sense, reading these admiring Russian readers of Bazin, that the French critic compelled them to reflect again on the "native" montage tradition, and enabled them to enliven their own considerations of it. Bazin led them to consider how montage, too, might generate or be thought in terms of ambiguity, rather than the univocal imparting of "information" or stimulus; to think about how a cinema grounded in montage, such as that of the Soviet 1920s, fit into the history of film style more generally; and to ponder how cinema might be related to the other arts, above all to the novel. (Of course, in all these respects, the Soviets had before them, for comparison and contrast, the colossal and motivating example of Sergei Eisenstein's theoretical work, also appearing in the 1960s in new editions. Serious comparison of the theories of Bazin and Eisenstein, going beyond the montage/anti-montage dichotomy and employing the new Bazin archive and the newest Eisenstein editions, is long overdue.) The Russo-Soviet responses to Bazin, largely unknown outside of Russia and only sketchily and partially summarized here, are thus important sites of transnational and transhistorical film-theoretical comparison, and worthy of recovery for this reason alone.

One of the earliest significant Russian-language articles on Bazin, entitled "On the Development of Sound Cinema (Eisenstein, Bazin and Contemporary Cinema)," was written by the Bulgarian critic Nedelcho Milev and appeared in *Problems of Film Art* (the predecessor to *Film Studies Notes*) in 1967.[15] Milev, still an active film scholar in Sofia who has published in both Russian and Bulgarian, begins by distinguishing Bazin the critic—enormously interesting and insightful, in Milev's view—from Bazin the theorist, whose undialectical valorization of long takes and deep space in the name of "realism" leads to the counterintuitive conclusion that (for instance) Pudovkin's *Mother* (1926) or Eisenstein's *Potemkin* (1925) are non-realist, while Hitchcock's *Rope* (1948) is realist. Milev's primary focus, however, is on Bazin's version of film history, which he aims to complicate in various ways.

Bazin had claimed that cinema achieved all the hallmarks of a classical art by 1938; the "art" intended by Bazin, Milev notes, must be a "verbal-narrative" one, for cinema had already achieved the status of a classical "visual-poetic" art by the mid-1920s. This "visual-poetic" line, which Milev aspires to defend and which he tacitly associates with the avant-garde, seemed to vanish after the war, to be replaced by the "documentary" aesthetic of neorealism and the theatrical mannerism of much French "quality" cinema of the postwar period. At present, however—that is, in the mid-1960s—Milev detects an incipient return of the "visual-poetic" tendency in the work of filmmakers like Chris Marker, Alain Resnais, and Jean-Luc Godard, who are experimenting with "generalizing, musical-intellectual [modes of] organizing the film," against the narrative sound-cinema norms identified by Bazin.

On a different front, Milev argues that Bazin, no doubt out of honest ignorance, fails to take into account the later development of montage theory, and especially its refinement in the 1930s through concepts such as "vertical montage." He notes Eisenstein's increasing interest, especially as expressed in the 1945 monograph *Nonindifferent Nature*, in assimilating the strategies of "intellectual montage" to a realistic mise-en-scène (in contrast to, say, the more abstract critical études inserted into *October* [1928]), and his discussion, in the same volume, of Welles' *Citizen Kane* (1941) as aspiring to a new complexity of montage construction rooted, as in the case of Joyce's collagist yet mainly character-grounded prose, in point of view.

In many ways, indeed, Milev seems to articulate a kind of space of convergence between Eisenstein and Bazin on the plane of theory and across the history of film style. He concludes his article by arguing that that the real cinematic event of the late '50s-early '60s had not been any increasing dominance of deep space mise-en-scène but the appearance of interior monologue—theorized by Eisenstein as early as 1932—in films like Andrei Tarkovsky's *Ivan's Childhood* (1962), Mikhail Romm's *Ordinary Fascism* (1965), Ingmar Bergman's *Wild Strawberries* (1957), Resnais and Duras' *Hiroshima Mon Amour* (1959), and Fellini's *8 ½* (1963). These films' use of interior monologue manages—in a distinctly Bazinian way, Milev argues—both to "materialize" their protagonists and to make the films themselves more novel-like.

Although Milev refers to *Ivan's Childhood*, he doesn't discuss Andrei Tarkovsky specifically, whose work from *Andrei Rublev* (1966) onward might be characterized as a kind of late-Soviet *bazinism*. It seems somehow more than merely coincidental that Tarkovsky's first and most important theoretical article, "Imprinted Time," appeared alongside Milev's in the very same issue of *Problems of Film Art*, offering its now well-known argument that, with the cinema the human being received the matrix of *real time*. Seen and affixed, time could now be preserved in metallic cans for a long time (theoretically, forever). . . . The strength of cinema consists in the fact that [in it] time is seized in its real and unbreakable connection with the very material of reality that surrounds us every day and every hour.[16]

For all the work that has appeared on Tarkovsky in recent years, we still have surprisingly little rigorous reflection on the relationship between his thinking on cinema and Bazin's obviously related conceptions. It may be that such a reflection would be best commenced by re-embedding Tarkovsky's writings into that mid-1960s Soviet context when the arrival of Bazin reactivated considerations of montage and realism alike.

Milev's preoccupations lay with the larger arc of film history; it was left to Naum Kleiman in his 1968 article "The Shot as a Montage Cell" to engage, in a more direct and intensive way, with Bazin's efforts to place "montage under suspicion" (to borrow the first subtitle of Kleiman's essay).[17] Kleiman begins by noting that the recent interest in cinema's capacities of registering real sights and sounds seems to have emerged out of developments in documentary (Jean Rouch, Edgar Morin, Chris Marker) and sync sound technology. Yet he argues that the stress on registering some extrafilmic "real" is misleading to the extent that the difference between documentary and fiction has to be thought of in terms of discourse and intention, rather than "ontologically," on the basis of the kind of "material" the film contains. Alluding to Bazin's critical discussion of Frank Capra's war documentaries, Kleiman argues that Bazin erroneously generalizes a critique proper to documentary film—a critique centering on fidelity—to film in general, in large part because of an insufficient stress upon film's semantic-discursive aspects.

In his direct critique of Bazin's reading of the Kuleshov experiment, Kleiman notes two significant mistakes made by Bazin:

1. Bazin indicates that the actor Mozzhukhin was smiling, when in fact his face had a "peaceful," "indeterminate" expression, according to the authoritative accounts; and
2. Bazin contradicts his own argument that the juxtaposition of shots leads to the mere "abstract idea of pity" (face plus dead child equals pity), when he says that viewers perceived Mozzhukhin's facial expression as itself changing to one of "pity."

Dismissing the possibility that the Kuleshov effect operates through sympathy (i.e., that we simply "transfer" our own emotions onto the images as guided by the montage), Kleiman argues instead that in the experiment, the actor's face is best regarded as "the simultaneous copresence of potentially different expressions in a held-back, contained, undeveloped form." He also adds, however, that what is "in" the shot provides an assemblage of material—in Mozzhukhin's case: sunken cheeks, high cheekbones, thick, broken eyebrows—which then becomes relevant or not depending on what it is juxtaposed to. Thus, the reading of a montage linkage involves the transformation (in consciousness) of the semantic (rather than the "ontological") material within the shot. According to Kleiman, the big mistake made by most interpreters of the Kuleshov effect—and Kleiman reproaches both Pudovkin and Kuleshov himself here—is their assumption that the shot needs to be read as an "elementary unit," like a letter or phoneme.

> The idea conveyed by a montage phrase does not consist in shots as such, but is formed only through the participation of *certain components* of the heterogeneous material within a given shot.[18]

Those familiar with Eisenstein's thought will not be surprised that Kleiman goes on to mention Eisenstein's theories of "dominants" and "overtones" interacting within a shot. And to be sure, the quest for a "dialectical" montage, and a dialectical conception of montage, is also part of what is at stake here. Kleiman argues, citing Hegel and Lenin, that Bazin's derisive précis of the Kuleshov effect is a symptom of his failure to conceive of the relationship between shots in terms of the dialectic, where "concreteness" and "realism" are matters of the interconnectedness between things, rather than of unmediated presence.[19]

Summing up, Kleiman returns finally to montage's relationship to ethical questions of truth and falsity, and to the place of montage aesthetics within postwar cinema. He writes:

> The danger of falsification through montage is no greater than it is in the profilmic transformation of reality in fictional film, or even in the documentary filming of an object, which object either might not contain [by itself] parts or elements of substantial import for [that object's] conceptualization, or is simply capable of lying. . . . To suspect montage as a method and instrument of investigation is like rejecting a scalpel because it can end up in the hands of a murderer.[20]

As far as the history of style goes, Kleiman argues that if, according to Bazin, "a dramatic event can with the help of montage be analyzed differently and thus produce different films," then we must conclude, against Bazin's own view of a film like *Citizen Kane*, that *Kane* is nothing less than a macro-montage of such films, each of which is by itself relatively univocal yet constructed out of montage (that is, out of fragments associated with discrete narrators). Yet the end result is not authoritative meaning but ambiguity, or (in Kleiman's own resonant phrase) "indeterminacy opened up." Thus, writes Kleiman, it would be better to regard *Kane* or *Rashomon* (1950) as large-scale instances of the Kuleshov effect—now harnessed to an aesthetics of ambiguity—rather than as stylistic alternatives to it.[21] It is this novel conclusion—or, put more precisely, this reconsideration of the standard Soviet conception of montage under pressure from the Bazinian critique—that has made Kleiman's article a standard reference point in Russia for all later writing on montage, and on Bazin.

In the ensuing years—characterized by a deepening cultural and ideological conservatism—Soviet scholars moved from analysis of Bazin to tracking, usually with disapproval, the vicissitudes of his reception in light of contemporary developments in France. A fine example is a 1975 conspectus entitled "The Metamorphoses of *Cahiers du Cinéma*," where Viktor Ilich Bozhovich, a well-known scholar of French film and culture, offers a tendentious reading of that journal's turn against the thought of its founder, a reading that arguably reveals more about late Soviet ideology than it does about *Cahiers*.[22]

For many years, stresses Bozhovich, *Cahiers* was dominated by Bazin's "theoretical constructions," which had "placed in doubt the validity of active, idea-driven aesthetic interpretation of reality, because for him the basis of cinema was the principle of the self-unfolding of life on the screen." An apparent shift around 1968 toward "activist" politics and explicitly Marxist theorizing (under the influence of Althusser among others) led, on the cinematic front, away from Bazin to the work of Eisenstein and long studies of works such as the Popular Front omnibus *La Vie est à nous* (*Life Is Ours*, 1936) and Kozintsev and Trauberg's *New Babylon* (1929). Yet, Bozhovich insists, the new *Cahiers* "remains within the borders of Bazinian aesthetics, despite having rotated his orientation 180 degrees":

> The Bazinian postulate of ontological realism is rethought by *Cahiers'* advocates of "materialist cinema" [by arguing that] since the specificity of cinema lies in the objective reproduction of the reality around us, and because this reality is bourgeois, so cinema itself is a means of reproducing bourgeois ideology . . . because that "reality" is determined by the dominant ideology.[23]

Thus, Bozhovich continues, the dominant cinema is still regarded as "realist," indeed as automatically so by virtue of the mechanical nature of moving photographic registrations; but this realism is "now endowed with a minus sign rather than a plus sign."[24] The conclusion of the new *Cahiers* is that cinema must break away from deep space, sync sound, and so forth, and instead show the process of shooting, the material processes from which the film emerges.

> The new *Cahiers* authors are prepared to find in cinema anything at all—industry, ideology, sign systems, "theoretical practice"—anything, that is, except art.[25]

Needless to say, this lamentable shift is blamed not on Godard, Lacan, or even Althusser, but on Maoism, which had, Bozhovich reminds us, also infected the pages of *Tel Quel* by this time. Of particular concern to Bozhovich is the enlisting of Dziga Vertov—who had by now been given a decisively "realist" or "film-journalistic" gloss by Soviet criticism—by the new (and essentially Maoist) political antirealism in the work of Godard and others.[26]

　　This antagonism toward the ideology-focused theory, dominant in the 1970s and '80s, was largely extended into the immediate post-Soviet period. Meanwhile, however, Bazin's work found a new, highly receptive and even adulatory audience, one that took up Bazin's "idealism" and "metaphysics" as weapons with which to bludgeon Marxist materialisms, vulgar or otherwise. In an article in *Film Studies Notes* from 1993 on "André Bazin's Metaphysics," critic A. N. Doroshevich rebuked those French, British, and American theorists who had attacked Bazin as a kind of bourgeois authoritarian, going on to link those associated with the Althusserian wave of the '70s (like James Roy MacBean) with earlier Soviet pro-montage critics of Bazin, all of whom supposedly promoted the view that the naturalization of "realism" is the goal of all ideology.[27] Vis-à-vis Soviet Bazin criticism, this reproach is, as we have already seen, grossly inaccurate, and has far more to do with the post-1991 wholesale purgation of the cultural sphere of putatively "Marxist" residues than with any critique of "theory" as such. Doroshevich acknowledges, however, that MacBean is right in identifying a "religious underpinning" to Bazin's work, and that religion, rather than stylistic questions about deep focus mise-en-scène and the long take, should be at the center of discussions of Bazin's work.

　　He insists that according to Bazin, "a director has only to seize upon the metaphysical sense [of reality] and make the viewer feel it," adding with regret that neither atheistic semioticians like the otherwise "outstanding" Yuri Lotman nor the Nietzschean poststructuralists have been able to accept this Bazinian position.[28]

Discussing Bazin's treatments of Chaplin's *Monsieur Verdoux* (1947), Rossellini's *Europe' 51* (1952), and Bresson's *Diary of a Country Priest (Journal d'un curé de campagne,* 1951)— Bazin's essays on those three films were published in the same issue[29]—he claims that for Bazin, the "essence of the [truly cinematic] composition consists" in the "indissoluble unity of physical presence and metaphysical meaning," in contrast to "left" art of the Eisenstein type, which "looked in a pragmatic direction, and regarded art as a way to program human behavior." At the same time, Bazin's "religious approach to artistic forms," claims Doroshevich in allusion to Paul Claudel, "is [ultimately] directed 'beyond' 'signifiers'—to the invisible."[30] Doroshevich doesn't characterize the "religion" inherent in Bazin's perspective very clearly, even if the historical motivations for his attempting to do so seem obvious enough. Writing at a time (1993) of large-scale economic and social collapse in Russia, he advocates Bazin's religious humanism and the Bazinian metaphor of the screen as a "window" on reality as more useful antidotes to "today's fog of deconstructive schemes" than either the structuralist "frame" or the poststructuralist "mirror," with their "labyrinths of mutual reflections."[31]

This mischief-making structuralist and poststructuralist thought did gradually make its way into Russian discussions of Bazin after 1991, and I would like to summarize in conclusion one brief and stellar example: Mikhail Iampolski's 1997 article, "Translation and Reproduction: André Bazin and the Aesthetics of the Remake."[32] Iampolski talks about two lesser-known Bazin articles, "A Propos de Reprises" from 1951 and also "Remade in USA" from 1952 (both published in *Cahiers*),[33] and detects there a remarkable anxiety vibrating within Bazin's evaluation of remakes. In the earlier essay, notes Iampolski, Bazin describes the remake as a kind of inauthentic cinephilia, a re-filming of an earlier script that fails even properly to acknowledge the existence of an original source. In the second, by contrast, the remake is more positively described as a "nostalgic attempt to transfer the original, the source, in all of its tiniest details."[34] Bazin gives as an example of such transference the playing of cup-and-ball in both Julien Duvivier's *Pepé le Moko* (1937) and its American remake, John Cromwell's *Algiers* (1938), by the character of "Jimmy" (played by Gaston Modot in Duvivier's original). Iampolski argues that it is precisely in the way that the remake scrupulously retains details of the "original" that it also participates in the fetishism of detail characteristic of cinephilia.

Yet in the remake, he notes, two additional things happen. First, the carrying-over of details from the previous film ends up undermining the stylistic wholeness of the text: Bazin, for instance, regrets the inclusion of "period" expressionist details in Joseph Losey's otherwise impeccably neorealist remake of Fritz Lang's *M* (1951). Secondly, in the remake, those details that were previously the exclusive cognitive property of the elite cinephile—the fetishist-in-the-know—are now placed in the foreground and made apparent to the broadest public. Iampolski's argument, then, is that the remake acts as a kind of psychoanalytic allegory of cinephilia itself, as well as an exposure of the madness of cinephilic fetishism, by revealing through a pastiche effect the distance between the spectator and the fetishized "original." Although I think that Iampolski might err slightly by making Bazin seem more "elitist" than he was— indeed, Bazin seems to support a "democratic cinephilia," rather than an exclusionary one— there is no denying the richness and acuity of his observations. "One cannot exclude the thought," concludes Iampolski, "that when Bazin speaks about the 'monstrous absurdity' of the remake, he exposes his own secret vice."[35]

A more complete survey of the post-Soviet Russian writing on Bazin would fill many more pages than I have at my disposal; to be sure, the work of philosopher Oleg Aronson, who has written with unusual sophistication about Bazin, Pasolini, Deleuze and many others, would figure prominently in any such expansion.[36] The basic message of my brief survey is, I hope, clear: Bazin has been a central figure in Russo-Soviet thinking about cinema for almost fifty years and across starkly different cultural conjunctures; he will no doubt continue to be remade in interesting ways by his Russian readers (even as he remakes them in turn).

Notes

1. A. Bazen, "Frantsuzskij Renuar," in *Zhan Renuar: Stat'i. Interv'iu. Vospominaniia. Stsenarii* (Moscow: Iskusstvo, 1972); A. Bazen, *Chto takoe kino?*, trans. V. Bozhovich and I. Epshtein (Moscow: Iskusstvo, 1972).

2. *Voprosy Kinodramaturgii*, 5 (1965), 313–23.

3. *Kinovedcheskie Zapiski*, 20 (1993), 145–85. Other articles on Bazin have appeared on the pages of this and other Russian film journals, to be sure.

4. André Bazin, *What Is Cinema?* vol. 1, trans. Hugh Gray (Berkeley: University of California Press, 1967), 25–26.

5. Ibid., 36, 38.

6. Generally, we might take Il'ia Vaisfel'd's attack (in his introduction to the 1972 collection) on Bazin's "neutralism" and scruples about "intervention" in the image as typical of the 1960s–1970s Soviet political critique of Bazin, a critique which Vaisfel'd in turn juxtaposes to "positive" features such as Bazin's insistence on "the need to reflect life on the screen" and on "cinema's democratic character," as well as his "criticism of formalism and superficiality" (*Chto Takoe Kino?* 36).

7. Bazin, "Mif Stalina v Sovetskom Kino," *Kinovedcheskie Zapiski* 1 (1988), 154–69.

8. Naum Kleiman, "Drugaia Istoriia Sovetskogo Kino (II)," in *Formula Finala: Stat'i, Vystupleniia, Besedy* (Moscow: Eizenshtein-Tsentr, 2004), 416–32; here 428.

9. Georgii Avenarius, "Ot 'Avangarda' k Narodnomu Frontu," *Iskusstvo Kino*, 8 (1938), 60–63.

10. André Bazin, *Jean Renoir*, ed. François Truffaut, trans. W.W. Halsey II and William H. Simon (New York: Simon and Schuster, 1973), 18.

11. Ilya Trauberg, "Fil'm Frantsuzskogo Naroda," *Iskusstvo Kino*, 9 (1938), 36–40.

12. The crucial text here is doubtless Lukács' 1938 "Realism in the Balance," in *Aesthetics and Politics*, ed. Ronald Taylor (London and New York: Verso, 1997), esp. 38–43. See also my essay "Disorganized Noise: *Enthusiasm* and the Ear of the Collective," at http://www.kinokultura.com/articles/jan05-mackay.html.

13. *Katalog Vystavki Rabot Aleksandra Mikhailovicha Rodchenko* (Moscow, 1961); S. Khan-Magomedov, "Traditsii i Uroki Konstruktivizma," *Dekorativnoe Iskusstvo*, 9 (1964), 25–29; B. I. Rostotskii, *O Rezhisserskom Tvorchestve V.E. Meierkhol'da* (Moscow: Vserossiiskoe Teatral'noe Obshchestvo, 1960); Dziga Vertov, *Stat'i, Dnevniki, Zamysli*, ed. S. Drobashenko (Moscow: Iskusstvo, 1966).

14. Rafail Gikov, "Zametki o Kinokhronike," *Iskusstvo Kino*, 3 (1940), 17–21. The article appeared in an issue devoted to nonfiction film, and a number of its neighboring essays (especially those by M. Slutskii and B. Iagling) similarly argue against the "arbitrariness" and abstraction of montage-based documentary, as exemplified by the works of Vertov, including *Three Songs of Lenin* (1934) and *Lullaby* (1937).

15. Nedelcho Milev, "O Razvitii Zvukozritel'nogo Kinematografa (Eizenshtein, Bazen i Sovremennoe Kino)," *Voprosy Kinoiskusstva*, 10 (1967), 129–52.

16. Andrei Tarkovsky, "Zapechatlennoe Vremia," *Voprosy Kinoiskusstva*, 10 (1967), 79–102; here 82.

17. Kleiman, "Kadr kak iacheika montazha," *Voprosy Kinoiskusstva*, 11 (1968). I am using here the version reprinted in Kleiman's *Formula Finala*, 254–89.

18. Kleiman, *Formula Finala*, 266.

19. Philip Rosen has powerfully demonstrated that Bazin's fundamental dialectic pertains to spectator and image (rather than to the relationships between shots) in his chapter "Subject, Ontology, and Historicity in Bazin," in *Change Mummified: Cinema, Historicity, Theory* (Minneapolis: University of Minnesota Press, 2001), 3–41.

20. Kleiman, *Formula Finala*, 282–83.

21. Ibid., 283–85, 287.

22. Viktor Bozhovich, "Metamorfozy 'Kaie diu sinema,'" *Voprosy Kinoiskusstva*, 16 (1975), 263–78.

23. Ibid., 265–66.

24. Ibid., 266.

25. Ibid., 267.

26. Ibid., 275.

27. A. N. Doroshevich, "Metafizika Andre Bazena," *Kinovedcheskie Zapiski* 17 (1993): 96–101. For MacBean on Bazin, see his *Film and Revolution* (Bloomington: Indiana University Press, 1975), 101–103 and *passim*.

28. Doroshevich, "Metafizika Andre Bazena," 97.

29. Bazen, "Iz kriticheskogo naslediia," *Kinovedcheskie Zapiski*, 17 (1993), 62–95.

30. Doroshevich, "Metafizika Andre Bazena," 99.

31. Ibid., 100–101.

32. Mikhail Iampol'skii, "Perevod i vosproizvedenie (Andre Bazen i estetika rimeika)," in *Iazyk-Telo-Sluchai* (Moscow: Novoe Literaturnoe Obozrenie, 2004), 286–99. I cite this republished version here; the article first appeared in English, in slightly different form, as "Translating Images . . ." *Res*, 31 (Autumn 1997).

33. Bazin, "A propos des reprises," *Cahiers du Cinéma*, 5 (1951), 54–55; "Remade in USA," *Cahiers du Cinéma*, 11 (1952), 54–58.

34. Iampolski, op. cit., 292.

35. Ibid., 299.

36. On Bazin, see his "Kinematograficheskoe sobytie: K teorii glubinnoi mizanstseny Andre Bazena," in *Metakino* (Moscow: Ad Marginem, 2003).

29

From Ripples to Waves

Bazin in Eastern Europe

ALICE LOVEJOY

To Antonín J. Liehm

It was not until 1979 that a selection of translations from André Bazin's *Qu'est-ce que le cinéma?* was published in Czechoslovakia, making the country one of the last in Eastern Europe to release a volume of the critic's writings. Hungary had done so in 1961, with *Selected Studies in Film Aesthetics*,[1] and Poland soon after, with the 1963 *Film and Reality*.[2] The Soviet Union, as John MacKay discusses in this volume, published a version of *Qu'est-ce que le cinéma?* in 1972.[3] The belatedness of the Czechoslovak volume, *Co je to film?*, published by the state-adminis-tered Czechoslovak Film Institute (*Československý filmový ústav*), was due in part to the fact that individual essays had been available in translation previously; and in part, according to Miroslav Zůna in his introduction, to the existence of the Soviet volume, which many Czecho-slovak readers could access without difficulty. Yet this Soviet publication may have also signaled that it was acceptable for Czechoslovakia—its official loyalty to the Soviet Union renewed in the aftermath of the 1968 Warsaw Pact invasion—to follow suit with a local translation. Zůna dutifully attempts to frame Bazin as, despite his unfortunate Catholicism ("understandable in the context of the concrete historical situation and intellectual and cultural atmosphere of Europe between the two worlds"), an exemplar of socialist values. According to Zůna, Bazin is, above all, a devoted realist opposed to "formalism, schematism, stylization," and an intermediary who channeled Soviet avant-garde thought to the West—even if he misunderstood postwar Soviet film and drew certain "one-sided" conclusions about it.[4]

While this interpretation of Bazin reflects the degree to which discourse about cinema in "normalized" Czechoslovakia differed from that of the 1960s, its pigeonholing of Bazin into categories that don't quite fit points to the fact that the publication had effectively missed its moment. For Bazin *had* played a crucial role in Czechoslovak cinema and criticism at the same moment that the Hungarian and Polish volumes were published. During the early 1960s, Czechoslovakia's famous New Wave was emerging, spurred, on one hand, by domestic cine-matic and political developments (namely, destalinization—Czechoslovakia did not experience the large-scale "thaws" that Hungary, Poland, and the Soviet Union had in 1956), and on the other, by developments in international film culture. The French New Wave, to whose advent and form Bazin was so instrumental, was chief among these developments, and Czechoslovak filmmakers and critics avidly watched their Western colleagues' films at festivals, in film clubs, and in cinemas; they also kept up with essays by its filmmakers and critics (Bazin among them), in French or in translation. In short, Bazin's writings, and the films his writings helped create, encountered Czechoslovak cinema during an intensive period of reinvention that mirrored the recent reinvention in French cinema. And it is this parallel that tells us the most about Bazin's reception in Czechoslovakia, for it is almost as if the filmmakers and critics of the early 1960s were too busy doing what Bazin and his colleagues had done in France several years earlier to take his writings to heart in the same way their neighbors did.

Co je to film? was certainly not the first appearance of Bazin's criticism in Czech or Slovak; his writings had been translated sporadically from 1958. In this, the year of his death, *Panorama of Foreign Film Journalism* (*Panoráma zahraničního filmového tisku*), Czechoslovakia's biweekly collection of foreign film criticism (a specialist publication directed to film professionals and enthusiasts), published Bazin's and Charles Bitsch's interview with Orson Welles (from *Cahiers du Cinéma*).[5] In February of the following year, *Film a doba*, Czechoslovakia's nerve center of intellectual film criticism, translated "On Film and Television" ("O filmu a televizi"), a conversation between Jean Renoir, Roberto Rossellini, and Bazin.[6] While Bazin is largely an afterthought in these first two interviews, he figures more prominently in the March 1959 publication, also in *Panorama of Foreign Film Journalism*, of "Thoughts on Criticism" ("Úvahy o kritice"), one in a series of such articles translated from the French cinema-club magazine *Cinéma 58*.[7]

Bazin's canonical articles began to be published in April 1961, when an excerpt of "Théâtre et Cinéma" entitled "The Film Screen and the Realistic Operation of Space" ("Filmové plátno a realistické působení prostoru") appeared in *Film a doba*.[8] In May, *Panorama of Foreign Film Journalism* published a translation of "Peinture et Cinéma," an article conceived as a pair to *Film a doba's* version of "Théâtre et Cinéma."[9] Other key works followed several years later: in *Film a doba*, in March 1964, "Ontologie de l'image photographique" (translated by critic Drahomíra Novotná) and a review of the Polish anthology *Film and Reality* by Jan Svoboda, who characterized Bazin as a critical realist for whom film was a "life passion and a tool for truth."[10] The following month, a review of *Qu'est-ce que le cinéma?* appeared in *Film a doba*, and, finally, in 1966, Antonín J. Liehm translated "L'Evolution du langage cinématographique" for the magazine.[11]

In 1963, Bazin was framed in a different context, when a version of "Pour un cinéma impur" ("Obhajoba filmových adaptací") appeared in *Film Is Art: A Collection of Essays* (*Film je umění: sborník statí*), alongside articles by Balázs, Delluc, Moussinac, Clair, Eisenstein, Arnheim, Pudovkin, Grierson, Rotha, Barbaro, Kozlov, Lawson, Zavattini, Malraux, Chiarini, Kracauer, and Richter. The book's editors, Jaroslav Brož and Ljubomír Oliva, introduce Bazin favorably, as "the exemplary type of film critic and journalist who saw the main logic of his profession in everyday journalistic work," yet the essay is accessory to the book's more programmatic intention: to address the lack of a popular audience for any type of film criticism in Czechoslovakia.[12] "The state of Czechoslovak writing on film, both original and in translation, is bleak," the authors write. "If this anthology inspires interest . . . in film theory and aesthetics, if it contributes even a little bit to making the publication of original and translated film literature richer and more systematic . . . it will have fulfilled its goal."[13]

Nevertheless, the introduction to this translation is one of the very few Czechoslovak publications (the others being the *Panorama* translation of "Painting and Cinema" and the book reviews) to comment on Bazin's thinking, or explicitly grapple with his ideas.[14] Indeed, as they were published, Bazin's writings seem to have been naturally integrated into the transformation from classical to modernist cinema in Czechoslovakia that critics like Jan Žalman observed in the 1960s. In this sense, the book is very much a product of the year of its publication, for 1963 was a most extraordinary moment for Czechoslovakia, politically and culturally. This was the year when the country's politicians officially critiqued the Stalinist "cult of personality," when the 12th Congress of the Czechoslovak Communist Party exonerated the victims of the show trials of the early 1950s, and when the famous Kafka conference took place in the town of Liblice.[15] In the film world, the influx of foreign film criticism embodied in *Film Is Art* was balanced by the export of a new kind of cinema that marked Czechoslovak film's recovery from the setbacks it had suffered at the 1959 Banská Bystrica festival (at which a series of films produced during the brief "thaw" of 1956–1958 were sharply criticized). These new films were largely made by young directors, among them Věra Chytilová, whose *Something Different* (*O něčem jiném*, 1963) became a topic of excited discussion domestically and internationally after it won the Grand Prix at the Mannheim Film Festival, providing hard proof that something *was* indeed different in Czechoslovak cinema.[16]

The two elements in Bazin's writing most important to this emerging cinema—which would come to be called, after its French forebear, the Czechoslovak New Wave—were, first, his conception of realism, and second, precisely what *Film Is Art* represented: the broader cinematic world reflected in his criticism. These, in turn, are the elements that, in his 1964 article "On the Problems of Czechoslovak Cinematic Modernism" ("K problémům československé filmové moderny"), Žalman (a pseudonym for Antonín Novák, one of *Film a doba*'s editors) observes as central to the new films emerging in Czechoslovakia: "an attempt to break away from the exhausted, average and stiff Central European conventions, to enter into contact with trends in the modern world and bring to them our own, specific national contribution, which we have gained through an expanded space for experimentation," and "a deep truthfulness and nonconformist directness in speaking about the present moment, about society, and about man . . ."[17]

"Truthfulness" (with its natural links to reality and realism) was at the core of debates about Czechoslovak cinema in the early to mid-1960s, as critics and filmmakers attempted to come to terms with how a new form of cinematic realism—one that would still be socialist, but not socialist realist—might look. The pages of *Film a doba* and other publications were filled, as were Czechoslovak film festivals, with discussions of *cinéma vérité*, *kino-pravda*, and new, more "truthful," sociological approaches to filmmaking.[18] At the same time, critics saw the "reality" expressed in new fiction films as extending beyond the objective world: Galina Kopaněvová, for instance, wrote in 1967 that "the Czechoslovak film avant-garde has arrived at the domain of a new visualization of reality, one that exists in the world of the consciousness, ideas, and fantasies of the creator."[19]

These questions of realism were, in effect, a dialogue of sorts with Bazin, for we know from the controversy surrounding "The Stalin Myth in the Soviet Cinema" that he had already come to blows over socialist realism.[20] Seven years after the publication of the "Stalin" article, in a piece on the Polish School for *France observateur*, Bazin renewed his attack on the socialist realist aesthetic, and in the process of doing so, offered a model for a new kind of realism in Eastern Europe. Citing a *Cahiers du Cinéma* article by Jerzy Plazewski, Bazin writes:

> With regard to this alleged realism, in 1949, the Polish minister of culture even called the masterpieces of postwar Italian cinema "decadent naturalism, clearly having nothing

in common with nineteenth century naturalism and not reflecting objective truth in any detail." . . . This was also the time in which the famous Chiaourelli taught Polish filmmakers a lesson by explaining to them that it was neither decent nor sensible to show Julius Caesar blowing his nose.[21]

It is this, Bazin observes, "that inspires a certain mistrust in the young generation and that gives them the bravery and additional lucidity to build a new cinema, this time in real harmony with socialist society."[22]

Bazin, here, seems to call for the Polish School to engage with a kind of realism based on the everyday, a style that would depict life under state socialism in the same way that Italian neorealism depicted postwar Italian society. As he mentions in this article, Andrzej Wajda's *Kanal* (1957), set during World War II, could clearly not be expected to depict socialist society, but he notes that the film "testifies at least to some of the indispensable qualities that [such a cinema] would need to possess." The most important of these appears to be

> a certain, typically Warsovian psychology that Wajda depicts and puts in action through a series of characters with different natures and from different origins, placed on the same common denominator. These are indeed individual characters, but based on a particular national character. This depiction . . . leads to an optimism of self-knowledge. . . . This is . . . the concrete depiction of a very real social reality, a sort of self-analysis, if not a self-criticism of national historical behavior.[23]

Although it is unlikely that this article was ever translated into Czech or Slovak, we may imagine that this call for a cinema that speaks to a "particular national character" and embodies a fresh idea of realism was part of what made Bazin's writing appealing to Czechoslovak filmmakers and writers. For a "new cinema in real harmony with socialist society" was precisely what Czechoslovak filmmakers and critics were trying to build in the 1960s—and in this phrase, the faint echo of the leading axiom of the Prague Spring, "socialism with a human face," is apt. In Žalman's estimation, this is the crucial difference between the Czechoslovak and French New Waves. "The problem begins," he writes in "On the Problems of Czechoslovak Cinematic Modernism," "with assertions that our young people's resistance to the cult [*note:* Stalinism], which is inherently linked with the generation of our fathers, is the same resistance that youth in the West feel; that the refusal of any kind of responsibility for the 'sins of our fathers' is common to the young generation both there and here."[24] Films of the French New Wave, he writes, "sneer, hate, scandalize, speak about the 'right to debauchery' or about amorality, doubt everything except their right to doubt and contempt. They speak of isolation." Contra this, in Czechoslovakia, "we say NO to something so that we can say YES to something else. Something is—if we must use the term—destroyed, so that something even more refined, stripped of yesterday's husks, can be built more strongly and beautifully. . . . This is socialism, its ethos, its social relations, its material standard and its culture."[25]

The divergences that Žalman observes between the French and Czechoslovak situations may be overstated, for at the core of his article is an acknowledgement that something new was happening in both countries, and that there was a degree of dialogue (formal and otherwise) between them. And indeed, the parallels were clear between the situation Czechoslovak cinema found itself in during the early 1960s, and the situation out of which Bazin's writings themselves emerged.[26] Bazin's criticism was born in the film clubs and cinemas of postwar France, the festivals of the postwar world, and the editorial offices of *Cahiers du Cinéma*, where filmmakers and critics were in close contact, mapping a new understanding of cinema for a world that had changed fundamentally. These writings, in translation or in the films they inspired, bubbled up in the film clubs, cinemas, and editorial offices of a Czechoslovakia that was itself at something akin to a "year zero," the beginning of a social (and cinematic) experiment that would last until 1969. And this account of cinema reinventing itself in two, parallel spaces—not that of a much-delayed translation with its slightly off-key introduction—is perhaps the true story of Bazin's reception in Czechoslovakia. For, ironically, *Qu'est-ce que le cinéma?* might very likely have been published earlier had Czechoslovakia not been so (rightfully) enthralled by its own "miraculous" situation. If anything, Bazin's writings stand as an analogy to this situation, as Liehm intimates in his 1964 "Argument": "Somehow we still can't get our wits about us, we rub our eyes, we pinch our hands to convince ourselves that this isn't only a dream. But no, we are more or less conscious, fully aware, and the entirely unexpected ascent of our cinema in the last two years is an indisputable reality."[27]

Notes

1. *Válogatott filmesztétikai tanulmányok*, ed. and trans. Deszö Baróti (Budapest: M. Filmtud. Int. és Filmarchívum, 1961).

2. *Film i rzeczywistość*, ed. and trans. Bolesław Michałek (Warsaw: Wydawnictwa Artystyczne i Filmowe, 1963).

3. John MacKay, infra.

4. André Bazin, *Co je to film?* ed. and trans. Ljubomír Oliva (Prague: Čs. filmový ústav, 1979), 9. All translations in this article are my own.

5. Bazin and Charles Bitsch, "Rozmluva s Orsonem Wellesem," *Panoráma zahraničního filmového tisku* (September 9, 1958), 724–31.

6. Jean Renoir and Roberto Rossellini, trans. E. N., "O filmu a televizi," *Film a doba*, 2 (1959), 106–12. The French original, "Cinéma et télévision," was published October 23, 1958 (two weeks before Bazin's death) in *France observateur*. See Michael Cramer, infra for a discussion of this "conversation" about the media.

7. *Panoráma zahraničního filmového tisku* (March 3, 1959), 176–82.

8. Bazin, trans. M. D., "Filmové plátno a realistické působení prostoru," *Film a doba*, 4 (1961), 253–57.

9. *Panoráma zahraničního filmového tisku* (May 10, 1961), 438.

10. Bazin, trans. Drahomíra Novotná, "Ontologie fotografického obrazu," *Film a doba*, 3 (1964), 136–37; J. S., "Krátce ze zahraniční filmové literatury," *Film a doba*, 3 (1964), 159.

11. Bazin, trans. Antonín J. Liehm, "Vývoj filmové řeči," *Film a doba*, 2 (1966), 61–65.

12. Jaroslav Brož and Ljubomír Oliva, *Film je umění: Sborník statí* (Prague: Orbis, 1963), 201.

13. Ibid., 5–6.

14. According to Liehm, no major theoretical articles were published on Bazin at the time (Antonín J. Liehm, email communication, November 25, 2009). I thank Mr. Liehm, one of Bazin's original translators into Czech, for the precious information he has shared with me concerning the resonance of this critic in Eastern Europe.

15. These exonerations would culminate in 1968 with the government finally acknowledging its complicity in the trials. See H. Gordon Skilling, *Czechoslovakia's Interrupted Revolution* (Princeton, NJ: Princeton University Press, 1976), 49. For more on the resonances of 1963 for cinema, see Peter Hames, *The Czechoslovak New Wave*, Second Edition (New York: Wallflower, 2005).

16. Jana Hádková, "K filmové kritice šedesátých let," *Filmový sborník historický*, 2; *90 let vývoje čs. kinematografie-příspěvky z konference* (Prague: Československý filmový ústav, 1991), 273.

17. Jan Žalman, "K problemům československé filmové moderny," *Film a doba*, 5 (1964), 234.

18. See, for instance, Antonín Navrátil, "Dny krátkého filmu: Renesance dokumentárního filmu?" *Rudé právo* (March 27, 1964); and Drahomira Novotná, "Přistupte ke skutečnosti," *Film a doba*, 8 (1962), 488–94.

19. Galina Kopaněvová, "Kontexty nového československého filmu," *Film a doba*, 8 (1967), 396.

20. See Dudley Andrew, *André Bazin* (New York: Oxford University Press, 1978), 138–44. See also, Antoine de Baecque, infra.

21. Bazin, "Ils aiment la vie," *France observateur*, 410 (March 20, 1958).

22. Ibid.

23. Ibid.

24. Žalman, 232.

25. Žalman, 232, 234.

26. These parallels are, curiously, disregarded in a chapter on Bazin and Siegfried Kracauer in Slovak film theorist Peter Mihálik's 1983 book *Chapters From Film Theory* (*Kapitoly z filmovej teórie*). Mihálik regards Bazin's writings less as theory with broad international relevance, and more as criticism pertinent primarily to the historical situation in which it emerged. He writes: "The 'theoretical nature' of Bazin's approach is . . . debatable, for what was published at the end of his life and after his death offers a more or less complete critical conception, a certain critical ideal, an understanding of film . . . directed to a certain group of filmmakers, the members of the 'new wave,' for whom Bazin was the critic of a generation." Peter Mihálik, "Neštrúkturne koncepcie Bazina a Kracauera," *Kapitoly z filmovej teórie* (Bratislava: Tatran, 1983).

27. Antonín J. Liehm, "Argument," *Literární noviny* (April 25, 1964).

30

Bazin in Brazil

A Welcome Visitor

Ismail Xavier

In the period following World War II, the impact of neorealism was the central debate among Brazilian film critics, as in other countries. The dialogue with films, with Zavattini's texts, and with Italian critics marked the cultural and aesthetic atmosphere from which the generation that would later lead the *Cinema Novo* movement, beginning in 1959–1960, emerged. However, an equally decisive factor in the development of ideas both for the more experienced critics and the younger leaders of Brazilian modern cinema was the intensive reading of *Cahiers du Cinéma.*

For people like Glauber Rocha, Gustavo Dahl, Carlos Diegues and Paulo Cesar Saraceni, the "young turks" were an inspiration, specifically concerning the development of the *politique des auteurs.* At the same time, they were aware of how much these *Cahiers'* critics owed to André Bazin, the godfather who did not always agree with his pupils but who established the coordinates of a reflection on mise-en-scène that created the best parameters for the comparison between the styles of modern and classical cinema. Nevertheless, Bazin's ideas, although echoed in many ways in Brazilian criticism after 1950, with his articles mentioned by influential writers,[1] only took on a more defined shape for Brazilians after the publication in 1959 of the first volumes of *Qu'est-ce que le cinéma?* Still, it was only in the 1960s that one could scrutinize the consequences of his original conception of realism, recognizing how his reflections on the significance of the sequence-shot and depth of field projected an analysis of style onto the aesthetic-ontological plane. Thus, the dialogue between Brazilian critics and filmmakers with André Bazin passed through two distinct phases: before and after his books were available.

The 1950s and the Case of the *Revista de Cinema*

During the 1950s, critical debate in Brazil agreed on the need for a revision of classical theory. The new directions cinema was taking could no longer be seen as a confirmation of the legacy marked by montage theory as formulated in connection with the avant-gardes of the 1920s. The new postwar trends signaled that realism had become the question forming the axis of any new film aesthetics. Side by side with attention to neorealism and Orson Welles, Bazin's expression "impure cinema" was used by critics to deal with impressive adaptations, like those of Laurence Olivier, not to mention Welles' *Macbeth* (1948). But for Brazilian critics, a dialogue with their Italian counterparts predominated, because of questions of cinematic specificity and the consequent revision of classical montage theory. This debate was present throughout the 1950s, notably in one major site of theory in Brazil, *Revista de Cinema*, a journal published in the city of Belo Horizonte, which had national scope and contributors from many regions.[2]

The critics writing for this review proposed no hard-line endorsement of one particular type of cinema or theory; rather, they adhered to a general precept that the value of a film is directly connected to its exploration of film-specific resources. The central question concerned the different forms of realism and not the debate opposing narrative and experimental cinema. It is not by chance that Pudovkin was the greatest reference from the Soviet tradition, a choice mediated by Umberto Barbaro. Equilibrium was the goal, not more radical forms, such as the "exaggeration" of rapid montage (considered formalist). The formal concerns of the critics (rhythm, duration of shots, a new conception of the work of the actor) shared space with Bazin's ideas, but he was seldom quoted and his more specific notions took some time to be incorporated in these discussions.[3]

In general, the debate involving the critical wings of the review—marked by the oppositions between Catholics and Marxists, typical of the ciné-clubs at that time—did not center on form or on specific figures of language (sequence-shot, depth of field, etc.). Cyro Siqueira, the principal theorist at the review, concentrated most on the formal plane, but he distrusted the excessive appreciation of any figure of style. He preferred the principle of the functionality (economy) of form adjusted to content; his defense of neorealism was based on this principle and on the category of simplicity.

The leftist wing of the review took its cue from the Italian Marxists, Barbaro and Guido Aristarco. For his part, Siqueira was more aligned with phenomenological French criticism and praised Bazin because his aesthetic stance and formal concerns were not strongly inflected by ideological bias. His point of view found its supporters in 1957 when new contributors to the review—such as Maurício G. Leite, Flávio P. Vieira, and Haroldo Pereira—began to draw not only on *Cahiers* but also on well-known figures of French phenomenological thought (Merleau-Ponty and Sartre) and on film critics related to them, like Bazin and Amédée Ayfre.[4] Brazilian film theory now paid more attention to figures of style: the refusal of the shot/counter-shot and of classical *découpage*, with references to William Wyler and Antonioni. Since Bazin's central notions referred to these subjects, his views became increasingly visible. But only in the 1960s would discussion of form really take hold.

Salles Gomes

In 1957 Paulo Emilio Salles Gomes' book on Jean Vigo was published in France,[5] where he had conducted his research and writing from 1949 to 1952. Although he was in close contact with Henri Langlois at the Cinémathèque Française, he only met Bazin two or three times while composing it. Still, the French critic would write a rave review of this work upon its publication, stressing its importance as an exhaustive and exemplary work on an auteur.[6] Bazin praised the author's method, especially the way he connected the filmmaker's life and work, as well as his passion for objectivity which he described as a kind of acute sense of the "poetics of facts," akin to Vigo's own sensibility.

Salles Gomes had returned to Brazil earlier in the decade, and he was one of the organizers of the 1954 Festival de Cinema in São Paulo, to which Bazin was invited [figure 30.1]. The critic's stay in Brazil generated two articles: one in which he wrote of his experience at the festival,[7] and the other, "De la difficulté d'être Coco," in which he recounted the saga of his return trip with the parrot he purchased as a souvenir. The latter article, extraordinary for its portrait of a personality, was published in the special issue of *Cahiers* on the occasion of the death of Bazin, the same issue in which Salles Gomes' touching testimony on the critic appeared [figure 16.1].[8]

As for the presence of Bazin's writings in Brazil, "Peinture et cinéma" ["*O* cinema e a pintura"][9] was probably the first text published there. It came out in 1955 in the catalog "Films on Art," which documented an exhibition that ran during the Third Biennial of Art in São Paulo.

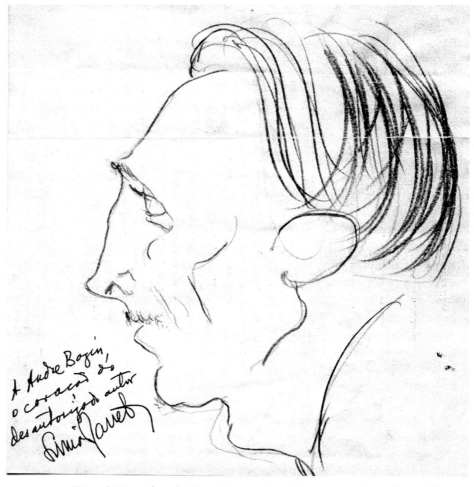

FIGURE 30.1: "To André Bazin, from the Heart of an unauthorized Auteur, Lima Barreto (cineaste)" Sao Paulo, 1954 (Florent Bazin collection)

For the catalog published by the Cinemateca Brasileira, *História do cinema francês 1895–1959*, on the occasion of the Fifth Biennial of Art in São Paulo (1959), Salles Gomes wrote an introductory note with the title "French cinematographic ideologies," in which he evokes the evolution of criticism from Louis Delluc to André Bazin. In this note, he stressed the role of the French Cinémathèque, Georges Sadoul's research on film history, and the critical work of Bazin. For Salles Gomes, the latter was responsible for what he called the "airing out of criticism," a milestone in overcoming that demand for purity in cinema from the classical tradition. He commented on Bazin's appropriation of "ambiguity" as an ontological category related to the existential form of human presence in space-time, a category that supports an aesthetics particular to the cinema, and that has the additional virtue of interacting with formulations from literary and art criticism, offering a new way to insert cinema into culture.

That same year, Salles Gomes wrote two articles expressly to honor Bazin. The first sympathetically outlined the biography of an extraordinary man.[10] The second provided an introduction to the critic's thought, in which he expressed his conviction that while Bazin and Eisenstein were the two greatest minds of the theory of cinema, the French critic was unique as a writer. Salles Gomes mentions Bazin's conceptual inventions, especially his analysis of the historical-aestethical implications of techniques such as depth of field. Above all, he points to Bazin's sharp focus on "what is there," both in the world and in artistic works, not what "should be there," emphasing Bazin's understanding of method in the etymological sense of *quest*: an approach to films not attached to fixed rules, but undertaken as a genuine interaction with images and sounds, an open exploration in perception and critical thought.[11]

Cinema Novo and Criticism in the 1960s

The dialogue between two key national film movements, the Cinemanovistas and the Nouvelle Vague, inevitably brought Bazin and his ideas into prominence right after his death. When asked about the significance of Bazin for the Cinema Novo generation, Gustavo Dahl claimed that it had been the first volumes of *Qu'est-ce que le cinéma?* that revealed the entire dimension and the depth of a theory that helped his group develop their projects and begin discussions with a new group of influential Brazilian critics that came to the foreground, such as Jean-Claude Bernardet, José Carlos Avellar, Paulo Perdigão and Sérgio Augusto.[12] Since this was at the moment of the debate related to Cinema Novo, this dialogue with international critics was adjusted so as to bear intensely on the topics of the national debate concerning the direction cinema was taking.

From the Cinema Novo group, David Neves gave most credit to Bazin as an inspiration.[13] This in contrast, for example, to Leon Hirszman, aligned more with the thinking of Eisenstein. Glauber Rocha read *Cahiers* and developed his own thoughts on the sequence-shot, typical of his future style, but he maintained a tense relationship with Bazin. Godard and Buñuel were more central for him, along with the inspiration he felt from Brecht and Eisenstein.[14] One important anthology, *Cinema Novo, cinema moderno* (1966), creates a profile of references for thinking about the new cinema, and three of its contributors, Gustavo Dahl, Norma Bahia Pontes and the critic Paulo Perdigão, specifically appeal to Bazin's ideas to explain aspects of the new aesthetics.[15]

In addition to the texts that directly relate to the defense of the *Cinema Novo*, there are examples of commentaries on the work of Bazin by such critics as José Lino Grunewald and

Enéas de Souza who were not engaged in that debate, yet who completely identified with Godard and Resnais. In 1966 Souza published "Pensamento crítico de André Bazin,"[16] where he commented succinctly on such ideas as cinema's means of fighting against time and death, the ontology of the photographic image, and the relations between cinema and theater. When he comes to discuss the dramatic implications of depth of field, he works out his own formulations, based on ideas elaborated by Bazin. Souza treats Bazin at a philosophical level, as a *penseur*, rather than as a critic and essayist which is how Salles Gomes had praised him. And he ends his piece quoting Michel Mourlet, who described Bazin as a man who did more than lay out aesthetic hierarchies but actually captured the essence of cinema in his thought.

In the 1960s phase of *Revista de Cinema*, Cyro Siqueira resumed his argument in defense of realism (and simplicity), expressing his objections to the "formalist" New Wave, which he took to be a "new consumer item" for cinephiles. Again he praises Bazin's phenomenological approach as a milestone in film theory but sees him adopting too radical a stance when he links realism to a specific formal procedure. Given Siqueira's concern for content, the idea of "montage prohibited," taken as a precept, went too far in its inversion of montage theory. Consequently, it had been appropriated by the young New Wave critics-filmmakers, to justify some of their more dogmatic statements as well as the particular taste inscribed in the *politique des auteurs*.[17]

The Emergence of Academic Film Scholarship in Brazil

In the late 1960s and throughout the 1970s, criticism everywhere was punctuated by extreme antirealist postures coming in the form of attacks on the illusionism of the cinematographic image. In Brazil this shift in ideas of film and film style was simultaneous with a radicalization promoted by the generation of post–Cinema Novo filmmakers who took a more aggressive position, breaking with narrative codes and returning to the spirit of an earlier avant-garde. Deconstruction became a key word, though its use by film critics did not always involve all the aspects of Apparatus theory which had a growing presence among scholars elsewhere in the 1970s, a period during which graduate programs in film studies were created in Brazilian universities. These programs would define the progress of academic research, a new source of theoretical thought and criticism with its specific goals and methods, a segment of film culture that, in Brazil, would maintain a connection with urgent debates between filmmakers and critics.

Apart from ongoing film historical research, university studies in Brazil initially followed the semiological strains of Christian Metz and C. S. Peirce. Semiology's linguistic basis in the analysis of the image-sign and its codes involves a critique of Bazin's idealism, a critique radicalized by Apparatus theory. However, in Brazil, Metz's own phenomenological tendency opened a debate on his affinities with Bazin, particularly when the semiologist addressed the question of the indexical and iconic properties of the film image. These properties created the so-called phantom of analogy, which referred to a methodological hindrance in the linguistic turn. Quite successful in its approach to narrative structures, semiology encountered difficulties when dealing with more refined aspects of style and form which, because cinematic time and duration depend on specific formal choices, resist the general terms of semiology. Moving images have distinct material connections to their referents, different from those established by words, and the old question of the "reality effect," although it doesn't cover everything involved in the process of semiosis, plays a major role in it as Bazin had suggested in his critical essays.

I mention this discussion from the 1970s to evoke a single example of the well-known process by which ideas that have presumably been overcome are not erased by "epistemological breaks" (an expression à la mode at that time); new ideas in film theory often call for a reexamination of seminal thinkers like Bazin, Eisenstein, and Epstein.

Although there is currently no research group studying Bazin's thought specifically, focusing on his legacy as a whole, Brazilian film scholars share a reiterated sense of his place as one among other indispensable references. Situating his thought on the level of cinema's foundational characteristics, where technique and aesthetics meet, he has been a mandatory link in the analysis of film styles and an inspiration with respect to his critical starting point. The consolidation of academic research has greatly improved the discussion of Bazin's work in Brazil, helping to make his texts available in Portuguese from 1983 on.[18]

Generally speaking, the theoretical trends over the last few decades, including the influential theoretical-philosophical continent opened by the books of Gilles Deleuze, have encouraged in Brazilian universities a renovated dialogue with Bazin concerning modern cinema, time, and film form. More specifically, the recent "return of the real" in art forms and film styles, reinforced by contemporary cinema, is a research topic that has also heated up the dialogue between Brazilian scholars and the French critic.[19] Bazin's strong presence is clear in a variety of research areas: cinema and other arts (painting, theater), the question of voice-over and literary adaptation, studies that focus on the notion of mise-en-scène reworked in recent books by Jacques Aumont, studies on the question of the film essay, taking into account his observations in his 1957 review of Chris Marker's *Lettre de Sibérie*.[20]

These research topics can be found in the books, film journals, and presentations at the Annual Conference of the Brazilian Society for Cinema Studies. The specific field of documentary studies has received a new impulse in Brazil in connection with contemporary Brazilian cinema and with the new conceptual framework provided by specific studies and new taxonomies. Here again, Bazin remains a significant reference in the analysis of relations between image and reality, camera and characters, frame and open space, moving image and duration; or in the analysis of the dialectics of performance and authenticity in filmed interviews.[21] His thought also inflects today's more systematic discussion of the nature of the documentary, as it involves a revision of older concepts in relation to the genesis and the properties of the cinematographic image.[22]

This overview cannot be complete without mentioning the importance of Bazin for the development in Brazil of the critical essay as a form. Jean-Claude Bernardet,[23] author of a seminal book on the documentary, and himself one of the principal essayists since the 1960s, notes that Brazilian critical thought developed through exploring specific topics, studying genres, and analyzing films, rather than through the creation of a systematic work of general theory. In tune with Bazin's style of intervention, many Brazilian scholars and critics try to keep in mind the lesson of the extraordinary essayist who left us the spirit that Salles Gomes described so well in his 1959 testimony: "My greatest admiration for him came from observing how this man, gifted with exceptional ability for great, rigorous theoretical constructions, opened his mind voluntarily when watching films, scrupulously avoiding imposing on the films any pre-established system and loyally granting them all opportunities for revelation. . . . Each of Bazin's critical writings is an adventure and what is common to all of them is the passion to understand and explain."[24]

And then, of course, there are the cineastes and their films, from Nelson P. dos Santos, Paulo C. Saraceni and Eduardo Coutinho to Walter Salles, João Moreira Salles, Karim Ainouz and Luiz Fernando Carvalho, but that is another (Bazinian/Brazilian) story.

Notes

1. Almeida Salles, Moniz Vianna, Paulo Gastal, and Walter da Silveira are among them. Silveira has cited Bazin since 1954 and was emphatic in affirming his debt to him. See *Walter da Silveira, o eterno e o efêmero*, ed. José Umberto Dias (Salvador: Oiti Editora, 2006).

2. Alex Viany, Ely Azeredo, Salyano Cavalcanti de Paiva, Almeida Salles, Rudá de Andrade, and Paulo Emilio Salles Gomes contributed to the review.

3. The debate on neorealism and the revision of the theory of montage started in the first issue (April 1954) and lasted until its ninth issue (December 1954), involving Cyro Siqueira, Guy de Almeida, Fritz Teixeira de Salles, Alex Viany, and Salvyano Cavalcanti de Paiva.

4. *Revista de cinema*, 25 (December 1957).

5. Paulo Emilio Salles Gomes, *Jean Vigo* (Paris: Seuil, 1957).

6. André Bazin, "Présence de Jean Vigo," in *France observateur*, 380 (August 22, 1957).

7. Bazin, "Un festival de la culture cinématographique," *Cahiers du Cinéma*, 54 (April 1954).

8. Bazin, "De la difficulté d'être Coco," *Cahiers du Cinéma*, 91 (January 1959). See Seung-hoon Jeong, infra.

9. This text seems to be a translation of the long article Bazin had published in *Revue du cinéma*, 19–20 (October,1949), republished in *Qu'est-ce que le cinéma?* and translated into English as "Painting and Cinema" in *What Is Cinema?* vol. 1, trans. Hugh Gray (Berkeley: University of California Press, 1967), 164–69. The next Bazin text to be translated in Brazil was his preface for Jean-Louis Rieupeyrout's *Le Western ou le cinéma américain* par excellence (Paris: Editions du Cerf, 1953), which came out through Editora Itatiaia in 1963.

10. Salles Gomes, "Descoberta de André Bazin," *O Estado de São Paulo* (March 21, 1959). See the collection *Paulo Emilio: crítica no Suplemento Literário* vol. 2 (Rio de Janeiro: Editora Paz e Terra, 1982).

11. Salles Gomes, "O crítico André Bazin," *idem* (April 4, 1959). Also included in the collection of Salles Gomes' articles published by Editora Paz e Terra.

12. Recent interview conducted by the author. For Dahl's reception of Bazin's book, see the quotations in his article "Da Nouvelle Vague" in *O Estado de São Paulo* (September 19, 1959).

13. For Neves' reading of Bazin, see "A técnica de Orson Welles," in *O Metropolitano* (March 22, 1959), and "Max Ophuls: cinco filmes," *idem* (October 25, 1959); articles included in *David Neves-Telégrafo visual: crítica amável de cinema*, ed. Carlos Augusto Calil (São Paulo: Editora 34, 2004).

14. Rocha's words concerning Bazin were "respect and disagreement," but he became more caustic from the late 1960s on. See "Il faut revenir à Eisenstein," in *Le siècle du cinéma* (Crisnée Belgium: Yelow Now, 2006), originally published in *Il Messagero* (February 1969). Rocha's letter to Salles Gomes, January 26, 1976, was published in *Glauber Rocha: cartas ao mundo*, ed. Ivana Bentes (São Paulo: Companhia das Letras, 1997), 583.

15. Flávio Moreira da Costa, ed., *Cinema Moderno, Cinema Novo* (Rio de Janeiro: José Álvaro Editor, 1966).

16. Enéas de Souza, *Trajetórias do cinema moderno e outros textos* (Porto Alegre: Secretaria Municipal de Cultura, 2007), 241–49.

17. Siqueira refers to Luc Moullet, Truffaut and Chabrol. See "Cinema, estética do consumo," *Revista de Cinema*, 4 [new series] (September–October 1964).

18. Bazin's "Mort tous les après-midi," "Ontologie de l'image photographique," and "En marge de l'érotisme au cinema" were included in *A experiência do cinema*, ed. Ismail Xavier (Editora Graal, 1983). Bazin's books in Brazil include: *O cinema – ensaios* (São Paulo: Brasiliense, 1989), translation of *Qu'est-ce que le cinéma?*; *O cinema da crueldade* (São Paulo: Martins Fontes, 1989); *Charles Chaplin* (Rio de Janeiro: Jorge Zahar, 2004); *Orson Welles* (Rio de Janeiro: Jorge Zahar, 2006).

19. A research group focusing on the "recoveries of the real" is coordinated by Denilson Lopes (Brazil), Jens Andermann (UK), Álvaro Fernández Bravo (USA), Gabriela Nouzeilles (USA), and Maurício Lissovsky

(Brazil). Brazilian scholars such as Lúcia Nagib (University of Leeds) and Ivone Margulies (CUNY), who focus on the question of realism and Bazin's critical essays, have contributed to that group.

20. Jacques Aumont, *Cinéma et la mise en scène* (Paris: Colin, 2006); Laura Rascaroli, *The Personal Camera: Subjective Cinema and the Essay Film* (London: Wallflower, 2009).

21. Consuelo Lins, Cláudia Mesquita, Cezar Migliorin, Ismail Xavier, and Elinaldo Teixeira have done research work focusing on documentary films. The review *Devires* 5:2, 2008, coordinated by César Guimarães, offers a significant collection of essays on documentary by other scholars.

22. See Fernão Pessoa Ramos, *Mas, afinal . . . o que é mesmo o documentário?* (São Paulo: Editora SENAC, 2008). Ramos develops his dialogue with Bazin in a balance of theories of the cinematographic image, which includes a chapter dedicated to Bazin and analyzes texts not included in *Qu'est-ce que le cinéma?* In a historical approach to the documentary film, Silvio Da-Rin, *O espelho partido: tradição e transformação do documentário* (Rio de Janeiro: Azougue Editorial, 2004), also discusses Bazin's texts.

23. Jean-Claude Bernardet, *Cineastas e imagens do povo* (São Paulo: Companhia das Letras, 2003 [first edition 1985]).

24. Salles Gomes, "O crítico André Bazin," op. cit., endnote 11.

31

Bazin and the Politics of Realism in Mainland China

CECILE LAGESSE

André Bazin was first introduced in Mainland China on March 3, 1962, when a series edited by the Film Bureau—*Digest of Film Translations* (*Dianying yishu yicong*)—published several articles about Eisenstein's montage theory. One of them was "Montage Interdit" ("Mengtaiqi yunyong de jiexian," today known as "Bei jinyong de mengtaiqi") by a certain "Andelei Bashan"[1] who, the translator noted in a postscript, was "one of the most influential film critics among the French bourgeoisie." The next year, China Film Press (Zhongguo dianying chubanshe) published translations of works written by Western film theorists, and among these was *Esthétique du cinéma* (1959),[2] whose author, Henri Agel, referred often to Bazin, his mentor. Bazin's name was however hardly noticed at a time when the Chinese film community was more concerned with, and bound by, domestic politics of the most dramatic sort. Only after the Cultural Revolution and the beginning of the Reform Era in 1978 did his writings resurface in Mainland China.

It is thus with a delay of several decades that the Chinese[3] film community had a chance to be affected by Bazin's writings. His approach to cinematic realism would allow filmmakers and critics to rethink cinema's relationship to reality after the Cultural Revolution and to free cinema from its former role as an ideological conduit. A dialogue was established between Bazin's notions and the reigning Chinese realist tradition, which set the terms for a deep reflection on Chinese reality and on film that has shaped an important sector of Chinese filmmaking in the subsequent three decades.

An Alternative to Socialist Realism

In its first issue of 1979, *Film Art* (*Dianying yishu*) published Bai Jingsheng's "Discussion on the Evolution of Montage" ("Tantan mengtaiqi de fazhan"). The author, a professor at the Beijing Film Academy, was the first to directly discuss Bazin's cinematic realism. Two issues later, *Film Art* brought out "On the Modernization of Film Language" where Li Tuo and director Zhang Nuanxin overtly referred to Bazin as well as to Italian neorealism and the French New Wave. In 1980, Li Tuo published another article in *Film Culture* (*Dianying wenhua*)—"A School of Thought on Film Aesthetics Worth Paying Attention To: On the 'Long Take Theory'"

("Yige zhide zhongshi de dianying meixue xuepai—guanyu 'chang jingtou lilun'")[4]—this time cowritten with Zhou Chuanji, one of the professors of the future Fifth Generation at the Beijing Film Academy.

Li Tuo and Zhang Nuanxin's understanding of Bazin was directly influenced by American scholar Brian Henderson's article "Two Types of Film Theory,"[5] which distinguished two opposed approaches to film: one that aligned itself with Eisenstein's montage theory and the other that shared Bazin's conception of cinematic realism. Henderson's distinction played a significant role in the debates that continued into the '80s. At the time, Chinese film was still dominated by a strong tradition of socialist realism inherited from the Soviet film school and applied to all Chinese official art forms. The concept of "montage" in China [*mengtaiqi*] directly refers to Soviet cinema and not to the connotations that the French word possesses. As a result, one's opposition to the use of montage in film is not merely aesthetic but inevitably political: "*montage interdit*" must be taken as a riposte to the official conception of film art. The Chinese film community, in need of theoretical and formal renewal, welcomed Bazin's approach as the most promising alternative to socialist realism.

In 1981, China Film Press published the translation of Siegfried Kracauer's *Theory of Film: The Redemption of Physical Reality* (1960),[6] on which Shao Mujun had already worked back in the 1960s. According to Hu Ke,[7] Shao Mujun and other scholars understood Kracauer's and Bazin's theories as closely linked to each other. The "realism" they both advocated was then translated as *xieshizhuyi* rather than *xianshizhuyi*, a more accurate translation in Chinese. *Xieshi* means "writing or painting realistically," drawing attention to method rather than subject matter. In Hao Jian's view,[8] such a translation not only expresses a deep misunderstanding of Bazin's philosophical, aesthetic, and cultural background, it also results from a deliberate attempt to distance Kracauer's and Bazin's realisms from socialist realism, commonly translated as *shehuizhuyi xianshizhuyi*. Equally, this term might help erect a bridge between Bazin's realism and an earlier Chinese social realism—translated as *shehui xieshizhuyi*—that characterized most of Shanghai film production from the 1920s to the 1940s. This social realism in fact bears striking resemblance to the Italian neorealism that Bazin trumpeted: an attention to social issues and to the everyday life of ordinary people, a concerted if nonsystematic effort to shoot on location, the use of natural light and naturalistic acting. However, Chinese social realism departs from Bazinian realism—though not from certain neorealist films—in the sense that it unabashedly promotes the political views of its leftist directors. It is also built on melodrama and classical narrative structure, far beyond what operates in even the most commercial neorealist efforts.

As film production stabilized in the '80s, filmmakers and theorists looked for an aesthetic theory that could coexist with official ideology, while allowing creative independence, including a dialogue with Western ideas. Such a theory had to address the very nature of cinema, and yet be flexible enough to be adapted to new contexts. Bazin's notions, already partly available, seemed able to blend into China's social realist heritage and so served this role. A series of simplified catchphrases cropped up that were indebted to his ideas, without directly translating his formulations: *jishi meixue*, meaning "aesthetic of the report" or "'on the spot' aesthetic," *zhenshi meixue*, meaning "aesthetic of the truth" or "aesthetic of the real," and *changjingtou lilun*, meaning "theory of the long take." These became the watchwords of a whole generation of film theorists.

A New Cinematic Language

The Fourth Generation of Chinese filmmakers[9] helped bring about this "translation" of Bazin's realism into Chinese terms, putting theory into practice after 1979. Their earliest works—Zhang Zheng's *Little Flower* (*Xiaohua*, 1980), Yang Yanjin's *Troubled Laughter* (*Kunao ren de xiao*, 1979), Wu Tianming and Teng Wenji's *Reverberations of Life* (*Shenghuo de chanyin*, 1979), and Han Xiaolei's *Cherries* (*Ying*, 1979)—express an unmistakable desire to renew film language. They pursued their experiments in 1981 and 1982 with a more systematic use of the long take, natural light, on-site shooting, naturalistic acting, and with innovative and relatively complex strategies of narration. These elements are apparent in Zhang Nuanxin's *Drive to Win* (*Sha Ou*, 1981), Zheng Dongjian and Xu Rongming's *Neighbor* (*Linju*, 1981), Yan Jianjin's *The Alley* (*Xiao jie*), Huang Shuqin's *Contemporary People* (*Dangdairen*, 1981), Han Xiaolei's *Lawyer on Probation* (*Tianxi lüshi*, 1982), Huang Jianzhong's *As You Like It* (*Ruyi*, 1982), Teng Wenji's *The Village in the City* (*Dushi li de cunzhuang*, 1982), Ding Yinnan's *Countering, Lights* (*Ni Guang*, 1982), and Wu Yigong's *My Memory of Old Beijing* (*Chengnan jiushi*, 1983).

By the middle of the decade, no one contested that Fourth Generation filmmakers had definitely become theoretically informed, pointing to Ding Yinnan's *He is in a Special Zone* (*Ta zai tequ*, 1984), Guo Baochang's *Fogbound* (*Wujie*, 1984), and Zhang Nuanxin's *Sacrificed Youth* (*Qingchun ji*, 1985). After all, this latter director had coauthored the key article "On the Modernization of Film Language" that had served as the manifesto of the era. Yet none of these directors ever directly paid tribute to Bazin or mentioned him in discussing their work. Furthermore, they put into practice mainly the technical aspects of his approach to realism (camera work, editing, and narrative structure), not his ideas about subject matter and the depiction of human relationships. Such a privileging of form over content aimed to renew film language by pulling cinema away from the theatricality and literary forms that had hampered Chinese cinema all along. Attention to film language not only asserted film's maturity and independence, it underwrote the idea of personal directorial expression in this medium. In this respect, realism rapidly proved too limited an approach, and Chinese directors intensified and developed their own repertoire of formal experiments. As Zhang Wei argued in "The Fundamental Shortcomings of the 'On the Spot' Aesthetic and Filmmakers' Personal Expression" ("Jishi meixue de genben yu dianying yishujia de gexing fangxie"),[10] the Fourth Generation needed more stylistic freedom. Realism was a mere stage.

The superficiality of the Fourth Generation's interpretation of Bazin is partially explained by how few of his essays had been translated in the early 1980s. But the main reason for their simplification and "misunderstanding," according to Dai Jinhua, stems from a strategic adaptation of his ideas to China's political context:[11] by privileging form over content, style over expression, Fourth Generation directors were able to avoid taking a political stance. They traded realism for artistic independence, historical responsibility for personal style.

Their focus on innovation brought the Fourth Generation into line with other artists during this period of drastic change when so many were breaking out of the repressive mentality of the Cultural Revolution era. In literature, such a break emerged with "scar" literature and the linguistic innovations in fiction and poetry that rapidly followed. In cinema, it took the Fifth Generation directors to bring this renewal to its apogee. From 1978 to 1982, the directors of the future Fifth Generation were studying at the Beijing Film Academy mostly under the supervision of Fourth Generation directors whom they wished to surpass. Taking their aspirations even further, and inspired both by Western films they saw at the Academy and by the Western literature and theories that were quickly being introduced in translation, they developed a distinctive artistic opposition to earlier forms of Chinese cinema. In particular, they took over where the Fourth Generation left off with regard to countering film's dependence on literature, and created a much more daring formal language. Stylistic expressivity marks the very first works of this group: Zheng Junzhao's *One and Eight* (*Yige he bage*, 1983); Chen Kaige's trilogy *Yellow Earth* (*Huang tudi*, 1984), *King of Children* (*Haizi wang*, 1987), and *The Big Parade* (*Da yue bing*, 1986); and Zhang Yimou's *Red Sorghum* (*Hong gaoliang*, 1987). These revolutionary works only came about after years of reflection on the nature of cinema; Bazin played a serious role in those reflections.

A Direct Relationship Between Film and Reality

Bazin's conception of an ontological relationship between film image and pro-filmic reality provided Chinese filmmakers with the best way to free themselves from their former political straitjacket, for it acknowledged the camera's capacity to record the real beyond human interference, thus undermining the conception of cinema as an inevitably ideological medium. Reality can be represented "as it is," not through the lens of ideology, and the filmic image can be "true to life" [*bizhen*], that is, close to one's own experience and conditions. Hence the value that suddenly accrued to individual expression: reality is seen through subjective eyes, and the testimony of one's own direct relationship to reality does not obviate the work of the objective lens that grasps the light coming through it without human interference. Subjectivity is a guarantee of authenticity, which in turn subtends realism. This new "on the spot" aesthetics [*jishimeixue*] claimed to break up the old way of thinking, since visual innovation would inevitably encourage innovation in conceptual thinking. It also broadened and democratized the representation of reality, expressing an appetite for the ordinary life of ordinary people that emerged within the Chinese art world at the end of the 1970s. The amateur photography exhibition "Nature-Society-Humanity," organized in Beijing Zhongshan Park in April 1979, had actually launched a general movement in Chinese arts toward this more basic kind of realism, a return to nature and to the everyday.

The first half of the 1980s witnessed a full flowering of this discourse on the relationship between film and reality.[12] It was not until the end of the decade, however, that Chinese theorists and filmmakers started to grasp the whole magnitude of Bazin's thought on the subject. Until then it had been understood as a simple recovery of material reality, sometimes critiqued for not being able to penetrate the nature of the underlying social framework of everyday life; now several articles tried to correct this misunderstanding and question the relation of "'On the spot' realism" to Bazin's theory.[13] This gradual maturing of views of Bazin could be anticipated since many of his texts were at last available. *World Cinema* (*Shijie dianying*) had brought out translations (mostly by Cui Junyan) of "L'Evolution du language cinématographique," "Ontologie de l'image photographique," "Le Mythe du cinéma total," and "Une grande oeuvre: *Umberto D.*,"[14] while articles discussing his notions were translated by Zhou Chuanji, Hu Bin, Bao Yuheng, and Dan Wanli. One could also now find a flourishing discourse about Bazin, right up to the moment of the Tiananmen Square incident,[15] including the translation of the chapter of Dudley Andrew's *André Bazin*[16] that details his intellectual roots. The cornerstone of this turn to Bazin was without question the translation of *What Is Cinema?*[17] by Cui Junyan for China Film Press, in 1987.

Ironically, all this publishing activity rolled off the presses just as his prestige among intellectuals in the Chinese film world had started to go into eclipse. In August 1984, two Chinese scholars, Cheng Jihua and Chen Mei, organized a seminar on Western contemporary theory in Beijing (the first of a series of five) that introduced structuralist semiotics, psychoanalysis, ideological critique, and feminism to the Chinese film community.[18] That summer, Nick Brown gave a talk on contemporary film theory[19] in which he argued that Bazin's approach had been superseded by these current theories. As a result, Chinese film theorists turned to the most recent Western ideas as the next step in their evolution toward international standards. Actually, their initial interest in Bazin had been triggered by this very urge to catch up to classical film theory after the Cultural Revolution. Even though this first phase had been animated by heated debates, the pace both of the country's reforms and of its cultural growth was such that classical theory soon found itself unable to satisfy the intellectual appetite of China's film theorists even before the key classical writings had been properly analyzed and digested.

Bazin's Heritage

Despite the decline of classical theory in the face of newer trends, Bazin's writings would continue to have an effect on Chinese film production right up to today. First, we must credit his influence, albeit not exclusive, on the works of the Fifth Generation up through the Tiananmen Square incident: most of their early works are characterized by narrative ambiguity, elusiveness, a yearning for authenticity, and the use of both the long shot and the long take. Directors such as Tian Zhuangzhuang, Li Shaohong and Ning Ying even developed an approach inspired by Italian neorealism—and thus by Bazin—that would continue to shape their later films.[20]

However, it would be at the turn of the decade that Bazin's influence on Chinese cinema took on a new dimension, one that moved away from the Fifth Generation. Right after Tiananmen, China's marginal art world expressed a strong desire for truth, authenticity, and individual expression in art. Following the impulse initiated by the "new realist" literature at the very end of the 1980s, an independent documentary movement emerged in the early 1990s with directors such as Wu Wenguang, Kang Jianning, Duan Jichuan, Wang Guangli, Shi Jian, and Jiang Yue.[21] Furthermore, the Sixth Generation of Chinese directors revived, in their feature films, the "on the spot" aesthetics that had been inspired by Bazin's writings and tentatively developed by the Fourth Generation a decade earlier. Zhang Yuan, Wang Xiaoshuai, Lou Ye, He Jianjun and others[22] in fact claimed to reveal the contradictions inherent within Chinese society by laying bare its raw, underlying reality thanks to a direct, unmediated relation to the real. The so-called post-socialist realism[23] of their work drew simultaneously, even if not always consciously, on Bazin's ideas and on Chinese social realism.

Director Jia Zhangke's work represents a very specific evolution of Chinese cinematic realism à la Bazin visible at the turn of the century. According to Jason McGrath,[24] while Jia Zhangke's first projects were characteristic of the 1990s post-socialist realism, his following films, starting from *Platform* (*Zhantai*, 2000), can be inscribed in the broader tradition of international art cinema. These present a type of aestheticized long-take realism that has become prominent in the global film festival and art-house circuit—a neo-Bazinian realism that pushes the limits of Bazin's approach.

Jia Zhangke benefited from the undeniable improvement in the understanding of Bazin's theory within the Chinese academic world during his studies at the Beijing Film Academy in the 1990s. He explicitly adapted the French critic's approach not only to the new social, political, and aesthetic context of China in the twenty-first century but also to the new technology of the digital camera.[25] With this device, he aimed to establish a new relationship between the image and the real: realism is no longer guaranteed by the automatic, mechanical link between image and pro-filmic referent assured by light imprinting itself on celluloid; it is rather the intimacy of the director's presence at the center of the filmed reality—made possible by the small digital camera—that guarantees realism. This presence expresses itself simultaneously both as "immediate" rapport with the referent and as "distanciation" from the referent. The spectator's perception of reality comes through the link that the director makes between his camera and the real. Such a conception relies on an ethic that underlies Bazin's conception of film and life.

Jia Zhangke perpetuates the relationship that Chinese theorists and filmmakers have maintained with Bazin's writings since 1979. Bazin's realism has supported a recurring critique of entrenched political and artistic views, instigating alternatives. While the Fourth and Fifth Generations drew on his theory to reject a rigid and moribund socialist realism and to work toward a more independent and expressive art form, the Sixth Generation relied on their own understanding of Bazin's realism to condemn both the allegorical cinema of the Fifth Generation and the ideological representation of reality that still informs all official images. As for Jia Zhangke's neo-Bazinian realism, it offers an alternative to both Hollywood and Chinese entertainment cinema.

In advocating a pre-ideological attention to the magma of the real, Bazin appears to have been a key support for a succession of Chinese new waves and trends—not only in Mainland China but also in Taiwan and Hong Kong.[26] His conception of a privileged relationship between the film image and its referent, although systematically subject to reassessment and disavowal, has encouraged a constant renewal of film language, supporting a continuing critique of social reality and its representations.

China may have been among the last places to catch wind of André Bazin, but she can be counted the first to commemorate the fiftieth anniversary of his death, indicating just how far his presence has penetrated the film culture of the P.R.C. In June 2008, Shanghai University cosponsored a conference on "Bazin in China" with *Cahiers du Cinéma*. Gathering there were Jia Zhangke and Xie Fei from the Mainland, Hou Hsiao-hsien from Taiwan, and Ann Hui from Hong Kong, all eloquently holding forth about Bazin's relation to their films. That same spring, *Contemporary Cinema (Dangdai Dianying)* brought out a special issue on Bazin featuring articles by Chinese scholars.[27] Clearly, his impact on Chinese film and film culture has not abated; it seems especially needed at this crucial moment when vast transformations are underway in every cinema sector (technology, techniques, distribution, exhibition) on the Mainland and throughout the "Chinas."

Notes

1. "Bazin" was translated as "Bashan" in the 1960s, then as "Bashang" in the late 1970s, and as "Bazan" today.
2. Henri Agel, *Esthétique du cinéma* (Paris: Presses Universitaires de France, 1959).

3. "Chinese" is understood as "Mainland Chinese" here as in the rest of this essay.

4. In the first edition of *Film Culture* (*Dianying wenhua*), published by China's Social Sciences Press (Zhonguo shehui kexue chubanshe) in 1980.

5. Brian Henderson. "Two Types of Film Theory," *Film Quarterly*, 24:3 (Spring 1971).

6. Siegfried Kracauer, *Theory of Film: The Redemption of Physical Reality* (New York: Oxford University Press, 1960).

7. Hu Ke, "André Bazin's Influence and the Concept of Truth Film in China" ("Zhongguo dianying zhenshi guannian yu Bazan yingxiang"), *Contemporary Cinema* (*Dangdai dianying*), 145 (April 1, 2008).

8. Hao Jian. "André Bazin in China: Spoken of and Forgotten" ("Andelei Bazan zai Zhongguo: bei yanshuo yu bei xiaojian"), *Contemporary Cinema* (*Dangdai dianying*), 145 (April 1, 2008).

9. Chinese film history is commonly and conveniently divided into generations. The "Fourth Generation" refers to filmmakers who experienced the Cultural Revolution and started making films in 1978. The "Fifth Generation" was the first to graduate from the Beijing Film Academy in 1982 after the institution reopened its doors in 1978, and the "Sixth Generation" started making films after 1989. Although this terminology is contested by film scholars and more often by filmmakers, I follow it in this essay to track the evolution of Chinese cinema in relation to Bazin's realism.

10. Published in *Contemporary Cinema* (*Dandai Dianying*), 5 (1985).

11. Dai Jinhua. "Leaning Tower: Focus on the Fourth Generation" ("Xieta: zhongdu disidai"), *Film Art*, 4 (1989).

12. See Zheng Xuelai, "Views On Different Schools of Thought In Contemporary Film Aesthetics" ("Dui xiandai dianying meixue sichao de jidian kanfa"), *Research in Literature and Art* (*Wenyi yanjiu*), 4 (1981); Yang Ni, "Tchekov and Montage: On Montage Metaphors in Contemporary Films" ("Qikefu yu mengtaiqi – qiantan xiandai dianying zhong de mengtaiqi yinyu"), *Film Art* (*Dianying yishu*), 5 (1981); Luo Huisheng, "Analyzing 'Total Realism': On Bazin's Understanding of Film Aesthetics" ("'Zongti xianshizhuyi' pouxi – guanyu Bazan de dianying meixue sixiang"), *Research in Literature and Art* (*Wenyi yanjiu*), 1 (1984); Chen Xihe, "On Bazin's Conception of Film Truth" ("Lun Bazan de dianying zhenshi guannian"), *Contemporary Cinema* (*Dangdai diaying*), 1 (1984).

13. Shao Mujun, "Random Thoughts and Report on Film Aesthetics" ("Dianying meixue suixiangji yao"), *Film Art* (*Dianying yishu*), 1 (1984); Hao Dazheng, "Film Theory and Today's Works" ("Dianying guannian yu dangqian chuangzuo"), *Film Art*, (*Dianying yishu*), 3 (1985); Deng Zhufei, "Notes on the Nature of the Report" ("Jishixing zhaji"), *Film Art* (*Dianying yishu*), 8 (1986).

14. "L'Evolution du langage cinématographique" appeared in *World Cinema* (*Shijie dianying*), 2 (1980); The other four essays appeared in *World Cinema* (*Shijie dianying*), 6 (1981).

15. Yao Xiaomeng, "Interpreting Bazin" ("Chanshi Bazan"), *Contemporary Cinema* (*Dangdai dianying*), 5 (1989); Xu Zengjing, "A Question Elaborated by History: What Is Cinema" ("Lishi de shewen: dianying shi shenme"), *Contemporary Cinema* (*Dangdai dianying*), 1 (1990); Pan Xiutong and Wan Liling, "Classification and Analysis of the Long Take" ("Chang jingtou bianxi"), *Contemporary Cinema* (*Dangdai dianying*), 1 (1990); Zhang Sun, "Bazin's Ideal Aesthetics" ("Bazan de meixuelixiang"), *Film Art* (*Dianying yishu*), 5 (1992); Liu Yunzhou, "Philosophical Concept in Bazin's Film Theory" ("Bazan dianying lilun zhexueguan"), *Contemporary Cinema* (*Dangdai dianying*), 3 (2000); Jin Danyuan, "On the Philosophical Background of the Theory of the 'Long Take' and its Signification Today" ("Lun 'changjingtou' lilun beihouzhexue qiji dangxia yiyi"), *Film and Theater* (Xiju yishu), 6 (2000); Tian Song, "Achievement and End of the Myth of 'Total Cinema'" ("'Wanzheng dianying' shenhua de shixian yu zhongjie"), *Contemporary Cinema* (*Dangdai dianying*), 6 (2000).

16. Dudley Andrew, *André Bazin* (New York: Oxford University Press, 1978).

17. Cui Junyan translated, from the French, all the essays that the French volume contains.

18. Contemporary theory was first introduced to China in the early 1980s with Li Youzheng's article "Structuralism and Film Aesthetics" ("Jiegouzhuyi yu dianying meixue"), published in *Digest of Film Translations* (*Dianying yishu yicong*), 3 (1980). The same issue of the magazine published an article entitled "An Introduction to Metz's Film Semiotics" ("Meici dianying fuhaoxue shuping"), translated by Wu Hanqing. It was brought in however as a complete theoretical system in 1984 through the seminars organized by Cheng Jihua and Chen Mei. The interest in Western contemporary theory peaked in China in the late 1980s. Dudley Andrew aimed to integrate Bazin into contemporary trends in a series of lectures at the Beijing Film Academy in fall 1988.

19. The exact title of Nick Brown's talk was "Some questions concerning contemporary film theory and the history of Western film theory."

20. Other Fourth and Fifth Generation directors made realist urban films in the 1990s. These were however isolated and uncharacteristic efforts.

21. Important works are: Wu Wenguang's *Bumming in Beijing: The Last Dreamers* (*Liulang Beijing: zui hou de mengxiang zhe*, 1990), Kang Jianning's *Sand and Sea* (*Sha yu hai*, 1990), Duan Jichuan and Wen Pulin's *The Sacred Site of Ascetism* (*Qingbuku xiuzhe de shengdi*, 1992), Wang Guangli and Shi Jian's *I Graduated* (*Wo biye le*, 1992), and Jiang Yue's *The Other Shore* (*Bi an*, 1993).

22. In films such as Zhang Yuan's *Mum* (*Mama*, 1990), *Beijing Bastards* (*Beijing zazhong*, 1993), Lou Ye's *Weekend Lovers* (*Zhoumo qingren*, 1993), *Don't Be Young* (*Weiqing shaonü*, 1995), Wang Xiaoshuai's *The Days* (*Donchun de rizi*, 1992), and He Jianjun's *Postman* (*Youchai*, 1995).

23. Jason McGrath appropriately uses this term to define the Sixth Generation's early works in *Postsocialist Modernity: Chinese Cinema, Literature, and Criticism in the Market Age* (Stanford, CA: Stanford University Press, 2008), 132.

24. McGrath, *Postsocialist Modernity*, 130–36.

25. Jia Zhangke, remarks at Shanghai University conference on "Bazin in China," June 17, 2008.

26. Bazin's realism undeniably influenced Hong Kong's and Taiwan's cinemas, particularly in the 1980s. The history of these influences differs from that of Mainland China. For a valuable presentation of the impact of Bazin's realism on Taiwanese cinema, see Ru-Shou Robert Chen's article "André Bazin from the Lens of Taiwan Cinema" ("Cong Taiwan dianying guankan Bazan xieshizhuyi lilun"), *Film Appreciation Journal* (*Dianying xinshang xuekan*), 138 (March 2009).

27. *Contemporary Cinema* (*Dangdai dianying*), 145 (April 1, 2008).

32

Japanese Readings
The Textual Thread

Kan Nozaki

Before the Translation of *What Is Cinema?*

In the 1950s and 1960s, *Film Criticism* (*Eiga Hyōōron*) was the most ambitious and influential film journal in Japan. Founded in 1926, at the end of the Taisho era, the journal experienced a considerable revival after World War II. Bringing together critics like Tadashi Iijima and Tadao Satō, as well as writers, poets, and young directors like Yasuzō Masumura and Nagisa Ōshima, the journal represented a new way of thinking about film in Japan. In December 1959, it published a special edition, "Japanese Cinema's New Wave," sparking the first talk of the fledgling movement emerging from the young directors at Shōchiku Studios.

So it was in keeping with the guiding principles of the journal that it would publish an article by Susumu Okada and Yuriko Mayama's in 1960 with the title: "*Qu'est-ce que le cinéma?* d'André Bazin."[1] This is, to my knowledge, the first appearance of Bazin's name in the Japanese press. In this article, discussing the first two volumes of Bazin's collected work, the authors underline the fundamental importance of Bazin's criticism which, according to them, "tries to shed light on the *raison d'être* of cinema, with even more vehemence than Sartre in his *What Is Literature?*" In the same issue as this excellent introductory article, the journal published the scenario for *Rokudenashi* (*Good-for-Nothing*, 1960), the first film by Kijū Yoshida, one of the figureheads of the Japanese New Wave.

One year after this first appearance, Bazin's name comes up in an article by Yuriko Mayama, "L'époque du scénario,"[2] published in *Scénario*, the official journal of the Japan Writers Guild. In this article, Mayama describes "For an Impure Cinema: Defense of Adaptation" emphasizing the "pragmatic" aspect of Bazin's ideas: by considering cinema's use of literary works as a means of enrichment, Bazin could encourage "the talented directors who are currently confronted with big problems" in Japan. With these two articles, Bazin's theories received confirmation in the cinematic world of Japan during an era of its profound transformation.

The Poet Kokai Translates Bazin

Soon after the publication of *Qu'est-ce que le cinéma?* in France, a Japanese poet began to translate all four volumes of Bazin's *magnum opus* on his own. Eiji Kokai was born in 1931 in Tokyo. After completing his studies in the French literature department at the University of Tokyo, he first became a teacher at a middle school, then at a high school in Tokyo, before obtaining a position at the University of Fine Arts in Tama. Appointed professor at the National University of Yokohama in 1966, he taught in its faculty of education sciences for nearly thirty years, retiring in 1995.

Best known as a poet—he authored several collections and was for a time president of the Japanese Society of Contemporary Poets—Kokai was equally an active pedagogue, editing numerous manuals on the Japanese language. But he has also passionately devoted himself to the translation of Francophone and Spanish poets, especially Henri Michaux and Federico García Lorca. Bazin, himself a talented pedagogue and poetry enthusiast, found in Kokai the ideal translator.[3]

Kokai's work as a translator is indeed exemplary for his dedication and his fidelity to the original work. The translation that he offered is not an abridged version of *Qu'est-ce que le cinéma?*; it is a genuinely *integral* translation that does not omit any text contained in the four volumes of the original.

When one considers that Kokai carried out this immense work all alone, while also translating Henri Michaux's *Complete Works* in four volumes, one cannot help but be struck by his immense productive capacity. Changing the order of the volumes "for the personal reasons of the translator and of the publishing house" (according to the afterword to the second volume of the translation), Kokai published the first Japanese volume of *What Is Cinema?* in 1967. This corresponded to tome 3 of the original, *Cinéma et Sociologie*, while the second Japanese volume (1970) corresponds to Bazin's tome 1. The third volume on neorealism appeared in 1973; and the final Japanese installment (tome 2, "Cinema and the Other Arts") finally arrived in 1976, bringing to a close a full decade of dedicated labor.

This translation was part of the "Fine Arts Collection," a series undertaken in the '60s and '70s by *Bijutsu-shuppansha* (The Fine Arts publishing house) primarily devoted to contemporary and avant-garde art, but also open to film criticism. In addition to *What Is Cinema?*, one can find in this series a book by Susumu Okada called *The Image*,[4] and the Japanese translation of *Surréalisme au cinéma* by Ado Kyrou.

In the postface of the first volume, Kokai admits: "The translation of this book demanded a lot of effort. The style of Bazin is not always very easy, dotted with expressions that do not translate easily into Japanese." Kokai adds, "There must remain numerous rocky phrases. In addition, I surely have made mistakes in spite of myself. I am thus very grateful to readers who might inform me of them." Of course, we can find faults and errors in Kokai's work, as is normal when a translation of such a scale is at stake. It goes without saying that at the time, not a single video or DVD of the films was available. Translating articles on films that one has not seen is a challenge. We can say that Kokai stood up to this challenge very well. Across his chiseled and poetically dense Japanese sentences, the literary qualities of Bazin's writing clearly reveal themselves. Though not a specialist in cinema, Kokai nevertheless possesses profound knowledge of the cinematic art, which must have aided him greatly in his work.

Under the Leadership of Yamada and Hasumi

Soon after the full *What Is Cinema?* was available in Japanese, a fairly new phenomenon appeared in Japan: *la cinéphilie*, in the French sense of the term. Two great critics, both extremely francophile, played a decisive role in this.

Kōichi Yamada was born in Jakarta in 1938. His stay in Paris in the middle of the 1960s, as a student on scholarship from the French government, allowed him to meet the young critics and directors of *Cahiers du Cinéma*, with whom he collaborated actively. Upon his return, he evoked his memories in books and essays. A close friend of François Truffaut—we can trace their friendship thanks to letters published in the director's *Correspondance*[5]—Yamada translated, with Shigehiko Hasumi, Truffaut's *The Films In My Life* in 1979.[6] Published in two volumes, with footnotes that contain valuable information, this work became the guidebook for Japanese directors (and those who aspired to the title). Truffaut's lead article entitled "What do Critics Dream About?" was especially important as the author recounts his childhood memories and cites the words of Bazin, his benefactor. We can add to this an entire series of articles and books by Yamada about Truffaut and the French New Wave, written in a charming style and with a contagious passion, culminating in *Truffaut, A Cinematic Life* (*Truffaut, aru eigateki jinsei*), published by Heibonsha, a book that was honored with the Bunkamura-Deux Magots literary prize in 1991. "François Truffaut, superstar au Japon": this is the title of an article in the French daily *Libération*.[7] Yamada played a significant role in helping the Japanese discover and appreciate Truffaut's films. And thanks to his writings, the image of André Bazin as Truffaut's adoptive and spiritual father has become familiar.

Despite all this, Bazin's theories have not exercised as striking an influence in Japan as in China: there, soon after the end of the Cultural Revolution era, Bazin was considered the indisputable *maître à penser*, originator of a cinematic realism that liberated China from its hardened communist aesthetic. In Japan, it is instead Bazin the man (to the detriment of Bazin the theorist) who drew the attention of cinephiles as an appealing personality in French film history. Somehow, despite the already-existing integral translation—which admittedly disappeared quickly from bookstores and became unobtainable except in libraries and secondhand bookstores—the Japanese were far from conscious of the theoretical impact of Bazin's thoughts on cinema.

One factor may be that Shigehiko Hasumi, the most powerful figure in film and literary criticism in Japan, author of innumerable books in these fields who exerted (and continues to exert) enormous influence over devotees of cinema, has always revealed himself to be quite reticent on the subject of Bazin. Hasumi himself admits that as an unconditional admirer of John Ford films, he has never been able to forgive Bazin for neglecting the incomparable genius of that director.[8] Having at his disposal an entire arsenal of critical concepts elaborated through dialogue with Barthes, Deleuze, and Foucault, but going beyond these with his immense love of cinema and his "moving body sight" capable of delving into the most secret details of a film, Hasumi has never had a particular need to turn to Bazin to form his arguments.[9]

From *Cahiers du Cinéma Japon* to University Research

During the 1990s, *Cahiers du Cinéma Japon* played a remarkable role amongst cinephiles nourished by Yamada's and Hasumi's books. The Japanese editors of this version of the famous French journal were not content with publishing only translations of the French articles; they took the initiative to publish texts on their own, engaging young Japanese critics, among them the future directors Kiyoshi Kurosawa, Shinji Aoyama, Akihiko Shiota and Kunitoshi Manda, all former students at Rikkyō University who had taken Shigehiko Hasumi's filmology course.

The one who played the role of Bazin for this group was Yōichi Umemoto, professor at the National University of Yokohama who, with Kokai, organized a ciné-club at the Franco-Japanese Institute and was a fervent defender of the auteurs of world cinema. When he was a student in Paris, very moved by *Le Dernier Métro* (1980), Umemoto wrote a long letter to Truffaut, who responded to it straight away by sending along one of Bazin's books. On that day, Truffaut lit the path for the young man who determined to become a film critic.[10] Completely attached to the *Cahiers* values, Umemoto instilled the contemporary spirit of French criticism in young Japanese cinephiles with his energetic language, drawing especially on the writing of Serge Daney, whose book *Persévérance* he translated into Japanese.[11] Umemoto and his colleagues, without directly examining Bazin's work, greatly contributed to circulating the style of watching a film from a post-Bazinian point of view, since the French critics who served as their reference points, starting with Daney, were all more or less the heirs of the Bazin tradition.

Meanwhile, Bazin's work in its entirety began to be an object of university study during the 1990s. Before this, there had only been one serious analysis: *The Filmic System of the New Wave* by Tadashi Iijima.[12] Iijima, professor at Waseda University and one of the pioneers of film criticism in Japan, paraphrased Bazin's books at length in the first volume of his trilogy on the theoretical history of the French New Wave. To the presentation of Bazin's articles were added reviews of articles concerning Bazin, beginning with Jean Laurence (*Le Cinéma et le temps*, 1954) through Dudley Andrew ("André Bazin," an article published in *Film Comment* in 1973), by way of Rohmer, Sadoul, and Metz. If Iijima's work constitutes a sort of summary of readings that bring together valuable bibliographic information, this was part of the effort at the university level in the 1990s to finally confront André Bazin's articles themselves, attempting to detect the original ideas in their nascent state, and to seize their essential dynamism.

Kiyoshi Takeda, professor at Waseda University, launched the academic study of Bazin with his article "Rethinking André Bazin,"[13] which highlights the idea of "self-representability" that lies at the heart of Bazin's criticism. Within the film study group directed by Takeda at Waseda, Chié Niita wrote an article on *French Cinema of the Occupation and Resistance*, a book that had gone unnoticed in Japan. I myself devoted a series of articles to Bazin entitled "A Man Who Believed in Cinema," an attempt to shed light on the evolution of Bazin's thought across several of his key notions.[14] Finally, the translation of Gilles Deleuze's monumental books *Cinéma 1* and *Cinéma 2*[15] helped in this renewal of interest in Bazin, as the philosopher often renders homage to the critic, underlining the decisive importance of Bazin's theories for the cinematic thought of today.

Toward a New Translation

What assessment can we give of the reception of André Bazin in Japan after fifty years? We could certainly note that his name continues to appear in film and academic journals, indicating a lasting interest in the man and his ideas, especially in the context of the history of the French New Wave. But his influence has always seemed to limit itself to the realm of critics and Francophile academics. What's regrettable is the lack of any Japanese directors who claim

Bazin's influence. This contrast is accentuated when we think of the exaltation that "the revelation of Japanese cinema"[16] had provoked among French criticism in Bazin's day.

However, we must not hastily conclude from this that Bazin's work does not hold sway among Japanese directors. During a colloquium that I organized in 2009 to commemorate the semicentennial of Bazin's death,[17] the director Nobuhiro Suwa gave a talk on "The Ontology of Ambiguity" and cited an extract of his new film *Yuki and Nina* (2009) to show how much the aesthetic aspect of Bazin's theory can enlighten a filmmaker in the quest for genuine expression. Dialogue, then, between Japanese directors and André Bazin is still open. Even if his theories have generally not won over key directors, Bazin's attitude toward cinema stimulates and encourages them.

And from a critical point of view, Japanese cinema offers a nearly limitless field of investigation for those searching for inspiration from Bazin, since the cinema of Japan distinguishes itself by the existence of numerous auteurs known for the "one-scene one-cut" style of shooting advocated by Bazin. Indeed, from Mizoguchi to the young contemporary filmmakers, through Tatsumi Kumashiro and Shinji Somai, masters of this form abound. Without being able to speak of Bazin's direct influence, we can always examine their distinctiveness by referring to Bazin's concepts.[18]

The most desirable way to pull Bazin from the intellectual "ghetto" would be the publication of a new translation, not necessarily of the entirety of the four volumes of *Qu'est-ce que le cinéma?*, but of his foundational articles, starting with "Ontology of the Photographic Image" and "The Myth of Total Cinema." Rendering Bazin's fundamental texts accessible to Japanese readers, in a renewed translation and in pocket format, is a project that I have considered for a long time, and which is now in the midst of being realized. The Kobunsha Press, which has had great success in its new translations of classic articles, has now added Bazin to its collection. The new English translation by Timothy Barnard, accompanied by his extremely valuable notes, will help us greatly clarify the text. Bazin's work, represented in its quintessence, will thus meet a large Japanese readership, inviting it to think of the cinema and its audiovisual culture by confronting it with ideas professed over half a century ago, which still remain incredibly strong and pertinent.

Notes

1. Susumu Okada and Yuriko Mayama, "*Qu'est-ce que le cinéma?* d'André Bazin," *La Critique cinématographique (Eiga hyōron)*, July 1960, 64–70.
2. Yuriko Mayama, "L'époque du scénario," *Scénario*, June 1961, 84–87.
3. Kokai's works are gathered in the eight volumes of *Oeuvres choisies* (Tokyo: Maruzen, 2007).
4. In this book about the link between man and the visual image, a chapter devoted to "Langage cinématographique renouvelé" contains remarks on Bazin's theories on Italian neorealism; Susumu Okada, *L'Image* (Tokyo: Bijutsu-shuppannsha, 1969), chapter 4.
5. Letters of exchange between the director and his friend Yamada are found in François Truffaut, *Correspondence 1945–1984* (New York: Cooper Square, 1990), 399–400, 406. Published in French as *Correspondance* (Paris: Hatier, 1990).
6. François Truffaut, *Mes films, ma vie* (*Waga eiga, waga jinsei*); *Rêve de cinéma, critique de rêve* (*Eiga no yume, yume no hihyō*), trans. Kōichi Yamada and Shigehiko Hasumi (Tazawa-shobō, 1979).
7. *Libération*, June 18, 2003.
8. Shigehiko Hasumi, *Notes sur le cinématographe* (Tokyo: University of Tokyo Press, 2008), 410.

9. As a cross-section of his critical writings, see the monographic study on Ozu, translated into French (Shigehiko Hasumi, *Yasujiro Ozu* [Paris: Cahiers du Cinéma, 1998]).

10. See *Libération*, June 18, 2003.

11. Serge Daney, *Persévérance*, trans. Yōichi Umemoto (Tokyo: Film Art, 1996).

12. Gathering articles published in the journal *Le Décade du cinéma* (Kinema junpō) in 1975, the first tome of Tadashi Iijima, *Le Systeme cinématographique de la Nouvelle Vague* (Tokyo: Tōjusha, 1980), is devoted to Bazin, but also to Alexandre Astruc.

13. Kiyoshi Takeda, "Repenser André Bazin" (André Bazin saikō), *Filmologie* (Eigagaku), 1 (1987).

14. Kan Nozaki, "Un homme qui croyait au cinéma: introduction à la pensée cinématographique d'André Bazin," *Cultura philologica* (Tokyo: Hitotsubashi University Press, 1995). Three other articles followed this one, all published in this journal in 1996, 1997, and 1998, and now accessible on the Internet (CiNii).

15. Gilles Deleuze, *Cinéma*, vol. 1: *L'Image-temps*, trans. Kuniichi Uno et al.; vol. 2: *L'Image-mouvement*, trans. Osamu Zaitsu and Susumu Saitō (Tokyo: Hōsei University Press, 2006 and 2008).

16. André Bazin, "La leçon de style du cinéma japonais," in *Le cinéma de la cruauté* (Paris: Flammarion, 1987), 204–205.

17. The international colloquium "André Bazin et l'origine de la pensée moderne du cinéma," included the following speakers: Ronald Chen, Tamaki Tsuchida, Nobuhiro Suwa; moderator: Kan Nozaki; January 28, 2009, the University of Tokyo.

18. Cf. My essay which proposes a reading of Hayao Miyazaki's animated films with the critical tools of Bazin: Kan Nozaki, "Miyazaki cinéaste bazinien," *Cahiers du Cinéma*, December 2008, 82–83. To complete this partial list of Japanese works related to Bazin, we must cite the translation by Toyomaru Satō and Yukiko Nishimura of *Cinéma de la cruauté* (Shinjusha, 2003), and Kuniichi Uno, *Traité sur image et corps* (Misuzu, 2008), which devotes two chapters to Bazin to accentuate the evolution of reflections on cinema in France that led to Deleuze's oeuvre.

Japanese Lessons

Bazin's Cinematic Cosmopolitanism

Ryan Cook

André Bazin's writing on Japanese cinema has been preserved for posterity primarily thanks to the 1975 volume *Cinéma de la cruauté*,[1] edited by François Truffaut, which brings together four of his most significant essays on the subject. Appearing there under the somewhat too-narrow rubric of an auteur profile of Akira Kurosawa, these essays cull insights from a quantity of reviews and articles by Bazin on Japanese films shown in Europe during the 1950s, and synthesize his positions on the Japanese cinema and on world cinema more generally. But while these canonized essays offer something like a reflective summation of his thinking in this area, there is I think intimacy and further evidence to be gained by looking to the additional materials contained in his full archive.

Indeed from the "revelation" of Kurosawa's *Rashomon* (1950) at the 1951 Venice Film Festival through the ensuing near-decade, Bazin wrote frequently and enthusiastically on Japanese cinema. From the start, this enthusiasm was not a response only to a great film, nor only to a great auteur, but to the discovery all at once of a world-class cinema hitherto unknown, or at least "delayed" in Europe by the war (Japanese films had in fact screened in recent memory at Venice under Mussolini, but these had reached Bazin only by word of mouth).[2] More than a great film, *Rashomon* was a glimpse of uncharted territory, of an exterior to the closed circuit of European-American film festivals and distribution, and, to be sure, of a cinematic Orient.

A consistent theme of the many articles that Bazin devoted to the exploration of this new terrain is its "instructive" value. These films were ripe with lessons for Bazin: lessons of style, as he makes clear, but also significantly, and I think compellingly today, lessons in cinematic cosmopolitanism. Bazin elegantly likened the arrival of Japanese films in Europe to the arrival of starlight in the eye of an observer on earth, which is to say at a delay, out of sync with its origin, and necessarily dual. These films inspired him to write in broad strokes, not of the films themselves, but of a whole cinema that shimmered before the eyes even as it remained obscure. Illusory though this cinema may be in Bazin's formulation, he nonetheless shows himself determined to find instruction in what, with less indulgence, might go by names like exoticism or orientalism. I take the lessons that Bazin found in the Japanese cinema as my guides through this corner of the archive.

First the "lessons of style." It goes without saying that Bazin was interested in the realism of Japanese films, to the extent that he proposed a Japanese brand of neorealism in kinship with that of Italy. But what he finds remarkable here is the coexistence of realism with the conventions of traditions in the plastic arts, notably in what he sees as the influence of painting and the Nō theater, among other traditions, on cinematic style in Japan. These conventions impose refining constraints on cinematic naturalism, and he thus identifies a principle of artificially disciplined realism throughout his writings on Japanese cinema and along several fronts: with respect to the effects of genre when he writes of the surprising continuity between the staged samurai period piece and the "neorealist" modern social drama; with respect to tonality and performance when he writes of the tempering of violence with restraint and of the submission of passion to ritual; and in some of his final writing on Japanese cinema in 1958, with respect to the eroticism of Kō Nakahira's *Crazed Fruit* (1956), when he writes of the modulation of sexual frankness with modest reserve.[3] In a related vein, Bazin often expresses his surprise over the paradoxical "authenticity" of melodrama in the Japanese cinema. In contrast to Europe where the dead form of melodrama only resurfaces to "intolerable" and "vulgar" effect, melodrama in Japan maintains for Bazin a living connection to dramatic tradition. In an association that looks forward to the cosmopolitan lessons of the Japanese cinema, this mutual accommodation of melodrama and realism is moreover something that Japanese cinema shares with other non-European cinemas in Bazin's view, notably those of Mexico and India.[4]

The notion of tradition as discipline that Bazin draws from the peculiar realism of Japanese films points to the greater stylistic lesson at hand, which is a model of the relation between the work of art and the civilization in which it takes form. He writes that "good" cinema emerges from the "conjunction of a high civilization with a great theatrical tradition and a great plastic tradition."[5] Japanese cinema, which seems to "ascend back into the night of time" of the traditional arts of theater, painting, and literature,[6] stands in this respect as an ideal or a principle. Unlike in France, where cinema encounters a historical rupture between bourgeois traditions and popular arts,[7] the cinema that it pleases Bazin to imagine in Japan is cut from the cloth of its civilization. (Jean Renoir is an exception to the situation Bazin sees in France, where he says there are only French *films* by individual auteurs and no common French *cinema*; citing the Japanese example, Bazin argues that Renoir is a sole exception, his films being of a piece with French culture and society.)[8] For analogy he invokes salt crystals, any fragment of which, including the smallest, shares the geometry and chemistry of the whole crystallized body. Elegant though this image may be, the somewhat contrived quality of Bazin's linkage of art and civilization is better avowed by other analogies, in which he considers a "vulgar" Japanese film to be as improbable as spilt tea in a Japanese tea ceremony, or as unlikely as the presence of a poorly trimmed cherry tree anywhere on the archipelago. This willful disregard of imperfection speaks to the instructional function that Japanese cinema serves for Bazin in the 1950s: it is a hypothetical model and an ideal.

The second lesson, that of cinematic cosmopolitanism, is concerned less with intrinsic stylistic value than with what value Japanese films are to have within an increasingly international film culture. This lesson has two addressees. First, it aims to instruct critics regarding how to evaluate foreign films. On this point, Bazin considers the notion of "critical relativity." Conceding, in a 1954 essay devoted to Teinosuke Kinugasa's *Gate of Hell* (1953), that his admiration for that film might be informed by an "exoticism" proportionate to what he does not know of the art and civilization of the Far East, and by what he cannot know of the Japanese film industry given the small number of titles released in France, he allows for the fact that foreign films are subject to a changing critical optic not only in their circulation between cultures, but even within the outlook of a single critic whose judgment might be in need of recalibration with time. But in defiance of those who reject exoticism as naïve, Bazin defends what he calls critical "errors of perspective" in the evaluation of foreign films, and sees in his pleasure, however uninformed, an entitlement as well as a critical response with positive value, as much for himself as for those culturally in the know.[9] In the same 1954 essay he formulates an analogy, later reprised in an essay collected in *Cinéma de la cruauté*: his naïve appreciation for Japanese films is comparable to the prestige of Marcel Pagnol among American critics who tend to admire precisely the *wrong* films of the oeuvre, which is to say the films considered the most "vulgar" in Paris. But Bazin refers to this "error" only to demonstrate how correct these American critics in fact are insofar as they admire *The Welldigger's Daughter* (*La Fille du puisatier*, 1940) not as a discrete work, but for the "freedom of mise en scène" which speaks to Pagnol's total oeuvre, and arguably to a tendency of the French cinema as a whole. While the critical optic in New York may be out of sync with that of Paris or Tokyo, it is not altogether invalid or without value. In fact, it contributes to the general value of cinema across time zones, and enriches those cosmopolitan centers at Cannes and Venice, which Bazin credits for promoting a world cinema neglected by regimes of commercial distribution.

The lesson of cosmopolitanism is also addressed to cinema itself. Japan has challenged Western cinema to come to terms with a cinematic other. With *Rashomon*, world cinema has had its baptism. World cinema refers of course not to just another selection of foreign films sharing Paris screens with titles from Sweden, Germany, and England, but to the cinema of other "civilizations," as we have seen, and of discrete distribution networks.[10] On the one hand, Bazin seems to advocate a certain normalization of world cinema that would make of it, in a sense, as ordinary a product as English cinema. To this end he frequently commends or chastises distributors and exhibitors for their efforts or failures to make films accessible. It is a measure of his pragmatism in this respect that Bazin occasionally complains of films that present the viewer with too many "Asiatic faces" or that are too immersed in cultural "complexities"[11] to enjoy wide circulation in France. But these are highly exceptional remarks, and reflect his pre-*Rashomon* speculation over an invisible cinema presumed too specific in its cultural and racial composition for export;[12] far more than a marketably normalized or unmarketably racial Japanese cinema, it is the aforementioned idealism that preoccupies Bazin. After *Rashomon*, it is no longer Japanese films that must adapt to the world, but the world that must accommodate Japanese films. The idealism which they represent for Bazin invariably turns a discussion of any individual film toward a discussion of the Japanese cinema as a whole, and furthermore inspires associations, again and again, of Japan with the other provinces of world cinema, especially Egypt and India. These associations only reinforce Japan's status as an instructive model. Just as modern Turkey's founder, Mustapha Kemal Atatürk, had to exchange his fez for a cap, writes Bazin, the Egyptian cinema has sought national inspiration while facilely imitating Hollywood.[13] On the contrary, the cinema of Japan, like modern Japanese civilization, has taken what it pleased of Hollywood and submitted it to the discipline of its own traditions.

What then does Bazin want from world cinema? What in this respect is his investment in this principle of Japanese cinema? Clearly, his interest is not only touristic or ethnographic.

Indeed, Bazin defiantly deems knowledge of Japan irrelevant to his pleasure in Japanese cinema. But this is also not a humanist valorization of the universal at the expense of the particular. Bazin's agenda does not lie in pursuing a strictly universal language of cinema, not even one like that cited by Jacques Rivette who claims that the only language of importance in Japanese cinema is not Japanese, but mise-en-scène.[14] Rather, what Bazin valorizes through the hypothetical notion of the unity of art and civilization, I argue, is an integrity that can be said to set the ideal condition for membership in a cosmopolitan cinema. This membership entails a dialectic of universalism and particularity. The language of Japanese cinema is mise-en-scène, but it is also Japanese.

Interesting in this respect is the *Cahiers du Cinéma* polemic over the respective merits of Kurosawa and Mizoguchi that took place once *Rashomon* was followed in France by other Japanese films that exceeded Kurosawa's in the "purity" of their cinematic vision. It is Mizoguchi whom Rivette champions for his purity of style in this debate, not as a Japanese director but as an auteur. The Bazin of 1957 acknowledges his own preference for the style of Mizoguchi as well but finds himself revisiting his initial 1952 reaction to *Rashomon* for what it had already contained of the aforementioned dialectic. Bazin originally concedes with regard to *Rashomon* that a traveling shot is a traveling shot in Paris as in Tokyo, but what interests him is the peculiar "rhythm" with which the shot travels[15] and, I would add, what it means that there are traveling shots and traveling shots. In this sense, it is clear that Bazin was drawn from the beginning to Kurosawa's negotiation of "particular inspiration" with the "universal signification" of cinema. With time, once Kurosawa had been accused of "reverse exoticism" in borrowing the cinematic and genre conventions of Hollywood—and of committing his own "errors of judgment," though toward the West—Bazin would find himself faced with an interesting choice between the evidently purer Mizoguchi and the relatively impure Kurosawa. By 1957, it seems that his ideal of Japanese cinema is reframed somewhat, so that it is precisely the impurity of Kurosawa that now appeals to Bazin. To be "impure" is in a sense what it means to claim membership in the world of world cinema, and Bazin seems to say that Kurosawa will teach his own Japanese cinema this very lesson in "indicating" its future through his own "dialectical progress."[16]

To speak of membership and of East and West, or in Bazin's terms of tradition versus modernity as seen in his comments on Turkey and Egypt, lends a political dimension to Japan's idealized cultural integrity. But this Japan, as I have emphasized, is above all an instructional model. It stands foremost not for the possibility of dissolving frontiers, as some would have it, but of crossing them even as they remain intact. Writing on *Gate of Hell*, for example, Bazin processes the idealized integrity of the Japanese cinema, which is to say its particularity, through Paul Valéry's distinction between classical and modern narrative, to account for one of its more "traditional" elements: namely, the tendency to narrate stories already well-known to the intended audience. Bazin says that classical narrative for Valéry operates on the principle of anticipation, whereas modern narrative functions on the principle of surprise. In Bazin's ideal Japanese cinema, the audience already knows what will happen. It is a matter of tradition. The film thus becomes a ritual, an "economy of expression" more than an exposition on a structure of narrative revelation.

The problem, and simultaneously the pedagogical *possibility*, that this classicism poses to world cinema is that no one but an initiated spectator can partake of this particular kind of film experience. Bazin in response proposes a kind of pedagogical exercise in responsible spectatorship:

uninitiated spectators should see the film multiple times in order to neutralize the effect of unfamiliarity and gain access to the film's ideal form of address. We may never learn anything about Japan no matter how many times we watch *Gate of Hell*, but successive viewings, Bazin seems to say, will teach us how to respect a cinematic world that challenges our look. For Bazin, Japan supplies the model for a principled world cinema.

Notes

1. André Bazin, *Le Cinéma de la cruauté: De Buñuel à Hitchcock*, ed. François Truffaut (Paris: Flammarion, 1975); translated as *The Cinema of Cruelty: From Buñuel to Hitchcock* (New York: Seaver Books, 1982). The following four articles are reprinted in that volume, though not necessarily in the exact form in which they originally appeared. Nearly a third of the *Rashomon* article is omitted in the reprint: "La Leçon de style du cinéma japonais," *Arts*, 504 (March 9, 1955); "Un Film japonais: *Rashomon*," *France observateur*, 102 (April 24, 1952), 23; "Les Sept samouraïs," *France observateur*, 291 (December 8, 1955), 19; "Petit journal du cinéma: *Vivre*," *Cahiers du Cinéma*, 69 (March 1957).

2. Bazin, "Un Film japonais: *Rashomon*," *France observateur*, 102 (April 24, 1952).

3. See Bazin, "*Rashomon*. . .une révélation," *Parisien libéré*, 2366 (April 22, 1952); "*La Vie d'O'Haru*," *France observateur*, 196 (February 11, 1954), 22–23; "*Les Enfants d'Hiroshima*: Pèlerinage de l'apocalypse," *Parisien libéré*, 2952 (March 10, 1954), 6; "Leçon japonaise," *Les Journées*, 9 (March 19, 1955), 1; "*Les Bateaux de l'enfer*: Un *Potemkin* japonais," *Parisien libéré*, 3870 (February 19, 1957); and "*Passions juvéniles*," *Parisien libéré*, 4235 (April 23, 1958).

4. On melodrama, see Bazin, "*Le Cheval et l'enfant*: Le Poney. . .jaune," *Parisien libéré*, 3692 (July 24, 1956); "*Le Démon doré*: Surprenant Japon," *Parisien libéré*, 3260 (March 5, 1955), 6; and "*La Vie d'O'Haru*," *France observateur*, 196 (February 11, 1954), 22–23.

5. Bazin, "*Les Sept Samouraïs*," *France observateur*, 291 (December 8, 1955), 19.

6. Bazin, "*La Porte de l'enfer*," *France observateur*, 216 (July 1, 1954), 21–22.

7. Bazin, "Leçon japonaise," *Les Journées*, 9 (March 19, 1955).

8. Bazin, *Jean Renoir* (New York: Da Capo Press, 1992), 135.

9. Bazin, "*La Porte de l'enfer*." Bazin makes a similar point elsewhere in his review of Keigo Kimura's 1952 film *The Beauty and the Thief* (*Bijo to tōzoku*): "*La Belle et le voleur*," *France observateur*, 232 (October 21, 1954), 22.

10. In a review of Mikio Naruse's 1952 film *Mother* (*Okasan*), for example, Bazin notes the exoticness of Japanese films in France but is happy to observe that they are increasingly received by a habituated foreign film audience: "*Okasan*: Le néo-réalisme japonais," *Parisien libéré*, 3190 (December 14, 1954), 6.

11. Bazin, "*Les Bateaux de l'enfer*: Un *Potemkin* japonais." In the case of Keigo Kimura's film *Princess Sen* (*Senhime*, 1954), Bazin suggests that cultural "complexities" which hinder his understanding of the film are nonetheless of formal interest inasmuch as psychological drama of "Racinian simplicity" is eschewed for the discipline of history and ritual: "*Princesse Sen*," *France observateur*, 301 (February 16, 1956), 15.

12. Bazin, "Initiation au cinéma. . .égyptien," *Parisien libéré*, 600 (July 19, 1946).

13. Bazin, "*La Porte de l'enfer*." For other instances in which Bazin considers Egyptian and Indian cinema with reference to Japan, see for example: "Journée géographique au Festival de Cannes avec des films égyptien, australien, hindou et brésilien," *Parisien libéré*, 3312 (May 5, 1955); "*Calcutta, ville cruelle* (*Deux hectares de terre*): Néo-réalisme hindou," *Radio, Cinéma, Télévision*, 277 (May 8, 1955); "Le Soleil est venu couronner l'Inde et le Japon," *Parisien libéré*, 4039 (September 6, 1957); and "L'Inde remporte le Lion d'or avec *L'Invaincu*," *Parisien libéré*, 4041 (September 9, 1957).

14. Rivette, Jacques, "Mizoguchi Viewed from Here," in *Cahiers du Cinéma, The 1950s: Neo-Realism, Hollywood, New Wave*, ed. Jim Hillier (Cambridge: Harvard University Press, 1985), 264.

15. Bazin, "*Rashomon*," in *Cinéma de la cruauté: De Buñuel à Hitchcock*, 214.

16. Bazin, "Petit journal du cinéma: *Vivre*" in *Cinéma de la cruauté*, 222.

Notes on Contributors

Dudley Andrew, Professor of Film Studies and Comparative Literature at Yale, has recently published *What Cinema Is!: Bazin's Quest and Its Charge*. His biography, *André Bazin,* is being reissued with a new introduction from Oxford University Press.

Diane Arnaud is Maître de conferences in Cinema Studies at the University of Paris-Denis Diderot. She has authored *Figures d'enfermement: Le cinéma de Sokourov* (2005) and *Kiyoshi Kurosawa: Mémoire de la disparition* (2007).

Antoine de Baecque, Professor of the History of Cinema at the University of Nanterre, is the biographer of both François Truffaut and Jean-Luc Godard, as well as the author, among many other books, of *Cahiers du Cinéma: Histoire d'une revue.* He served as editor in chief at *Cahiers* from 1996 to 1998 and cultural editor and critic at *Libération* from 2001 to 2006.

Jean-François Chevrier is Professor in the History of Contemporary Art at the École nationale supérieure des Beaux-Arts in Paris. Examining photography's place between the fine arts and media, he has recently brought out an expanded edition of his *Proust et la photographie,* a monograph on Jeff Wall, and the first three volumes of his collected writings and interviews (1978–2009).

Tom Conley is Professor of French and of Film at Harvard University. His film books include *Film Hieroglyphs: Ruptures in Classical Cinema* (1991) and *Cartographic Cinema* (2007).

Ryan Cook is a doctoral candidate in Film Studies and East Asian Languages and Literatures at Yale. He has published on Oshima and on Japanese film theory and is completing a dissertation concerning cinephilia in postwar Japan.

Ludovic Cortade, who studied at the École Normale Supérieure de Saint-Cloud (Bazin's alma mater), is Assistant Professor of French at NYU and the author of *Le Cinéma de l'immobilité* (Paris: Publications de la Sorbonne, 2008).

Michael Cramer is completing a dissertation at Yale on cinema and pedagogy, focusing on Godard, Peter Watkins, and especially Roberto Rossellini.

Monica Dall'Asta is Professor of Film Studies at the University of Bologna where she teaches film theory, historiography, and feminism. Her books focus on silent cinema, including serials and pioneer women filmmakers.

Angela Dalle Vacche, Professor of Cinema at Georgia Institute of Technology, has authored *The Body in the Mirror* (1992), *Cinema and Painting* (1996), and *Diva: Defiance and Passion in Early Italian cinema* (2008).

Thomas Elsaesser, Professor Emeritus at the University of Amsterdam and Visiting Professor at Yale, has authored over a dozen books, most recently, *Film Theory: An Introduction Through the Senses*.

Rochelle Fack is a critic and teacher of cinema in Paris working principally on Stephen Dwoskin and Hans-Jurgen Syberberg. She has also published on Rainer Fassbinder, Marco Ferreri, and Jean-Marie Straub.

Jean-Michel Frodon, editor in chief of *Cahiers du Cinéma* from 2003 to 2009, has recently published *Le Cinéma français de la Nouvelle Vague à nos jours* and *Le Cinéma d'Edward Yang*. He also edited *Cinema and the Shoah* (SUNY, 2010).

Tom Gunning, Professor of Cinema and Media Studies at the University of Chicago, has published books on D. W. Griffith and Fritz Lang. He recently received the Mellon Distinguished Achievement Award.

Seung-hoon Jeong is Assistant Professor of Cinema Studies at New York University Abu Dhabi. His doctoral dissertation in Film Studies and Comparative Literature concerns "Cinematic Interfaces."

Hervé Joubert-Laurencin is Professor of Cinema and Director of the Arts Research Center at the University of Picardie-Jules Verne (Amiens). He has written copiously on Bazin, while building an archive and database. He is also a leading French exponent and translator of Pasolini, as well as the author of a key text on animation, *La Lettre volante*.

Cecile Lagesse holds degrees from the Sorbonne and the National Institute of Oriental Languages and Civilizations in Paris. She is a doctoral candidate at Yale, specializing in Chinese cinema, particularly the urban generation.

Alice Lovejoy is Assistant Professor in the Department of Cultural Studies and Comparative Literature at the University of Minnesota. A former editor at *Film Comment*, she specializes in the relationship between cinema and the state and in East European cinema.

Colin MacCabe, Distinguished Professor at the University of Pittsburgh and Professor at Birbeck College, University of London, is the author of *Godard, Portrait of the Artists at Seventy*. He has also produced feature films and documentaries on the history of the cinema.

John MacKay is Professor of Film Studies and of Slavic Languages and Literatures at Yale. His study of the life and work of Dziga Vertov is forthcoming from Indiana University Press.

Ivone Margulies is Associate Professor in the Department of Film and Media Studies at Hunter College and the CUNY Graduate Center. She is the author of *Nothing Happens: Chantal*

Akerman's Hyperrealist Everyday (1996) and editor of *Rites of Realism: Essays on Corporeal Cinema* (2002).

Daniel Morgan is Assistant Professor at the University of Pittsburgh. He is author of "Rethinking Bazin: Ontology and Realist Aesthetics" (*Critical Inquiry* 2006) and is currently completing a book on Jean-Luc Godard's work since the late 1980s.

Kan Nozaki, Professor of French Literature at the University of Tokyo, is the translator of a forthcoming Japanese edition of Bazin's *Qu'est-ce que le cinéma?*

Philip Rosen, author of *Change Mummified: Cinema, Historicity, Theory* (2001), is Professor of Modern Culture and Media at Brown University.

Noa Steimatsky, Associate Professor of Cinema and Media Studies at the University of Chicago, is the author of *Italian Locations: Reinhabiting the Past in Postwar Cinema* (2008).

Jeremi Szaniawski is completing a doctorate at Yale on Alexander Sokurov with whom he published an interview in *Critical Inquiry* (2006).

James Tweedie is Assistant Professor of Cinema Studies in the Department of Comparative Literature at the University of Washington. Coeditor of *Cinema at the City's Edge: Film and Urban Networks in East Asia* (2010) he is completing a book on new wave cinemas around the globe.

Steven Ungar, Professor of Cinema and Comparative Literature at the University of Iowa, is the author of *Cleo de 5 à 7* (2008) and coauthor of *Popular Front Paris and the Poetics of Culture* (2005).

Marc Vernet is Professor of Cinema at the University of Paris-Diderot and serves as adviser for film heritage at the Institut National du Patrimoine.

Philip Watts, Associate Professor of French at Columbia University, has authored *Allegories of the Purge: How Literature Responded to the Postwar Trials of Writers and Intellectuals in France* (Stanford, 1999) and has coedited *Jacques Rancière: History, Politics, Aesthetics* (Duke, 2009).

Grant Wiedenfeld, a doctoral candidate in Film Studies and Comparative Literature at Yale, researches French and American avant-gardes in literature and cinema.

Ismail Xavier is Professor of Film Theory and History at the University of São Paulo. His *Allegories of Underdevelopment* (1997) is a standard text on Brazilian cinema.

Index (Names)

Index (Films)

Note: Films are alphabetized under English language titles except when commonly known by the original title.

Index (Terms)

Note: Frequently cited articles by Bazin are listed under his name.

Indexes complied by Liam Andrew

Lightning Source UK Ltd.
Milton Keynes UK
UKOW020504221212

204009UK00002B/84/P